Lecture Notes in Computer Scie

Edited by G. Goos, J. Hartmanis and J. van I

T0250825

Springer

Berlin
Heidelberg
New York
Barcelona
Hong Kong
London
Milan
Paris
Singapore
Tokyo

Joseph Sventek   Geoffrey Coulson (Eds.)

Middleware 2000

IFIP/ACM International Conference
on Distributed Systems Platforms
and Open Distributed Processing
New York, NY, USA, April 4-7, 2000
Proceedings

Springer

Series Editors

Gerhard Goos, Karlsruhe University, Germany
Juris Hartmanis, Cornell University, NY, USA
Jan van Leeuwen, Utrecht University, The Netherlands

Volume Editors

Joseph Sventek
Agilent Laboratories Scotland
Mailstop SQFRD3, South Queensferry
West Lothian, EH 30 9TG, UK
E-mail: sventek@labs.agilent.com

Geoffrey Coulson
Lancaster University
Distributed Multimedia Research Group
Lancaster LA1 4YR, UK
E-mail: geoff@comp.lancs.ac.uk

Cataloging-in-Publication Data applied for

Die Deutsche Bibliothek - CIP-Einheitsaufnahme

Middleware 2000 : proceedings / IFIP-ACM International Conference on
Distributed Systems Platforms and Open Distributed Processing, New
York, NY, USA, April 4 - 7, 2000. Joseph Sventek; Geoffrey Coulson
(ed.). - Berlin ; Heidelberg ; New York ; Barcelona ; Hong Kong ;
London ; Milan ; Paris ; Singapore ; Tokyo : Springer, 2000
  (Lecture notes in computer science ; Vol. 1795)
  ISBN 3-540-67352-0

CR Subject Classification (1991): C.2.4, D.4, C.2, D.1.3, D.3.2, D.2

ISSN 0302-9743
ISBN 3-540-67352-0 Springer-Verlag Berlin Heidelberg New York

Springer-Verlag is a company in the BertelsmannSpringer publishing group.

©2000 IFIP International Federation for Information Processing, Hofstrasse 3, A-2361 Laxenburg,Austria
Printed in Germany

Typesetting: Camera-ready by author, data conversion by DA-TeX Gerd Blumenstein
Printed on acid-free paper   SPIN 10720092   06/3142   5 4 3 2 1 0

Preface

Middleware is everywhere. Ever since the advent of sockets and other virtual-circuit abstractions, researchers have been looking for ways to incorporate higher-value concepts into distributed systems platforms. Most distributed applications, especially Internet applications, are now programmed using such middleware platforms.

Prior to 1998, there were several major conferences and workshops at which research into middleware was reported, including ICODP (International Conference on Open Distributed Processing), ICDP (International Conference on Distributed Platforms) and SDNE (Services in Distributed and Networked Environments). Middleware'98 was a synthesis of these three conferences.

Middleware 2000 continued the excellent tradition of Middleware'98. It provided a single venue for reporting state-of-the-art results in the provision of distributed systems platforms. The focus of Middleware 2000 was the design, implementation, deployment, and evaluation of distributed systems platforms and architectures for future networked environments.

Among the 70 initial submissions to Middleware 2000, 21 papers were selected for inclusion in the technical program of the conference. Every paper was reviewed by four members of the program committee. The papers were judged according to their originality, presentation quality, and relevance to the conference topics. The accepted papers cover various subjects such as caching, reflection, quality of service, and transactions.

We would like to express our deepest appreciation to the authors of the submitted papers and the program committee members for their diligence in reviewing the submissions. We would also like to thank IFIP and ACM for their technical sponsorship and financial support, respectively. Finally, we would like to thank the members of the steering committee and the other organizing committee members for their efforts towards making Middleware 2000 a successful conference.

April 2000   Joseph Sventek and Geoffrey Coulson

Organization

Middleware 2000 was organized under the auspices of IFIP TC6 WG6.1 (International Federation for Information Processing, Technical Committee 6 [Communications Systems], Working Group 6.1 [Architecture and Protocols for Computer Networks]).

Steering Committee

Gordon Blair, Lancaster University, UK
Jan de Meer, GMD-Fokus, Germany
Peter Honeyman, University of Michigan, USA
Guy Leduc, University of Liege, Belgium
Kerry Raymond, DSTC, Australia
Alexander Schill, TU Dresden, Germany
Jacob Slonim, Dalhousie University, Canada

Sponsoring Institutions

 IFIP (International Federation for Information Processing)
http://www.ifip.or.at/

 ACM (Association for Computing Machinery)
http://www.acm.org

Supporting Companies

 Agilent Technologies
http://www.agilent.com

 BBN Technologies
http://www.bbn.com

 Cisco Systems
http://www.cisco.com

 IBM
http://www.ibm.com

 Siemens
http://www.siemens.com

Organizing Committee

General Chair: Douglas C. Schmidt,
                            Univ. of California at Irvine, USA
Co-program Chair: Joseph Sventek , Agilent Technologies, UK
Co-program Chair: Geoffrey Coulson, Lancaster University, UK
Tutorials Chair: Douglas C. Schmidt,
                            Univ. of California at Irvine, USA
Publicity Chair: Guruduth Banavar,
                            IBM TJ Watson Research, USA
Local Arrangements Chair: Francis Parr , IBM TJ Watson Research, USA

Program Committee

Jean Bacon, Cambridge University, UK
Bela Ban, Cornell University, USA
Martin Chapman, ebeon, Ireland
Naranker Dulay, Imperial College, UK
Frank Eliassen, University of Oslo, Norway
Rachid Guerraoui, EPFL, Switzerland
Teruo Higashino, Osaka University, Japan
Peter Honeyman, CITI, University of Michigan, USA
Doug Lea, SUNY at Oswego, USA
Peter Linington, University of Kent at Canterbury, UK
Claudia Linnhoff-Popien, RWTH Aachen, Germany
Silvano Maffeis, Softwired, Inc., Switzerland
Louise Moser, UCSB, USA
Elie Najm, ENST, France
Kerry Raymond, DSTC, Australia
Richard Soley, OMG, USA
Jean-Bernard Stefani, CNET, France
Robert Strom, IBM TJ Watson Research, USA
Robert Stroud, Newcastle University, UK
Maarten van Steen, Vrije Universiteit, The Netherlands
Gregor von Bochmann, University of Ottawa, Canada

Table of Contents

Implementing a Caching Service for Distributed CORBA Objects*

Gregory V. Chockler[1], Danny Dolev[1], Roy Friedman[2], and Roman Vitenberg[2]

[1] Institute of Computer Science, Givat Ram,
The Hebrew University, Jerusalem Israel
{grishac,dolev}@cs.huji.ac.il
http://www.cs.huji.ac.il/{~grishac,~dolev}
[2] Computer Science Department
Technion - Israel Institute of Technology, Haifa Israel
{roy,romanv}@cs.technion.ac.il
http://www.cs.technion.ac.il/{~roy,~romanv}

Abstract. This paper discusses the implementation of CASCADE, a distributed caching service for CORBA objects. Our caching service is fully CORBA compliant, and supports caching of active objects, which include both data and code. It is specifically designed to operate over the Internet by employing a dynamically built cache hierarchy. The service architecture is highly configurable with regard to a broad spectrum of application parameters. The main benefits of CASCADE are enhanced availability and service predictability, as well as easy dynamic code deployment and consistency maintenance.

1 Introduction

One of the main goals of modern middlewares, and in particular of the CORBA standard [45], is to facilitate the design of interoperable, extensible and portable distributed systems. This is done by standardizing a programming language independent IDL, a large set of useful services, the Generic InterORB Protocol (and its TCP/IP derivative IIOP), and bridges to other common middlewares. Thus, CORBA compliant middlewares combined with the global connectivity of the Internet, creates a potential for truly global services that are available for clients anywhere in the world.

However, the long and unpredictable latencies of the Internet as well as its unreliability, complicate the realization of this potential. We conducted a simple test using the UNIX ping program to measure the Internet delays. The results of this test demonstrate the variance of latencies incurred by the Internet: Pinging a local host in the same LAN takes less than one millisecond, pinging a host in the Hebrew University from the Technion takes about 11ms, while pinging a machine in the USA takes almost 600ms. Therefore, the difference in the response

---

* This work was supported in part by the Israeli Ministry of Science grant number 1230-1-98.

J. Sventek and G. Coulson (Eds.): Middleware 2000, LNCS 1795, pp. 1–23, 2000.

time in accessing objects spread over the Internet might be dramatic, regardless of the Object Request Broker (ORB) being used.

This calls for caching solutions for improving availability and predictability of distributed services. In this paper we propose to enrich CORBA middleware systems with generic caching service. We developed Caching Service for CORBA Distributed objEcts (CASCADE) which offers a scalable and flexible framework for general CORBA objects. CASCADE facilitates scalable application design by building cache hierarchies for the objects it manages. The hierarchy construction is dynamically adaptive with respect to service demand. As different applications have different consistency, security, and persistence requirements, our architecture is highly configurable with regard to a broad spectrum of application parameters. CASCADE allows client applications to fully control many aspects of object caching, by specifying a variety of *policies* for cache management, consistency maintenance, persistence, security, etc.

Our work is based on a high abstraction level provided by standard, commercially available CORBA compliant ORBs, and is aimed at preserving native programming models wherever possible. Furthermore, as discussed in Section 3, CASCADE design strictly follows the standard CORBA services design principles outlined in [46].

CASCADE caches both object data and code. Code caching allows us to preserve the standard CORBA programming model: The application works with the cached copy through the same interface it would have worked with the original object. In addition, all object methods (including updates) can be invoked locally eliminating the need to contact the remote object.

In this paper we report on the implementation of CASCADE, its performance, and the lessons learned from the implementation experience.

2   Related Work

2.1   Object Caching in CORBA Compliant Systems

To the best of our knowledge, there is no any programming framework provided by commercially available ORBs that allows for caching general CORBA objects. A very limited solution is provided by the so called *smart stub* mechanism provided by some existing CORBA implementations (e.g., Orbix [26] and VisiBroker). This mechanism allows an application programmer to override automatically generated client stubs. Using smart stubs it is possible to cache results of method invocations so that the subsequent method invocations will return locally cached values without invoking the remote operation. This framework, however, is not general enough for implementing a generic caching mechanism that will allow for caching true CORBA objects and not just some method-specific information. Moreover, with smart stub based caching the burden of maintaining coherency of cached object copies lies entirely on the application programmer.

MinORB [37] is a research ORB that allows caching partial results of read method invocations at the client side. Since this system is conceptually similar to a caching solution that can be built using smart stubs, it bears the limitations incurred by this approach (see above).

The ScaFDOCS system [32] is another research project concerned with the object caching service for CORBA compliant systems. ScaFDOCS provides multiple consistency levels for copies of cached objects. This system supports several protocols for various cache consistency semantics [31]. However, it does not support caching of active CORBA objects (both data and code). In addition, though cache consistency protocols used in this system scale relatively well, the system architecture is not hierarchical and is not aimed to operate in wide area networks.

2.2   The Service Approach to Caching and Migration

Java^{TM} [11] enables writing mobile programs that run on different hardware platforms and operating systems. Recently, several distributed systems and architectures (e.g., Voyager [43], FarGo [1] etc.) that utilize these features to provide a transparent or application-controlled object migration have emerged. Yet, these systems dictate their own programming model to the application.

In contrast, our work is based on a higher abstraction level provided by standard, commercially available CORBA compliant ORBs, and is aimed at preserving native programming models wherever possible.

2.3   Consistency in Shared Memory and Distributed Systems

Our caching service is highly configurable with respect to a great variety of consistency disciplines that can be enforced on the cached object copies. Here we benefited from the vast amount of research that was dedicated to implementing shared memory systems with various consistency guarantees, including *sequential consistency* (sometimes referred to as *strong consistency*) [33], *weak consistency* [25], *release consistency* [19], *causal consistency* [3,4], *lazy release consistency* [29], *entry consistency* [14], and *hybrid consistency* [22]. In contrast to our service, such systems are geared towards high-performance computing, and generally assume non-faulty environments and fast local communication. We refer the reader to [7,8,22,53] for other applied and theoretical studies of consistency strategies.

The Globe system [49] follows an approach similar to CASCADE by providing a flexible framework for associating various replication coherence models with distributed objects. Among the coherence models supported by Globe are the PRAM coherence, the causal coherence, the eventual coherence, etc.

The recent LOTEC protocol [24] maintains consistency for nested object transactions. This protocol spares the programmer the burden of explicitly specifying synchronization operations needed for transactional processing. Finally, the novel Millipage [27] technique enables efficient control over the granularity of a shared unit, thus enabling applications to achieve good performance while maintaining sequential consistency.

Object-based shared memory systems, in which consistency guarantees are given per object, have also been studied. Orca [10] supports object replication and migration with strong consistency guarantees. However, all objects in this system must be written in a special Orca language.

Spring [41] is a distributed operating system that provides a unified caching architecture that can be used for caching different types of remote objects. However, this system does not provide generic support for a variety of consistency and other requirements inherent for object caching. In order to address the requirements of a specific object type, the application developer must reimplement the object itself.

2.4   Object-Oriented Database Systems (OODS)

Some OODS have been designed to provide persistent storage for objects that include methods, e.g., O2 [21], GemStone [16] and Thor [35]. For example, the Thor system [35] supports highly-reliable and highly-available access to storage. For this purpose its object repositories (ORs) can be replicated, and objects can migrate from one OR to another. This system also supports client-side caching, providing a mix of consistency guarantees that can be determined by the user. It uses a variant of copying garbage collection [9] to manage the cache. In order to achieve *type-safe sharing*, all object implementations in Thor are required to be written in the Theta [36] programming language.

2.5   Web Caching

Caching web pages is nowadays a hot research topic (see, e.g., [2,5,12,17,38,39,44] [47,51,52]). Web caching is intended for use in wide area internets, similarly to our caching service, and scalability is also a major concern here. However, the web caching model is limited to data objects (HTML pages) only and does not deal with general objects that include executable code. Moreover, the contents of caches can change only as a result of a primary copy update.

The idea of *Active Web Caching* [18] can be considered a step towards active object caching. This work proposes to attach an applet to each web document. When a document (or its cached copy) is retrieved, the applet is executed.

Another point to be stressed about web caching is that the user has extremely limited control over caching decisions. The work of [42] describes several typical Enterprise network scenarios when incorrect caching decisions eliminate any improvements in response time gained from using web caching. In contrast, caching decisions in our service are application-controlled. Therefore, proper application choice can eliminate all of the above mentioned problems.

3   CASCADE and the Standard CORBA Services

The CORBA standard specifies a collection of object services, called *CORBAservices* that support basic functions for using and implementing objects [46]. These services are needed to support meaningful and productive communication at the application level and are useful for any CORBA applications regardless of their specialization. The most prominent examples of the CORBA services implemented by almost any ORB vendor are the Naming Service, the Event Service and the Transaction Service.

In this respect our design goal was twofold: to preserve the programming framework provided by the standard CORBA services, and to allow co-existence and cooperation with these services. To achieve this, we strictly followed the standard CORBA services design principles outlined in [46] (see below). Thus, our caching service can be viewed as another useful object service aimed to improve responsiveness and availability of any CORBA-based application independent of application domain.

The following is a summary of the CASCADE features that place it in line with the standard CORBA services:

- The design of CASCADE uses and builds on CORBA concepts: separation of interface and implementation, object references are typed by interfaces, clients depend on interfaces, not implementations, etc.
- The service provided by CASCADE is generic with respect to cached object types.
- CASCADE allows local and remote implementations: The caching service is structured as a CORBA object with an OMG IDL interface and can be implemented as either an application library or a standalone server.
- CASCADE does not depend on any global identifier service or global id space in order to function. All the internal CASCADE components that require some kind of identification rely on ids generated internally by CASCADE. These ids are unique only within the caching service scope and are invisible for the client applications.
- Finding the caching service is at a higher level and orthogonal to using the service. Since the caching service is structured as an object, all that is needed for accessing the service is its interoperable object reference (IOR). The latter can be found using any general purpose service (e.g., the Naming Service).

4 CASCADE System Overview

Our caching service is designed along the following lines (see Figure 1): The service is provided by a number of servers each of which is responsible for a specific *logical* domain. In practice, these domains can correspond to geographical areas. We call these servers *Domain Caching Servers (DCSs)*. Cached copies of each object are organized into a hierarchy. A separate hierarchy is dynamically constructed for each object. The hierarchy construction is driven by client requests. The construction mechanism ensures that for each client, client's local DCS (i.e., the DCS responsible for the client's domain) obtains a copy of the object. In addition, this mechanism attempts to guarantee that the object copy is obtained from the nearest DCS having a copy of this object (see Section 6.1 for further details). Once the local DCS has an object copy, all client requests

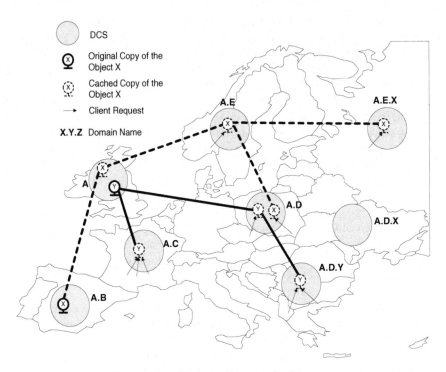

Fig. 1. The Caching Service Architecture

for object method invocation go to this DCS, so that the client does not have to communicate to a far server.

The DCS that holds an original object becomes the *root* for this object cache hierarchy. It plays a special role in building the hierarchy and in ensuring consistency of the cached copies, as described below.

Hierarchies corresponding to each object are superimposed on the DCS infrastructure: Different object hierarchies may overlap or be completely disjoint. Also overlapping object hierarchies do not necessarily have the same root. For example, in Figure 1 the original copy of the object X is located in the DCS of domain $A.B$. This DCS is the root of the X's hierarchy. The cached copies of X are located in the DCSs of domains A, $A.E$, $A.D$ and $A.E.X$. Note that, in addition to being the holder of the cached copy of X, the DCS of domain A also serves as the root of the object Y hierarchy. Further, the $A.D$'s DCS contains only cached object copies and the $A.D.X$'s DCS does not contain objects at all.

Compared with other distributed architectures, using a hierarchy has the following advantages:

Conserved WAN bandwidth consumption : The bandwidth consumption of communication over a tree is low because each message is sent only $|V|-1$ times, where V is the number of nodes in the tree.

Improved scalability : The stateful communication over a hierarchical architecture is known to be scalable because of the low number of simultaneously opened node to node connections and because of the small communication state kept at each node.

Reduced initial response time : Since an object copy is obtained from the nearest member of the object hierarchy, it takes less time on average to bring this copy to a local DCS than to obtain the copy from the original object holder. Thus, the client waits less for the result of its first request addressed to this object.

Easy management : It is easier to add or to remove a server in a tree than in other distributed architectures. In addition, a tree can be relatively easily reconfigured (a root of the tree can be moved etc.).

Easy consistency maintenance : If strong consistency among cached copies is required, a universally known root of the hierarchy can impose a total order on object updates.

The main disadvantage of a tree is its vulnerability to node failures. A single node failure can disconnect the whole branch of the tree. This problem can be solved, for example, by local replication of each DCS using a primary backup approach (see, e.g., [15]).

Note that the communication between DCSs is also implemented via CORBA, so that each DCS provides a service for other DCSs and implements a well defined IDL interface for internal requests. Thus, the inter-DCS communication benefits from all CORBA advantages: interoperability, portability, reliability guarantees for communication, and a wide spectrum of services which can be used, e.g., for secure communication and for name resolution. It is also important to emphasize that there is only one central object at each DCS implementing this interface for internal requests and not one object per each cached object. This reduces the number of stubs used for DCS to DCS communication to one, rendering the system more scalable.

In the framework of the caching service we introduce two policy classes: *per-object* policies and *per-request* policies. The per-object policies do not change over the object life time, whereas the per-request policies specify a particular request semantics. In order to provide an adequate interface for configuring the system, we introduce the notion of a *policy object*, which is associated with either an object or a request. These policies are used to specify the required behavior of the caching service in terms of consistency guarantees, security, persistence, etc.

5 CASCADE System Modules

5.1 The Client Structure

The client structure is depicted in Figure 2. It consists of the following elements:

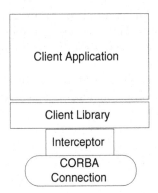

Fig. 2. The Client Structure

Interceptor [1]: This module is responsible for interception of client invocations of cached object methods and for altering the content of the request transparently for the client application. This module is used for passing implicit request parameters and invocation semantics (see Section 6.2). It is also used for encryption, decryption and authentication of client requests (see Section 6.5).

Client Library : The client library is aimed at facilitating the interaction between the client application and the caching service. In particular, the library hides the interceptor from the application. Thanks to the client library, the application interacts with the cached object in the same way as it would do with an ordinary CORBA object.

5.2   The DCS Structure

Figure 3(a) shows the DCS breakdown into modules. The DCS object consists of three parts:

Object cache : This is where objects cached in the local DCS actually reside. Each cached object is wrapped into a *proxy object* whose structure is depicted in Figure 3(b) and discussed in Section 5.3 below.

Policy implementations : This is a collection of implementations of various per-object policies. Each policy implementation is shared among all cached objects. However, for each cached object a policy implementation is parameterized by the corresponding *policy object*. Policy objects are located within the object proxy (see Figure 3(b) and Section 5.3).

Common task implementations : This part includes the implementations of the cache manager, the class loader and the hierarchy manager. The cache

---

[1] Interceptors are a common way of gaining access to CORBA's communication protocol; they are a part of the CORBA 2.3 standard [40]. While they are to undergo a technical revision in CORBA 3, no conceptual changes are anticipated.

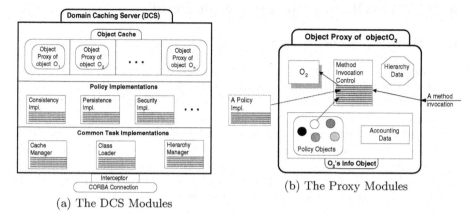

(a) The DCS Modules   (b) The Proxy Modules

Fig. 3. The CASCADE System Modules

manager controls insertion/deletion of objects to/from the object cache. Its implementation is based on a particular cache replacement policy implemented by the DCS (see Section 6.4). The class loader is responsible for loading the cached objects' code into the Java virtual machine. Finally, the hierarchy manager controls the hierarchy construction for all objects cached within the DCS (see Section 6.1).

In addition, there is an interceptor object underneath the DCS that intercepts client requests to cached objects. This is used to extract the implicit request parameters added by client side interceptors (see Section 5.1).

5.3   The Proxy Object Structure

Figure 3(b) shows the internal structure of the proxy of a cached object O_2. It consists of the following elements:

The cached copy of O_2 : This includes the copy of O_2's state and code.

O_2's info object : This object consists of two parts: O_2's policy objects and O_2's accounting data. There is one policy object for each policy defined for O_2. The policies are configured when O_2 is first registered with the CASCADE system. O_2's accounting data includes various run-time statistics that are collected during its life-time.

O_2's Hierarchy Data : The knowledge of this proxy node about its location in the object hierarchy: its father node, its children nodes etc.

The method invocation control : This module processes incoming method invocations based on the policies defined for the object: Whenever a method is invoked on the cached object, it is forwarded to the object proxy. The invocation is then processed by the method invocation control module that passes control to the appropriate policy implementations and supplies the requested invocation semantics (per-method policy) and the per-object policies as parameters.

6   CASCADE Implementation in Detail

6.1   Hierarchy Construction

A hierarchy construction is started when a client calls *register_object* in order to create a new hierarchy for the object (or for the group of objects). This call registers the object (or the group of objects) with the local client's DCS which becomes the root of the new hierarchy. In the following description we call it a *root DCS* for this hierarchy. It keeps the knowledge of the whole hierarchy and it is responsible for the hierarchy construction. The root DCS also plays a special role in achieving consistency among the cached copies of the object, as we explain in Section 6.2. In addition, the root DCS registers itself with the naming service as a caching service provider for its cached object (or the group of objects).

Figure 4 shows the sequence of operations executed when a new DCS joins the hierarchy. When a client wishes to start working with a cached object, it calls *copy_object* on its local DCS. Unless the local DCS has this object already cached, it finds the root DCS for this object with the aid of the naming service. Then it contacts the root DCS with a request to join the hierarchy for this object. This request also contains the domain of the new DCS.

When the root DCS receives such a join request from a DCS of domain D, it finds a domain D' in the existing hierarchy such that D' is the closest to D. Then, the root DCS sends a reply specifying the location of the D''s DCS to the local client's DCS. Upon receiving this reply, the latter sends a request to its designated father node in order to register as its son in the hierarchy and in order to obtain a cached copy of the object. The father node registers the new son and sends its cached copy, thus, completing the join protocol.

The notion of a distance between different domains is still an open question. Currently, we use symbolic domain names to determine the distance between domains, e.g., we assume that domain $a.b.c$ is closer to $a.b$ than to $x.y.z$. This approach works well for some Internet domain names, e.g., domain *technion.ac.il* is indeed closer to *huji.ac.il* than to *whitehouse.gov*. On the other hand, this scheme cannot differentiate between the enormous number of *.com* domains, and thus, we are also going to investigate other approaches.

The hierarchy construction protocol guarantees that for each client there is a local DCS that has a cached copy of the object; the local DCS handles the client's requests. It is this fact and the hierarchical architecture of the system that allow to significantly reduce the response time, to distribute the load on DCSs and to render the caching service scalable.

The disconnection from the hierarchy is currently supported only for leaves. If some object is no longer used, and some intermediate DCS node wants to leave the hierarchy for this object, this DCS should wait for its sons to disconnect first.

When a leaf DCS node D wishes to disconnect from the object hierarchy, it first informs the root about this, so that the root updates its knowledge about the hierarchy. Then D sends its father a request to detach it from the hierarchy. Only when D receives a reply, it can safely disconnect.

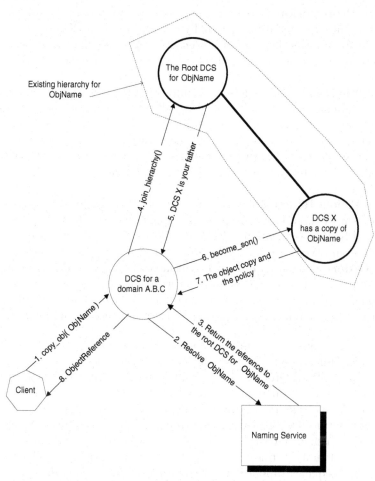

Fig. 4. Joining the hierarchy

It should be emphasized that CASCADE takes care of all synchronization problems that arise during joining and leaving the hierarchy.

6.2   Implementation of Cached Copies Consistency

When the system concurrently maintains several copies of the same object, it should also guarantee mutual consistency of these copies. Different levels of consistency are widely known, e.g., [13,14,23,28,33]. In general, the stronger the consistency level, the higher latency its implementation incurs [8].

In order to make our service as flexible as possible, we support several *consistency policies*. The set of supported policies is motivated by the guarantees presented in [48] and [30]. Following [48] we present 6 consistency guarantees that can be combined together to form a consistency model.

Update Propagation This requirement, called also update dissemination, ensures that each update is eventually received by each DCS.

Read Your Writes This condition ensures that the effects of every update made by an application are visible to all subsequent queries of this application.

Monotonic Reads This condition requires that the effects of every update seen by an application query are visible to all subsequent queries of this application (unless overwritten by later updates). The Monotonic Reads guarantee implies that the observed object is increasingly up-to-date over time.

Monotonic Writes (FIFO ordering) This requirement guarantees that two updates initiated by the same application are applied in order of their issuance.

Writes Follow Reads This condition entails that the updates whose effects are seen by an application query are applied before all subsequent updates issued by this application. The Writes Follow Reads requirement along with Monotonic Writes ensure *causal ordering of updates* [34].

Total Ordering This requirement guarantees that all updates are applied in the same order by all GCSs. In other words, it implies that there is a global sequence of updates. Total Ordering entails Writes Follow Reads (see [50] for a discussion about the relation of different ordering properties).

CASCADE always guarantees eventual Update Propagation. Other requirements are fulfilled only if requested by the application.

The use of Total Ordering is determined by the object policy. It affects the way method invocation requests are applied and/or propagated through the hierarchy: While queries are always locally executed at the DCS of a client, updates might need to be propagated through the hierarchy before being applied at the DCS which initiates them. If total ordering is required, updates first ascend through the hierarchy towards the root. The root of the hierarchy orders the updates in a sequence, applies them and propagates ordered updates through the hierarchy downwards towards the leaves. At this point there are two possibilities (the choice is policy configurable): the root DCS can either propagate the request itself or the resulted version of the object, whichever is shorter. Of course, if the request has a side effect of updating another, non-cached object through the network (e.g., updating a non-distributed database), then the root can only propagate the new object version.

If total ordering is not deployed, updates are first applied locally and then propagate through the hierarchy. This shortens the latency of updates, and reduces the load imposed on the root DCS. However, different updates may be applied in different order at different DCSs.

Other consistency requirements (i.e., Read Your Writes, Monotonic Reads, Monotonic Writes and Writes Follow Reads) are part of a per-request policy. This is more flexible than specifying the required set of these guarantees once for the whole client session as implemented in Bayou. [20] contains a detailed description of how these consistency requirements are implemented. It should be noticed that in some cases (in particular when total ordering is not used) their implementation implies a cooperation of the client. Along with a method invocation request, a client should provide consistency information such as the last update the client has seen. This can be done either explicitly through a special purpose interface or transparently for the client application by using interceptor library (see [20] for a detailed description of the client interface).

As noted in [48], these four consistency conditions (required by all the clients) in conjunction with total ordering guarantee the classical *strong* or *sequential* consistency [33].

Object Group-Based Consistency The above mentioned consistency policies apply to an individual object. However, some applications might wish to impose sequential consistency across several objects. To address this, we introduce *object group-based* consistency policy. With this policy, a group of objects, each one having its own hierarchy, are to be maintained in a strongly consistent manner. We impose a restriction for this policy that these hierarchies must have a common root. Without such a limitation the algorithms for achieving group consistency become prohibitively expensive.

This policy is implemented in the following way: The common root introduces a total order on the updates of all the objects in the group. Then, updates of each object are propagated through its own hierarchy. However, if some DCS has cached copies of more than one object in the group, this DCS does not apply updates to any object before it applies all other preceding updates, including updates of other objects.

6.3   Support for Atomic Operations and Locking

Sometimes several requests are to be executed *atomically*, without being interrupted by the execution of other requests. CASCADE provides the client a possibility to specify several update operations in one request. Each DCS applying this request atomically processes the specified sequence of update operations. When an object group-based consistency is used, and the client's local DCS has cached copies of two objects X and Y belonging to the same group, then the client can invoke *update_object* on X, and include an update of Y into the atomic operation request.

Locking can be a very useful functionality for applications that deploy a caching service with strong consistency semantics. When the local DCS possesses a lock for an object, its clients can be sure that they work with the most updated object copy. In addition, locking can be used for implementing *distributed transactions*, even for objects with different root DCSs.

CASCADE supports three types of object locks defined in the specifications of CORBA Concurrency Control Service [46]: *Write* lock conflicts with any other lock, *read* lock conflicts only with a write lock, and *upgrade* lock conflicts with a write lock and with other upgrade locks.

A lock is assigned to the client application following its request. Normally, a lock is released also upon a client request. However, since CASCADE cannot rely on the reliability of the client, special care should be taken so that the object would not remain locked forever. Therefore, the DCS that obtained the locks releases them automatically after a given timeout unless it receives another lock request for the same object. Thus, if the client intends to continue updating the object, it should issue another lock request before the timeout elapses.

6.4   Overview of Cache Management in CASCADE

Since the size of the cache is limited, a DCS can hold only a limited number of cached copies. When a cached copy is to be brought to a DCS but there is no more space in the cache, some other object is to be evacuated from the cache. However, not all cached objects are suitable for evacuation. In particular, objects locked by this DCS and/or objects whose methods are currently being executed are never replaced. In addition, since each object registered with CASCADE should remain available until it is explicitly unregistered, objects for which this DCS is the root of the hierarchy are also never evacuated from the cache.

In order to prevent the uncontrolled growth of the total size of registered objects, CASCADE imposes two limits: (1) on the maximal number of objects registered at each DCS, and (2) on the maximal size of each registered object. If the total number of registered objects reaches the limit, new register requests are rejected. In addition, whenever the size of some registered object grows beyond the limit, it is unregistered and its hierarchy is destroyed.

If some previously evacuated object is required later by a client, it will be acquired again from the father node transparently for this client. In turn, if the father node also does not have a copy of the requested object, it will try to acquire it from its father node. This way the request ascends all the way up along the hierarchy until the DCS that has a copy of the object is reached. (In the worst case, the chain reaches the root of the hierarchy). The object copy then descends along the hierarchy back to the request originator.

When an object copy is evacuated from the cache, the DCS continues to keep a small record needed for information dissemination along the hierarchy. This record is finally removed only when (1) no client has issued a request for the object during a pre-defined timeout, and (2) this DCS becomes a leaf of the object hierarchy. When this occurs, the DCS undertakes the steps detailed in Section 6.1 in order to disconnect from the hierarchy.

In the current version of CASCADE, the decision about which objects to evacuate from the cache is made by the LRU algorithm driven by client requests to objects. That is, whenever a new or previously evacuated object O is to be brought into the cache, currently cached objects are evacuated according to the LRU criterion until there is enough space to accommodate O.

We intend to study the applicability of other cache replacement algorithms (see [20] for a discussion of potential alternatives).

6.5   Support for Security

CASCADE offers support for securing cached object access and communication between clients and cached objects. This is done by encrypting and signing communication and deploying object access control. Which of these measures are undertaken is determined by means of per-object *security policy* that can be specified by the object creator when the object is registered with CASCADE.

We are currently working on DCS protection from malicious objects and malicious clients. [20] provides a more detailed description of these and other issues related to security in CASCADE.

7   Applications

In this section we describe three typical applications that can benefit from our caching service.

7.1   Yellow Pages Service

An example of a typical application that requires only Update Propagation and Monotonic Updates consistency guarantees is a yellow pages service. The object to be cached here is a catalogue of named information items. Clients can register their names along with the information they would like to publish about themselves. They can update information about themselves and they can also query information about some particular name or search the catalogue for some particular information.

Under the realistic assumption that no two clients will try to register under the same name, updates from different clients are not interrelated. While synchronous catalogue update provides better fairness, it will usually be permissible for two clients to temporarily see different views of the catalogue. After all, even the phone company does not deliver a new yellow pages book at the same time to all houses. In addition, if the DCS hierarchy reflects the geographical location of the servers, then, according to the principle of locality, if some client registers information at some DCS, it is more probable that queries about this information will be issued to the same DCS. Thus, additional consistency guarantees are not required for this type of application.

7.2   Tickets Reservation Service

In contrast to the Yellow Pages Service, this service requires the classical strong consistency [33]. The object to be cached here is a ticket reservations database. Clients can book a ticket and they can also query information about ticket availability. The service should not allow two clients to book the same ticket. This implies that all reservation requests should be totally ordered.

This service can deploy a distributed transaction for booking a group of tickets. In addition, this service can make use of a dirty query mechanism explained below. Consider the following situation: Some client reserves a ticket at some DCS, and then another client attempts to reserve the same ticket at the same DCS before the previous update has been propagated. Then a dirty query can already show that this ticket is not available before the actual update propagation. Note that the probability that the second client contacts the same DCS is relatively high because of the above mentioned principle of locality.

Note also that our caching service can be used for both airline ticket reservations and theater reservations. Here, again, the fact that we cache active objects is instrumental as the rules for performing reservations in both cases are different. For example, airlines allow for over-booking, but over-booking might not be acceptable in theaters.

It should be noticed that queries in a ticket reservation service can benefit from *dirty copy consistency* [6]. Loosely speaking, a dirty copy consistency query returns a value resulted from all locally known updates, even if some of these updates were not ordered in the global sequence yet. Suppose, for example, that a number of clients connect to their regional DCS and request to book a seat in the same flight. Suppose also that as a result of all these booking requests the flight gets overbooked. Now another client connects to the same DCS in order to book a seat. It first wants to figure out the situation so it issues a dirty copy query request and immediately learns that the flight is overbooked and therefore, the chance for it to get a seat is small. The client can then go and try to book a ticket for another flight to the same destination.

7.3   Distributed Bulletin Board

In a distributed bulletin board, users can post events, or poll the board for recently posted events. Also, it is possible to define topics, in which case a user may look for postings in a specific category, or get a listing of all postings. An additional requirement from a bulletin board is to preserve causality [34] of event postings so that a follow-up posting is always seen after the original posting it is referring to. Thus, this application requires Update Propagation, Monotonic Writes, Writes Follow Reads and Monotonic Reads consistency guarantees.

8   CASCADE Performance

In order to assess CASCADE performance we conducted a simple test involving two DCSs: one running on a machine connected to the Hebrew University of Jerusalem CS department LAN and another running on a machine connected to the Haifa Technion CS department LAN. Both CS departments are connected to the Israeli Academic and Research network and separated by 7 hops. Both hosts are Intel architecture machines (Pentium II 300 Mhz with 128 MB RAM) running Windows NT 4.0 operating systems. The ORB used in testing environment was Visibroker 3.2 for Java.

Our goal was to evaluate the effect of using CASCADE on method invocation time of a CORBA object. To achieve this, we measured the method invocation time twice: once for a standard CORBA remote invocation and another time for an invocation when the object was cached with CASCADE. The test was conducted with a 10 KB CORBA object whose interface consisted of both updates and queries. Method argument data types were of small size and therefore their marshaling/demarshaling had a little effect on overall invocation times. The object consistency policy included only the Update Propagation guarantee (see 6.2).

Tables 1 and 2 summarize our results (all the times are given in *ms*).

Table 1. Method invocation profiling on a DCS

Operation	Avg. time	Std. deviation
Processing in interceptors	< 1	< 1
Request processing by proxy	0.83	2.87
Proper invocation time	2.4	6.59
Full invocation time	11.1	25

Table 2. Method invocation profiling on a client

Operation	w/o CASCADE		using CASCADE	
	Avg. time	Std. deviation	Avg. time	Std. deviation
Marshaling/demarshaling	1.32	4.1	1.49	3.91
Client interceptors	N/R	N/R	< 1	< 1
Request invocation	93	8	46.78	15.7

We measured the following times at a DCS:

Processing in interceptors - time spent on request processing by server interceptors. It was always close to 0 because of the weak consistency policy we chose. However, even when we measured this time for strong and group consistency policy, it was never more than few milliseconds.

Proper invocation time - time spent in the *invoke* function of the cached object. It was only few milliseconds for our lightweight object.

Request processing by proxy - time taken by an object proxy to process the request in order to satisfy consistency and other policy requirements.

Full invocation time - this is the sum of the above times and the time of the request processing by ORB. The latter includes the times of marshaling/demarshaling.

We measured the following times at a client application:

Marshaling/demarshaling - time spent in the stubs on marshaling the *in* parameters and demarshaling *out* parameters. It was few milliseconds because of the small size of parameter types.

Client interceptors - time spent on request processing by client interceptors. All explained about time spent in server interceptors applies here as well.

Request invocation - time taken by *request.invoke()*. It consists of the time spent in client interceptors, the full invocation time at the DCS, additional request processing by ORB, and the network latency.

The results shown in the tables clearly indicate that the network latency is the most influential factor in the overall invocation time. Since use of CASCADE significantly reduces the network latency, it leads to a 2 times speedup for our settings. Furthermore, taking into consideration that a ping from Israel to the US or to Europe takes about 600ms, we expect the magnitude order of a speedup to be 20-30 times for far objects.

In future we intend to conduct tests for a larger number of DCSs and cached objects, for objects of different sizes and for more data transmitted during request invocation. We expect the speedup for bigger requests to be even greater because the time of their transmission over the network will overweigh the difference in marshaling time.

9   Lessons Learned from CORBA Experience

Object by Value CORBA has the advantage over many commercial RPC systems in that it allows object references to be manipulated as regular data type values in a straightforward manner. In particular, an object reference can be passed as an argument of a method invocation on another object. However, other parameter passing semantics are not supported by CORBA. Specifically in CASCADE, there is a need to pass objects by value when the object is cached at some DCS. Currently, this is implemented with the aid of Java serialization. The shortcomings of this approach are that (a) we are limited in the choice of programming language, and (b) the object state is passed as a sequence of bytes. This does not stay in line with object-oriented approach.

While CORBA 2.3 introduced the object-by-value standard to tackle this problem, this standard is not mature enough and its implementations are rare. Furthermore, CORBA lacks the ability to forward an incoming request to another server, i.e., to pass it by value. This ability is important for CASCADE that executes the same update request at multiple locations and totally orders update requests in order to achieve consistency. Below we explain how we circumvent the lack of this ability with the aid of interceptors.

Interceptors Use of interceptors is vital for CASCADE implementation. Interceptors allow CASCADE to perform a set of operations transparently to the client applications: to encrypt and sign requests and replies, to maintain consistency and to pass implicit per-request policy parameters.

Unfortunately, the interceptor standard of CORBA is to undergo a major revision, and there are no implementations of the current standard. Therefore, we used proprietary Visibroker 3.2 interceptors which conceptually correspond to the standard of message-level interceptors. Per-request policies and consistency parameters were passed through the service context field of a standard GIOP request message header. Unfortunately, Visibroker (and even the CORBA standard) defines no means for encapsulating typed data into service context, so we had to implement marshaling/demarshaling by ourselves.

An additional use of interceptors in CASCADE is for forwarding an incoming request to another DCS. This was implemented in the following way: when DCS A receives a request to be propagated to its parent DCS B, A calls an internal DCS interface method on B and passes the GIOP request message body as a parameter (see [20] for a description of the internal DCS interface). If B is to apply this request, it creates an instance of CASCADE class that implements *CORBA::ServerRequest* and that is initialized with a GIOP request message body.

However, in some ORBs, this solution could lead to little endian - big endian incompatibilities: If A and B have the same endian order, the standard CORBA input/output streams are used for marshaling/demarshaling: The request message body is written to the *CORBA::portable::OutputStream* by calling *write_octet_array*, *CORBA::portable::InputStream* is created out of the OutputStream, and the typed data is read from this InputStream. However, if A and B have different endian order, we had no choice but to use input and output streams implemented in CASCADE.

An alternative way of redirecting a request would be to use request-level interceptors, to demarshal request parameters into *any*s, and to call an appropriate method on B, passing the list of these *any*s. However, in this solution the types of *any*s would be also passed on the wire, while these types would be absolutely unnecessary.

10   Future Work

CASCADE is a rapidly evolving system that is under permanent development. As part of our future work we intend to evaluate applicability of several existing protocols for reliable multicast and dynamic resource discovery in the Internet for improved hierarchy construction and update propagation. Other research directions include evaluating cache replacement policies, working out the security model, adding fault-tolerance, conducting thorough performance tests etc.

Another interesting problem to be addressed is whether the hierarchical cache architecture employed by CASCADE is most adequate for wide area distributed settings. To answer this question we intend to examine other possibilities for replicating and caching CORBA objects. For example, an interesting option to examine would be a hybrid architecture that combines replication of CORBA objects at limited number of powerful servers with light-weight cache servers at the end-user sites.

Also, it would be interesting to identify features provided by various CAS-CADE components that are generic enough in order to be incorporated independently into the CORBA standard. For example, consistency policy implementations can be beneficial for a wide range of distributed applications that involve object replication for improved availability and fault-tolerance.

We are also working on development of various wide area CORBA based distributed applications that will utilize CASCADE for improved availability and service time predictability. Among the applications currently under development are a distributed news facility and a shared whiteboard. These applications will help us to assess the CASCADE impact on the service quality and to identify the features that should be added to CASCADE in order to better meet the application needs.

References

1. FarGo home page. http://www.dsg.technion.ac.il/fargo/. 3
2. Marc Abrams, Charles R. Standridge, Ghaleb Abdulla, Stephen Williams, and Edward A. Fox. Caching proxies: limitations and potentials. In *Proceedings of the 4th International WWW Conference*, December 1995. Available at http://www.w3.org/pub/Conferences/WWW4/Papers/155/. 4
3. M. Ahamad, P. Hutto, and R. John. Implementing and programming causal distributed shared memory. Technical Report TR GIT-CC-90-49, Georgia Institute of Technology, December 1990. 3
4. M. Ahamad, G. Neiger, P. Kohli, J. Burns, and P. Hutto. Causal memory: Definitions, implementation, and programming. *Distributed Computing*, 9(1), 93. 3
5. Virgílio Almeida, Azer Bestavros, Mark Crovella, and Adriana de Oliveira. Characterizing reference locality in the WWW. In *Proceedings of the IEEE Conference on Parallel and Distributed Information Systems (PDIS)*, December 1996. Available at http://cs-www.bu.edu/faculty/best/res/papers/pdis96.ps. 4
6. Y. Amir. *Replication Using Group Communication Over a Partitioned Network*. PhD thesis, Institute of Computer Science, The Hebrew University of Jerusalem, Israel, 1995. 16
7. H. Attiya and R. Friedman. A correctness condition for high-performance multiprocessors. In *Proc. of the 24th ACM Symp. on the Theory Of Computing*, pages 679–690, May 1992. Revised version: Technical Report #767, Department of Computer Science, The Technion. Submitted for publication. 3
8. H. Attiya and J. Welch. Sequential consistency versus linearizability. *ACM Transactions on Computer Systems*, 12(2):91–122, May 1994. 3, 11
9. Henry Baker. List processing in real time on a serial computer. *Communications of the ACM*, 21(4):280–294, April 1978. 4
10. H. Bal, F. Kaashoek, and A. Tanenbaum. Orca: A language for parallel programming of distributed systems. *IEEE Transaction on Software Engineering*, 18(3):190–205, March 1992. 3
11. H. J. Bekker. The Java Platform, A White Paper. JavaSoft, Sun Microsystems. Available at http://www.javasoft.com/docs/white. 3
12. H. J. Bekker. Survey on caching requirements and specifications for prototype. DESIRE European project deliverable D4.1. Available at http://www.ruu.nl/~henny/desire/survey.html. 4
13. J. Bennett, J. Carter, and W. Zwaenepoel. Munin: Distributed shared memory based on type-specific memory coherence. In *Proc. of the 2nd ACM Symp. on Principles and Practice of Parallel Processing*, pages 168–176, 1990. 11

14. B. N. Bershad, M. J. Zekauskas, and W. A. Sawdon. The Midway distributed shared memory system. In *Proc. of the 38th IEEE Intl. Computer Conf. (COMPCON)*, pages 528–537, February 1993. Available at http://www-cgi.cs.cmu.edu/afs/cs/project/midway/WWW/CompCon93.ps. 3, 11

15. K. P. Birman. *Building Secure and Reliable Network Applications.* Manning Publishing Company and Prentice Hall, December 1996. 7

16. P. Butterworth, A. Otis, and J. Stein. The GemStone database management system. *Communications of the ACM*, 34(10), October 1991. 4

17. Pei Cao and Sandy Irani. Cost-aware WWW proxy caching algorithms. In *Proceedings of the 1997 Usenix Symposium on Internet Technologies and Systems (USITS-97)*, December 1997. Available at http://www.cs.wisc.edu/ cao/papers/gd-size.ps.Z. 4

18. Pei Cao, Jin Zhang, and Kevin Beach. Active cache: Caching dynamic contents on the web. In *IFIP Intl. Conference on Distributed Systems Platforms and Open Distributed Processing (Middleware '98)*, pages 373–388, 1998. 4

19. J. B. Carter. *Efficient Distributed Shared Memory Based on Multi-Protocol Release Consistency.* PhD thesis, Department of Computer Science, Rice University, September 1993. 3

20. G. Chockler, D. Dolev, R. Friedman, and R. Vitenberg. Cascade: Caching service for corba distributed objects. Technical report, Department of Computer Science, The Technion, October 1999. In preparation. 12, 13, 14, 15, 19

21. O. Deux et al. The story of O2. *IEEE Transactions on Knowledge and Data Engineering*, 2(1):91–108, March 1990. 4

22. R. Friedman. *Consistency Conditions for Distributed Shared Memories.* PhD thesis, Department of Computer Science, The Technion, 1994. 3

23. K. Gharachorloo, D. Lenoski, J. Laudon, P. Gibbons, A. Gupta, and J. Hennessy. Memory consistency and event ordering in scalable shared-memory multiprocessors. In *Proc. of the 17th International Symposium on Computer Architecture*, pages 15–26, May 1990. 11

24. Peter Graham and Yahong Sui. LOTEC: A Simple DSM Consistency Protocol for Nested Object transactions. In *ACM Symposium on Principles of Distributed Computing (PODC)*, 1999. To appear. 3

25. P. Hutto and M. Ahamad. Slow memory: Weakening consistency to enhance concurrency in distributed shared memories. Technical Report TR GIT-ICS-89/39, Georgia Institute of Technology, October 1989. 3

26. IONA. *Orbix Programming Guide.* IONA Technologies Ltd., November 1995. 2

27. Ayal Itzkovitz and Assaf Schuster. MultiView and Millipage — Fine-Grain Sharing in Page-Based DSMs. In *Proc. of the 3rd Symp. on Operating Systems Design and Implemen tation (OSDI'99)*, New Orleans, February 1999. To appear. 3

28. K. L. Johnson, M. F. Kaashoek, and D. A. Wallach. Crl: High-performance all-software distributed shared memory. In *15th ACM SIGOPS Symposium on Operating Systems Principles (SOSP)*, pages 213–228, December 1995. 11

29. P. Keleher. *Lazy Release Consistency for Distributed Shared Memory.* PhD thesis, Department of Computer Science, Rice University, December 1994. 3

30. A. M. Kermarrec, I. Kuz, M. van Steen, and A. S. Tanenbaum. A Framework for Consistent, Replicated Web Objects. In *Proceedings of the 11th International Conference on Distributed Computing Systems (ICDCS'98)*, Amsterdam, The Netherlands, May 1998. 11

31. R. Kordale and M. Ahamad. A scalable technique for implementing multiple consistency levels for distributed objects. In *16th International Conference on Distributed Computing*, 1996. 3

32. R. Kordale, M. Ahamad, and M. Devarakonda. Object caching in a corba compliant system. *USENIX Computing Systems Journal*, 9(4), 1996. 3

33. L. Lamport. How to make a multiprocessor computer that correctly executes multiprocess programs. *IEEE Trans. on Computers*, C-28(9):690–691, 1979. 3, 11, 13, 15

34. L. Lamport. Time, clocks, and the ordering of events in a distributed system. *Communications of the ACM*, 21(7):558–565, July 78. 12, 16

35. B. Liskov, A. Adya, M. Castro, M. Day, S. Ghemawat, R. Gruber, U. Maheshwari, A. Myers, and L. Shrira. Safe and efficient sharing of persistent objects in Thor. In *ACM SIGMOD International Symposium on Management of Data*, pages 318–329, June 1996. 4

36. Barbara Liskov, Dorothy Curtis, Mark Day, Sanjay Ghemawhat, Robert Gruber, Paul Johnson, and Andrew C. Myers. *Theta reference manual.* Programming Methodology Group Memo 88, MIT Lab. for Computer Science, feb 1994. Also available at http://www.pmg.lcs.mit.edu/papers/thetaref/. 4

37. P. Martin, V. Callaghan, and A. Clark. High Performance Distributed Objects using Caching Proxies for Large Scale Applications. In *Proceedings of the IEEE International Symposium on Distributed Objects and Applications (DOA'99)*, Edinburgh, Scotland, September 1999. 2

38. Ingrid Melve. Web caching architecture. DESIRE European project. Available at http://www.uninett.no/prosjekt/desire/arneberg/. 4

39. Ingrid Melve, Lars Slettjord, Henny Bekker, and Ton Verschuren. Building a Web caching system - architectural considerations. In *Proceedings of the 1997 NLANR Web Cache Workshop*, June 1997. Available at http://ircache.nlanr.net/Cache/Workshop97/Papers/Bekker/bekker.ps. 4

40. P. Narasimhan, L.E. Moser, and P.M. Melliar-Smith. Using interceptors to enhance CORBA. *IEEE Computer*, 32(7):62–68, July 1999. 8

41. M. N. Nelson, G. Hamilton, and Y. A. Khalidi. A framework for caching in an object-oriented system. SMLI TR 93-19, Sun Microsystems Laboratories, Inc., October 1993. 4

42. Thomas Nolle. To cache or not to cache. http://www.nwfusion.com/columnists/1109nolle.html (registration required). 4

43. ObjectSpace. Voyager home page. http://www.objectspace.com. 3

44. Katia Obraczka, Peter Danzig, Solos Arthachinda, and Muhammad Yousuf. Scalable, highly available Web caching. Technical Report 97-662, USC Computer Science Department, 1997. Available at ftp://usc.edu/pub/csinfo/tech-reports/papers/97-662.ps.Z. 4

45. OMG. *The Common Object Request Broker: Architecture and Specification.* OMG, 1995. 1

46. OMG. *CORBA services: Common Object Services Specification.* OMG, 1995. 2, 4, 5, 13

47. Guillaume Pierre and Mesaac Makpangou. Saperlipopette!: a distributed Web caching systems evaluation tool. In *Proceedings of the 1998 Middleware conference*, September 1998. Available at http://www-sor.inria.fr/publi/SDWCSET_middleware98.html. 4

48. D.B. Terry, A.J. Demers, K. Petersen, M.J. Spreitzer, M.M. Theimer, and B.B. Welsh. Session guarantees for weakly consistent replicated data. In *Proceedings of the IEEE Conference on Parallel and Distributed Information Systems (PDIS)*, pages 140–149, Austin, TX, September 1994. 11, 13

49. M. van Steen, P. Homburg, and A. S. Tanenbaum. Globe: A Wide-Area Distributed System. *IEEE Concurency*, 7(1):70–78, January-March 1999. 3

50. R. Vitenberg, I. Keidar, G. Chockler, and D. Dolev. Group communication specifications: A comprehensive study. Technical Report MIT-LCS-TR-790, Massachusetts Institute of Technology, Laboratory for Computer Science, October 1999. Also: Technical Report CS #0964, Department of Computer Science, The Technion. 12

51. Philip S. Yu and Edward A. MacNair.   Performance study of a collaborative method for hierarchical caching in proxy servers.   In *Proceedings of the 7th International WWW Conference*, April 1998.   Available at http://www7.conf.au/programme/fullpapers/1829/com1829.htm.   4

52. Lixia Zhang, Sally Floyd, and Van Jacobson. Adaptive web caching. In *Proceedings of the 1997 NLANR Web Cache Workshop*, June 1997. Available at http://ircache.nlanr.net/Cache/Workshop97/Papers/Floyd/floyd.ps.   4

53. R. N. Zucker and J.-L. Baer. A performance study of memory consistency models. In *Proc. of the 19th International Symposium on Computer Architecture*, pages 2–12, May 1992. 3

A Middleware System Which Intelligently Caches Query Results

Louis Degenaro[1], Arun Iyengar[1], Ilya Lipkind[2], and Isabelle Rouvellou[1]

[1] IBM Research, T. J. Watson Research Center
P. O. Box 704, Yorktown Heights, NY 10598, USA,
{degenaro,aruni,isabelle}@watson.ibm.com
[2] Courant Institute of Mathematical Sciences, New York University,
New York, NY, USA,
lipkind@cs.nyu.edu

Abstract. This paper describes how caching was used to improve performance in the Accessible Business Rules framework (ABR) for IBM's Websphere. ABR is a middleware system which enables application writers to build applications where the time and situation-variable parts of their business logic are externally applied entities known as business rules. The cache significantly reduced the number of queries to remote databases by storing query results. A key problem we faced was how to keep the cache current after database updates. This was solved using data update propagation (DUP). Two enhancements we made to DUP were to employ an update strategy which considers the values of database updates in order to perform intelligent cache invalidations and to automatically compute dependencies using compile and run-time analysis. Our techniques can be applied to other caching environments besides ABR. We show how our cache invalidation strategies perform for applications with database updates having queries similar to those in the Set Query benchmark.

1 Introduction

Caching is critical for improving the performance of many middleware applications. In order for an application to benefit from caching, it must repeatedly use data which is expensive to calculate or fetch. By caching such data, the application only needs to calculate or fetch the data once. Whenever the data is needed after it has been cached, the application can fetch the data from the cache instead of recalculating it or fetching it from a remote location.

This paper describes how caching is used to improve performance in the Accessible Business Rules framework (ABR) for IBM's Websphere. ABR is a middleware system which enables application writers to build applications where the time and situation-variable parts of their business logic are externally applied entities known as business rules.

The techniques we have used for caching in ABR can be applied to other applications as well. The General-Purpose Software cache (GPS cache) which

J. Sventek and G. Coulson (Eds.): Middleware 2000, LNCS 1795, pp. 24–44, 2000.

we used is designed to be plugged into different applications. The GPS cache has also been successfully deployed in a Web server accelerator. The GPS cache has very efficient code for storing data in memory, on disk, or both. It also has optimized support for invalidating objects based on expiration times and for logging cache transactions.

The GPS cache, as applied in ABR, stores the results of queries ultimately made to a database. A key problem with caching query results is determining which queries are affected by changes that occur to the database. In order to keep caches current after database updates, we use an enhanced version of data update propagation (DUP) [2]. A query result may depend on several attributes, and these dependency relationships are represented by an *object dependence graph* (ODG).

DUP has been previously used to cache dynamic Web data. We made two key innovations to DUP for caching in ABR. When attributes change, we consider the old and new values of the attributes in order to determine how to update the cache. This *value-aware* update policy is implemented by annotating edges of ODG's with values based on queries.

When DUP was used for caching dynamic Web data, an application program was responsible for generating the ODG. The second key innovation we made to DUP for ABR was to automatically generate ODG's from the queries within an ABR application.

Our techniques for caching queries in ABR can be deployed in other query-based environments as well. This paper examines how our update policies perform under different update rates for queries similar to those used by the Set Query benchmark.

The remainder of the paper is structured as follows. Section 2 presents an overview of the ABR system which utilized our cache. Section 3 describes the general-purpose software cache used to improve the performance of ABR. Section 4 describes the techniques we used to keep cached data current in the presence of updates. Section 5 discusses the performance of our cache update schemes on applications with queries similar to those in the Set Query benchmark. Section 6 discusses related work. Finally, Section 7 summarizes our main results and conclusions.

2   Overview of the Accessible Business Rules Framework (ABR)

The techniques for intelligent query caching described in this paper were developed to improve performance for the Accessible Business Rule framework (ABR), one of the e-business application frameworks available on IBM's Websphere middleware [4]. ABR enables application writers to build applications where the time and situation-variable parts of their business logic are externally applied entities called business rules. The structure of the application then matches the built in core behavior with variations specified, managed, and applied externally. Customizable services and features (such as web personalization) can also be built on top of ABR. An ABR rule is a persistent object encapsulating code implementing variable behavior as well as a number of attributes defining the business context in which this behavior applies. ABR defines structured exit points from the main application logic which are referred to as *variability points* or *decision points*. The code in decision points selects the particular business logic (rule or rules) to be executed via a query. A query statement is a constraint on the context attributes of the rule objects which reflect the business criteria and context used to select the rules. Some contexts are fixed and represent a static business situation (i.e. not dependent on run-time data). They are captured in ABR with either a simple direct name (e.g. ComputeRateQuote) or a compound name when the context is hierarchical (e.g. Vehicle::isEligible). Some contexts are situational; the correct rules then partly depend on a business context computed or derived at run time (e.g. category of the customer accessing this web page, season of the year). More details on ABR can be found in [19,9].

Externalizing business rules from the main code has invaluable benefits for the clarity of the application and its ease of maintenance. However, this externalization, as first implemented, had significant overhead which largely resulted from querying. Performance profiling clearly correlated the performance bottleneck with the overhead introduced by querying the persistent store (typically a database) where the rules are stored.

Because business rules do not change very often, though much faster than the core of the applications they are attached to, the benefits of caching the query results in that context were apparent. However, because queries were dependent on multiple objects in nontrivial ways, there was a need for a general cache invalidation mechanism to avoid using stale objects when caching of query results was desired.

Figure 1 depicts a Websphere system including an ABR Rule Server. This configuration contains three cloned instances of the Rule Application Server distributed on two different nodes (i.e. a physical system on which the application server runtime is installed). Multiple server instances are defined and active on a node, and each server is a single, multithreaded process. The three rule server instances are in a Rule Server Group (i.e. a named collection of server instances) and are all connected to the same database (IBM's DB2). The Rule Server Group is defined for availability and performance reasons, but client applications see only a a single logical server instance. The figure shows two types of clients: a rule administrator client which would typically be within the same Intranet as the Rule Server and other browser-based clients accessing different rule-based Web applications. Although not shown in the figure, clients may also have caches.

3   Caching Software Used by ABR

Caching is an extremely useful technique for improving performance in a variety of software applications. We have used caching to significantly improve performance of ABR and numerous Web applications [2,17,13]. In order to achieve performance improvements for multiple applications, we have implemented a

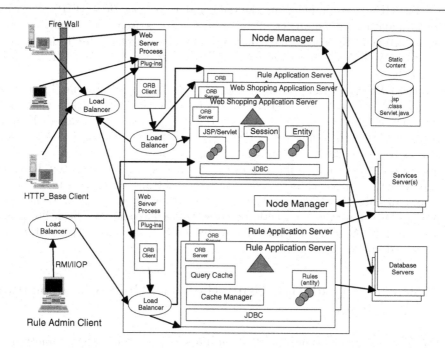

Fig. 1. The ABR architecture

General-Purpose Software cache (GPS cache). The GPS cache is a POSIX-compliant [18] C++ library. In order to use the GPS cache, an application uses the GPS cache application program interface (API) to manage the cache and is linked with the GPS cache library. Applications add, delete, and query the cache via a set of API function calls. The GPS cache has been used to improve performance in ABR and in a Web server accelerator [17].

Software designers without something similar to a GPS cache would have to write their own caches for each application requiring one. This could require considerable extra effort. A hastily designed cache is likely to have inferior performance and less functionality than the GPS cache.

We would like to see the GPS cache or something similar to it become widely available in operating systems or software development libraries. This would allow software developers to easily improve performance via caching. Ideally, a common API for invoking caching functions could be agreed upon.

The GPS cache can be configured to store data in memory, on disk, or both. A common mode of operation is to use disk as secondary storage for cached data which cannot fit in memory due to the presence of other cached data which are accessed more frequently.

Cached objects can have expiration times associated with them after which they are no longer valid. The GPS cache implements an efficient algorithm for invalidating objects based on expiration times.

The GPS cache implements the data update propagation (DUP) algorithm for invalidating cached objects [2,14]. This feature is useful for keeping complex data current in the cache. DUP has proved to be extremely useful for caching dynamic Web pages. Future sections of this paper describe how DUP was used for ABR.

The GPS cache allows cache transactions to be logged in a file. In order to reduce the overhead for logging, the frequency with which buffers containing transaction information are flushed to the file system can be varied. If every transaction record is flushed to disk as soon as it is generated, log files will always be up to date, and no logs will be lost if the cache process fails. The overhead for immediately flushing every transaction log is substantial, however. An alternative approach is to accumulate several transaction records in a buffer before flushing the buffer to disk. This approach has lower overhead. If the cache process fails, however, transaction records which have not yet been flushed to disk are lost. A detailed description of the GPS cache and its performance is contained in [12].

4   Cache Invalidation Using the Data Update Propagation Algorithm

Data update propagation (DUP) determines how cached data are affected by changes to underlying data which determine the current values of the data. For example, if a cache is storing results from querying databases, a method is needed to determine which query results are affected by updates to the database. Such a method could synchronize caches with databases so that the caches do not contain stale data. Furthermore, the method should associate cached data with parts of the database in as precise a fashion as possible. Otherwise, objects whose values have not changed may be mistakenly invalidated or updated from a cache after a database change. Such unnecessary updates to caches can increase miss rates and hurt performance.

DUP maintains correspondences between *objects* which are defined as entities which may be cached and *underlying data* which periodically change and affect the values of objects. In the ABR system, the objects being cached are query results and the underlying data are parts of the database. We have also employed DUP for caching Web data in which the objects being cached are Web pages.

The system maintains data dependence information between objects and underlying data. When the system becomes aware of a change to underlying data, it examines the dependence information which it has stored in order to determine which cached objects are affected. Caches use dependency information to determine which objects need to be invalidated or updated as a result of changes to underlying data.

Data dependencies between underlying data and objects are represented by a directed graph known as an *object dependence graph (ODG),* wherein a vertex usually represents an object or underlying data. An edge from a vertex v to another vertex u, denoted (v, u), indicates that a change to v also affects u.

Node v is known as the *source* of the edge, while u is known as the *target* of the edge. For example, if node $go2$ in Figure 2 changes, then nodes $go5$ and $go6$ also change. By transitivity, $go7$ also changes.

Edges may optionally have weights associated with them which indicate the importance of data dependencies. In Figure 2, the data dependence from $go1$ to $go5$ is more important than the data dependence from $go2$ to $go5$ because the former edge has a weight which is 5 times the weight of the latter edge. Edge weights can be used to quantitatively determine how obsolete a cached object is. In some cases, it is acceptable to keep around a cached object which is not too obsolete. Retaining slightly obsolete versions of cached objects results in better performance than updating or invalidating an object every time it changes.

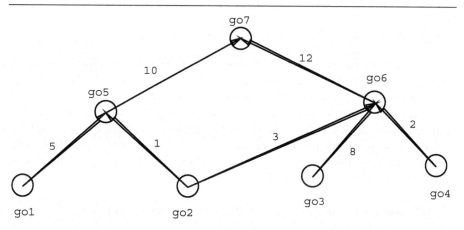

Fig. 2. An object dependence graph (ODG). Weights are correlated with the importance of data dependencies

For most situations in ABR, the object dependence graph is a *simple object dependence graph* having the following characteristics:

- Each vertex representing underlying data does not have an incoming edge.
- Each vertex representing an object does not have an outgoing edge.
- All vertices in the graph correspond to underlying data (nodes with no incoming edges) or objects (nodes with no outgoing edges).
- None of the edges have weights associated with them.

Figure 3 depicts a simple ODG.

4.1   Constructing ODG's from Queries

We now give an example of constructing an ODG from a query. The query:

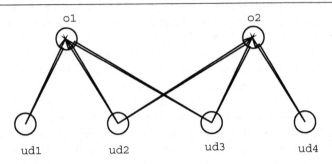

Fig. 3. A simple object dependence graph

```
select A where A.x > 2 and A.x < 9 and A.z = B.y
```

would generate the ODG shown in Figure 4. Each class.attribute term in the query has a corresponding vertex in the ODG. Edges are drawn from each class.attribute vertex to the query result objects it affects.

A key enhancement that we have used in applying DUP to ABR over previous implementations of DUP is the use of annotations of graph edges in order to achieve a *value-aware* invalidation scheme. For example, the annotation of the edge originating from the A.x vertex indicates that if A.x changes, query result Q1 would only be affected if either:

1. A.x was previously between 2 and 9 and is no longer in this range
2. A.x was previously not between 2 and 9 but now is in this range

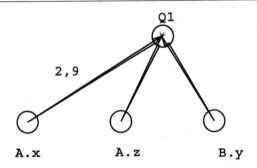

Fig. 4. The ODG resulting from the query *select A where A.x > 2 and A.x < 9 and A.z = B.y*. The annotation of the edge from *A.x* to *Q1* allows more selective invalidations

There are no annotations of edges originating from A.z and B.y. This indicates that value-aware invalidation is not being used for these edges, and any change to A.z or B.y might affect the value of $Q1$.

ODG's constructed in this fashion are stored in the GPS cache. The GPS cache has an efficient algorithm for traversing ODG's in order to locate all cached query results affected by changes to underlying data.

4.2   DUP Implementation in ABR

As mentioned in Section 2, ABR applications contain decision points which query the ABR Rule Server for the collection of rules that presently apply. Once retrieved, these rules are "fired", resulting in the appropriate application behavior at this decision point (note that the "variable behaviors" encapsulated in rules range from constraint checking to derivation of a particular value). Ordinarily, such a query would be pushed down to the persistent store (typically a database). Caching improves performance by avoiding the persistent store in many cases.

We now describe how ABR handles queries extracted from a particular rule-based Web shopping application. This application serves pages to browsers. The pages are created with "holes" which get filled with dynamic content (e.g. URLs or images) according to business rules that are managed externally. The selection of the content is typically situational (e.g. category of the customer accessing this web page, season of the year). We focus below on a particular hole which is to be filled with a product promotion based upon classification of the shopper's status into Gold, Silver, or Bronze. The code interacting with the ABR server issues two queries. The first query, Q1, retrieves classifier rules which when fired return the classification(s) of the current shopper. The second query, Q2, retrieves promotion content rules defined for the current shopper classification as established when firing the classifier rules returned by Q1.

Q1 and Q2 are shown below:

```
Q1 :
    SELECT * FROM RULEUSETABLE WHERE
                CONTEXTID         LIKE 'customerLevel'
        AND     TYPE              LIKE 'classifier'
        AND     COMPLETIONSTATUS LIKE 'ready'

Q2(userClassification):
    SELECT * FROM RULEUSETABLE WHERE
                CONTEXTID         LIKE 'promotion'
        AND     CLASSIFICATION    LIKE $1
        AND     TYPE              LIKE 'situational'
        AND     COMPLETIONSTATUS LIKE 'ready'
```

Q1 is a static SQL statement for which the ODG is completely generated at compile time. Q2 is a parametrized statement ($1 represents a variable whose value isn't known statically) for which all of the ODG, except for annotations of edges dependent on parameters, is generated at compile time. Such annotations are determined at run-time. In our example, the run-time work is limited to setting a parameter and thus introduces minimal overhead. The ODG generated from Q1 and Q2 is shown in Figure 5.

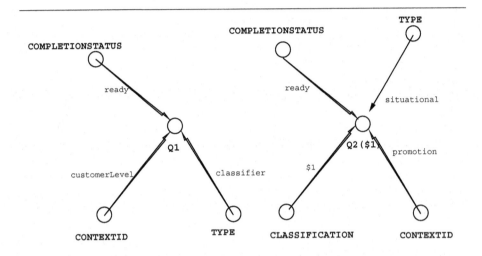

Fig. 5. The ODG generated statically from the two ABR queries given in the text. The actual value of "$1" is determined at run-time

The ABR Server API offers 23 queries for use in ABR-enabled applications. These queries are constraints on all or a subset of the 13 attributes of the rule. All but one of the queries are similar to the ones shown above and are therefore either static or parameterized. ODG's for dynamic SQL statements can be created from scratch by the system at run-time.

Selective invalidation of the cache is triggered by invalidation code in the attribute setter, creation and deletion methods. The code is automatically generated at compile time. Invalidation tokens need to be partially computed at run-time in order to allow value-aware invalidation. Just as with parameterized queries, much of the token is known statically, and the run-time computation just involves determining a parameter, a process which usually introduces little overhead.

Figure 6 shows the invalidation code in a set method. In this example, if a new classifier establishing customer level is introduced (e.g. a Platinum level is created, resulting in new classifier rules of ContextId "CustomerLevel"), Q1 will be invalidated. Cached Q2 query results corresponding to the old classification are still valid and don't need not to be invalidated.

```
void RuleUse.setContextId(String inContextId)
{
// Cache begin invalidate

if (!contextId.equals(inContextId)) {
    cache.invalidate("RuleUse.contextId", inContextId);
}

// Cache end invalidate

contextId = inContextId;
...
}
```

Fig. 6. The invalidation code in a set method

Figure 7 shows how the ABR caching system works for two typical scenarios. The first one is initiated by a client of a rule-enabled application; the second one is initiated by a rule administration client.

In the first scenario, a client invokes the Web Shopping application which runs until it encounters an ABR dynamic content decision point. This triggers a (1) find to be requested for a set of rules to classify the current situation. The query processor attempts a (2) cache lookup to retrieve the requested (3) result from cache and returns it to continue the second phase of the decision point processing for displaying dynamic content based upon classification. Each individual RuleUse returned in the query result is interrogated via (7) get for desired attributes. Then each RuleUse is fired to produce the current classification, which is then used to locate and fire more RuleUses to render the dynamic content. If not found in the cache, then the result is obtained via (4) database access, followed by caching of (3) the result, which causes the appropriate ODG to be constructed. Finally, the result is returned, and processing continues as above. Future requests for the same result will be obtained from the cache until the result is invalidated.

In the second scenario, a rule administration client has already performed one or more queries to obtain collections of RuleUses. Now the administrator decides to change one of the RuleUse attributes via (5) set attribute. This action causes (6) invalidate to occur which will precipitate (10) result discard or update of zero or more dependent query results from the cache, as prescribed by the ODG. A similar invalidation sequence occurs when the administrator decides to (8) create or (9) delete one or more RuleUses.

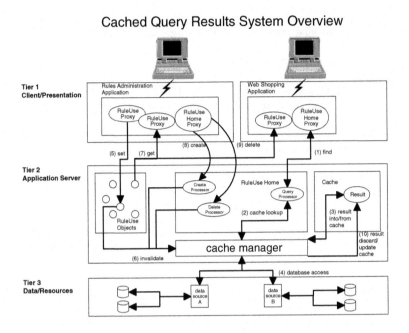

Fig. 7. Typical interaction sequences with the ABR caching system

5   Performance of Query Caching Techniques

DUP with value-aware invalidations can be applied to a variety of query caching environments and not just ABR. In order for DUP to show significant improvement over conventional caching methods, some query results must change over time. Our approach is particularly important for *set queries* which need to refer to data from a potentially large set of table rows for an answer. Such queries are common in document searching, direct marketing, and decision support.

To determine the quantitative benefits of using our caching techniques, we have run a series of experiments designed to evaluate cache hit rates under different workload scenarios using the Set Query benchmark [10]. This benchmark emphasizes set queries and is designed to model queries encountered in document searching, direct marketing, and decision support. The benchmark includes nine different types of queries. All of them are run against a single table of a million entries that has thirteen different attributes. Each attribute spans a different set of values ranging from 2 to 1,000,000 unique values. Queries involve multiple attributes and ranges of values. A complete list of the queries is contained in the Appendix.

The original benchmark designed to test the performance of the database server did not contain any updates. Since we wanted to show how caches that use our invalidation scheme perform under different update rates, we introduced updates into the mix of transactions.

In general, three types of events can potentially invalidate the results of a query. They include change in the attribute value of a particular object, object creation, and object deletion. From the perspective of the invalidation scheme, object creation and deletion are equivalent to resetting all of the object's attributes. We varied two factors: the percentage of update transactions in the total mix and the percentage of attributes updated per update transaction. The attributes to update were chosen uniformly from the set of all attributes, while the update value was chosen uniformly from the full range of possible values for a specific attribute.

The experiments were conducted for three different invalidation policies. The first policy (Policy I) invalidated all cached data after any update. Policy II used the basic DUP algorithm described in [2] to invalidate query results. We refer to this policy as being *value-unaware* because it uses only object dependency information without considering the values involved in the update. Policy III, the *value-aware* policy, uses the enhanced DUP algorithm with edge annotations on the ODG (Figure 4).

We now give an illustrative example of how Policies II and III work for a query of type Q3A. Generalization of this example to the other query types is straightforward. Query Q3A is of the form:

```
Q3A: SELECT SUM(K1K) FROM BENCH
     WHERE KSEQ BETWEEN 400000 AND 500000 AND KN = 3;
```

For each $KN \in \{K100K, ..., K4\}$. Figure 8 shows the ODG for the case where $KN = K100K$. Using Policy II, any update to KSEQ or K100K would cause the cached query result to be invalidated. Using Policy III, the cached query result would only be invalidated if:

1. An update to KSEQ moved it from inside the range of 40000 and 50000 to outside this range or vice versa.
2. An update to K100K changed it from 3 to something else or vice versa.

Figure 9 shows the hit rates for different types of queries. Queries 1, 2A and 2B involve one or two attributes and testing for specific values which explains the high hit rates, especially for the value-aware invalidation scheme. Queries 3A, 3B, 4A and 4B involve ranges of values for combinations of different attributes, and the performance numbers show that our techniques can be effectively used for range type queries as well. Query 5 returns a count of records which fall in cells of a two-dimensional array, determined by the specific values of each of two fields. For this type of query, Policy II and III are equivalent and result in the same hit rates. Finally, queries of Type 6 involve relationships between two different attributes (A.x > A.y), where both Policy II and III are also equivalent. The difference in hit rate for those queries is explained by the presence of additional conditions of the type exhibited in Queries 1,2,3 and 4.

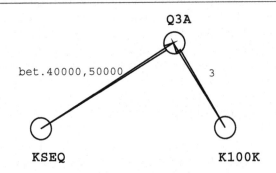

Fig. 8. An ODG resulting from a query of type Q3A

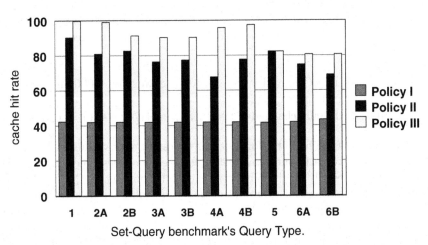

Fig. 9. Cache hit rates for different types of queries. Two percent of the transactions are updates. Each update transaction modifies one attribute

Overall, we see that the value-aware scheme improves performance significantly for single value or range type queries (i.e low selectivity), and both are vastly superior to Policy I.

The experimental results summarized in Figure 10 show the performance of the cache under different update rates. The results demonstrate that that the value-aware policy results in reasonably high hit rates even in the presence of frequent updates.

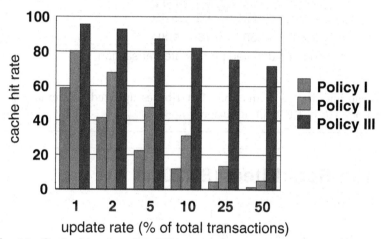

Performance for different update rates (update size fixed at 15%)

Fig. 10. Cache hit rates for different update rates. Update rates are expressed as the percentage of transactions which are updates. Each update transaction modifies two attributes

Figure 11 show the effect of the percentage of attributes modified per update transaction. Here the benefits of using value-aware invalidation increase with the proportion of attributes being updated per transaction.

Figure 12 shows the effect of hot spots. For the data plotted in this figure, 80% of the accesses were uniformly distributed among 20% of the data. The other 20% of accesses were uniformly distributed among the remaining 80% of the data. Updates were uniformly distributed. Only one bar is shown for Policy I because cache hit rates didn't vary much in the presence of hot spots. Policy II and III achieve more significant performance gains in the presence of hot spots than when accesses are uniformly distributed. The advantages of these policies increase with the update rate.

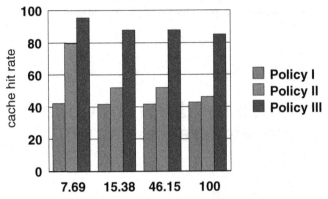

Fig. 11. Cache hit rates as a function of attributes updated per update transaction. Two percent of the transactions are updates

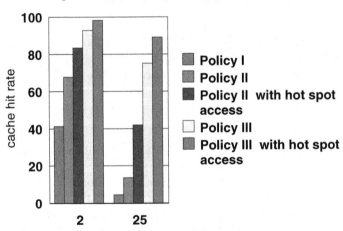

Fig. 12. Cache hit rates in the presence of hot spots. Each update transaction modifies two attributes. Since hit rates for Policy I are similar with and without hot spots, only one bar for Policy I is shown

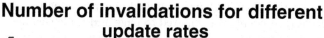

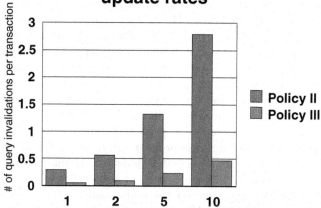

Fig. 13. Average number of query invalidations per transaction as a function of update rate. Update rates are expressed as the percentage of transactions which are updates. Each update transaction modifies two attributes

In our system, the cache runs on one machine, so the number of invalidations per update does not affect the performance of the system in any significant way. However, distributed caches running on clustered servers or even clients might require some coherence traffic for invalidations. Figure 13 shows the number of invalidations per transaction for Policies II and III. Under Policy I, we assume that the cache can be purged completely in a single instruction, so the number of invalidations doesn't affect the coherence traffic. The average number of invalidations per transaction for the two invalidation schemes can be used for predicting the invalidation traffic if a remote cache is used.

5.1   Other Benchmarks

We have also looked at how our cache invalidation techniques affect cache hit rates for the commonly used benchmarks TPC-C and TPC-D [5]. TPC-C models on-line transaction processing applications and has a high percentage of update transactions. We did not see significant improvements in cache hit rates when our methods were applied to TPC-C. TPC-D is a commonly used benchmark which models data warehousing applications. Queries tend to be aggregations of large amounts of data. Updates to such data tend to be done periodically in large batches or not at all. For such situations, having a sophisticated invalidation strategy such as ours is not important.

6   Related Work

A number of previous papers have examined query caching in various contexts. Semantic caching at clients is compared to page and tuple caching in [6]. Clients maintain semantic descriptions of cached data instead of maintaining a list of physical pages or tuple identifiers. Query processing makes use of the semantic descriptions to determine what data are locally available in cache, and what data are needed from servers. Usage information for replacement policies is maintained in an adaptive fashion for *semantic regions,* which are associated with collections of tuples. Maintaining a semantic description of cached data enables the use of sophisticated value functions that incorporate semantic notions of locality for cache replacement. The paper demonstrates advantages that semantic data caching has compared with page and tuple caching. The use of data replication and query caching to improve performance in client-server database architectures is examined in [7]. A system known as DynaMat that dynamically materializes information at multiple levels of granularity in order to match the demand but also takes into account the maintenance restrictions for the warehouse is presented in [16]. DynaMat unifies view selection and view maintenance under a single framework that takes into account both the time and space constraints of the system. Query caching and optimization in distributed mediator systems is analyzed in [1]. A predicate-based caching scheme for client-server database architectures is presented in [15]. A query optimizer which integrates query matching into optimization and generates more efficient query plans using cached results is presented in [3]. The query optimizer features data and pointer caching, alternative cache replacement strategies, and different cache update methods. Caching multidimensional queries using chunks is discussed in [8]. This paper doesn't focus on how to keep cached query results current in the event of updates, however. Loading a cache with query results is discussed in [11]. This paper also doesn't focus on how to keep cached query results current in the event of updates. The use of distributed query result caching to evaluate queries for parallel data mining algorithms is discussed in [20].

The DUP algorithm used to keep caches updated was first deployed for caching dynamic Web data [2]. We have generalized DUP for caching query results which are not necessarily part of Web applications. Previous implementations of DUP require application programs to manually construct object dependence graphs. The DUP implementation for ABR automatically constructs object dependence graphs. We have also extended DUP to employ a value-aware invalidation scheme which improves cache hit rates over previous implementations.

ABR is presented in [19,9]. Neither of these references discuss caching, however.

7   Summary and Conclusions

We have described how caching is used to improve performance in the Accessible Business Rules framework (ABR) for IBM's Websphere. ABR is a middleware system which enables application writers to build applications where the time and situation-variable parts of their business logic are externally applied entities known as business rules.

The General-Purpose Software cache (GPS cache) used by ABR is designed to be plugged into different applications. The GPS cache, as applied in ABR, stores the results of queries ultimately made to a database. A key problem with caching query results is determining which queries are affected by changes that occur to the database. In order to keep caches current after database updates, we use an enhanced version of data update propagation (DUP). A query result may depend on several attributes, and these dependency relationships are represented by an object dependence graph (ODG).

DUP has been previously used to cache dynamic Web data. We made two key innovations to DUP for caching in ABR. When attributes change, we consider the old and new values of the attributes in order to determine how to update the cache. This value-aware update policy is implemented by annotating edges of ODG's with values based on queries.

When DUP was used for caching dynamic Web data, an application program was responsible for generating the ODG. The second key innovation we made to DUP for ABR was to automatically generate ODG's from the queries within an ABR application.

Our techniques for caching queries in ABR can be deployed in other query-based environments as well. We examined how our update policies perform under different update rates for queries similar to those used by the Set Query benchmark.

References

1. S. Adali, K. Candan, Y. Papakonstantinou, and V. Subrahmanian. Query Caching and Optimization in Distributed Mediator Systems. In *Proceedings of ACM SIGMOD*, 1996. 40

2. J. Challenger, A. Iyengar, and P. Dantzig. A Scalable System for Consistently Caching Dynamic Web Data. In *Proceedings of IEEE INFOCOM'99*, March 1999. 25, 26, 28, 35, 40

3. C. Chen and N. Roussopoulos. The Implementation and Performance Evaluation of the ADMS Query Optimizer: Integrating Query Result Caching and Matching. In *Proceedings of the 4th International Conference on Extending Database Technology*, 1994. 40

4. IBM Corporation. IBM Software : Application Development : Component Broker : Overview. http://www.software.ibm.com/software/ad/cb/. 25

5. Transaction Processing Performance Council. Welcome to the TPC Main Page! http://www.tpc.org/. 39

6. S. Dar, M. Franklin, B. Jonsson, D. Srivastava, and M. Tan. Semantic Data Caching and Replacement. In *Proceedings of the 22nd VLDB Conference*, 1996. 40

7. A. Delis and N. Roussopoulos. Performance and Scalability of Client-Server Database Architectures. In *Proceedings of the 18th VLDB Conference*, 1992. 40

8. P. Deshpande, K. Ramasamy, A. Shukla, and J. Naughton. Caching Multidimensional Queries Using Chunks. In *Proceedings of ACM SIGMOD*, 1998. 40

9. D. Ehnebuske, B. Mc Kee, I. Rouvellou, and I. Simmonds. Business Objects and Business Rules. In *Proceedings of the OOPSLA '97 Business Object Workshop*, 1997. 26, 40

10. J. Gray and R. Cattell. *The Benchmark Handbook*. Morgan Kaufmann Publishers, Inc., second edition, 1993. 34

11. L. Haas, D. Kossmann, and I. Ursu. Loading a Cache with Query Results. In *Proceedings of the 25nd VLDB Conference*, 1999. 40

12. A. Iyengar. Design and Performance of a General-Purpose Software Cache. In *Proceedings of the 18th IEEE International Performance, Computing, and Communications Conference (IPCCC'99)*, February 1999. 28

13. A. Iyengar and J. Challenger. Improving Web Server Performance by Caching Dynamic Data. In *Proceedings of the USENIX Symposium on Internet Technologies and Systems*, December 1997. 26

14. A. Iyengar and J. Challenger. Data Update Propagation: A Method for Determining How Changes to Underlying Data Affect Cached Objects on the Web. Technical Report RC 21093(94368), IBM Research Division, Yorktown Heights, NY, February 1998. 28

15. A. Keller and J. Basu. A Predicate-based caching scheme for client-server database architectures. *The VLDB Journal*, 5:35–47, 1996. 40

16. Y. Kotidis and N. Roussopoulos. DynaMat: A Dynamic View Management System for Data Warehouses. In *Proceedings of ACM SIGMOD*, 1999. 40

17. E. Levy, A. Iyengar, J. Song, and D. Dias. Design and Performance of a Web Server Accelerator. In *Proceedings of IEEE INFOCOM'99*, March 1999. 26, 27

18. D. Lewine. *POSIX Programmer's Guide*. O'Reilly & Associates, 1991. 27

19. I. Rouvellou, L. Degenaro, K. Rasmus, D. Ehnebuske, and B. Mc Kee. Externalizing Business Rules from Enterprise Applications: An Experience Report. In *Practitioner Reports in the OOPSLA '99 Companion*, 1999. 26, 40

20. M. Taylor, K. Stoffel, J. Saltz, and J. Hendler. Using Distributed Query Result Caching to Evaluate Queries for Parallel Data Mining Algorithms. In *Proceedings of the International Conference on Parallel and Distributed Techniques and Applications*, 1998. 40

A   Appendix: Queries from the Set Query Benchmark

– A COUNT of records with a single exact match condition, known as query Q1:

```
Q1: SELECT COUNT(*) FROM BENCH
    WHERE KN = 2;
```

(Here and in later queries, KN stands for any member of a set of columns. Here,
$$KN \in \{KSEQ, K100K, ..., K4, K2\}.$$

The measurements are reported separately for each of these cases.)

– A COUNT of records from a conjunction of two exact match conditions, query Q2A:

```
Q2A: SELECT COUNT(*) FROM BENCH
     WHERE K2 = 2 AND KN = 3;
```

For each $KN \in \{KSEQ, K100K, ..., K4, K2\}$
or an AND of an exact match with a negation of an exact match condition: query Q2B:

```
Q2B: SELECT COUNT(*) FROM BENCH
     WHERE K2 = 2 AND NOT KN = 3;
```

For each $KN \in \{KSEQ, K100K, ..., K4\}$
- A retrieval of data (not counts) given constraints of three conditions, including range conditions, (Q4A), or constraints of five conditions, (Q4B).

```
Q4: SELECT KSEQ, K500K FROM BENCH
    WHERE constraint with (3 or 5) conditions ;
```

- A query where a SUM of column K1K values is retrieved with two qualifying clauses restricting the selection.

```
Q3A: SELECT SUM(K1K) FROM BENCH
     WHERE KSEQ BETWEEN 400000 AND 500000 AND KN = 3;
```

For each $KN \in \{K100K, ..., K4\}$
- In addition, Query Q3B captures a slightly more realistic (but less intuitive) OR of several ranges corresponding to a restriction of Zip-codes:

```
Q3B: SELECT SUM(K1K) FROM BENCH
     WHERE (KSEQ BETWEEN 400000 AND 410000
            OR KSEQ BETWEEN 420000 AND 430000
            OR KSEQ BETWEEN 440000 AND 450000
            OR KSEQ BETWEEN 460000 AND 470000
            OR KSEQ BETWEEN 480000 AND 500000)
     AND KN = 3;
```

For each $KN \in \{K100K, ..., K4\}$
The SUM aggregate in queries Q3A and Q3B requires actual retrieval of up to 25,000 records, since it cannot be resolved in index by current commercial database indexing methods; thus, a large data retrieval is assured.
- A query which returns counts of records which fall in cells of a 2-dimensional array, determined by the specific values of each of two fields.

```
Q5: SELECT KN1, KN2, COUNT(*) FROM BENCH
    GROUP BY KN1,KN2;
```

For each $(KN1, KN2) \in \{(K2, K100), (K10, K25), (K10, K25)\}$
- Queries Q6A and Q6B exercise the join functionality that would be needed when data from two or more records in different tables must be combined.

```
Q6A: SELECT COUNT(*) FROM BENCH B1,BENCH B2
     WHERE B1.KN = 49 AND B1.K250K = B2.K500K;
```

For each $KN \in \{K100K, K40K, K10K, K1K, K100\}$

```
Q6B: SELECT B1.KSEQ, B2.KSEQ FROM BENCH B1,BENCH B2
     WHERE B1.KN = 99
     AND B1.K250K = B2.K500K
     AND B2.K25 = 19;
```

For each $KN \in \{K40K, K10K, K1K, K100\}$

Distributed Object Implementations for Interactive Applications *

Vijaykumar Krishnaswamy, Ivan B. Ganev, Jaideep M. Dharap, and
Mustaque Ahamad

College of Computing, Georgia Institute of Technology, Atlanta, GA 30332
{kv,ganev,jaideep,mustaq}@cc.gatech.edu

Abstract. As computers become pervasive in the home and community
and homes become better connected, new applications will be deployed
over the Internet. Interactive Distributed Applications involve users in
multiple locations, across a wide area network, who interact and cooperate by manipulating shared objects. A timely response to user actions,
which can potentially update the state of the objects, is an important
requirement of interactive applications. Because of the inherent heterogeneity of the environment, distributed applications are built using technologies like distributed objects. Central server based implementations
of distributed objects cannot meet the response time needs of interactive users because invocations are always subject to communication latencies. Our approach is to extend these technologies with aggressive
caching and replication mechanisms to provide interactive response time
and to improve scalability. A flexible caching framework is presented,
where objects can be cached in an application specific manner. It provides multiple consistency protocols that enable tradeoffs between the
consistency of a cached object's state at a particular client, and the
communication resources available to the client. At runtime, clients can
specify their consistency requirements via a Quality of Service specification interface that is meaningful at the application level. This paper
presents the caching framework, its implementation and some preliminary performance results.

Keywords: Remote Method Invocation(RMI), Caching, Consistency
Protocols, Timeliness, Quality of Service.

1 Introduction

As computers become pervasive in the home and community and homes become better connected, a new class of applications will emerge in the wide-area
distributed computing environment. We consider applications that we call *interactive distributed applications*. These applications involve users in multiple
locations who interact and cooperate with each other by manipulating shared

---

* This work was supported in part by NSF grants CCR-961937 and a grant from the
Southeastern Universities Research Association.

J. Sventek and G. Coulson (Eds.): Middleware 2000, LNCS 1795, pp. 45–70, 2000.

objects. Examples of such applications include collaborative design, distributed games, and group oriented educational applications.

The system support that will enable interactive distributed applications must address a number of challenges. First, because the applications are interactive, it is necessary to provide quick response to a user's action even when the remote users with whom he or she is interacting with are connected by a high latency communication network. Users must also observe remote actions in a timely fashion, and the timeliness requirements could vary across users due to differences in available resources, or because of the differing roles users play in the application. Finally, users must have a consistent view of the shared objects that are manipulated by them.

Interactive distributed applications can be built using technologies such as distributed objects (e.g, Java RMI, CORBA or DCOM). Although these technologies are attractive for building such applications in heterogeneous environments, they require that shared objects be implemented by common servers, and users must access such an object by remotely invoking it at the server node. Such centralized servers are undesirable because response time for user actions that manipulate the objects cannot be independent of the communication latencies in the system. Although proxy technology that allows a client site to cache an object has been explored[24], many issues that arise when dynamically changing state is cached have not been addressed. We are exploring an approach that retains the ease of programming benefits of distributed objects while providing interactive response time to the invocations made to them. This is done by replication and caching of object state where it is accessed. Consistency requirements arise across the multiple copies that are created when replication and caching are employed. We develop a quality of service (QoS) interface that allows applications to specify their consistency needs. For example, a client can specify timeliness requirements to ensure that it learns of a remote update to a cached object within a certain time period after the write is done.

We present a framework for caching Java distributed objects at client sites. Since we want applications to control the level of consistency of a cached object via a simple QoS interface, we chose BBN's Quality Object (QuO) framework[28] to specify shared state QoS metrics that are are meaningful at the application level. The following are the primary contributions of the paper.

1. We develop a framework that allows clients to invoke cached objects transparently. If a user action results in the invocation of one or more objects, often their cached copies can be invoked and hence response time independent of communication latencies can be provided. The clients only need to specify their consistency needs for the cached object copies, which is done at a high level using QuO's contract object facility.

2. We implement consistency protocols that are particularly well-suited for a heterogeneous environment. In particular, they offer consistency vs. resource usage tradeoffs, and different clients may request different levels of consistency.

3. We develop a prototype system and use it to evaluate the costs of consistency protocols. Using the prototype, we show that invoking a locally cached copy is fifty times cheaper than a remote invocation at the server even in a local area network. We also evaluate the impact of varying timeliness based consistency on the response time of object invocation with a synthetic workload for interactive applications.

Section 2 describes an interactive distributed application and some interesting properties of such applications. Section 3 presents a brief overview of the system architecture. The consistency protocols and their implementation in the caching framework is described in Sect. 4. We present performance results in Sect. 5. Related work is discussed in Sect. 6 and the paper is concluded in Sect. 7.

2   Interactive Applications

Interactive applications process user input and respond to user actions on a continuous basis. We consider distributed interactive applications that involve several users in different locations. The actions issued by one user could impact other users and hence their actions. Many such distributed interactive application scenarios can be developed easily. We briefly describe the AquaMoose[6] system that is currently being developed at the Georgia Institute of Technology. AquaMoose supports an online community of children interested in educational activities. These children can be geographically distributed and can share and manipulate a virtual world representing an ocean. A user can create various entities in the world and entities created by different users may have rich interactions. For example, two fish can race in trajectories defined by their creators and the bigger fish may eat the smaller one. The virtual world visualization at each user is driven by the state of the entities in the world (e.g., fish) including their location and direction of movement. The entity state changes dynamically as the virtual world evolves.

A closer study of AquaMoose and other such applications reveals some very interesting properties. These applications have state that is highly dynamic. Also, for these applications to perform well, the response time to the user actions should be bounded. For example, a delay of more than 100ms in a direct manipulation interface is perceptible. As the delay for these user actions increases, the user satisfaction with these applications worsens. If the participants in these applications are connected via a wide area heterogenous network, network latencies could be much larger than this threshold. One approach for developing such applications is to maintain a replica of the shared application state on the local machine and keep it consistent with the replicas at other participating sites by using consistency protocols. This way invocations made by user actions can be executed with the local copy. Also, different user actions may require different levels of consistency for their replicas. For instance, in the AquaMoose example, if two fish are far away from each other and are controlled by two geographically separated users, the updates made to their attributes (e.g. locations) can be disseminated relatively slowly to the other sites. But if these fish are in close proximity, then the updates made to their locations should be quickly transferred to the other site for acceptable execution behavior of the application. In the following sections we will explore the system support for developing such highly interactive and dynamic distributed applications.

3   System Architecture

In a distributed object system, invocation to a remote object requires communication with the server that implements the object. To provide acceptable performance for user actions in interactive applications, it is desirable that latencies associated with method invocations be minimized. In wide area systems, a major portion of the invocation time can be attributed to network latencies. This overhead can be avoided by locally caching the state of the objects used for building these applications. Caching can be effective in such applications because of two reasons. First, GUI based visualization of the application is driven by the state of the shared objects. Hence, their state is frequently accessed. Second, updates to cached object state can be disseminated periodically, depending on the consistency requirements of the applications. For example, in the AquaMoose application, cached state (or computed state using techniques such as dead reckoning[13]) can be used until a new update for a fish's position is received.

We have developed a caching framework for distributed objects that can transparently cache the objects at the clients that invoke them. The consistency requirements can differ depending on application needs and where the application is deployed. The framework that we have developed addresses this by providing facilities for dynamic specification of consistency protocols and its parameters. The *Quality Objects*(QuO)[28] project offers a framework for creating applications that adapt to different Quality of Services (QoS) offered by the underlying system. Rather than developing a new QoS specification interface from ground up for our caching framework., we chose to use QuO to explore shared state QoS. In the following section we will briefly discuss the support that we have added to QuO for specifying and maintaining the QoS of an object's cached state.

3.1   QuO Framework

QuO is a framework that has been developed to support distributed applications with QoS requirements. QuO provides the ability to specify, monitor, and control QoS in an application. In a traditional CORBA application, a client makes a method call on a remote object through its functional interface. The call is processed by an object request broker (ORB) on the client's host, delivered to an ORB on the object's host, and executed by the remote object. The client sees it strictly as a functional method call. A QuO application adds additional steps to this process for QoS evaluation. As shown in Fig. 1, all QuO application consists of the following additional components.

- A QoS contract between the client and the object. This specifies the level of service desired by the client, the level of service the object expects to provide, operating regions indicating possible measured QoS, and actions to take when the level of QoS changes.
- A smart delegate of the remote object. The delegate provides a functional interface identical to the remote object, but can trigger contract evaluation upon each method call and return. The QoS developer can provide alternative behaviors and a dispatch statement based on the current state of the contract.
- System condition objects interface between the contract and resources, objects and ORBs in the system. These are used to measure and control QoS. They are shown as the polygons with Syscond label in Fig. 1.

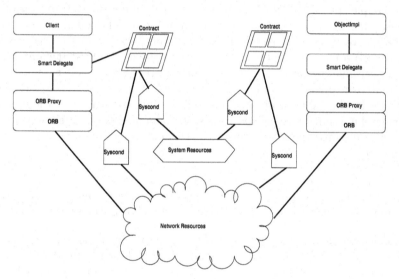

Fig. 1. The Quality Object Framework

A suite of Quality Description Languages (QDL) for describing contracts, system condition objects and the adaptive behavior of objects and delegates is provided by the QuO system. QDL consists of a Contract Description Language (CDL) and a Structure Description Language (SDL). CDL is used to describe the QoS contract between a client and an object. SDL describes the internal structure of delegate's implementations, such as implementation alternatives, and the adaptive behavior of object delegates. The object delegate generator creates client-side and server-side object delegate code from SDL, CDL, and IDL code. When a client calls a remote method, the call is passed to the object's smart delegate instead. The delegate can trigger contract evaluation, which accesses the current values of system condition objects. More details on QuO's architecture can be found in [28].

We show how QuO's contract facility can be used to manage the QoS of the shared state of an interactive application such an AquaMoose. The entities (fish) in the application are exclusively owned by users who create them. The attributes of these entities are only changed by the owners, while other users who are in the vicinity of these entities in the virtual world would like to observe these changes. Thus, one set of users mostly read the shared state of the object while the other one actively modifies it. Hence one set of users (i.e., the owners) would like to have active control of the object, while passive reading would be fine with the rest. These QoS requirements can be mapped onto the QuO's quality of service specification interface (i.e, the contract) as shown in the Fig. 2. A user who modifies the state of a shared object negotiates for the `ActiveUser` QoS region. `PassiveUser` region can be negotiated for by a user who mostly reads the state of the shared object.

A simple contract `CacheStateContract`, specifying the QoS regions of operation for the example application is shown in Fig. 2. The different QoS levels of operation are specified as regions in the contract. This contract is used to continuously monitor the current state of a cached object. `CacheStateContract` has several variable declarations. The variable `ClientExpectedStaleness` is used to specify the current timeliness QoS required by the user. `ClientCallback` is a handle to the callback object. This will be invoked whenever there is a discrepancy between the requested QoS and available QoS. `CacheMonitor` object is used to monitor the attributes of the caching framework that are of interest to the clients.

As shown in Fig. 2, the contract is divided into a series of regions. The users specify the desired region of operation through the variable `ClientExpectedStaleness` (different users can choose different regions).

In this particular contract example, the *negotiated* regions are `ActiveUser` and `PassiveUser`. A writer can choose the `ActiveUser` region while the readers can choose `PassiveUser` as their QoS region of operation. As seen from the sample code fragment in Fig. 2, the specification of a negotiated region triggers a sequence of events. For example, if the user negotiates for the ActiveUser region, then the transition $any-> ActiveUser$ invokes the `setProtocol` method in the `CacheMonitor` object. This sets the consistency policy to the one that guarantees immediate dissemination of the new object values. Transition into `PassiveUser` region will also trigger events as in the `ActiveUser` region.

The available QoS for a resource at a given time is represented by a *reality* region. The QoS in a negotiated region can transition between the reality regions. In our example, the reality regions are `Xclusive`, `Shared` and `Stale` for the `ActiveUser` region. They correspond to the state in which the object is currently cached. `Green`, `Orange` and `Red` are the reality regions for the `PassiveUser` region. They indicate current age (potential staleness) of the cached object. Transition to any reality region triggers handlers in the callback object, which can be used to inform the client application.

```
/*Example Contract that monitors the state of the cached object*/
contract CacheStateContract (
  syscond ValueSC InitializedValueSCImpl ClientExpectedStaleness;
  syscond ValueSC CacheStateSCImpl CacheMonitor;
  callback CacheStateCallback ClientCallback ){
  /* The three names in a syscond variable declaration refer to*/
  /*interface, implementation and the name of the variable respectively*/
   /* Negotiated region -- ActiveUser, Reality regions -- Xclusive, Shared, Stale*/
  region ActiveUser (ClientExpectedStaleness == 0) {
    region Xclusive ( CacheMonitor == 1 ){}
    region Shared ( CacheMonitor==2 ) {}
    region Stale ( CacheMonitor== 3 ) {}
    transition any->Xclusive { synchronous {ClientCallback.nowXclusive();} }
    transition any->Shared { synchronous {ClientCallback.nowShared();} }
    transition any->Stale { synchronous {ClientCallback.nowStale();} }
  }
  /*Negotiated region -- PassiveUser, Reality regions -- Green, Orange and Red */
  /*Timeliness value less than 10 seconds is represented by the reality region green */
  /*Orange represents a timeliness value between 10 and 20 seconds */
  /* Anything over 20 seconds is region Red */
  region PassiveUser( ClientExpectedStaleness >= 1 ) {
    region Green ( CacheMonitor >= 1 && CacheMonitor <= 10000) {}
    region Orange ( CacheMonitor >=10000 && CacheMonitor <= 20000 ) {}
    region Red ( CacheMonitor >= 20000) {}
    transition any->Green { synchronous {ClientCallback.nowGreen();} }
    transition any->Orange{ synchronous {ClientCallback.nowOrange();} }
    transition any->Red{ synchronous {ClientCallback.nowRed();} }
  }
  transition any->ActiveUser {
    synchronous {
       /*Choose a STRICT consistency protocol */
      CacheMonitor.setProtocol(Consistency.STRICT,0);
     }
  }
  transition any->PassiveUser {
    synchronous {
      /*Choose a TIME-BASED consistency protocol */
      CacheMonitor.setProtocol(Consistency.TIMEBASED,ClientExpectedStaleness);
    }
  }
}
```

Fig. 2. A simple contract that exports the current state of the cached object to an application defined *Callback* object

3.2   Adding Caching to the QuO Framework

In order to cache objects locally at client sites and provide consistency guarantees defined by the contract, the framework should address several important issues.

- How and when to cache an object? It should be possible to enable and disable caching dynamically based on locality of access and resource availability.
- How does the system guarantee the consistency QoS requirements of an application? How are the QoS levels associated with the appropriate consistency protocol and its parameters such as the timeliness threshold?
- The consistency actions executed by the protocols depend on the type of access, i.e., if an invocation results in reading of an object's state or the state is also updated. How is read/write access information for the object member functions inferred?

The caching framework developed by us tries to address these issues. Our current prototype has been developed in Java. Some of the objects that make up the caching framework on the server and client sides are shown in Fig. 3.

The caching subsystem on the client side consists of a CConsistencyObject which is responsible for maintaining the consistency of a cached implementation or implementations. The policy for the CConsistencyObject can be specified through a contract. The caching framework is accessed through SmartDelegate that is specifically created by QuO's stub generators for caching purposes. The SmartDelegate has two references to the remote object. The first one is a direct reference to the cached implementation. This is used whenever an invocation is executed with the locally cached implementation. The second one is a *Java RMI* remote object interface to the actual object implementation at the server. This is used to invoke the object at the remote location when caching is disabled. Assume that objects O_1, O_2, ..., O_n are currently cached at the client. The objects, RW_1, RW_2, .., RW_n in Fig. 3 have the read/write access information for all the member functions of the implementations O_1, O_2, ..., O_n. These objects are generated from compile time tags associated with method definitions in the implementations. They are transferred along with object definitions to a client's address space, when the objects are cached for the first time at the client. The caching subsystem has a TransportObject which is used for communication with other clients and the server.

The server side of the framework consists of a SConsistencyObject. This orders the invocations that take place at the server with the ones that are executed with cached copies at client sites. Further, it serves as a rendezvous point for incoming clients, providing them with information to setup their caching framework. If the consistency policy happens to be server based, then SConsistencyObject plays a more active role in keeping the client copies consistent. The ServerDelegate redirects all the direct invocations made on the implementation at the server to SConsistencyObject, thus ensuring consistency when both cached and non-cached invocations are executed. RemoteClassLoader is used by the framework to remotely load the definitions of the implementations O_1, O_2, ..., O_n, the read-write access information objects RW_1, RW_2, ..., RW_n, and other objects that are referred to by the implementations in the server process. `RemoteClassServer` is the server side component that serves the class definition requests from the `RemoteClassLoader`.

The following are sequence of actions that are performed when an invocation $o.m()$, is made on the cacheable object, o.

1. The application invokes the method $m()$ in the `SmartDelegate`.
2. QuO semantics dictate a pre-method and a post-method evaluation of the contract. The delegate does a pre-method evaluation of the contract object to determine the current QoS region of operation. This can be used to determine the current state of the cached object, staleness value, ownership etc.
3. The contract checks with the system condition objects to determine the status of the cached object and if necessary, it also communicates with the callback object.
4. The delegate consults the consistency object to ensure that the cached object is in a consistent state with respect to the invocation. An invocation on the object can either read or modify the object state. Invocation mode can hence be either read or a write. Objects can be cached in shared or in exclusive mode. If the object is not valid or if the invocation mode does not match with the current mode in which the copy is cached, then the delegate asks the consistency object to perform the necessary consistency actions to bring the cached implementation to a consistent state. It also temporarily locks the implementation for the duration of the call thus providing method level atomicity.
5. The delegate invokes the method on the local object copy.
6. The delegate then makes a request to the the consistency object to free up the resources held by the call, to allow any pending consistency actions to be executed.
7. During the post-method evaluation, the delegate once again communicates with the contract to determine the active region.
8. The contract probes the system condition objects for new values. This can be useful for post method operations like starting new consistency actions in the background without blocking the application.
9. The delegate finally returns the results to the application.

4   Consistency Protocols

Consistency protocols ensure that client invocations are executed with local object copies that have consistent state. The consistency of a cached copy of an object can be defined along two dimensions, namely *orderliness* and *timeliness*. The orderliness property specifies how updates to the object done at various nodes are ordered and viewed by read operations. For the convergence of an object's state (e.g., a unique final state of the object is obtained after the execution of the invocations), it is essential that all writes to it are ordered. Weaker

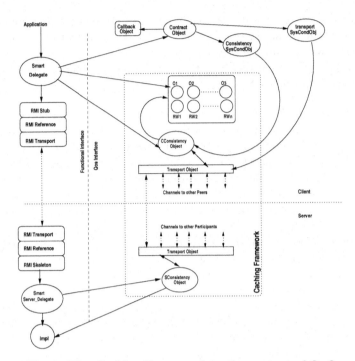

Fig. 3. The Caching Framework in the context of QuO

orderings are possible (e.g., causal[2]) when concurrent writes are rare or other mechanisms can be used to fix divergent object state.

The timeliness property specifies the time interval after which an update to an object must become visible at sites that are caching it. By controlling the timeliness interval, updates can be propagated to remote sites with decreased frequency which reduces the number of consistency messages. These two dimensions of consistency are independent. For example sequential consistency provides strong ordering but no timeliness guarantees.

In this section we describe some of the consistency protocols that we have implemented in the caching framework. The first one is an invalidation based protocol (SC_{inv}) and the second one, LC_{set}, is the local consistency (LC) protocol which is based on invalidation sets. The two protocols present different approaches for maintaining cache consistency. SC_{inv} is an example of a strong consistency protocol that provides a unique ordering for all the writes in the system while providing immediate timeliness for the reads. It is used widely in shared memory systems [8,16] as well as in file systems[9,19,22]. LC_{set} allows the timeliness threshold to be varied, but orders writes as in SC_{inv}. By changing the timeliness threshold for reads, LC_{set} allows the consistency overhead of cached objects to be varied.

Because our framework works at the object level, for the following discussion we consider method invocations on cached objects as writes or reads, depending on whether the method modifies the object or not. We now proceed to describe the details of the SC_{inv} and the LC_{set} protocols.

4.1 Server Based Invalidation Protocol (SC_{inv})

The SC_{inv} protocol allows either a single writer or multiple readers at a given time. We refer to the client that caches an object copy in exclusive mode as its *owner*. The algorithm for this protocol is presented in the Fig. 4.

When a client P_i attempts to read an object copy and experiences a read-miss, it communicates with the server. If no other client caches the object copy in exclusive mode, then the server returns its copy to the client and adds the client to its reader set. Otherwise, the server downgrades the owner's copy to read-only mode and provides P_i the latest copy from the owner. For a client P_i to perform a write operation on an object x, it needs to cache it in an exclusive mode. If x's copy has not been already cached or, if a copy has been cached in the shared mode, P_i experiences a write-miss,[1] forcing it to communicate with the server. The server returns its copy of x, immediately, if the object is currently not cached by other nodes. If x's copies exist at other nodes in shared mode, then the server invalidates all such copies, and returns x to client P_i in an exclusive mode. If another node happens to cache x in an exclusive mode, then the server gets the recent state from that node, invalidates that copy and finally sends the most recent copy to the requester. Although this protocol orders all writes and provides immediate timeliness, its scalability, however, is limited because of the high communication costs of synchronous invalidations for update operations. The protocol presented next attempts to alleviate some of these problems.

4.2 Invalidation-Set Protocol (LC_{set})

The basic LC_{set} protocol was first presented in [1] but we have improved it in a number of ways. For example, we explore the timeliness aspect of consistency in LC_{set}, which was not explored in earlier work. Similar to SC_{inv}, LC based protocols also assume a single writer for an object at a time, but there are some important differences between the invalidation protocol and those based on LC.

The LC_{set} protocol permits control over the timeliness aspect of the consistency of cached objects. The protocol orders all writes that are executed on a group of related objects. However, it allows a writer to update the object state while other clients are accessing the older state of the object in read only mode. The writes are not immediately propagated to all the remote sites that are caching a copy of the object. This delay may result in the reads at the remote sites returning older values of the object state. The protocol guarantees that the reads will never return a value for the object that is older than the timeliness

---

[1] There are two cases: Write-miss and Write-fault. Write-fault occurs when the client does not have a locally cached copy of the object and a write-miss occurs when the local copy is in shared mode and needs to be upgraded. The consistency actions are similar in the two cases and we do not consider them separately.

ACTIONS AT CLIENT P_i :

```
readmiss(x)
    x = x.server.access(x, P_i)
    x.access = read

writemiss(x)
    x = x.server.chngOwner(x,P_i)
    x.access = write

downgrade(x)
    x.access = read
    return (x)

invalidate(x)
    x.state = invalid
    if(x.owner = self)
        return(x)
```

ACTIONS AT SERVER :

```
access(x, P_i)
    if( x.owner ≠ self)
        x = x.owner.downgrade(x)
        readerset.add(x.owner)
        x.owner = self
    readerset.add(P_i)
    return (x)

chngOwner(x, P_i)
    if(x.owner ≠ self)
        x = x.owner.invalidate(x)
        x.owner = P_i
    else
        for each client P_j≠P_i caching x
            P_j.invalidate(x)
        readerset = ∅
    return (x)
```

Fig. 4. Central Server Invalidation protocol (SC_{inv})

threshold specified for the protocol. The client accesses that return older cached copies are serialized before the writes that create the new values. An LC based protocol orders all accesses to related objects by introducing new object copies into the node's cache in a systematic manner. At the time a new object copy is added to a node cache, the node performs local consistency actions to ensure that currently stored copies of shared objects are valid with respect to the information received with the newly fetched object. Such consistency actions are carried out based on meta-data received from the server and require no communication.

The server maintains meta-data about updates to objects and sends it to a client whenever the client communicates with it. There are two cases in which it becomes necessary for the client to communicate with the server. First, all misses require communication with the server. The server does not send messages to invalidate other copies in the system when a write-miss request is received. Instead, information about the object that needs to be invalidated is recorded in an invalSet (for invalidation set). Because invalset stores the identities of those objects which have been updated but the update related consistency messages have not been propagated to the caching clients, invalset continuously evolves as objects are updated and communication takes place between the nodes. We can associate a time with each member of invalset. This can be used to determine when updates to certain objects were done. The functions update and merge in Fig. 5 are used to update an invalset. update adds an object to invalset when the object is updated and also includes the time at which this change to the invalset is made (if the object is already in invalset, then only the time is changed). The merge function merges two invalidation sets by keeping the information about the most recent update to each object listed in the two sets. The newerthan function in the algorithm uses timing information to order updates to an object. The function newWrite is called during each write operation (say on x) to update `invalset` (the entry corresponding to x) to indicate that a more recent update has been done.

ACTIONS AT CLIENT P_i :

```
readmiss(x)
<x, receiveSet> =
          x.server.access(x,Pᵢ)
for each Obj in receiveSet
    if ((receiveSet.state(Obj)
       newerThan invalSetᵢ.state(Obj))
       and (Obj.owner ≠ self))
          Obj.state = invalid
    invalSetᵢ.merge(receiveSet)
    x.state = valid

writemiss(x)
<x, receiveSet> =
          x.server.chngOwner(x,Pᵢ);
for each Obj in receiveSet
    if ((receiveSet.state(Obj)
       newerthan invalSetᵢ.state(Obj))
       and (Obj.owner ≠ self))
          Obj.state = invalid
    invalSetᵢ.merge(receiveSet)
    x.owner = self

downgrade(x)
    x.owner = server
    return <x.value,
                invalSetᵢ>

fetchCopy(x)
    newState[x] = false
    return <x.value,
                invalSetᵢ>
```

```
timelinessCheck(x)
    if (x.owner ≠ self and
       Time_current - x.Time_cached > T)
          x.state = invalid;


newWrite(x)
    if (newState[x] = false)
       invalSetᵢ.update(x)
       newState[x] = true
```

ACTIONS AT SERVER S :

```
access(x, Pᵢ)
    if (x.owner ≠ self)
       <xval,receiveset> =
             x.owner.fetchcopy(x)
       invalSet_S.merge(receiveSet)
       x.value = xval
    return (<x, invalSet_S>)

chngOwner(x, Pᵢ)
    if (x.owner ≠ self)
       <xval,receiveSet> =
             x.owner.downgrade(x)
       invalSet_S.merge(receiveSet)
       x.value = xval
       x.owner = Pᵢ
    return (<x, invalset_S>)
```

Fig. 5. Invalidation-Set protocol (LC_{set})

As shown in the `chngOwner` and the `access` methods in Fig. 5, if a client node's (say P_i's) request for an object x results in the server contacting the owner of the object, and if the server determines that the recent copy of x from the owner is newer than its copy, then this information is used to update the `invalSet`. When P_i's request returns, `invalSet` is piggybacked with the result of the request. The second case when a client communicates with the server is when the client timeliness threshold for an object expires. In this case the client invalidates the cached object copy, but it does not immediately communicate with the server to request the new copy of the object. A subsequent invocation on this object triggers communication with the server.

Read misses are handled as in SC_{inv} except that the owner node's copy is not downgraded. Instead the server gets the latest copy of the object from it and allows it to continue as the owner. Also, the `invalset` is returned to the client as in the case of write misses. When a client receives an `invalset` from the server, it invalidates the cached copies of objects listed in the `invalset` that have been overwritten. Thus, object copies at a client are invalidated only when the client communicates with the server and not when the object is written.

There are two different ways in which the server can maintain the `invalset`. It can either maintain the set on a per-client basis or can have a single `invalset` for all the clients. We chose the latter approach in our protocol to improve scalability and to reduce the computation costs associated with updating each client's `invalset`, when an object is updated. The `invalset` can be viewed as a table of records indexed by the object-id. Each record in the table is the tuple { *modify-bit, epoch*}. A value of 1 for the modify-bit indicates that the object is currently cached in an exclusive mode by a client. If the `invalset` does not contain an entry for an object, then it means that either the object has not been cached by any client or is being cached in read-only mode by all the clients. The epoch number can be considered as a generation identifier indicating how old the object is. The server increments this epoch number whenever it receives a new copy of the object from its current owner. The clients locally maintain an epoch vector for all the objects they cache. Whenever a client receives the invalidation set, it compares the epoch received for each object with its local epoch number and it invalidates the cached copy only if the new epoch number is greater than the local one. This ensures that the client does not invalidate an object if it has the latest copy of the object.

An example of how the `invalset` is used by LC_{set} to ensure ordering is shown in Fig. 6. There are three clients C_1, C_2 and C_3 and the server S. The application has three shared objects, O_1, O_2 and O_3 that get instantiated at the server at the start. The figure also shows the sequence of operations executed at the clients. The table in Fig. 6 gives a possible global serialization order of the operations as provided by the LC_{set} protocol, the consistency action description, the state of the cached objects at the clients before and after the execution of consistency actions, and the value of the epoch numbers in the `invalset` at the clients after the completion of consistency actions. The clients first populate their caches with the initial state of O_1, O_2 and O_3 which are respectively v_1, u_1, and z_1. As seen from the figure, the operation $c_1{:}w(O_1)v_2$ at client C_1 triggers the consistency action $C_1 \rightarrow S$ (from C_1 to S), which grants the exclusive ownership of O_1 to C_1 . It also changes the `invalset` at C_1 and S to *100*, indicating that O_1 has been modified. During the write operation $c_2{:}w(O_2)u_2$ at C_2, the consistency operation $C_2 \rightarrow S$, modifies the `invalset` at C_2 to *[110]*. Since the epoch of O_1 in the received `invalset` is higher than the locally stored epoch, C_2 invalidates its local copy of O_1. During the next operation $c_2{:}r(O_1)v_2$, C_2 experiences a read miss. The consistency action $C_2 \rightarrow S \rightarrow C_1$ brings the new state of O_1 to C_2 from C_1. Also during this transfer, a new invalidation set *110* is propagated to C_1. Again C_1 invalidates O_2 because of the higher epoch number received. When C_3 writefaults during the operation $c_3{:}w(O_3)z_2$, S sends the `invalset` *[110]* to C_3. C_3 invalidates the local copies of O_1 and O_2 because their new epoch numbers are greater than the local epoch values. Subsequent read operations on them experience read misses and the new states of O_1 and O_2 are brought in from C_1 and C_2.

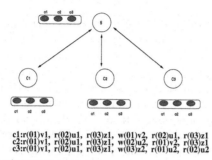

c1:r(01)v1, r(02)u1, r(03)z1, w(01)v2, r(02)u1, r(03)z1
c2:r(01)v1, r(02)u1, r(03)z1, w(02)u2, r(01)v2, r(03)z1
c3:r(01)v1, r(02)u1, r(03)z1, w(03)z2, r(01)u2, r(02)u2

Global Order provided by LC_set	State Before Action				Consistency Actions	New invalidation-set at				State After Action			
	At	O1	O2	O3		C1	C2	C3	S	At	O1	O2	O3
c1:r(01)v1	C1	U	U	U	C1→S	⊡	null	null	⊡	C1	S	U	U
c1:r(02)u1	C1	S	U	U	C1→S	⊡	null	null	⊡	C1	S	S	U
c1:r(03)z1	C1	S	S	U	C1→S	⊡	null	null	⊡	C1	S	S	S
c2:r(01)v1	C2	U	U	U	C2→S	⊡	⊡	null	⊡	C2	S	U	U
c2:r(02)u1	C2	S	U	U	C2→S	⊡	⊡	null	⊡	C2	S	S	U
c2:r(03)z1	C2	S	S	U	C2→S	⊡	⊡	null	⊡	C2	S	S	S
c3:r(01)v1	C3	U	U	U	C3→S	⊡	⊡	⊡	⊡	C3	S	U	U
c3:r(02)u1	C3	S	U	U	C3→S	⊡	⊡	⊡	⊡	C3	S	S	U
c3:r(03)z1	C3	S	S	U	C3→S	⊡	⊡	⊡	⊡	C3	S	S	S
c1:w(01)v2	C1	S	S	S	C1→S	⊡	⊡	⊡	⊡	C1	X	S	S
c1:r(02)u1	C1	X	S	S	None	⊡	⊡	⊡	⊡	C1	X	S	S
c1:r(03)z1	C1	X	S	S	None	⊡	⊡	⊡	⊡	C1	X	S	S
c2:w(02)u2	C2	S	S	S	C2→S	⊡	⊡	⊡	⊡	C2	I	X	S
c2:r(01)v2	C2	I	X	S	C2→S→C1	⊡	⊡	⊡	⊡	C2	S	X	S
c2:r(03)z1	C2	S	X	S	None	⊡	⊡	⊡	⊡	C2	S	X	S
c3:w(03)z2	C3	S	S	S	C3→S	⊡	⊡	⊡	⊡	C3	I	I	X
c3:r(01)v2	C3	I	I	X	C3→S→C1	⊡	⊡	⊡	⊡	C3	S	I	X
c3:r(02)u2	C3	S	I	X	C3→S→C2	⊡	⊡	⊡	⊡	C3	S	S	X

U - Uncached   X - Exclusive   S - Shared   I - Invalid

Fig. 6. An example of Invalidation-set protocol. The figure shows the new invalidation-sets at the three clients C_1, C_2 and C_3 and the server S when the shared objects O_1, O_2 and O_3 are read or written

Clients that do not communicate with the server, will continue to read the copies cached by them. To guarantee that the cached copy of an object does not remain stale for more than the specified timeliness threshold, periodic communication between the client and the server is necessary. This could be ensured in the following two ways.

– The server could maintain a global time clock and after every refresh-period force the clients to invalidate the locally cached copies, by sending them the latest invalset. This is a push based approach.

- In a pull based approach, each client can locally timeout when the communication has not taken place with the server for a certain period of time. The client can then locally invalidate the objects with expired timeliness so that the next invocation on them will result in the client communicating with the server and getting a more recent `invalset`.

We chose the second option to provide clients control over when to fetch the object. Also, this way different clients can choose different timeliness thresholds for their cached copies based on their needs and bandwidth availability. In our implementation, whenever an object state is renewed at the client, it also gets timestamped. The function `timelinessCheck` called during each invocation checks if the time since the last communication with the server for that particular object exceeds its timeliness bound. If so, then the object is marked invalid. This will trigger a `readmiss` or a `writemiss`, forcing the client to communicate with the server to retrieve the latest copy. The client will also receive the `invalset` for the entire set of cached objects.

4.3   Implementation of Consistency Protocols

This section describes some implementation specific issues of the caching framework. In particular, the programming interface to the caching system. The consistency protocols are all implemented as Java classes and have a generic parent class defining methods that are common to all the protocols. The parent class also implements interfaces through which the consistency protocol objects may be accessed from outside. The actual definitions of the methods in these interfaces may be delegated to the consistency policy class implementing a particular consistency protocol. The details are as follows.

Consistency protocols implemented by the consistency objects on both the client and server sides extend the *ConsistencyModel* class. They also implement the *ConsistencyScheme* interface. The *ConsistencyModel* Class has a generic set of routines that are suitable for any consistency protocol. The *ConsistencyScheme* interface defines methods, through which the consistency object is accessed. In addition, the client side consistency object implements the *ConsistencyScheme_Client* interface and the server side object implements the *ConsistencyScheme_Server* interface. These interfaces contain methods specific to the client side and the server side of the caching framework.

The *ConsistencyModel* is an abstract class. It contains definitions for the methods that are common to all the consistency protocols and abstract methods which are more protocol specific. Some of these methods are the following.

- *setProtocol* - It is used to set the consistency policy of the caching framework.
- *fetchLatestCopy* - It ensures that the reference to the cached copy is in a valid state. It is an abstract method, whose definition is delegated to a particular consistency protocol object.
- *takeActions* - It is invoked when a request for a consistency action is received from other consistency objects at server or at other clients. The actual definition of the method is delegated to the protocol object.

The *ConsistencyScheme* interface provides access points through which the caching framework can be accessed from the outside (e.g. delegate). It declares the following two functions:

- *guard*- It is invoked before the actual method invocation. This method locks the object so that no consistency related actions are performed on the object during the execution of the method.
- *relax* - It is invoked after the execution of the method is completed. It releases the lock acquired during the guard method .

We chose an approach in which the framework provides synchronized access to object state rather than delegating it to the object implementor. By allowing the framework to control synchronization, we can allow invocations that only read the object state to execute simultaneously at a node, increasing parallelism.

The *ConsistencyScheme_Client* interface declares the method *cacheObject*, which is called once when the object is cached for the first time at the client node. The method adds the object to the set of objects cached at the client. The *ConsistencyScheme_Server* interface declares the *cacheObject* method which is called once when an object is exported at the server node.

5   Performance

So far we have discussed the architecture of the caching system and the consistency protocols that have been implemented to ensure that operations are executed with consistent object state. The goal of this section is to experimentally evaluate the performance of the caching system to quantify the improvements that can be achieved by caching, and the impact of the consistency protocols on the performance of caching. We first measure the costs associated with the basic operations in the system such as the overhead imposed by the caching framework to execute invocations that read or write the state of the invoked object. This is followed by a more detailed evaluation of the system with a synthetic workload derived from attributes of an interactive distributed application.

The experiments were conducted on a cluster of 248 MHz Sparc Ultra-30's connected by a 100 Mb Ethernet. The machines were all equipped with 128 MBytes of memory. The Java virtual machine used was Java2 from Javasoft and we used it with the just-in-time (JIT) option enabled. There were no other applications running on the machines when the experiments were conducted and hence the numbers generated were repetitive. We ran each of the experiments three times and the numbers presented here are averaged across multiple runs and over multiple clients. It was difficult to generate numbers that were repetitive for a wide-area configuration. This was primarily due to our lack of control on the network. Because of this reason, we are only presenting the measurements for the local-area environment in this paper. In the future, we plan to repeat these with widely distributed sites connected by the Internet, possibly using an Internet emulation testbed.

In our experiments clients invoked an object O implemented by the server. The definition of O has two member functions: *read()*, and *write()*. The read method has a null body while the write method increments the state of a shared counter. Since little time is spent in the execution of the methods, the average invocation time obtained in the experiments is a direct measure of the communication and computation costs associated with the caching framework.

5.1 Basic Performance of Caching

Object caching enables a remote invocation to be completed locally when the cached object is in a valid state and in proper mode. If the cached copy is not consistent, the invocation will result in the client communicating with the server to fetch the current copy which could generate one or more messages between the server and clients. To measure the cost of completing a remote invocation in different situations, we decided to measure the cost of invocations in the following cases.

- The object is invoked remotely at the server without caching it locally. Thus, this will be the base case where the existing Java RMI framework is used to make the invocation at the remote server.
- The object is cached locally and is in a valid state and correct mode. This invocation is local and will not result in any communication with the server. This is the best case for caching.
- The object is locally cached but is not in a valid state, but a valid copy can be found at the server. This will result in the client communicating with the server, fetching the new copy from it.
- The object is locally cached and is not in a valid state. A valid copy can be found at some other remote client C_n. This will result in the client communicating with the server followed by the server communicating with C_n, which will return a copy via the server to the requesting client.
- The object is cached locally in shared mode and the invocation needs an exclusive copy. The client has to communicate with the server, and the server with other remote clients depending on the consistency protocol.

Table 1. Comparison of the time per invocation in milliseconds averaged over 10,000 invocations. The invocations were executed at the server and with locally cached copies. The size of the object was 1024 bytes and a group of 8 related objects were used

Invocation Execution	Invocation Time in milliseconds
At remote server	1.244
At locally cached copy	0.025

Table 2. Comparison of time per invocation in milliseconds averaged over 10,000 invocations. The invocations were executed at the cached object with a write-miss resulting in the new state being fetched from the server. The size of the object was 1024 bytes and the group had 8 objects. The *Reader-set* size corresponds to the number of other clients in the system that had the object cached in the shared state

Consistency actions for Invocation Execution	Protocol	Number of Clients caching the object			
		0	2	4	8
With write-miss and	SC_{inv}	3.286	5.631	8.124	13.532
copy fetched from server	LC_{set}	3.575	3.575	3.575	3.575

Table 1 compares the costs of executing an invocation at the server and on the locally cached copy. Eight objects, each of size 1024 bytes were used in the evaluation. The average cost of a local invocation is about 25 microseconds, while it takes 1.244 milliseconds for the remote execution to take place at the server. Thus, there is a fifty fold improvement in performance if the execution can be done locally. Table 2 compares the costs of similar actions, for cached invocations when SC_{inv} and the LC_{set} protocols are employed for consistency maintainence. For a reader to fetch a new copy from a writer via the server, it costs about 3.575 milliseconds when using the LC_{set} protocol. If every two out of three invocations can be executed locally, then the total time spent on the invocations is about 3.625 milliseconds, while the three remote invocations at the server require 3.732 milliseconds. So for a hit-ratio greater than 67%, the performance of LC_{set} is better than executing the invocations at the server.

Table 2 also shows an interesting difference in the two consistency protocols. As the size of the reader-set increases, there is an increase in the invocation time for SC_{inv}, while it does not change for the LC_{set} protocol. This is because SC_{inv} allows either one exclusive owner or multiple shared readers to co-exist. Therefore, before it can grant access to an exclusive copy for a write-miss, it has to invalidate all the clients of the reader-set. The LC_{set} allows one exclusive writer and multiple shared readers to co-exist at the same time. A request for write-miss does not result in any immediate invalidation messages from the server to the reader clients. Hence the invocation cost does not vary with the number of clients caching the object in the shared mode.

Table 3 compares the invocation cost for the LC_{set} protocol for objects of different sizes (8 bytes and 1024 bytes). There is a 20% increase in the invocation time when the size of the invalidation-set is increased from 1 to 16 objects. This can be attributed to the additional computation and communication costs involved in marshalling and unmarshalling larger invalidation-set objects.

Table 3. Time per invocation in milliseconds averaged over 10,000 invocations for the LC_{set} protocol

Consistency actions for Invocation Execution	Object Size in bytes	Invalidation-Set Size in objects				
		1	2	4	8	16
With read-miss and	8	2.902	2.961	2.900	3.112	3.525
copy fetched from server	1024	3.296	3.309	3.401	3.575	3.955
With read-miss and copy fetched	8	5.477	5.482	5.488	5.830	6.421
from remote client via the server	1024	5.859	5.952	5.959	6.328	6.912

5.2 Workloads

Workload Modeling The cost of basic operations in the caching framework clearly reveals that significant improvements can be achieved if invocations are executed with cached copies. However, locality of access, which determines when the cached copies can be used, depends on the behavior of the applications. Hence, it is desirable to evaluate the system using actual distributed applications. Unfortunately currently available traces are mostly from the distributed file system [5,9,10,19,22] and the world-wide web [20,21] domains. The read/write sharing patterns for these are more coarse grained and often there is a single writer for a given object. Hence we chose not to use these traces to evaluate our system. Since interactive applications can involve actual users and their behavior can depend on response time for their actions, it is difficult to create real traces [4]. We decided to use synthetically generated workloads based on important parameters of interactive applications like Aquamoose described earlier. Our synthetic workload can be described by the following parameters. The values associated with the parameters below were those used in generating the traces.

Number of Objects: There are N shared objects O_1, O_2, ..., O_n each of size S_1, S_2, ..., S_n bytes that are governed by the consistency protocol. They are all instantiated at the same server. In our experiment we assigned a value of 32 to N and all of S_1, S_2, ..., S_n were assigned a value of 64.

Number of Clients: There are C clients that can make invocations on the objects. We assigned a value of 8 to C.

Number of Invocations per Client: Each client makes K invocations. K was chosen to be 10,000.

Read Frequency: Assuming that interactive applications are visual and require frequent screen updates, we generated read request to the objects once in every 30 milliseconds.

Write Frequency: The writes in these applications may be because of user actions or because of movement of autonomous entities (e.g., movement of fish in a predetermined trajectory). We also assumed that a user does not recognize events happening in a time period less than 100ms. So the lower limit for the

time between writes is 100ms (for autonomous entity movement) and the higher
limit was fixed at 3 seconds (for user actions). The writes were generated at
random with the above mentioned higher and lower time bounds.

Ownership: The ownership was assumed to be static for this trace. This is a
reasonable assumption because in many distributed applications like the virtual
world, the changes to object state are made only by the users who created them.

We use a trace generated based on the above parameters to evaluate the two
protocols.

Performance Evaluation The performance metrics that are of interest are
the average invocation time and the number of cache misses and server requests.
The experiments were conducted in the same lab environment in which the basic
benchmark tests were done.

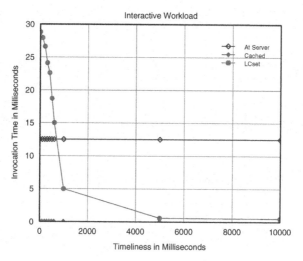

Fig. 7. The invocation time averaged over 10000 invocations with 8 clients and
32 objects. The invocation time for the method execution at the server is 12.52
milliseconds while the invocation time for the method execution on the local
copy is 25 microseconds

Fig. 7 shows the average execution times for invocations at the server, locally
cached invocation and local invocation with the LC_{set} protocol, for different values of the timeliness threshold. The average invocation time for execution at the
server is 12.52 milliseconds. This is different from the micro-benchmark results
and can be explained by the increase in server load because of 8 clients operating simultaneously while the average invocation time for a locally cached copy
is only 25 microseconds. The invocation time for the LC_{set} protocol is an exponentially decreasing curve. It is about 28.84 milliseconds when the timeliness

threshold is 0 and reduces to about 746 microseconds as the timeliness threshold value is increased to 5 seconds. This can be explained from the way the protocol works. The clients invalidate their local copies whenever they receive an invalidation-set from the server or whenever the timeliness threshold expires. When the timeliness threshold is set to 0, the object copy expires as soon as it is locally cached. Hence all the invocations find the copy invalid, leading to consistency actions. This accounts for higher method execution times. However, when the timeliness threshold is increased, such invalidation and the resulting communication decreases The system initially invalidates the objects when it receives the invalidation-sets. As the steady state is reached, the cache gets populated with objects in valid state. Thus, invalidation frequency due to the receipt of invalidation-set decreases and beyond a point, the invalidations are only due to the expiration of the timeliness threshold. This explains why the number of cache-misses decrease as the timeliness threshold is increased, leading to much smaller execution times for the invocations.

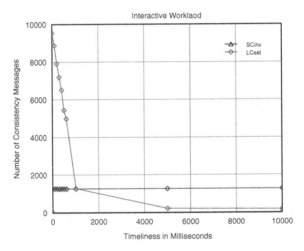

Fig. 8. The number of cache misses for 10000 invocations with 8 clients and 32 objects. The cache misses generated for the SC_{inv} protocol is 1267

Fig. 8 shows the number of cache misses for the protocols SC_{inv} and LC_{set}. The number of consistency messages generated by the SC_{inv} protocol does not depend on the timeliness value. While for the LC_{set} protocol, it is an exponentially decreasing curve. At a timeliness threshold of 0, every invocation other than writes (because of the exclusive ownership assumption) will result in a cache-miss for reasons explained earlier. This is why we experience 9532 cache misses for the 10000 invocations executed during the experiment. As timeliness threshold is increased, a lot more invocations are completed with the cached object and hence the cache misses decrease.

6   Related Work

Rich interactive distributed applications like *Spline*[3], *Aquamoose* [6] and other virtual reality (VR) applications have been developed in the recent past which could involve large numbers of geographically distant users interacting in real time. In addition to interacting with each other, users also interact with computer simulations which range from the very simple (e.g., a revolving door) to the very complex (e.g., a human-like robot). These applications also allow users to make temporary and permanent modifications and extensions to the environment while they are running, so that the content of an environment can dynamically change. For reasons of efficiency, consistency and scalability, these applications are built with abstractions provided by a distributed communication infrastructure. Some examples of such infrastructures include the *MR* toolkit [26] and the *dVS* system [12]. They assume a client-server topology, where a client is represented by a collection of processes. It uses message passing paradigm to disseminate information between the participants. Any change in the state at a client is propagated by the client's *network process* to every other client's network process. *DIVE* [15] uses shared memory paradigm and uses object abstractions for shared state. An ownership protocol and multicast mechanisms are used to maintain the consistency of the state. *SIMNET* [7] and *NPSNET* [18] are used to develop military battlefield simulations. They use a combination of shared memory and message passing mechanisms. They use best-effort broadcast or multicast to communicate user actions to remote sites. Scalability is achieved by locally maintaining a copy of remote state and simulating remote actions through one of the allowed set of behaviors of the application. *High Level Architecture (HLA)* [11] is a system where messages across nodes can be ordered at the receiver using one of the following ordering types: receive order, priority order, causal order, time stamp order etc. Our distributed object caching system also provides a platform that can be used by the applications mentioned earlier. But it differs from them by allowing clients to specify their timeliness constraints through a high level QoS interface. By separating out the QoS interface from the functional part of the application, our system can execute the same application program at different locations, but in different QoS domains. For example, different clients can define different timeliness thresholds based on their need and resources available to them. At the same time, the system can provide consistency via its consistency protocols. It also tries to optimize communication overhead based on consistency policies used. The system can adaptively change its timeliness requirements at runtime based on available resources and application needs.

Commercial ORBs like *Orbix*[24] from Iona and *Visigenic*[23] from Borland have a proxy technology that can be used to add caching to their remote object framework. These are called *smart proxies* in Orbix and *interceptors* in Visigenic. We could have used these systems but we chose QuO because QuO proxies are generated from a high level QoS description language. Thus, it was easy to add shared state QoS to the QuO framework. Other object systems such as *Globe*[25] have multiple physical copies of an object residing on different machines. Clients may contact any copy to get methods executed without knowing the internal structure and protocols used by the object implementation. This scheme allows different objects to use different algorithms for data partitioning, replication, consistency, and fault tolerance, in a way transparent to the users. We focus on object caching and the consistency aspects of the cached copies in a QoS framework.

A lot of consistency related work has been done in the areas of distributed shared memory, distributed file systems and the world-wide web. Consistency protocols for the web are described in [14,17,27]. Weak consistency protocols based on time to live (TTL) for timeliness are presented in [14]. Although these weaker consistency protocols provide better scalability and enhance system performance, their notions of consistency are too weak to support interactive applications. Stronger notions of consistency based on invalidation and polling for the web are presented in [17]. Different distributed file systems like *XFS* [9] employ caching and replication to enhance performance. The invalidation based consistency protocols used by them disallow the co-existence of readers and writers and are more expensive to implement. The LC_{set} protocol described in this paper provides strong consistency but allows readers and a writer to co-exist, and explicitly addresses the timeliness dimension of consistency, providing consistency vs. cost tradeoffs.

7   Conclusions

In this paper we have presented the architecture of an object caching system that transparently caches objects. The framework is configurable and multiple consistency protocols are used to govern the state of the cached objects based on application requirements and resource availability. The high level specification of the consistency requirements is done through the Quality Object's Quality Description Languages. We also presented the details of the caching framework for the specification and governance of the consistency QoS requirements.

We have implemented two consistency protocols, a server based strict consistency protocol, SC_{inv} which provides a strict serialization order for all the reads and writes in the system and the LC_{set} protocol which provides a more relaxed ordering for reads depending on the value of the timeliness threshold. The LC_{set} protocol provides better response time for invocations, almost as small as an invocation on a local object, for interactive workloads, for a timeliness threshold value greater than 1 second. Also, the number of consistency messages needed for the LC_{set} protocol is much lower than the the SC_{inv} protocol for higher timeliness thresholds.

In the future we would like to develop additional consistency protocols for the framework providing different levels of guarantees based on the timeliness and the ordering requirements. Also, we would like to develop synthetic workloads for interactive applications. Actual experiments and simulations driven by the workloads will allow us to perform a detailed evaluation of the protocol implementations. We are also interested in developing some applications with which we can drive the framework, to determine the effectiveness of the system.

References

1. M. Ahamad and R. Kordale. Scalable Consistency Protocols for Distributed Services. *IEEE Transcations on Parallel and Distributed Systems*, 1999. 55
2. M. Ahamad, G. Neiger, J. E. Burns, P. W. Hutto, and P. Kohli. Causal Memory: Definitions, Implementation and Programming. *Distributed Computing*, 9:37–49, 1995. 54
3. D. W. Anderson ,J. W. Barrus, J. W. Barrus, J. W. Howard, C. Rich, C. Shen, and R. C. Waters. Building Multi-User Interactive Multimedia Environments in MERL. *IEEE Multimedia*, 2(4):77–82, 1995. 66
4. S. Bhola and M. Ahamad. Workload Modeling for Highly Interactive Distributed Applications. Technical Report GIT-CC-99-2, College of Computing, Georgia Institute of Technology, 1999. 64
5. M. Blaze. *Caching in Large-Scale Distributed File Systems*. PhD thesis, Princeton, 1992. 64
6. A. Bruckman. Community Support for Constructionist Learning. In *Proc. of the 7th ACM Conference on Computer Supported Cooperative Work*, 1998. 47, 66
7. J. Calvin, A. Dickens, B. Gaines, P. Metzger, D. Miller, and D. Owen. The SIMNET Virtual World Architecture. In *Proceedings of the IEEE VRAIS*, pages 450–455, 1993. 67
8. J. Carter, J. Bennett, and W. Zwaenepoel. Implementation and Performance of Munin. In *Proceedings of the Thirteenth Symposium on Operating Systems Principles (SOSP)*, pages 152–164, October 1991. 54
9. M. D. Dahlin, R. Y. Wang, T. E. Anderson, and D. A. Patterson. Cooperative Caching: Using Remote Client Memory to Improve File System Performance. In *Proc. of ACM SIGMETRICS*, 1994. 54, 64, 67
10. J. H. Howard. et.al. Scale and Performance in Distributed File Systems. *ACM Transactions on Computer Systems*, Feburary 1988. 64
11. R. M. Fujimoto and R. M. Weatherly. Time Management in the DoD High Level Architecture. In *Proceedings of the Tenth Work-shop on Parallel and Distributed Simulations*, pages 60–67, 1996. 67
12. S. Ghee. DVS: A Distributed VR Systems Infrastructure. In *ACM SIGGRAPH Course Notes*, 1995. 66
13. R. Gossweiler, R. J. Laferriere, M. L. Keller, and Paush. An Introductory Tutorial for Developing Multiuser Virtual Environments. *Presence: Teleoperators and Virtual Environments*, 3(4), 1990. 48
14. J. Gwertzman and M. Seltzer. World-Wide Web Cache Consistency. In *Proc. of the 1996 USENIX Technical Conference, Jan 1996*, 1996. 67
15. O. Hagsand. Interactive Multiuser VES in the DIVE System. *IEEE Multimedia*, 1996. 67
16. K. Li and P. Hudak. Memory Coherence in Shared Virtual Memory Systems. *ACM Transactions on Computer Systems*, 1989. 54
17. C. Liu and P. Cao. Maintaining Strong Consistency in the World-Wide Web. In *Proc. of the International Conference on Distributed Computing Systems*, 1997. 67
18. M. R. Macedonia, M. Z. Zyda, D. R. Pratt, P. T. Barham, and S. Zeswitz. NPSNET: A Network Software Architecture for Large-Scale Virtual Environments. *Presence*, 3(4):265–287, 1990. 67

19. M. N. Nelson, B. B. Welch, and J. K. Osterhout. Caching in Sprite File Sytem. *ACM Transactions on Computer Systems*, 1988. 54, 64

20. P. Cao. *A Collection of Web Proxy/Client Traces.* http://www.cs.wisc.edu/ cao/icache/proxytrace.html. 64

21. P. Cao. *A Collection of Web Server Traces.* http://www.cs.wisc.edu/ cao/icache/trace.html. 64

22. R. Sandberg, D. Boldberg, S. Kleiman, D. Walsh, and B.Lyon. Design and Implementation of Sun Network Filesystem. In *Proc. of the Summer Usenix Conference*, 1985. 54, 64

23. Borland Technologies. *The VisigenicC++ Programmer's Guide.* http://www.visigenic.com/techpubs/books/vbj/vbj40/framesetindex.html. 67

24. Iona Technologies. *The Orbix C++ Programmer's Guide.* http://www.iona.com/products/orbix/manuals/index.html. 46, 67

25. M. van Steen, P. Homburg, and A. Tanenbaum. Globe: A Wide-Area Distributed System. *IEEE Concurrency*, pages 70–78, January-March 1999. 67

26. Q. Wang, M. Green, and C. Shaw. EM - An Environment Manager for Building Networked Virtual Environments. In *Proceedings of IEEE VRAIS*, 1995. 66

27. K. Worrell. Invalidation in Large Scale Network Object Caches. Master's thesis, University of Colarado, 1994. 67

28. J. Zinky, D. Bakken, and R. Schantz. Architectural Support for Quality of Service for CORBA Objects. In *Theory and Practice of Object Systems*, pages 41–49, 1997. 46, 48, 49

MIMO – An Infrastructure for Monitoring and Managing Distributed Middleware Environments[*]

Günther Rackl, Markus Lindermeier, Michael Rudorfer, and Bernd Süss

LRR-TUM
Lehrstuhl für Rechnertechnik und Rechnerorganisation, Institut für Informatik
Technische Universität München, 80290 München, Germany
rackl@in.tum.de

Abstract. This paper presents the MIMO MIddleware MOnitoring system, an infrastructure for monitoring and managing distributed, heterogeneous middleware environments. MIMO is based on a new multi-layer-monitoring approach for middleware systems, which classifies collected information using several abstraction levels. The key features of MIMO are its openness, flexibility, and extensibility. MIMO's research contribution is to enable easy integration of heterogeneous middleware platforms, to be suited for large classes of online tools covering both monitoring and management functionality, and therefore to be applicable for tools supporting the complete software lifecycle. In addition to the core MIMO system we outline exemplary instrumentation techniques for integrating CORBA and DCOM platforms, and present the MIVIS visualization tool demonstrating the features of the MIMO infrastructure.

1 Introduction and Overview

Developing and maintaining large distributed software environments is one of the major challenges in computer science at the time. The usage of middleware platforms abstracting from diverse and heterogeneous computing platforms is a common approach to handle the complexity of such systems. Middleware platforms include general purpose distributed object-computing environments [1] like CORBA or DCOM, message-oriented middleware (MOM), transaction processing monitors (TPMs), or meta-computing infrastructures like Globus [2].

A main drawback deploying all kinds of these platforms is the lacking support for online tools which allow to monitor and manage the environments, especially when various types of middleware products are combined within one computing environment. Monitoring and management tools should cover the whole software lifecycle, i.e the development and the deployment phases of middleware-based software products.

In the past, several monitoring systems have been developed for specific kinds of middleware products [3,4]. But, most systems are limited to one single type

---

[*] Research supported by German Science Foundation (DFG) SFB 342 (TP A1).

J. Sventek and G. Coulson (Eds.): Middleware 2000, LNCS 1795, pp. 71–87, 2000.

of middleware platform, only concentrate on specific aspects of these platforms, and are therefore only suited for a small class of tools.

This paper presents the MIMO MIddleware MOnitor infrastructure, a monitoring and management system that addresses the following issues:

- *Support for the whole software lifecycle:* In order to be able to build tools for the complete software lifecycle, information on all abstraction levels of the system has to be gathered. This includes low-level information, e.g. needed for debugging purposes during software development, as well as high-level information for application management issues during software deployment. MIMO solves this problem by introducing a multi-layer-monitoring model that is used to classify data collected from the observed system.
- *Integration of monitoring and management functionality:* Supporting the complete software lifecycle allows us to use a single system for monitoring and management tasks; as the term "monitoring" is mostly used for low-level aspects, and "management" rather for high-level administrative tasks, the multi-layer-model makes it possible to build both kinds of tools only using MIMO[1].
- *Integration of heterogeneous middleware platforms:* MIMO is designed to enable monitoring of different middleware platforms simultaneously. This is done by introducing a generic interface for middleware platforms to MIMO, such that heterogeneous systems can be easily integrated. As interoperable applications are getting more and more popular (see e.g. CORBA-COM bridges), the ability to observe heterogeneous systems simultaneously is one of the key features for future monitoring systems.

As requirements for monitoring and management tools are very diverse, especially when allowing to observe heterogeneous components simultaneously, there is no common definition of tool functionality or behavior. Therefore, the MIMO approach is based on defining a general infrastructure, i.e. a *framework* [5] for tools. This framework consists of basic monitoring system components which offer defined and generic interfaces both for tools and middleware platforms. Furthermore, access patterns defining how to make use of the components and interfaces are defined. This combination of components and patterns makes it possible to keep MIMO very generic and configurable, and thus allows to use it for very diverse purposes without altering the core MIMO implementation.

This paper is organized as follows: Section 2 introduces the multi-layer-monitoring approach on which MIMO is based. Section 3 presents the core MIMO infrastructure, section 4 explains how information can be gathered from various middleware platforms, and section 5 presents the MIVIS visualization tool, an example for a fundamental tool making use of MIMO. Section 6 outlines an example scenario showing the usage of MIMO and MIVIS, and section 7 finally summarizes and concludes the paper.

---

[1] In the following, we will not distinguish between the term "monitoring" and "management" anymore; we will mostly use the term "monitoring", which shall cover both classes of systems and tools.

Related Work

Basic work on monitoring systems has be done in the OMIS project [6]. However, OMIS is mainly aimed at lower-level monitoring of parallel applications using a message-passing communication paradigm.

For CORBA, there are several management systems, which are mostly commercial products tied to specific CORBA implementations. These include e.g. ObjectObserver by Black&White Software, CORBA-Assistant by Fraunhofer Institute, or IONA's OrbixManager. An overview of these systems can be found in [4]. The main drawback of all these products is the lacking genericity which allows to deal with heterogeneity in a way MIMO does, because they are mostly tailored to one specific middleware product. Moreover, all of them only allow to monitor the server-side of CORBA applications, client-side activity cannot be observed explicitly.

2 Multi-Layer-Monitoring

This section describes the system model and multi-layer-monitoring approach, on which the MIMO system is based.

2.1 Distributed Middleware Environment Model

Figure 1 shows an illustration of a typical distributed middleware environment that we consider. The system to be monitored consists of six abstraction layers, from which the monitor collects information and provides it to tools only by means of the tool-monitor interface.

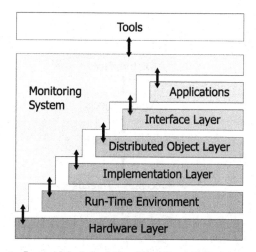

Fig. 1. Layer Model of the Distributed Environment

The highest abstraction level within the system is the application level. Here, only complete applications are of interest for the monitoring system. Within an application, the whole functionality exported by the components is described by interfaces. These interfaces are defined in an abstract way in the interface layer. The implementation of the behavior described by these interfaces is done by objects within the distributed object layer. These objects may still be considered as abstract entities residing in a global object space. In order to enable communication between the distributed objects, some type of middleware is required. Especially, a mechanism to define and uniquely identify objects within the object space is needed. All commonly used middleware standards use some kind of globally unique object references. For example, CORBA uses Interoperable Object References (IORs) to identify CORBA objects [7], Sun's Java Remote Method Invocation RMI uses Uniform Resource Locators (URLs), and Microsoft DCOM [8] generates so-called Globally Unique Identifiers (GUIDs) or monikers. As objects on the distributed object level are still abstract entities, they need to be implemented in a concrete programming language. This implementation of the objects is considered in the subsequent implementation layer. Obviously, objects may be implemented using some O-O language, but also non-O-O languages may be used, e.g. for integrating legacy code. Finally, the implementation objects are executed within a run-time environment which can be an operating system or a virtual machine on top of an operating system that is being executed by the underlying hardware nodes.

For various middleware platforms, this abstract model can be mapped to concrete entity types related to the respective middleware environments like e.g. CORBA or DCOM; Figure 2 shows the CORBA mapping of the MLM, where the main entities of interest are CORBA objects; see [9] for details.

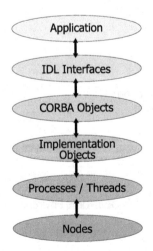

Fig. 2. CORBA Mapping

2.2 Multi-Layer Monitoring

For the monitoring system, two aspects are important: First, it has to be possible to gather data on all abstraction levels in order to serve as an information source for all kinds of online tools. And secondly, the mappings between the different layers are of great importance. As all entities within a specific layer are mapped onto appropriate entities within the layer on the next lower level until the hardware layer is reached, keeping track of these mappings is essential because the relationships between entities in two adjacent layers are not necessarily one-to-one relationships.

Tools making use of the monitoring system may be very diverse and therefore operate only on specific abstraction levels (e.g. a visualizer might be interested in interfaces and CORBA objects). For other tools, mappings between layers can be of special interest (e.g. for performance analysis, the process distribution on the nodes can be decisive).

As a consequence, a *multi-layer monitoring* (MLM) approach [9] which closely reflects the structure of distributed object-environment is well suited for a large class of online tools. For obtaining information from all abstraction layers, specialized modules adapted to requirements of the layer to be observed can be inserted into the monitoring system. Thus, the monitor is kept very modular and flexible and can easily be adjusted to changes of the distributed environment.

3 MIMO

This section introduces the principle design of MIMO's components and interfaces. An important issue for the overall design of MIMO was the genericity of the approach; this means that MIMO is kept open to integrate various types of middleware platforms, and to make it suitable for building any kind of tool. As requirements for different middleware and tools can be very diverse, MIMO itself is designed to depend as little as possible on concrete implementations and semantics of events. Hence, only little information about common entities within the environment is stored by MIMO, and flexibility is gained by tools and intruders being adjusted to each other.

MIMO itself is completely implemented in Java (Java 2 platform), making use of the ORBacus 3.2 [10] CORBA implementation.

3.1 Monitoring and Management Scenario

The MIMO MIddleware MOnitor provides a framework for online monitoring and management tools which is compliant to the multi-layer-monitoring approach. The fundamental architecture relies on the separation of the tools from the monitoring system and the observed applications [6]. Figure 3 illustrates the resulting 3-tier model, which shows tools making use of MIMO by means of a tool-monitor-interface, while MIMO collects information from the monitored applications by means of intruders or adapters which communicate with

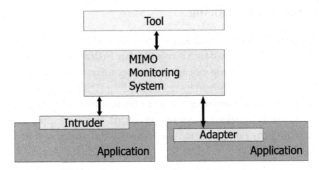

Fig. 3. 3-Tier Model of the Monitoring Architecture

MIMO through a intruder-monitor-interface. The difference between intruders and adapters is that intruders are transparently integrated into the application (without rebuilding the application), while adapters might be built by inserting code into the application (and rebuilding it).

An important aspect in this context is that MIMO makes it possible to monitor both the client- and server-side of distributed applications. Most of the existing management tools are limited to server-side monitoring and administration; MIMO's approach in contrast is layed out for client-side instrumentation too, which in most cases is implemented by proxy-instrumentation techniques.

Finding and Accessing MIMO Communication with MIMO is exclusively handled by CORBA communication. So, when tools or intruders/adapters are being started, they first need to get an IOR for the respective MIMO interfaces in order to be able to communicate with MIMO. Therefore, every running MIMO instance publishes its IOR at a CORBA naming service whose IOR is being stored at a fixed URL which the clients need to access via http; this URL is kept constant, so that clients can even find MIMO and the appropriate naming service when they get restarted with different IORs over time. As multiple instances of MIMO might be running at the same time, every registration at the naming service includes the hostname on which the MIMO instance is running; thus, client (tools, intruders/adapters) can easily choose a local MIMO instance, if it exists.

3.2   MIMO Architecture

An illustration of the basic MIMO architecture is shown in Figure 4. Every instance of MIMO keeps information about the current system state, i.e. data about the applications currently attached to this instance via the intruders/adapters. Furthermore, information about currently attached tools and their active requests is stored. Information can also be exchanged between various MIMO instances, but it is only stored once at the MIMO instance whose intruder/adapter provided the data.

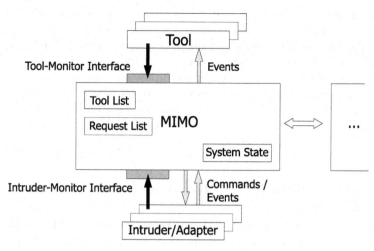

Fig. 4. MIMO Communication: Interfaces and Event Channels

Tool-Monitor-Interaction The only entrance point for tools to MIMO is the tool-monitor-interface, which is a CORBA IDL interface that basically provides methods for attaching to and detaching from MIMO, and for starting and stopping requests.

When requests are started, the result can either be returned synchronously if this is possible (e.g. for system state queries), or in an event-based manner, which is necessary for passing results of asynchronously occurring events (e.g. interactions between entities). Events are passed from MIMO to the tool through a CORBA event channel which is set up during the attachment of the tool. For example, a tool might issue the simple command

$$request("get\_objects", < appl1, appl2 >, objList),$$

which provides a list of all objects belonging to applications `appl1` and `appl2` as an out parameter in `objList`. Or, as an asynchronous request, the tool might get notified whenever `obj2` makes use of the interface `ifc1` with the request

$$start\_request(tid, "get\_interactions", < ifc1, obj2 >),$$

where `tid` is the tool-identifier which is needed to select the corresponding event channel for passing the interaction-events from MIMO to the tool.

Intruder/Adapter-Monitor-Interaction The entrance point for adapters and intruders is the intruder-monitor-interface, which provides methods for attaching and detaching intruders/adapters. After initialization, communication between MIMO and the clients is only handled via two CORBA event channels which are set up at startup. Event channels are mandatory because an asynchronous way of interaction is needed in order to influence the observed system as little as possible. Whenever an "interesting" event occurs within the monitored application, the intruder builds a CORBA event and passes it to MIMO via the monitor-intruder event channel. Similarly, whenever MIMO needs to pass information to the intruder, e.g. for configuring the intruder, it passes a CORBA event to the intruder via its intruder-monitor event channel. This way of communication results in a decoupled intruder/adapter-MIMO interaction scheme. Moreover, it is very flexible due to the standardized protocol which allows for easy integration of different types of middleware platforms which need to be attached by very different intruder/adapter implementations.

4   Instrumentation of CORBA and DCOM Platforms

Enabling different middleware platforms to be observed by MIMO needs some kind of instrumentation to get information out of the respective applications. Instrumentation techniques can be very diverse, and consequently no general approach that is suitable for all kinds of middleware products can be given, but some basic mechanisms are shown here. Nevertheless, MIMO is kept open and allows for using other instrumentation techniques, whenever they provide information in the standardized way through the interfaces and event channels.

This section outlines two exemplary approaches to connect CORBA or DCOM applications to MIMO; however, the general techniques can easily be transferred to other similar middleware environments. Fundamental data to be collected from CORBA and DCOM applications contain information about all existing instances of distributed objects (i.e. CORBA or DCOM objects) within the system, and their interactions (i.e. method calls to such objects). The following examples concentrate on gathering these data.

4.1   Instrumenting CORBA Applications

As mentioned above, data collection in MIMO can either be done by an adapter or an intruder. Here, we outline both approaches for instrumenting CORBA applications.

CORBA Adapter The CORBA adapter basically consists of a Java class providing a library of methods for communicating with MIMO. This includes functions for attaching and detaching to/from MIMO easily, and for sending and receiving CORBA events to and from MIMO. Events can be any kind of information sent to MIMO, but for common tasks the following predefined functions exist:

- Object creation and deletion
- Interaction between objects
- Any other calls to CORBA middleware functions

These event types can easily be generated from within the application code by calling the MIMO adapter functions. Adapters can be useful when the source code is available, and when knowledge about the application domain can be used to instrument the application manually in a way to get specifically interesting events.

CORBA Intruder When the application cannot be rebuild, or instrumentation needs to be inserted transparently, the CORBA intruder can be used. It is based on the instrumentation of the used CORBA library (in our case the ORBacus C++ library). With this technique, *wrapper functions* for the original CORBA methods are created and inserted into the library. The original functions are renamed and called by the MIMO wrappers. The approach is implemented by using symbol replacement inside the CORBA library.

The problem with this approach is to find the appropriate CORBA methods which need to be wrapped in order to get the required information. For our CORBA intruder, the idea is as follows:

– For startup purposes, CORBA initialization functions like `ORB::init` need to be wrapped for enabling the attachment to MIMO.
– To get information about newly created or deleted objects, keeping track of the reference counter functions (duplicate and release) is a convenient way; when the reference counter reaches zero, the CORBA object gets deleted. Furthermore, observing the creation of client-side proxies is also possible by looking at the `string_to_object` operation which instantiates a proxy for a given CORBA object.
– Interactions between objects finally result in a call to a CORBA request's `invoke` (or related `send_oneway` and `send_deferred`) method. Thus, wrapping this method allows us to observe all method calls to any CORBA objects.
– Any other CORBA method call can be instrumented, if given circumstances need to access it.

Hence, this proceeding enables to monitor different aspects of CORBA systems. The advantage is that information can be gathered at different *levels of detail*, depending on the granularity required by a given tool.

Performance data evaluating the overhead introduced by the CORBA intruder will be available for a final version of the paper.

4.2   Instrumenting DCOM Applications

In DCOM, no direct way exists to get information about method calls to DCOM objects. While there is no difference implementing objects for in-process, out-of-process or remote access, there is a big difference in how they are called. Out-of-process and remote calls base on the RPC protocol and a pair of proxy and stub, in-process calls are direct procedure calls without any participation of the COM library. Gathering information about all kinds of COM calls requires other mechanisms than instrumenting the COM library.

DCOM Wrapper The best way to achieve this goal is to use a wrapper for each monitored object. This provides scalability because only calls of interest are recorded. The wrapper has to provide hooks for requests orthogonal to the method call. These requests could not only be auditing requests but also security checks etc[2]. The approach applied in MIMO is based on a universal delegator object [12,13], and trace hooks [14]. To work properly, the wrapper has to be called instead of the original object, such that it can process the call first. Therefore, the registry is manipulated to set up a special class factory for the monitored object. This class factory first creates the monitored object using the original class factory, then creates and initializes the wrapper with the object and gives back a pointer to the wrapper. Once this is set up, the wrapper analyzes the call stack every time a method call is received. Then it checks whether only to pre-process the call or to pre- and postprocess it. It sends the required information to the hook and forwards the call to the original object after changing the return address to itself. The wrapper and the hook themselves are in-process objects tied to the original object's thread (Figure 5).

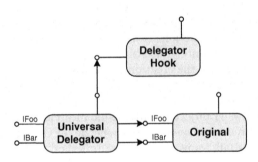

Fig. 5. DCOM Delegator

To work with MIMO, some additional work is required. Therefore, a universal framework was designed which supports any kinds of information sources and any kinds of information processors. One component is a CORBA-COM bridge-object, which provides the interface to MIMO. The main information source is the combination of the wrapper (Universal Delegator) and the hook (Trace-Hook). Other sources could be objects reading the event log or performance data. The overall scenario is showh in Figure 6.

Performance and Limitations Performance tests have been carried out to get an evaluation of the overhead of this solution. As the wrapper approach implies a process switch during the call, it is only applicable for out-of-process or remote calls, and not for in-process calls (as the overhead in this case would

---

[2] In COM+, which ships with Windows2000, such a wrapper will be integrated into the COM+ event service [11].

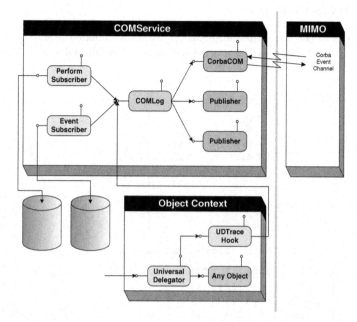

Fig. 6. Overview of the DCOM Instrumentation Approach

be tremendous). The measured overhead of the DCOM wrapper framework was 2.9 for out-of-process (but still local) calls, and 1.6 for remote calls. These values show that it might not be useful to collect all available data, but to build a more "intelligent" wrapper which only gathers information on request; this issue is an implementation problem which will be solved in a future version of the wrapper. More details can be found in [15].

5 MIVIS Visualization Tool

Here we describe the visualization tool MIVIS (MImo VISualizer). Our goal was to develop a visualization tool that is based upon the multi-layer-monitoring concept described earlier. It interacts with MIMO and presents data it receives in an advantageous way to the user. Amongst the requirements for MIVIS were scalability, uncomplicated extensibility, platform independence, an ergonomic user interface, and the possibility of having several displays at a time.

A general problem of visualization is scalability: Huge amount of data have to be presented in a way which allow the observer to keep track of the information offered. Thus, there has to be the possibility to reduce data by means of filtering mechanisms. MIVIS realizes this reduction by its selection mechanism which provides a kind of filtering based on the multi-layer-monitoring model.

5.1 MIVIS Concepts

All entities in the monitored application are shown inside the selection frame (see Figure 7). Each layer of the multi-layer-monitoring model is represented in one

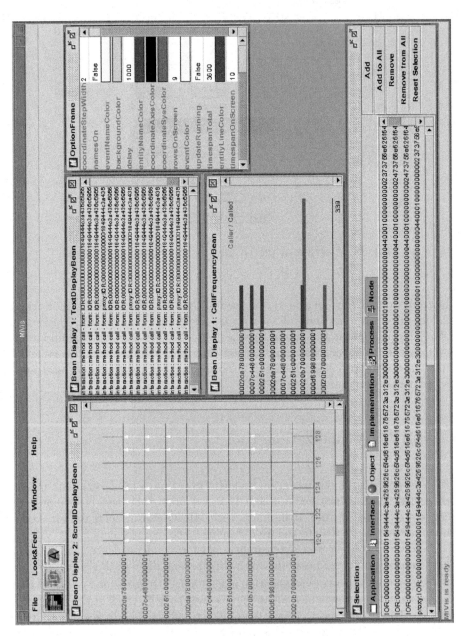

Fig. 7. MIVIS Displays

tab of a tabbed pane. The user can select entities within the different layers and thus control the granularity of his visualization. To gain an overall survey she can monitor the system on the application layer or the hardware layer without being bothered by details. To get more insight in the internals of the application she can pick out a few interesting entities and go up or down to adjacent layers to get more detailed information;

5.2   Implementation

To fulfill the requirement of uncomplicated extensibility of the visualization tool, it is split into a main program and several JavaBeans software components. The main program takes care of the communication with MIMO and the processing of the data, and the JavaBeans do the graphical display.

All JavaBeans are discovered by MIVIS at startup time, and get dynamically integrated into the GUI. If a different type of display is needed, a user can program that display type using Java and turn it into a JavaBean. This component is placed into a specific directory so that MIVIS can find and use it. The main program does not have to be changed at all, the only requirement is that the JavaBean implements a minimal interface that enables the main program to communicate with the bean.

The bean-specific properties can be set by the user. MIVIS knows about these properties by means of the introspection mechanism and provides editors to change the settings of these properties. Additional editors for properties of a special data type can be placed inside the JavaBean and used instead of the standard editors. All properties together with their editors are shown inside the Option Frame (see Figure 7). Hence, MIVIS allows the user to edit properties which the tool itself does not know from the beginning. This approach offers a very dynamic and flexible way to configure the behavior of various display types; the concept of separating the display types from the main program makes it very easy to generate new display types for MIVIS without the need of changing the original code.

5.3   MIVIS Displays

So far, three display types have been implemented: text display, scroll display and call frequency display. These three displays types can be seen in Figure 7.

- The text display prints out the events that are monitored in plain text, what can basically be used for logging purposes; details that might not be visible in a graphical display can be looked up here at a later time.
- The scroll display visualizes communication between entities. The selected entities are displayed on the y-axis in a coordinate system. The x-axis shows the time. When an entity communicates with another entity, an arrow between the two is shown in the coordinate system.
- The call frequency display visualizes communication in a different way: Only cumulative data containing the number of calls are of interest are shown as a vertical beam for each caller and for each called entity.

These displays are only fundamental aspects of an application that might be of interest, but others can easily be added by programming new JavaBeans.

In this sense, MIVIS can be seen as a general *framework for GUI-based MIMO-tools* which provides the basic monitoring functionality, and can be extended with additional JavaBeans to fulfill any further monitoring requirements.

More details about MIVIS can be found in [16].

6   Example Scenario

To test MIVIS in a real-world scenario we picked a simple library application, which represents a 3-tier client-server application with distributed data.

- The first tier consist of clients that can do various operations, such as searching for books, inserting new book into the library etc; these clients can be located on different machines.
- The second tier keeps the client interfaces which provide the business logic of the application; they basically process the client requests, make database queries to the third layer, assemble the results, and pass them back to the clients. Client interfaces can also be located on several machines.
- The third tier contains library managers, which contain the actual library databases. Different managers store information about different books. Again, the library managers can be distributed over a set of nodes.

When a client starts a request, for example a search for a certain book, the following things occur: The client selects a free client interface at random to process the request. The client interface contacts all library managers that are known to it and requests the information about the book. It waits for the answers of the library managers and combines all answers to the final result which is sent back to the client.

In our test scenario, clients periodically start search requests. Each call from a client to a client interface is followed by several calls from the selected client manager to all library managers. In our example we have three library managers, so there are three calls from the client interface for each client request. In Figure 7, every call is displayed as an arrow from the caller to the called entity. As the time between the calls is very short, all arrows for one request seem to be one line in this coarse illustration. In Figure 8, we can see that the vertical beam for the calls from the client interface is three times the size of the one for the calls from the client and for each library manager (because for each client call, the client interface invokes every library manager).

Hence, his example briefly demonstrates how to use MIVIS to visualize the behavior of distributed middleware applications. Clearly, in practice more sophisticated scenarios have to be analyzed, but the general approach to investigate request sequences in n-tier client-server applications is a very important and helpful feature, either for debugging, performance analysis, or management purposes.

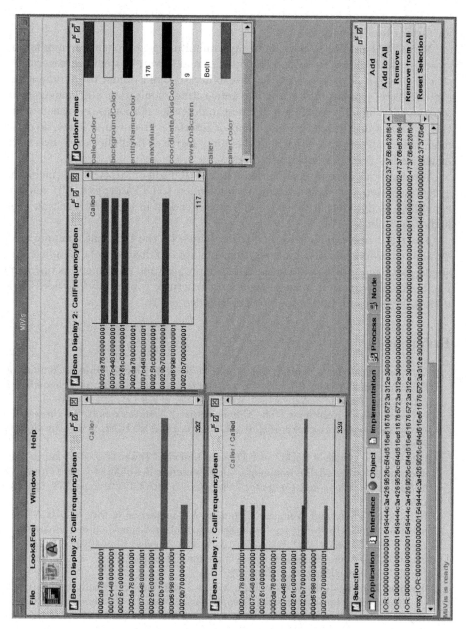

Fig. 8. MIVIS 3-tier Library Example

7 Conclusion

In this paper, we have presented the MIMO infrastructure for monitoring and managing distributed middleware environments, and the MIVIS visualization tool demonstrating basic MIMO functionality, and which serves as a framework for further tool extensions.

MIMO is based on a new multi-layer-monitoring approach for middleware systems which allows us to handle complex middleware systems on several abstraction levels. This provides the possibility to build online tools supporting the complete software lifecycle while integrating monitoring and management functionality. The integration of different middleware platforms is reached by introducing a standardized intruder-monitor-interface. To our knowledge, no other monitoring infrastructure reaching this high degree of flexibility over several dimensions has been developed up to now.

What still needs to be completed is the distribution of MIMO itself (including synchronization and event ordering issues, similar to OCM project [17]), and the capability to dynamically insert code into intruders in order to reach an even higher flexibility.

The main research contribution is motivated by the fact that common middleware environments and tool requirements are too diverse to be handled by a single, static monitoring system. Instead, we propose and implement an open and flexible monitoring and management infrastructure, which only provides basic monitoring services, but is open to be extended easily.

References

1. Günther Rackl, Ivan Zoraja, and Arndt Bode. Distributed Object Computing: Principles and Trends. In *International Conference on Software in Telecommunications and Computer Networks – SoftCOM '99*, pages 121–132, Oct 1999. 71
2. I. Foster and C. Kesselman. The Globus project: A status report. In *Proceedings of the Heterogeneous Computing Workshop*, pages 4–18. IEEE Computer Society Press, 1998. 71
3. Ivan Zoraja, Günther Rackl, and Thomas Ludwig. Towards Monitoring in Parallel and Distributed Environments. In *International Conference on Software in Telecommunications and Computer Networks – SoftCOM '99*, pages 133–141, Oct 1999. 71
4. Bernfried Widmer and Wolfgang Lugmayr. A Comparison of three CORBA Management Tools. In Wolfgang Emmerich and Volker Gruhn, editors, *Engineering Distributed Objects (EDO'99)*, pages 12–21, Los Angeles, May 1999. 71, 73
5. Ralph E. Johnson. Frameworks = (components + patterns). *Communications of the ACM*, 40(10):39–42, Oct 1997. 72
6. Thomas Ludwig, Roland Wismüller, Vaidy Sunderam, and Arndt Bode. *OMIS — On-Line Monitoring Interface Specification (Version 2.0)*, volume 9 of *Research Report Series, Lehrstuhl für Rechnertechnik und Rechnerorganisation (LRR-TUM), Technische Universität München*. Shaker, Aachen, 1997. 73, 75
7. OMG (Object Management Group). The Common Object Request Broker: Architecture and Specification — Revision 2.2. Technical report, February 1998. 74
8. Microsoft Corporation. DCOM Architecture. Technical report, 1998. 74
9. Günther Rackl. Multi-Layer Monitoring in Distributed Object-Environments. In Lea Kutvonen, Hartmut König, and Martti Tienari, editors, *Distributed Applications and Interoperable Systems II — IFIP TC 6 WG 6.1 Second International Working Conference on Distributed Applications and Interoperable Systems*

(DAIS'99), pages 265–270, Helsinki, June 1999. Kluwer Academic Publishers. 74, 75

10. Object Oriented Concepts Inc. ORBacus, Nov 1999. http://www.ooc.com/ob/. 75

11. David S. Platt. *Understanding COM+*. Microsoft Press, 1999. 80

12. Keith Brown. Building a Lightweight COM Interception Framework, Part 1: The Universal Delegator. *Microsoft Systems Journal*, Jan 1999. 80

13. Keith Brown. Building a Lightweight COM Interception Framework Part 2: The Guts of the UD. *Microsoft Systems Journal*, Feb 1999. 80

14. Simon Fell. Activation tricks. WWW, July 1999. http://www.zaks.demon.co.uk/com/activation.htm. 80

15. Bernd Süss. Konzepte und Mechanismen zum on-line Monitoring von DCOM-Anwendungen. Diploma thesis, Technische Universität München, 1999. In german. 81

16. Michael Rudorfer. Visualisierung des dynamischen Verhaltens verteilter objektorientierter Anwendungen. Diploma thesis, Technische Universität München, 1999. In german. 84

17. Roland Wismüller, Jörg Trinitis, and Thomas Ludwig. OCM — A Monitoring System for Interoperable Tools. In *Proc. 2nd SIGMETRICS Symposium on Parallel and Distributed Tools SPDT'98*. ACM Press, 1998. 86

Gateways for Accessing
Fault Tolerance Domains*

P. Narasimhan, L. E. Moser, and P. M. Melliar-Smith

Department of Electrical and Computer Engineering
University of California, Santa Barbara, CA 93106
priya@alpha.ece.ucsb.edu {moser,pmms}@ece.ucsb.edu

Abstract. Enterprise applications can be structured as domains, where each domain contains objects that are replicated for fault tolerance, with the replication being managed by a fault tolerance infrastructure local to the domain. Gateways can allow unreplicated clients to benefit from the fault tolerance services of the replicated servers, without compromising replica consistency within the fault tolerance domain. For CORBA-based enterprise applications, the gateway mechanisms can be implemented transparently to the ORB and to the application using interception; specific enhancements to existing ORBs make it possible for unreplicated clients to enjoy a higher degree of reliability.

1 Introduction

Applications are increasingly spanning enterprises across the Internet, with the application objects within one enterprise communicating with, and performing operations on, the application objects of another enterprise. The reliability of the application as a whole depends on the reliability of the objects in each of the communicating enterprises, which are separated possibly by a considerable distance, as shown in Fig 1. Each enterprise is likely to be, and indeed should be, responsible only for the reliability of the objects under its control, but each enterprise must nevertheless allow the objects of a different enterprise to communicate with its own objects without compromising the consistency of the replicated objects of either enterprise. The domain of control of the fault tolerance infrastructure of each enterprise constitutes a *fault tolerance domain*; different fault tolerance domains can be connected through a *gateway*.

The concepts of fault tolerance domains and gateways are not restricted to communication between enterprises. Internet-based applications such as stock trading involve customers using Web browsers (typically unreplicated thin clients) to communicate with the servers (typically replicated for fault tolerance) of a stock trading company. The unreplicated Web browser should not

---

* Research supported by the Defense Advanced Research Projects Agency in conjunction with the Office of Naval Research and the Air Force Research Laboratory, Rome, under Contracts N00174-95-K-0083 and F3602-97-1-0248, respectively.

J. Sventek and G. Coulson (Eds.): Middleware 2000, LNCS 1795, pp. 88–103, 2000.

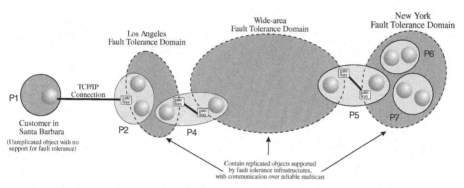

Fig. 1. Gateways bridge fault tolerance domains, and allow objects in one fault tolerance domain to communicate with those in another. P_i represents a processor hosting some application objects

need to be aware of the replication of the stock trading servers, but can nevertheless benefit from the fault tolerance of the servers. The unreplicated clients (the Web browsers) can be made to communicate with the replicated servers (the stock trading servers) through a gateway that hides the replication of the servers. The replicated servers are managed by the fault tolerance infrastructure of the stock trading company, and the gateway serves as the "entry point" into the fault tolerance domain. The gateway is a crucial element because it must "understand" the reliability mechanisms inside the fault tolerance domain, as well as the unreliable semantics of the external client, and must bridge these different semantics and mechanisms, without compromising the reliability of the objects within the fault tolerance domain.

A different motivation for a fault tolerance domain is that an application might have a large number of objects that require replication, and it might not be a scalable or feasible solution for a single fault tolerance infrastructure to manage the replication of all of these objects. Instead, it would be preferable to decompose the application into smaller collections of objects, with each collection of objects being managed by a distinct fault tolerance infrastructure, and therefore constituting a fault tolerance domain.

Regardless of the motivation for a fault tolerance domain, the gateway mechanism is identical and essential. In this paper, a gateway mechanism is described in the context of applications developed using the Common Object Request Broker Architecture (CORBA) [9] distributed object standard established by the Object Management Group (OMG). While CORBA currently does not provide support for fault tolerance, efforts [8] are underway within the OMG to standardize interfaces for fault-tolerant CORBA.

A key issue in fault tolerance for CORBA will be the mechanisms to support interaction of non-fault-tolerant CORBA systems with fault-tolerant CORBA systems. The gateways described in this paper address the issues in the implementation of such mechanisms, the problems in building those mechanisms using

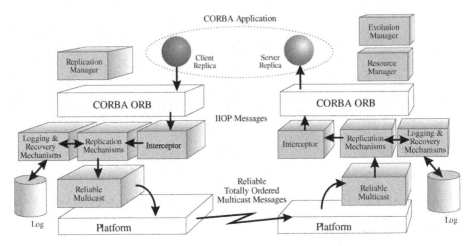

Fig. 2. The Eternal system – the fault tolerance infrastructure within the fault tolerance domain

existing ORBs, and enhancements to existing ORBs that might overcome these deficiencies.

2   The Fault Tolerance Infrastructure

The Eternal system [5,6] constitutes the fault tolerance infrastructure (within the fault tolerance domain) that provides reliability for applications running over commercial-off-the-shelf implementations of CORBA. The mechanisms implemented in different parts of the Eternal system work together efficiently to provide strong replica consistency with low overheads, and without requiring modification of either the application or the ORB.

In the Eternal system, the client and server objects of the CORBA application are replicated, and the replicas are distributed across the system. Active replication and passive replication of both client and server objects are supported. To facilitate replica consistency, the Eternal system conveys the Internet Inter-ORB Protocol (IIOP) messages of the CORBA application using an underlying reliable totally ordered multicast group communication system, such as Totem [4].

The structure of the Eternal system is shown in Figure 2. The Eternal Replication Manager replicates each application object, according to user-specified fault tolerance properties (including the choice of replication style – stateless, cold passive, warm passive, active, active with voting) and distributes the replicas across the system. The Eternal Resource Manager monitors the system resources, and maintains the initial and minimum number of replicas.

The Eternal Interceptor captures the IIOP messages (containing the client's requests and the server's replies), which are intended for TCP/IP, and diverts them instead to the Eternal Replication Mechanisms for multicasting via Totem. The Eternal Replication Mechanisms, along with the Eternal Logging-Recovery Mechanisms, maintain the consistency of the replicas, detect and provide recovery from faults. The Replication Mechanisms and the Totem protocols run on every processor within a fault tolerance domain.

The Eternal Evolution Manager exploits object replication to support upgrades to the CORBA application objects. The Replication Manager, the Resource Manager and the Evolution Manager are themselves implemented as collections of CORBA objects and, thus, can themselves be replicated and thereby benefit from Eternal's fault tolerance capabilities. They need not be present on every processor; their replicas can run on any processor within the fault tolerance domain.

The technology of Eternal formed the basis of our response [2] to the Object Management Group's Request for Proposals [8] on fault-tolerant CORBA. With our close involvement in the ongoing OMG standardization process, it appears likely that the technology of Eternal will form the basis of the forthcoming OMG standard for fault tolerance for CORBA.

2.1   Transparency via Interception

The Eternal Interceptor [7] is a non-ORB-level, non-application-level component that transparently "attaches" itself to every executing CORBA object, without the object's or the ORB's knowledge, and is capable of modifying the object's behavior as desired. Because of its location underneath the ORB, Eternal's Interceptor is transparent to the ORB and to the application, and can be implemented in an ORB-independent manner.

Current operating systems provide "hooks", such as library interpositioning, that can be exploited to develop interceptors. Using library interpositioning, the Eternal Interceptor can transparently override the default definitions for the symbols in any dynamically linked library, without requiring modification of the ORB, the CORBA application or the operating system.

The library routines that an interceptor is made to redefine in a library-interpositioning implementation, depends on the extent of the information that the interceptor must extract (from the ORB or the CORBA application) to enhance the application with new features. The interceptor may capture all, or a particular subset, of the library routines used by the CORBA application, depending on the feature being added. The library interpositioning approach used by Eternal's Interceptor has no overheads in the path of message transmission, and can be deployed with various ORBs.

2.2   Strong Replica Consistency

The Replication Mechanisms, operating in concert with the Logging-Recovery Mechanisms, provide for strongly consistent replication of the CORBA application objects. Eternal provides support for the detection and suppression of duplicate invocations and duplicate responses, and for state transfer to new and

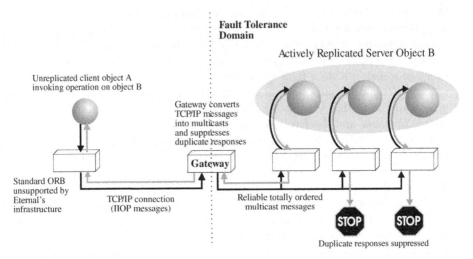

Fig. 3. Eternal's gateways allow unreplicated clients to communicate with replicated objects

recovering replicas for both actively and passively replicated objects. Most commercial applications and/or ORBs use multithreading, a significant source of non-determinism. To ensure strong replica consistency even for multithreaded CORBA objects that are replicated, Eternal employs special Interceptor-level mechanisms to enforce determinism for multithreaded CORBA applications, without requiring them to be modified.

While the fault tolerance infrastructure ensures strong replica consistency within the fault tolerance domain, it is the responsibility of the gateway to ensure that unreplicated clients wishing to contact replicated objects within the fault tolerance domain (through the gateway) do not compromise the replica consistency of those replicated objects.

3   Gateways to Fault Tolerance Domains

Eternal must allow the CORBA applications that it supports to communicate with unreplicated objects that are outside the fault tolerance domain, *i.e.*, Eternal's domain of control. Some of these unreplicated objects (*e.g.*, a Web browser on a personal computer that provides no fault tolerance) may not be supported by, or have access to, Eternal's fault tolerance infrastructure, and may run over standard IIOP-enabled ORBs.

Eternal ensures that these unreplicated objects outside the fault tolerance domain can nevertheless communicate with the replicated objects that are under Eternal's control inside the fault tolerance domain. Eternal makes this communication possible without the unreplicated object ever being aware of the existence of a fault tolerance domain, of the replication of the objects within the fault tolerance domain, or of Eternal itself. Thus, Eternal extends the replication transparency that it provides to the application objects within the fault tolerance domain equally to unreplicated objects outside Eternal's control.

The gateways that the Eternal system provides serve as the "entry point" for unreplicated clients into the fault tolerance domain, and allow unreplicated external objects to invoke replicated Eternal-managed objects.

Within a fault tolerance domain:

- All objects are replicated, with the replication managed by Eternal's fault tolerance infrastructure. Each replicated object is assigned a unique object group identifier.
- Communication between replicated objects occurs through a reliable totally-ordered multicast protocol, thereby facilitating replica consistency, as described in Section 2.2. The Replication Mechanisms hosting the replicas of an object are addressed by multicasting messages to the object's group identifier.
- Replicated clients do not use the TCP/IP {host, port} information within the Interoperable Object Reference (IOR) of any of the server replicas to contact the replicated server. Instead, the Eternal Interceptor transparently diverts the socket establishment routines at every client replica to form a connection to the local Eternal Replication Mechanisms, which then multicast the notification of the connection establishment to the Replication Mechanisms hosting the server replicas.

Outside a fault tolerance domain:

- Objects are unreplicated, and are unaware of the internal mechanisms of, and the replication within, the fault tolerance domain
- Communication occurs through CORBA's TCP/IP-based Internet Inter-ORB Protocol (IIOP)
- Clients use the TCP/IP {host, port} information within the Interoperable Object Reference (IOR) of the target server to establish a connection with the server.

Unreplicated objects outside the fault tolerance domain must never be allowed to access the replicated objects within the fault tolerance domain directly. Such direct communication, if permitted, would violate replica consistency. The reason is that the unreplicated client can communicate only through TCP/IP, thereby implying that it would contact only *one* of the server replicas, and invoke an operation on that replica alone.

If the server is actively replicated, and only the single invoked server replica performs the operation, it may have a different state from that of the other replicas of the server object, resulting in inconsistent replication. If the server is passively replicated, and the single primary replica is invoked, the primary replica might itself invoke nested operations as a result of the original invocation. If the primary fails before it receives the results of the nested invocations, a new primary server replica will be elected. However, because the new primary (formerly a backup replica) did not receive the original invocation, it will not be able to handle the returned responses from the nested invocations and to return a response to the original invocation. Thus, to ensure replica consistency, the replicas of an object are contacted through a reliable totally-ordered multicast, and not individually through TCP/IP.

Additional mechanisms are provided by Eternal so that an IOR published by a replicated object within the fault tolerance domain "point" the external clients in the direction of the IIOP-enabled gateway, rather than the target replicated object. However, the external client that uses this IOR is unaware of this. When using the information in the IOR for connection establishment, the client implicitly assumes that the endpoint is the real server and, thus, sends IIOP invocations (destined for the server) to the gateway.

Note that the gateway is not a CORBA object, but constitutes part of the mechanisms provided by the fault tolerance infrastructure of Eternal. However, by receiving the unreplicated client's IIOP invocations without returning exceptions, and by forwarding the replicated server's IIOP responses to the unreplicated clients, the gateway appears to the client to be a remote CORBA server object.

To perform the invocation (response) forwarding into (out of) the fault tolerance domain, the gateway must be able to interpret the IIOP messages sent over TCP/IP connections from outside the fault tolerance domain, as well as the reliable totally-ordered multicast protocol messages within the fault tolerance domain, and must provide the necessary translation between them. This functionality of the gateway is shown in Figure 3.

Another aspect of the gateway is that it must "hide" the replication of the servers from the external client. This involves detecting duplicate responses returned by the replicas of the server, and filtering out only a single distinct response to the external client. In addition, the gateway must itself be reliable so that it does not constitute a single point of failure.

3.1 Connection Establishment

When a gateway is used, every unreplicated external client must continue to "believe" that the remote endpoint to which it connects (using the information in the server IOR) is the server when, in fact, the remote endpoint is the gateway. This can be done by ensuring that the addressing information in the IOR is the {gateway_host, gateway_port} and that the gateway always returns the expected IIOP responses to the client's IIOP invocations so that the client never suspects otherwise.

Eternal replaces the {server_host, server_port} in the IOR of each server replica with the {gateway_host, gateway_port} through the use of its Interceptor. The intent of the Interceptor is to interpose at the point that the server-side ORB queries the operating system for the host and the port information, *prior* to publishing the IOR. By modifying the *getsockname()* call and/or the *sysinfo()* call (with the SI_HOSTNAME command) to return the gateway_host and the gateway_port instead of the server_host and the server_port, respectively, the IOR

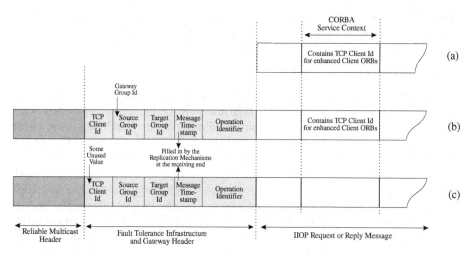

Fig. 4. Messages sent (a) between an unreplicated client and the gateway, (b) from the gateway to a replicated object within the fault tolerance domain, and (c) between replicated objects within the fault tolerance domain

that the server-side ORB publishes automatically contains the {gateway_host, gateway_port}. This eliminates the effort of having to parse the IOR string to do the replacement, and also results in fewer undesirable interceptions. The gateway_host and the gateway_port are dedicated choices that are supplied to the interceptor at system configuration time.

When an unreplicated client uses this IOR, the client-side ORB, implicitly assuming that the host and port in the IOR refer to the server object, connects the client to the gateway. The gateway now becomes the recipient of every IIOP message sent by the unreplicated client, which continues to "believe" that the gateway is indeed the target server object. By extracting the server's object key (which the client-side ORB inserts into IIOP invocations to identify the target server), the gateway identifies the target server, multicasts the client invocation to the server object group. The gateway inserts sufficient information into the multicast messages to enable it to associate the server's response with the client's invocation.

The gateway process must be continuously listening for connections from unreplicated clients on its dedicated {gateway_host, gateway_port}. For each new client that contacts the gateway, the gateway spawns a new TCP/IP socket to communicate solely with that client, and uses the original socket to listen for further clients. The additional spawned sockets are destroyed when the connection between the unreplicated client and the gateway terminates.

Note that the replacement of the {server_host, server_port} in the IOR does not affect connection establishment or communication within the fault tolerance domain. Replicated clients wishing to communicate with replicated servers within the fault tolerance domain never use this TCP/IP-specific addressing information, but use instead the server's object group identifier to contact the replicated server through the fault tolerance infrastructure.

3.2   Encapsulation of IIOP into Multicast Messages

A gateway must encapsulate the IIOP invocations from the external unreplicated clients into multicast messages for transmission to the target replicated server object within the fault tolerance domain. Similarly, the IIOP responses, encapsulated within the multicast messages returned by the replicated server object, must be extracted by the gateway and returned to the unreplicated clients.

When an IIOP-encapsulating message is multicast by the gateway into the fault tolerance domain, the message contains the gateway_group_id as the sender group, and the server_group_id (determined by the gateway from the server's object key embedded in the client's IIOP invocation) as the destination group. The message is received in total order by the Replication Mechanisms hosting each of the server replicas. The replicated server performs the operation, and the fault tolerance infrastructure multicasts the results to the gateway. The replicated server assumes that the gateway that sent the IIOP invocation is a CORBA client object. Eternal's transparency through interception effectively ensures that neither the unreplicated client, nor any of the server replicas, is ever aware of communicating through the fault tolerance infrastructure using reliable multicast. The gateway (and, of course, the fault tolerance infrastructure itself) is the only party in the chain of communication that is aware of the reliable multicast and the fault tolerance infrastructure.

When the replicated server returns the response to the gateway, the IIOP response from each server replica is encapsulated by the Replication Mechanisms hosting that replica into a multicast message. The message contains the server_group_id as the sender group, and the gateway_group_id as the destination group. This information is insufficient for the gateway to route the IIOP response to the client replica that invoked the operation because multiple unreplicated TCP/IP-based clients may have invoked the same replicated server through the gateway. The gateway has no way of discriminating between these clients.

Thus, every multicast message must contain additional information, inserted by the gateway to identify each TCP/IP client that contacts the gateway. The resulting multicast messages have the structure shown in Figure 4. For every multicast message exchanged between replicated objects within the fault tolerance domain, the TCP/IP client identification is set to some unused value. The gateway (as well as the fault tolerance infrastructure) uses the destination group identifier, the source group identifier and the TCP/IP client identifier *collectively* to route every message to its intended destination.

Ideally, the client identification information ought to be supplied by the client-side ORB, as discussed in Section 3.5. Because this is not the case with current ORBs, the gateway maintains a simple counter, one for each destination server group. For each incoming TCP/IP client, the gateway first determines the server_group_id from the first IIOP message received from the client. The

```
for (every received IIOP message)          for (every received multicast message)
{                                          {
    Obtain TCP client identifier               Extract operation identifier
    Map socket to client identifier            Examine if message is a duplicate
    Generate operation identifier              if (non-duplicate message)
    Generate header containing:                {
      – TCP client identifier                      Extract TCP client identifier
      – Gateway group identifier                   Find corresponding socket
      – Server group identifier                    Extract IIOP message
      – Operation identifier                       Send IIOP message to the
    Convey header and IIOP message                   client over the socket
      via a multicast message                  }
    Send multicast message into the          else
      fault tolerance domain                     Discard duplicate message
}                                          }
```

(a)   (b)

Fig. 5. Actions of the gateway for incoming messages from (a) external un-replicated clients outside the fault tolerance domain, and (b) replicated objects within the fault tolerance domain

gateway then uses the value of the counter corresponding to that server group as the TCP/IP client identifier. The counter is then incremented, to serve as the identifier for the next TCP/IP client for the same replicated server. The disadvantage of the gateway-assigned client identifiers, over identifiers supplied by the client-side ORB, is discussed in Section 3.4.

Figure 5 shows the sequence of steps that the gateway executes for incoming IIOP messages from outside the fault tolerance domain, and incoming multicast messages from within the fault tolerance domain.

3.3   Duplicate Detection and Suppression

To ensure replica consistency, duplicate detection and suppression mechanisms are used by Eternal throughout the fault tolerance domain; the gateways also employ these mechanisms for filtering duplicate responses from the replicated server objects within the fault tolerance domain. The gateway returns only a distinct copy of each response to the invoking external client. The duplicate copies of each response, if not suppressed, would be delivered to the client object, and may cause the client object's state to be corrupted.

To detect duplicate copies of each response, both the fault tolerance infrastructure and the gateway prepend an *operation identifier* to each message that is multicast within the fault tolerance domain, as shown in Figure 4. The operation identifier takes the form of either an *invocation identifier* for all multicast messages that encapsulate IIOP invocations, or a *response identifier* for all messages that encapsulate IIOP responses.

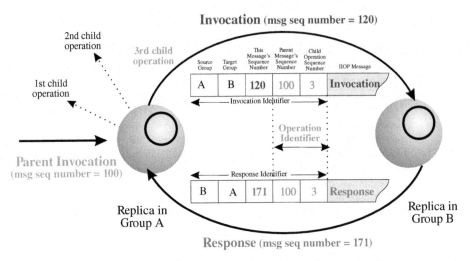

Fig. 6. Assignment of invocation, response and operation identifiers

Operation Identifiers For each outgoing IIOP invocation received by the gateway from an unreplicated client, the gateway generates the invocation identifier as shown in Figure 6. The gateway then inserts the invocation identifier into the Eternal-specific header of the message that it multicasts into the fault tolerance domain. The timestamp of this multicast message, which forms a part of the invocation identifier, is filled in by the fault tolerance infrastructure at the receiving end, when the message is delivered. The timestamp information is derived from the totally-ordered message sequence numbers assigned by the multicast group communication system.

For each outgoing IIOP response sent by a server replica, Eternal "remembers" and reuses a portion of the invocation identifier that was sent with the corresponding invocation. The portion of the invocation identifier that is reused in its counterpart response identifier is the *operation identifier*, which completely and uniquely identifies the operation consisting of the invocation-response pair. Both the invocation and the response identifiers have the same operation identifier fields. Furthermore, the operation identifier is identically determined at every server replica.

The gateway, on receipt of multiple copies (one copy for each server replica that returns a response) of a response to an IIOP invocation that it multicasts into the domain, can deliver the first copy that it receives, and discard all subsequently received copies by simply comparing the response identifier fields of the Eternal-specific header.

An invocation identifier has the form $(T_{B_{inv}}, (T_{A_{inv}}, S_{A_{inv}}))$, where $T_{A_{inv}}$ is the timestamp of the message containing the invocation of group A, $T_{B_{inv}}$ is the timestamp of the message containing the invocation of the group B, and $S_{A_{inv}}$ is the sequence number of the invocation of B in the sequence of invocations by group A. Similarly, a response identifier has the form $(T_{B_{res}}, (T_{A_{inv}}, S_{A_{inv}}))$, where $T_{B_{res}}$ is the timestamp of the message containing the response by group B to group A and the other two fields are the same as for the invocation identifier. These invocation and response identifiers are contained in the multicast messages.

Note that the timestamps $T_{A_{inv}}$, $T_{B_{inv}}$ and $T_{B_{res}}$ are derived from the totally-ordered message sequence numbers assigned by the Totem multicast group communication system. The system-wide uniqueness of these timestamps (as a result of the total ordering) contributes to the uniqueness of the operation identifiers, and thus, to the detection of duplicate messages.

In the example of Figure 6, $T_{A_{inv}}$ corresponds to 100, $S_{A_{inv}}$ corresponds to 3, $T_{B_{inv}}$ corresponds to 120 and $T_{B_{res}}$ corresponds to 171. In the case of the gateway, A represents the gateway_group and B represents the target replicated server that the unreplicated client (that connects to the gateway) wishes to contact.

3.4   Using Existing ORBs

Existing ORBs do not have the capability to traverse a list of profiles, and select the next profile if the first one fails on connection. The disadvantage of this is that redundant gateways are not possible. Clients may experience disconnection if the processor hosting the gateway fails, and does not recover. The processor hosting the gateway is a single point of failure. If the client ORB has the capability to understand only the first IIOP profile (the standard TAG_INTERNET_IOP profile), and if the gateway to which it connects using the first profile fails, the client has no alternative but to abandon the request. Furthermore, the client does not know the status of any invocations that it has already sent, for which it is still awaiting responses.

An alternative to using multiple gateways might be to have a cold passively replicated gateway. In this case, the gateway's state should be checkpointed often enough to allow it to be recovered. However, clients will still be disconnected from the gateway if it fails, and must have mechanisms to allow them to reconnect to the gateway, when it recovers.

In the case of redundant gateways, the new gateway to which the client connects (on failure of the first gateway) has no way of "knowing" that this is the same client. The simple counter mechanism, described in Section 3.2, is insufficient in this case to identify the client. This means that, even if the new gateway receives the response for an outstanding invocation sent by the client through the first gateway, the new gateway does not know which of its connected clients should receive this response. Secondly, if the client were now to re-issue all of the pending invocations to the new gateway, the new gateway may, in turn, re-issue these invocations to the replicated objects within the fault tolerance domain, thereby corrupting their state.

Thus, due to lack of client-side identification provided by the ORB, the gateway cannot prevent duplication of client requests if

- The unreplicated client fails, recovers and resends its request (this is outside the fault tolerance domain's and the gateway's control, and cannot be handled without extending some of the fault tolerance mechanisms to the unreplicated client)
- The gateway process fails, and then recovers, and the client reconnects to the gateway
- Redundant gateways are used, and the original gateway fails, and the client switches to the next operational gateway

3.5   Enhancements to Existing ORBs

If only a single gateway is provided for a fault tolerance domain, it is insufficient to guarantee the level of reliability that customers of Internet-based applications have come to expect. For instance, if a customer uses an unreplicated Web browser to connect to a replicated stock trading server through a gateway, the failure of the gateway could leave the customer wondering about the status of any outstanding invocations issued on the stock trading server. Because the gateway constitutes a single point of failure, the benefits of the server replication are lost to the customer.

The use of redundant gateways requires additional intelligence on the part of the client-side ORB to exploit the multiple gateways. Unfortunately, the required mechanisms are not part of the current CORBA standard. In the absence of the required support in current ORBs, we have implemented a thin client-side interception layer that mimics the support that an enhanced client-side ORB would provide to allow unreplicated CORBA clients to benefit from fault tolerance. As discussed in Section 3.5, we envisage that the functionality of this interception layer will eventually incorporated into the client-side ORB itself.

According to the current CORBA standard, a profile contains addressing information within an IOR. An object's IOR can contain multiple profiles, with each profile designating an alternative address for contacting the object. To allow the addressing information for the multiple gateways to be made available to unreplicated clients, the Eternal Interceptor "stitches"' together the addressing information for each gateway into a single multi-profile IOR.

On the client side, the thin interception layer has the capability of traversing the profiles within the multi-profile IOR, should this be required. The interception layer connects the client object to the first gateway listed in the multi-profile IOR, and inserts a unique TCP/IP client identifier into the service context field (a part of the IIOP request and reply messages), where the user may insert information; if a receiving ORB cannot interpret this information, it will ignore it) of each IIOP message sent out by the client. The advantage of using the service context field is that it can be safely ignored (as is the case here) by a server ORB that does not understand it. It is intended purely for the consumption of the gateway.

For each IIOP request message that a gateway receives from a client, the gateway first multicasts the message to the group of gateways. This is done so that every gateway in the group has a record of the invocation in case the first connected gateway fails. The gateway group then multicasts the message into the fault tolerance domain, and the gateway group (and not the connected gateway alone) receives the response.

If the first gateway fails to respond, the client-side interception layer transparently skips to the next profile in the multi-profile IOR, and connects the client to the next operational gateway, and reissues any pending invocations. If the client object sent an invocation for which a response was expected from the first gateway, the client-side interception layer obtains it from the next operational gateway. This is possible because the client-side interception layer supplies the same unique client identifier for each of its requests, along with a unique request identifier, which would make it possible for the new gateway to detect reinvocations due to reconnection of the client-side interception layer to a different gateway. The reason for the reinvocations is two-fold: firstly, it allows the client-side interception layer to communicate the client's unique identifier to the gateway, and secondly, the client-side interception layer has no way of knowing if the first invocation ever reached the original failed gateway. Each gateway also contains the intelligence to inform all of the other gateways in the event that the client fails. In this case, the gateways can delete any state that they may have stored on behalf of the client.

Eternal's duplicate detection and suppression mechanisms described in Section 3.3, along with the unique client identifier, and CORBA's existing request identifier mechanisms, enable the gateway to preserve the replica consistency within the fault tolerance domain, as well as to protect the unreplicated client outside the fault tolerance domain from having its state corrupted. Furthermore, the redundant gateways scheme enables the unreplicated client to benefit from the fault tolerance of the server.

4   Related Work

Other systems have addressed issues related to consistent object replication and fault tolerance for CORBA applications. The Object Group Service [3] provides replication for CORBA applications through a set of CORBA services. Replica consistency is ensured through group communication based on a consensus algorithm implemented through CORBA service objects. Mechanisms have been provided for duplicate detection and suppression, and for state transfer of application state.

The Maestro toolkit [12] includes an IIOP-conformant ORB with an open architecture that supports multiple execution styles and request processing policies. The replicated updates execution style can be used to add reliability and high availability properties to client/server CORBA applications in settings where it is not feasible to make modifications at the client side, as in the case of unreplicated clients contacting replicated server objects. The Maestro toolkit addresses some of the issues in the implementation of gateways.

The AQuA architecture [1,10] is a CORBA-based dependability framework that provides object replication and fault tolerance. AQuA exploits the group communication facilities and the ordering guarantees of the underlying Ensemble and Maestro toolkits to ensure replica consistency for the application. The AQuA gateway translates CORBA object invocations into messages that are transmitted via Ensemble. Duplicate invocations and duplicate responses are detected and filtered by the gateway.

The Distributed Object-Oriented Reliable Service (DOORS) [11] provides fault tolerance through a CORBA-compliant service approach. DOORS consists of CORBA objects that detect, and recover from, replica and processor faults. The system provides support for management of resource and reliability requirements based on the needs of the CORBA application. DOORS employs libraries for the transparent checkpointing of applications; however, duplicate detection and suppression are not addressed.

5   Conclusion

The Eternal system allows applications to span multiple enterprises over the Internet, with the application being decomposed into fault tolerance domains, with the mechanisms of Eternal providing strong replica consistency within each fault tolerance domain. In addition, Eternal provides gateways to allow unreplicated clients and other fault tolerance domains to communicate with the replicated server objects within a fault tolerance domain, without compromising the replica consistency within any fault tolerance domain. Through the use of interception, Eternal provides this fault tolerance transparently to the CORBA application and to the ORB. The gateway mechanisms are crucial to today's applications, where clients are unreplicated, but nevertheless wish to benefit from the fault tolerance provided for the servers.

References

1. M. Cukier, J. Ren, C. Sabnis, W. H. Sanders, D. E. Bakken, M. E. Berman, D. A. Karr, and R. Schantz. AQuA: An adaptive architecture that provides dependable distributed objects. In *Proceedings of the IEEE 17th Symposium on Reliable Distributed Systems*, pages 245–253, West Lafayette, IN, October 1998. 101
2. Eternal Systems and Sun Microsystems. Fault tolerant CORBA using entity redundancy: Initial joint submission. OMG Technical Committee Document orbos/98-04-08, October 1998. 91
3. P. Felber, R. Guerraoui, and A. Schiper. The implementation of a CORBA object group service. *Theory and Practice of Object Systems*, 4(2):93–105, 1998. 101
4. L. E. Moser, P. M. Melliar-Smith, D. A. Agarwal, R. K. Budhia, and C. A. Lingley-Papadopoulos. Totem: A fault-tolerant multicast group communication system. *Communications of the ACM*, 39(4):54–63, April 1996. 90
5. L. E. Moser, P. M. Melliar-Smith, and P. Narasimhan. Consistent object replication in the Eternal system. *Theory and Practice of Object Systems*, 4(2):81–92, 1998. 90
6. P. Narasimhan, L. E. Moser, and P. M. Melliar-Smith. Replica consistency of CORBA objects in partitionable distributed systems. *Distributed Systems Engineering*, 4(3):139–150, 1997. 90

7. P. Narasimhan, L. E. Moser, and P. M. Melliar-Smith. Using interceptors to enhance CORBA. *IEEE Computer*, pages 62–68, July 1999. 91
8. Object Management Group. Fault tolerant CORBA using entity redundancy: Request for proposals. OMG Technical Committee Document orbos/98-04-01, April 1998. 89, 91
9. Object Management Group. The Common Object Request Broker: Architecture and specification, 2.3 edition. OMG Technical Committee Document formal/98-12-01, June 1999. 89
10. R. Schantz, J. Zinky, D. A. Karr, D. Bakken, J. Megquier, and J. Loyall. An object-level gateway supporting integrated-property quality of service. In *Proceedings of the IEEE 2nd International Symposium on Object-Oriented Real-Time Distributed Computing*, pages 223–234, Saint Malo, France, May 1999. 101
11. J. Schonwalder, S. Garg, Y. Huang, A. P. A. van Moorsel, and S. Yajnik. A management interface for distributed fault tolerance CORBA services. In *Proceedings of the IEEE 3rd International Workshop on Systems Management*, pages 98–107, Newport, RI, Apr. 1998. 102
12. A. Vaysburd and K. Birman. The Maestro approach to building reliable interoperable distributed applications with multiple execution styles. *Theory and Practice of Object Systems*, 4(2):73–80, 1998. 101

An Architecture for Distributed *OASIS* Services

John H. Hine[1,*], Walt Yao[2,**], Jean Bacon[2], and Ken Moody[2]

[1] School of Mathematical and Computing Sciences
Victoria University of Wellington
[2] Computer Laboratory
University of Cambridge

Abstract. Role based access control promises a more flexible form of access control for distributed systems. Rather than basing access solely on the identity of a principal the decision also takes into account the roles that the principal currently holds. We present a distributed architecture that supports the *OASIS* role based access control model. The *OASIS* model is based on certificates held by the client and validated by credential records held by servers. We wish to replicate and distribute the credential records to support high availability and reduce latency for certificate validation. Protocols are presented for maintaining replicated credential databases and coping with both server and network failures.

1 Introduction

Role based access control promises a more flexible form of access control for distributed systems. Rather than basing access solely on the identity of a principal the decision also takes into account the roles that the principal currently holds. This set of roles can change dynamically. Indeed the identity of the principal and the roles held can be thought of as constituting a protection domain [7]. Proponents of role based access control also argue that a formal representation of roles can significantly improve the management of access control policies [10,2,12].

The concept that a principal should hold access control rights dates from the development of capabilities [11]. The key problem with roles or capabilities when compared with access control lists is the management of the distributed representation of access control rights. To date there have been few designs for role based access control that have adequately addressed this issue. In [2] the authors describe a limited cgi-script based system for an organisational web server. In [4] and [5] the authors describe an Open Architecture for Secure Interworking Services, *OASIS*, a proposal for a more general design of a role based access control system.

---

* The work described here was undertaken while John H. Hine was a visiting research fellow in the Computer Laboratory, Cambridge University. The work was supported by the U.K. Engineering and Physical Sciences Research Council, grant no. GR/M37592.
** Walt Yao was supported by the U.K. Engineering and Physical Sciences Research Council, grant no. GR/M75686.

J. Sventek and G. Coulson (Eds.): Middleware 2000, LNCS 1795, pp. 104–120, 2000.

In this paper we present a distributed architecture for the *OASIS* service. The distributed architecture increases availability and reduces latency. Both features are critical to the successful deployment of role based access control into real systems. We present a protocol using weak consistency that is sufficient for maintaining the integrity of the access control policies; a protocol for recovering from a server crash or network partition is also presented.

The following two sections provide an overview of *OASIS*, its major components and operation. We then present the design of a distributed architecture to support *OASIS* services. This is followed by consideration of the implications of server failure and network partition faults. We conclude with a summary of additional work that remains to be undertaken.

2   Policy, Roles, Certificates and Credentials

A claimed advantage of role based access control is the management of access control policy. *OASIS* includes a Role Definition Language (RDL) for the representation of policy. RDL supports the formal specification of the requirements for all aspects of role membership: entry, retention and revocation. RDL specified policy can be translated into a compact form for interpretation by *OASIS* servers. A full discussion of RDL is beyond the scope of this paper. See [4] and [5] for details.

For our purposes it suffices to note that access control policy specifies the necessary requirements for:

1. The entry of a principal into a role and continued possession of that role.
2. The allocation, by one principal to another, of entry to a role and the subsequent revocation of that role.
3. A principal's use of a role to access a service.

A principal requests entry to a role by presenting an *OASIS* server with the prerequisite credentials. If the server is satisfied it grants the principal entry to the requested role by returning a role membership certificate (RMC). The RMC validates membership in the role and may subsequently be presented to an *OASIS* aware service as part of the access control process.

It is important to note that the access control policy specifies both preconditions for role entry and conditions which must remain true for a role to remain valid. For example, it may be required for the principal *Susan* to hold the role DOCTOR-ON-DUTY in order to be admitted to the role WARD-CHARGE-DOCTOR. We would also expect that for *Susan* to continue in the role WARD-CHARGE-DOCTOR she must also retain the role DOCTOR-ON-DUTY. The formal nature of RDL allows *OASIS* to represent these dependencies as a proof tree ensuring that if a certificate becomes invalid other certificates depending on it will also be invalidated. For example if *Susan* loses the role DOCTOR-ON-DUTY her certificate for role WARD-CHARGE-DOCTOR would also become invalid. Role membership certificates may be parameterised. We would expect the certificate for WARD-CHARGE-DOCTOR to be parameterised by the ward identifier.

OASIS also enables a principal holding a suitable role to request auxiliary credentials that can be passed to a third party. In requesting an auxiliary credential the principal may specify pre-conditions, such as roles held, for its use. These are then built into an *auxiliary credential certificate* (ACC), taking advantage of *OASIS*'s existing functionality. The principal may also introduce an arbitrary decision process in deciding which other principals will be passed the ACC. Such a credential may be used by the recipient to obtain entry to additional roles provided the specified pre-conditions are met.

We will use an example to demonstrate the flexibility of auxiliary credentials. Some authority such as a hospital or government health service might issue *Susan* with an auxiliary credential, *doctor*, asserting her medical qualifications. The auxiliary credential certificate would be valid only when used in conjunction with some authenticated principal representing *Susan*, for example at a workstation whose reader held her personal ID-card. Once issued the ACC would be retained across sessions and so allow the DOCTOR-ON-DUTY role to be entered whenever *Susan* logged in.

These auxiliary credentials, which can be used for traditional delegation amongst other purposes, were referred to as *delegation certificates* in [5]. Specific to each ACC the issuer retains a *revocation certificate*, which allows the credential to be revoked at any time. The mechanism allows an appropriate authority to issue and withdraw credentials that control role entry on the basis of alternative decision making processes, possibly external to the computer based system.

3   Overview of *OASIS*

In this section we look at how a principal interacts with a single *OASIS* secured service and how that service manages its role certificates and access control. A *principal* is a process or thread acting on behalf of a particular user or organisation. We assume that each principal has been issued with a unique identifier by an underlying operating system.

Figure 1 shows a single principal interacting with a single service that is secured with *OASIS* role based access control. Role entry and access control are separate functions. As the role entry function issues each role membership certificate a *credential record* supporting the RMC is stored for subsequent use by the access control function.

It is not necessary that the components of Fig. 1 be combined within a single application. For example, an *OASIS aware service* has only the access control function and the secured service. It relies on a separate *OASIS* service to validate certificates presented to it. At the other end of the spectrum an *OASIS* issuing service has responsibility only for managing the access control policy by performing the role entry function, storing credential records and validating certificates for various access control functions. Frequently, such an *OASIS* issuing service will be set up to meet the specialized requirements of an application do-

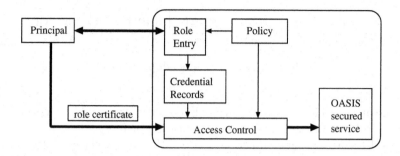

Fig. 1. An *OASIS* service and client

main in which access to particular functions will be controlled on the basis of the roles established.

3.1 Role Entry

In most cases a policy will require that an applicant for entry to a role already holds one or more other roles. The applicant must present appropriate certificates to prove membership of these roles.

Each principal must be able to obtain its first certificate(s) without presenting other certificates. Like Kerberos [14] we assume the existence of some form of initial login server. The user interacts with the login server using a password, swipecard or similar technology to authenticate the user's initial principal. Once authenticated that principal is allowed to enter the role LOGGED-IN-USER and is granted a *LoggedInUser* certificate which may be used to enter further roles.

The role entry function will need to verify the principal and certificates as described below. After the server has confirmed that a certificate is valid and current the role entry function is able to issue a new membership certificate for the requested role.

3.2 Certificates

Figure 2 shows the format of a role membership certificate. The first field identifies the role for which this RMC grants membership. This is followed by a set of N parameters for this role.

The next field is a certificate identifier (CID) that uniquely identifies this certificate. The CID has two components, an identifier of the issuing service and a unique identifier for the certificate within the service. The CID may be used to create an audit trail of access control decisions. The next field is a credential record reference (CRR). The combined CID and CRR fields are used by an access control mechanism to locate the credential record held by the service that issued the certificate. The CID identifies the issuing service and certificate and the CRR provides a hint to locate the credential record.

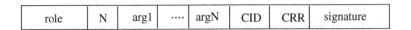

| role | N | arg1 | .... | argN | CID | CRR | signature |

Fig. 2. A role membership certificate

The final field is a digital signature. Each certificate is held by a principal and may be subject to theft, malicious modification or fabrication. This is guarded against by using a hashing function such as MD5 to sign the certificate [15]. The issuing *OASIS* service uses a secret known only to itself in hashing the certificate to produce the signature. The fields that are hashed include the identity of the principal. When the certificate is presented for use it is returned to the issuer for verification. This is done by repeating the hash function and comparing the result with the signature.

3.3   Credential Records

When an *OASIS* server issues a role membership certificate or an auxiliary credential certificate it creates and stores a matching *credential record*. The credential record identifies the certificate and holds state relating to its validity.

The structure of stored credential records establishes a proof tree for each RMC and ACC. Figure 3 demonstrates with a simple example. In this example we assume that *doctor* is an auxiliary credential that has been issued to *Susan*. Assume that entry to the role DOCTOR-ON-DUTY requires both this auxiliary credential and the role LOGGED-IN-USER. *Susan* requests the role DOCTOR-ON-DUTY by presenting her ACC for *doctor* and her RMC for LOGGED-IN-USER. This enables the role entry function and the servers holding the existing credential records to create the proof tree of Fig. 3. A pointer to the new credential record is included with the credential records corresponding to the credential *doctor* and the role LOGGED-IN-USER. (Note that both of these certificates would be parameterised with a persistent identifier for the doctor.)

An acyclic credential record graph is created with some of its links pointing from the credential record database of one service into the credential record database of another. To revoke one of its certificates a service locates the corresponding credential record and sets state to flag the certificate as invalid; it then finds links to the credential records of all immediate dependants. These certificates can then also be revoked. The process continues, recursively invalidating a sub-tree of the credential record database.

3.4   Role Use

A principal uses a role by presenting one or more role membership certificates to the access control mechanism when requesting service. Since the certificate has been held by the principal the access control mechanism must make the following checks:

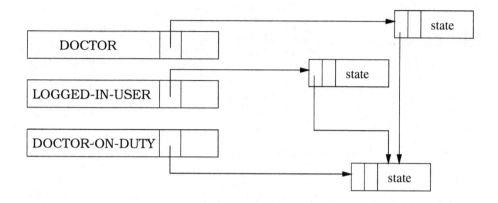

Fig. 3. The certificates held by principal *Susan* and their credential record tree

1. Authenticate the identity of the principal presenting the certificate.
2. Verify that the certificate has not been tampered with.
3. Verify that the certificate has not been revoked and that all necessary conditions for its use remain true.

The principal may be authenticated using a conventional authentication service [9]. The process is completed by referring the certificate and the principal's identity to the *OASIS* service that issued the certificate. The service is identified from the CID. Each service will only recognize certificates issued by services which are explicitly identified within its access control policy. The issuing server recomputes the digital signature using the principal identity supplied. If the signature is correct it uses the CRR to locate the credential record for the certificate in order to ensure that it has not been revoked.

Once the certificate and principal have been verified the access control mechanism uses the identity of the principal, the certified role, and any parameters included in the certificate to determine whether or not to grant the access requested.

3.5   Auxiliary Credentials

An important aspect of *OASIS* role based access control is the ability of one principal to use auxiliary credentials to control another principal's ability to enter a role. Policy for role entry expressed in RDL can require the presentation of an auxiliary credential certificate in addition to one or more role membership certificates. The ACC may give details of additional RMCs required together with any constraints on their parameters. It can therefore be used to extend the role entry policy stored at the *OASIS* server.

Let us develop the example of Fig. 3. It is possible that a hospital manager would appoint charge doctors for the various wards. This could be done by supplying an auxiliary credential, *charge*, to the doctor, *Susan*, and requiring

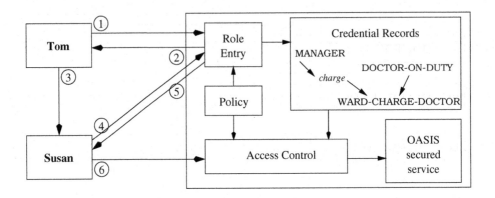

Fig. 4. Creation and use of auxiliary credentials

that she present the *charge* ACC along with her DOCTOR-ON-DUTY RMC in order to enter the role WARD-CHARGE-DOCTOR.

OASIS manages auxiliary credentials with two additional classes of certificates, the auxiliary credential certificate and the revocation certificate. Figure 4 shows the basic steps that would be used in our example. The six messages are:

1. Principal *Tom* requests entry to a role, MANAGER, that can distribute auxiliary credential certificates *charge*. *Tom* would need to satisfy the policy requirements to enter MANAGER. *Tom* is issued with a role membership certificate for MANAGER and a credential record is stored.
   While *Tom* holds the role MANAGER he may request ACCs, *charge*, for entering role WARD-CHARGE-DOCTOR. When requesting an ACC *Tom* may specify pre-conditions for its use when entering the role. These include roles and constraints on parameters of those roles. These conditions are embedded within the ACC and protected by the digital signature.

2. *Tom* allocates the right to enter role WARD-CHARGE-DOCTOR to *Susan*, following a negotiation. Arbitrary information such as references or past experience can be taken into account. *Tom* now requests an ACC *charge* for *Susan*, specifying any pre-conditions agreed during the negotiation. In our example, the ACC *charge* would require an accompanying RMC for DOCTOR-ON-DUTY. These conditions are in addition to any imposed by the role entry policy for the role WARD-CHARGE-DOCTOR.
   When certificate *charge* is issued *Tom* also receives a matching revocation certificate, *revoke*. A credential record for the ACC is stored. There is no credential record for *revoke*.

3. *Tom* allocates the right to enter role WARD-CHARGE-DOCTOR to *Susan* by sending her the ACC, *charge*. *Tom* retains the revocation certificate, *revoke*.

4. *Susan* presents the ACC *charge* and the other prerequisites requesting entry to role WARD-CHARGE-DOCTOR.

5. Assuming entry to role WARD-CHARGE-DOCTOR is granted an appropriate RMC, *WardChargeDoctor*, is returned to *Susan*. A credential record for

this RMC is stored such that it is dependent on the credential record for the auxiliary credential certificate *charge*.

6. *Susan* presents the RMC *WardChargeDoctor* requesting an operation from the service.

The auxiliary credential certificate contains the usual reference (CID plus CRR) to its own credential record. The revocation certificate contains two fields, the first a reference to the credential record for the ACC *charge*, and the second the role MANAGER (possibly parameterised) under which it was issued.

The auxiliary credential may be revoked using the revocation certificate. This must be presented together with an RMC for the role MANAGER. The CRR for the ACC *charge* is used to locate the credential record and the certificate is then invalidated. Any RMC *WardChargeDoctor* that depends on the ACC *charge* will also be revoked.

Using auxiliary credentials it is possible to extend policy expressed in RDL. First, before applying for an ACC the issuer may base the decision on arbitrary logic, including human intervention. Secondly, the issuer can use the ACC to specify roles and constraints on those roles that must be met by any principal.

4   A Distributed Architecture

The *OASIS* service shown in Fig. 1 implies a monolithic service including role entry, access control and the service being secured. We mentioned earlier that this need not be the case and there are strong arguments for separating an *OASIS* aware service (access control, access policy and service) from an *OASIS* certificate issuing and validation service (role entry, role entry policy, credential record storage and certificate validation).

1. The functions of the certificate issuing and validation service are common and can be shared amongst many *OASIS* services.
2. These functions are the foundation of the system's security and should be resident in a physically secured environment.
3. Validation of a certificate requires authenticated communication with other *OASIS* services. By sharing validation services the number of servers is drastically reduced and much of the communication becomes localised within a server.
4. Similarly, the reduced number of servers reduces administration problems.

The deployment of *OASIS* within an enterprise requires consideration of availability and performance. If the *OASIS* issuing service is not available the entire distributed environment will come to a halt. The approach to take is a question of scale. In a smaller organisation where a single server can provide good performance a hot back up can be used to achieve availability. This technique is common and well understood. In a larger enterprise a single server may not meet performance requirements and/or the complexities of the network may invalidate the use of backup for high availability. The architecture presented in

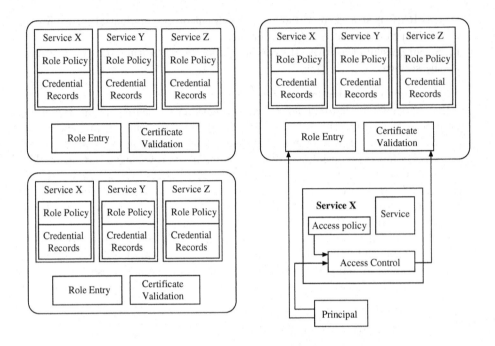

Fig. 5. An architecture for distributed *OASIS* servers

this section is designed for a single enterprise that requires a more robust and complex solution.

Our design allows the *OASIS* certificate issuing and validation servers (here after simply called servers) to be arbitrarily replicated. The algorithms below assume the credential database for each *OASIS* service is replicated on all of the *OASIS* servers. Figure 5 shows three servers with the replicated databases of three services. The service X which uses *OASIS* role based access control may use any server to validate certificates. Clients use the role entry function of the servers to obtain new certificates.

By replicating a service across several machines high availability can be achieved, and by providing multiple points of access we decrease the latency through increased concurrency and the possibility of local access. To further ensure good concurrency, our design does not depend on locking protocols to maintain consistency of the distributed data structure.

These federated servers are identical from the users' viewpoint. That is, the same result is obtained regardless of the server to which a request is addressed. We achieve this using a weak consistency model which tolerates limited transient inconsistency amongst distributed data structures at any instant in time.

Replication of the credential record graph leads to several problems that must be addressed by any solution.

Concurrent Update. Requests to update the CR graph for a particular service may occur independently and concurrently on different servers. For example, two clients may request entry to roles at the same time.

Propagation Delay. Race conditions may arise involving the propagation of a change to a CR graph and the use of that change by a client.

Partial Failure. In many systems the goal of replication is to increase availability and reduce latency. Algorithms that address partial failure are intended to restore an inoperable or disconnected server to operation. *OASIS* servers face the same problem but must also consider the implications of partial failure on access control decisions.

The following assumes that a reliable transport protocol is available between pairs of servers. Each server is assumed to have a persistent store capable of withstanding machine crashes. We assume that a technique such as a redo log allows updates to the credential database to be done atomically [8].

4.1 Distributing Updates

Each server maintains a full and complete replica of each service's credential record graph. This enables each server to validate any certificate issued by any *OASIS* service. The next concern is the maintenance of consistency across the servers. Although it would be possible to use a reliable multicast protocol, see [3], the present application does not require causal ordering of messages.

Our consistency protocol is based on an update-notify model. Each server may make modifications to its own credential database at any time. The server then reliably broadcasts an update message communicating the change to the other servers in the federation. An update message will indicate either an addition or a removal of a CR. A functional definition of these messages is:

```
add ((CID, CRR), new CR, parent list [(CID, CRR) list])
revoke ((CID, CRR))
```

An **add** message carries a new CR, its CID and CRR, and a list of CID and CRR pairs indicating the certificates upon which this CR depends. The server is required to insert the new CR and a new pointer from each CR on which it depends. No existing information is modified.

A **revoke** message carries the CID and CRR pair of the CR which is to be removed from the tree. This CR and any CRs that depend on it are removed.

Each server maintains a sequential count of the updates it initiates. This count is included in each update message broadcast to other servers. Each server maintains a list of the update messages it has seen from all other servers. The sequence count is also used in creating the CID whenever a new certificate is created. As a consequence we have a partial ordering of all messages and CIDs.

Upon receiving an update message, a server is expected to update the appropriate graph to maintain consistency with its peers. Generally speaking the **add** and **revoke** operations are idempotent and may be independently executed in any order. However, there are two situations that can lead to one or more of the CID/CRR pairs in an update message referring to a non-existent CR in the current server's graph 1) the referenced CR has been concurrently revoked, or 2) the pair refers to a new CR which has not yet been notified to this server. In the prior case, the server should simply discard the update message since the earlier revocation implies that the current tree is already the updated version. In the latter case, the server should retain the update message until it receives the update message notifying the creation of the referenced CR.

These cases can be distinguished by comparing the sequence number in the CID with the messages seen from the originating server. If the CID has a higher sequence number it refers to a new certificate for which no CR yet exists at this server. If the CID is smaller it implies that the CR has been deleted.

4.2   Support for Fault Tolerance

In general replication is used to increase availability by allowing service to continue despite a failure. In replicating a security system great care must be taken that operation during a partial failure does not jeopardise system security. The protocol described below is designed to deal with server crashes and network partitions of both a transient and persistent nature.

We assume a fail-silent system in which a crashed server simply stops sending messages, rather than generates erroneous messages. Our aim is to provide support for fault tolerance in the protocol level in order to maintain consistency across replicated servers.

Failure Cases. The protocol described in Sect. 4.1 requires update information to be broadcast to all servers to enable them to update their credential database to reflect the current state of the service. Inconsistency is introduced if a server does not receive one or more messages. The effect of this inconsistency is possible ambiguity observed by the clients. For example, a certificate may be incorrectly rejected if the validation is done by a server that has not received notification of creation of the certificate.

Network partitioning presents a particularly difficult situation for a service supporting security. If a partition separates a set of servers into two groups, while all servers are functional in their own right, updates made to servers on one side of the partition will not be reflected in servers on the other side. The servers are active but have an inconsistent view of the state of the credential records. This has two implications:

1. The creation or invalidation of certificates on one side will not be noticed on the other side until the partition is repaired.
2. It may not be possible to revoke a role entered on the basis of an auxiliary credential if the allocator resides on one side of the partition while the holder is on the other.

We have designed protocols to address each issue. A heartbeat is used to allow lazy consistency, but also detect failures and partitions. We recognise that many failures are transient and provide reliable messaging to overcome these. For more persistent failures that result in a server's database becoming significantly out of date we restore the full database from an agreed checkpoint.

Finally, we address the question of how an operating server should respond to a partial failure by deferring to policy. Some services may be prepared to operate in a partitioned state. Other services may judge that this is too great a risk. The correct place to make this decision is in the policy of each individual service. We accomplish this by providing a simple variable representing the current operational state of each server within the system. The variable may be used in expressing policy allowing decisions to include constraints such as "all servers operating" or "a majority of servers operating". Observe that while it is quite feasible to make decisions on the validity of a certificate it would be unwise to allow copies of the database on both sides of the partition to be updated. Our recovery protocol for persistent failures will not merge two separate databases.

Recovery Protocols. We use separate protocols for recovering from transient and permanent failures. Transient failures are addressed by introducing reliable message logging [1] to the messaging protocol of Sect. 4.1. Where a long term failure occurs the inconsistency of the database may be such that it is more appropriate to download the entire database from another server or to introduce a new replacement server. At this point we switch to a recovery protocol that is a form of active replication [13].

We define five states which describe the state of a server at any given instant.

Normal The server is operating normally. It believes all its peer servers are also alive and share a weakly consistent state.

Replay Logging A server enters this state when it has detected a failed server amongst its peers. It maintains a redo log of all messages which have not been delivered to the failed servers for replay in the future.

Down A server enters this state if it is crashed.

Recovering A server enters this state when it has rebooted following a crash, or network communication to its peers is restored after network partitioning.

Coordinating A recovering server nominates a server to coordinate its recovery phase. The nominated server enters this state.

Short term failures that cause update messages not to be delivered are handled using reliable message logging. In handling a client request to add or revoke a credential record, the server delays the reply until the update is fully logged in its persistent store. It then broadcasts the updates to the other servers. It retains a persistent copy of each broadcast message until it receives an acknowledgement from all other servers.

A heartbeat protocol amongst the servers is used to maintain the currency of connections. Where data is transmitted the heartbeat is piggybacked to avoid unnecessary traffic. When a server detects that another server is down it enters the Replay Logging state, maintaining a structured log of messages not acknowledged by the failed or disconnected server. In this state all update messages are

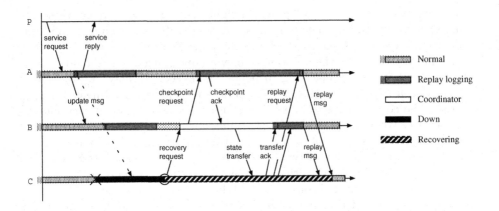

Fig. 6. Recovery from a server crash

saved until the failed server rejoins the federation or a decision is made that any future recovery will be made using a full restore.

If and when the failed server restarts it enters the Recovering state. In this state it uses the last sequence numbers seen from each server to request that all subsequent messages be resent. Once these messages have been received and acknowledged all servers can return to the Normal state of operation.

If a server remains unavailable for a sufficient period of time recovery from structured logs may be abandoned. If this happens all messages that are queued for this server only may be deleted. If this empties the queue of logged messages the server may return to a Normal state.

Where a long term failure occurs the inconsistency of the database may be such that it is more appropriate to download the entire database from another server. In this case other servers discard their redo logs and assume that if the server returns it will recover by doing a full transfer. This allows the same algorithm to support the introduction of an entirely new server and a restart of the failed server.

The full restoration of a server consists of three operations: agreement on a state, $\mathcal{S}$, to be transferred, transfer of $\mathcal{S}$, and transmission of messages arising after the establishment of $\mathcal{S}$. The new server selects one of the operating servers as the coordinator of the recovery process.

Figure 6 demonstrates this recovery protocol. A, B and C are replicated servers, and the state of each server is denoted by S_A, S_B and S_C. Initially, S_A, S_B and S_C are identically equal to $\mathcal{S}$. Let P be a principal requesting a certificate from A. A validates the request and creates a certificate c for P. It will then send an update message $upd(c)$ to both B and C. Now, suppose C crashes before receiving $upd(c)$. Detecting the loss of contact with C, both A and B will move from Normal state to Replay logging state, and log subsequent messages for forwarding to C.

At this point, we know there is some failure in our federation of replicated servers. It is possible the failure is transient. If C resumes while A and B are in Replay logging state, the recovery only involves re-sending any logged messages. However if C remains down for an extended period of time, A and B will abandon this and return to the Normal state. A serious fault has been detected and C has left the federation.

When C returns it enters the Recovering state and broadcasts a message seeking a partner to coordinate its recovery. It accepts one reply, in this example B. B is responsible for coordinating all operating servers to ensure that state S_C is consistent at the end of the recovery protocol. B enters the Coordinator state.

On assuming the role of coordinator, B broadcasts a checkpoint request to all other operational servers, in this example, A. The checkpoint request indicates that C is recovering. Each server responds to the checkpoint request by providing to the Coordinator the sequence number of the last message that it broadcast and entering the Replay Logging state on behalf of the recovering server, C.

The Coordinator awaits the responses from all servers. When these have arrived it confirms that its own database contains all the updates less than or equal to the checkpoints it has received. (The assumption of an underlying reliable messaging protocol implies that this should have happened as a matter of course.) At this point it transfers its entire database to the recovering server, C. When this is acknowledged the Coordinator has finished. It now enters the Replay Logging state, logging any further updates.

The recovering server, C, now completes the recovery process as it would recover from a transient fault. It requests all logged messages from each server specifying the sequence number reached in its database. This is just the sequence number provided by the server to the Coordinator and all subsequent updates are now provided directly to C.

4.3 Analysis

Our protocol solves the concurrent update problem by ensuring the consistency of the final state after all updates. Take the simple example shown in Fig. 7. Suppose we have two servers, A and B, replicating a CR tree. The initial state is shown in (a). Assume a request is made to A to revoke CR4, and simultaneously another request is made to B to create CR6 dependent upon CR4. Both A and B would proceed with their individual requests, producing a temporarily inconsistent state, as shown in (b).

However, A and B will send each other an update message after the local modification has been made. A will notice that CR4 is no longer valid because it was revoked, and it will discard the update message. A will also increment its view of B's current sequence number, since B has used the sequence number to create CR6. B will remove CR4 as a result of receiving the update message from A, producing a tree which is identical to A's. This is the final state of the consolidated CR tree, as shown in (c).

One may argue that there is a window of chance that the certificate for which CR6 is a credential will be used before the revocation of CR4 takes place. If the

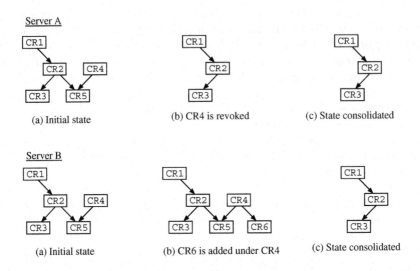

Fig. 7. Resolution for concurrent updates

certificate is presented to A, it would treat it as a new unknown certificate. After the reception of the update message from B, it will learn that the certificate depends on a revoked CR, therefore the use of this certificate will be rejected. If this certificate is presented to B, B will authorise its use if the update message from A has not been received. We argue that this problem is an example of a race condition. Even in a single server situation, the order of arrival of the requests determines the exact consequences. There would still be a chance that certificate CR6 may be used before it is revoked.

Our protocol also solves the problem of delayed propagation. The servers' sequence numbers allow each server to determine whether a missing CR has been revoked or is new. The servers can take appropriate action. For example, a certificate issued by A may be sent for validation before B receives the update message. If B has been asked to validate this certificate, it can determine that this is a new CR. In this case it would wait for the update message from A.

Correctness of the Recovery Protocol. The recovery protocol is correct because the update operations are commutative, and every update made is recorded by at least one server within the federation. The strategy depends on a weak consistency model.

Updates made to a CR tree are either an addition of a new CR or a removal of an existing one, with removal invalidating all dependent CRs. It is trivial to see the commutativity if two updates are made on unrelated CRs. If two updates are made on related CRs, this property still holds. Consider adding a CR that depends on a CR which is being revoked. The addition will fail since there is no valid CR for the new one to depend on in the tree. If the two operations are done in reverse order, the final result would still be the same. This is exactly the case illustrated in Fig. 7.

Consider the case where two additions are made concurrently to a server, with one creating a CR that depends on the CR created by another. If the dependent CR has not been processed by the server, the addition will be left pending until it has been created. This in effect guarantees a consistent final state by serialising the addition operations. The last case involves two removal operations made on related CRs. Removing a node of an inverted tree and its dependents and subsequently removing a second node that the first depended on results in exactly the same tree as removing just the second node.

The commutativity of update operations is crucial, since our recovery protocol must achieve the same result regardless of the order of replaying messages.

The requirement that a server must fully log an update before replying to the client ensures that no orphan state can exist [1,6]. Therefore recovery is a straightforward transfer of state followed by a resend of update messages. This scheme also works in multi-node failure situations.

5   Conclusion

We have presented a description of *OASIS* role based access control and a distributed architecture for supporting it. Work continues on both the functionality of *OASIS* and on the architecture. Our understanding of auxiliary credentials and the different ways in which they may be applied is still evolving. This will improve with experience applying role based access control in different contexts.

The protocols employed in the architecture presented here retain a relatively high level of efficiency at the cost of replicating all services on each server. This constrains the scale that can be achieved in several ways. The cost of updates is proportional to the square of the number of servers. Partial failures may cause some services to stop functioning when they could have functioned quite happily with a smaller number of replicas all on operating servers. A next goal is to produce a design that allows a subset of services to be replicated at each server.

An implementation of the distributed model is under way. It will be used to address questions about the cost of protocols and the system's ability to scale. It will also be used to gain experience with the organisation of roles. We are also investigating the use of *OASIS* role based access control in areas of electronic health records and network management.

Role based access control promises a number of advantages for security in large, complex distributed systems. In this paper we have presented a distributed architecture that supports a resilient, highly available access control service based on the *OASIS* model. This includes protocols supporting weak consistency and recovery from server and network failures.

References

1. L. Alvisi, B. Hoppe, and K. Marzullo. Non-blocking and orphan-free message logging protocols. *23rd Int. Conf. on Fault-Tolerant Computing (FTCS-23)*, pages 145–154, 1993. 115, 119

2. David F. Ferraiolo, John F. Barkley, and D. Richard Kuhn. A role-based access control model and reference implementation within a corporate intranet. *ACM Transactions on Information and System Security*, 2(1):34–64, Feb 1999. 104

3. S. Floyd, V. Jacobson, and S. McCanne. A Reliable Multicast Framework for Light-weight Sessions and Application Level Framing. In *Proc. of the 1995 ACM SIGCOMM Conference*, pages 342-356, Cambridge, MA, Aug 1995. 113

4. Richard Hayton. *OASIS An Open Architecture for Secure Interworking Services.* PhD thesis, Computer Laboratory, University of Cambridge, Mar 1995. 104, 105

5. Richard Hayton, Jean Bacon, and Ken Moody. Oasis: Access control in an open, distributed environment. In *Proc. of IEEE Symposium on Security and Privacy*, pages 3–14, Oakland, CA, May 1998. IEEE. 104, 105, 106

6. D. B. Johnson and W. Zwaenepoel. Sender-based message logging. *17th Int. Symp. on Fault-Tolerant Computing*, pages 14–19, 1987. 119

7. B. W. Lampson. Protection. In *Proc. Fifth Princeton Symposium on Information Sciences and Systems*, pages 437–443, March 1971. reprinted in Operating Systems Review, 8, 1 (Jan. 1974) pp. 417-429. 104

8. Tobin J. Lehman and Michael J. Carey. A recovery algorithm for a high-performance memory-resident database system. In *Proceedings of ACM SIGMOD Annual Conference on Management of Data*, San Francisco, May 1987. ACM. 113

9. R.M. Needham and M.D. Schroeder. Using encryption for authentication in large networks of computers. *Communications of the ACM*, 21(12):993–999, Dec 1978. 109

10. Matunda Nyanchama and Sylvia Osborn. The role graph model and conflict of interest. *ACM Transactions on Information and System Security*, 2(1):3–33, Feb 1999. 104

11. J. H. Saltzer. Naming and binding of objects. In R. Bayer, R.M. Graham, and G. Seegmuller, editors, *Operating Systems, An Advanced Course*, pages 99–208. Springer-Verlag, Berlin, 1979. 104

12. Ravi S. Sandhu, Edward J. Coyne, Hal L. Feinstein, and Charles E. Youman. Role-based access control models. *IEEE Computer*, 29(2):38-47, Feb 1996. 104

13. F. B. Schneider. Implementing fault-tolerant services using the state machine approach: A tutorial. *ACM Computing Surveys*, 22(4):299–319, Dec 1990. 115

14. J.G. Steiner, C. Neuman, and J.I. Schiller. Kerberos: An authentication service for open network systems. In *USENIX*, Dallas, TX, 1988. Uniforum. 107

15. Gene Tsudik. Message authentication with one-way hash functions. In *IEEE Infocom 1992*. IEEE Press, May 1992. 108

Monitoring, Security, and Dynamic Configuration with the *dynamicTAO* Reflective ORB*

Fabio Kon**, Manuel Román, Ping Liu, Jina Mao, Tomonori Yamane, Luiz
Claudio Magalhães, and Roy H. Campbell

Department of Computer Science
University of Illinois at Urbana-Champaign
{f-kon,mroman1,pingliu,jinamao,yamane,magalhae,rhc}@cs.uiuc.edu
http://choices.cs.uiuc.edu/2K/dynamicTAO

Abstract. Conventional middleware systems fail to address important
issues related to dynamism. Modern computer systems have to deal
not only with heterogeneity in the underlying hardware and software
platforms but also with highly dynamic environments. Mobile and distributed applications are greatly affected by dynamic changes of the environment characteristics such as security constraints and resource availability. Existing middleware is not prepared to react to these changes.
In many cases, application developers know when adaptive changes in
communication and security strategies would improve system performance. But often, they are not able to benefit from it because the middleware lacks the mechanisms to support monitoring (to detect when
adaptation should take place) and on-the-fly reconfiguration.
dynamicTAO is a CORBA-compliant reflective ORB that supports dynamic configuration. It maintains an explicit representation of its own
internal structure and uses it to carry out runtime customization safely.
After describing *dynamicTAO*'s design and implementation, we discuss
our experience on the development of two systems benefiting from the
reflective nature of our ORB: a flexible monitoring system for distributed
objects and a mechanism for enforcing access control based on dynamic
security policies.

> There is nothing permanent except change.
> *Heraclitus of Ephesus (535-475 BC)*

1 Introduction

One of the major motivations for the development of middleware is the high
degree of hardware and software heterogeneity encountered in existing systems.
Middleware systems like CORBA are able to hide the specifics of the underlying
platform and provide a uniform high-level interface for application developers.

---

* This research is supported by NSF grants 98-70736 and 99-70139.
** Fabio Kon is supported in part by a grant from CAPES-Brazil, proc.#1405/95-2.

J. Sventek and G. Coulson (Eds.): Middleware 2000, LNCS 1795, pp. 121–143, 2000.
© Springer-Verlag Berlin Heidelberg 2000

However, the diversity in modern computer systems is not limited to differences in the underlying hardware and operating system. One must not forget that even machines with the same hardware type and operating system may be configured with extremely different resources (e.g., Ethernet versus ATM networking, different amounts of RAM and disk space) and with different software packages.

Besides this "diversity in space", we also find a huge "diversity in time", i.e., a single machine typically experience drastic variations in CPU, memory, disk, and network availability. Mobile computers experience changes in connectivity, bandwidth, and error patterns as they move from one area to another. Laptops are subject to different security policies as they are connected to different domains.

Existing middleware systems are not ready to deal with these two kinds of diversity. They are usually optimized to a particular architecture and to a particular configuration. But, computing environments are getting increasingly dynamic; if the next generation middleware is not capable of managing the dynamic variations in the environment properly, a large amount of computing resources will be wasted and application performance will be greatly affected.

In order to cope with these variations and still maintain a good performance level, middleware and application components must be able to detect changes in the environment and reconfigure themselves to optimize their performance under the new conditions. We addressed this problem by adding support for reconfiguration and runtime extensibility within TAO, an open source CORBA Object Request Broker (ORB).

2   *dynamicTAO*

In order to deal with the highly dynamic environments described in the previous section, our group is developing the *2K* distributed operating system [16], which is based on a dynamically configurable middleware layer compatible with CORBA. Rather than implementing a new ORB from scratch, we realized that it would be more productive to modify an existing ORB to add the dynamism we needed.

After carefully studying existing ORBs, we came to the conclusion that the TAO ORB [29] would be the best starting point for developing our infrastructure. TAO is a portable, flexible, extensible, and configurable ORB based on object-oriented design patterns. It is written in C++ and uses the *Strategy* design pattern [6] to separate different aspects of the ORB internal engine. A configuration file is used to specify the strategies the ORB uses to implement aspects like concurrency, request demultiplexing, scheduling, and connection management. At ORB startup time, the configuration file is parsed and the selected strategies are loaded.

TAO is primarily targeted for static hard real-time applications such as Avionics systems. Thus, it assumes that, once the ORB is initially configured, its strategies will remain in place until it completes its execution. There is very little support for on-the-fly reconfiguration.

The *2K* project, on the other hand, seeks to build a flexible infrastructure to support adaptive applications running on dynamic environments. On-the-fly adaptation is extremely important for a wide range of applications including the ones dealing with multimedia, mobile computers, multiple security domains, and other kinds of dynamically changing environments. We achieved the desired level of configurability with *dynamicTAO*, our extension of TAO that enables on-the-fly reconfiguration of its strategies.

2.1   A Reflective ORB

dynamicTAO is our first complete implementation of a CORBA reflective ORB. As pointed out in [31,32], a *reflective* system is a system that gives a program access to its definition and evaluation rules, and defines an interface for altering them. In an ORB, client requests represent the "program" to be evaluated by the system. The ORB implementation represents the "evaluator", and "evaluation" is simply remote method invocation. A reflective ORB makes it possible to redefine its evaluation semantics.

dynamicTAO is a reflective ORB because it allows inspection and reconfiguration of its internal engine. It achieves that by exporting an interface for (1) transferring components across the distributed system, (2) loading and unloading modules into the ORB runtime, and (3) inspecting and modifying the ORB configuration state. The infrastructure can also be used for dynamic reconfiguration of servants running on top of the ORB and even for reconfiguring non-CORBA applications.

Reification in *dynamicTAO* is achieved through a collection of entities known as *component configurators* [12,13]. A component configurator holds the dependencies between a certain component and other system components. Each process running the *dynamicTAO* ORB contains a component configurator instance called `DomainConfigurator`. It is responsible for maintaining references to instances of the ORB and to servants running in that process. In addition, each instance of the ORB contains a customized component configurator called `TAOConfigurator`.

`TAOConfigurator` contains hooks to which implementations of *dynamicTAO* strategies are attached. Hooks work as "mounting points" where specific strategy implementations are made available to the ORB. We currently support hooks for different kinds of strategies such as Concurrency, Security, Monitoring, and the like. The association between hooks and component implementations can be changed at any time, subject to safety constraints.

Figure 1 illustrates this reification mechanism in a process containing a single instance of the ORB. If necessary, individual strategies can use component configurators to store their dependencies upon ORB instances and other strategies. These configurators may also store references to client connections that depend on the strategies. With this information, it is possible to manage strategy reconfiguration consistently as we explain in section 2.3.

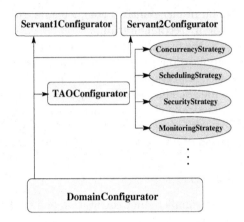

Fig. 1. Reifying the *dynamicTAO* structure

Component implementations are shipped as dynamically loadable libraries, so they can be linked to the ORB process at runtime. They are organized in *categories* representing different aspects of the ORB internal engine (which are associated with *dynamicTAO* hooks) or different types of servant components. In future implementations, we intend to support category type-checking using ANSI C++ runtime type information (RTTI).

The *dynamicTAO* architectural framework is depicted in figure 2. The *Persistent Repository* stores category implementations in the local file system. It offers methods for manipulating (e.g. browsing, creating, deleting) categories and the implementations of each category. Once a component implementation is stored in the local repository, it can be dynamically loaded into the process runtime.

A *Network Broker* receives reconfiguration requests from the network and forwards them to the *Dynamic Service Configurator*. The latter contains the DomainConfigurator (shown in figure 1) and supplies common operations for dynamic configuration of components at runtime. It delegates some of its functions to specific component configurators (e.g., *TAOConfigurator* or a certain *ServantConfigurator*).

We minimized the changes to the standard ACE/TAO distribution by delegating some of the basic configuration tasks to components of the ACE framework such as the ACE_Service_Config (used to process startup configuration files and manage dynamic linking) and the ACE_Service_Repository (to manage loaded implementations) [9].

This architectural framework enables the development of different kinds of persistent repositories and network brokers to interact with the Dynamic Service Configurator. Thus, it is possible to use different naming schemes when storing category implementations and different communication protocols for remote configuration as described below.

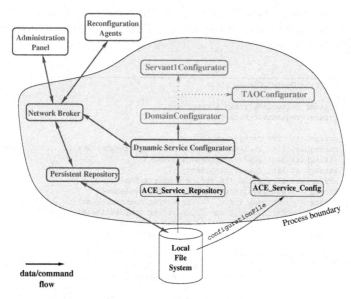

Fig. 2. *dynamicTAO* Components

We built the *dynamicTAO* components using the ACE wrappers [5] for operating system services. Thus, *dynamicTAO* runs on the several different platforms to which ACE was ported.

2.2   Reconfiguration Interface

dynamicTAO supports three distinct forms of reconfiguration interfaces. In general terms, they all provide the same functionality but each of them has characteristics that makes it more or less appropriate for certain situations. A description of the interfaces follows.

1. The **DCP Broker** is a customized subclass of the *Network Broker* shown in Figure 2. It listens on a TCP port, waiting for connection requests from remote clients. Once a connection is established, a client can send inspection and reconfiguration commands using DCP, our Distributed Configuration Protocol [11]. This interface is particularly good for debugging and for fast interaction with an ORB since the user can access the configuration interface simply by establishing a telnet connection to the DCP Broker.
2. The **Reconfiguration Agent Broker** is also a customized subclass of the *Network Broker*, it is useful for configuring a distributed collection of ORBs as we describe in section 2.4.
3. The **DynamicConfigurator** is a CORBA object that exports an IDL interface with operations equivalent to the ones offered by the DCP protocol. It is the most convenient of the three interfaces for programmatic interactions since all the communication aspects are hidden by the CORBA middleware.

We now use the DynamicConfigurator IDL specification presented in figure 3 to explain the functionality of the *dynamicTAO* reconfiguration interfaces[1].

```
interface DynamicConfigurator
{
 typedef sequence<string> stringList;
 typedef sequence<octet> implCode;

 stringList list_categories ();
 stringList list_implementations (in string categoryName);
 stringList list_loaded_implementations ()
 stringList list_domain_components ();
 stringList list_hooks (in string componentName);
 string     get_impl_info      (in string implName);
 string     get_comp_info      (in string componentName);
 string     get_hooked_comp    (in string componentName,
                                 in string hookName);
 string     get_latest_version (in string categoryName);

 long load_implementation (in  string categoryName,
                           in  string impName,
                           in  string params
                           in  Configuration::Factory factory,
                           out Configuration::ComponentConfigurator cc);
 void hook_implementation (in string loadedImpName,
                           in string componentName,
                           in string hookName);

 void suspend_implementation   (in string loadedImpName);
 void resume_implementation    (in string loadedImpName);
 void remove_implementation    (in string loadedImpName);
 void configure_implementation (in string loadedImpName,
                                in string message);

 void upload_implementation    (in string categoryName,
                                in string impName,
                                in implCode binCode);
 void download_implementation (in string categoryName,
                               inout string impName,
                               out implCode binCode);
 void delete_implementation    (in string categoryName,
                                in string impName);
};
```

Fig. 3. The *DynamicConfigurator* interface

The *DynamicConfigurator* interface specifies the operations that can be performed on *dynamicTAO* abstractions, namely, categories, implementations, hooks, and configurable components. The first nine operations in the interface are used to inspect the dynamic structure of that domain and retrieve information about the different abstractions. A *category* represents the type of a component; each category typically contains different *implementations*, i.e., dynamically loadable code stored in the Persistent Implementation Repository. For example, a category called Concurrency contains the three threading models

---

[1] To make figure 3 more clear, we omitted the exceptions that each operation can raise.

that *dynamicTAO* currently supports: `Reactive_Strategy`, `Thread_Strategy`, and `Thread_Pool_Strategy`.

Once an implementation is loaded into the system runtime, it becomes a *loaded implementation* and can be associated with a logical *component* in the ORB domain. Finally, components have *hooks* that are used to represent inter-component dependence; if a component *A* depends upon component *B* then this dependence is represented by attaching *B* to a hook in *A*.

`load_implementation` dynamically loads and starts an implementation from the persistent repository. `hook_implementation` attaches it to a hook in one of the components in the domain.

The next four methods allow operations on loaded implementations. It is possible to suspend and resume their main threads, remove them from the process, and send them component-specific reconfiguration messages.

`upload_implementation` allows an external entity to send an implementation to be stored in the local Persistent Repository, so that it can be linked to a running process and attached to a hook. Conversely, `download_implementation` allows a remote entity to retrieve an implementation from the local Persistent Repository. Finally, `delete_implementation` is used to delete implementations stored at the ORB Persistent Repository.

Consider now the scenario in which a user wants to change the threading model at runtime by using an implementation of the Concurrency strategy called *Thread_Pool Strategy*. Assuming that the user wants to start with a thread pool of size 20, the required configuration steps are the following.

1. Load the implementation into memory:
   ```
   version = load_implementation("Concurrency","Thread_Pool_Strategy",
   "20", 0, cc)
   ```
2. Attach the implementation to the *Concurrency* hook in TAO:
   ```
   hook_implementation("Concurrency":version,"TAO",
   "Concurrency_Strategy")
   ```

After the new implementation is attached, the ORB starts using it. In section 2.3, we discuss what happens if a different concurrency strategy is in use.

Figure 4 shows C++ code that uses the Dynamic Configurator to retrieve and print some information about the ORB internal configuration. The code obtains a reference to the *DynamicConfigurator* object through the ORB's *resolve_initial_references()* method.

To facilitate interactive configuration, we developed *Doctor*, a Dynamic ORB Configuration Tool. As shown in figure 5, *Doctor* is a Java graphical user interface that lets users manipulate both the ORB persistent repository and the runtime configuration interactively. The tool establishes a connection to the ORB DCP Broker and let users send DCP messages by using the mouse.

2.3   Consistency

Reconfiguring a running ORB while it is servicing client requests is a difficult task that requires careful consideration. There are two major classes of problems.

```
CORBA::Object_var          dcObj;
DynamicConfigurator_var    dynConf;
CORBA::ORB_var             orb;

orb     = CORBA::ORB_init (argc, argv);
dcObj   = orb->resolve_initial_references ("DynamicConfigurator");
dynConf = DynamicConfigurator::_narrow (dcObj.in ());

stringList *list = dynConf->list_implementations ("Concurrency");

printf ("Available concurrency strategies:");
printStringList (list);

char *ret = dynConf->get_hooked_comp ("TAO", "Concurrency_Strategy");

printf ("Now, using the <%s> concurrency strategy.", ret);
```

Fig. 4. Inspecting the ORB internal state

Consider the case in which *dynamicTAO* receives a request for replacing one of its strategies (S_{old}) by a new strategy (S_{new}). The first problem is that TAO strategies are implemented as C++ objects that communicate through method invocations; thus, before unloading S_{old}, the system must be sure that no one is running S_{old} code and that no one is expecting to run S_{old} code in the future. Otherwise, the system could crash. Thus, it is important to assure that S_{old} is only unloaded after the system can guarantee that its code will not be called.

The second problem is that some strategies need to keep state information. When a strategy S_{old} is being replaced by S_{new}, part of S_{old}'s internal state may need to be transfered to S_{new}. Both problems can be addressed with the help of the *TAOConfigurator*.

Consider, for example, the three concurrency strategies supported by *dynamicTAO*: single-threaded reactive, thread-per-connection, and thread-pool. If the user switches from the reactive or thread-per-connection strategies to any other concurrency strategy, nothing special needs to be done. *dynamicTAO* may simply load the new strategy, update the proper *TAOConfigurator* hook, unload the old strategy, and continue. Old client connections will complete with the concurrency policy dictated by the old strategy. New connections will utilize the new policy.

However, if one switches from the thread-pool strategy to another one, we must take special care. The thread-pool strategy we developed maintains a pool of threads that is created when the strategy is initialized. The threads are shared by all incoming connections to achieve a good level of concurrency without having the runtime overhead of creating new threads. A problem arises when one switches from this strategy to another strategy: the code of the strategy being replaced cannot be immediately unloaded. This happens because, since the threads are reused, they return to the thread-pool strategy code each time a connection finishes. This problem can be solved by a *ThreadPoolConfigurator* keeping information about which threads are handling client connections and destroying them as the connections are closed. When the last thread is destroyed the thread-pool strategy signals that it can be unloaded.

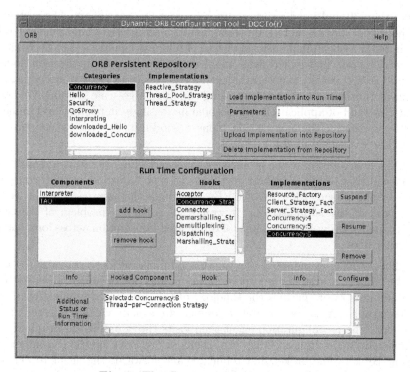

Fig. 5. The *Doctor* configuration tool

Another problem occurs when one replaces the thread-pool strategy by a new one. There may be several incoming connections queued in the strategy waiting for a thread to execute them. The solution is to use the *Memento* pattern [6] to encapsulate the old strategy state in an object that is passed to the new strategy. An object is used to encapsulate the queue of waiting connections. The system simply passes this object to the new strategy which then takes care of the queued connections.

2.4   Reconfiguration Agents

After implementing the first version of *dynamicTAO* we noticed that a significant limitation it presented was that, in order to configure a particular ORB, it required a point-to-point connection between the administration node (e.g. running *Doctor*) and the ORB process. Thus, if a system administrator needed to upgrade a certain component of an on-line service composed of ten replicas located in different countries, it was necessary to connect to each replica separately, upload the new implementation of the component, and reconfigure the replica. This process was extremely laborious and tiresome.

Our group had experience with the deployment of a large-scale Multimedia Distribution System to broadcast live video and audio through a network of more than 30 multimedia servers spread across five continents. The system ran 24 hours per day for more than three months and delivered multimedia streams to more than one million users in dozens of different countries [14]. The difficulty in carrying out that experiment (managing more than 30 application nodes in a wide-area network) exposed the extreme necessity of flexible mechanisms for efficient runtime reconfiguration of long-running, large-scale systems. We believe that this kind of application will become increasingly important and numerous on the Internet in the next decade. Thus, a good infrastructure to support them would be extremely useful.

As a first solution to the problem we considered implementing a management front-end that would allow administrators to type sequences of DCP commands that would be sent to a list of ORBs. Although this approach would simplify the work of the administrator, it would not solve the problem of bandwidth waste, i.e., sending large amounts of duplicated information across long-distance Internet lines.

The solution we adopted was to allow administrators to organize the nodes of their Internet systems in a hierarchical manner for reconfiguration purposes. The administrator specifies the topology of the distributed application as a directed graph and creates a mobile *reconfiguration agent* which is injected into the network. The reconfiguration agent then visits the nodes of this graph of interconnected ORBs. In each ORB, the agents are received by the Reconfiguration Agent Broker. The broker first replicates and forwards the agent to neighboring nodes, then processes the DCP commands locally, and finally, collects the reconfiguration results, sending them back to the neighboring agent source.

Using this approach, the administrator can organize the reconfiguration hierarchy to optimize the data flow between distant application nodes. The reconfiguration commands are executed in parallel in the various nodes, improving response time. If desired, the graph may contain different levels of redundancy so that the system can tolerate the failure of some of the nodes in the reconfiguration network.

Administrators use a Java graphical administrative front-end for specifying reconfiguration graphs and for assembling and sending reconfiguration agents. Given the large variations on Internet line speeds, administrators should have an approximate idea of the available bandwidth in each edge of the reconfiguration graph. With this information it is possible to organize the graph to minimize the transmission over low-bandwidth and congested Internet lines.

The administrator selects those ORBs that will be part of the reconfiguration graph (see figure 6) and draws directed edges connecting the graph nodes (see figure 7). Each time a new ORB is selected from the list on the left-hand side of figure 6, a new node is added to the graph in figure 7.

Once the reconfiguration graph is defined, a new window assists the administrator to build a list of DCP commands that are codified into a reconfiguration agent. Finally, the administrator instructs the graphical front-end to send the agent to an initial node in the graph. Figure 8 shows the composition of an agent

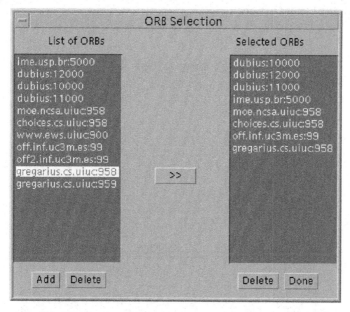

Fig. 6. Selecting the nodes of the reconfiguration graph

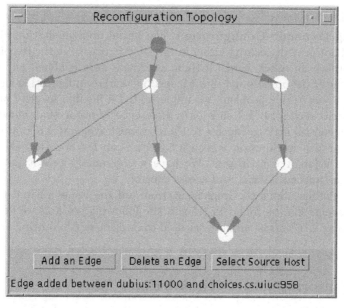

Fig. 7. Defining the reconfiguration topology

with three DCP commands: `list_categories`, `list_loaded_implementations`, and `list_implementations`.

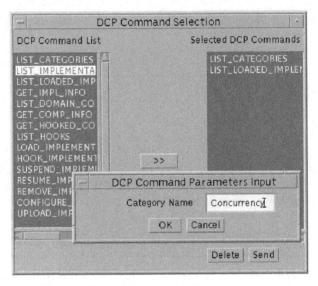

Fig. 8. Composing a reconfiguration agent

Securing Dynamic Configuration The initial implementation of *dynamic-TAO* did not provide security either in the DCP Broker or in the Reconfiguration Agent Broker. In other words, if these interfaces were enabled, any user could contact one of the brokers and inject inspection and reconfiguration agents freely. In order to solve this problem, we implemented a flexible security architecture described in section 4. It relies on a Reference Monitor that allows for very fine-grain control over the access to the *DynamicConfigurator* operations.

We are also working on a security mechanism for both the DCP and the Reconfiguration Agent Brokers. We have a preliminary prototype supporting encryption, authentication, and access control.

More details about the implementation and the issues related to reconfiguration agents can be found in [15]. In the following sections we describe how the *dynamicTAO* infrastructure was used to implement Monitoring and Security services.

3   Monitoring Object Interactions

To support the construction of effective adaptable applications and systems, the middleware must provide a way to detect when adaptation should take place. In the previous section, we showed **how** *dynamicTAO* could be used to adapt an application. In this section, we show how an application can know **when** it is time to adapt.

We built the *2K* Monitoring Service [21] as a dynamically loadable component that can be attached to and detached from *dynamicTAO* at any time by using the configuration interfaces described in the previous section. It is able to collect and consolidate information about the interactions (i.e., method invocations) among CORBA objects in the distributed system. By using the Monitoring Service in conjunction with the *2K* Resource Manager (which provides dynamic information about hardware resource availability), a program can be completely aware of the dynamics of the environment in which it is inserted.

By knowing the nature and magnitude of the interactions between components, a system can reconfigure itself in order to adapt to different situations and improve its performance. Moreover, if the information about component interaction is exported to applications, they become capable of implementing their own adaptation policies. Finally, exporting this information to system administrators and users in a way that they can easily understand, might help them to identify bottlenecks in their system. For example, by showing that applications spend most of their time waiting to access the local file system might indicate that the administrator should install a faster hard disk or that the system should adopt a more effective caching policy.

We developed this service following having two major goals in mind: minimum performance degradation and minimum interference. First, the Monitoring Service should not slow down any part of the system significantly. Second, it should not change the dependency relations among other system and application components. That means that when the service is deactivated, it should be as if the service did not exist. And when the service is activated, the system and application components should not be aware of the service unless it needs to use it.

3.1   Architecture

The Monitoring Service uses the reflective ORB *DynamicConfigurator* interface for dynamically loading (and unloading) its modules. Once the service is loaded, it is inserted into the invocation path by using a request-level interceptor[2]. Unloading it from memory or suspending its execution temporarily causes its removal from the invocation path. When the service is not active, the overhead for the interceptor is negligible (simply checking the nullity of a pointer).

Our architectural framework, shown in Figure 9, is composed of the *Monitoring Interceptor*, which collects information about selected client requests and one or more *Storage Servers*, which are responsible for saving the data into a persistent store and for processing queries about the stored data. In addition, the *dynamicTAO DynamicConfigurator* is used to dynamically configure the interceptor behavior. The Monitoring Service user depicted in Figure 9 is either

---

[2] The interceptor mechanism is defined in the CORBA specification, chapter 18 [22].

a computer program responsible for detecting special conditions in the environment or a programmer or system administrator using a text-based or graphical front-end.

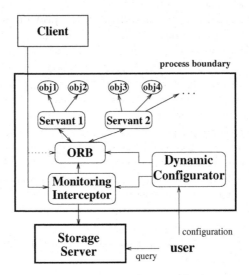

Fig. 9. The Monitoring Service Architecture

Upon initialization, the interceptor contacts the Name Server to locate a Storage Server in the network. Users can then configure the monitoring process through the *configure* method of the *dynamicTAO DynamicConfigurator* interface. It is possible to specify (1) the name of the objects that should be monitored, i.e., which objects should have their requests information sent to the Storage Server, (2) which operations of each object should be monitored, and (3) some interceptor internal parameters such as how often it sends the collected information to the Storage Server.

Every time the interceptor detects a client request that should be sent for storage, it creates a record containing five kinds of information about that request: client machine address, target object name, target operation name, timestamp, and server-side duration. The records are grouped in a local buffer and a different thread sends them to the Storage Server periodically.

The Storage Server stores its data either in a file system or in a database management system and exports two interfaces. The first is used by the monitoring interceptor to publish the collected information and the second is used by users to send queries about the collected information. The query interface provides support for a wide range of query types. Users can ask, for example, "When was the last call to operation A on object X?", "What is the average completion time for calls to operation A on object X from host P?", "How many times did object X receive requests between time t_0 and t_1?", and so on.

3.2   Performance Measurements

We measured the latency on calls to a CORBA object in three different stages. In stage one, we measured the latency on each of the method calls without using the Monitoring Service. In stage two, we measured the latency after the Monitoring Service was loaded and attached to the interceptor, but without having it monitoring this particular object. In the last stage, we measured the latency when the object is being monitored by the Monitoring Service. For each stage, we tested both local and remote method calls. Table 1 shows the average of the results for 50 experiments ran between a Sun Ultra2 and Ultra60 machines running Solaris 2.6 and connected by fast Ethernet. Each experiment consists of measuring the round-trip time for a call on a *getHello()* operation that simply returns a 12-character CORBA string to the client.

Table 1. Monitoring Service overhead (in ms)

getHello calls	Without Monitoring	Monitoring Disabled	Monitoring Enabled
Local	0.781	0.803	0.941
Remote	1.252	1.277	1.379

As can be seen from Table 1, the overhead of the Monitoring Service on an object that was being monitored was 20% and 10% for local and remote calls, respectively. The overhead was reduced to 2.8% and 2.0% when the Monitoring Service was active but not monitoring that particular object.

We are certain that there are still opportunities for optimizations that would make the overhead smaller. However, it is important to notice that the *getHello* operation is almost the worst case scenario because it has no parameters and its returned value is very small. In common cases, CORBA operations carry a large number of arguments that must be marshalled and demarshalled. In those cases, the relative overhead of the Monitoring Service would be much smaller.

4   Dynamic Security

The second service we implemented on top of the *dynamicTAO* infrastructure was the Reference Monitor [17], a flexible mechanism for enforcing access control based on dynamic security policies. This work consisted on deploying the Cherubim security framework [2] in the *dynamicTAO* environment and adding support for audit logging and caching of security decisions.

As we described in section 2.1, the *TAOConfigurator* contains a hook to which security strategies can be dynamically attached. When this happens, the new security strategy has the opportunity to add message-level interceptors (to encrypt/decrypt the message contents and authenticate communication peers) and request-level interceptors (to control the access to CORBA objects).

When using our *Cherubim_Security_Strategy*, applications are able to choose from a large range of security models including Discretionary Access Control (DAC), Double Discretionary Access Control (DDAC), and Mandatory Access Control (MAC) [28]. Cherubim adopts the general CORBA Security Reference Model and the OMG Security Service interfaces [23].

We are currently extending our implementation to support Role-Based Access Control (RBAC) [26] and message-level authentication and encryption. The new security system resulting from this effort will be the basis for security in the *2K* distributed environment.

4.1   Architecture

The Cherubim security framework supports access control by using *Active Capabilities* [2], pieces of Java bytecode that have the same role as conventional capabilities but that carry objects instead of just data. Active Capabilities are protected by digital signatures and encryption and are generated by an administrative tool that has access to a trusted secure store. All the information about user (or principal) roles and privileges are maintained in a secure store object called a *credential*. A single active capability can carry credentials for several objects and, since it contains interpretable code, it can support dynamic, flexible security policies, making decisions based on changing attributes such as location, resource availability, and other situation-specific parameters.

When a principal wants to access an object, it must first present the active capability and then send the desired requests. In our model, clients access secured objects by first installing an active capability into the Reference Monitor and then using the objects without having to worry about security. Alternatively, the active capabilities may be installed by a third party like an administrative tool, or fetched transparently by the Reference Monitor so that the application can be totally unaware of security. In our experiments, we adopted the last approach, which works with security-unaware applications.

Figure 10 shows the major components of our Reference Monitor architecture. If the *Cherubim_Security_Strategy* is attached to the *Server_Security_Strategy* hook in the *TAOConfigurator*, then all client requests are intercepted and delivered to the *Reference Monitor* module.

Before forwarding the call to the ORB, the Reference Monitor must check if the principal associated to the client sending the request is allowed to call that particular operation, on that particular object, with those particular arguments. The Reference Monitor first checks whether that security decision is available in the *Authorization Cache*. If the decision is cached, then it either forwards the call to the ORB (if the security decision is to grant access) or throws a CORBA *NO_PERMISSION* exception.

If the security decision is not available in the Cache, the Reference Monitor contacts the *Active Capability Evaluator*. If necessary, the Active Capability Evaluator contacts the *Policy Server* to fetch the active capability from the *Secure Store*. After the active capability is evaluated, the security decision is stored in the *Authorization Cache* for future use. If any credential in an active

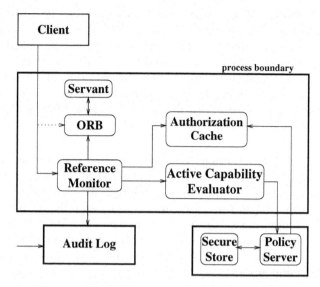

Fig. 10. The Reference Monitor Architecture

capability is revoked, the Policy Server contacts the Authorization Cache to update its list of security decisions.

If desired, security decisions can be stored in the *Audit Log.* The log can be used as a record of all security-sensitive operations performed in the system, assisting in the detection of attempted security violations.

The possibilities for dynamically configuring the security subsystem that *dynamicTAO* provides are very useful for a wide range of applications in several situations. As an example, consider a mobile computer moving from a corporate intranet towards a wireless satellite network. It may be acceptable to use lightweight encryption and soft access control in the intranet but it may be required to apply strong encryption and very tight access control policies when switching to the wireless network.

Each rectangle in figure 10 is a separate component that may be running on a separate machine. Thus, the system is subject to network partitions and to failures in individual components. Our current implementation requires that all the components be available, otherwise, it denies the access by throwing a security exception. The service could be extended to support different behaviors in the presence of network outages such as relying on a local versions of the policy server with limited functionality, and logging the events locally while the remote Audit Log is unreachable.

5   Componentizing the ORB

After our experience in developing applications with both open source and commercial ORBs, we came to the conclusion that typical applications utilize just a very small fraction of the services and functionalities provided by common ORBs. Besides, one of the criticism that CORBA often receives is that it is too big and heavy-weighted to be used in small devices and embedded systems. Although *dynamicTAO* can be configured dynamically, its memory footprint is never less than a Megabyte. It would be extremely difficult, if not impossible, to run it on a PDA such as the PalmPilot III. This motivated us to develop *LegORB*, which can be customized dynamically to adapt to resource availability and to accommodate the requirements of different applications and devices at different moments.

Mies van der Rohe's dictum "Less is more" is *LegORB*'s major tenet. It is a component-based ORB that can be configured at runtime so that it loads just enough components to provide the middleware services required by each application. Applications can select from a range of different implementations for each ORB component category and, as in *dynamicTAO*, replace components on-the-fly. To achieve minimal code size and high performance, we are writing the whole ORB source code from scratch, having small devices and componentization as our fundamental goals.

Unlike *dynamicTAO*, *LegORB* was designed having componentization and dynamic reconfiguration as a fundamental premise. We had embedded systems and PDAs in mind since the very beginning, which allowed us to achieve surprising results in terms of code size. A minimal configuration of LegORB containing just the basic infrastructure and a simple IIOP client engine that is able to send CORBA requests to standard ORBs occupies only around 6Kbytes on the PalmOS operating system for the PalmPilot. The server side includes extra functionality to receive and process client requests. Still, its size can be limited to around 10 to 20Kbytes. These LegORB instances are able to interoperate with traditional ORBs such as Orbix, ORBacus, and Washington University's TAO.

LegORB has a basic skeleton with a set of hooks to which infrastructure components are attached. These components then collaborate to offer ORB functionality. The set of hooks can be extended to accommodate situation specific functionality like real-time processing. Even though the categories are already defined, each category has different implementations. Combining different kinds of categories leads to different ORB behaviors.

The current implementation of the client side of the LegORB defines seven different categories: Invocation Interface, Connector, GIOP, IIOP, MIOP, Marshaler, and Demarshaler. Each category defines a standard interface that implementations of that category must provide. In addition to that, each implementation can add more functionality by offering a more detailed interface to be used by components that are aware of it.

One of the scenarios in which we are applying *2K* is in the context of *active spaces* such as smart rooms. These rooms contain computers, printers, video cameras, projectors, microphones, digital white boards, as well as other kinds of electric and electronic devices. In our preliminary experiments, we "CORBArized" some devices by implementing IDL interfaces that control video cameras, light switches, and even a microwave oven. By using well-defined interfaces and CORBA as a common communication substrate, we were able to integrate all these highly heterogeneous devices into the distributed system and interact with them not only by using powerful workstations running full CORBA implementations but also by using hand-held PalmPilot computers running our minimal ORB.

6 Related Work

Recent research in middleware have identified limitations on existing CORBA implementations, which led to ORB extensions for dealing with specific aspects such as real-time [7], group communication [20], and fault-tolerance [19]. Our goal, on the other hand, is to provide a generic infrastructure in which different kinds of customizations can be performed using reflection [18].

Other research groups have addressed the problem of middleware customization by using different approaches. The Operating Systems group at the Friedrich-Alexander University of Erlangen-Nürnberg is developing AspectIX [8], a configurable middleware architecture based on the fragmented object model. AspectIX clients would interact with a fragment of the global object (the fragment implementation) by using an interface (the fragment interface). The global object could be configured by using "profiles" which in turn specify "aspects" that must be supported by the fragment implementations. AspectIX Aspects can be compared to *dynamicTAO* category implementations with the difference that *dynamicTAO* implementations can be added on-the-fly. The AspectIX group plans to implement a prototype of their model where each object running within a single ORB would be able to specify its own policies and protocols. In *dynamicTAO*, a similar effect could be achieved by using different ORBs inside a single process and configuring each of the ORBs in a different way. In the *LegORB* model, on the other hand, the ORB can be configured to support any of the two approaches.

The Distributed Multimedia Research Group at the Lancaster University has proposed a reflective architecture for next generation middleware [1,4]. They developed a prototype using the Python interpreted language in which the programmer is able to inspect and change the implementation at runtime. The level of reflection is much higher than in *dynamicTAO* since, in their Python system, it is possible to add or remove methods from objects and classes dynamically and even change the the class of an object at runtime. Their research has emphasized dynamic configurability through a well-defined *open binding* model which allows multiple reflective levels. In contrast, our research concentrates on a simpler reflective model, focusing on high performance. In our model, the reflective mechanisms are not included in the normal flow of control, they are only invoked when needed.

The Distributed Adaptive Run-Time (DART) [25] provides a framework where applications can modify their internal behavior as well as the behavior of services that they are using. It distinguishes between internal application adaptation (*Adaptive Methods*) and adaptation of the application's environment

(*Reflective Methods*). In the case of Adaptive Methods, applications offer several implementations of each method. A special entity called *selector* chooses the most effective one at each invocation. In its turn, reflective methods allow adaptation of the runtime environment. When calling a reflective method, the call is redirected to a set of meta-level objects that manage run-time services. A *DART manager* (which can be compared to the *dynamicTAO* DomainConfigurator) stores adaptation information and references to applications and policies. Reconfiguration is triggered and controlled by using events that are also used to maintain consistency. Entities known as *policies* have the knowledge required to reconfigure applications. Policies use the DART manager to access applications as well as the meta-objects associated with them.

COMERA [34] (COM Extensible Remote Architecture) provides a framework based on Microsoft COM that allows users to modify several aspects of the communication middleware at run-time. It relies on the *Custom Marshaler* interface exported by COM, as well as the componentized architecture design that allows the use of user-specified components. By using COMERA, system developers can customize the middleware according to application requirements.

Previous work in system instrumentation and monitoring developed significant contributions that could be applied in the context of CORBA. The Pablo research group at the University of Illinois has developed a powerful framework for performance analysis and visualization [27]. In this framework, raw performance data is processed by performance visualization, correlation, evaluation, and interaction tools. Data is then correlated with appropriate network and computation components, both hardware and software, in order to highlight performance problems in meaningful ways.

The Distributed Object Visualization Environment (DOVE) [10] supports monitoring and visualization of applications and services in heterogeneous distributed systems. DOVE implements a flexible framework where DOVE-enabled applications use *application proxies* to send collected information to DOVE *agents*, which monitor and publish the information to DOVE-enabled browsers.

Unfortunately, most of the existing tools require that the applications be modified to include calls to the instrumentation libraries or monitoring agents. In our reflective approach, the monitoring system can be dynamically loaded into *dynamicTAO* and start to collect information selectively according to the user needs. There is absolutely no change required either in the application code or in the Monitoring Service code.

Our work on security builds on previous and ongoing work in standards for encryption, authentication, and access control [28,26,33]. Commercial products providing security for CORBA systems are starting to appear. However, to the best of our knowledge, no other implementation of the CORBA Security Service provides the degree of flexibility and dynamic configurability that our security architecture provides.

7   Future Work

We are currently developing new components for *LegORB*. Our long-term goal is to support full CORBA functionality through a component-based ORB. Fortunately, the *LegORB* architecture allows us to have working versions of the ORB from its early stages. Now, our work is to add new components incrementally until we achieve the complete functionality we desire. We are currently working on *LegORB* components supporting quality of service for multimedia applications [35] and fault-tolerance in real-time systems [30].

Our Monitoring Service currently does not provide support for visualizing the data that it captures. We will investigate the possibility of utilizing existing tools, like some of the DOVE components, to provide an interactive graphical interface to visualize the data and to configure the monitoring process without loosing the benefits of our system, namely, transparency, flexibility, and dynamic configurability.

Finally, we are extending the security architecture to add support for encryption and role-based access control for the *2K* distributed system by using UIUC Sesame [3] and scalable, dynamic security mechanisms [24].

8   Conclusions

Computing devices tend to become more and more pervasive in our society. Users will no longer tolerate having to adapt to different environments each time they interact with a computer. On the contrary, users expect the computer software to adapt itself to provide the service they need.

These highly dynamic environments with mobile computers, mobile software, and mobile users require a new paradigm for software development and deployment. Heraclitus argued change is the only constant. Middleware systems must be ready to adapt to change.

The ideas and architecture introduced by *dynamicTAO* provide a solid base for supporting safe dynamic reconfiguration of scalable, high-performance distributed systems. We are convinced that our reflective approach to middleware design provides the agility that modern applications require. Even though we are still far from having a complete solution for every aspect of the problem, preliminary results indicate that we are moving in the right direction.

The complete source code for *dynamicTAO* can be obtained from the *2K* web site at http://choices.cs.uiuc.edu/2k/dynamicTAO.

References

1. Gordon Blair, Geoff Coulson, Philippe Robin, and Michael Papathomas. An Architecture for Next Generation Middleware. In *Proceedings of Middleware '98*, Lake District, England, November 1998. 139

2. Roy Campbell and Tin Qian. Dynamic Agent-based Security Architecture for Mobile Computers. In *Proceedings of the Second International Conference on Parallel and Distributed Computing and Networks (PDCN'98)*, pages 291–299, Australia, December 1998. 135, 136
3. Monika Chandak. Implementation of Sesame in Java. Master's thesis, Department of Computer Science, University of Illinois at Urbana-Champaign, 1999. 141
4. Fabio Costa and Gordon Blair. A Reflective Architecture for Middleware: Design and Implementation. In *Proceedings of the ECOOP'99 Workshop for PhD Students in Object Oriented Systems*, Lisbon, June 1999. 139
5. Schmidt Douglas C. The ADAPTIVE Communication Environment. In *Proceedings of the Sun User Group Conference*, San Jose, California, December 1993. 125
6. E. Gamma, R. Helm, R. Johnson, and J. Vlissides. *Design Patterns, Elements of Object-Oriented Software.* Addison-Wesley, 1995. 122, 129
7. Timothy H. Harrison, David L. Levine, and Douglas C. Schmidt. The Design and Performance of a Real-time CORBA Object Event Service. In *Proceedings of the OOPSLA*. ACM, October 1997. 139
8. F. Hauck, U. Becker, M. Geier, E. Meier, U. Rastofer, and M. Steckmeier. AspectIX: A Middleware for Aspect-Oriented Programming. In *Object-Oriented Technology, ECOOP'98 Workshop Reader, LNCS 1543*, pages 426–427. Springer-Verlag, 1998. 139
9. Prashant Jain and Douglas C. Schmidt. Dynamically Configuring Communication Services with the Service Configuration Pattern. *C++ Report*, 9(6), June 1997. 124
10. Michael Kircher and Douglas C. Schmidt. DOVE: A Distributed Object Visualization Environment. *C++ Report*, 11(3):42–51, March 1999. 140
11. Fabio Kon. Distributed Configuration Protocol. Project home page: http://choices.cs.uiuc.edu/2k/DCP, June 1998. 125
12. Fabio Kon and Roy H. Campbell. Supporting Automatic Configuration of Component-Based Distributed Systems. In *Proc. 5th USENIX Conference on Object-Oriented Technologies and Systems (COOTS'99)*, pages 175–187, San Diego, CA, May 1999. 123
13. Fabio Kon and Roy H. Campbell. Dependence Management in Component-Based Distributed Systems. *IEEE Concurrency*, 2000. To appear. 123
14. Fabio Kon, Roy H. Campbell, See-Mong Tan, Miguel Valdez, Zhigang Chen, and Jim Wong. A Component-Based Architecture for Scalable Distributed Multimedia. In *Proceedings of the 14th International Conference on Advanced Science and Technology (ICAST'98)*, pages 121–135, Lucent Technologies, Naperville, April 1998. 130
15. Fabio Kon, Binny Gill, Roy H. Campbell, and M. Dennis Mickunas. Secure Dynamic Reconfiguration of Scalable CORBA Systems with Mobile Agents. Technical Report UIUCDCS-R-99-2131, Department of Computer Science, University of Illinois at Urbana-Champaign, December 1999. 132
16. Fabio Kon, Ashish Singhai, Roy H. Campbell, Dulcineia Carvalho, Robert Moore, and Francisco J. Ballesteros. 2K: A Reflective, Component-Based Operating System for Rapidly Changing Environments. In *ECOOP'98 Workshop on Reflective Object-Oriented Programming and Systems*, Brussels, Belgium, July 1998. 122
17. Ping Liu. The Design and Implementation of a Reference Monitor for the 2K Operating System. Master's thesis, Department of Computer Science, University of Illinois at Urbana-Champaign, July 1999. 135
18. P. Maes and D. Nardi, editors. *Meta-Level Architectures and Reflection.* North-Holland, 1987. 139

19. Silvano Maffeis. Adding Group Communication and Fault-Tolerance to CORBA. In *Proceedings of the 1995 USENIX Conference on Object-Oriented Technologies*. The USENIX Association, June 1995. 139

20. Silvano Maffeis and Douglas C. Schmidt. Constructing reliable distributed communication systems with CORBA. *IEEE Communications Magazine*, 14(2), February 1997. 139

21. Jina Mao. Monitoring and Analyzing Method Invocations in the 2K Operating System. Master's thesis, Department of Computer Science, University of Illinois at Urbana-Champaign, May 1999. 133

22. OMG. *CORBA v2.2 Specification*. Object Management Group, Framingham, MA, February 1998. OMG Document 98-07-01. 133

23. OMG. Security Service Specification (revision 1.2). Technical Report ptc/98-01-02, The Object Management Group, November 1998. 136

24. Tin Qian. *Dynamic Authorization Support in Large Distributed Systems*. PhD thesis, Department of Computer Science, University of Illinois at Urbana-Champaign, November 1999. 141

25. P.-G. Raverdy and R. Lea. DART: A Distributed Adaptive Run-Time. In *Work-in-progress presented at the IFIP International Conference on Distributed Systems Platforms and Open Distributed Processing (Middleware'98)*, September 1998. 139

26. Ravi S. Sandhu, Edward J. Coyne, Hal L. Feinstein, and Chlarles E. Youman. Role-based Access Control Models. *IEEE Computer*, 29(2):38–47, February 1996. 136, 140

27. Daniel A. Reed and Randy L. Ribler. *Performance Analysis and Visualization*, chapter in the book "Computational Grids: State of the Art and Future Directions in High-Performance Distributed Computing". Morgan-Kaufman Publishers, August 1998. 140

28. Ravi S. Sandu and Pierangela Samarati. Access Control: Principles and Practice. *IEEE Communications Magazine*, 32(9):40–48, September 1994. 136, 140

29. Douglas C. Schmidt and Chris Cleeland. Applying Patterns to Develop Extensible ORB Middleware. *IEEE Communications Magazine Special Issue on Design Patterns*, 1999. 122

30. Lui Sha, R. Rajkumar, and M. Gagliardi. Evolving Dependable Real Time Systems. In *Proceedings of the IEEE Aerospace Applications Conference*, pages 335–346, Aspen, CO, February 1996. IEEE Computer Society Press. 141

31. Ashish Singhai, Aamod Sane, and Roy Campbell. Reflective ORBs: Supporting Robust Time-Critical Distribution. In *Proceedings of the ECOOP'97 Workshop on Reflective Real-Time Object-Oriented Systems*, pages 55–61, Finland, June 1997. ECOOP'97 Workshop Reader, LNCS 1357. 123

32. Ashish Singhai, Aamod Sane, and Roy Campbell. Quarterware for Middleware. In *Proc. 18th International Conference on Distributed Computing Systems (ICDCS)*, pages 192–201. IEEE, May 1998. 123

33. M. Vandenwauver, R. Govaerts, and J. Vandewalle. Overview of Authentication Protocols: Kerberos and SESAME. In *Proceedings of the 31st Annual IEEE Carnahan Conference on Security Technology*, pages 108–113, 1997. 140

34. Y. M. Wang and Woei-Jyh Lee. COMERA: COM extensible remoting architecture. In *Proceedings of the 4th Conference on Object-Oriented Technologies and Systems (COOTS)*. Usenix, April 1998. 140

35. Dongyan Xu, Duangdao Wichadakul, and Klara Nahrstedt. Multimedia Service Configuration and Reservation in Heterogeneous Environments. In *Proceedings of the 20th International Conference on Distributed Computing Systems (ICDCS'2000)*, Taipei, Taiwan, April 2000. 141

Customization of Object Request Brokers by Application Specific Policies

Bo Nørregaard Jørgensen[1*], Eddy Truyen[2**], Frank Matthijs[2**], and Wouter Joosen[2**]

[1]The Maersk Mc-Kinney Moller Institute for Production Technology,
University of Southern Denmark, Odense Campus,
DK-5230 Odense M, Denmark.
bnj@mip.sdu.dk

[2]Computer Science Department, Katholieke Universiteit Leuven
Celestijnenlaan 200A, B-3001 Leuven Belgium
{Eddy.Truyen, Frank.Matthijs, Wouter.Joosen}@cs.kuleuven.ac.be

Abstract. This paper presents an architectural framework for customizing
Object Request Broker (ORB) implementations to application-specific
preferences for various non-functional requirements. ORB implementations are
built by reusing a domain-specific component-based architecture that offers
support for one or more non-functional requirements. The domain-specific
architecture provides the mechanism that allows the ORB to reconfigure its
own implementation at run-time on the basis of application-specific
preferences. This mechanism is based on a run-time selection between
alternative component implementations that guarantee different service-levels
for non-functional requirements. Application-specific preferences are defined in
policies and service-level guarantees are defined in component descriptors.
Policies and component descriptors are expressed using descriptive languages.
This gives application programmers an easy and powerful tool for customizing
an ORB implementation. To validate the feasibility of our architectural
framework we have applied it in the domain of robotic control applications.

1 Introduction

The success of distributed object technology in time-critical distributed systems, such
as robotic manufacturing systems, depends on the advent of Object Request Brokers
(ORBs) that integrate support for non-functional requirements. Non-functional
requirements pertain to requirements that are not directly included in the functionality
of the application (i.e. what the application does) but rather express additional

---

* This research was supported in part by the A. P. Møller and Chastine Mc-Kinney Møller
Foundation, The Danish National Centre for IT Research and …
** … by a grant from the Flemish Institute for the advancement of scientific-technological
research in the industry (IWT).

J. Sventek and G. Coulson (Eds.): Middleware 2000, LNCS 1795, pp. 144-163, 2000.

characteristics that the application should have. In industrial settings such additional requirements include reliability and real-time.

In robotic manufacturing systems various non-functional requirements have effect on the exchange of control messages. Control messages can be simple activation and deactivation commands or commands containing isochronous data. Isochronous data is characterized by being equidistant in time and requiring processing at equal time intervals. In advanced model-based robotics [1] motion planning and joint control result in control messages that contain isochronous data. Distributing these messages in a timely manner requires real-time support from the ORB. By now, it is well known that conventional ORBs like CORBA [2], DCOM [3], Java RMI [4] are not designed to cope with real-time requirements [5].

The development of ORBs that support vertical integration of non-functional requirements from the application level all the way down to the network layer is crucial for successful application of distributed objects in robotic manufacturing systems. To deal with the wide range of non-functional requirements, ORBs are required that can be customized to application-specific preferences. Application-specific customization of an ORB requires some level of flexibility and openness in its implementation. Previous work has shown that meta-level architectures are a powerful technique for opening the ORB's implementation to the application programmer [6]. However, full-scale meta-level architectures make the customization process more complex than most application programmers can comprehend. This results from the inherited complexity of reflective systems and the non-trivial protocols and algorithms used to implement an ORB. As a result, it is very hard for application programmers, who are typically not experts in meta-level architectures or ORB development, to create specialized ORBs that satisfy their needs [7]. One way of solving this problem is to provide tools that allow the application programmer to customize an ORB without requiring him to understand the inner working of an ORB.

The approach we propose is based on architectural support for dynamic reconfiguration of ORB implementations. Reconfiguration of the ORB is based on policies that describe the non-functional requirements specific to the application and descriptors that specify how non-functional requirements are supported by the alternative implementations available for each ORB component. Policies and component descriptors are defined with a specific language for expressing non-functional requirements. At run-time the ORB interprets the policies and descriptors to select the right components for configuring its implementation.

An important characteristic of our approach is that it does not enforce a particular ORB architecture on the ORB developer but allows him to create the ORB architecture that is most appropriate for his specific application domain. The rationale behind this thought is that one size does not fit all. On the contrary, some application domain may require some ORB components that are not present in other domains. For example, embedded systems need compact ORBs with a small footprint, while e-commerce applications need ORBs that support data integrity, authentication, and authorization of remote method invocations.

This paper is organized as follows: section 2 gives an overview of the proposed approach. Section 3 describes each of the elements of our architectural framework. In section 4 we exemplify our architecture by showing how it can be used to create a customized ORB for a robotic control system. Related work is described in section 5. Finally, section 6 concludes.

2   Overview of Our Approach

Traditionally, object oriented analysis and design only focus on the entities within the problem domain, their relationships, and how they interact with external actors. This is all part of describing the functional requirements of the system. However, non-functional requirements, such as reliability, availability, performance, security, or real-time are equally important for establishing a system that can deliver the expected quality of service. Non-functional requirements should be dealt with during analysis and design and should not be postponed until the implementation phase. During use-case analysis some considerations about non-functional requirements often come up. For instance, when describing the use-case for an ATM Cashier system the domain expert may very well ask himself whether or not the transaction responsible for money withdrawal should use a secure line to the main server. By extending the use-case analysis phase to include the specification of non-functional requirements, the domain expert can record non-functional requirements together with the functionality they apply to.

This paper presents an architecture that offers an easy but powerful way for integrating those non-functional requirements into ORB implementations. In the rest of this section we describe the important features of our work.

2.1   Architectural Framework for Domain Specific ORBs

Since distributed technologies are nowadays applied in almost every application domain, one general ORB architecture that is put forward as a fit for all applications, is not realistic. Instead ORBs should be developed for a specific application-domain or for a family of applications, incorporating support for only those non-functional requirements that are relevant for that specific application domain or family of applications.

Our approach supports this idea by providing the ORB developer with a domain-specific component framework that defines a basic ORB architecture that is tailored for a specific application domain or family of applications. The ORB developer uses this basic architecture to build an ORB implementation that realizes all the non-functional requirements recorded during the use-case analysis phase. However, since the non-functional behavior is not necessarily the same for all parts of the application, it is essential that the ORB implementation can be dynamic reconfigured with respect to how non-functional requirements are realized. To enable this, we define the basic ORB architecture in terms of architectural entities that abstract away from concrete implementation details. This is possible by differentiating between the notions of *component types* that constitute such architectural entities and *component instances* that realize implementations of component types. Each component type defines a set of contractually specified interfaces that describe the external characteristics of the architectural entity, without stating anything about its implementation. The architecture of an ORB is then defined as a static composition of component types that are connected appropriately through their respective interfaces. A component instance provides a specific implementation for a specific component type. There can be more than one component instance per component type: various component instances can differentiate in the non-functional requirements they support and how this support is implemented.

Building an ORB implementation that realizes flexible support for the subset of non-functional requirements, identified in use-case analysis, is then a matter of instantiating the basic architecture with those component instances that provide the expected service-level for each non-functional requirement.

2.2   Policies and Component Descriptors for QoS Specification

A second feature of our approach is that we use a descriptive language for specifying Quality of Service (QoS) expectations of applications and QoS guarantees delivered by component instances. QoS expectations reflect application specific preferences to how well the system must perform with respect to a specific non-functional requirement. QoS guarantees describe the service-level of a component instance for one non-functional requirement. In our approach, QoS expectations are defined in a policy, while QoS guarantees are specified in a component descriptor. For each non-functional requirement, a separate descriptive language is used. Hence policies and component descriptors are defined per non-functional requirement.

The application programmer defines specific policies for each method that takes part in realizing the use-cases. An application specific policy specifies how the non-functional requirement should be handled for the method that it applies to. Hence, an application specific policy will be enforced per remote method invocation. Similarly the ORB component developer defines component descriptors for the component instances that he implements.

2.3   Dynamic Reconfiguration of ORB Implementation

Dynamic reconfiguration of an ORB implementation is supported by a run-time selection mechanism between alternative component instances. This mechanism is implemented within the component type as a generic variation point. A detailed discussion of variation points can be found in [8]. The variation point performs the selection on a per method invocation basis by comparing policies with component descriptors. In our approach, method invocations are reified as typed objects that offer introspection facilities for accessing parameters, method names, destination, invocation context attributes, etc. This is done by stub objects, which also attach to the reified method invocation the policies for that method. This provides the variation point with the information it needs to make appropriate tradeoffs when selecting between alternative component instances. Each variation point bases its choice of component instance on a comparison between the application specific policies associated with the remote method invocation and the component descriptors provided by the alternative component instances.

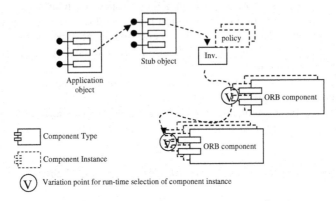

Fig. 1. Flow of reified invocation and policy object

Consequently, the customization of the ORB is controlled at runtime by the application specific policies associated with the methods in the application objects. Fig. 1 shows how the remote method invocation reified by the stub object traverses through the ORB together with its associated policy objects. Propagating the policy objects along with the reified remote method invocation allows all variation points to make the proper choices with respect to the selection of the suitable component instance.

3   Architecture for Customization of Object Request Brokers

In this section we discuss each of the basic building blocks of our architectural framework in detail.

3.1   Variable Features in ORB Design

In general, the implementation of an Object Request Broker can be described as a collection of features. A feature corresponds to an identifiable part of the ORB functionality. Examples of such features are marshalling, invocation scheduling, routing of invocations, etc.

In conventional ORB design, ORBs are viewed as black boxes. This information hiding principle helps during ORB development, but it locks in decisions that can effect QoS, after which those decisions are not readily reexamined. For instance, in robotic manufacturing systems, some remote method invocations have strict timing requirements. Hence the choice of scheduling algorithm in the ORB can effect whether the ORB implementation is acceptable for such systems. In our opinion, an ORB implementation must be designed for change by allowing different variants of the implementation for one or more of its specific features. In the rest of this section we give a non-exhaustive list of features that we believe are subject to variability, limiting the scope to those features that are related to the implementation of remote method invocation. The list of features covers ORBs as well as protocol stacks.

Invocation dispatching Invocation dispatching refers to the process of calling the method corresponding to the invocation on the servant that implements the remote object. Dispatching provides an interception point for reflecting on invocations at the server side.

Marshalling Refers to the process of taking a collection of objects and assembling them into a form suitable for transmission in a message. During marshalling objects can be replaced, like it is the case with stubs in Java RMI. Furthermore marshalling can be extended to perform data compression or encryption.

Unmarshalling This is the reverse process of marshalling. Unmarshalling is the process of disassembling a marshalled message to produce an equivalent collection of objects at the destination. When resolving an object during unmarshalling, it can have its attributes modified or it can be replaced with an equivalent object.

Invocation Context This is a reification of the runtime context in which the invocation takes place. The invocation context is often used to associate non-functional requirements with the invocation, such as security context, priority, user preferences, etc. In the CORBA specification the functionality of an invocation context is provided by the Context object abstraction [2].

Invocation semantics In distributed systems asynchronous invocation semantics can be preferable, since synchronous invocation semantics can result in unnecessary delay at the caller side. Therefore both synchronous and asynchronous invocation semantics should be supported by the ORB.

Invocation scheduling The decision on whether or not an invocation is to be executed may depend on different factors, such as, the state of the servant (preconditions), the priority associated with the invocation if any, the CPU load of the node (resource admission control), etc.

Threading The number of threads available for executing object invocations determines the degree of concurrency within the system. If only one thread is available for executing object invocations, a purely sequential system is the result. In contrast, multiple threads result in a truly concurrent system.

Channel Handle the responsibility of maintaining a session between two address spaces. Session management comes in many flavors, for example object to object, node to node (multiplexed), one per invocation.

Reliability The kind of transport protocols available for transferring the invocation may vary depending on the underlying network technology or according to application domain specific requirements.

Routing According to the non-functional requirements of the application certain types of network technologies may be preferable. This includes Ethernet, ATM, Firewire, Canbus, etc. The availability of network technology is strongly dependent on the application domain. For instance, the use of Canbus is common in industrial automation.

3.2   Architectural Reuse in ORB Design

To facilitate the ORB development for a specific domain, a component framework is used that offers a component-based ORB architecture that is tailored for that specific domain. The architecture defines a set of component types and how these component types cooperate together. In order to support variability, each component type reflects upon a particular variable feature of an ORB in an implementation-independent manner. In the implementation of the component type the variable feature is exploited at a variation point. For each component type, the ORB developer selects one or more component instances. The alternative component instances are characterized by different service-levels for each non-functional requirement.

For example, in the context of a robot control project [1] we have build an ORB component framework that defines an architecture tailored to real-time applications. This architecture is explicitly represented by a composition of Java Beans, where each component type is implemented as a separate Java Bean and component types cooperate together through various classes of events. Fig. 2 gives an overview of the architecture. It consists of the following component types:

ReferenceBean provides the support for the synchronous and asynchronous invocation semantics.

MarshallerBean is responsible of marshalling outgoing invocations and replies, and unmarshalling incoming invocations and replies.

ChannelBean is responsible for session management between address spaces.

TransportBean transmits messages containing invocations and replies between address spaces.

InvocationSchedulerBean determines the order in which to dispatch incoming invocations on the corresponding servant objects.

TaskSchedulerBean controls the threading strategy for executing all computations within the system. This includes computations related to the basic functionality of the

ORB (e.g. listening for incoming requests) as well as computations related to method execution on servant objects.

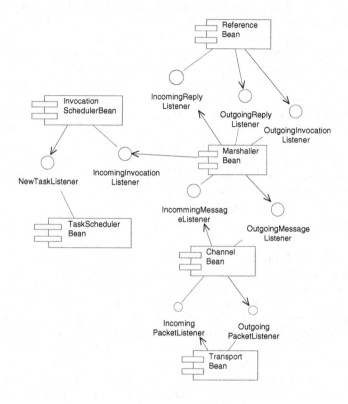

Fig. 2. Bean model of the ORB architecture.

A real-time ORB implementation is constructed as an instantiation from this architecture. The ORB developer just provides the component instances that have to be available for each component type and glue code within each component type connects a component instance - once selected - into the ORB implementation.

Component instances are also implemented as separate Java Beans that implement one feature of the ORB. The design decisions made by the component developer determine its QoS-level for the different non-functional requirements.

3.3   ORB Customization Through Descriptive Languages

ORBs have to take application-specific information into account, to achieve optimal performance. In our approach, application-specific QoS expectations with respect to the implementation of a specific non-functional requirement are defined in a policy. The ORB implementation tries to offer the requested QoS expectations by integrating those components that guarantee the expected service level for that non-functional requirement. In this way, by choosing appropriate individual components, the overall ORB implementation is tailored to the application-specific QoS expectations. QoS guarantees provided by a specific component are defined in component descriptors that are packaged together with the component. As for policies, component descriptors are specified per non-functional requirement.

The definition of policies is the task of the application programmer, whereas the definition of component descriptors is the task of the ORB component developer. However, they are both declared at a high level of abstraction in the same specialized language. The vocabulary of such a language is defined by the ORB developer as a general template. Application-specific policies and component descriptors are then defined using this template. This means that their interpretation is done in terms of the vocabulary defined by the template. The use of templates keeps the variation point independent of specific characteristics of non-functional requirements, as well as component instance implementations. As a consequence, a generic mechanism for realizing variation points can be offered to the ORB developer. Note that the ORB developer has to define a template for each non-functional requirement that he wants to take into account.

3.3.1   Defining Templates, Policies and Component Descriptors

A template defines the vocabulary of a language for describing one specific non-functional requirement. The vocabulary is defined as a set of parameters that can be used to specify QoS expectations and guarantees for one non-functional requirement. The possible service-levels available for each parameter are defined as an enumeration. Each service-level can be further refined by associating it with a number of attributes. For example, for reliability you could define a parameter called *tolerance* that can have three different service-levels: "NONE", "NOT_TRANS-PARENT", "TRANSPARENT". The service-level "TRANSPARENT" has an attribute for specifying the number of faults that are allowed. Another parameter is the *fault type*. For this parameter three different service-levels can be defined: "FAIL_STOP", "BYZANTINE", and "TIME".

Defining a policy from a template consists of specifying the service-level for one or more parameters and setting the associated attributes. A policy only has to define the number of parameters from its template that are necessary to specify the QoS expectations of its associated application method. Parameters that are not defined are assigned a default service-level, by default this is the first service-level from the parameter's enumeration in the template. The process for defining a component descriptor is similar. Each component implementation can have more than one component descriptor, since it can have been built to support more than just one specific non-functional requirement. For instance, a marshalling component can provide support for real-time requirements as well as security requirements, but it doesn't has to do so. Examples for defining policies and component descriptors are given in section 4.

Policies and component descriptors are transformed into objects by parsing their definitions. The corresponding class diagram is shown in Fig. 3.

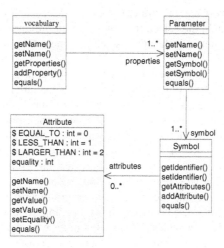

Fig. 3. Class diagram for representing policies and descriptors

3.3.2   Matching Policies with Component Instances

At run-time, all application specific policies that apply to a method are grouped together. The variation points within the ORB component types traverse this group to find the policy objects that influence their choice of implementation.

To make the best match the variation points apply a mapping function to the application specific policies provided for the method and the component descriptors of the component instances of the implicated component type. At each variation point that component instance is selected whose component descriptors make the "best match" with the application specific policies. The best match for an application specific policy is the component descriptor that has the most parameters that match the parameters in the policy. Matching is based on the notion of equality; that is, a component descriptor matches a policy if the attributes associated with the service-levels of its parameters equal with the corresponding attributes of the service-levels defined by the policy. For instance, assume that the value of an attribute in a component descriptor always has to be larger than the value of the attribute in the corresponding policy. This relationship is expressed by setting the equality relation of the attribute in the component descriptor to LARGER_THAN and the equality relation of the attribute in the policy to LESS_THAN. The matching function will then verify that the relation holds for the actual attribute values. An appropriate set of keywords is provided for specifying such equality relations when defining policies and descriptors.

The advantage of the 'best match' strategy is its generality. It is implemented once and for all in one variation point and this variation point can immediately be used in any component type. However, when dealing with more complex cases, the 'best match' strategy may not be sufficient. Examples include the cases where none or more than one component instance fails to completely match all QoS parameters for a non-functional requirement. In these cases, different selection strategies could be preferable over the 'best match' strategy. For instance, when no component instance makes a complete match, the selection strategy could prefer an instance that performs weakly on some parameters rather than selecting one which fails completely on one parameter.

Another complex situation occurs when combining non-functional requirements that are not orthogonal. Non-functional requirements that are not orthogonal introduce constraints that have to be taken into consideration by specialized variation points that are able to enforce these constraints. For instance, when policies for real-time and security are applied simultaneously for a method, an invocation of the method may miss its deadline due to the additional overhead induced by encryption and decryption. This constraint can be taken into account if the framework architect constructs a third template that defines the vocabulary for expressing such a constraint. Using this template the application programmer can for example specify a desired upper limit for encryption overhead, leading to the definition of a third 'overlapping' policy. This provides the variation point with the information it needs to make a good choice between component instances, without breaking the constraint. Here again, different specialized selection strategies can be used. For example, one variation point could decide - when the constraint is violated - to decrease the required security level in favor of the timeliness requirement. One could also consider a variation point that is able to customize its component instances by forwarding the constraint information via a contractually specified meta-interface that the component instances export. Which selection strategy is best, is however often not determinable until the time of instantiating a specific ORB implementation from the ORB component framework. Hence, component types must offer hooks that allow different variation point implementations to be plugged in.

4   Applying the Approach to a Time-Critical Application

In this section we show how our approach can be used to customize an ORB for a distributed robot controller application. The robot controller is part of the SmartController project that addresses the development of a generic robot controller for arbitrary robotic manipulators [1]. The robot controller is built as a component framework, based on an extension of the JavaBeans model [9].

Basically, there are two primary functional aspects that a non-trivial robot controller should take care of. First, there is the task of generating collision free motion for the robot within the work cell. The robot should not collide with itself or with the work piece. Secondly, there is the planning of the work that the robot has to perform on the work piece. This work is described by a process description that specifies the speed by which the robot should move over the surface of the work piece to perform the work correctly. Deviation from the specified speed will have an impact on the quality of the performed work. For instance in spray painting, deviation in the speed by which the spray gun is moved over the surface of the work piece will either result in a thinner or ticker layer of paint.

4.1   Defining a Template for Temporal Behavior

Object interactions within a real-time system can be characterized along the dimensions of timeliness, temporal behavior, and invocation precedence. Timeliness expresses whether an object interaction is time constrained. Temporal behavior specifies how often an object interaction occurs. Finally, invocation precedence specifies whether the next invocation of a method by the same caller is more important than the present one. Invocation precedence is useful when old information becomes obsolete as soon as new information is available. One example is proximity sensors. In robotics, proximity sensors provide information about the distance to nearby obstacles. The actuality of this information is crucial for collision avoidance.

In the context of this paper, timeliness of object interactions is classified by the two values:

REALTIME Response must be timely; that is, within a specified deadline. A late response will have undesirable consequences in the application domain.
NEUTRAL No timing constraint is imposed on the object interaction.

Timeliness says nothing about the magnitude of a timing constraint; it can be microseconds or weeks. The temporal behavior of object interactions is classified as:

PERIODIC Object interactions that take place at regular time intervals and that execute for a fixed amount of time. Each interaction has to finish before the end of its period.
SPORADIC Object interactions triggered by external events or internal state changes.

The precedence of subsequent invocations of the same method is classified as:

NEXT The next invocation has precedence over the present. The present invocation can be skipped if it has not begun execution before the next one arrives.
CURRENT The current invocation has to be finished before the next one is allowed to execute.

Based on these classifications we can define a template for specifying application specific policies for temporal behavior. Fig. 4 shows the template definition.

```
template TemporalBehavior {
    parameter timeliness enum NEUTRAL,REALTIME;
    parameter temporal enum SPORADIC,PERIODIC;
    parameter precedence enum CURRENT,NEXT;
    REALTIME attributes DEADLINE Long;
    PERIODIC attributes PERIOD Long;
}
```

Fig. 4. Template for specifying temporal behavior

4.2   Defining an Application Specific Policy for Temporal Behavior

To illustrate how application specific policies are instantiated from the temporal behavior template we apply it to two methods of the JointController component from our robot controller framework. The result is shown Fig. 5. The JointController component is responsible for applying the forces that describe the robot motion to the robot's joint actuators.

```
TemporalBehavior JointController.
    addSensorDataSubscriber(SensorDataSubscriber) {
    timeliness NEUTRAL;
    temporal SPORADIC;
    precedence CURRENT;
}
TemporalBehavior JointController.onForceReady(Force) {
    timeliness REALTIME attribute DEADLINE 100;
    temporal PERIODIC attribute PERIOD 100;
    precedence NEXT;
    relation DEADLINE larger than;
    relation PERIOD larger than;
}
```

Fig. 5. Temporal policy applied to an application class

The first part of the policy specifies that the method addSensorDataSubscriber is only invoked sporadically and that there is no timing constraint on the execution of the method. The second part specifies that the method onForceReady is invoked periodically and that the execution of each invocation is constrained in time. The precedence parameter tells that new force values are preferable over old ones. The equality relation for the deadline and the period attribute specifies that it must always be larger than the corresponding attribute provided by a component descriptor.

4.3   Defining Component Descriptor for Temporal Behavior

The ORB components that directly influence the temporal behavior of a distributed application are the components responsible for executing and transmitting remote method invocations. In our case these components are the TaskSchedulerBean and the TransportBean. Before we show the descriptors for these components, we describe each component in more detail to give the basis for understanding the meaning of these descriptors.

4.3.1   TaskSchedulerBean
Predictions about the system's temporal behavior can only be made if the execution of all computations within the system is coordinated. Coordination ensures that all computations advance, as they are required to. Introducing the concept of a task enables this. A task represents the basic unit of computation. Examples of tasks within

the ORB include listening for and receiving messages from the network, dispatching invocations to servant objects, etc. Hence, all execution within the ORB and its application is represented as tasks that are scheduled by the TaskSchedulerBean. The application programmer is not allowed to create threads within the application, since they will interfere with the scheduling done by the TaskSchedulerBean. Component instances of the TaskSchedulerBean can provide different scheduling guarantees. One component instance can be used for tasks that only require best-effort scheduling and execution; whereas, another component instance can be used for tasks that require real-time scheduling. Here real-time scheduling refers to either Early-deadline-first or Rate-monotonic scheduling [10].

The rationale for encapsulating the threading feature in the TaskSchedulerBean is the fact that if a time-critical application is built on top of an ORB that does not apply any strategy for coordinating the execution of threads, it can result in missed deadlines for important operations. In the task-based approach this situation is avoided by using a component instance which implements a real-time scheduling algorithm for executing time constrained tasks and a component instance that implements a non real-time scheduling algorithm for executing tasks that only require best-effort service. The execution of tasks scheduled by the real-time scheduling algorithm will be done in a thread given a real-time priority whereas execution of non real-time tasks will be done in a thread with normal priority. Component descriptors for two component instances of the TaskSchedulerBean that implements these different scheduling strategies are shown in Fig. 6. In our current prototype, the RealtimeTaskSchedulerBean uses a thread running at the highest priority.

```
TemporalBehavior FifoTaskSchedulerBean {
    timeliness NEUTRAL;
    temporal SPORADIC;
    precedence CURRENT;
}
TemporalBehavior RealtimeTaskSchedulerBean {
    timeliness REALTIME attribute DEADLINE 10;
    temporal PERIODIC attribute PERIOD 10;
    precedence NEXT;
    relation DEADLINE less than;
    relation PERIOD less than;
}
```

Fig. 6. Component descriptor for TaskScheduler component instances

4.3.2   TransportBean

The TransportBean is responsible for transferring object invocations to a different address space. The most interesting case is when the source and destination address spaces are located on different hosts. In that case, the object invocations are sent over the network, which is an important factor affecting the overall QoS guarantees an ORB is able to make. The TransportBean is implemented as a specialized instantiation of our DIPS protocol stack framework [11]. The framework can instantiate dynamic protocol stacks which can cope with variability in much the same way as the global ORB architecture. The TransportBean is in itself a component framework with its own variation points. This nested structure has the advantage that each variation point inside this Bean can be individually described, while the TransportBean still fits in the global ORB architecture as one component which supports the global QoS concerns. The designers of the TransportBean have to determine which non-functional concerns they will support. For each non-functional aspect they support, they have to provide a component descriptor. In the case of our example, they will support the TemporalBehaviour template. The example of the TransportBean is interesting in that it shows what happens when an ORB component is itself built from components. In this case, the TransportBean consists of two component types, namely the RoutingBean and the ReliabilityBean. The rest of the TransportBean structure and functionality is not relevant for the discussion in this paper. We like to stress, though, that as the TransportBean is built with a flexible protocol stack framework, new versions can be built which expose additional internal component types, should the need arise.

We now describe the function of each of the two nested component types in more detail.

RoutingBean The RoutingBean is responsible for selecting the underlying network technology. A selection is made based on the application requirements and on the capabilities of the underlying communication technology. This resource-aware routing is a variation point in the TransportBean, therefore the TransportBean exposes the RoutingBean type. Depending on the type of remote method invocation that has to be sent over the network, a specific RoutingBean instance will be chosen. For example, a real-time invocation with a short deadline will be sent over a communication channel which can guarantee timely delivery, such as IEEE 1394 Firewire. Neutral invocations are sent over another channel if possible, for example, a cheap Ethernet connection, to avoid unnecessary usage of precious resources. The cases discussed in this example are handled by the FirewireRoutingBean and the EthernetRoutingBean component instances, respectively.

ReliabilityBean Many remote method invocations require reliable transmission. The TransportBean therefore includes a ReliabilityBean for managing acknowledgements and retransmissions. The retransmission strategy is an important ingredient of this component which has a strong impact on the ability of the TransportBean to provide QoS. Therefore, the TransportBean includes a variation point for the retransmission strategy by exposing the ReliabilityBean component type. As a result, a specific ReliabilityBean instance is chosen depending on the properties of the object invocation at hand. For example, for a periodic remote method invocation for which the precedence parameter has the value "NEXT", the strategy takes into account the period of the invocation and it does not perform retransmissions when the next invocation is imminent. For sporadic invocations, a retransmission strategy such as the one included in TCP is more suitable. These cases are handled by the PrefernextReliabilityBean and the NormalReliabilityBean component instances, respectively.

In order to support the automatic component instance selection, the TransportBean component developer has to provide a component descriptor for every instance of both the RoutingBean and the ReliabilityBean. See Fig. 7 for the descriptors of the component instances from our example. The FirewireRoutingBean can cope with remote method invocations with real-time constraints, whether they are sporadic or periodic. The EthernetRoutingBean can only handle neutral sporadic invocations. The ReliabilityBean instances can each handle a different kind of precedence.

```
TemporalBehavior FirewireRoutingBean {
    timeliness REALTIME attribute DEADLINE undefined;
    temporal SPORADIC,PERIODIC attribute PERIOD undefined;
    relation DEADLINE less than;
    relation PERIOD less than;
}
TemporalBehavior EthernetRoutingBean {
    timeliness NEUTRAL;
    temporal SPORADIC;
    precedence CURRENT;
}
TemporalBehavior PrefernextReliabilityBean {
    precedence NEXT;
}
TemporalBehavior NormalReliabilityBean {
    precedence CURRENT;
}
```

Fig. 7. Component descriptors for the RoutingBean and the ReliabilityBean

In addition, the TransportBean itself needs a descriptor that describes its capabilities to the rest of the ORB. This descriptor is simply the combination of the capabilities of all internal component instances that make up the TransportBean. The result is given in Fig. 8.

```
TemporalBehavior TransportBean {
    timeliness NEUTRAL, REALTIME attribute DEADLINE undefined;
    temporal SPORADIC, PERIODIC attribute PERIOD undefined;
    precedence CURRENT, NEXT;
    relation DEADLINE less than;
    relation PERIOD less than;
}
```

Fig. 8. Component descriptor for TransportBean component implementation

This descriptor basically means that our TransportBean instance can cope with all kinds of remote method invocations. Its internal variation points and nested components will take care of it. Note that the values for the deadline and period attributes are left out for the TransportBean. This means that the values are dynamically determined at run-time by the component instances.

4.4   Mapping Temporal Behavior to Component Instances

To exemplify how reconfiguration of the ORB works, we will discuss the invocation of two methods with different temporal behavior. Both methods belong to the JointController component from our SmartController framework.

When the method addSensorDataSubscriber is invoked on the JointController stub, the invocation is reified and the application specific policies associated with the method are retrieved. In the present case only one application specific policy has been associated with the method, namely an instance of the TemporalBehavior template. Its policy object is now propagated along with the invocation down through the ORB. When the invocation arrives at the TransportBean at the client side, the RoutingBean and the ReliabilityBean within the TransportBean decide to transmit the invocation to the destination address space using the component instances EthernetRoutingBean and NormalReliabilityBean, respectively. The TransportBean makes this decision based on the value of the timeliness parameter, which is "NEUTRAL". At the server side, the TaskSchedulerBean assigns the Task responsible for executing the invocation is the component instance FifoTaskSchedulerBean. This assignment is based on the same reasoning.

Invocation of the method onForceReady leads to different choices within the TransportBean and the TaskSchedulerBean, due to the different values of the policy properties. Now the TransportBean chooses to use the component instances FirewireRoutingBean and PrefernextReliabilityBean for transmitting the invocation. This choice is made because the value of the timeliness parameter is "REALTIME". Similarly, the TaskSchedulerBean, at the server side, chooses to use the RealtimeTaskSchedulerBean component instance. In general terms the temporal nature of the method onForceReady can be characterized as isochronous. This is specified by setting the timeliness parameter to "REALTIME", the temporal parameter to "PERIODIC", and the precedence parameter to "NEXT". The retransmission algorithm within the PrefernextReliabilityBean can utilize this information to optimize its performance for transferring the force information. Here optimization consists in skipping retransmission of the current invocation in case of transmission failures if the next invocation has become available in the meanwhile.

This example illustrates that the temporal behavior of a method depends on its function within the application. Accordingly the ORB can not just handle all method invocations equally. Run-time reconfiguration of the ORB is necessary to meet the requirements of different methods.

5   Related Work

Related projects investigate ways of adding support for non-functional requirements to distributed object systems, although many of them are concentrating on specific application domains, such as ReTINA [12] (telecommunications), or restrict themselves to non-functional requirements only concerning bandwidth and throughput, such as TAO [5]. The ReTINA project has developed a distributed processing environment for telecommunication applications that complies with the Telecommunications Information Networking Architecture (TINA) standard. ReTINA provides real-time audio and video, and network QoS guarantees. TAO is a real-time CORBA compliant ORB that provides end-to-end QoS by vertically integrating the ORB middleware with communication protocols and network subsystems. TAO is the first real-time ORB supporting end-to-end QoS over COTS platforms and ATM networks. Our research goals are much broader than the goals of those projects, since we believe the dynamic reconfiguration offered by our framework is applicable to a wide range of non-functional requirements.

Other related work, are projects where reflection and component-based techniques are used to achieve open Object Request Brokers. Researchers at APM have developed an experimental middleware platform called FlexiNet [13]. This platform allows the programmer to tailor the underlying communications infrastructure by inserting/removing meta-level components. Researchers at Illinois have developed dynamicTAO [14], a CORBA compliant reflective ORB that supports run-time reconfiguration. DynamicTAO maintains an explicit representation of its own internal structure and uses it to carry out dynamic reconfiguration. Reconfiguration is implemented by a so called TAOConfigurator that contains hooks to which implementations of dynamicTAO strategies are attached. In our opinion, policies can here be used to drive the configuration process implemented within the TAOConfigurator. At Lancaster University researchers conduct research about a generic reflective architecture for constructing open middleware platforms [6]. They define three distinct meta-object protocols that reify specific aspects of the middleware architecture: encapsulation, composition and environment. In their approach they build an ORB at the base-level, that can customize itself through the deployment of these three MOPs. However, a general problem of applying meta-level programming for application-specific customization, is that it's too complex for the average application programmer to comprehend [7]. We address this problem by introducing application-specific policies together with a reconfigurable ORB architecture. However, we think that our work is also complementary to this related work, since policies can be applied there as well.

Researchers at HPLabs have developed a general-purpose language for QoS, called QML [15]. QML has three main abstraction mechanisms for QoS specification: contract type, contract and profile. Although these abstractions are more generic than ours, the first abstraction is similar to a template and the last two abstractions are captured by a policy. They show how QML can be used to build a QoS-based trader that matches client requirements with QoS properties of services [16]. In this case, they don't use QML for customization of the underlying distributed platform.

6   Conclusion

In this paper we presented an architectural framework that can be used to implement domain specific ORBs that can be dynamically configured to support different quality of service levels for non-functional requirements. An important characteristic of the ORB architecture is that it allows each remote method invocation to be treated differently. This is particularly important in time-critical applications where some remote method invocations have timing constraints and others don't. For other applications, such as e-commerce the situation is similar. Here security is an issue for some remote method invocations and for others it is not. This variation between methods is easily expressed by defining policies that describe how non-functional requirements impact the invocations of each method. Our experiences with applying policies for constructing open communication systems [17][11], and customizable metalevel programs for non-functional requirements [7] have given us confidence in the feasibility of our architecture.

To validate our ORB architecture we developed a prototype that integrates the protocol stack with the ORB. We chose not to differentiate between the ORB and the protocol stack like conventional ORB implementations, where the protocol stack is a black-box because of the real-time requirements of our robot controller application. Only by integrating the protocol stack with the rest of the ORB can we be sure that the real-time requirements of the robot controller application are effectively enforced at all levels.

The approach we have presented provides a simple but powerful tool for customizing ORBs to support non-functional requirements. The approach divides the responsibility for the different parts of the customization process to the people who have the necessary knowledge to perform it. In future work we will investigate how XML can be used for expressing policies and component descriptors. Using XML will make our architecture more accessible since XML is becoming the universal language for specifying meta-data.

References

1.   Joosen W., Jørgensen B.N., Linder S.M., Olsen M.M., Perram J.W., Petersen H.G., Ruhoff P.T., Sørensen A., Sørensen A.S. and Wagenaar J.M., "Towards a generic controller for arbitrary robotic manipulators", Submitted to ICRA2000.
2.   Object Management Group, "The Common Object Request Broker: Architecture and Specification", 2.2 ed., Feb. 1998.
3.   D. Box, "Essential COM", Addison-Wesley, Reading, MA, 1997.
4.   A. Wollrath, R. Riggs, and J. Waldo, "A Distributed Object Model for the Java System", USENIX Computing Systems, vol. 9, November/December 1996.
5.   Douglas C. Schmidt, David L. Levine, and Chris Cleeland, "Architectures and Patterns for High-performance, Real-time ORB Endsystems", Advances in Computers, Academic Press, Ed., Marvin Zelkowitz, to appear in 1999.
6.   Blair, G.S., Coulson, G., Robin, P., Papathomas, M., "An Architecture for Next Generation Middleware", Proc. IFIP International Conference on Distributed Systems Platforms and Open Distributed Processing (Middleware '98), pp 191-206, Springer, 1998.

7. Bert Robben, Bart Vanhaute, Wouter Joosen, Pierre Verbaeten, "Non-Functional Policies", In Proceedings of the Second International Conference on Metalevel Architectures and Reflection, Saint-Malo, France, July 1999.
8. Jacobsen I., Griss M., Jonsson P., "Software Reuse; Architecture, Process and Organization for Business Success", Addison Wesley 1997, ISBN 0-201-92476-5.
9. B. N. Jørgensen, W. Joosen, "Classifying Component Interaction in Product-line Architectures", Proceedings of TOOLS PACIFIC 99, Melbourne, Australia, IEEE, 1999.
10. Liu C., Layland J., "Scheduling Algorithms for Multiprogramming in a Hard-Real-Time Environment", JACM, vol. 20, pp. 46-61, January 1973.
11. Frank Matthijs, "A framework for the domain of protocol stacks: methodology, conception and applications", PhD thesis, Katholieke Universiteit Leuven, 1999.
12. Bosco, P.G., Dahle, E., Gien, M., Grace, A., Mercouroff, N., Perdigues, N., and Stefani, J.B., "The ReTINA project: an overview", ReTINA Technical Report, 1996.
13. Hayton R., "FlexiNet Open ORB Framework", APM Technical Report 2047.01.00, APM Ltd., Poseidon House, Castle Park, Cambridge, UK, October 1997.
14. Manuel Román, Fabio Kon and Roy Campbell, "Design and Implementation of Runtime Reflection in Communication Middleware: the dynamicTAO Case", in proceedings of the ICDCS'99 Workshop on Middleware. Austin, Texas. May 31 - June 5, 1999
15. Svend Frølund, Jari Koistinen, "Quality-of-Service Specification in Distributed Object Systems", in Distributed Systems Engineering Journal, volume 5, number 4, December 1998.
16. Svend Frølund, Jari Koistinen, "Quality-of-Service Aware Distributed Object Systems", in proceedings of the 1999 USENIX Conference on Object-Oriented Technologies and Systems (COOTS).
17. Eddy Truyen et. al., "Open Implementation of a Mobile Communication System", In Proceedings of the ECOOP' 98 Workshop on Mobility and Replication, July 1998, Brussels, Belgium. http://www.cs.kuleuven.ac.be/~eddy/mp/smove.html

The Role of Software Architecture in Constraining Adaptation in Component-Based Middleware Platforms

Gordon S. Blair[1], Lynne Blair[1], Valérie Issarny[2], Petr Tuma[3], Apostolos Zarras[2]

[1]Distributed Multimedia Research Group, Computing Department, Lancaster University, Bailrigg, Lancaster, LA1 4YR, U.K.
{gordon,lb}@comp.lancs.ac.uk

[2]Solidor Research Group, INRIA-Rocquencourt, Domaine de Voluceau, Rocquencourt - BP 105, 78153 Le Chesnay Cédex, France.
{Valerie.Issarny,Apostolos.Zarras}@inria.fr

[3]Distributed Systems Research Group, Department of Software Engineering, Faculty of Mathematics and Physics, Charles University, Prague, Czech Republic.
tuma@nenya.ms.mff.cuni.cz

Abstract. Future middleware platforms will need to be more *configurable* in order to meet the demands of a wide variety of application domains. Furthermore, we believe that such platforms will also need to be *re-configurable*, for example to enable systems to adapt to changes in the underlying systems infrastructure. A number of technologies are emerging to support this level of configurability and re-configurability, most notably middleware platforms based on the concepts of open implementation and reflection. One problem with this general approach is that widespread changes can often be made to the middleware platform, potentially jeopardizing the integrity of the overall system. This paper discusses the role of *software architecture* in maintaining the overall integrity of the system in such an environment. More specifically, the paper discusses extensions to the Aster framework to support the re-configuration of a reflective (component-based) middleware platform in a constrained manner. The approach is based on i) the formal specification of a range of possible component configurations, ii) the systematic selection of configurations based on a given set of non-functional properties, and iii) the orderly re-configuration between configurations, again based on formally specified rules.

1 Introduction

Middleware technologies such as CORBA and DCOM are now established as central elements in modern computer systems, offering portability and interoperability through their platform independent programming models. However, with the rapid deployment of such platforms, there is an increasing demand to introduce more configurability and re-configurability into middleware. For example, configurability is important to meet the often conflicting requirements in areas such as embedded systems, real-time systems, telecommunications, digital libraries, etc. Similarly, re-configurability is increasingly important to cope with rapidly fluctuating environmental conditions as found, for example, in mobile computing. In addition, re-

J. Sventek and G. Coulson (Eds.): Middleware 2000, LNCS 1795, pp. 164-184, 2000.

configurability can help enormously in supporting systems evolution, as functional or non-functional requirements change over time (e.g. the scaling up of a system to deal with an order of magnitude increase in activity).

A number of researchers have investigated issues of configurability and re-configurability in middleware platforms. Such solutions often involve the selective replacement or tailoring of key components of the system, e.g. parts of the protocol stack. However, a more general solution is offered by emerging reflective middleware platforms, exploiting the concepts of open implementation and reflection to offer a more principled access to the underlying virtual machine. A number of such platforms have been developed, including Open-ORB [Blair98], Dynamic TAO [Román99], Open CORBA [Ledoux97], and Flexinet [Hayton97]. Such platforms offer great flexibility in terms of meeting the needs of a wide range of application domains. However, they all suffer from the problem of offering too much flexibility, i.e. it is possible to compromise the overall integrity of the system by allowing unbridled access to details of implementation. This paper examines this issue in depth. In particular, the paper considers the role of software architecture in constraining adaptation in reflective middleware platforms. More specifically, the paper examines the results of the Aster Project [Issarny96] and considers the potential of Aster tools and techniques to ensure robust adaptation in the context of Open-ORB (although the results are equally applicable to a range of other reflective middleware platforms). Some important extensions are suggested for Aster to ensure more seamless support for adaptation in such environments.

The paper is structured as follows. Section 2 presents some background information on reflective middleware in general, and the Open-ORB Project in particular. Emphasis is given to the component-based design of this platform. Section 3 then examines the key results of the Aster Project, illustrating how Aster can be used to support the automatic synthesis of middleware platforms from statements of the required non-functional properties (cf configurability). Following this, section 4 provides a more in-depth examination of the adaptation process, highlighting 4 key phases that must be supported. Our solution is then discussed in section 5. This section also includes an explicit statement of the required extensions to Aster, including exploitation of the specifics of reflective middleware. Finally, related work and concluding remarks are given in sections 6 and 7 respectively.

2   Background on Open-ORB

2.1   Why Reflective Middleware?

The concept of reflection was first introduced by Smith in 1982 [Smith82]. In this work, he introduced the reflection hypothesis which states:

> "In as much as a computational process can be constructed to reason about an external world in virtue of comprising an ingredient process (interpreter) formally manipulating representations of that world, so too a computational process could be made to reason about itself in virtue of comprising an ingredient process (interpreter) formally manipulating representations of its own operations and structures".

The importance of this statement is that a program can access, reason about and alter its own interpretation. Access to the interpreter is provided through a *meta-object protocol (MOP)* which defines the services available at the *meta-level* [Kiczales91]. Access to the meta-level is provided through a process of *reification*. Reification effectively makes some aspect of the internal representation explicit and hence accessible from the program.

The primary motivation of a reflective language or system is to provide a principled (as opposed to ad hoc) means of achieving open engineering. In contrast, the present-day approach to developing middleware platforms is generally to adopt a *black box* philosophy, whereby implementation details are hidden from the platform user (cf. distribution transparency). There is increasing evidence though that the black box philosophy is becoming untenable. For example, the OMG have recently added internal interfaces to CORBA to support services such as transactions and security. The recently defined Portable Object Adapter is another attempt to introduce more openness in their design. Nevertheless, their overall approach can be criticised for being rather ad hoc. Similarly, a number of ORB vendors have felt obliged to expose selected aspects of the underlying system (e.g. filters in Orbix or interceptors in COOL). These are however non-standard and hence compromise the portability of CORBA applications and services. The authors believe that the solution is to provide flexible middleware platforms through application of the principle of reflection.

2.2   The Open-ORB Architecture

In the Open-ORB architecture, we adopt a *component-based* model of computation [Szyperski98]. A middleware platform is then viewed as a particular configuration of components, which can be selected at build-time and re-configured at run-time. We therefore provide an open and extensible library of components, and component factories, supporting the construction of such platforms, e.g. protocol components, schedulers, etc. The use of components is important given the trend towards the application of this technology in open distributed processing, e.g. CORBA v3 [OMG99] and DCOM. Note however that these technologies exploit component technology at the application level; we extend this approach to the structuring of the middleware platform itself. Our particular component model includes features to support multimedia applications, and is derived from previous work on the Computational Language from RM-ODP [Blair97]. One notable feature of this component model is that communications channels are explicitly represented by components. Such components are referred to as bindings and have the important role in supporting inspection and adaptation of communications related aspects. A fuller description of the component model can be found in [Blair97].

Each component (or more strictly, each interface) has an associated meta-space, offering access to meta-level for the component, i.e. the underlying virtual machine supporting the execution of this component. Because of the complexity of distributed systems, this meta-space is partitioned into a number of orthogonal *meta-space models*. This approach was first advocated by the designers of AL-1/D, a reflective programming language for distributed applications [Okamura92]. The benefit of this approach is to simplify the interface offered by the meta-space, by maintaining a separation of concerns between different system aspects. Currently, four meta-space models are supported in Open-ORB as discussed below.

1. *The Encapsulation Meta-model.* This meta-model provides access to the representation of a particular interface in terms of its set of methods and associated attributes, together with key properties of the interface. This is equivalent to the introspection facilities available, for example, in the Java language, although we go further by also supporting adaptation.

2. *The Compositional Meta-model.* In reality, many components will in fact be *composite*, using a number of other components in their construction. In recognition of this fact, we also provide a compositional meta-model offering access to such constituent components. In the meta-model, the composition of a component is represented as a *component graph*, in which the constituent components are connected together by *local bindings*[1]. The interface offered by the meta-model then supports operations to inspect and adapt the graph structure, i.e. to view the structure of the graph, to access individual components in the graph, and to adapt the graph structure and content. This meta-model is particularly useful when dealing with binding components [Blair98]. In this context, the composition meta-model reifies the internal structure of the binding in terms of the components used to realise the end-to-end communication path. For example the component graph could feature an MPEG compressor and decompressor and an RTP binding component. The structure can also be exposed recursively; for example, the composition meta-model of the RTP binding might expose the peer protocol entities for RTP and also the underlying UDP/IP protocol. It is argued in [Fitzpatrick98] that open bindings alone provide strong support for adaptation.

3. *The Environmental Meta-model.* The environmental meta-model supports the reification of activity related to a particular interface of a component. In terms of middleware, this equates to functions such as message arrival, enqueueing, selection, unmarshalling and dispatching (plus the equivalent on the sending side) [Watanabe88, McAffer96]. At present, our architecture offers a simple environmental meta-model enabling the insertion of pre- and post- methods. Such a mechanism can then be used to introduce, for example, additional levels of distribution transparency (such as concurrency control) or to insert functions such as security managers or compression components.

4. *The Resources Meta-model.* Most reflective languages and systems restrict their scope to the above styles of reflection. In experiments, however, we have identified a significant weakness of this approach, namely that we have no means of accessing the level of resources and resource management in the system. This is a particular problem for mobile, multimedia and real-time systems where it is often important to be aware of the resources currently available at a given node (e.g. if it is intended to introduce a new software compression component). We therefore introduce a fourth meta-model, referred to as the resource meta-model [Blair99a].

---

[1] The RM-ODP inspired concept of local binding is crucial in our design, providing a language-independent means of implementing the interaction point between interfaces within a given address space.

This meta-model supports the reification of resource creation, scheduling and, more generally, management. The meta-model provides access to a set of components representing resources, together with the associated managers. As with other meta-models, it is then possible to either inspect or adapt activity associated with resources. For example, it is possible to insert monitors to capture statistics on the effectiveness of a thread scheduling policy and then possibly change this policy based on the information collected.

The first two meta-space models support what is often referred to as structural reflection in the literature, whereas the latter two models offer behavioural reflection [Watanabe88].

The complete Open-ORB architecture is summarised in figure 1. This highlights the recursive nature of the architecture in that each meta-space is populated by components that, consequently, have their own meta-space models, etc.

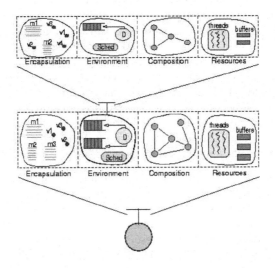

Fig. 1. The Structure of Meta-Space in Open-ORB

An implementation of the Open-ORB architecture has been carried out using Python. In addition, a second implementation is now underway using a lightweight and efficient reflective component model, based on COM. Further information on the reflective middleware architecture and associated implementation work can be found in the literature [Blair98, Blair99a, Costa98].

2.3   Analysis

The Open-ORB architecture described above provides a principled means of supporting both inspection and adaptation of the underlying middleware platform. Through inspection, the programmer can discover information about the structure of a component, together with any sub-components used in its construction. The programmer can also analyse the behaviour of key parts of the system and resource usage through the insertion of monitoring behaviour. Based on this, the programmer can then make a number of fine or course grained changes to the underlying platform. For example, the programer can locate a key compression component and request a change to the compression strategy (e.g. drop B-frames in MPEG). Alternatively, he/she can change the compression and matching decompression component completely (e.g. to H.263). Other strategies include allocating more resources or changing the resource management policy for a subset of resources, or extending the system with new capabilities (e.g. encryption).

As can be seen, this *procedural* approach provides great flexibility to the programmer. Indeed, as argued in the introduction, there is often too much flexibility. At present, this is constrained only by (run-time) type checking on creating a local binding between components. While offering a degree of safety, this is clearly not sufficient. What we therefore require is a mechanism that i) can delegate responsibility for adaptation to a (trusted) management entity or entities, ii) can offer a more declarative view of adaptation, and iii) can ensure the architectural integrity of the system before, during and after re-configurations. This is precisely the problem that is addressed in this paper, where we investigate the role of software architecture, in general, and the Aster techniques and tools, in particular, in providing this level of robust adaptation management.

3   Software Architecture for Component-Based Middleware

3.1   What is Software Architecture?

Research effort in the software architecture domain aims at reducing costs of developing large, complex software systems. Towards that goal, formal notations are being provided to describe software architectures, replacing the usual informal description of software architectures in terms of box-and-line diagrams [Perry92]. These notations are generically referred to as *Architecture Description Languages* (ADLs). Basically, an ADL allows the developer to describe the gross organisation of the system in terms of coarse-grained architectural elements, thus abstracting away from implementation details. Prominent elements of a software architecture subdivide into the three following categories:

1. *components* that abstractly define computational units written in any programming language,
2. *connectors* that abstractly define types of interactions between components (*e.g.*, pipe or client-server), and
3. the *configuration* that defines an application structure in terms of the interconnection of components through connectors.

The interested reader is referred to [Medvidovic97] for a survey of existing ADLs and associated CASE tools.

3.2   The Aster Approach

The main goal of the Aster Project is to apply ideas from the software architecture community to the field of component-based middleware. More specifically, the aim of the work is to support the systematic synthesis of middleware configurations from architectural descriptions. Through this approach, it is then possible to match the services offered by the middleware platform to the demands of a given application domain. In more detail, the input of the synthesis process is an architectural description of the application that, apart from specifying the overall structure of the application in terms of components and connectors, also includes a specification of the required properties of the middleware connectors that mediate the interaction among the components, i.e. *non-functional properties* required by the application (such as scalability, real-time performance, etc). The output of the process is a middleware configuration (e.g. a component graph as exposed by the compositional meta-model associated to the middleware in terms of Open-ORB) consisting of components implementing services (e.g. OMG's CORBA services, Open-ORB's constituent components) that are interconnected through a specific connector that corresponds to the underlying middleware platform (e.g. OMG's Object Request Broker, Open-ORB's base binding components). Interestingly, the whole configuration can also be viewed as a connector (with added value) as it serves to support interactions between application components (e.g. Open-ORB's binding components defined through composition). Given this, a recursive approach to architectural description is required as already illustrated by the definition of the Open-ORB's compositional meta-model.

In more detail, the Aster environment for the systematic synthesis of middleware relies on the following key elements:

1. *An ADL for the description of both application and middleware software architectures.* Any architecture description may further embed the specification of the non-functional properties that are either provided or required by the constituting software elements, using the framework given below.

2. *A framework for the formal specification of properties offered by middleware configurations.* The framework is based on linear temporal logic and has been used so far for the specification of properties relating to dependability [Saridakis99], security [Bidan98] and transactions [Zarras98]. This framework is central to the Aster environment as it forms the basis for reasoning about the matching of available middleware configurations to the properties required by applications. Basically, a middleware configuration matches application requirements if the properties enforced by the configuration, as specified by the corresponding logic formula, imply the non-functional properties required by the application. In addition, the framework is used for structuring a *repository* of available middleware architectures according to a lattice structure, which encodes the refinement relationship holding over properties provided by available middleware elements. This repository effectively provides a pool of tried and tested software architectures offering a variety of non-functional behaviour.

3. *A tool for the integration of a chosen middleware configuration retrieved from the repository with the application that initiated the search.*

As an example of Aster usage, consider an application that requires transactional support from the underlying middleware. Given this, it is necessary to search the Aster repository for an appropriate match. A possible repository structure is depicted in figure 2. In this repository, all the architectures at the bottom of the figure match the application's requirements, with each corresponding to a different middleware style (i.e. EJB, CORBA, DCOM). In the remainder of this paper, we will be using the CORBA-style architecture of transactional middleware for illustration purpose. This architecture is composed of the CORBA ORB together with OTS (Object Transaction Service) and CCS (Concurrency Control Service) services. Due to the lack of space, we do not provide here the Aster ADL description of the above architecture nor formal specification of related non-functional properties; the interested reader is referred to the aforementioned references for detail. However, let us notice that property specifications within the ADL are given in terms of textual names in order to simplify the developer's task. However, these should have a corresponding formal definition within the Aster environment, which stores each property as a pair giving the name of the property and the corresponding temporal logic formula.

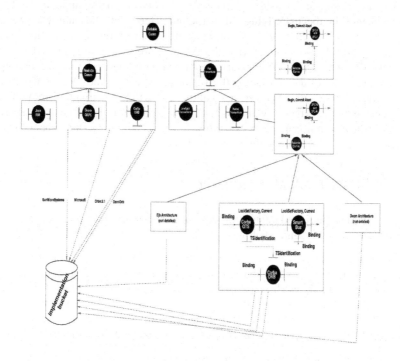

Fig. 2. A Middleware Repository

Each middleware architecture available within the repository may actually represent a number of concrete middleware configurations, depending on available implementations for the constituting components. Such configurations are stored within the *implementation bucket*, as depicted in figure 2. When multiple configurations implement a retrieved middleware architecture, the designer is requested to select the one that best suits the application regarding environmental parameters such as available resources.

3.3   Analysis

Since the early design of the Aster environment presented in [Issarny96], prototype implementation has been carried out so as to assess the proposed approach. The current Aster prototype relies on the STeP theorem prover [Bjorner98] for the implementation of property matching when either inserting or seeking an element in the middleware repository. Experimentation has generally been carried out within the CORBA framework. Although work is still needed for improving the environment's usability (*e.g.* the use of formal methods by software designers may be seen as a challenge), our experience shows that the approach actually eases the construction of middleware, contributes to software robustness, and fosters software and design reuse.

The Aster approach has focussed on the synthesis of middleware platforms whose properties are defined at design time. However, it does not deal with the adaptation of middleware at run-time, resulting either from evolution of the application design or from changes in the underlying infrastructure. Hence, it does not yet provide the mechanisms we seek for reflective middleware architectures (as identified in section 2.3 above). We believe though that the Aster approach *a priori* provides a way to alleviate the penalty of middleware adaptation. Furthermore, the Aster approach naturally extends to accommodate the seamless nature of the Open-ORB reflective architecture, i.e. the use of components above and within the middleware platform. In particular, we have already seen how the recursive nature of architectural description in Aster can accommodate such structures. Before examining extensions to Aster, it is helpful, however, to examine the issue of adaptation more closely.

4   A Closer Look at Adaptation

In order to manage the adaptation process, it is necessary to provide support for each of the four phases presented below.

1. *Identifying conditions for initiating middleware changes.* We consider two separate triggers for middleware adaptation: i) revision of the requested middleware properties, and ii) modification of the environment. The former type of change typically follows evolution of the application's design. The latter type of change results from the evolution of either the execution or the software environment, requiring the corresponding revision of the middleware implementation.

2. *Computing the middleware architecture complying to a requested change.* Once it has been determined that a change must take place, it is then necessary to compute the corresponding impact on the middleware configuration. Note that such changes may range from trivial component/connector exchanges to major structural changes, including revision of the middleware architecture.

3. *Detecting when it is safe to actually change the current middleware platform.* The adaptation process must ensure that an application remains in a consistent state throughout the adaptation of the underlying middleware configuration. For

example, in the case of a platform offering transactional support, the changes to the configuration should not disrupt the execution of ongoing transactions. As such, it is necessary to detect when it is safe to carry out such changes. In doing so, the primary design concern is to find the right trade-off between minimal application disruption and timely exchange.

4. *Adapting the current middleware.* This step is highly dependent on the support provided by the underlying middleware platform, e.g. in terms of reflective facilities (if available). In terms of Open-ORB, for example, the adaptation process would exploit the different meta-space models, as appropriate. For example, the adaptation may require access to a compositional meta-model to exchange one component for another. Adaptation may also require additional support in terms of, for example, the transfer of state information between configurations. Again, this can often be supported by underlying reflective facilities.

We consider the support provided for each of these phases in some detail below.

5   Extensions to Aster to Support Architectural Adaptation

5.1   Overall Approach

There are a number of ways of approaching the problem of adaptation as defined above. The most constraining solution consists of allowing only planned changes. In such a case, the application designer must provide a specification of the range of middleware configurations, together with the conditions for switching between configurations. In such an approach, the number of possible configurations is clearly finite and pre-determined. In contrast, the less constraining solution consists of tolerating any change at runtime, almost independently of design decisions. We believe that both these solutions are unsatisfactory. The former is impractical, as there is no way to exhaustively anticipate changes to the middleware that may be required. The latter option is more flexible from the standpoint of supported changes. However, this is at the expense of software robustness because there is no way to guarantee that the middleware adaptation still complies to the application design. It seems then necessary to constrain the range of accepted changes at runtime whilst not requiring an exhaustive list of supported changes.

This debate relates very closely to research in the area of dynamic reconfiguration [Edler92]. Briefly stated, work in this area investigates support for expressing and achieving reconfiguration of applications at runtime. Within this field, two general approaches have been proposed: *programmed* and *evolutionary reconfiguration²*. Programmed reconfiguration is a form of planned evolution where the set of possible changes and conditions for changing are prescribed at design time (typically by associating state predicates with each system configuration, e.g. see [Barbacci93]). In evolutionary reconfiguration, in contrast, a configuration manager responds to requests for reconfiguration (typically from the user) and ensures that the necessary changes are carried out. Our proposal is for an evolutionary approach whereby a form

---

² A number of hybrid solutions have also been defined.

of configuration manager, which we refer to as an *adaptation manager*, takes
responsibility for all changes and also ensures that architectural integrity is
maintained. Further details of the role of the adaptation manager will emerge from the
discussion below.

5.2   The Four Steps Revisited

5.2.1   Conditions for Initiating Changes

Technical Approach
As stated above, there are two distinct cases that must be considered, i.e. revision of
the requested non-functional properties and modification of the environment.

Revision of non-functional properties can only be made known to the adaptation
manager through user interaction (typically, designer intervention) and hence this
requires a corresponding GUI tool. Such changes are expected to be infrequent as
they map on to evolution of the general design. Architectural constraints are
maintained by extending applications architectural descriptions with denotations of
the *weakest properties* that must be satisfied by the middleware configuration
supporting a given application. The adaptation manager can then accept such changes
as long as the required weakest properties remain satisfied. Note that, if we set the
weakest properties to true, then any changes will be tolerated. However, allowing
such flexibility is under the responsibility of the application's designer who decides to
not constrain changes and hence to favor flexibility over robustness. In general terms,
this proposal favors software robustness without unduly restricting adaptation;
essentially, the application designer, based on knowledge of the application domain
and environmental conditions, determines the right trade-off between flexibility and
robustness.

In contrast, modifications of the environment can be initiated either through user
intervention or, more likely, as a result of events generated by underlying monitoring
components. Crucially, such monitoring components can be inserted dynamically into
the middleware configuration using reflection. For example, a monitor can be inserted
in the resource meta-space to report on the current processor load. Similarly, the
compositional meta-space can be used to insert a monitor into a binding object to
report on inter-arrival times of video frames. The frequency of such changes is
expected to be somewhat greater than that for non-functional properties.

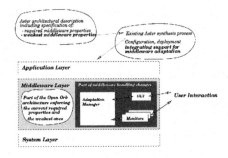

Fig. 3. Support for Initiating Change

Figure 3 summarises the support required for initiating middleware adaptation (with highlighting in boldface).

Required Changes to Aster
The first change is the incorporation of *weakest properties* specifications into the Aster framework. This can easily be achieved. The Aster ADL already supports the specification of non-functional properties required from a middleware configuration (as used by the synthesis process). Given this, it is sufficient to enrich such a description with a clause prescribing the weakest properties that should always be enforced by the middleware platform (written using temporal logic). The middleware properties specified at design time should imply the weakest ones, a condition that can easily be checked using the Aster toolset.

The proposed changes also require the introduction of an *adaptation manager*. While the provision of such a manager relates more to the middleware infrastructure than to the Aster environment, we present it here as an Aster extension as it is central to the adaptation process.

5.2.2   Computing the New Middleware Configuration

Technical Approach.
Once the adaptation manager has checked the required properties, the corresponding middleware architecture must be computed. This is easy to achieve using Aster, as it amounts to exploiting the *synthesis process*. In general, though, this is a difficult problem, potentially requiring complex analysis of the current configuration, the desired non-functional properties, and the set of possible changes that can be made to achieve such properties. Considering the Open-ORB infrastructure, this requires us to identify the necessary updates within the current component graph managed by the compositional meta-model. This is also made more difficult because of potential dependencies between components in the current configuration, e.g. in the example of transactional middleware in section 3.2., the OTS and CCS services are closely inter-related at the implementation level. The Aster approach does not enable us to directly deal with such dependencies due to the highly abstract description of middleware properties. In addition, the synthesis process would need to be adapted so as to integrate computation of a middleware configuration with respect to both an existing configuration and required properties and not just middleware properties. Investigation of this is an area for future work. Currently, we adopt a more pragmatic approach, in order to minimise Aster extensions whilst supporting robust middleware adaptation.

Dealing with changes in the required non-functional properties is quite straightforward. In this case, the synthesis process is carried out with the new abstract properties as input, the result being the target configuration. In other words, this means that the component graph managed by the compositional meta-model is fully replaced by the graph corresponding to the newly synthesized middleware configuration. Dealing with environmental changes is however more complex and requires further discussion. In this case, it is crucial to be able to distinguish between middleware configurations implementing a given architecture with given non-functional properties but differing in terms of *environmental parameters*[3]. For example, one architecture might be more appropriate in a resource rich environment with plentiful bandwidth, processing capacity, battery life, etc, whereas other solutions may be better in the cases of drops in bandwidth or problems with battery life. It is important not to place bounds on the criteria taken into account in the selection process of middleware configurations implementing a given architecture. The only prerequisite is to ensure that the various concrete middleware configurations implementing a single middleware architecture can be compared and hence all prescribe the same set of selection criteria (or at least have a set of common selection criteria). In addition, it should be possible to assess the environment features with respect to those common criteria so as actually be able to select the most suitable configuration. In the case where multiple configurations are still eligible, one is chosen randomly. We now consider the impact of this on Aster.

Required Changes to Aster.
The current Aster repository enables us to distinguish middleware architectures with respect to the abstract properties they provide. However, Aster does not enable us to distinguish between valid implementations that differ in terms of environmental parameters. In order to extend this, we introduce the concept of a *sub-repository* (possibly empty) which gives all the eligible configurations for implementing a given architecture, hence making the Aster repository close to a multi-dimensional database. A sub-repository is further defined by a vocabulary of selection criteria and, for each term of the vocabulary, a value needs to be specified for each embedded (concrete) configuration. More formally, let P denote the power set, a sub-repository is denoted by:

```
Concrete: P (CONFIGURATION)
Criteria: P (STRING)
Value: Criteria → TYPE
```

and each element of `Concrete`, which is a concrete configuration, is such that for all the elements of `Criteria`, it defines a function:

```
Valid: Criteria → ConfigElement → TYPE   ∪ ⊥
```

where `ConfigElement` is the set of configuration elements (i.e. component, connector implementations) and `TYPE` should be equal to `Value(c)` with c being the criterion under consideration. The `Valid` function then serves to identify for each relevant criterion, the value of the environment parameter that is required for each configuration element, ⊥ meaning that the criterion does not apply for this specific element.

As an example, let us consider the CORBA-based transactional middleware architecture that was discussed in Section 3.2. Although not part of the standard, we

---

[3] A second important consideration is the cost of adaptation. As stated earlier, this can vary between changing properties of a particular component, through to major reconstruction of the configuration. This should be taken into account in the decision making process, e.g. by associating a cost metric with each possible transition. This has not yet been addressed in our work, although this is a crucial area for future research.

may consider different implementations for the OTS service based on existing results in the area of transaction management: transaction commitment using either a 2-phase or a 3-phase protocol according to the frequency of failure occurrences, or transaction management supporting transaction execution over a disconnected laptop. These implementations relate to the same middleware architecture. However, the corresponding configurations differ depending on the following set of criteria: {*MTBF, ConnectionMode*}, where *MTBF* gives the Mean Time Between Failure of components and takes its values in the set of integers (i.e. Value(MTBF) = INT), and *ConnectionMode* gives the connection mode of components and takes its values in the set {*LAN, Wireless*} (i.e. Value(ConnectionMode) = {LAN, Wireless}). Hence, the middleware configuration made out of the OTS implementing the 2-phase commit protocol is valid as long as the value of the *MTBF* of each component exceeds a given threshold *t*, and the value of the ORB *ConnectionMode* is equal to *LAN*. In the same way, the 3-phase commit implementation is eligible when at least one of the *MTBF*s is lower than *t*, the value of ORB's *ConnectionMode* being still *LAN*. Finally, the middleware configuration composed of the OTS implementation supporting disconnected transactions is valid when the *ConnectionMode* is equal to Wireless, whatever are the values of the *MTBF*s.

5.2.3   Detecting When it is Safe to Adapt the Configuration

Technical Approach
Adaptation of the middleware configuration should be carried out in a way that maintains the overall system in a consistent state. At the time of middleware change, there might be requests, qualified as *pending*, which are issued through the old middleware and for which the requested properties (i.e. properties enforced by the old middleware) are not yet satisfied. For the middleware exchange to be correct, it must be ensured that, for all the requests pending at the time of the integration, the new middleware satisfies the non-functional requirements for those particular requests. A trivial pre-condition upon the middleware state for achieving exchange is then to have no pending request. Such a state is qualified as *idle*. Requiring an idle state for the middleware prior to carrying out adaptation is at the expense of timeliness. Although the execution environment may enforce reaching an idle state by selectively blocking requests (as long as this does not prevent termination of ongoing requests) [Kramer90], this may take quite a long time. A weaker pre-condition is then to require a *safe state*, which guarantees that for all the pending requests at the time of the exchange, these requests will eventually be terminated and their non-functional properties will be satisfied.

Middleware exchange under safe state detection requires the following capabilities from the middleware, so as to ensure the correct termination of pending requests: i) the non-functional properties provided by the new middleware should imply the properties of the current configuration, and ii) part of the state of the current middleware configuration relating to pending requests should be mapped onto the state of the new middleware. The former condition always holds when the middleware adaptation is due to environmental changes. On the other hand, adaptation due to new non-functional requirements must be dealt with on a case-by-case basis. The latter condition requires the middleware to be able to import and export its state (e.g. [Hofmeister93]), a function that can be directly supported by reflective middleware (e.g. see [Killijian99]). Note that meeting this condition is specific for each pair of middleware configurations involved in the exchange (regarding implementation of the state mapping function). We cannot afford the definition of an exhaustive mapping function, covering all the possible middleware adaptations, due to either changing non-functional requirements or environmental parameters. However, such a function may be devised for the specific case of environmental changes: the range of middleware adaptations is bounded in this case by the number of configurations stored within the corresponding sub-repository. Consequently, middleware adaptation due to environmental changes is carried out under safe state detection while idle state detection is used in the other cases.

Required Changes to Aster

Support for either safe or idle state detection does not require changes to Aster per se, apart from enriching sub-repository management for storing and retrieving *state mapping functions*. However, this imposes a number of requirements upon the middleware infrastructure, which are easy to handle given a reflective middleware.

State mapping functions should be introduced within sub-repositories for pairs of configurations; these functions are then used whenever the middleware changes relate to the corresponding pairs. A *safe state detector* should also be provided with each mapping function. This safe state detector can then be installed when the change is requested, so as to detect when the safe state is reached. In the absence of this information, idle state detection should be carried out by default.

Unlike safe state, the definition of idle state depends only on the properties of the old middleware configuration. Hence, it is possible to build the required middleware configuration with an *idle state detection* mechanism already in place. A second important property of the idle state definition is that it is based only on predicates that qualify the interaction between the middleware configuration and the application components, which derives from the definition of middleware properties that are always given in terms of component interactions. This makes it possible to implement a module that detects whether a middleware is in an idle state with respect to a specific property only by monitoring the interaction between the middleware and the components. Since such an idle state detector is independent of the specific middleware configuration, it can be stored in the middleware repository together with each architecture, and integrated into the middleware configuration during the middleware synthesis.

We do not further detail the implementation of idle and safe state detectors. These exploit the meta-space models for inspecting the middleware state.

5.2.4   Carrying out the Adaptation

Technical Approach

Once the above adaptation decision has been taken, the task of re-configuration is quite straightforward. In terms of implementation, re-configuration will make extensive use of the different meta-space models in carrying out the required adaptation. For example, for fine-grained adaptations, the compositional meta-model can be used to identify encapsulated components. Once identified, direct changes of the properties of a given component can then be made. For more course-grained adaptations, changes to the component graph can be requested. Note that support is provided to enable *smooth* transition between different configurations. For example, consider the transaction example given in section 5.2.2. In this example, support is provided to enable the new configuration to be constructed and primed in parallel with the operation of the old configuration. A hand-over can then be made as a single action, thus minimizing the disruption to service. Further information on such facilities can be found in [Fitzpatrick99].

Required Changes to Aster
The main change is to associate an *adaptation script* for pairs of configurations in the sub-repository. This is then invoked when changes are due to environmental conditions. For other changes (i.e. those due to evolving non-functional requirements), it must be assumed that the code for adaptation is provided by the user/ designer. Note that, if an adaptation script is not provided for a given pair, then it is necessary for the Aster environment to replace completely the old configuration with the new one. In this respect, adaptation scripts can be viewed as an important optimisation. For example, in many cases the adaptation could be quite lightweight, e.g. changing the properties of a single component. It would then not make sense to build a complete new configuration. Note also that this adaptation script should invoke the state mapping function (as appropriate) as part of its operation.

5.3   Analysis

This section has considered extensions to Aster to deal with adaptation, both in terms of the overall evolution of the design, e.g. to include new non-functional properties, or in response to changes in the underlying environment. Briefly, the required changes are as follows:

1. the incorporation of weakest properties specifications into architectural descriptions, to place constraints on the range of possible responses to new requirements,
2. the inclusion of environmental parameters in architectural descriptions to support the selection of the most appropriate configuration following changes in environmental conditions, through the introduction of a sub-repository of configurations per middleware architecture.
3. the introduction of an adaptation manager as a key middleware service,
4. the definition of safe state or idle state detectors, again provided through the sub-repositories, to indicate when it is safe to change,
5. the provision of a set of associated state mapping functions in sub-repositories to perform the required state transfers between pairs of configurations, and
6. the provision of adaptation scripts, again in sub-repositories, to carry out the necessary steps to switch between pairs of configurations.

Let us further recall that the proposed extensions have been addressed assuming a reflective middleware platform, which gives the necessary support for actually changing middleware configurations in an efficient way. We believe that this approach provides a good compromise between flexibility and robustness. In particular, it enables the designer to constrain the supported middleware changes with respect to the application's requirements, and it relieves the application programmer from writing code specific to middleware adaptation.

6   Related Work

Among existing ADLs, DARWIN [Magee92], DURRA [Barbacci93], and C2 [Medvidovic96] support dynamic configuration of applications. DARWIN provides language primitives allowing the user to describe the dynamic instantiation, removal and re-binding of ports. A DARWIN specific configuration manager is used to apply changes into a running configuration. The basic language primitives that describe dynamic instantiation and port re-binding can be used by both the application components and the application administrator. In DURRA, runtime configuration changes are modeled in terms of reconfiguration rules. A reconfiguration rule describes a transition from one configuration to another. Possible transitions are described at design time and are applied at runtime by a set of configuration managers, with each manager being responsible for changing a particular cluster of component instances. In C2, configuration changes are modeled as sequences of primitive reconfiguration actions like component creation, removal, welding, etc. The language provides corresponding primitives for the expression of such reconfiguration actions. All the aforementioned ADLs provide support for creating, removing and re-binding components of the application. However, none of them confronts changes in the middleware connector that mediates the interactions among the components.

There are many projects investigating adaptation/ dynamic QoS management in middleware platforms. BBN's QuO (QUality Objects) project [Vanegas98] is perhaps the closest in approach to our own work in that it adopts a similar open implementation philosophy. QuO, however, adopts an approach reminiscent of aspect-oriented programming [Kiczales97] to specify different aspects of QoS support using a range of specialised (high-level) languages. As such, it provides a more declarative, as opposed to procedural, approach to QoS management. Similarly, researchers at the University of Illinois have developed a task control model to support dynamic reconfiguration in middleware platforms [Li99]. This project is complementary to the Dynamic Tao project mentioned earlier [Román99], exploiting the openness of this underlying platform for more fine-grained control. Their approach is based on the use of a fuzzy logic inference engine together with a rule base of possible adaptations. The crucial difference between these projects and our proposals is that our work introduces overall architectural constraints based on explicit modeling of the software architecture. In previous research, the Lancaster authors have also developed a QoS management scheme for adaptation based on the use of timed automata [Blair99b]. While providing some support for adaptation, this work does not have the breadth of coverage of the work described in this paper. Finally, a number of other middleware projects include important elements of configurability and re-configurability including DIMMA [Donaldson98], Tao [Schmidt97] and Jonathan [Dumant97], again, however, with limited coverage of the range of issues raised by adaptation.

7   Concluding Remarks

This paper has argued that the next generation of middleware platforms will need to be more configurable and re-configurable. Furthermore, it is argued that reflection, together with component technology, provide the right technical solution to meet these requirements. However, such approaches have significant problems in terms of maintaining the integrity of the underlying configuration. We argue that such problems can be overcome by adopting ideas from the software architecture community.

More specifically, we have explored the role of the Aster framework in supporting dynamic adaptation in the context of the Open-ORB middleware platform. Following a detailed examination of adaptation, it was concluded that Aster could usefully be extended to meet our requirements. The key extensions to Aster include the incorporation of weakest properties and environmental parameters in architectural descriptions to accommodate re-configurations due to changing non-functional parameters and environmental conditions respectively.

The most significant contributions of this paper are:

1. the development of techniques to constrain changes in an open environment, and
2. the extension of software architecture techniques to accommodate dynamic change.

The work also has a more general contribution to make to the automatic synthesis of component-based configurations, and their subsequent monitoring and adaptation, based entirely on architectural descriptions.

The Aster toolkit is fully developed, although the changes described above have not yet been incorporated. In addition, as mentioned above, prototype implementations of Open-ORB have been developed. Although the proposed framework still needs to be integrated within Aster for further validating our approach, it is our belief that such an integration should not pose any difficulty, although it would be demanding in terms of implementation effort. However, work is still needed for a thorough assessment of our approach from a practical standpoint. In particular, despite the benefits of our approach with respect to sofware system robustness, it should be demonstrably efficient for it to be used in practice. We are currently working on such an issue by further investigating support for efficient middleware adaptation regarding both the implementation of the Aster extensions and the OpenORB infrastructure. We are also investigating the application of our framework to multimedia systems which are among the most demanding in terms of middleware adaptation due to their highly demanding resource usage and increasing use over heterogeneous platforms ranging from powerful workstations to wireless PDAs.

Acknowledgements

Research in the Open-ORB Project is partly funded by CNET, France Telecom (CNET Grant 96-1B-239) and partly by the EPSRC together with BT Labs (Research Grant GR/K72575). We would like to thank our collaborators for their support. Particular thanks are due to Jean-Bernard Stefani and his group at CNET, and also Ian Fairman, Alan Smith and Steve Rudkin at BT Labs. We would also like to acknowledge the contributions of a number of researchers at Lancaster to the Open-ORB Project, namely Mike Clarke, Fabio Costa, Geoff Coulson, Tom Fitzpatrick, Hector Duran, Nikos Parlavantzas and Katia Saikoski.

Research in the Aster project has been partly funded by CNET, France Telecom, and partly by the Esprit LTR C3DS project. Particular thanks are due to former members of the Aster project, namely C. Bidan and T. Saridakis.

Finally, this joint paper would not have been possible without the support of INRIA, which enabled Gordon and Lynne Blair to visit the Solidor Group during Easter, 1999.

References

[Barbacci93] Barbacci, M., C. Weinstock, D. Doubleday, M. Gardner, R. Lichota, "DURRA: A Structure Description Language for Developing Distributed Applications", Software Engineering Journal, pp 83-94, March 1993.

[Bidan98] Bidan, C., V. Issarny, "Dealing with Multi-Policy Security in Large Open Distributed Systems", Proceedings of the 5th European Symposium on Research in Computer Security, pp 51-66, September 1998.

[Bjorner98] Bjorner N., A. Browne, M. Colon, B. Finkbeiner, Z. Manna, M. Pichora, H.B. Sipma, T.E. Uribe, "STeP: The Stanford Temporal Prover Educational Release", Stanford University, 1.4-a edition, July 1998.

[Blair97] Blair, G.S., J.B. Stefani, "Open Distributed Processing and Multimedia", Addison-Wesley, 1997.

[Blair98] Blair, G.S., G. Coulson, P. Robin, M. Papathomas, "An Architecture for Next Generation Middleware", Proc. IFIP International Conference on Distributed Systems Platforms and Open Distributed Processing (Middleware'98), Springer, 1998.

[Blair99a] Blair, G.S., F. Costa, G. Coulson, H. Duran, N. Parlavantzas, F. Delpiano, B. Dumant, F. Horn, J.B. Stefani, "The Design of a Resource-Aware Reflective Middleware Architecture", Proc. of the 2nd Int. Conference on Meta-Level Architectures and Reflection (Reflection'99), St-Malo, France, Springer-Verlag, LNCS, Vol. 1616, pp 115-134, 1999.

[Blair99b] Blair, G.S., A. Amdersen, L. Blair, G. Coulson, "The Role of Reflection in Supporting Dynamic QoS Management Functions", Proceedings of the IEEE/IFIP International Workshop on Quality of Service (IWQoS'99), London, June 1999.

[Costa98] Costa, F., G.S. Blair, G. Coulson, "Experiments with Reflective Middleware", Proceedings of the ECOOP'98 Workshop on Reflective Object-Oriented Programming and Systems, ECOOP'98 Workshop Reader, Springer-Verlag, 1998.

[Donaldson98] Donaldson, D., M. Faupel, R. Hayton, A. Herbert, N. Howarth, A. Kramer, I. MacMillan, S. Waterhouse, "DIMMA - A Multi-media ORB", Proc. Middleware '98, The Low Wood Hotel, Ambleside, England, September 1998.

[Dumant97] Dumant, B., F. Horn, F. Dang Tran, J.B. Stefani, "Jonathan: An Open Distributed Processing Environment in Java", Proc. IFIP International Conference on Distributed

Systems Platforms and Open Distributed Processing (Middleware'98), Springer, September 1998.

[Edler92] Edler, M., J. Wei, "Programming Generic Dynamic Reconfiguration for Distributed Applications", Proceedings of the International Workshop on Configurable Distributed Systems, pp 68-79, March 1992.

[Fitzpatrick98] Fitzpatrick, T., G.S. Blair, G. Coulson, N. Davies, P. Robin, "Supporting Adaptive Multimedia Applications through Open Bindings", Proceedings of the 4th International Conference on Configurable Distributed Systems, IEEE, 1998.

[Fitzpatrick99] Fitzpatrick, T., "Open Multimedia Component Middleware for Adaptive Distributed Applications", PhD Thesis, Computing Department, Lancaster University, Bailrigg, Lancaster, LA1 4YR, UK, September 1999.

[Hayton97] Hayton, R., "FlexiNet Open ORB Framework", APM Technical Report 2047.01.00, APM Ltd, Poseidon House, Castle Park, Cambridge, UK, 1997.

[Hofmeister93] Hofmeister, C., J. Purtilo, "Dynamic Reconfiguration for Distributed Systems, Adapting Software Modules for Replacement", Proceedings of the 13th IEEE International Conference on Distributed Computing Systems (ICDCS'93), May 1993.

[Issarny96] Issarny, V., C. Bidan, "Aster: A Framework for Sound Customization of Distributed Runtime Systems", Proceedings of the 16th IEEE International Conference on Distributed Computing Systems (ICDCS'96), May 1996.

[Kiczales91] Kiczales, G., J. des Rivières, D.G. Bobrow, "The Art of the Metaobject Protocol", MIT Press, 1991.

[Kiczales97] Kiczales, G., J. Lamping, A. Mendhekar, C. Maeda, C. V. Lopes, J-M. Loingtier, J. Irwin, "Aspect-Oriented Programming", Proceedings of the European Conference on Object-Oriented Programming (ECOOP), Finland, Lecture Notes in Computer Science, Vol. 1241, Springer-Verlag, June 1997.

[Killijian99] Killijian, M.O., J.C. Ruiz-Garcia, J.C. Fabre, "Using Compile-Time Reflection for Objects' State Capture", Proceedings of the 2nd International Conference on Meta-Level Architectures and Reflection (Reflection'99), St-Malo, France, Springer-Verlag, LNCS, Vol. 1616, pp 150-152, 1999.

[Kramer90] Kramer, J., J. Magee, "The Evolving Philosophers Problem", IEEE Transactions on Software Engineering, Vol. 15, No. 1, pp 1293-1306, November 1990.

[Ledoux97] Ledoux, T., "Implementing Proxy Objects in a Reflective ORB", Proc. ECOOP'97 Workshop on CORBA: Implementation, Use and Evaluation, Jyväskylä, Finland, 1997.

[Li99] Li, B. and K. Nahrstedt, "Dynamic Reconfiguration for Complex Multimedia Applications, Proceedings of the IEEE International Conference on Multimedia Computing and Systems (IEEE Multimedia Systems '99), Florence, Italy, June 7-11, 1999.

[Magee92] Magee, J., N. Dulay, J. Kramer, "Structuring Parallel and Distributed Systems", Proc. of the International Workshop on Configurable Distributed Systems, March 1992.

[McAffer96] McAffer, J., "Meta-Level Architecture Support for Distributed Objects", In Proceedings of Reflection 96, G. Kiczales (end), pp 39-62, San Francisco; Also available from Department of Information Science, The University of Tokyo, 1996.

[Medvidovic96] "ADLs and Dynamic Architecture Changes", Proceedings of the 2nd ACM SIGSOFT International Software Architecture Workshop (ISAW-2), pp 24-27, October 1996.

[Medvidovic97] N. Medvidovic, R. Taylor, "A framework for classifying and comparing architecture description languages", Proc. of the Joint European Software Engineering - ACM SIGSOFT Symposium on Foundations of Software Engineering, pp 60-76, September 1997.

[Okamura92] Okamura, H., Y. Ishikawa, M. Tokoro, "AL-1/d: A Distributed Programming System with Multi-Model Reflection Framework", Proceedings of the Workshop on New Models for Software Architecture, November 1992.

[OMG99] The Common Object Request Broker: Architecture and Specification versions 3.0., available at http://www.omg.org/.

[Perry92] D. E. Perry, A. L. Wolf, " Foundations for the Study of Software Architecture ", ACM SIGSOFT Software Engineering Notes, 17(4), pp 40-52, October 1992.

[Román99] Román, M., F. Kon, R. Campbell, "Design and Implementation of Runtime Reflection in Communication Middleware: the dynamicTAO Case", Proceedings of the ICDCS'99 Workshop on Middleware, Austin, Texas, May-June 1999.

[Saridakis99] Saridakis, T., V. Issarny, "Developing Dependable Systems Using Software Architecture", Proceedings of the 1st Working IFIP Conference on Software Architecture, pp 80-104, February 1999.

[Schmidt97] Schmidt, D.C., R. Bector, D. Levine, S. Mungee, G. Parulkar, "An ORB End System Architecture for Statically Scheduled Real-Time Applications", Proceedings of the Workshop on Middleware for Real-Time Systems and Services", IEEE, San Francisco, 1997.

[Smith82] Smith, B.C., "Procedural Reflection in Programming Languages", PhD Thesis, MIT, Available as MIT Computer Science Technical Report 272, Cambridge, Mass., 1982.

[Szyperski98] Szyperski, C., "Component Software: Beyond Object-Oriented Programming", Addison-Wesley, 1998.

[Vanegas98] Vanegas, R., J. Zinky, J. Loyall, D. Karr, R. Schantz, D. Bakken, "QuO's Runtime Support for Quality of Service in Distributed Objects", Proc. IFIP International Conference on Distributed Systems Platforms and Open Distributed Processing (Middleware'98), Springer, September 1998.

[Watanabe88] Watanabe, T., A. Yonezawa, "Reflection in an Object-Oriented Concurrent Language", In Proceedings of OOPSLA'88, Vol. 23 of ACM SIGPLAN Notices, pp 306-315, ACM Press, 1988; Also available as Chapter 3 of "Object-Oriented Concurrent Programming", A. Yonezawa, M. Tokoro (eds.), pp 45-70, MIT Press, 1987.

[Zarras98] Zarras, A., V. Issarny, "A Framework for Systematic Synthesis of Transactional Middleware", Proc. IFIP International Conference on Distributed Systems Platforms and Open Distributed Processing (Middleware'98), pp 257-272, Springer, September 1998.

Exploiting IP Multicast in Content-Based Publish-Subscribe Systems

Lukasz Opyrchal[1], Mark Astley[2], Joshua Auerbach[2], Guruduth Banavar[2], Robert Strom[2], and Daniel Sturman[2]

[1] Dept. of EECS, University of Michigan,
1301 Beal Avenue, Ann Arbor, MI 48109, USA
[2] IBM T.J. Watson Research Center,
30 Saw Mill River Rd., Hawthorne, NY 10532, USA

Abstract. Publish-subscribe systems are evolving toward using content-based subscription rather than subject-based subscription. A key problem in implementing such systems is that a straightforward mapping from matching sets to multicast groups produces a number of groups that rapidly grows beyond practical limits. This paper proposes a set of alternative algorithms for solving this problem, by: (1) using a smaller set of overbroad multicast groups, judiciously chosen to minimize imprecision; (2) issuing multiple multicasts to appropriately chosen clusters; or (3) sending an event over multiple hops each involving a multicast to a set of neighbors. We evaluate these algorithms on a simulated wide-area network. We find that (1) a simple flooding algorithm is viable over an extensive range of conditions; and (2) under conditions of high selectivity and high regionalism of subscriptions, the other approaches mentioned above perform significantly better; however, the specific algorithm to use depends upon the economics of deployment.

1 Introduction

Publish-subscribe systems provide a convenient approach for interconnecting applications on a distributed network. Publish-subscribe middleware is currently being deployed for application integration in many domains including financial, process automation, and transportation. In the publish-subscribe paradigm, information providers publish units of information called *events*, and information consumers subscribe to particular categories of events. The middleware ensures the timely delivery of published events to all interested subscribers.

The earliest publish-subscribe systems used *subject-based* subscription. In the past decade, systems supporting this paradigm have matured significantly, resulting in several academic and industrial strength solutions [3,16,18,19,21]. In subject-based subscription, each event is classified and labeled by the publisher as belonging to one of a fixed set of subjects (also known as groups, channels, or topics). Consumers subscribe to all the events within a particular subject or set of subjects. Except for the subject identifier, the information content of events is opaque to the middleware. A strength of this approach is the potential

J. Sventek and G. Coulson (Eds.): Middleware 2000, LNCS 1795, pp. 185–207, 2000.

to easily leverage group-based multicast techniques to provide scalability and performance, by assigning each subject to a multicast group.

An emerging alternative to subject-based subscription is content-based subscription [1,2,20]. These systems support an *event schema* defining the type of information contained in each event. For example, applications interested in stock trades may use the event schema [issue: string, price: dollar, volume: integer]. A content-based subscription is a predicate against the event schema, such as (issue="IBM" & price < 120 & volume > 1000). With content-based subscription, subscribers have the added flexibility of choosing filtering criteria along multiple dimensions, without requiring pre-definition of subjects. In our stock trading example, a subject-based subscriber is forced to select trades by issue name. In contrast, a content-based subscriber is free to use an orthogonal criterion, such as volume, or indeed a collection of criteria, such as issue, price and volume.

While content-based subscription is the more general and flexible paradigm, providing efficient and scalable implementations of such systems is still an open problem. In particular, existing group-based multicast techniques cannot readily be applied to this problem. Each subscriber may have a unique subscription, and therefore, each event may go to a widely varying group of subscribers. To naively map these subscribers into groups may require a number of groups exponential in the number of subscribers (i.e. 2^N).

In this paper, we explore a number of approaches for exploiting group-based multicast for event delivery in content-based publish-subscribe systems. In particular, we focus on being able to exploit widely available, best effort multicast such as IP Multicast [8], or reliable multicast techniques built on top of IP Multicast such as SRM [9].

We explore three approaches to reducing the number of groups needed: (1) reducing precision: i.e., sending to overly broad groups where brokers may receive events for which they have no client subscriptions, (2) multiple sends: i.e., sending an event on multiple multicast groups instead of making a single multicast, or (3) multi-hop routing: i.e. sending an event over a set of multiple hops each of which entails a multicast to a set of intermediate brokers.

We define and evaluate five algorithms – traditional flooding, plus four newly proposed algorithms – each of which exploits one or more of the above approaches. Each of the techniques we present in the paper is compared to an abstract algorithm which we call "ideal multicast." Ideal multicast assumes that a perfect multicast group can be determined for each event. Ideal multicast provides a lower bound on network bandwidth utilization and latency.

We evaluate these algorithms on a simulated wide area network (WAN). This network consists of 100 multicast-enabled routers supporting 88 publish-subscribe servers (a.k.a. *brokers*), which include eight brokers with publishers and 80 brokers with a total of 10,000 subscribers.

The remainder of the paper is organized as follows. In Sect. 2, we describe all the evaluated algorithms. In Sect. 3, we provide details of the simulation setup that we use to evaluate the various algorithms, and we summarize our findings.

In Sect. 4, we review some of the previous work on event distribution systems using content-based subscription, and on applications of group multicast. Finally, Sect. 5 discusses conclusions of these experiments and suggests future directions for our work.

2   Group Multicast Algorithms

As mentioned earlier, the naive use of group-based multicast for implementing content-based publish-subscribe may require as many as 2^N groups where N is the number of communication end-points. Rather than treating each subscribing client as a communications end-point, we assume that the communication end-points are *brokers*, which are servers that manage client connection and event distribution. Brokers reduce the complexity of routing events by reducing the total number of endpoints known to the distribution system. Each end-point broker performs a local matching operation before forwarding the event to the subscribing clients. The local matching operation determines the set of interested clients connected to that broker. An implementation of matching for content-based subscription is described in [1] and shown to take time sub-linear in the number of subscriptions.

The current IPv4 specification for IP Multicast provides a maximum of 2^{24} locally scoped multicast addresses. The practical limit is smaller, since routing table space in backbone routers is a scarce resource [4]. Thus, it is important to reduce the number of groups needed. However, multicast technology is evolving rapidly, so it is difficult to know how few is "few enough." Rather than setting an arbitrary limit (other than the architected limit of 2^24), we examine ways to reduce the number of groups needed for a given number of brokers, favoring approaches that use fewer groups over those that use greater numbers. We explore three general approaches to reducing the number of groups needed.

1. *Reduce group precision.* In this approach, events are sent to multicast groups that may contain brokers that do not have subscriptions for the event. In the extreme case, messages are sent to all brokers (Sect. 2.2). Another way to reduce precision is to combine groups to form larger groups until the number of groups is within an acceptable limit. This approach is explored in Sect. 2.6.
2. *Send multiple multicasts.* In this approach, the set of end-points is divided into mutually exclusive subsets, thereby reducing the total number of required groups. For example, if N endpoints are divided into two equal subsets, the number of groups required in each subset is $2^{N/2}$, and the total number of groups required is $2 \times 2^{N/2}$. However, each event must be sent to two groups in this case. This approach is explored by the algorithm in Sect. 2.3.
3. *Send over multiple hops.* In this approach, each publisher sends to a small subset of neighboring brokers, which in turn forward the event to their neighbors, and so on. This approach is explored in Sect. 2.5.

Hybrid approaches that combine more than one of the above approaches are also possible; one such algorithm, explored in Sect. 2.4, combines approaches 1 and 2 above.

2.1   The Ideal Algorithm

In an environment where we could have as many groups as we need, we could assign a multicast group to every required subset of the set of brokers. Every such group may be reached using a single multicast, and every event published is always sent to the group which contains exactly those brokers subscribing to the event. We call this the *Ideal* algorithm.

Of course, for any system with non-trivial size, the ideal algorithm requires an impractical number of multicast groups. This makes the ideal algorithm useless in practice. Nonetheless, the ideal algorithm provides a useful benchmark for evaluation – we expect the ideal algorithm to provide a lower bound on the performance of each of our multicast strategies.

2.2   Flooding

A simple solution to the problem of content-based routing is to send every published event to all brokers. In this approach, only one multicast group is needed consisting of all the brokers in the system.

A simple optimization to avoid sending events that do not match any subscribers is to first perform a matching operation at the publishing broker against all subscriptions. The additional overhead of this matching step (on the order of 100 microseconds for 10,000 subscriptions) is not significant relative to overall network latencies (on the order of a hundred milliseconds).

2.3   Clustered Group Multicast (CGM)

The CGM algorithm is based on the use of *clusters*: mutually exclusive subsets of brokers where each subset has its own set of multicast groups. We observe that if we divide N endpoints into 2 clusters, we reduce the number of groups in each cluster to $2^{N/2}$ groups, and the total number of groups to $2 \times 2^{N/2}$. The cost of this approach, however, is that it may be necessary to multicast an event twice: once to a group in each cluster. In general, if we divide N into C clusters, the total number of groups needed is given by $g = C * 2^{N/C}$. Figure 1 shows, for a given number of groups and number of clusters, the number of endpoints that can be supported. For example, if we have 2^{13} multicast groups available, we can support 80 broker end-points by dividing them into 8 clusters of 10 brokers each. Since the groups within a cluster enumerate all possible combinations of brokers, each broker must join half these groups (those that include the broker) at system configuration time.

Each broker contains an instance of the subscription matching engine with entries for all client subscriptions in the system. When an event is published,

Max Groups	# Clusters	# Endpoints
2^{24}	8	168
2^{24}	4	88
2^{17}	8	112
2^{17}	4	60
2^{13}	8	80
2^{13}	4	44

Fig. 1. Number of endpoints supported by CGM

the publisher's broker matches the event against all subscriptions, and sorts the resulting list of brokers by cluster. It then looks up the group in each cluster that contains exactly those brokers destined to receive the event. The publisher's broker then performs up to C multicasts, where C is the number of clusters. Some clusters may have no matching brokers and are therefore skipped.

The choice of cluster assignment has a significant impact on performance. For example, brokers that match a single subscription, but that are spread over multiple clusters will require multiple multicasts. One approach builds clusters by grouping brokers with similar subscription sets. Another uses geographic (or network) location data to group brokers into clusters. The algorithms described here use the latter approach.

2.4 Threshold Clustered Group Multicast (TCGM)

The CGM algorithm described above requires a number of groups that may be prohibitively large for many applications. The number of groups required may be reduced by reducing the precision of the algorithm. One approach to reducing the precision is to flood a cluster when more than a threshold number of brokers within that cluster need to receive an event. That is, the algorithm behaves like CGM unless the number of destinations in a cluster exceeds a threshold, at which point the event is multicast to the entire cluster. We call this algorithm Threshold CGM (or TCGM).

For each cluster, we pick a threshold $T < K$, where K is the size of the cluster. If an event matches more than T endpoints, the event is sent to all brokers in one cluster. Otherwise, the event is sent only to the brokers subscribed to the event (as in CGM). This algorithm requires multicast groups for all subsets of brokers in a cluster of size T or smaller, plus one additional multicast group for all brokers in the cluster. A closed form expression for the number of groups required is given in Fig. 4. Figure 2 compares group requirements for CGM and TCGM for three different values of threshold T, and for different numbers of brokers and clusters. The group requirement for TCGM is many orders of magnitude smaller than in the case of CGM.

Nodes	CGM	TCGM, T = 5	TCGM, T = 4	TCGM, T = 3
168, 8 clusters	16,777,216	223,168	60,376	12,496
112, 8 clusters	131,072	27,784	11,768	3,760
112, 4 clusters	1,073,741,824	489,756	96,632	14,732
88, 4 clusters	16,777,216	141,776	36,436	7,176

Fig. 2. Group requirements of CGM vs. TCGM

2.5   The Neighbor Matching Algorithm

The neighbor matching algorithm is derived from our earlier work [2]. In this approach, each broker designates a number of nearby brokers as "neighbors." Each broker performs just enough tests of the event content to determine which subset of its neighbors are on the next hop to a final destination broker.

There is one major difference between the earlier work and the use of neighbor matching in this paper: In the earlier work, we assumed a point-to-point link to each neighbor (which is why in that work, the algorithm was named "link matching"). In this paper, we are assuming that there is a multicast group for each possible combination of neighbor brokers. When an event arrives at a broker, the broker computes the set of brokers on the "next hop" and forwards the event to the corresponding group.

There are a number of potential advantages of this approach. First of all, it is more scalable as the number of brokers in the system grows. Each broker has to know about only its immediate neighbors, not about all the brokers. For k neighbors, a broker can have a maximum of 2^k groups. Furthermore, the knowledge of those group names does not need to be widely disseminated; only neighbors need to subscribe to a group.

The disadvantages of the approach are that there is extra processing required on brokers, extra bandwidth required on the links between brokers and the network, and potential extra delay from publisher to subscriber because of the extra hops required.

2.6   Group Approximation Algorithm

The group approximation algorithm is a single multicast approach which reduces the number of groups required by combining actual groups to approximate groups. This approach reduces precision because an approximate group often contains a superset of the brokers which match an event. That is, some brokers may receive *waste* events: events which do not match any subscription held by a broker. The volume of waste events can affect system performance. Thus, an important aspect of this technique is to construct approximate groups which minimize the volume of waste events received by each broker, given a fixed number of multicast groups.

One way to choose approximate groups is to make use of the information contained in the subscriptions stored at each broker. In particular, we may require a separate group for each disjoint *matching set* entailed by a collection of subscriptions. The matching set of a subscription is the set of events which satisfy the constraints of the subscription. Figure 3 gives example subscriptions and corresponding matching sets. Note that the ideal algorithm creates a multicast group for each disjoint matching set.

The intuition behind the group approximation algorithm is the observation that, in systems with large event schemas, many groups have a relatively low probability of receiving events. Therefore, combinations of such groups also have a relatively low probability of introducing wasted events.

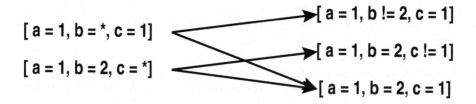

Fig. 3. Example subscriptions (on the left) and their corresponding disjoint matching sets (on the right) for the simple event schema [a: integer, b: integer, c: integer]. The events in the first set match the first subscription, events in the second set match the second subscription, and events in the third set match both

The group approximation algorithm operates as follows. Let g be the desired number of groups, then:

1. Determine the set of required multicast groups and their probability of receiving an event.
2. Combine pairs of groups until there are no more than g groups in the system.

The choice of groups to combine at each step has a significant impact on the waste generated by approximation. This waste may be characterized as follows. Given a multicast group G_i, define:

p_i The probability that G_i will receive an event.
l_i The loss factor of G_i. That is, the expected number of events wasted for each multicast to G_i.
b_i The set of brokers with a subscription containing the matching set represented by G_i.

The expected waste induced by a group G_i is $p_i \times l_i$. The *net waste induced* (NWI) by combining two groups G_1 and G_2 is given by the expression $\text{NWI}(1,2) = (p_1 + p_2) \times l_{1,2} - p_1 \times l_1 - p_2 \times l_2$ where $l_{1,2}$ is given by:

$$l_{1,2} = \left(\frac{p_1}{p_1 + p_2}\right) \times (|b_2 - b_1| + l_1) + \left(\frac{p_2}{p_1 + p_2}\right) \times (|b_1 - b_2| + l_2)$$

and $|b_i - b_j|$ is the number of brokers in set b_i but not in b_j. Note that for the combined group $G_{1,2}$ we also have $p_{1,2} = p_1 + p_2$ and $b_{1,2} = b_1 \cup b_2$, where the former follows from the fact that G_1 and G_2 represent disjoint matching sets. Reducing the equations above, $NWI(1, 2)$ may be expressed as $p_1 \times |b_2 - b_1| + p_2 \times |b_1 - b_2|$.

Typically, the set of disjoint matching sets is exponential in the number of subscriptions (several million for the simulations described in the next section). Moreover, the order in which we combine groups is significant. Therefore, an ideal group reduction involves a search over all possible orders of combining groups, and is therefore exponential in the size of the initial group set. Thus, heuristics are the only practical approach for deriving approximate groups using the expressions above. However, even in the case of polynomial heuristics, the exponential size of the initial group set is still a limiting factor[1].

In this paper, we use a hybrid approach where we approximate the set of initial groups, and then use a heuristic to reduce to a final group set. We approximate the initial group set by reducing the selectivity of subscriptions by eliminating rare attributes of the schema. We then combine groups to form an approximate group set by first sorting the initial groups from least to greatest according to probability of receiving an event. Groups with the same probability are further sorted from greatest to least according to the expression $|b_i| - l_i$. We then compute $NWI(i, j)$ for each combination of the first 100 groups, and combine the pair with the minimal net waste induced. The combined group is reinserted and the algorithm is repeated until we have reduced to the desired number of groups.

The motivation for sorting the groups is that groups with small probability pay less of a penalty for non-optimal combinations. In the case of the second sorting term, the intuition is that groups with many members but little waste are more likely to overlap in a productive manner. As a further check, we find the best pair of groups to combine by considering the first 100 groups, rather than simply combining the first two groups in sorted order. This algorithm is $O(log\ n)$ for each combination step.

Note that some error is introduced by only considering a subset of subscription attributes. In particular, it is possible to discover an actual group at run-time which has no corresponding approximate group. In this case, we dynamically map the actual group to the smallest approximate group which is a superset of the actual group.

---

[1] One simple heuristic is to use a greedy algorithm which combines pairs of groups with minimal NWI. This algorithm is $\approx O(n^3)$ which is still prohibitively expensive for group sets with size in the millions.

2.7   Summary

Each of the algorithms described above makes specific tradeoffs in order to exploit multicast. While a common goal is to reduce the number of groups, there are several other criteria by which these algorithms may be categorized:

- *Precision:* Defined as the ratio $\frac{\#\ matched\ brokers}{\#\ receiving\ brokers}$. Precision is one measure of the amount of waste in the system.
- *Number of Multicasts:* The number of multicast sends required in order to distribute an event.
- *Total Number of Groups:* A bound on the total number of groups required in the system.
- *Groups Per Broker:* A bound on the number of groups each broker is required to join.
- *Configuration:* The stage at which multicast groups must be created. "Static" means that groups can be created before the subscription set is known.
- *Manageability:* An indication of the complexity and ease of management of a particular algorithm.

	Ideal	Flooding	CGM	TCGM	Neighbor	Approx
Precision	1	$\mathcal{P}_b$	1	$[\frac{T+1}{K}, 1]$	1	$1 - \frac{W}{N}$
# Mcasts	1	1	1...C	1...C	1 per hop	1
Groups	2^N	1	$C \times 2^B$	$C \times \sum_{i=0}^{T} \binom{B}{i}$	$N \times 2^k$	Configurable
Grps/Broker	2^{N-1}	1	2^{B-1}	$\sum_{i=0}^{T-1} \binom{B-1}{i}$	$k \times 2^{k-1}$	Variable
Config.	Static	Static	Static	Static	Static	Dynamic
Manag.	Hard++	Trivial	Moderate	Moderate	Moderate	Hard

Fig. 4. Summary of event distribution algorithms where N is the number of brokers, k is the average number of neighbors of each broker, $\mathcal{P}_b$ is the probability that an arbitrary broker will match an event, C is the number of clusters, B is the number of brokers in each cluster, T is the threshold value for TCGM, and W is the total waste induced by the group approximation algorithm

Figure 4 summarizes the characteristics of each of the algorithms under consideration. Note that the ideal algorithm is infeasible to implement in most systems and is only presented for comparison purposes.

3   Evaluation

We have implemented the multicast algorithms described in the previous section and tested them on a simulated network topology. The goals of our simulations were:

1. To measure the bandwidth utilization characteristics of the algorithms we developed as well as the simple flooding algorithm and the ideal algorithm.
2. To measure the latency characteristics for the same set of algorithms. We define latency as the delay from the time an event is published to the time it is delivered to a subscribing client.

It should be noted that if subscriptions are uniformly distributed over a geographic region, then for a high enough probability of match between a random event and a random subscription, and a small enough set of brokers, it follows from straightforward probability theory that most events will be required by all brokers, and thus the behavior of ideal multicast and the behavior of flooding will be the same. Therefore, we concentrate on evaluating other algorithms only where these conditions do not occur, or in other words, where the following conditions do occur:

1. *High selectivity.* The subscriptions are sufficiently selective that the average probability of a match is very low; or
2. *High regionalism.* The subscriptions are sufficiently non-uniform that certain kinds of events will have high interest in certain parts of the network and low interest in other parts of the network.

3.1   Simulated System

We simulate an eighty-eight broker publish-subscribe network deployed across a WAN. The WAN topology used in the simulations was generated using the Georgia Tech Internetwork Topology Models [5]. We used the transit-stub topology model [26] which approximates wide-area networks. The generated topology is shown in Fig. 5. It consists of three kinds of nodes: eighty broker nodes with only subscribing clients (rectangles), eight broker nodes with only publishing clients (double circles), and one hundred multicast-enabled router nodes (circles). Links between these nodes are of three types: backbone links (bold lines) that are OC-12 class (622Mbit), intermediate links (normal lines) that are OC-3 class (155Mbit), and fringe links (dotted lines) that are high-speed LAN class (100Mbit). Latencies are labeled on individual links.

The multicast routers in the network are state of the art *wire-speed* routers. That is, they are able to forward messages at the maximum bandwidth of their incoming links. However, for each outgoing link, there is an output queue for messages that are yet to be consumed by that link. Routers and links in the network are also loaded with traffic unrelated to publish-subscribe traffic. This ambient load is 25% of the link capacity on average, uniformly across the network[2].

Each of the eighty brokers with subscribing clients has twenty five clients connected to it, with an average of five subscriptions per client (giving 10000 total subscriptions). Subscriptions are generated randomly using an event schema

---

[2] We leave the study of a more realistic non-uniform ambient load as future work.

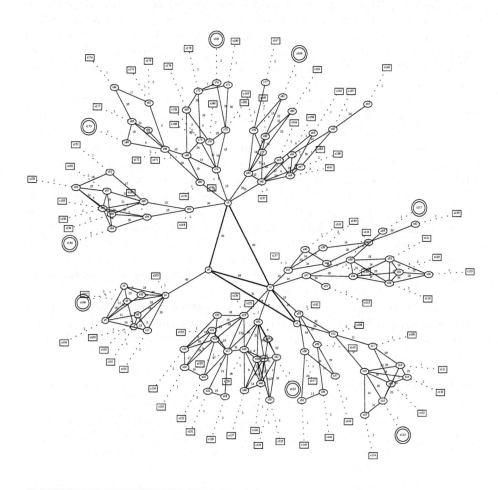

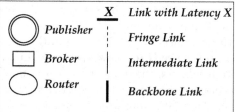

Fig. 5. Simulated network topology

with fifteen attributes, where each attribute has four possible values. For each attribute, a subscription gives either a concrete value chosen from a Zipf distribution, or a "don't care" value, which matches events with any value for the attribute. Subscriptions are generated randomly in such a way that the first attribute is a concrete value with probability of 0.98, and this probability decreases from the first to the last attribute. We vary the rate of this decrease to obtain results for different subscription match rates. For example, if the probability that an attribute is a concrete value decreases at the rate of 78%, each event matches about 2.24% of subscriptions. If the probability of a concrete value decreases at the rate of 88%, each event matches about 0.21% of subscriptions.

There are also 8 publishers in the network that publish events tracked by the simulator. Events are generated randomly, with attribute values in a Zipf distribution. Events arrive at the publishing brokers according to a Poisson distribution with mean arrival rate of 200 μs. The size of each event is 1KB.

When an event is published, it is matched at the publishing broker and then one of the previously described algorithms is used to forward it towards other brokers. Along the way, it incurs latency delays along different links as well as queuing delays at router output queues. Receiving brokers also perform a matching operation before forwarding to clients or to other brokers (in the case of neighbor matching). The brokers' CPU utilization for performing the matching operations is also modeled.

Simulations were run for all multicast algorithms described above with each run consisting of 5000 published events. In all cases, this number of events guarantees less than a 1% error rate (with 99% confidence) for the bandwidth measurements.

Additional Setup for Specific Algorithms

For the purposes of the neighbor matching algorithm of Sect. 2.5, the topology described above also specifies a "neighbor" relation between brokers, as shown in Fig. 6. Each circle in Fig. 6 corresponds to one of the broker nodes (rectangle or double circle) in Fig. 5. Latencies between neighbors represent latencies on the shortest path between corresponding brokers. In the particular experimental configuration tested here, we assign neighbor relationships based upon proximity in the network topology. We limit the number of neighbors so that the total number of groups used in the system is approximately 2^{13}. We chose 2^{13} to match the number of groups used in the simulation of CGM-8 and in the group approximation algorithm. Because no broker needs to know about any groups other than those used by its immediate neighbors, the number of groups known to any one broker is small — on the average a broker needs to know 100 groups to which it can send, and needs to join 325 groups from which it can receive an event.

For the purposes of the CGM algorithm of Section 2.3, we manually assigned each broker to one of the required number of clusters, based on its geographical location and its proximity to other brokers in the same cluster.

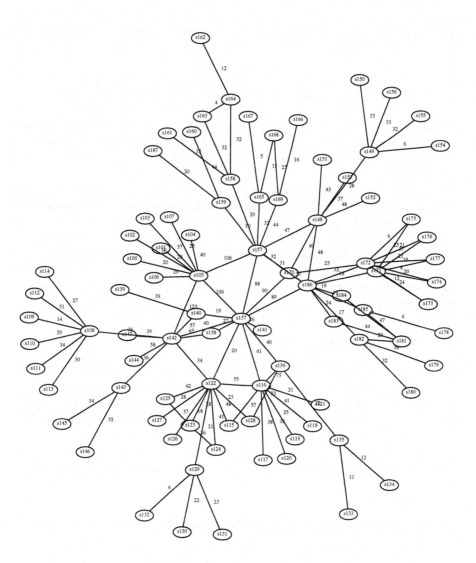

Fig. 6. Broker "neighbor" relations

Subscription Distributions

We ran simulations for two kinds of subscription distributions: non-regional, and regional. In the non-regional distribution, the subscriptions are assigned randomly with a uniform distribution, without regard to the location of the subscribing client. In the regional distribution, topologically nearby clients are more likely to be interested in the same events. This is achieved by assigning one attribute of the event schema as the "regionalism" attribute. The value of the regionalism attribute is a number between one and four, corresponding to its "cluster" as determined by the CGM clustering algorithm (with 4 regions) described above. With probability p, a subscription for a client in region i specifies an interest in an event with value i for the regionalism attribute; otherwise it specifies a don't-care for this attribute. This probability p is a simulation parameter we call the *degree of regionalism*. At $p = 0$, the distribution is equivalent to the non-regional distribution. We refer to the distribution at $p = 1$ as "total regionalism".

The regionalism simulations were further refined according to whether or not publisher events are assigned a regionalism attribute based upon the location of the publisher. In one scenario, called "publisher regionalism", all events are assigned a regionalism attribute value equal to the publisher's region number; in the other scenario, the regionalism attribute is assigned randomly. As it turned out, the results of the simulations were not sensitive to publisher regionalism. We therefore present only the results with non-regional subscriptions and regional subscriptions.

3.2   Bandwidth Utilization Results

To study the bandwidth utilization of the multicast algorithms described earlier, we divide the links into three classes: backbone links, intermediate (router to router) links, and fringe (router to broker) links, corresponding to link types in Sect. 3.1. This classification is based not only on the bandwidth capacity, but also on economic and administrative considerations. For example, the cost of using a backbone link may be different from that of a fringe link. Similarly, economic decisions regarding fringe links may affect the way in which subscriptions on a broker are managed. For these reasons, we believe that these three classes of links must be studied separately.

Highly Selective Non-Regional Subscriptions

For non-regional subscriptions, the various approaches are only distinguishable when match rates are low (e.g., less than 3%). Figure 7 charts the mean bandwidth utilization per published event at various subscription match rates, for different classes of links. On backbone links, the graph shows that cluster-based algorithms use a factor of two or three more bandwidth on the backbone than the other algorithms. This is because these approaches send multiple messages for each published event. The other algorithms perform similar to each other on the backbone, and are close to ideal for almost all match rates. One interesting observation here is that the neighbor matching algorithm is slightly more efficient than the ideal algorithm even though it uses multiple sends, one per hop. This is because hops from neighbor to neighbor may use an optimal number of backbone links although a sub-optimal number of links overall.

On intermediate links, all the algorithms outperform flooding if the subscription set is highly selective. In particular, the neighbor matching and CGM-4 algorithms perform better than others (excluding ideal) for subscription match rates below 1.5%. Thus, if an application has a stable match rate in this region, one of these algorithms may prove to be suitable. However, at higher match rates, these algorithms perform worse than a simple flooding approach. Similarly, CGM-8 and TCGM perform worse than flooding for anything but the most highly selective subscriptions. The group approximation algorithm does no worse than flooding asymptotically, but offers a slight benefit for match rates below 0.5%.

On fringe links, bandwidth utilization is closely related to the precision of algorithms. Single-hop precise algorithms, such as the cluster-based algorithms perform similar to the ideal algorithm, the difference being the extra usage of fringe links from publisher brokers. Single-hop imprecise algorithms, such as TCGM and Approx utilize more bandwidth on the fringes, and quickly approach flooding. Neighbor matching, although precise, utilizes worse amounts of bandwidth on the fringes since it is based on multiple hops between brokers (which are always on the fringes).

As expected, all algorithms (even ideal) eventually converge to the same (or worse) bandwidth usage as the flooding approach. With 125 subscriptions per broker and 2% subscription match rate, the fact that subscriptions are uniformly distributed (as opposed to regionally distributed) gives a 92% probability that an arbitrary broker will have a subscription matching a particular event. This means that over 90% of the brokers receive each published event.

Regional Subscriptions

For regional subscriptions, all the algorithms have the same relative performance (with the exception of approx) but show a marked improvement over flooding as the degree of regionalism (as given in Sect. 2) is increased. Figure 8 illustrates the effect of regionalism on the various approaches at a fixed match rate of 3%. At the top of the figure, intermediate link utilization is plotted as a function of the degree of regionalism. It is interesting to note that none of the algorithms perform significantly better than flooding until regional correlation reaches 0.75. At this point, ideal, neighbor matching and CGM-4 begin to show successively better improvement as the degree of regionalism increases. CGM-8 and TCGM-4(3) also show improvement but do not compare favorably with flooding until regional correlation is close to 1. The one exception to this trend is the group approximation algorithm which does not improve because the set of required groups is approximated and regionalism is not accounted for. In

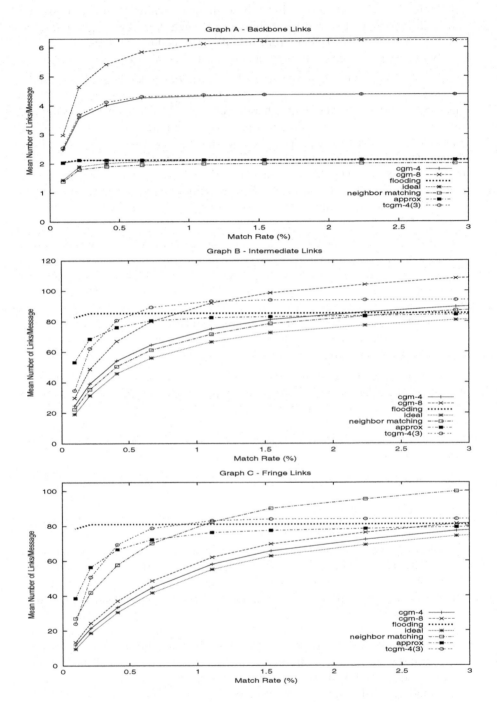

Fig. 7. Link utilization results for non-regional subscriptions

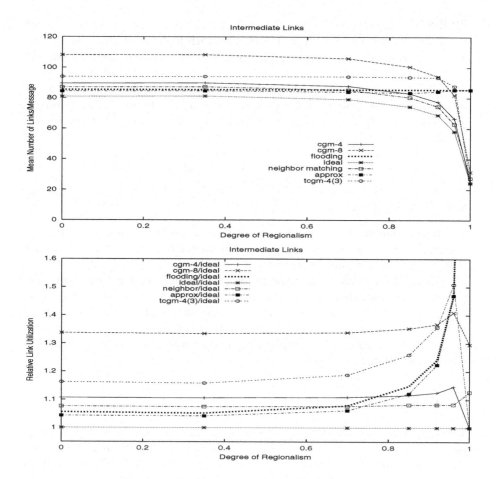

Fig. 8. Effect of regionalism on intermediate link utilization

particular, it is possible for groups from separate regions to be combined into a single group during the group combination phase[3].

The bottom of Fig. 8 illustrates the performance of each algorithm relative to the ideal algorithm. The peaks in the graph indicate regions where the ideal algorithm improves at a faster rate than the other algorithms. The CGM-4 and TCGM algorithms converge with ideal at total regionalism because the four regions used in the experiment correspond exactly with the four clusters used in these algorithms[4].

---

[3] The group approximation algorithm can be refined to take regions into account while combining groups in order to eliminate this effect.

[4] Also, under total regionalism, all matching subscriptions will be in the same region. As a result, a match rate of 3% gives a high probability that every broker in a cluster will require an event. Thus the flooding aspect of TCGM has no detrimental effect.

Summary

These results illustrate that in scenarios with high selectivity (match rates in the 1% range) or high regionalism (degree of regionalism greater than 0.8), the algorithm of choice will depend on the economics of deployment. If the cost of fringe links is the highest, a cluster-based algorithm may be feasible, provided that the number of groups required can be supported. If intermediate links are most expensive, that may suggest the neighbor matching approach. If backbone is expensive, anything but the cluster-based algorithms are acceptable. A weighted sum of the bandwidth utilizations, where the weights are based on the cost of using each class of links, will suggest the optimal algorithm.

3.3   Latency Results

The latency metric compares the average time taken by an event to travel from a publisher to all subscribers. It turns out that the latency of all algorithms except neighbor matching were virtually identical for all match rates. All these algorithms do not differ since the event publish rate used in our simulations was not high enough to induce queueing delays at the various routers. Even under regionalism, event rates were not sufficiently high to show any latency variation. In all cases, however, neighbor matching was about 25% slower because of the delays introduced by performing partial matching at broker nodes on intermediate hops.

4   Related Work

The background of this study, and work related to it, will be reviewed in two phases. First, we examine the event distribution algorithms of those systems that support non-trivial subscription languages, with respect to how (if at all) these systems exploit group multicast at the network level. Second, we examine algorithms that employ multiple IP multicast groups, with respect to how closely their semantics resemble those of content-based subscription systems.

4.1   Event Distribution Systems

Relatively few event distribution systems [25] allow subscriptions to be expressed as predicates over the entire message content. A few noteworthy examples of this emerging category are SIENA [6], READY [10], Elvin [20], JEDI [7], Yeast [12], GEM [15], and Gryphon [2]. All of these systems support rich subscription predicates, and thus face problems of scalability in their event distribution algorithms.

However, pure content-based systems are only one endpoint on a scale of subscription "richness," and an increasing number of publish-subscribe systems may be expected to experience aspects of the problem explored here. The Java Message Service (JMS) [22] enables the use of *message selectors*, which are predicates over a set of message *properties*. Message designers are free to store information in properties rather than the message body, making the resulting system behave more like a content-based system. The OMG Notification Service [17] describes structured events with a "filterable body" portion. Many vendors are implementing JMS, or the OMG Notification service, or both, which has the result of making this form of subscription more popular. The TIB/Rendezvous system [23] available from the TIBCO corporation has a hierarchy of subjects and permits subscription patterns over the resulting segmented subject field, also approximating some of the richness available with content-based subscription.

The actual event distribution algorithms employed by the "richer" systems vary. Some systems, such as Yeast [12] and Elvin [20], are centralized, with a single server to which all events are first sent. The server evaluates subscription expressions and sends the results to individual subscribers. Multicast is not used. The Elvin server supports a "quench" function, wherein publishers are able to find out if an event has any subscribers at all: such events are not sent to the server.

TIB/Rendezvous uses LAN broadcast to deliver all events, and performs event filtering in daemon processes at client machines. An extension to use IP multicast [8] instead of LAN broadcast has been accomplished and it is reportedly in use by some customers.[5] This extends the reach of the Rendezvous solution to a somewhat wider network, but the solution still employs a single group and is optimized for the LAN case, where the cost of multicast and unicast are similar.

Both SIENA [6], and our previous work in the Gryphon project [2] explored algorithms that delivered events over a logical network of brokers. These algorithms delivered events only to interested subscribers, employed only links that were along a path to an interested subscriber, and sent each message at most once over each link. Both papers characterized their algorithms as forms of multicast, but neither system actually exploited multicast services at the network level: their implementation assumed only point-to-point links.

READY [10] is a new, distributed version of Yeast. It offers two ways for publishers and subscribers to connect to event brokers, via TCP connections, or via a "reliable multicast" provider. However, what they mean by reliable multicast is itself an event-based middleware layer such as TIB/Rendezvous or IONA's OrbixTalk [11]. Whether or not network-layer multicast is exploited depends on how the underlying product achieves its reliable multicast semantics. READY employs a peer group of equivalent servers rather than a graph of servers as in SIENA or Gryphon.

Both READY and TIB/Rendezvous provide specialized routers between administrative domains (called "boundary routers" in READY and "routing daemons" in Rendezvous). The assumption is that the publishers and subscribers within an administrative domain have high levels of traffic, while messages cross domain boundaries less frequently. Elvin lists a similar function as future work [20].

As far as we can determine, all previous solutions either do not use group multicast at the network level, or employ a single group with filtering at the

---

[5] See **http://www.rv.tibco.com/faq.html**.

clients, or modify the second technique only at boundaries between administrative domains. We wish, in contrast, to use network-level multicast as a flexible building block in developing a specialized content-based multicast solution.

4.2 Other Algorithms That Exploit IP Multicast

Publish-subscribe systems are not the only domain in which information is periodically delivered to a set of clients whose membership may vary from delivery to delivery. IP multicast was, of course, designed for the case where the set of interested clients was the same for a large set of related deliveries. So, the need to use multiple, possibly overlapping, IP multicast groups may be expected to arise in numerous domains.

One domain where the use of multiple IP groups is becoming popular is web caching. The Adaptive Web Caching proposal [27] proposes a dynamically maintained mesh of overlapping multicast groups, over which trees are implicitly formed with web servers at their root and caches as nodes. A mixture of multicast and unicast transmissions are used in constructing the protocol. Caching is based on requests from clients, rather than pro-active "pushes" from servers, so the relevance of this proposal to publish-subscribe systems is limited.

Other web caching proposals, however, have used a model in which servers push content to proxy caches based on predictions concerning likely interest in particular pages. This is much more like a publish-subscribe system. MMO [14] and LPC [24] are two recent examples of multicast "push" caching proposals that assign caches to multiple IP multicast groups based on clusters of web pages that are expected to have "similar" hit patterns.

As far as we can determine, proposals in which web caches belong to multiple IP multicast groups have assumed that the number of groups will be modest, and that the limit of IP multicast addressing is not a factor in the scalability of the proposals. In contrast, the present study contemplates algorithms in which the number of groups can become a factor in scalability, and considers tradeoffs to minimize the number of groups.

5 Conclusions and Future Work

One important result of this study is that the flooding algorithm is viable over an extensive range of conditions. As pointed out earlier, when subscription patterns do not vary by location in the network, even a fairly low match rate guarantees that all or nearly all brokers will have some subscription matching each event. For instance, under our simulation parameters (10,000 subscriptions distributed among 80 brokers), with a match rate of about 3%, each event goes to over 91% of the 80 brokers. That is, there is less than 9% wasted work on the fringe links and in the destination brokers if that event were broadcast to all brokers (there is an even smaller percentage of wasted work on the other links). Even with a match rate as low as 1.5%, each event goes to over 77% of all brokers. Therefore, it is only useful to examine the non-flooding algorithms for cases with high selectivity (i.e., match rates are low or highly variable), or high regionalism (i.e., where the probability of match is biased according to the location of the broker).

The algorithms being studied here do not begin to perform significantly better than flooding until the match rate drops below 1%. CGM performs well in this region, but still requires a very large number of groups and does not scale well. Neighbor matching is the best of the candidates if intermediate link bandwidth is the most important, but suffers in terms of latency. The group approximation algorithm is potentially scalable but performs worse than neighbor matching in the low match-rate region.

The case in which subscriptions display what regionalism is an important one. In this case, flooding is less likely to perform well because subscriptions are localized and wide-scale dissemination of events will unnecessarily congest the network. Thus, it is not surprising that many of the approaches described in this paper begin to perform better than flooding when more than 75% of subscriptions have a regional correlation. In particular, CGM and neighbor matching may provide significant bandwidth savings in these highly regional scenarios. These results suggest a hybrid approach where our multicast techniques are only utilized during high regionalism conditions. In particular, an important future direction is to discover such conditions dynamically, and to exploit them in creating small numbers of groups tailored to the most likely patterns of event deliveries.

In evaluating multicast techniques, we have emphasized performance based on a static set of subscriptions, based on the assumption that events are published far more frequently than subscription changes. However, many systems are likely to experience a flux of subscriptions. Thus, multicast groups may need to be periodically reconstructed as subscription sets change. Of the approaches considered, flooding, CGM, and neighbor matching are the most resilient to subscription set changes, since these approaches organize brokers into multicast groups which are fixed at system configuration time. For group approximation, subscription changes may alter the waste incurred by existing groups. In the worst case, the entire set of approximate groups must be reconstructed from scratch. Some overhead may be reduced in each of these approaches by performing group reconstruction at idle times and using flooding for new subscriptions in the interim. On the other hand, if subscription regionalism is also a dynamic feature then both flooding and CGM may suffer in performance. Flooding, for example, does not account for regionalism. Similarly, CGM may suffer from an unfortunate choice of regions at configuration time. In contrast, the neighbor matching algorithm is more adaptable to dynamically forming regions.

Any practical solution is likely to incorporate a hybrid of technologies. It may be cost effective to incorporate a certain degree of higher-level function in routers. For instance, neighbor matching or group approximation may be combined with a form of network multicast that permits sending to a subset of a group, as in AIM [13]. Moreover, as broker networks are consolidated and grow into the hundreds of brokers, even clustering will not significantly reduce the number of required groups. Thus, it may be necessary to consider structuring the larger network hierarchically, using different multicast algorithms internally within the subnetworks and across subnetworks.

6 Acknowledgements

The authors wish to thank Arthur Goldberg for his comments and suggestions regarding the cluster multicast algorithm, and Dilip Kandlur for his help in understanding IP router characteristics. The authors also thank Sumeer Bhola and the reviewers for their comments.

References

1. Marcos K. Aguilera, Robert E. Strom, Daniel C. Sturman, Mark Astley, and Tushar D. Chandra. Matching Events in a Content-Based Subscription System. In *Proceedings of Principles of Distributed Computing (PODC '99)*, Atlanta, GA, May 1999. 186, 187
2. Guruduth Banavar, Tushar Chandra, Bodhi Mukherjee, Jay Nagarajarao, Robert E. Strom, and Daniel C. Sturman. An Efficient Multicast Protocol for Content-Based Publish-Subscribe Systems. In *International Conference on Distributed Computing Systems (ICDCS '99)*, June 1999. 186, 190, 202, 203
3. Ken P. Birman. The process group approach to reliable distributed computing. *Communications of the ACM*, 36(12):36–53, December 1993. 185
4. S. Bradner and A. Mankin. *The Recommendation for the IP Next Generation Protocol*. IETF. RFC 1752. 187
5. Ken Calvert, Matt Doar, and Ellen W. Zegura. Modeling Internet Topology. *IEEE Communications Magazine*, June 1997. 194
6. Antonio Carzaniga. *Architectures for an Event Notification Service Scalable to Wide-area Networks*. PhD thesis, Politecnico di Milano, December 1998. Available from http://www.cs.colorado.edu/~carzanig/papers/. 202, 203
7. G. Cugola, E. DiNitto, and A. Fuggetta. The JEDI event-based infrastructure and its application to the development of the OPSS WFMS. Submitted to Transactions on Software Engineering. 202
8. S. Deering. *Host Extensions for IP Multicasting*. IETF. RFC 1112. 186, 203
9. S. Floyd, V. Jacobson, C. Liu, S. McCanne, and L. Zhang. A Reliable Multicast Framework for Light-weight Sessions and Application Level Framing. *IEEE/ACM Transactions on Networking*, 5(6):784–803, December 1997. 186
10. R. Gruber, B Krishnamurthy, and E. Panagos. An Architecture of the READY Event Notification System. In *Proceedings of the Middleware Workshop at the International Conference on Distributed Computing Systems 1999*, Austin, TX, June 1999. 202, 203
11. IONA Corporation. *OrbixTalk Fact Sheet*. http://www.iona.com/products/messaging/talk/index.html. 203
12. B. Krishnamurthy and D. Rosenblum. Yeast: A general purpose event-action system. *IEEE Transactions on Software Engineering*, 21(10), October 1995. 202, 203

13. B. N. Levine and J.J. Garcia-Luna-Aceves. Improving internet multicast with routing labels. In *Proc. IEEE International Conference on Network Protocols*, pages 241–50, October 1997. 205

14. Dan Li and David R. Cheriton. Scalable Web Caching of Frequently Updated Objects Using Reliable Multicast. In *Proceedings of the USENIX Symposium on Internet Technology and Systems*, Boulder, Colorado, 1999. 204

15. M. Mansouri-Samani and M. Sloman. A Generalized Event Monitoring Language for Distributed Systems. *IEE/IOP/BCS Distributed Systems Engineering Journal*, 4(2), June 1997. 202

16. Shivakant Mishra, Larry L. Peterson, and Richard D. Schlichting. Consul: A Communication Substrate for Fault-Tolerant Distributed Programs. Technical Report TR 91-32, Dept. of Computer Science, The University of Arizona, November 1991. 185

17. Object Management Group. *Notification Service*. http://www.omg.org/cgi-bin/doc?telecom/98-06-15. 203

18. Brian Oki, Manfred Pfluegl, Alex Siegel, and Dale Skeen. The Information Bus - An Architecture for Extensible Distributed Systems. *Operating Systems Review*, 27(5), December 1993. 185

19. David Powell. Group Communication. *Communications of the ACM*, 39(4):50–97, April 1996. (Guest Editor). 185

20. Bill Segall and David Arnold. Elvin has left the building: A publish/subscribe notification service with quenching. In *Proceedings of AUUG97*, Brisbane, Australia, September 1997. 186, 202, 203

21. Dale Skeen. Vitria's Publish-Subscribe Architecture: Publish-Subscribe Overview. Technical report, Vitria Technology Inc., 1996. http://www.vitria.com. 185

22. Sun Microsystems. *Java Message Service*. http://java.sun.com/products/jms. 202

23. TIBCO. *TIB/Rendezvous White Paper*. http://www.rv.tibco.com/whitepaper.html. 203

24. J. Touch and A. S. Hughes. The LSAM Proxy Cache - a Multicast Distributed Virtual Cache. *Computer Networks and ISDN Systems*, 30(22–23), November 1998. 204

25. Workshop on Internet Scale Event Notification. See http://www.ics.uci.edu/IRUS/wisen/wisen98 for details. 202

26. Ellen W. Zegura, Ken Calvert, and S. Bhattacharjee. How to Model an Internetwork. In *Proceedings of IEEE Infocom '99*, San Francisco, CA, April 1996. 194

27. L. Zhang, S.Floyd, and V. Jacobson. Adaptive Web Caching. In *Proceedings of the 2nd NLANR Web Cache Workshop*, Boulder, Colorado, 1997. http://ircache.nlanr.net/Cache/Workshop97/Papers/Floyd/floyd.ps. 204

The Design and Performance of a Scalable ORB Architecture for CORBA Asynchronous Messaging*

Alexander B. Arulanthu, Carlos O'Ryan, Douglas C. Schmidt, Michael Kircher, and Jeff Parsons

Department of Computer Science
Washington University, St. Louis, MO 63130
{alex,coryan,schmidt,mk1,parsons}@cs.wustl.edu

Abstract. Historically, method-oriented middleware, such as Sun RPC, DCE, Java RMI, COM, and CORBA, has provided synchronous method invocation (SMI) models to applications. Although SMI works well for conventional client/server applications, it is not well-suited for high-performance or real-time applications due to its lack of scalability. To address this problem, the OMG has recently standardized an asynchronous method invocation (AMI) model for CORBA. AMI provides CORBA with many of the capabilities associated traditionally with message-oriented middleware, without incurring the key drawbacks of message-oriented middleware.

This paper provides two contributions to research on asynchronous invocation models for method-oriented middleware. First, we outline the key design challenges faced when developing the CORBA AMI model and describe how we resolved these challenges in TAO, which is our high-performance, real-time CORBA-compliant ORB. Second, we present the results of empirical benchmarks that demonstrate the performance benefits of AMI compared with alternative CORBA invocation models. In general, AMI based CORBA clients are more scalable than equivalent SMI based designs, with only a moderate increase in programming complexity.

1 Introduction

Motivation:

Historically, applications based on the standard CORBA [1] distributed object computing model have had to choose between three *invocation models*: one-way operations, synchronous two-way operations, and deferred synchronous operations using the dynamic invocation interface (DII). Unfortunately, these alternatives are often inappropriate for applications with stringent quality of service

---

* This work was supported by DARPA contract 9701516, NSF grant NCR-9628218, Siemens ZT, Sprint, Nortel, Boeing, SAIC, and Lucent.

J. Sventek and G. Coulson (Eds.): Middleware 2000, LNCS 1795, pp. 208–230, 2000.

(QoS) requirements. For instance, one-way operations lack well-defined semantics [2], which reduces their portability and suitability for applications with nontrivial reliability requirements. Likewise, synchronous two-way operations are not scalable because they require a client thread for each pending request/response invocation. Finally, the deferred synchronous model is inefficient and tedious to program due to its reliance on the DII [3], which allocates memory and copies data excessively.

To address these limitations, the OMG adopted a Messaging specification [4] for the CORBA standard. One of the key features in the CORBA Messaging specification is support for asynchronous method invocations (AMI).

Overview of CORBA AMI:

The CORBA AMI specification defines a *polling* model and a *callback* model, as described below:

• *Polling model:* In this model, each two-way AMI operation returns a `Poller` `valuetype` [5], which is very much like a C++ or Java class in that it has both data members and methods. Operations on a `Poller` are just local C++ method calls rather than remote CORBA operation invocations. The polling model is illustrated in Figure 1. The client can use the `Poller` methods to check the status

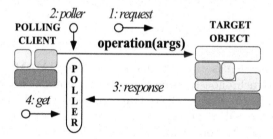

Fig. 1. Polling Model for CORBA Asynchronous Twoway Operations

of the request so it can obtain the server's reply. If the server hasn't replied yet, the client can either (1) block awaiting its arrival or (2) return to the calling thread immediately and check back on the `Poller` to obtain the `valuetypes` when it's convenient.

• *Callback model:* In this model, when a client invokes a two-way asynchronous operation on an object, it passes an object reference for a *reply handler* servant as a parameter. The reply handler object reference is not passed to the server, but instead is stored locally by the client ORB. When the server replies, the client ORB receives the response, and dispatches it to the appropriate callback

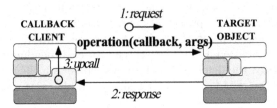

Fig. 2. Callback Model for CORBA Asynchronous Twoway Operations

operation on the reply handler servant provided by the client application, as shown in Figure 2.

Reply handler servants are accessed through normal object references. Therefore, it is possible for a client application to obtain an object reference for a remote reply handler servant and use that object reference to make AMI calls. In this case, replies for the asynchronous invocations will be handled in processes other than the client or the server involved in the original invocations. The most common use-case, however, is for the original client to process the response. In this case, therefore, client application developers must obtain, initialize, and activate reply handlers on a POA, which makes the application behave effectively as both a client and a server.

In general, the callback model is more efficient than the polling model because the client need not invoke method calls on a `valuetype` repeatedly to poll for results. Moreover, compared with CORBA's original invocation alternatives, the new AMI models provide the following benefits:

• *Simplified asynchronous programming model:* CORBA AMI allows operations to be invoked asynchronously using the *static invocation interface* (SII). Using SII for AMI eliminates much of the tedium, complexity, and inefficiency inherent in DII. In particular, DII requires programmers to allocate a new `Request` object explicitly and insert the operation parameters into a list of name value pairs, *i.e.*, an `NVList` pseudo-object. Conversely, in SII the IDL compiler can use an ORB's internal mechanisms to avoid extra memory allocations and data copies. Although deferred synchronous request implementations can exploit many AMI optimizations, such as better utilization of the network resources and improved parallelism, those improvements are hindered by DII's extra overhead, which often makes AMI a more attractive alternative.

• *Improved quality of service:* When implemented properly, AMI can improve the scalability of CORBA applications. For instance, it allows "pipelining" of twoway operations and minimizes the number of client threads that are otherwise required to perform two-way synchronous method invocations (SMI). In addition, AMI is important for real-time CORBA applications [6] because it helps to bound the amount of time a client spends blocking on two-way requests.

Synopsis of research contributions:

Our previous research has examined many dimensions of high-performance and real-time ORB endsystem design, including static [7] and dynamic [8] scheduling, event processing [9], I/O subsystem [10] and pluggable protocol [11] integration, ORB Core architectures [12], systematic benchmarking of multiple ORBs [13], patterns for ORB extensibility [14] and ORB performance [15]. This paper focuses on a previously unexplored dimension in the high-performance and real-time ORB endsystem design space: *the design and optimizations used to implement the standard CORBA asynchronous method invocation (AMI) callback model.*

The vehicle for our research on high-performance and real-time CORBA is TAO [7]. TAO is an open-source[1], CORBA-compliant ORB designed to address applications with stringent quality of service (QoS) requirements. In addition to being the first ORB with a standard Portable Object Adapter [15], TAO was the first ORB to implement the standard CORBA AMI callback model.

Related work:

The AMI polling model stems from research on programming language support for distributed computing. For instance, Futures [16] and Promises [17] are language mechanisms that decouple method invocation from method return values passed back to the caller when a method finishes executing. As with AMI `Poller`s, calls are invoked asynchronously, clients can rendezvous with a Future/Promise to obtain reply values when they become available.

Previous research on *method-oriented middleware* [9,18,19] has examined how the CORBA Event Service can be used to perform asynchronous communication between CORBA applications. However, the CORBA AMI specification provides a different programming model than the CORBA Event Service. For instance, since the CORBA Event Service allows single-point-to-multi-point and anonymous communication models, application developers must devise their own means to send replies from event consumers back to event suppliers. In contrast, AMI applications can receive replies that include multiple IDL types. Moreover, CORBA Event Service participants communicate using a single `Any` argument. Although Anys can send all IDL types, they incur significant marshaling and message footprint overhead. In contrast, AMI clients can send and receive multiple IDL types and IDL compilers [20] can generate efficient marshaling and demarshaling code for them.

Message-oriented middleware (MOM), such as the Isis [21] Message Distribution System, TIBCO Information Bus, and IBM's MQSeries, provide mechanisms that allow suppliers to reliably transmit messages asynchronously to one or more consumers. MOM systems typically consist of additional "router" processes that store and forward messages on behalf of application processes. If a consumer

---

[1] The source code and documentation for TAO can be downloaded from `www.cs.wustl.edu/~schmidt/TAO.html`.

happens to be unavailable due to scheduled downtime, a site crash, or a network partition, the router will attempt to deliver the message periodically until the consumer becomes available. The OMG Message specification defines similar routing capabilities via its Time-Independent Invocation (TII) feature [22,4]. Both the TII and MOM asynchrony mechanisms are too heavyweight, however, for many high-performance and real-time applications. Moreover, the message-oriented invocation mechanisms of MOM systems can be harder to program correctly due to the lack of strong typechecking.

The remainder of this paper is organized as follows: Section 2 outlines the general structure and dynamics an ORB requires to support AMI callbacks; Section 3 describes key design challenges faced when implementing the CORBA AMI callback model and explains how TAO resolves these challenges; Section 4 empirically analyzes the performance of AMI callbacks in TAO [7] and compares it with alternative communication models; and Section 5 presents concluding remarks that summarize the lessons learned from implementing AMI callbacks in TAO.

2   ORB Architectural Support for AMI Callbacks

This section outlines the general structure and dynamics an ORB requires to support AMI callbacks.

2.1   AMI Callback Features

To support AMI callbacks, an ORB should implement the following functionality:

1. AMI stubs: For each two-way operation in the IDL interface, an ORB's IDL compiler [20] should generate an *AMI stub* that applications can use to issue asynchronous operations. Each AMI stub is responsible for (1) setting up state in the ORB to receive the reply and dispatch it to the appropriate reply handler, (2) marshaling the in and inout arguments provided by the application, and (3) using the ORB Core to send the message to a remote ORB. High-quality IDL compilers should provide an option to suppress the generation of AMI stubs to reduce the footprint of applications that do not use them.

2. Manage pending invocations: The client ORB must store reply handler object references for all asynchronous invocations. If the reply handler servant is collocated with the client, the application developer must activate the reply handler implementation with the client's ORB POA. When a reply returns, the client ORB locates the reply handler servant and invokes the callback method on it. The client ORB delivers this new request to the reply handler servant using its regular invocation path, which allows an ORB's collocation optimizations [23] to be used to minimize dispatching overhead.

3. Explicit event loop methods: An ORB must implement the standard CORBA `work_pending` and `perform_work` operations. Clients can use these operations to invoke the CORBA event loop in a client explicitly. In addition, if asynchronous replies arrive while a client is blocked waiting for a synchronous reply, the ORB can use the blocked thread to dispatch the asynchronous reply.

2.2 Collaborations between ORB Components for Asynchronous Invocation

After an OMG IDL compiler generates the AMI callback stubs, the generated code must collaborate with internal ORB components to send and receive asynchronous invocations. To demonstrate how this works, Figure 3 depicts the general sequence of steps involved when an asynchronous two-way `get_quote` operation is executed.[2] As shown in this figure, the interactions between client ORB

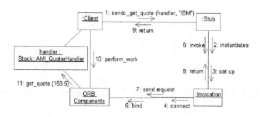

Fig. 3. Interactions Between Client ORB Components for Asynchronous Invocation

components for an asynchronous invocation consist of the following steps:

- The client application invokes the `sendc_get_quote` method on the `Stub` to issue the asynchronous operation (**1**). The client passes the `AMI_QuoterHandler` object reference, along with the name of the stock we're interested in, e.g., IBM.
- The `Stub` marshals its string argument into a buffer and instantiates an `Invocation` (**2**), which is a facade that delegates to internal ORB components that establish connections (**3**) & (**4**) with a remote server (if necessary), the ORB stores the `AMI_QuoterHandler` object (**5**), and send the requests (**6**) & (**7**) to the server.
- After the request is sent, `Invocation` returns control to the `Stub` (**8**), which itself returns control to the client (**9**).

---

[2] The names of certain objects in this discussion are specific to TAO, though the general flow of control and behavior should generalize to other ORBs that implement AMI callbacks.

- When a client application is prepared to handle callbacks, it calls the ORB's work_pending and perform_work (10) methods to receive and dispatch replies associated with asynchronous invocations.
- When the reply arrives, the ORB demarshals the reply and demultiplexes it to the callback method on the reply handler servant that was passed in by the application when the AMI method was invoked originally (11).

Section 3.2 revisits these steps in more detail after we've explained the components in TAO's ORB architecture.

3   The Design of TAO's AMI Callback Architecture

To make the discussion of ORB architectural support for AMI in Section 2 more concrete, this section describes our resolutions to key design challenges encountered when implementing TAO's AMI-enabled ORB architecture. Section 4 then illustrates the performance characteristics of TAO's AMI implementation compared to alternative SMI and DII deferred synchronous communication models.

3.1   Design Challenges and Resolutions

To assist developers of distributed object systems in making informed choices among alternative ORB middleware solutions, they should understand how the ORBs are implemented. Below, we (1) outline the key design challenges we faced when implementing AMI in TAO and (2) explain the patterns and components we used to resolve these challenges.

Challenge: How to Process Asynchronous Replies Efficiently

Context: Early TAO implementations supported only the Synchronous Method Invocation (SMI) model. In SMI, the calling thread that makes a two-way invocation blocks awaiting the server's reply. The client ORB can use the calling thread to process the response. For example, consider the *Leader/Followers* thread pool concurrency model [12] illustrated in Figure 4. TAO uses this concurrency model to support multi-threaded client applications efficiently, as follows:

- Each calling thread that invokes a two-way synchronous method (1) uses a connection to send the request (2).
- The client ORB designates one of the waiting threads the *leader* and the other threads as the *followers*. The leader thread blocks on the select operation (3); the follower threads block on semaphores (4).
- When a reply arrives on a connection, the leader thread returns from select. If the reply belongs to the leader, it continues to process the reply after first promoting the next follower to become the new leader. If the reply belongs to one of the followers, however, the leader signals the corresponding semaphore to wake up the follower thread (5).
- The awakened follower thread reads the reply (6), completes the two-way invocation (7), and returns to its caller.

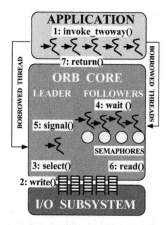

Fig. 4. Processing Synchronous Two-way Client Invocations using the Leader/Followers Concurrency Model

Problem: Although the Leader/Followers thread pool model described above works well for SMI, it does not work without modification for AMI. The problem stems from the fact that the calling stub goes out of scope as soon as the request is sent and control returns to client application code. Thus, the ORB must be prepared to process an asynchronous reply in another context, possibly within another client thread. Moreover, to complete the processing of server replies to asynchronous invocations, the ORB must maintain certain state information, such as reply handler object reference and a function to demarshal the reply (the so-called *reply-stub*).

Forces: The mechanisms provided to support AMI replies should add no significant run-time overhead to the existing SMI mechanisms.

Solution → Strategizing the reply dispatching mechanisms: The problem of processing asynchronous replies can be solved by *strategizing* the reply processing and dispatching mechanisms used for AMI and SMI calls. Figure 5 illustrates the components in TAO's `Reply Dispatcher` hierarchy. A `Synchronous Reply Dispatcher` is created by an `Invocation` object during a synchronous invocation on the local stack activation record. When the reply is received, the reply buffer, *i.e.*, TAO's `InputCDR` object, is placed in the dispatcher and control returns first to the `Invocation` object and then to the `Stub`. At this point, the `Stub` obtains the reply buffer from the `Invocation` object, demarshals the reply, and completes the invocation. Each `Reply Dispatcher` object maintains a `reply_received` flag that indicates if the reply has been received. This flag is set when the reply is dispatched to this object and the thread waiting for the reply returns to the `Stub`.

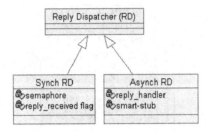

Fig. 5. Reply Dispatching Strategy

During an AMI call, an `Invocation` object creates an `Asynchronous Reply Dispatcher` on the heap[3] because the activation record where the `Invocation` object is created is exited before the reply is received. The AMI stub, *i.e.*, the `sendc_*` operation, stores the reply handler object reference provided by the client in the `Asynchronous Reply Dispatcher` object. In addition, the AMI stub stores the pointer to the appropriate reply-stub method in this object.

A Leader/Followers implementation using TAO's `Reply Dispatcher` architecture is illustrated in Figure 6 and behaves as follows:

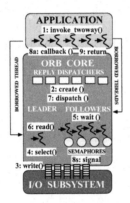

Fig. 6. TAO's AMI-enabled Leader/Followers Implementation

- When application threads make two-way invocations **(1)**, a `Reply Dispatcher` object is created for each invocation **(2)** and the request is sent **(3)**.
- The leader thread then blocks on the `select` call **(4)** and the follower threads block on the semaphores **(5)**.

---

[3] As an optimization, an ORB could use a pre-allocated pool to allocate these objects, thereby alleviating heap fragmentation [15].

- When a reply arrives on a connection, the leader thread itself reads the complete reply **(6)** and calls the `Reply Dispatcher` object that was created for that invocation to dispatch the reply **(7)**.
- For SMI calls, the `Synchronous Reply Dispatcher` signals **(8s)** the thread waiting for that reply and completes the invocation **(9)**. For AMI calls, however, the `Asynchronous Reply Dispatcher` object invokes the callback method in the reply handler servant **(8a)**.

Challenge: How to Minimize Connection Utilization

Context: Early implementations of TAO supported only a *non-multiplexed* connection model [12], which is not well-suited for hard real-time applications whose QoS requirements include highly predictable response times. In this model, a connection cannot be reused for another two-way request until the reply for the previous request is received. Figure 7 illustrates TAO's non-multiplexed connection model, where five threads make two-way invocations to the same server,

Fig. 7. One Outstanding Request Per-Connection

which creates five connections. TAO represents connections using a `Transport` object that provides a uniform interface to the TAO's `pluggable protocols framework` [11], this framework abstracts various underlying transport mechanisms, such as TCP, UNIX-domain sockets, and VME, implemented by TAO. TAO's pluggable protocols framework uses key patterns and components provided by ACE [24].

Problem: Non-multiplexed connection models are inefficient for CORBA AMI because client applications can issue hundreds or thousands of asynchronous requests before waiting for the replies. Thus, a non-multiplexed connection model would use a correspondingly large number of connections.

Forces:

1. An ORB should implement connection multiplexing so that multiple outstanding requests required to support the AMI model can be processed efficiently.
2. When multiple threads access a connection simultaneously, they should be synchronized so that requests are sent one-by-one and not corrupted through intermingled I/O calls.
3. To accommodate various use-cases and QoS requirements, applications should be able to configure multiplexed and non-multiplexed connection behavior both statically *and* dynamically.

Solution → Strategize the transport multiplexing mechanisms: To overcome the scalability limitations of a non-multiplexed connection architecture, we extended TAO to support a multiplexed connection option for both SMI and AMI. In this design, many requests can be sent simultaneously over the same connection, even when replies are pending for earlier requests. In general, multiplexing yields better use of connections and other limited OS resources [12], such as memory buffers.

To implement this design in TAO, we applied the Strategy pattern [25] and defined a new strategy called `Transport Mux Strategy` that supports both multiplexed and the non-multiplexed connections. The components in this design are illustrated in Figure 8.

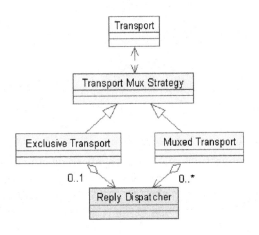

Fig. 8. Transport Mux Strategy

The `Exclusive Transport Strategy` implements the non-multiplexed connection strategy by holding a reference to a single `Reply Dispatcher` object. This strategy is "exclusive" because only one outstanding request at a time can pend on each connection. In contrast, the `Muxed Transport Strategy` uses a hash table that stores multiple `Reply Dispatchers`, each representing a request sent on the connection. As shown in Figure 8, the `Transport Mux Strategy` base class provides a common interface for these two different implementations. TAO uses the Service Configurator pattern [26] to allow applications to select between these two strategies and thereby configure TAO's `Transport Mux Strategy` either statically or dynamically.

To synchronize access to a multiplexed connection among multiple threads, the `Transport` object for that connection is marked as "busy" while one thread is sending a request. If during that time another thread tries to send a request, either a cached connection is recycled or a new connection is created. After the request is sent, the `Transport` object is marked as "idle" and is cached so it can be reused to send subsequent requests.

Challenge: How to Implement Scalable Reply Processing Mechanisms

Context: High-quality CORBA implementations should support "nested upcalls", in which an ORB processes incoming requests while it waits for replies. This support can be implemented using `select` to wait for both the reply and any incoming requests. This implementation can add unnecessary overhead, however, to "pure" clients that do not receive any incoming requests from servers. Therefore, TAO provides the following three reply processing strategies that allow developers to select the most appropriate mechanism for their application QoS requirements:

- Wait-on-Read: In this strategy, the calling thread blocks on `read` to receive the reply. This is a very efficient strategy for pure clients that need not receive requests or nested upcalls while waiting for server replies.
- Wait-on-Reactor: The Reactor [27] is a framework implemented in ACE [24] that provides event demultiplexing and event handler dispatching. In this strategy, a single-threaded `Reactor` is used to dispatch events, such as reply arrivals and upcalls. This strategy supports single-threaded client applications efficiently by having the waiting thread run the event loop of the Reactor to check for server replies. When there is input on a connection, the `Transport` object is notified and it reads the input message and dispatches the reply. The Wait-on-Reactor strategy also works with multi-threaded applications that use a Reactor-per-thread to minimize contention and locking overhead [12].
- Wait-on-Leader/Followers: If the application is multi-threaded and several threads are sharing the same Reactor, only one of them can run the Reactor's event loop at a time. Therefore, this strategy uses the Leader/Followers pattern [12] to synchronize access to the Reactor. In this pattern, the leader thread runs the event loop of the Reactor. All other threads wait on a semaphore. When a reply is available, the leader thread reads and dispatches the complete reply. If the reply is for an AMI request, it is dispatched to the callback method in the reply handler servant. For synchronous replies, the

reply buffer is transferred to the **Synchronous Reply Dispatcher** from the **Transport** object. If a reply belongs to the leader thread, it selects another thread as the leader and returns from the event loop. If the reply belongs to another thread, however, it signals this thread so it can wake up from the semaphore, return to its stub, and process the reply.

Problem: Pre-AMI-enabled versions of TAO implemented the three reply processing strategies described above as **Connection Handlers** within TAO's pluggable protocols framework, as shown in Figure 9. However, every **Transport**

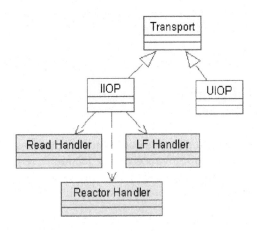

Fig. 9. Initial Design of TAO's Reply Processing Mechanisms

mechanism, such as IIOP and UNIX-domain sockets (UIOP), in TAO's pluggable protocols framework [11] required three **Connection Handler** implementations to support all the reply wait strategies in its **Transport** implementation. Not surprisingly, this approach did not scale up effectively when TAO incorporated additional transport mechanisms, such as VME, Fibrechannel, or TP4. TAO's original design also complicated the integration of the AMI callback model because changes to the reply wait mechanisms were necessary for *each* **Transport** implementation.

Forces: The semantics of the existing wait mechanisms, as well as the existing optimizations, must be maintained while integrating the AMI callback model. Moreover, applications should be able to configure TAO's reply wait mechanism according to their particular needs.

Solution → Refactor reply wait strategies: As part of our enhancement to TAO, we moved the reply wait mechanisms from the **Connection Handlers** to the new **Wait Strategy** and decoupled it from the underlying **Transport** and the

Connection Handler objects. TAO's new Wait Strategy architecture is illustrated in the UML class diagram in Figure 10. In TAO's enhanced architecture,

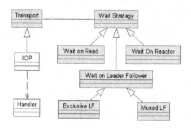

Fig. 10. Enhanced Design of TAO's Reply Processing Strategies

each **Transport** implements only one **Connection Handler**. Due to the patterns-based OO design [11] used in TAO, this modification required changes only to its **Transport** and **Connection Handler** implementations; no other ORB components were affected.

In addition to refactoring the wait strategies, a variation of the Leader/Followers implementation has been integrated into TAO's Wait-on-Leader/Followers strategy. This change was necessary because the original Leader/Followers implementation assumed non-multiplexed connections, *i.e.*, only one request at a time was sent per-connection. Therefore, state variables, such as semaphores, were kept in the **Transport** and the **Connection Handler** objects, which are per-connection objects. Although this implementation works for the **Exclusive Transport** strategy, it is unsuitable for **Muxed Transport**, where multiple threads may wait simultaneously for replies on a single connection.

To address the multiplexing problem, we enhanced the Leader/Followers model described earlier to create a variation called Muxed-Wait-on-Leader/Followers strategy. This new strategy uses the Thread-Specific Storage pattern [28] to store a per-ORB-per-thread condition variable. This condition variable is created on-demand just once, by a factory method in TAO's ORB Core. This factory method provides a facade [25] to all ORB strategies, helper classes, and global or thread-specific resources.

Challenge: How to Minimize Stub Footprint

Context: Earlier, we discussed the ORB components used by the client stub to set up the connection, create the **Reply Dispatchers**, send the request, keep track of the **Reply Dispatchers** and *reply-stubs*, wait for and process replies, and deliver the replies to target threads or reply handler servants. A stub can either invoke methods on these ORB components directly, or it can use helper classes that can be implemented as part of the ORB. Helper classes can interact with various ORB components on behalf of the stub and execute all functionality outlined above.

Problem: If stubs interact with the internal ORB components directly, the code size of the stub increases. In turn, this increases the footprint of the generated C++ code because TAO's IDL compiler creates stubs for each operation in the IDL interface.

Forces: There is a tradeoff between code size and performance [29]. In general, stubs could inline all the code required to complete their task [30]. However, inlining can cause unacceptably large memory footprint. Conversely, stubs could simply pass parameter data to a shared interpreter, such as a DSI/DII engine [31]. In this case, however, system performance would suffer.

Solution → Optimized invocation helper facades: To reduce memory footprint, stubs should use helper classes to factor out common code from the stubs into reusable ORB Core components. In TAO, these helper classes are called Synchronous Invocation and Asynchronous Invocation. They provide stubs with facades that encapsulate the details of various features implemented internally to the ORB to support both AMI and SMI.

When called by a stub on behalf of a client, the Synchronous Invocation class establishes a connection[4] to the remote host, sends the request, waits for a reply, receives the reply, and returns control to the stub once the reply is received. The Asynchronous Invocation class is similar, but it returns control to the stub as soon as it sends the request. Thus, the Synchronous Invocation object creates the Synchronous Reply Dispatcher on its local stack activation record, whereas the Asynchronous Invocation object creates the Asynchronous Reply Dispatcher on the heap.

As illustrated in Figure 11, TAO's synchronous and asynchronous variants inherit from a common Invocation class, which provides a uniform interface to other components in the ORB. Both classes delegate the tasks described above to other ORB components we discussed earlier.

3.2   Collaborations between Components in TAO's AMI-Enabled Architecture

Now that the preceding sections described TAO's ORB architecture components that process synchronous and asynchronous requests, we can present the overall AMI-enabled ORB architecture of TAO, which is shown by the UML class diagram in Figure 12. Moreover, Figure 13 reexamines the sequence of steps that occur when an application issues an AMI or SMI call. Each of these steps is described below:

---

[4] TAO uses connection caching [12] to avoid establishing new connections if one is already open to a particular ORB endpoint.

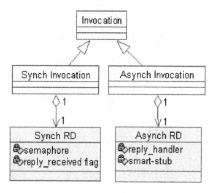

Fig. 11. Invocation Interface

- The `Client` calls the `Stub` to invoke an operation. In the case of an AMI call, it passes a reference to a reply handler servant (**1**).

- The stubs generated by TAO's IDL compiler are different for the SMI and AMI calls. In particular, the SMI and AMI stubs instantiate their corresponding `Invocation` objects (**2**).

- The `Invocation` object creates a `Synchronous` or `Asynchronous Reply Dispatcher`, depending on the type of the request (**3**). The `Invocation` object then binds the `Reply Dispatcher` object with the `Transport Mux Strategy` object (**4 & 5**).

- The `Invocation` object calls the `Transport` object, which in turn uses TAO's pluggable protocols framework [11] and ACE [24] to send the request (**6 & 7**).

- In the AMI model, the stub returns control to the application at this point. Later, the `Client` can wait for the server's reply. In the SMI model, conversely, the `Invocation` object calls the `Transport` to wait for the reply, which delegates this task to the `Wait Strategy` (**8**).

- When the reply arrives, the `Transport` object is notified to read the reply (**9**). It reads the complete reply and calls the `Transport Mux Strategy` to dispatch the reply (**10**). The `Transport Mux Strategy` uses the correct `Reply Dispatcher` object created for that invocation and calls its dispatch method (**11**).

- If a `Synchronous Reply Dispatcher` is used, it simply stores the reply buffer, sets the state variables within the object to indicate that the reply has been received, and then returns. Conversely, the `Asynchronous Reply Dispatcher` invokes the reply stub stored in the object, passing in the reply handler servant and the reply buffer, and dispatches the reply (**12**).

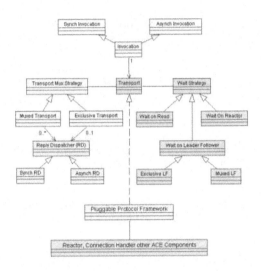

Fig. 12. AMI-enabled TAO ORB Architecture

4   Evaluating the Performance of TAO AMI Callbacks

4.1   Overview

As discussed in Section 1, AMI can help improve the scalability of CORBA applications by minimizing the number of client threads required to perform two-way invocations. In this section, we present empirical results that show how TAO's AMI implementation helps to increase application scalability by minimizing the number of client threads. We demonstrate the efficiency of the implementation by comparing both the latency and operation throughput of SMI and AMI two-way invocations in TAO.

All experiments were performed on two 400 Mhz quad-CPU Dell 6300 computers running Linux 2.2 and connected by a 100 Mbps Fast Ethernet. Each computer has 1 GB of RAM. The benchmarks were compiled using the GCC v. 2.95 compiler with the highest level of optimization.

The server implementation is held constant in all our benchmarks. Moreover, to minimize the overhead on the server, we use a simple interface that accepts a single argument and returns it. The argument is a 64-bit `unsigned long` that the client uses to send timestamps to the server to measure round-trip delays. To minimize jitter, all client and server benchmarking processes were run in the Linux real-time scheduling class.

4.2   Empirical Results

Two-way latency benchmark: In our first experiment, we compared the round-trip latency of 10,000 two-way calls in single-threaded applications using three

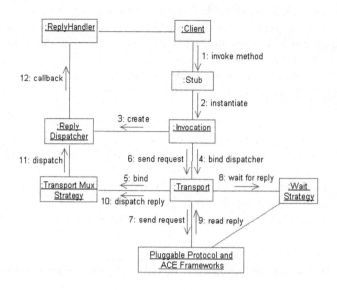

Fig. 13. Sequence of Steps in TAO's SMI & AMI Invocations

different invocation models: (1) SMI using the SII, (2) AMI using the SII, and (3) deferred SMI using the DII. For the DII and AMI benchmarks we sent the request and immediately waited for the asynchronous reply.

Table 1 compares the latency for the three invocation models. The best results

Table 1. μsecond Latency Results for Different Invocation Models

Test	Minimum	Average	Maximum	Jitter
SMI	455	497	684	2.7%
AMI	447	479	1,859	3.0%
DII	499	573	2,652	9.6%

are obtained using AMI requests, though the difference with respect to SMI is small (3%). This difference is within the error margins defined by the jitter measurements and is not significant. Compared to SMI, a larger amount of jitter was observed for AMI, resulting from the extra locking overhead required to dispatch the reply-stub. In contrast, the worst performance is obtained using the deferred synchronous model, which averaged 20% slower than AMI because it incurs additional DII processing overhead.

Operation throughput benchmark: In this experiment, we compared the throughput (in number of requests per second) of the different invocation models. To simulate asynchronous communication using ORBs without AMI support, applications have traditionally spawned additional threads. To compare this approach with an AMI application, therefore, the client process creates a new thread for each two-way SMI call, up to an OS imposed limit of 220.[5] The benchmark sends 10,000 requests on each thread.

In contrast to the heavily threaded SMI client, the AMI client uses only two threads. One thread sends as many two-way requests as required and the other thread runs the ORB event loop to dispatch replies to the appropriate reply handler. To match the number of calls performed by the SMI client, therefore, the AMI client performs 2,200,000 calls. Finally, we perform the same test using DII deferred synchronous requests.

The results of this experiment are shown in Figure 2. As shown by these

Table 2. Operation Throughput Results for Different Invocation Models

Test	Average Calls/sec.
SMI (220 threads)	1914
SMI (7 threads)	7080
AMI	8524
DII	3816

results, the AMI client not only provides a more scalable design than the multi-threaded SMI client, but also shows a significant performance improvement. This improvement stems from the fact that (1) the TCP/IP stack can send larger data packets containing multiple AMI requests, (2) the two threads in the AMI client can overlap request invocations and response processing, and (3) the AMI client fully utilizes the network resources, *i.e.*, it can completely fill TCP/IP windows because it can "pipeline" the two-way invocations.

In addition to scalability problems, the use of hundreds of threads in the SMI client also increases its synchronization overhead. Table 2 shows how reducing the number of threads in the SMI client test from 220 to 7 improved performance significantly. This solution has the adverse affect of reducing the number of simultaneous two-way calls, however, which increases average latency. In contrast, the AMI client do not suffer from this tradeoff.

Finally, note that that deferred synchronous requests can sometimes achieve better performance than a naively designed, heavily-threaded SMI client. It is unlikely, however, that the performance of deferred synchronous DII could ever

---

[5] Note that we were unable to create more than 220 threads before running out of resources on Linux. This illustrates one of the drawbacks of using threads to simulate asynchronous communication.

rival that of AMI, due to the inherent overhead of memory allocation and data copying. Moreover, DII's invocation model is more tedious and error-prone to program.

4.3 Summary of Results

The latency and operation throughput results presented above can be interpreted as follows:

- For simple applications that require few request-response interactions, SMI is almost as effective as AMI, with an insignificant difference in latency within the error margins. In addition, SMI has slightly less jitter because its implementation uses fewer locks.
- For more demanding applications, AMI applications can exhibit a measurable (20%) improvement in operation throughput compared with the best SMI results. These performance improvements illustrate how AMI clients can leverage network resources and inherent parallelism in distributed systems more effectively than SMI clients.

5 Concluding Remarks

Asynchronous method invocations (AMI) are an important feature that has been integrated into CORBA via the OMG Messaging specification [4]. A key aspect of AMI is that operations can be invoked asynchronously, while still using the static invocation interface (SII). The use of SII eliminates much of the complexity and inefficiency inherent in the dynamic invocation interface (DII)'s deferred synchronous model.

This paper explains how ORBs can be structured to support the CORBA AMI callback model efficiently and scalably. The following is a synopsis of the lessons learned developing TAO's AMI callback implementation:

AMI requires a scalable ORB architecture: An ORB should implement the AMI and SMI reply handling in a flexible and scalable manner. For instance, to support many simultaneous AMI requests efficiently, connection multiplexing optimizations should be supported in the ORB Core.

Optimizations should be guided by empirical measurements: AMI and SMI enhancements should be guided by systematic blackbox benchmarks and whitebox profiling so that existing optimizations in the ORB are preserved, while allowing applications to configure the ORB based on their specific QoS requirements. For example, during the validation phase of our AMI changes, we discovered that the SMI model was performing one memory allocation more than it did before the AMI changes. The problem was easily fixed, but it illustrates that careful, repeated whitebox analysis of the system and application of optimization principle patterns [15] is required to ensure and maintain its quality.

The ORB should adapt readily to different use-cases: Design patterns should be applied to configure ORBs with policies and mechanisms appropriate for particular application use-cases, while still preserving key optimizations necessary to support stringent QoS requirements. In particular, we repeatedly applied the Strategy pattern [25] to TAO's AMI implementation to support scalable connection multiplexing strategies, while retaining configurations that ensure the determinism required for hard real-time applications. Applications can select AMI or SMI strategies using the Service Configurator pattern [25], which makes the TAO framework dynamically configurable and therefore highly flexible.

Both AMI and SMI are important invocation models: Enhancements needed to support AMI should not add overhead to the ORB's SMI processing. Patterns like Strategy and Service Configurator can be used to make any additional overhead optional for applications that do not require it.

Programming AMI clients requires application developers to make design decisions: While developing our tests for the AMI implementations, we recognized that the AMI model, while more intuitive and easier to use than the DII deferred synchronous model, is more complex than simple SMI applications. For instance, client developers must decide how to handle the replies, *e.g.*, by using a separate thread, waiting for replies after a fixed number of replies, or adaptively waiting for replies. Developers must also decide how to connect the reply with the original request, *e.g.*, by using a different reply handler servant for each one, returning some kind of request id from the server, or using the POA dynamic activation mechanisms to distinguish between all the requests. Finally, client developers must be prepared to handle "inversion of control" in their applications, *i.e.*, by using a callback to handle the incoming reply.

These challenges should not be viewed as insurmountable problems, however. After developers master the appropriate patterns and idioms, AMI can be significantly easier to program than the CORBA deferred synchronous model. Moreover, it offers significant performance improvements over both SMI and DII calls. Thus, CORBA AMI is an important addition to the CORBA family of features and specifications.

References

1. Object Management Group, *The Common Object Request Broker: Architecture and Specification*, 2.3 ed., June 1999. 208
2. D. C. Schmidt and S. Vinoski, "Introduction to CORBA Messaging," *C++ Report*, vol. 10, November/December 1998. 209
3. D. C. Schmidt and S. Vinoski, "Programming Asynchronous Method Invocations with CORBA Messaging," *C++ Report*, vol. 11, February 1999. 209
4. Object Management Group, *CORBA Messaging Specification*, OMG Document orbos/98-05-05 ed., May 1998. 209, 212, 227
5. Object Management Group, *Objects-by-Value*, OMG Document orbos/98-01-18 ed., January 1998. 209

6. Object Management Group, *Realtime CORBA Joint Revised Submission*, OMG Document orbos/99-02-12 ed., March 1999. 210

7. D. C. Schmidt, D. L. Levine, and S. Mungee, "The Design and Performance of Real-Time Object Request Brokers," *Computer Communications*, vol. 21, pp. 294–324, Apr. 1998. 211, 212

8. C. D. Gill, D. L. Levine, and D. C. Schmidt, "The Design and Performance of a Real-Time CORBA Scheduling Service," *The International Journal of Time-Critical Computing Systems, special issue on Real-Time Middleware*, 2000. 211

9. T. H. Harrison, D. L. Levine, and D. C. Schmidt, "The Design and Performance of a Real-time CORBA Event Service," in *Proceedings of OOPSLA '97*, (Atlanta, GA), ACM, October 1997. 211

10. F. Kuhns, D. C. Schmidt, and D. L. Levine, "The Design and Performance of a Real-time I/O Subsystem," in *Proceedings of the 5 th IEEE Real-Time Technology and Applications Symposium*, (Vancouver, British Columbia, Canada), pp. 154–163, IEEE, June 1999. 211

11. C. O'Ryan, F. Kuhns, D. C. Schmidt, O. Othman, and J. Parsons, "The Design and Performance of a Pluggable Protocols Framework for Real-time Distributed Object Computing Middleware," in *Proceedings of the Middleware 2000 Conference*, ACM/IFIP, Apr. 2000. 211, 217, 220, 221, 223

12. D. C. Schmidt, S. Mungee, S. Flores-Gaitan, and A. Gokhale, "Software Architectures for Reducing Priority Inversion and Non-determinism in Real-time Object Request Brokers," *Journal of Real-time Systems*, To appear 2000. 211, 214, 217, 218, 219, 222

13. A. Gokhale and D. C. Schmidt, "Measuring the Performance of Communication Middleware on High-Speed Networks," in *Proceedings of SIGCOMM '96*, (Stanford, CA), pp. 306–317, ACM, August 1996. 211

14. D. C. Schmidt and C. Cleeland, "Applying Patterns to Develop Extensible ORB Middleware," *IEEE Communications Magazine*, vol. 37, April 1999. 211

15. I. Pyarali, C. O'Ryan, D. C. Schmidt, N. Wang, V. Kachroo, and A. Gokhale, "Applying Optimization Patterns to the Design of Real-time ORBs," in *Proceedings of the 5th Conference on Object-Oriented Technologies and Systems*, (San Diego, CA), USENIX, May 1999. 211, 216, 227

16. R. H. Halstead, Jr., "Multilisp: A Language for Concurrent Symbolic Computation," *ACM Trans. Programming Languages and Systems*, vol. 7, pp. 501–538, Oct. 1985. 211

17. B. Liskov and L. Shrira, "Promises: Linguistic Support for Efficient Asynchronous Procedure Calls in Distributed Systems," in *Proceedings of the SIGPLAN'88 Conference on Programming Language Design and Implementation*, pp. 260–267, June 1988. 211

18. Y. Aahlad, B. Martin, M. Marathe, and C. Lee, "Asynchronous Notification Among Distributed Objects," in *Proceedings of the 2 nd Conference on Object-Oriented Technologies and Systems*, (Toronto, Canada), USENIX, June 1996. 211

19. C. Ma and J. Bacon, "COBEA: A CORBA-Based Event Architecture," in *Proceedings of the 4rd Conference on Object-Oriented Technologies and Systems*, USENIX, Apr. 1998. 211

20. A. B. Arulanthu, C. O'Ryan, D. C. Schmidt, and M. Kircher, "Applying C++, Patterns, and Components to Develop an IDL Compiler for CORBA AMI Callbacks," *C++ Report*, vol. 12, Mar. 2000. 211, 212

21. K. Birman, "The Process Group Approach to Reliable Distributed Computing," Communications of the ACM, vol. 36, pp. 37–53, December 1993. 211

22. C. O'Ryan and D. C. Schmidt, "Applying a Real-time CORBA Event Service to Large-scale Distributed Interactive Simulation," in *5th International Workshop on Object-oriented Real-Time Dependable Systems*, (Monterey, CA), IEEE, Nov 1999. 212

23. N. Wang, D. C. Schmidt, and S. Vinoski, "Collocation Optimizations for CORBA," *C++ Report*, vol. 11, October 1999. 212

24. D. C. Schmidt, "ACE: an Object-Oriented Framework for Developing Distributed Applications," in *Proceedings of the 6th USENIX C++ Technical Conference*, (Cambridge, Massachusetts), USENIX Association, April 1994. 217, 219, 223

25. E. Gamma, R. Helm, R. Johnson, and J. Vlissides, *Design Patterns: Elements of Reusable Object-Oriented Software*. Reading, MA: Addison-Wesley, 1995. 218, 221, 228

26. P. Jain and D. C. Schmidt, "Dynamically Configuring Communication Services with the Service Configurator Pattern", *C++ Report*, vol. 9, June 1997. 219

27. D. C. Schmidt, "The Object-Oriented Design and Implementation of the Reactor: A C++ Wrapper for UNIX I/O Multiplexing (Part 2 of 2)," *C++ Report*, vol. 5, September 1993. 219

28. D. C. Schmidt, T. Harrison, and N. Pryce, "Thread-Specific Storage – An Object Behavioral Pattern for Accessing per-Thread State Efficiently," *C++ Report*, vol. 9, November/December 1997. 221

29. A. Gokhale and D. C. Schmidt, "Optimizing a CORBA IIOP Protocol Engine for Minimal Footprint Multimedia Systems," *Journal on Selected Areas in Communications special issue on Service Enabling Platforms for Networked Multimedia Systems*, vol. 17, Sept. 1999. 222

30. E. Eide, K. Frei, B. Ford, J. Lepreau, and G. Lindstrom, "Flick: A Flexible, Optimizing IDL Compiler," in *Proceedings of ACM SIGPLAN '97 Conference on Programming Language Design and Implementation (PLDI)*, (Las Vegas, NV), ACM, June 1997. 222

31. A. Gokhale and D. C. Schmidt, "Principles for Optimizing CORBA Internet Inter-ORB Protocol Performance," in *Hawaiian International Conference on System Sciences*, January 1998. 222

A Publish/Subscribe CORBA Persistent State Service Prototype

C. Liebig, M. Cilia[†], M. Betz, and A. Buchmann

Database Research Group - Department of Computer Science
Darmstadt University of Technology - Darmstadt, Germany
{chris,cilia,betz,buchmann}@dvs1.informatik.tu-darmstadt.de

Abstract. An important class of information dissemination applications requires 1:n communication and access to persistent datastores. CORBA's new Persistent State Service combined with messaging capabilities offer the possibility of efficiently realizing information brokers between data sources and CORBA clients. In this paper we present a prototype implementation of the PSS that exploits the reliable multicast capabilities of an existing middleware platform. This publish/subscribe architecture makes it possible to implement an efficient update propagation mechanism and snooping caches as a generic service for information dissemination applications. The implementation is presented in some detail and implications of the design are discussed. We illustrate the use of a publish/subscribe PSS by applying it to an auction scenario.

1 Introduction

The deployment of large scale information dissemination systems like Intranet and Extranet information systems, e-commerce applications, and workflow management and groupware systems, is key to the success of companies competing in a global marketplace and operating in a networked world. Applications like warehouse monitoring, auctions, reservation systems, traffic information systems, flight status tracking, logistics systems, etc. consist of a potentially large number of clients spread all over the world demanding timely information delivery. Many of these applications span organizational boundaries and are centered around a variety of data sources, like relational databases or legacy systems that maintain business data. The business logic may be spread over separate modules and the entire system is expected to undergo continuous extension and adaptation to provide new functionality.

Common approaches in terms of systems architecture can be classified into traditional 2-tier client/server, 3-tier TP-heavy using TP monitors and n-tier Object-Web systems.

In 2-tier client/server the client part implements the presentation logic together with application logic and data access. This approach depends primarily on RPC-like communication and scales well only if client and server are close together in terms of

---

[†] Also ISISTAN, Faculty of Sciences, UNICEN, Tandil, Argentina.

J. Sventek and G. Coulson (Eds.): Middleware 2000, LNCS 1795, pp. 231-255, 2000.

network bandwidth and access latency. However, it does not scale in the face of wide-area distribution. Moreover, the fat-client approach renders the client software dependent on the data model and API of the backend.

In a 3-tier architecture a middle-tier – typically based on a TP monitor - is introduced to encapsulate the business logic and to hide the data source specifics. TP monitors provide scalability in terms of resource management, i.e. pooling of connections, allocating processes/threads to services and load balancing. The communication mechanisms used in 3-tier architectures range from peer-to-peer messaging and transactional queues to RPC and RMI. TP monitor based approaches assume that the middle-tier has a performant connection to the backend data sources, because database access protocols for relational systems are request/response and based on "query shipping". In order to reduce access latency and to keep the load of the data source reasonably low, the application programmers are urged to implement their own caching functionality in the middle-tier. A well known example of such an architecture is the SAP system [21].

In n-tier Object-Web systems the clear distinction between clients and servers gets blurred. The monolithic middle-tier is split up into a set of objects. Middleware technology, such as CORBA, provides the glue for constructing applications in distributed and heterogeneous environments in a component-oriented manner. CORBA leverages a set of standard services [22] like Naming Service, Event and Notification Service, Security Service, Object Transaction Service, and Concurrency Control Service. CORBA has not been able to live up to expectations of scalability, particularly in the information dissemination domain, because of a limiting (synchronous) 1:1 communication structure and the lack of a proper persistence service. The new CORBA Messaging standard [23] will provide true asynchronous communication including time independent invocations. We argue, that the recently proposed Persistent State Service [14], which replaces the ill-fated Persistent Object Service, will not only play a key role as integration mechanism but also provides the opportunity to introduce efficient data distribution and caching mechanisms.

A straightforward implementation of the PSS relying on relational database technology is based on query shipping. The PSS must open a datastore connection to the server, then ships a query that is executed at the server side and the result set is returned in response. Such a PSS implementation realizes storage objects as stateless incarnations on the CORBA side, that act as proxies to the persistent object instance in the datastore. Operations that manipulate the state of objects managed by the PSS are described in datastore terms. This approach generates a potential bottleneck at the datastore side, because each operation request on an instance will result in a SQL query. Furthermore, for information dissemination systems, where the user wants to continuously monitor the data of interest, polling must be introduced which results in a high load at the backend, wasting resources and possibly delivering low quality of data freshness.

For information dissemination systems an alternate approach based on server-initiated communication is more desirable. Techniques ranging from cache consistency mechanisms in (OO)DBMSs [33,5] and triggers/active database rules [10] to broadcast disks [1] can be used to push data of interest to clients. In the context of the PSS a new publish/subscribe session is needed. A publish/subscribe session represents the scope of the objects an application is interested in, i.e. subscribes to. For those objects in a publish/subscribe session the cache is loaded and updated automatically. Additionally, this session provides notifications about insert, modify and delete events to the application. While publish/subscribe sessions currently are not part of the PSS specification they are definitely not precluded by it and would represent a useful extension to the spec.

In this paper we present an implementation of a PSS prototype that provides an intelligent caching mechanism and active functionality in conjunction with message oriented middleware (MOM) that is capable of 1:n communication. By removing two crucial bottlenecks from the CORBA platform we claim that highly scalable Object-Web systems become feasible.

In our PSS prototype[1] we take advantage of commercial publish/subscribe middleware that provides the paradigm of subject based addressing and 1-to-many reliable multicast message delivery. We show how a snoopy cache can be implemented for multi-node PSS deployment. We make use of a prototype of a database adapter for object-relational databases (Informix IUS, in particular) that was partially developed and extended in the scope of this project. The database adapter allows to use publish/subscribe functionality in the database and to push data to the PSS caches when update transactions are issued against the data base backend or when new data objects are created.

This paper concentrates on the basic infrastructure needed to provide scalability with respect to dissemination of information from multiple data sources. We explicitly exclude from the scope of this paper federated database and schema integration issues.

The remainder of this paper is organized as follows: Section 2 briefly introduces key concepts of the PSS specification and the multicast-enabled message oriented middleware; Section 3 provides an overview of the architecture of our prototype implementation of the PSS and identifies the main advantages of integrating the reliable multicast functionality of the TIBCO platform; Section 4 describes the implementation; Section 5 introduces auctions as a typical scenario for middleware-based Web-applications and Section 6 presents conclusions and identifies areas of ongoing research.

2   CORBA PSS and Messaging Middleware

2.1   CORBA Persistent State Service

The need for a persistence service for CORBA was recognized early on. In 1995, the Persistent Object Service was accepted but failed because of major flaws: the specification was not precise, persistence was exposed to CORBA clients, transactional access to persistent data was not covered, and the service lacks integration with other CORBA services. Recently, the Persistent State Service (PSS) was proposed to overcome those flaws. The goals of the PSS specification [14] are to make the state of the servant persistent, to be datastore neutral and implementable with any datastore, to be CORBA friendly, consistent with other OMG specifications

[1]   The work of this project is partially funded by TIBCO Software Inc., Palo Alto.

(Transactions, POA, Components, etc.) and also with other standards like SQL3 [18] and ODMG [7].

The PSS provides a single interface for storing objects' state persistently on a variety of datastores like OO-, OR-, R-DBMS, and simple files. The PSS provides a service to programmers who develop object implementations, to save and restore the state of their objects and is totally transparent to the client. Persistence is an implementation concern, and a client should not be aware of the persistence mechanisms. Therefore, the PSS specification does not deal with the external interface (provided by a CORBA server) but with an internal interface between the CORBA-domain and the datastore-domain.

Due to numerous problems with IDL valuetypes - used in previous proposals as requirement imposed by the RFP - the IDL was extended with new constructs to define storage objects and storage home objects. The extended IDL is known as Persistent State Definition Language (PSDL). Storage objects are stored in storage homes, which are themselves stored in datastores. In order to manipulate a storage object, the programmer uses a representative programming-language entity, called storage object *instance*. A storage object instance may be connected to a storage object in the datastore, providing direct access to the state of this storage object. Such a connected instance is called storage object *incarnation*. To access a storage object, a logical connection between the process and the datastore is needed. Such a connection is known as *session*.

There is also a distinction between abstract storage type specification and concrete storage type implementation. The abstract storage type spec defines everything a servant programmer needs to know about a storage object, while an implementation construct defines what a code generator needs to know in order to generate code for it. A given abstract specification can have more than one implementation and it is possible to update an implementation without affecting the storage objects' clients. So, the implementation of storage types and storage homes lies mainly in the responsibility of the PSS. An overview of these concepts is depicted in Figure 1.

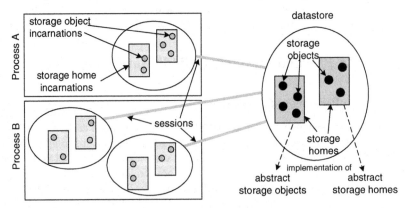

Fig. 1. PSS concepts [14]

A storage object can have both state and behavior, defined by the storage type : its state is described by attributes (also called state members) and its behavior is described by operations. State members are manipulated through equally named pairs of accessor functions. Operations on storage objects are specified in the same manner as with IDL. In addition to IDL parameter types, storage types defined in PSDL may be used as parameters. In contrast to CORBA objects, operations on storage objects are locally implemented and not remotely accessible.

A *storage home* does not have its own state, but it can have behavior, which is described by operations in the abstract storage home. A storage home can ensure that a list of attributes of its storage type forms a unique identifier for the storage objects it manages. Such a list is called a *key*. A storage home can define any number of keys. Each key declaration implicitly declares associated finder operations in the language mapping. To create or locate a storage object, a CORBA server implementor calls `create(<parameters>)` or `find_by_<some key>(<parameters>)` operations on the storage home of the storage type and in return will receive the according storage object instance.

The inheritance rules for storage objects are similar to the rules for interface inheritance in IDL. Storage homes also support multiple inheritance. However, it is not possible to inherit two operations with the same name; as well as to inherit two keys with the same name.

In the PSS spec the mapping of PSDL constructs to several programming languages is also specified. A compliant PSS tool must generate a default implementation for storage homes and storage types based on the given PSDL definition.

For the case that the underlying datastore is a database system, the PSS introduces a *transactional session* orchestrated by OTS through the use of the X/Open XA interface [34] of the datastore. Access to storage objects within a transactional session produces executions that comply with the selected isolation level i.e. *read uncommited, read commited*. Note that stronger isolation levels like *repeatable read* and *serializable* are not specified.

2.2 Multicast-Enabled MOM

We use COTS MOM [31] to build the PSS prototype, namely TIB/Rendezvous and TIB/ObjectBus products. TIB/Rendezvous is based upon the notion of the *Information Bus* [26] (interchangeable with the wording "message bus" in the following) and realizes the concept of *subject based addressing*, which is related to the idea of a *tuple space*, first introduced in LINDA [6]. Instead of addressing a sender or recipient for a message by its identifier, which in the end comes down to a network address, messages are published under a subject name on the *message bus*. The subject name is supposed to characterize the contents - i.e. the type - of a message. If a participant, who is connected to the *message bus*, is interested in some specific message types, she will subscribe for the subjects of interest and in turn be notified of messages published under the selected subject names. The subject name space is hierarchical and subscribers may use subject name patterns to denote a set of types to which they want to subscribe.

Messages are constructed from typed fields and can be recursively nested. Furthermore, messages are self-describing: a recipient of a message can inquire about the structure and type of message content. The abstraction of a bus inherently carries the semantic of many-to-many communications as there can be multiple publishers and subscribers for the same subject. The implementation of TIB/Rendezvous uses a lightweight multicast communication layer to distribute messages to all potential subscribers. On each machine, a daemon manages local subscribers, filters out relevant messages according to subject information and notifies individual subscribers. The programming style for listening applications is event-driven; i.e. eventually the program must transfer control to the TIB/Rendezvous library which runs an event-loop. Following the Reactor-Pattern [29] the onData() method of an initially registered callback object will be invoked by the TIB/Rendezvous library when a message arrives with a subject that the subscriber is listening to.

Message propagation can be configured to use IP multicast or UDP broadcast. In the latter case, a special message routing daemon must be set up in each subnet in order to span LAN (broadcast) boundaries. Optionally, TIB/Rendezvous can make use of PGM, a reliable multicast transport on top of IP multicast, which has been developed by Cisco Systems in cooperation with TIBCO and proposed to the IETF [30].

Two quality of service levels are supported by TIB/Rendezvous: reliable and guaranteed. In both modes, messages are delivered in FIFO order with respect to the publisher. There is no total ordering in case of multiple publishers on the same subject. Reliable delivery uses receiver-side NACKs and a sender-side in-memory ledger that buffers messages for some amount of time in case of retransmission requests. With guaranteed delivery, a subscriber may register with the publisher for a *certified session* or the publisher preregisters dedicated subscribers.

Strict group membership semantics must be realized at the application level if so required. However, atomic message delivery is not provided. The TIB/ Rendezvous library uses a persistent ledger in order to provide guaranteed delivery. Messages may be discarded from the persistent ledger as soon as all subscribers have explicitly acknowledged the receipt. In both variants, the retransmission of messages is receiver-initiated by sending NACKs.

The diagram in Figure 2 depicts, how the multicast messaging middleware is introduced to CORBA in ObjectBus, a CORBA 2.0 compliant ORB implementation.

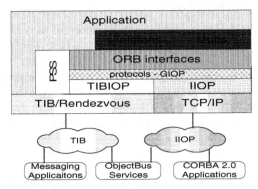

Fig. 2. ObjectBus Architecture

The General Inter-ORB Protocol (GIOP) is implemented both by a standard Internet Inter-ORB Protocol (IIOP) layer and a TIBCO specific layer (TIBIOP). When using

TIBIOP, the GIOP messages are marshaled into TIB/Rendezvous messages and published on the message bus on behalf of a specific subject. The CORBA (server) object may be registered with the ORB presenting an application specific subject name. In that case the returned Interoperable Object Reference (IOR) carries the subject name on behalf of the TIBIOP addressing profile. In order to preserve interoperability, server objects may be registered with both, TIBIOP and IIOP profiles at the same time. Additionally, CORBA applications may access the TIB/Rendezvous API directly to register listeners and publish messages on behalf of some subject. The PSS prototype implementation is mainly based on this TIB/Rendezvous messaging API.

3   Overview of the Prototype Architecture

In [13], the nodes in a general distributed information system are classified into: i) *data sources* which provide the base data that is to be disseminated, ii) *clients* which are net consumers of information and iii) *information brokers* (agents, mediators) that acquire information from data sources and provide the information to the clients. Data delivery mechanisms are distinguished along three main dimensions: push vs. pull, periodic vs. aperiodic and 1:1 vs. 1:n.

An analysis of the large, scalable, distributed applications that we are addressing reveals that they are best built using multi-tier architectures. The diagram in Figure 3 below shows this: clients can interact with an application either directly through an ORB or via a Web-server (optionally using an applet). Both periodic and aperiodic pull may be used to begin an interaction, while aperiodic notification and polling are required to propagate change to the users. At the integration-tier the application logic is realized through CORBA objects and services.

The interaction between the integration-tier and the backend-tier requires both pull and push communication to initiate individual requests and to update the caches, respectively. Further, aperiodic event-driven interaction is required and 1:n communication capabilities are essential for effective dissemination of updates and for snooping of load reply and *creation/deletion* events. Under these conditions, the PSS provides the means to efficiently realize CORBA objects as information brokers between data sources and CORBA clients.

In our prototype architecture of a publish/subscribe based PSS, we include a PSS Connector on the side of the integration tier and its counterpart, the DB Connector on the datastore. In terms of Object Oriented Database Systems architecture, the DB Connector plays the role of an object server, leveraging extended relational data base technology and the PSS Connector acts as the object manager.

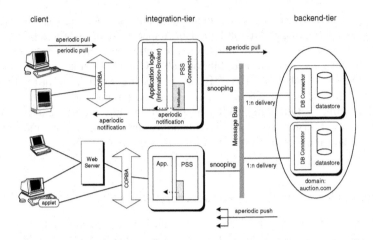

Fig. 3. Multi-tier Architecture for Information Dissemination Systems

We unbundle object caching and object-relational mappings and benefit from the reliable multicast messaging services provided by publish/subscribe MOM:

1. The PSS Connector at the CORBA side interacts with the data sources at the backend in *aperiodic pull* combined with *1:n* delivery. A storage object lookup request is initiated by some PSS Connector on application demand. The response is *published* by the DB Connector under an associated *subject* and all PSS Connector instances that have *subscribed* to that kind of object will snoop the resulting messages and possibly refresh or add a new incarnation to their object cache.

2. Updates to storage object instances result in *publishing* update notifications under an associated subject including the new state of the object, i.e. *aperiodic push* combined with *1:n* delivery. Again, the PSS Connector instances may snoop the update notifications to update the cached incarnation of the object and notify the application of the update.

3. In addition to update notifications, creation and deletion events can be signaled to the application by letting the PSS snoop the respective messages. The application is thus relieved from polling and may extend the chain of notification to the client-tier in order to facilitate timely information delivery.

4. The implementation of the PSS uses a hierarchy of subject names to address objects. Instead of addressing by location (i.e. IP number, DB listener socket address), *publish/subscribe* interactions use the paradigm of addressing content (i.e. *subject based addressing*). Thereby several data sources may be federated in a single data source domain. Additionally, a labeling mechanism can be introduced to support subscription to a collection of storage objects and simple subject-based queries.

Given the potential distribution of clients and caches we expect to benefit from reference locality not only in the scope of a single PSS instance but because of the snooping of load replies and update notifications we benefit from reference locality throughout the datastore domain across different PSS nodes.

4 Prototype Design & Implementation

The implementation consists of the realization of the PSS Connector and the DB Connector including the definition of the corresponding formats and protocols (FAP), provision of snoopy caching and active functionality, the mechanisms to adapt the database to the TIB/Rendezvous message bus, the mapping between PSDL and the (object-) relational data model, and last but not least the transactional semantics and correctness criteria that can be enforced.

4.1 Formats and Protocols between Connectors

In defining the FAPs we must specify the basic functionality to create, lookup, load, change/save and delete objects. More advanced features are snooping load replies, generating and snooping update notifications, and generating and snooping create/ delete events. Most important for the implementation of the advanced features on top of publish/subscribe messaging middleware is the definition of the subject namespace, i.e. the categories an application can subscribe to and under which to publish. Subjects must be chosen in a way that enables snooping load and update payload data, as well as detecting create/update/delete events and signaling them to the application. Appendix A presents the subject name space with respect to the FAP. Figure 4 below shows the basic functional units of the PSS prototype.

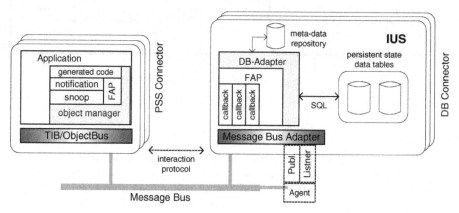

Fig. 4. PSS Prototype Components

The FAP is materialized by type-specific generated storage object (home) implementation on top of a general object manager library at the PSS Connector. At the DB Connector the FAP is implemented using callback handlers (external SQL UDR, see also 4.2). Additionally we must provide a DB Adapter that maps the payload data to the constructs of the datastore as reflected in the metadata repository.

4.1.1 Loading a storage object in a publish/subscribe session

An application gets access to one or more storage object incarnations through its respective storage home. Storage homes are managed by a publish/subscribe session, which also defines the scope of the object cache. Before actually accessing a storage object, the application must retrieve a handle to the object incarnation using find_by_pid() or some other key-based finder operation, or using find_by_label(). In the first case, the application is returned a handle to the storage object incarnation. In the second case the storage home will return a sequence of handles (see also ItemHome in Appendix C).

As the prototype is restricted to C++, the handle is realized by a C++ pointer. The actual implementation of state and of the corresponding accessor functions is delegated to a "data container" object. Thus the handle represents a smart-pointer [12] to the actual storage object incarnation This approach is somewhat similar to Persistence [28] and other OODB systems.

Although the handle is returned by the finder operation after the object lookup returned successfully, the data container part is not populated by pulling the datastore immediately. Instead, the respective delegate data container object subscribes to the storage object's subject name and snoops the message bus for LOADREPLY and UPDATENOTIFY messages.

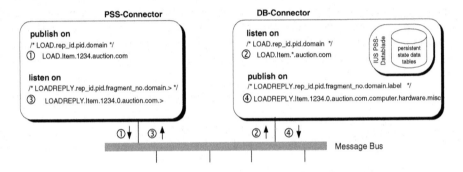

Fig. 5. Object load with publish/subscribe

At the time the application accesses the storage object incarnation - by calling an accessor method - we either have snooped the state in the meantime and can save pulling the object from the data store, or we run into an object fault and initiate a synchronous load request. Figure 5 depicts the object fault situation for a storage object of type Item with identifier *1234* in the data store domain *auction.com*. Other nodes running a publish/subscribe session may benefit from snooping message number 4 – an example scenario is presented later in Section 5.

The proposed mechanism is realized by the object manager in the PSS Connector and is transparent to the user. The proposed object faulting technique extends lazy swizzling to the accessed root object, compared to lazy swizzling restricted to contained references [20]. Fetching through collections of objects and navigating through an object tree are typical scenarios where lookup and access are separated in time and thus benefit most from the lazy swizzling with snooping.

As mentioned above, the publish/subscribe PSS provides a supplementary finder operation find_by_label() which returns a collection of handles to storage object incarnations. Storage object instances can be assigned a label, which will become a postfix of the subject name in DB Connector reply messages as depicted in Appendix A. The labeling mechanism presents the subject-based addressing paradigm to the server implementor to explicitly take additional advantage of publish/subscribe capabilities of the PSS implementation. By labeling a collection of related objects, the application can issue subject-based queries to find all storage objects with a given label. In contrast to traditional object server approaches, the result returned by the DB Connector is a set of subject names merely representing the storage object instances. The data container part of the incarnations is eventually filled by snooping on the message bus. As labels can be hierarchically structured, storage objects can be hierarchically categorized. The simple subject-based query mechanism is not supposed to replace a full fledged query service, but comes with our prototype implementation for no additional cost.

4.1.2   Snooping and state reassembling

As mentioned before, the data container of a storage object incarnation implements the snooping algorithm. In order to collect the state of an storage object the data container may subscribe to LOADREPLY as well as to UPDATENOTIFY messages.

Depending on the storage type definition, the storage object state may be mapped to different tables in the data store (see 4.3) and published on the message bus in different fragments per mapped table respectively. The data container reassembles the fragments according to a common *request_id* which identifies a particular request/reply interaction and which is enclosed in the message payload data (see Appendix A).

Given a specific incarnation, the data container object subscribes to the message bus using an appropriate *subject mask*. For example, to snoop for update notifications on storage object of type Item with identifier *1234* in data store domain *auction.com* the subject mask to use is "UPDATENOTIFY.Item.1234.*.auction.com.>". The subject mask for snooping load replies for the same storage object instance is "LOADREPLY.Item.1234.*.auction.com.>".

Figure 6 summarizes the swizzling with snooping mechanism implemented by any data container in the object manager. Initially the handle to the incarnation is unswizzled and snooping to loads and updates is initiated. Eventually, snooping the collection of fragments is completed and the incarnation is switched to the valid state or an accessor is called beforehand. In the former case, the storage object state members can be accessed without going back to the data store. In the latter case, a blocking load request is published – in turn, replies to this request may be snooped by other PSS nodes. Once in a valid state, the storage object incarnation continuously tracks updates by snooping UPDATENOTIFY fragment messages.

The construction of a valid state is possible only if the collection of incoming fragments is complete and all fragments are *compatible*. We say, that two fragments of a storage object instance are compatible if they carry the same *request_id* and thus are published on behalf of the same interaction. Thereby we assure that we assemble the object state belonging to the same snapshot of the object. The fragment buffer needs only one slot for each fragment, as we are only interested in one version of the object, i.e. the one that represents the latest snapshot.

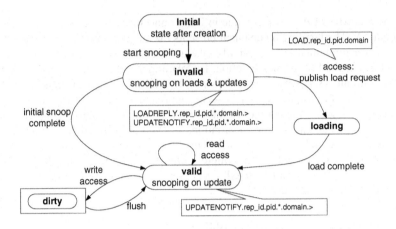

Fig. 6. Snooping states of the data container

As the snooping functionality is executed in an asynchronous thread with respect to the application, we have to synchronize the application access on storage objects with the snooping handler. In order to guarantee snapshot consistency (see also Section 4.4), even if the fragment buffer is complete, we may not unconditionally switch to a new snapshot of the object state in some situations:

- the incarnation is marked as *pinned*: do not switch to a new state until the object is unpinned; continue snooping in the background.
- a read accessor function is currently being executed: switch to the new state on return of the accessor.
- the incarnation is marked as *dirty*: do not switch, until
- the incarnation has been updated and flushed: switch not before a corresponding SAVEREPLY message is received.

4.1.3   Active functionality in PSS

So far, snooping and updating storage objects in the cache has been transparent to the user. To enable the application to reactively monitor significant events like *create*, *update*, *delete*, we extend the PSS API with a notification-channel-like interface.

Each storage home implementation acts as a push-style supplier. It exports the ProxyPushSupplier [24] interface, extended with label-based filtering (see ItemHomeImpl in Appendix C). An application may register a PushConsumer object (IOR) with a storage home, to receive *create* (*update*, *delete*) events, when they occur on any managed storage object whose label matches the given subject predicate. The event parameter of the push(Any e) notification carries the type of event (*create*, *update*, *delete*) and the identifier of the affected object. The notification may then trigger appropriate reactions of the application. The addition of a push channel to the PSS interfaces really enables to build CORBA based information brokers in information dissemination systems.

For example, the application could proactively collect instances of objects of some category - identified by label. To do so, the application registers a PushConsumer with an appropriate label predicate. Each time a new instance appears the event is pushed to the application. As a reaction, the application could then issue a find_by_pid() using the event payload data and thus proactively start snooping on the recently created object's state. Optionally, the application may itself act as a push-style supplier on behalf of an external notification channel which is connected to the front-end application (e.g. implemented as Java applet).

4.2   Message Bus Adapter

The Message Bus Adapter provides the means to connect a relational database to the Rendezvous message bus and thereby to provide transactional publish/subscribe functionality in the database. We use a prototype for Informix Universal Server (IUS) that initially was developed by TIBCO [8] and has been modified and extended by the authors to suit the needs of the project. At the time of this writing, TIB/Adapter ActiveDatabase [32] has been announced. This product shares many features with our prototype of the Message Bus Adapter (see Figure 4).

The API is provided through SQL User Defined Routines which are implemented as external routines in a datablade [15,16]. It is possible to publish row-type data using EVBSendRow() as well as results of (restricted) queries using EVBSendSQL() on a specific predefined subject.

Publishing is executed on behalf of a database transaction. The data is effectively published iff the publishing transaction commits. If the transaction commits, the published messages are guaranteed to be delivered to all (certified) subscribers eventually. In *certified* mode, the implementation uses *event-tables* to intermediately queue published messages which will be selected and sent on the message bus by a dedicated publication agent process, which runs outside of the server. We added functionality to publish in *reliable* mode directly out of the in-blade UDR, without the overhead of persistently queuing events and switching to the agent process. The reliable delivery multicast is more "lightweight" than the guaranteed delivery multicast on the message bus [9]. In fact, nearly all DB Connector messages are published using *reliable* mode, *certified* mode is used for incoming SAVE messages that contain the state of updated storage objects - SAVE messages are also used when creating an object to initialize its state.

As it is not possible to start a foreign event-loop in a datablade, there is the need for a listener agent process, that subscribes to the message bus on behalf of listeners and the associated subjects in the database. Our Message Bus Adapter provides support to register callback handlers, i.e. SQL UDRs, that will be executed when the subscribed subject is encountered for an incoming message. To implement the logic that is needed to drive the data protocol (i.e. create, find, load, save, delete), we register dedicated handlers for the respective subjects. The handlers are themselves implemented as external UDR in a separate datablade.

A particular problem in the implementation of the DB Connector for the PSS prototype is the need for extended trigger functionality in the database. In order to publish UPDATENOTIFY messages, containing the new state of an object - be it, because it was saved out of a PSS Connector or because the tables were modified directly through SQL - we would like to implement so called *sequential causal dependent* coupling [4] between the triggering transaction and the update notification transaction. This coupling between transactions would assure that the notification is only sent out if the update transaction is successfully committed and that no other update transaction can modify the data before having sent out the new state. Such a coupling mode is not supported for SQL3 triggers [18] (as well as Informix SQL [17] and SQL92 [11]). There are different ways to tackle this problem. One is to make use of database server extensions that allow to register callback handlers for transaction state changes in database extension modules like datablades in Informix [16]. This way, the DB Connector is able to detect the commit of an update transaction and act accordingly. The IUS 9.14 version, however, does not allow to pass closure data to a transaction state change handler and it is thus hardly feasible to know for which object to send out an update notification. A working (and more portable) solution for us is to let the listener agent run another callback handler after dispatching a save handler. Doing so, situations might occur, when an older update is overwritten before the next update on a storage object and only the latest state of the object will be notified to the PSS connectors. As an effect, a writer may not be able to read its own update, but already receives a more recent version of the storage object.

4.3   Mapper

This task is well understood in the database community [3,19]. Automated mapping from PSDL to object-relational therefore is straightforward. However, the derivation of an OO model from a relational schema may need user intervention. In our prototype we implemented the PSDL-to-relational mapping at first and made sure, that the meta-data and the algorithms allow to cope with relational-to-PSDL mappings.The mapping mechanism consists basically of two phases: configuration at compile-time and the mapping process at run-time. The first one is carried out by the PSDL compiler, which maps the definition of storage objects into tabular structures (here, we describe only the PSDL-to-relational mapping). This mapping process involves the following issues:

- inheritance hierarchy: each storage type is mapped into a separate table that contains only the specialized (new) state members, not the inherited ones;
- recursive storage object types: flattened into one table using an attribute as self reference;
- constructed types (`array`, `sequence`, `enum`, `union`, etc.): mapped into separate tables carrying a reference (primary key) of the related object;
- primitive types: mapped based on a predefined correspondence description between PSDL primitive types and basic SQL types;
- complex SQL types (`date`, `interval`, `blob` etc.): predefined library of storage types (homes) and their implementation.

The result of the configuration process populates the meta-data repository in the data store, which contains all necessary information to transform an object into a tabular structure and vice versa. Based on this meta-data repository the relational schema is generated. Additionally, the mapper creates the messages types, subjects, senders and listeners needed for the FAP in the Message Bus Adapter. One important consequence of the mapping in conjunction with the way, the message bus adapter defines message types is, that the state of a storage object might be fragmented into several messages which have to be published separately. This is the case for derived storage object types and storage object types containing sequences or unions. We are investigating, in how far we can benefit from object-relational mappings to increase efficiency of data shipping.

Once the configuration is established, the second phase is carried out at run-time when the mapping algorithm is executed in the database adapter i.e. called by some callback handler. We have to unmarshal the payload data of the incoming message, e.g. a fragment of a save request, and update the storage object's tabular representation accordingly.

4.4   Transaction Properties

Accessing a state member of a storage object incarnation is guaranteed to return a consistent value. The implementation of an accessor method is realized as atomic unit of access isolated from concurrent updates on the same storage object in that same publish/subscribe session and isolated from update notifications snooped from the message bus, as described in Section 4.1.2. Using the pin() operation on a storage object incarnation allows to extend the unit of isolation with respect to update notifications until the unpin() operation is called. Thereby it is possible to bracket several read accessor calls to the same storage object incarnation in order to read a consistent snapshot of the object [2].

Note, that we do not use a lock based implementation of isolation as it would require interaction with the DB Connector. As one consequence, the prototype does not support bracketing access to more than one storage object incarnation for snapshot consistency. Without locking, this would require the PSS Connector to assure a quiescent state [27] of the objects in the readset. In fact, deciding quiescence depends on a bounded transmission delay of update notifications [27], which we think is not realistic in the envisaged scenarios. As another consequence, concurrent updates to the same storage object from different sessions are possible. Updates to the same storage object will be serialized by the DB Connector in reception order. Updates are propagated to the datastore on session flush() using certified message delivery. The save handler in the DB Connector updates all the state fragments of the storage object in one database transaction and thus assures the atomicity of writes. Again, this is restricted to single storage objects, there is no transaction bracketing provided. In Section 4.2, we discussed a restriction imposed by the particular message bus adapter: it is not guaranteed that each update on a storage object will result in the publication of an update notification but two updates might be collapsed into one update notification. Nevertheless, snapshot consistency is preserved, as the application will never see an older update after a newer one.

The PSS prototype described in this paper does not support the notion of transactions as proposed for *transactional sessions* in the PSS specification, which is targeted to integration with OTS [25] and X/Open DTP XA compliant data bases [34]. Instead we define a *publish/subscribe session*. We argue that for many applications the object instance is a sufficient granularity of isolation, especially for long-running read-only applications with monitoring semantics. In that respect we trade serializability of computations for timely delivery and freshness of data.

5   Putting It all Together: An Auction Application Scenario

A worldwide person-to-person auction system (à la eBay) is the basic scenario. We assume the reader is familiar with the basic auction process. Figure 7 depicts the infrastructure of this application.

Beginning from the back-end, the DB Connector interacts with the datastore(s), where all auction entities are stored. The middle-tier encapsulates the auction business logic (see Appendix D) and the access to persistent auction entity instances through use of a publish/subscribe PSS (see Appendix B). In this scenario, there are multiple middle-tiers organized by region, providing similar functionality, and more important, accessing common storage objects of the auction.com datastore domain. At the front-end, clients use a browser interface, where auction applets are running that in turn are connected to the "nearest" application through an ORB. To refresh the data in the front-end, the user can configure the applet to automatically refresh the data when it receives the corresponding change/update notifications (aperiodic push/pull combination); the user can schedule a periodic refresh, e.g. every 5 minutes (periodic polling) or can refresh information on mouse-click (aperiodic polling).

We present a few characteristic interactions that illustrate the operation of the PSS in the context of the auction application. Space limitations preclude a more detailed analysis.

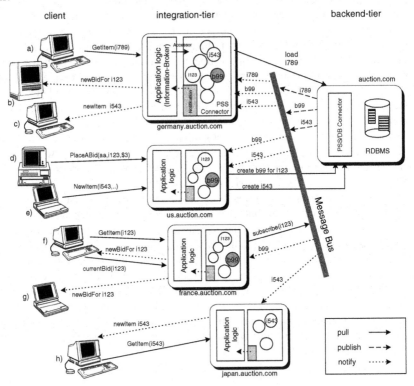

Fig. 7. Auction application scenario

- A German user on client (a) is interested on item i789, the applet calls the operation GetItem(i789) through the ORB on the application, which itself issues a find_by_item_id() on ItemHome (see Appendix C). Given that the object is not in the cache, the application will run into an object fault when reading the state of item i789, causing a load request to be published. The responsible DB Connector looks up the storage object instance and selects corresponding tabular data and publishes the fragments on the message bus. As no sessions exist on other nodes that hold an incarnation for i789, the item i789 is only loaded by the German middle-tier.

- The user on client (d), playing the role of a bidder, places a bid issuing a PutABid(aa,i123,$3) operation call on the application. This operation involves the creation of the bid instance b99 with label "i123" for the item i123. The BidHome creates this instance on the datastore by publishing a CREATE request. The responsible DB Connector of the particular datastore domain, maps the corresponding Bid storage object instance into its tabular structure, creates the required types and subjects in the Message Bus Adapter, and publishes a CREATEREPLY as well as the object state (after commit) on the message bus. All BidHome instances in PSS Connectors for which the application has registered a *PushConsumer* for create events with label "i123", snoop the message bus and signal the creation of bid b99 to the application. The respective storage homes will proactively create a storage object incarnation in the cache, which instantaneously snoops the new state. In the scenario, the PSS Connectors in Germany, U.S.A. and France have subscribed to "i123" labeled bids. On notification, the corresponding applications in turn read the new b99 storage object - which should already be in the cache – and send a *newBidFor i123* notification to clients (b), (f), and (g).

- An American seller, in front of client (e), wants to sell an item. She requests an item number and fills out all the required information (title, category, description, duration, first bid, etc.) and when completed the NewItem operation is called on the application. This method creates a new item instance (through ItemHome) identifying it with i543 and category label "comp.misc", as explained before. All applications that registered with a respective ItemHome for *create* events with label "comp.misc" again receive a *create* notification from the PSS, while the item incarnation is already snooped and placed in the cache. Since bidders can specify their interest in categories to the application, all new items under the selected categories can be notified to them. That is the case of germany.auction.com and japan.auction.com, where notifications are sent to the clients (c) and (h). The latter one pulls i543 item description calling GetItem on the application.

6   Summary and Future Work

We discussed the need for supporting information dissemination applications by integrating relational databases in a fully distributed Object-Web system. We have shown that this can easily be done in a CORBA framework through the use of a publish/subscribe Persistent State Service. In this paper we introduced an architecture that combines the reliable multicast capabilities of COTS middleware with the requirements of the new PSS specification. We presented implementation details of a prototype implementation based on Informix IUS 9.14 and TIBCO's TIB/Rendezvous and discussed the main implementation issues: design of PSS and DB Connectors and the associated formats and protocols, realization of an object manager that provides lazy swizzling with snooping techniques, the mechanisms for adapting a DBMS to interact with the messaging middleware and how active event signaling capabilities were built into the DBMS extensions, the mapping procedures between PSDL and the relational model and the required session and transaction semantics. We illustrated the use of the publish/subscribe PSS through an auction scenario and a few characteristic user interactions and the dissemination of the pertinent information.

The main advantage of our publish/subscribe PSS is the ability to support both client- and server-initiated interactions in contrast to typical client-initiated approaches based on query shipping. By exploiting the reliable multicast capabilities of the middleware we provide a scalable generic caching mechanism that enables the application developer to concentrate on application development rather than on the reimplementation of basic functionality. The prototype of our CORBA Persistent State Service is well suited to build n-tier information dissemination systems that require timely delivery of data and exhibit access patterns that are typical of monitoring applications. The introduction of a push channel in the PSS interface makes it possible to notify applications whenever an event of interest occurs. Through the use of lazy swizzling combined with message-bus snooping and subject-based addressing we provide the means to achieve efficient data staging across data stores.

The current PSS implementation is a good platform for further experimentation. On the one hand, future research includes the deployment in a realistic testbed for performance evaluation and the use of this platform in large-scale e-commerce application scenarios. On the other hand, PSS capabilities must be expanded and the interactions with other CORBA services must be tested. Specific issues to be resolved in our ongoing research include the use of timestamp-ordering consistency protocols, the extension of the caching mechanism to do proactive caching, replication among data stores, the integration with query, notification, and transaction services, and tool support for handling heterogeneous data stores.

Acknowledgements
We would like to thank Arvola Chan for his support and constructive feedback.

References

1. S. Acharya, R. Alonso, M. Franklin and S. Zdonik, *Broadcast Disks: Data Management for Asymmetric Communications Environments*. In Proceedings of the International Conference on Management of Data (SIGMOD 95), pp. 199-210, San Jose, June 1995.
2. H. Berenson, P. Bernstein, J. Gray, J. Melton, E. O'Neil, P. O'Neil, *A critique of ANSI SQL Isolation Levels*. In Proceedings of the International Conference on Management of Data (SIGMOD 95), pp. 1-10, San Jose, June 1995.
3. M. Blaha, W. Premerlani and H. Shen, *Converting OO Models into RDBMS Schema*. IEEE Software, Vol. 11, No. 3, pp. 28-39, May 1994.
4. H. Branding, A. Buchmann, T. Kurdass and J. Zimmermann, *Rules in an Open System: The REACH Rule System*. In Proceedings of Intl. Workshop on Rules in Database Systems (RIDS 93), pp. 111-126, Edinburgh, Scotland, September 1993.

5. M. Carey, M. Franklin, M.Livny and E. Shekita, *Data Caching Tradeoffs in Client-Server DBMS Architectures*. In Proceedings of the International Conference on Management of Data (SIGMOD 91), pp. 357-366, Denver, May 1991.

6. N.Carriero and D. Gelernter. *Linda in Context*. Communications of the ACM, Vol. 32, No. 4, April 1989.

7. R.G.G. Cattell et al (Editors). *The Object Database Standard: ODMG 2.0*. Morgan Kaufmann Publishers, 1997.

8. A. Chan. *Transactional Publish / Subscribe: The Proactive Multicast of Database Changes*. In Proceedings of the International Conference on Management of Data (SIGMOD 98), pp. 520, Seattle, Washington, 1998.

9. D.R. Cheriton and D. Skeen. *Understanding the Limitations of Causally and Totally Ordered Communication*. In 14th ACM Symposium on Operating System Principles, Asheville, NC, December 1993.

10. U. Dayal and A. Buchmann and D. McCarthy. *Rules are Objects too: a knowledge model for an active, object-oriented database system*. In Proceedings of the 2nd Intl. Workshop on Object-Oriented Database Systems, Lecture Notes in Computer Science 334, Springer, 1988.

11. C. Date and H. Darwen, *The Guide of SQL Standard*, 4th edition, Addison-Wesley, 1997.

12. D. Edelson, *Smart Pointers: They're Smart, but not They're Not Pointers*. Technical Report UCSC-CRL-92- 27, Baskin Center of Computer Engineering & Information Science, University of California, Santa Cruz, 1992.

13. M. Franklin and S. Zdonik, *"Data in your Face": Push Technology in Perspective*. In Proceedings of the International Conference on Management of Data (SIGMOD 98), pp. 516-519, Seattle, June 1998.

14. Fujitsu, Inprise, IONA Technologies, Objectivity, Oracle, Persistence Software, Secant Technologies, Sun Microsystems and TIBCO, *Persistent State Service 2.0, Joint Revised Submission*. OMG Document orbos/ 99-07-07, ftp://www.omg.org/pub/docs/orbos/99-07-07.pdf, August 1999.

15. Informix Inc., *Extending Informix Universal Server, User-Defined Routines*, 1997.

16. Informix Inc., *DataBlade API Programmers Manual*, 1997.

17. Informix Inc., *Informix Guide to SQL:Syntax*, Version 9.1, 1997.

18. ISO-ANSI, *Working Draft Database Language SQL (SQL / Foundation SQL3)*. Part 2, X3H2-94-080 and SOU-003, 1995.

19. A. Keller, R. Jensen and S. Agrawal, *Persistence Software: Bridging Object-Oriented Programming and Relational Databases*. In Proceedings of the International Conference on Management of Data (SIGMOD 93), pp. 523-528, Washington, May 1993.

20. A. Kemper and G. Moerkotte, *Object-Oriented Database Management: Applications in Engineering and Computer Science*, Prentice Hall, 1994.

21. R. Munz, *Usage Scenarios for DBMS*. Keynote, International Conference on Very Large Data Bases (VLDB 99), www.dcs.napier.ac.uk/~vldb99/IndustrialSpeakersSlides/SAPVLDB.pdf, Edinburgh, September 1999.

22. Object Management Group (OMG), *CORBA Services Specification*. OMG Document formal/98-12-09, ftp:/ /www.omg.org/pub/docs/formal/98-12-09.pdf, Famingham, MA, December 1998.

23. Object Management Group (OMG), *CORBA Messaging*, OMG Document orbos/98-05-05, ftp:// www.omg.org/pub/docs/orbos/98-05-05.pdf, Famingham, MA, May 1998.

24. Object Managment Group (OMG), *CORBA Notification Service*, OMG TC Document telecom/99-07-01, ftp://www.omg.org/pub/docs/telecom/99-07-01.pdf, Famingham, MA, August 1999.

25. Object Management Group (OMG), *Transaction Service Specification*, in *CORBA Services Specification*, Chapter 10, Famingham, MA, May 1998.

26. B. Oki, M. Pfluegl, A. Siegel and D. Skeen, *The Information Bus - An Architecture for Extensible Distributed Systems*. In Proceedings of SIGOPS 93, pp. 58-68, December 1993.

27. E. Pacitti, P. Minet and E. Simon. *Fast Algorithms for Maintaining Replica Consistency in Lazy Master Replicated Databases*. In Proceedings of the Intl. Conference on Very Large Data Bases (VLDB99), pp. 126- 137, Edinburgh, UK, September 1999.

28. Persistence Software, *Persistence PowerTier: A Technical Overview*. White Paper, www.persistence.com/ Sources/Download/WP_Technical.pdf.

29. D.C. Schmidt. *Reactor -- An Object Behavioral Pattern for Event Demultiplexing and Event Handler Dispatching*. Proceedings of the First Pattern Languages of Programs Conference in Monticello, Illinois, August, 1994.

30. T. Speakman, D. Farinacci, S. Lin and A. Tweedly. *PGM Reliable Transport Protocol Specification*. Internet Draft <draft-speakman-pgm-spec-02.txt>, Cisco Systems, August 1998.

31. TIBCO Software Inc. *TIB/Active Enterprise*.
http://www.tibco.com/products/active_enterprise/index.html, TIBCO Software Inc., Palo Alto, USA.

32. TIBCO Software Inc. *TIB/Adapter for ActiveDatabase*.
http://www.tibco.com/products/adapter_adb/whitepaper.html, TIBCO Software Inc., Palo Alto, USA.

33. W. Wilkinson and M. Neimat, *Maintaining Consistency of Client-Cached Data*. In Proceedings of the Intl. Conference on Very Large Data Bases (VLDB 90), pp. 122-133, Brisbane, Australia, August 1990.

34. X/Open DTP, *Distributed Transaction Processing: Reference Model, The XA Specification*, Reading, Berkshire, England, X/Open Ltd., 1991.

Appendix A. Subject Namespace

Table 1. Subject Namespace.

Task	Subject	participant	*	mask	content**
Create	CREATE.rep_id. domain	storagehome	P	CREATE.rep_id.domain	rep_id, [pid|{(key,value)}*] label, request_id
		DB-Connector	S	CREATE. *.domain	
	CREATEREPLY.rep_id. domain.label	DB-Connector	P	CREATEREPLY.rep_id. domain.label	rep_id, pid, request_id,label, result
" snoop		storagehome	S	CREATEREPLY.rep_id. domain.>	
		storagehome	S	CREATEREPLY.rep_id. domain.label	
Delete	DELETE.rep_id.domain	storagetype	P	DELETE.rep_id.domain	rep_id, pid, request_id
		DB-Connector	S	DELETE.*.domain	
	DELETEREPLY.rep_id. pid.domain.label	DB-Connector	P	DELETEREPLY.rep_id.pid. domain.label	rep_id, pid, request_id,label, result
" snoop		storage_type	S	DELETEREPLY.rep_id.pid. domain.label	
		storagehome	S	DELETEREPLY.rep_id.*. domain.label	
Find	FIND.rep_id.domain	storagehome	P	FIND.rep_id.domain	rep_id, pid, request_id, {(key, value)}*, label
		DB-Connector	S	FIND. *.domain	
	FINDREPLY.rep_id. Domain	DB-Connector	P	FINDREPLY.rep_id.domain	(rep_id, pid, label) collection, request_id
		storagehome	S	FINDREPLY.rep_id.domain	
Load	LOAD.rep_id. Pid.domain	storagetype	P	LOAD.rep_id.pid. domain	rep_id, pid, request_id
		DB-Connector	S	LOAD. *. *.domain	
	LOADREPLY. rep_id. pid. fragment_no. domain.label	DB-Connector	P	LOADREYPL.rep_id. pid. fragment_no.domain.label	fragment data
" snoop		storagetype	S	LOADREPLY.rep_id.pid.*. domain.>	
		storagetype	S	LOADREPLY.rep_id. pid.*. domain.>	
Update notification	UPDATENOTIFY. rep_id.pid. fragment_no. domain.label	DB-Connector	P	UPDATENOTIFY.rep_id.pid. fragment_no.domain.label	fragment data
" snoop		storagetype	S	UPDATENOTIFY.rep_id.pid. *.domain.label	
Save	SAVE.rep_id. pid.domain	storagetype	P	SAVE.repid.pid.domain	Fragment data, request_id
		DB-Connector	S	SAVE.*.*.domain	
	SAVECOMPLETE. rep_id.pid.domain	storagetype	P	SAVECOMPLETE.rep_id. pid.domain	rep_id, pid, request_id
		DB-Connector	S	SAVECOMPLETE.*.*. domain	
	SAVEREPLY. rep_id.pid.domain	DB-Connector	P	SAVEREPLY.rep_id. pid. domain	rep_id, pid, request_id, result
		storagetype	S	SAVEREPLY.rep_id.pid. domain	

* P:publisher, S:subscriber

** rep_id: repository identification; pid:persistent state object identification.

Appendix B. PSDL (Auction Example)

```
abstract storagetype User {
    //...
};
abstract storagetype Category {
    //...
};

abstract storagetype Item;
typedef sequence<ref<Item>> item_seq;

abstract storagetype Bid{
    readonly state long bid_no;
    state ref<User> bidder;
    state ref<Item> item;
    state date when;
    state money amount;
}

typedef sequence<ref<Bid>> bid_seq;
enum item_state {sold, cancelled, active, inactive};

abstract storagetype Item {
    readonly state long item_no;
    state string title;
    state string description;
    state ref<ItemDetails> details;
    state ref<Category> cat_no;
    state date from;
    state date until;
    state string location;
    state ref<User> seller;
    state item_state thestate;
};

abstract storagetype ItemDetails {
    state ref<Item> item;
    state string longdescription;
    state blob image;
};

storagetype ItemImpl implements ItemDescription{};
storagetype ItemDetailsImpl implements ItemDetails{};
storagetype BidImpl implements Bid{};
// ...

abstract storagehome ItemHome of Item {
    key item_no;
};
abstract storagehome BidHome of Bid {
    key bid_no;
};
abstract storagehome ItemDetailsHome of ItemDetails {};

storagehome BidHomeImpl of BidImpl implements BidHome {;
    primary key bid_no;
};
storagehome ItemHomeImpl of ItemImpl implements ItemHome {;
    primary key item_no;
};
storagehome ItemDetailsHomeImpl of ItemDetailsImpl implements
    ItemDetailsHome { };
```

Appendix C. PSS derived code (Auction Example)

```
// language mappings for special storagetypes date, money, blob
#include "sqltypes.h"

class Item : public virtual CosPersistentState::StorageObjectBase {
public:
    virtual CORBA_Long item_no() = 0;
    virtual const char* title() const = 0;
    virtual void title( const char* s ) = 0;
    virtual void title( char* s ) = 0;
    virtual void title( CORBA::String_var& s ) = 0;
    virtual const char* description() const = 0;
    virtual void description( const char* s ) = 0;
    virtual void description( char* s ) = 0;
    virtual void description( CORBA::String_var& s ) = 0;
    virtual ItemDetails* details() const =0;
    virtual const ItemDetailsRef
        details(CosPersistentState::YieldRef yr) const =0;
    virtual void details(ItemDetails* id) = 0;
    virtual void details(const ItemDetailsRef id) = 0;
    //...
}

class ItemHome : public virtual CosPersistentState::StorageHomeBase {
public:
    virtual Item* create(CORBA_Long item_no, const char* title,
        const char* description, const ItemDetailsRef& idr,
        const CategoryRef& cr, const date& from, const date& until,
        const char* location, const UserRef& seller, item_state is,
        const char* label)=0;
    virtual ItemRef create(CORBA_Long item_no, const char* title,
        const char* description, const ItemDetailsRef& idr,
        const CategoryRef& cr, const date& from, const date& until,
        const char* location, const UserRef& seller, item_state is,
        CosPersistentState::YieldRef yr, const char* label,)=0;
    // suppl. subscription based finder methods:
    virtual item_seq* find_by_label(in string label)=0;
    // finder methods for keys
    virtual Item* find_by_pid( const CORBA_OctetSeq& pid ) = 0;
    virtual Item* find_by_item_no( CORBA_Long item_no ) = 0;
    virtual ItemRef find_by_pid( const CORBA_OctetSeq& pid,
        CosPersistentState::YieldRef yr) = 0;
    virtual ItemRef find_by_item_no( CORBA_Long item_no,
        CosPersistentState::YieldRef yr ) = 0;
}

class ItemImpl : public virtual Item {
public:
    // accessors
    CORBA_Long item_no();
    const char* title() const;
    void title( const char* s );
    void title( char* s );
    void title( CORBA::String_var& s );
    const char* description() const;
    void description( const char* s );
    void description( char* s );
    void description( CORBA::String_var& s );
    ItemDetails* details() const;
    const ItemDetailsRef
        details(CosPersistentState::YieldRef yr) const;
    void details(ItemDetails* id);
    void details(const ItemDetailsRef id);
    // ...
```

```
        // methods inherited from StorageObjectBase:
        void _add_ref();
        void _remove_ref();
        void destroy_object();
        CORBA_Boolean object_exists();
        CORBA_OctetSeq* get_pid();
        CORBA_OctetSeq* get_short_pid();
        StorageHomeBase_ptr get_storage_home();
        void pin();
        void unpin();
    private:
        ItemImpl() {};
        ItemImpl( StorageHomeBase_ptr home, const CORBA_OctetSeq& pid,
            OBCM_Session *obrvcm_session );
        // ...
        StorageHomeBase_ptr _home;
        ItemImplData* _ptr;
}

class ItemHomeImpl : public virtual ItemHome {
    Item* create(CORBA_Long item_no, const char* title,
        const char* description, const ItemDetailsRef& idr,
        const CategoryRef& cr, const date& from, const date& until,
        const char* location, const UserRef& seller, item_state is,
        const char* label);
    virtual ItemRef create(CORBA_Long item_no, const char* title,
        const char* description, const ItemDetailsRef& idr,
        const CategoryRef& cr, const date& from, const date& until,
        const char* location, const UserRef& seller, item_state is,
        CosPersistentState::YieldRef yr, const char* label,);
    // suppl. notification channel interface, inherited from
    // StorageHomeBase:
    virtual void connect_any_push_consumer(notification_type nt,
        const char* label, const PushConsumer& pc);
    virtual void disconnect_any_push_consumer(notification_type nt,
        const char* label,const PushConsumer& pc);
};
```

Appendix D. IDL Interfaces (Auction Example)

```
// data structures for user, bid, item etc.
struct bid {...};
typedef sequence<bid> bid_seq;
struct item {...};
// ...

interface User
{
    string NewUser(in string name, in string email,
        in string password, in string address);
    boolean LogIn(in string UserId, in string password);
    boolean LogOut(in string UserId);
    void ItemOfInterest(in string UserId, in string ItemNo);
    void CategoryOfInterest(in string UserId, in long category);

// Seller:
    string NewItem(in string title, in string descr,
        in string details, in long category, in string seller,
        in short days, in string location);
    item_seq GetItemsForSale(in string UserId);

// Bidder:
    boolean PlaceABid(in string Bidder, in string ItemNo,
        in double amount);
    item_seq GetInterests(in string UserId);

    // ...
};

interface DataRetrieval
{
    item GetItem(in string ItemNo);
    itemDetails GetItemDetails(in string ItemNo);
    item_seq SearchItem(in string text);
    bid firstBid(in string ItemNo);
    bid currentBid(in string ItemNo);
    bid_seq BidHistory(in string ItemNo);
    cat GetCategory(in long catNo);
    user GetUser(in string UserId);
    // ...
}
```

QualProbes: Middleware QoS Profiling Services for Configuring Adaptive Applications*

Baochun Li and Klara Nahrstedt

Department of Computer Science
University of Illinois at Urbana-Champaign
{b-li,klara}@cs.uiuc.edu
http://cairo.cs.uiuc.edu

Abstract. It is widely accepted that in order to deliver the best Quality-of-Service (QoS), applications need to be adaptive to the fluctuating computing and communication environments. The middleware layer may assist by controlling the behavior of the applications so that they adapt and reconfigure themselves. In this paper, we present *QualProbes*, a set of middleware *QoS Probing and Profiling* services to discover such relationships at run-time. Our approach focuses on meeting the requirements of the *critical performance criterion* in the application. Such criterion may be affected by changes in more than one application-specific QoS parameters, and these parameters have diversely different resource usage patterns. *QualProbes* services are able to precisely capture the effects made to the critical performance criterion when resource availability varies, and thus enable more effective control of the application to adapt to resource variations. Our case study with *OmniTrack*, an omni-directional visual tracking application, provides solid proof that QualProbes significantly enhance our capabilities to satisfy the critical performance criterion, the *tracking precision*, while controlling the adaptation process of the application.

1   Introduction

Recent research advances in Quality-of-Service (QoS) and resource management have brought forth numerous solutions to support QoS-aware applications, so that their demands for both end system and network resources are met. Two major categories of such solutions have evolved. First, *reservation-based systems* employ various resource reservation and admission control mechanisms to enforce the delivery of requested QoS to the applications. Such enforcement may be deterministic or statistical, depending on the policies involved for resource reservation. One drawback of this approach is that many reservation mechanisms demand major overhaul in the design of prevalent operating systems in use today, such as Windows NT, or networking protocols, such as TCP/IP. In

* This research was supported by the Air Force Grant under contract number F30602-97-2-0121, NASA Grant under contract number NASA NAG 2-1250, and National Science Foundation Career Grant under contract number NSF CCR 96-23867.

J. Sventek and G. Coulson (Eds.): Middleware 2000, LNCS 1795, pp. 256–272, 2000.

contrast, *adaptation-based systems* operate based on best-effort environments, and attempt to adapt themselves or the applications for the purpose of providing the *best possible* QoS under available resource conditions, and of achieving the most graceful quality degradation in case of scarce resources.

It is advantageous to implement such *adaptation-based systems* in the middleware level, since it does not require tight integration or modifications to the best-effort services in OS kernel and network protocol stack, which is the major advantage of adaptation-based systems over reservation-based systems. Indeed, notable examples of adaptation-based systems, such as the *QuO* [1] and *Da CaPo++* [2], implement adaptation-based services in the middleware. Naturally, since both middleware components and the actual QoS-aware applications may be reconfigured to adapt to the changing environment, two approaches exist with two distinctive focuses. One approach is to dynamically reconfigure the middleware itself so that it can transparently provide a stable and predictable operating environment to the application. This approach is attractive since it does not require any modifications to the application, any legacy application can be deployed with little efforts and with a certain level of QoS assurance. However, since it can only provide a generic solution to all applications, a set of highly application-specific requirements cannot be addressed. Alternatively, the middleware may be *active*, and exert strict control of the adaptation behavior of QoS-aware applications, so that these applications adapt and reconfigure themselves under such control. This approach enjoys the advantage of knowing exactly what are the application-specific adaptation priorities and requirements, so that appropriate adaptation choices can be made to address these requirements. However, it lacks an easy way to manifest the relationship between application-specific adaptation choices and the actual changes in resource demands, caused by reconfiguring an adaptive application. We take the latter alternative in our approach.

Since the primary objective common to all adaptation-based approaches is to provide the *best possible* QoS with the current resource availability in a swiftly changing environment, the problem comes to the proper choice of a certain *criterion* that can assist the judgment of "What is best?". Most applications have more than one QoS parameters that are application-specific, and any changes in these parameters contribute to an increase or degradation of the delivered quality. In this paper, we focus on the *critical performance criterion*, which concentrates on the satisfaction of requirements related to the most critical application QoS parameter. The quality of other non-critical parameters can be traded off. For example, in our case study of *OmniTrack*, an omni-directional visual tracking application, the *tracking precision*[1] is the most critical QoS parameter in the tracking application. The *critical performance criterion*, therefore, is to keep the tracking precision accurate and stable.

In this paper, we present *QualProbes*, a set of middleware QoS probing and profiling services, that are uniquely designed to address the following problems:

---

[1] The *tracking precision* is a quantitative measurement of the collective performance of all concurrently running tracking algorithms, also referred to as *trackers*.

(1) How do changes in non-critical application QoS parameters relate to the critical QoS parameter, and thus the critical performance criterion? (2) How do the changes in application QoS parameters relate to changes in resource demands or consumption? (3) How do the solutions to the previous problems translate to appropriate control actions activated by the middleware, so that the critical performance criterion, e.g., a stable tracking precision, are satisfied and maintained? Once we have solved these problems, we are able to control the adaptation process within the application from the middleware, so that under any circumstances in a best-effort environment and with fluctuating resource availability, the application is able to maintain the *best possible* quality-of-service, in the sense that the *critical performance criterion* is always satisfied.

The rest of the paper is organized as follows. Section 2 briefly introduces the design and architecture of *Agilos* (**Agile QoS**), a middleware control architecture that actively controls the application's adaptation behavior. The *QualProbes* services are introduced and serve as critical core components in the *Agilos* architecture. Section 3 presents our theoretical and practical solutions to the above problems, forming the basis of *QualProbes*. Section 4 shows a detailed experimental analysis of the control effectiveness from the middleware, with and without the assistance of *QualProbes*. We use *OmniTrack*, our omni-directional visual tracking application, as an example of complex applications. Section 5 discusses related work and Section 6 concludes the paper.

2   *Agilos* Middleware: A Background Introduction

The ultimate objective of *Agilos*, our middleware control architecture, is to control the adaptation process within the application so that it is steered towards the satisfaction of application-specific *critical performance criterion*. In order to accomplish the objective, the core middleware components of *Agilos* consist of application-neutral *Adaptors* and application-aware *Configurators*, which reflect a two-level hierarchy of middleware control. In the application-neutral level, each Adaptor corresponds to a single type of resource, e.g., CPU Adaptors or network bandwidth Adaptors. Though the Adaptors are specific to resources, they are not aware of the semantics of individual applications. In contrast, the *Configurators* in the application-specific level are fully aware of the application-specific semantics, and thus each Configurator only serves one application. This hierarchical design of the *Agilos* architecture is illustrated as in Figure 1.

Though the Adaptors and Configurators form the basis of the *Agilos* architecture, three additional components are necessary to complete the design and to achieve the desired functionality. First, the *Negotiator* is responsible for all communications among *Agilos* middleware components on different end systems. Second, the *Observer* is responsible for monitoring resource availability and inspecting any application-specific parameters. Third, *QualProbes* provide QoS probing and profiling services so that application-specific mappings between the two adaptation levels can be derived. This paper focuses on the algorithm design of the *QualProbes* services.

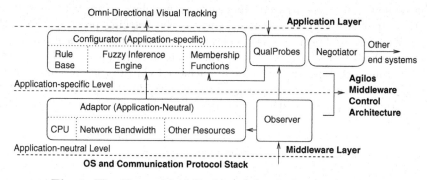

Fig. 1. The Hierarchical Design of the *Agilos* Architecture

QualProbes are designed to assist controlling the applications so that control actions are generated with better awareness of application's behavior and resource demands. To achieve this goal, the results of *QualProbes* are utilized in replacing the "fuel" of the Configurator. As detailed in previous work [3], the Configurator is designed as a rule-based fuzzy control system. As illustrated, the Configurator can be partitioned into three parts: the *Fuzzy Inference Engine*, *Membership Functions* and *Rule Base*. While *fuzzy inference engine* is application-neutral, the "fuel", namely the *rule base* and *membership functions* of associated linguistic variables, are application-specific. Such model guarantees that discrete adaptation choices and a wide variety of resource/application QoS mappings can be addressed easily with a replacement of the rules and membership functions in the rule base.

Rules in the rule base are written using linguistic variables and values. In *OmniTrack*, examples of variables are *cpu_demand* and *throughput_demand*, and examples of values are *below_average* or *very_low*. These values are uniquely characterized by *membership functions*, so that the inference engine can have exact definitions of these values. The design of the rule base involves the generation of a set of conditional statements in the form of if-then rules, such as *if* **cpu_demand** *is very_high and* **throughput_demand** *is below_average then* **configuration** *is compress*.

Apparently, the role of *QualProbes* is to capture the run-time relationships between application QoS and their resource demands, so that the above rules are activated with appropriate timing.

3   *QualProbes:* Investigating Application-Specific Behavior

Since the ultimate objective is to steer adaptations towards satisfaction of the critical performance criterion, the primary goal of QualProbes services is to devise mechanisms that best facilitate such optimal steering of adaptation decisions. To achieve this goal, QualProbes need to address the following issues.

First, QualProbes need to accurately capture the relationships between the most critical application QoS parameter, such as the tracking precision, and other non-critical ones. This is crucial to perform tradeoffs of non-critical parameters. Second, QualProbes need to capture the resource demands of each non-critical QoS parameters. Both of the above are achieved via run-time probing and profiling mechanisms. Finally, such profiling results should be used to assist the generation of application-specific control rules, which are integrated in the Configurator.

We address the above issues in the following sections. We illustrate our solutions with actual examples derived from *OmniTrack*.

3.1   Relations Among QoS Parameters and Resources: The Dependency Tree Model

As previously noted, the application-specific QoS parameters can be classified as *critical* (usually one parameter such as the tracking precision) and *non-critical*. In addition, the changes of each parameter in the *non-critical* collection may cause and be dependent on the changes of zero, one, or multiple types of resources.

Assume that we study m different resource types, and the current observation of consumed resources are $R_1, R_2, \ldots, R_m$, measured with their respective units. Typically in *OmniTrack*, $m = 2$, and R_{cpu} is measured with the CPU load percentage, while R_{net} is measured with bytes per second.

In addition, assume that there are n unique non-critical QoS parameters that may influence the critical parameter, p_c, in the application. These parameters are p_i, $i = 1, \ldots, n$. For p_i, $\forall i$, there are l of resource types related to p_i, where $l \leq m$. In the *OmniTrack* example, if p_i is *frame rate*, its changes correspond to R_{net} and R_{cpu}. In contrast, if p_i is the *object velocity*, it does not directly correspond to any resources, though p_c, the tracking precision, depends on its variations.

The Application Model In all subsequent discussions about application QoS parameters and resource types, we assume a *Task Flow Model* for distributed applications. A complex distributed application can be modeled as several *tasks*, each task generates output for the subsequent task, which can be measured by one or more *output QoS* parameters. Such output forms the input of subsequent tasks. In order to process input and generate output, each task requires a specific amount of resources. An acyclic task graph, as shown in Figure 2 can be used to illustrate such a model.

With such a conceptual model, we note that there may be various definitions of the concept *application task*, distinguished among themselves by the *granularity* of functional partitions in the application. Since we attempt to optimize the adaptation behavior of the application to achieve a performance goal, we divide the applications with *coarse granularity*, and demand that each task must present a one-to-one mapping to an individual executable component within the application. Static or dynamic linked library objects (such as codec or encryption modules) and individual working threads are not tasks themselves, though

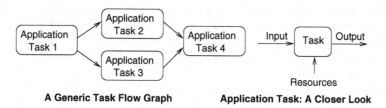

Fig. 2. Illustration of The Task Flow Model

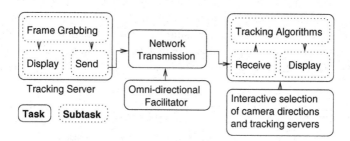

Fig. 3. The Task Flow Model of *OmniTrack*

they may be partitioned as *subtasks*. As an example, the Task Flow Model of *OmniTrack* is shown in Figure 3.

A Dependency Tree for Application QoS Parameters Although each p_i corresponds to resources R_i, $i = 1, \ldots, l$, we observe that such dependencies are generally hard to capture directly. We take the parameter *frame rate* in *Omni-Track* as an example. Naturally, the frame rate of video streaming depends on network bandwidth availability. However, the nature of such dependence is non-deterministic: For the same available bandwidth, the frame rate varies diversely for compressed video versus uncompressed video; different CPU load may limit the capacity that trackers can consume the frames, thus limiting the frame rate. Similar situation applies to other parameters.

Such observations illustrate that each p_i, in addition to being *directly* dependent on resource types, depends directly on a subset of p_j, $j \neq i$, and via its dependence with this subset of parameters p_j, *indirectly* corresponds to resources. We define that if p_i is *dependent* on p_j, then changes in p_j can cause changes in p_i. Ideally, a generic model for capturing the dependencies is by using an acyclic directed dependency graph, with the critical parameter p_c as the source, and resources R_i, $i = 1, \ldots, m$ as the sink. For simplicity reasons, we only consider a special case that all but the bottom levels of such a dependency graph is a directed *binary tree*, with p_c as the root of the tree, and resources as the leaves. Each p_i depends on zero, one or two other parameters or resources.

There are two key characteristics in such a dependency tree [2]. First, the resource types R_i, $i = 1, \ldots, l$ are always leaf nodes of the tree. This is based on a simplified assumption that the changes of each resource type never depend on any other resources, i.e., that resource types are independent with each other. Second, we note that in addition to demanding resources of certain types, the changes of an application QoS parameter may change the resource availability of some other resource types, without demanding them. For example, while changing the *compression ratio* in *OmniTrack* demands CPU resources, its changes will have significant effects on available network bandwidth also, since less data is necessary to be transmitted. This case is presented by a directed arrow from the resource node R_i to the QoS parameter node p_j, showing that the availability of R_i relies on p_j, rather than the usual case that p_j demands and relies on R_i. An illustration of our directed dependency tree model and an real-world example with *OmniTrack* is given in Figure 4.

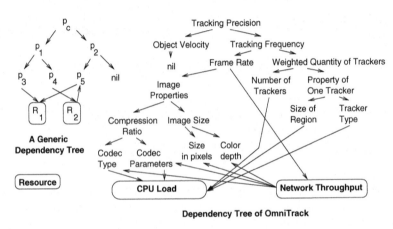

Fig. 4. The Dependency Graph for Application QoS Parameters

Characterizing the Relationship between Dependent Nodes Once we have established the dependency tree of QoS parameters for an application [3], the relationship between dependent nodes needs to be characterized appropriately. We assume that for $\forall i$, $\forall t$, there exists $\{p_i\}_{min}$ and $\{p_i\}_{max}$ such that $\{p_i\}_{min} \leq p_i(t) \leq \{p_i\}_{max}$, any values beyond this range is either not possible or not meaningful. For example, the *frame rate* may vary in between $[1, 30]$ fps. Assume the parent node p_i depends on two descendant nodes p_x and p_y. The dependency can thus be characterized by a function $f_{i,x,y}$, defined as:

---

[2] To be exact, it is only a binary tree without considering the bottom level related to resources. Otherwise, it is more of a lattice.

[3] Such establishment is application-specific, and may be derived based on knowledge of a specific application.

$$\Delta p_i = f_{i,x,y}(\Delta p_x, \Delta p_y)$$
$$p_k = \{p_k\}_{min} + \Delta p_k, \text{ with } k \in \{i, x, y\}$$
$$0 \leq \Delta p_k \leq \{p_i\}_{max} - \{p_i\}_{min} \tag{1}$$

where Δp_k is a normalized value of p_i. Function $f_{i,x,y}$ defines the dependence relationship between the parent node p_i and its descendant nodes p_x and p_y. If p_i only depends on one node p_x, then $f_{i,x,y}$ is equivalent to $f_{i,x}$, where $\Delta p_i = f_{i,x}(\Delta p_x)$. If one or two of the descendant nodes are resource types R_x and R_y, then we define f_{i,r_x,r_y} so that $\Delta p_i = f_{i,r_x,r_y}(\Delta R_x, \Delta R_y)$. Note that for the special case that the availability of resource type R_i depends on changes in p_j, i.e., there is a directed link from R_i to p_j, we define $f^r_{r_i,j}$ such that $\Delta R_i = f^r_{r_i,j}(\Delta p_j)$. Figure 5 visually shows the above characterization.

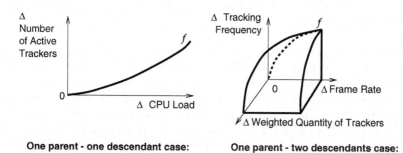

One parent - one descendant case:
Two-Dimensional Characterization

One parent - two descendants case:
Three-Dimensional Characterization

Fig. 5. Characterization of Dependencies among QoS Parameters

If we obtained all $f_{i,x,y}$ in the dependency tree via probing and profiling services, the relationship of any application QoS parameter p_i and its related resources can be characterized by a series of substitutions. As an example, for the generic dependency tree in Figure 4, we have

$$\Delta p_c = f_{c,1,2}(\Delta p_1, \Delta p_2)$$
$$= f_{c,1,2}(f_{1,3,4}(\Delta p_3, \Delta p_4), f_{2,5}(\Delta p_5))$$
$$= f_{c,1,2}(f_{1,3,4}(f_{3,r_1}(\Delta R_1), f_{4,r_2}(\Delta R_2)), f_{2,5}(f_{5,r_1}(\Delta R_1))) \tag{2}$$

and

$$\Delta R_2 = f^r_{r_2,5}(\Delta p_5) \tag{3}$$

which characterizes the relationship between p_c and resources R_1 and R_2.

3.2 QualProbes Services Kernel: The QoS Profiling Algorithm

QualProbes services are responsible for run-time capturing of the relationships f and f^r between dependent nodes in an application-specific dependency tree,

and for properly storing the results in profiles. QualProbes services are middleware components, and implement a *QoS Probing and Profiling* algorithm as
the kernel in each component. The QualProbes services kernel is designed to be
application-neutral, thus we require that all related application QoS parameters
should present the following properties:

1. *Observable.* Their run-time values at any instant can be obtained in a timely
   manner. Implementation-wise, we utilize the CORBA Property Service. Applications report values of their QoS parameters as CORBA properties to the
   Property Service when initializing or when there are changes, while Qual-
   Probes services kernel retrieves these values from the Property Service when
   necessary.
2. *Tunable.* They should be either directly or indirectly tunable from outside
   of the application. Since the application exports interfaces to the middleware Configurator for such tuning and reconfiguration, QualProbes services
   only need to reuse these interfaces to control the QoS parameters in the
   application.

Having ready "read/write" access to the application QoS parameters, Qual-
Probes services execute a *QoS Profiling* algorithm in their kernel. The algorithm
traverses the dependency tree from leaves up to the root, and attempts to discover the function f and f^r previously defined by tuning the values in descendant QoS parameters or resource types and measuring those of the parent QoS
parameter. If f is three-dimensional, a nested loop involving both descendant
parameters is executed. Figure 6 demonstrates the QoS profiling algorithm in
the pseudo-code form. In this algorithm, function **tune** executes recursively in
order to tune an application QoS parameter indirectly.

As an concrete example, Figure 7 illustrates the results of tuning the QoS
parameters *object velocity* and *tracking frequency* in order to measure the tracking
precision. The output of the inner loop (by only tuning tracking frequency) is
shown as bold dotted lines.

3.3   Towards Better Middleware Control

The design of QualProbes services in previous sections addresses the problem
of discovering relationships between the critical performance criterion and resource demands of an application. In order to complete the solutions provided
by QualProbes, we need to address the issue of bridging the obtained profiles
with actual membership functions and inference rules in the Configurator.

The Inference Rules Based on our extensive experiences with the real-world
application *OmniTrack*, we believe that the inference rules inside the rule base
cannot be generated automatically. Such rules need to be written by the application developer for a specific application. The reasons are two-fold: First, a rule
base customized by the application developer is best in exploiting all available

for each resource leaf node R_i in the dependency tree:

    if link$(R_i \rightarrow p_j)$ or link$(p_j \rightarrow R_i)$ exists
    for $k = \{p_j\}_{min}$ to $\{p_j\}_{max}$ step $\{p_j\}_{increment}$
        tune(p_j,k); log observed R_i

for each non-leaf node p_i in the dependency tree (nodes on descendant levels first):

    if p_i has one descendant parameter node p_x
    for $k = \{p_x\}_{min}$ to $\{p_x\}_{max}$ step $\{p_x\}_{increment}$
        tune(p_x, k); log observed p_i
    else if p_i has two descendant parameter node p_x and p_y
    for $k_1 = \{p_x\}_{min}$ to $\{p_x\}_{max}$ step $\{p_x\}_{increment}$
        for $k_2 = \{p_y\}_{min}$ to $\{p_y\}_{max}$ step $\{p_y\}_{increment}$
            tune(p_x, k_1); **tune**(p_y, k_2); log observed p_i

tune$(p_i,$ value$)$

    if p_i is directly tunable via exported interface
        call application exported interface to set $p_i =$ value
    else
        assume descendant nodes of p_i are p_x and p_y
        for $k_1 = \{p_x\}_{min}$ to $\{p_x\}_{max}$ step $\{p_x\}_{increment}$
            for $k_2 = \{p_y\}_{min}$ to $\{p_y\}_{max}$ step $\{p_y\}_{increment}$
                tune(p_x, k_1); **tune**(p_y, k_2);
                if ((observed p_i) $==$ value) **return;**

Fig. 6. QualProbes Services Kernel Algorithm

adaptation choices and best optimize the rich semantics of these choices, naturally integrating the relative priorities of different application QoS parameters. In other words, the application developer should decide the set of QoS parameters to be traded off in the event of quality degradation. Second, the rules are not constant. It should be tuned towards the needs and user preferences in different occasions where the application is executed.

***Thresholds*: Towards Better Membership Functions** Even though the rules can not be generated automatically, the profiles discovered by QualProbes services are of significant assistance in the process of determining the membership functions of linguistic values in the inference rules. In order to demonstrate such assistance, we take one inference rule in *OmniTrack* as an example:

    if *cpu_demand* **is** *very_high* **and** *throughput_demand* **is** *very_low* **then** *configuration* **is** *compress*

This inference rule operates as follows. First, it takes the output of *CPU adaptor* and *Network Bandwidth Adaptor* in the application-neutral level as input. When the CPU is idle, the *CPU adaptor* will apply its application-neutral control algorithm and suggests that the application under its control to demand more CPU resources. This yields a high *cpu_demand* value. Similarly, when the network is congested and there are very low bandwidth available, the network

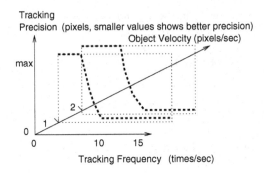

Fig. 7. QualProbes Services: An Example

bandwidth adaptor suggests that the application demand less network bandwidth, thus yielding a low value in *throughput_demand*. Second, the inference rule decides that if *cpu_demand* is high and *throughput_demand* is low, the application should reconfigure itself and add compression to its video streaming. Third, the actual definitions, made via the membership functions, of linguistic values *very_high* and *very_low* decide the activation timing of such reconfiguration choice.

The question is: How "high" is *very_high* for this specific rule? As we have observed in our experiences with OmniTrack, very frequently the discovered profiles by QualProbes services are non-linear, and contain certain *threshold* values. For example, by switch codec type from "uncompressed" to "Motion JPEG", we observe that ΔR_{cpu} steps up abruptly by a certain amount, e.g., 60%, while ΔR_{net} steps down by about 90% of the original value. The *threshold*, thus, can be determined by the profiles obtained from QualProbes services. For example, *very_high* can be defined as higher than 60%, while *very_low* can be defined as lower than 90% of $\{R_{net}\}_{max}$.

As another example, let us examine the profiles obtained related to the top level of dependency tree, the tracking precision. Such profiles are illustrated in Figure 7. One of the corresponding inference rule is:

if *tracking_frequency* **is** *low* **and** *object_velocity* **is** *medium* **then** *configuration* **is** *remove_tracker*

As illustrated by Figure 7, QualProbes services have discovered an approximate threshold value for tracking frequency at respective object speed levels. If the tracking frequency drops below such threshold values, we could speculate that tracking precision may degrade. In order to keep the tracking precision, which is the critical performance criterion for OmniTrack, we define the membership function of linguistic value *low* to cover the values lower than the threshold value that we have discovered, e.g., 10 iterations per second. When this definition is applied to the above inference rule, the configuration choice of *remove_tracker* will be activated when the tracking frequency falls below the critical threshold value. This ensures that the tracking precision is kept stable at all times.

4   Case Study: OmniTrack

4.1   *OmniTrack*: An Introduction

As a case study, we have developed *OmniTrack*, a distributed omni-directional visual tracking system, using tracking algorithms in the *XVision* [4] project. *OmniTrack* is a flexible, multi-threaded and client-server based application, which adopts complex tracking capabilities in multiple dimensions, such as visual object tracking, camera tracking and switching, and features full integration of user preferences. This application illustrates the coexistence of multiple adaptation possibilities, ranging from image properties, codec choices, server selections, to tracker quantities and variety. The actual adaptation choices are based on a combination of user preferences and decisions made by the underlying *Agilos* middleware control architecture. An illustration of *OmniTrack* architecture is shown in Figure 8.

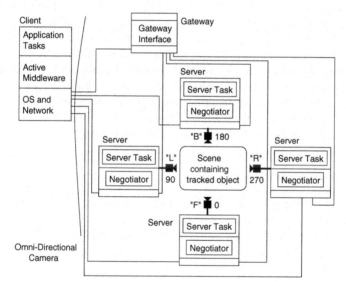

Fig. 8. *OmniTrack*: A Distributed Omni-Directional Visual Tracking System

OmniTrack is implemented in Windows NT, deployed under the control of Agilos middleware. *OmniTrack* exports a *control interface* which is clearly defined in IDL. All control commands made by the Agilos middleware is carried out through such a control interface via CORBA. This ensures that Agilos middleware architecture is generic and not bound to any specific applications. Besides exporting the control interface, *OmniTrack* reports on-the-fly observations of its application-specific QoS parameters to the CORBA Property Service, so that they are always observable from the middleware's point of view.

4.2   Experiments with OmniTrack

We have carried out a series of experiments with *OmniTrack*. In our experimental setting, while the basic inference rules in the Configurator are hand-tuned, we have been successful in applying the threshold values extracted from the profiles discovered by QualProbes services. Without QualProbes, it has been very difficult to specify appropriate membership functions to complete the definitions for the "fuel" of Configurator, let alone to put the Configurator in active service. With QualProbes services enabled and QoS profiles generated, such tasks have been straightforward. We feel that with QualProbes services, we are able to "see through" the internal behavior of the *OmniTrack* application. Such transparency has provided us with unparalleled assistance in our understanding of *OmniTrack*, as well as its control optimally. The following preliminary results are obtained in two different experimental scenarios.

(1) An animated video sequence is streamed from the server to the client using Motion-JPEG compression. The animated sequence is 320*240 pixel frame size video sequence. Within this scenario, we illustrate basic adaptation possibilities by adapting the image size. We measure the tracking precision and show that the tracking precision remains stable with fluctuating bandwidth availability.

(2) Live video is streamed from the active server to the client in a omni-directional setting. The content of the live video is captured by the digital camera and an image grabber. We use 320*240 pixel frame size for the default initial properties of the live video. Within this scenario, we illustrate both throughput-related and CPU-related adaptation in action simultaneously, such as compression and dropping trackers. We finally measure the tracking precision and show that it remains stable with fluctuating CPU availability.

4.3   Experimental Results

Scenario 1 In Figure 9, we illustrate basic adaptations by adapting the image size on a Motion-JPEG compressed video stream. We show from the results that, despite the fluctuating network bandwidth availability, the tracking precision remains stable under the control of Agilos middleware.

Scenario 2 Figure 10 and Table 1 show the experimental results. With respect to parameter-tuning adaptations, Figure 10(b) shows the result of Adaptors and Tuners by changing image size during the fluctuation of network bandwidth shown in Figure 10(a). With respect to reconfiguration alternatives, Figures 10(c), 10(d) and Table 1 show the Configurator in action. In this experiment, Figure 10(c) shows the CPU load fluctuation, while Table 1 shows the control actions generated by the Configurator at various time instants, and executed by the application. Figure 10(d) shows the actually measured tracking precision. The first tracker tracks a more important object, so if a `drop_tracker` event is signaled, later trackers should be dropped. We note that the tracking precision stays stable in a small range, which shows that the adaptation efforts are

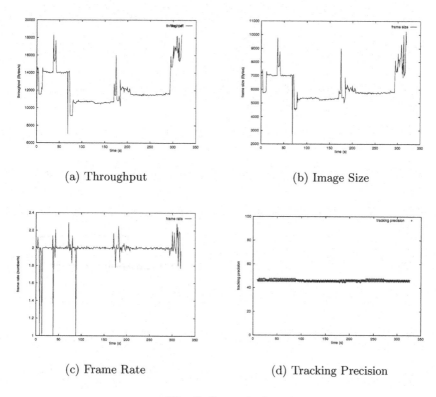

(a) Throughput

(b) Image Size

(c) Frame Rate

(d) Tracking Precision

Fig. 9. Scenario 1

successful to lock the trackers on the objects, before they are dropped for more important trackers.

5   Related Work

It has been widely recognized that many QoS-constrained distributed applications need to be adaptive in heterogeneous environments. Recent research work on resource management mechanisms at the systems level expressed much interests in studying various kinds of adaptive capabilities. Particularly, in wireless networking and mobile computing research, because of resource scarcity and bursty channel errors in wireless links, QoS adaptations are necessary in many occasions. For instance, in the work represented by [5][6], a series of adaptive resource management mechanisms were proposed that applies to the unique characteristics of a mobile environment, including the division of services into several service classes, predictive advanced resource reservation, and the notion of cost-effective adaptation by associating each adaptation action with a lost in network revenue, which is minimized. As another example, Noble et al. in [7] investigated

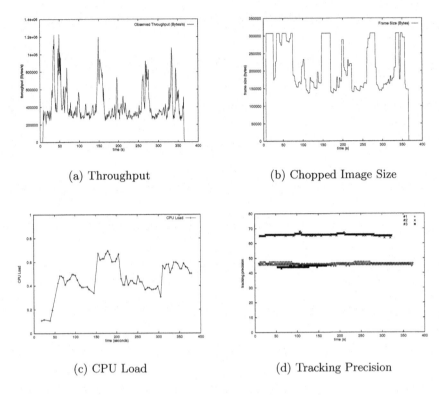

(a) Throughput

(b) Chopped Image Size

(c) CPU Load

(d) Tracking Precision

Fig. 10. Scenario 2

in an application-aware adaptation scheme in the mobile environment. Similarly to our work, this work was also built on a separation principle between adaptation algorithms controlled by the system and application-specific mechanisms addressed by the application. The key idea was to balance and tradeoff between performance and data fidelity.

Another related group of previous work studies the problem of dynamic resource allocations, often at the operating systems level. Noteworthy work are presented in [8][9][10]. The work in [8] focuses on maximizing the overall *system utility* functions, while keeping QoS received by each application within a feasible range (e.g., above a minimum bound). In [9], the global resource management system was proposed, which relies on middleware services as agents to assist resource management and negotiations. In [10], the work focuses on a multi-machine environment running a single complex application, and the objective is to promptly adjust resource allocation to adapt to changes in application's resource needs, whenever there is a risk of failing to satisfy the application's timing constraints.

Recently, in addition to studies in the networking and resource management levels, many active research efforts are also dedicated to various adaptive func-

Table 1. Control Actions produced by the Configurator (follow the time scale in Figure 10(c))

Time (sec)	Control Action from Configurator
28.22	`uncompress`
51.24	`add_tracker`
67.37	`compress`
167.7	`drop_tracker`
320.4	`drop_tracker`

tionalities provided by middleware services. For example, [11] proposes real-time extensions to CORBA which enables end-to-end QoS specification and enforcement. [1] proposes various extensions to standard CORBA components and services, in order to support adaptation, delegation and renegotiation services to shield QoS variations. The work applies particularly in the case of remote method invocations to objects over a wide-area network. The work noted in [12] builds a series of middleware-level agent based services, collectively referred to as *Dynamic QoS Resource Manager*, that dynamically monitors system and application states and switches *execution levels* within a computationally intensive application. These switching capabilities maximize the user-specified benefits, or promote fairness properties, depending on different algorithms implemented in the middleware.

In contrast, our approach is both unique and orthogonal in the following aspects. First, in defining QualProbes services, we defined a novel layered model for application-specific QoS parameters, for the purpose that the relationships between such parameters and system resource usage can be probed and profiled with ease. Second, our *Agilos* middleware is *active*, in the sense that rather than attempting to transparently provide adaptive services, it actively controls the applications themselves so that the applications, *not* the middleware components, are the ones to adapt. Third, our work is orthogonal in the sense that we leverage the advantages of any service enabling platforms, including both standard CORBA services or those with customized ORBs. Fourth, we attempt to develop mechanisms that are as generic as possible, applicable to applications with various demands and behavior. Finally, we attempt to provide support in the Agilos middleware with respect to multiple resources, notably CPU and network bandwidth.

6   Conclusion

This paper has presented new mechanisms with respect to investigating the behavior of the application, for the purpose of generating best control actions for the application to adapt itself to the environmental variations. A detailed analysis of *QualProbes* services is presented, including the application model, the dependency tree model for application QoS parameters, and the QoS profiling algorithm implemented in the QualProbes services kernel. The key contribution of this paper is that we have provided a unique approach to "see through" the behavior of the application, especially when environmental or requirement changes may occur. In addition, we have presented some preliminary experimental results with *OmniTrack*, a complex multimedia application that we have developed, in order to verify that our approaches are effective in assisting the understanding of the application, and generating the "fuel" of the Configurator, a key component in the *Agilos* architecture.

References

1. J. Zinky, D. Bakken, and R. Schantz, "Architectural Support for Quality of Service for CORBA Objects," *Theory and Practice of Object Systems*, 1997. 257, 271
2. B. Stiller, C. Class, M. Waldvogel, G. Caronni, and D. Bauer, "A Flexible Middleware for Multimedia Communication: Design, Implementation, and Experience," *IEEE Journal on Selected Areas in Communications*, vol. 17, no. 9, pp. 1580–1598, September 1999. 257
3. B. Li and K. Nahrstedt, "Dynamic Reconfigurations for Complex Multimedia Applications," in *Proceedings of IEEE International Conference on Multimedia Computing and Systems*, 1999. 259
4. G. Hager and K. Toyama, "The XVision System: A General-Purpose Substrate for Portable Real-Time Vision Applications," *Computer Vision and Image Understanding*, 1997. 267
5. S. Lu, K.-W. Lee, and V. Bharghavan, "Adaptive Service in Mobile Computing Environments," in *Proceedings of 5th International Workshop on Quality of Service '97*, May 1997. 269
6. V. Bharghavan, K.-W. Lee, S. Lu, S. Ha, J. Li, and D. Dwyer, "The TIMELY Adaptive Resource Management Architecture," *IEEE Personal Communications Magazine*, 8 1998. 269
7. B. Noble, M. Satyanarayanan, D. Narayanan, J. Tilton, J. Flinn, and K. Walker, "Agile Application-Aware Adaptation for Mobility," in *Proceedings of the 16th ACM Symposium on Operating Systems and Principles*, Oct. 1997. 269
8. R. Rajkumar, C. Lee, J. Lehoczky, and D. Siewiorek, "A Resource Allocation Model for QoS Management," in *Proceedings of 18th IEEE Real-Time System Symposium*, 1997. 270
9. J. Huang, Y. Wang, and F. Cao, "On developing distributed middleware services for QoS- and criticality-based resource negotiation and adaptation," *Journal of Real-Time Systems, Special Issue on Operating System and Services*, 1998. 270
10. D. Rosu, K. Schwan, S. Yalamanchili, and R. Jha, "On Adaptive Resource Allocation for Complex Real-Time Applications," in *Proceedings of 18th IEEE Real-Time System Symposium*, 1997. 270
11. D. Schmidt, D. Levine, and S. Mungee, "The Design and Performance of Real-Time Object Requests," *Computer Communications Journal*, 1997. 271
12. S. Brandt, G. Nutt, T. Berk, and J. Mankovich, "A Dynamic Quality of Service Middleware Agent for Mediating Application Resource Usage," in *Proceedings of 19th IEEE Real-Time Systems Symposium*, Dec. 1998, pp. 307–317. 271

Structuring QoS-Supporting Services with Smart Proxies

Rainer Koster and Thorsten Kramp

Distributed Systems Group, Dept. of Computer Science
University of Kaiserslautern, P.O. Box 3049, 67653 Kaiserslautern, Germany
{koster,kramp}@informatik.uni-kl.de
http://www.uni-kl.de/AG-Nehmer/Projekte/Squirrel

Abstract. While middleware platforms have been established in best-effort environments nowadays, support for QoS-sensitive services is still found lacking. More specifically, due to the high diversity of QoS requirements, the abstractions provided for QoS-unaware services cannot be maintained and the developer has to face the difficulties of low-level networking in heterogeneous environments again. In this paper, we therefore propose the notion of *smart proxies* as an effective means for making the use of QoS-sensitive services for the client-application developer as comfortable as the use of QoS-unaware services. This is achieved without imposing restrictions on the internal mechanisms and protocols used by an QoS-sensitive service to guarantee an agreed on level of QoS. Basically, smart proxies encapsulate service-specific code which is downloaded dynamically to the client during binding establishment. The benefits of this model are discussed in general and exemplified in a case study.

1 Introduction

Today's middleware platforms such as CORBA [17], DCOM [2], and DCE [4] have emerged as key components in heterogeneous environments with best-effort requirements. For QoS-sensitive application domains, however, the abstractions provided are still insufficient at best and prohibitively unsuitable at worst. In general, middleware platforms allow developing client and server applications independently of each other, with abstract interface specifications that are written in a language-independent *interface definition language* (IDL) and represent the link between client and server programmers. Aside from the interface specification neither the client programmer needs to know how the servers used by his client are implemented nor the server programmer needs to know about the internals of the clients that will access her server. Stubs, skeletons, and communications protocols in concert, directed by the middleware core, shield the client programmer from the low-level details of heterogeneous networking. Moreover, while performance issues, additional failure modes, and restricted parameter-passing rules tell the client that a service might be remotely located, it remains unaware of the exact location of the service.

J. Sventek and G. Coulson (Eds.): Middleware 2000, LNCS 1795, pp. 273–288, 2000.
© Springer-Verlag Berlin Heidelberg 2000

This model works well for best-effort application domains, yet applications with more stringent QoS requirements are not adequately supported. In fact, considering the vast diversity of QoS requirements imposed on middleware platforms by, for example, next-generation multimedia applications or within mobile environments (Fig. 1), it is highly unlikely that a single middleware platform will meet all these requirements equally well— specifically since, besides traditional remote invocations, time-constraint messages and continuous media streams are becoming more important. The latter demand protocols with predictable latency and strictly controlled jitter while the respective mechanisms necessarily vary with the underlying network technologies. For example, with a QoS-supporting network such as ATM, bandwidth reservations can be easily mapped onto native network parameters, whereas a best-effort network requires a feedback mechanism and buffering on top to effectively control the stream according to given QoS constraints. Moreover, bandwidth limitations often enforce data compression with an appropriate codec whose choice also depends on the processing time and buffer space available at the client and the server. Consequently, CORBA, for instance, does not attempt to define a one-size-fits-all streaming protocol but only prescribes generic control and management interfaces for streams [16]. Since QoS inherently is an end-to-end issue, this leaves it to both the client *and* the server application-developers to implement the low-level protocols needed which, of course, cannot be generated automatically from an IDL description.

In this paper, we therefore propose the use of *smart proxies* as a structuring mechanism for QoS-sensitive services. Basically, any service-specific code needed at the client side is encapsulated in a smart proxy, which replaces the traditional stub and provides to the client the same high-level service-centred interface as if its remote server would be co-located with the client. This high-level interface, in turn, can be described in an IDL and may provide for high-level QoS negotiation in terms of, for example, frame rate or resolution, leaving it to the smart proxy and the server to map service-level parameters to corresponding resource requirements and low-level mechanisms. Access to a QoS-supporting service then becomes as easy for the client programmer as it is to a conventional service that does not need particular QoS provisions.

As a consequence, all low-level service-specific development efforts are shifted to the service developer, who implements both the server and its smart proxies using whatever protocol functionality and communications patterns are appropriate. Transparently to the client, different implementations may be tailored for particular environments. The service interface, however, is unaffected by the internal implementation and remains constant, shielding the client from all low-level technicalities. Of course, while the client so far can be implemented without knowing what service implementations it will connect to, all eligible proxies still must be available at the client side beforehand. We therefore propose that smart proxies are loaded dynamically from the server during binding establishment. The middleware platform downloads the smart proxy to the client machine and dynamically links its code to the client application on demand; from then on, the smart proxy handles the communication to its server.

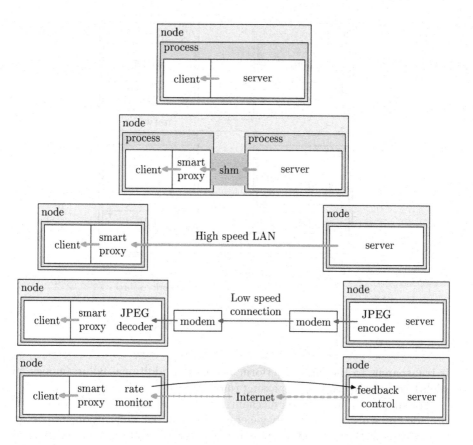

Fig. 1. Various Communication Scenarios

The remainder of this paper is structured as follows. Section 2 introduces the notion of smart proxies in more detail. Sections 3 and 4 then discuss the effects of downloading smart proxies dynamically at run time and what support is required from the middleware platform, respectively, followed, in Section 5, by a case study. Related work is summarised in Section 6 before the paper closes with conclusions and a brief outlook on future work in Section 7.

2   Smart Proxies

A *smart proxy* is service-specific code added to a client application. The client communicates with the smart proxy — and, thus, indirectly with the remote server — through a local interface as it would do with a co-located server, including QoS negotiation where appropriate. Whether the server is actually located within the client address space, on the client machine, or on a remote machine

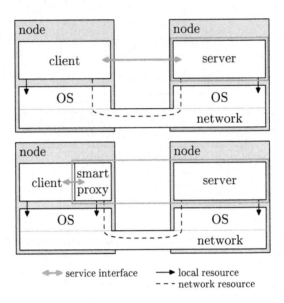

Fig. 2. Service Abstractions

is transparent to the client (performance issues, additional failure modes, and slightly restricted parameter passing rules aside).

For simple communication mechanisms, this functionality is identical to that provided by stubs automatically generated from an IDL description, as employed in CORBA or DCE, for instance. These stubs are limited to marshalling and unmarshalling of parameters, and sending requests via the standard protocols provided by their request broker. A smart proxy, in contrast, can also provide arbitrary functionality such as compression and sophisticated service-specific QoS management, although it must be developed specifically for each service instead of being automatically generated.

Since there is no one-size-fits-all protocol for applications that require particular performance optimisations or QoS functionality, it is highly unlikely that a single platform can satisfy all these requirements. In cases in which the platform's default protocol proves insufficient, client and server then need to communicate directly, that is, the low-level protocol used by the service actually becomes the service interface or at least part of it (Fig. 2). Hence, server implementations providing the same functionality but using different internal protocols essentially become different services and require different client software. This problem can be mitigated by supporting a set of protocols at both sides and choosing one in both sets during connection establishment. The CORBA telecoms specification relies on this approach for streaming by merely defining compatibility of stream endpoints [16]. The client, however, still needs to know how the internal communication works, what capabilities are provided by the server, and where the server is located.

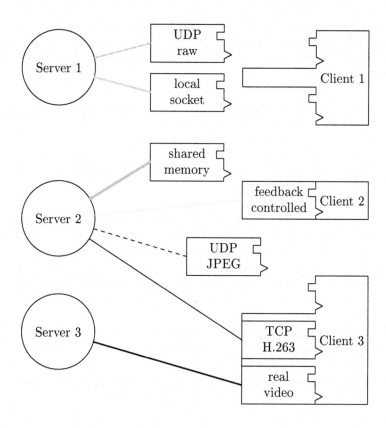

Fig. 3. Exemplified Smart Proxy Usage

By integrating and hiding complex communication mechanisms in smart proxies, the level of abstraction as provided by middleware platforms for QoS-unaware remote invocations can also be achieved for QoS-supporting services. There may be a variety of specialised server implementations and servers may provide different communication mechanisms for different connections (Fig. 3). For instance, a server could use shared memory locally, a compression mechanism and UDP across the Internet, or raw Ethernet on a dedicated LAN. In any case, the corresponding smart proxy implements the client side of the communication link, while, from the point of view of the client application, offering the same service-oriented high-level interface.

Note that the development of a smart proxy is not an additional effort. If complex functionality is required at the client and the server to appropriately handle a connection, this functionality unavoidably must be implemented manually and cannot be automatically generated from an abstract interface specification. Without smart proxies, however, the client developer as well as the service developer need to know the details of the communication protocol, whereas with smart proxies, the low-level details are hidden from the client developer and only the service developer, who is more likely to be familiar with low-level aspects of the service anyway, implements the low-level communication with the additional benefit of having both ends of the connection under control. The latter is particularly important for QoS control, which inherently is an end-to-end issue; in this case, both sides of a client/server connection must tightly cooperate to provide the negotiated level of QoS.

Consider, for instance, a video-streaming service. Its interface could include some high-level QoS parameters such as frame rate and resolution. With smart proxies the mapping of different QoS settings to low-level resource reservations and communication protocols can be handled transparently for the client developer:

1. If the underlying system supports resource reservation, the smart proxy can map these parameters to low-level resource requirements for the local node and the network connection in terms of CPU capacity and network bandwidth, for instance. Then, the smart proxy can obtain local resources and negotiate a guaranteed QoS with the server. This QoS then is reported to the client application, again in terms of high-level parameters such as frame rate and resolution.
2. If only a best-effort transport protocol is available, sophisticated feedback mechanisms are frequently used for QoS adaptation to guarantee an agreed on level of QoS. Such feedback loops, however, can be employed internally between the smart proxy and server without affecting the client application.
3. If the client and server happen to be in the same address space, no smart proxy is needed at all and the client can directly negotiate with the server what quality can be achieved with the resources available at this node. Substituting the server for the smart proxy again is transparent for the client since both share the same high-level interface.

In each of these example scenarios, the actual QoS management is hidden from the client application, whereas, without smart proxies, every client would need to handle all these cases itself. As a consequence, each client developer usually would have to implement the functionality for each connection type and server implementation himself.

Furthermore, smart proxies can also be beneficial for improving other non-functional aspects. They may, for instance, implement caching or prefetching strategies, which require service-specific knowledge about access patterns and appropriate consistency models.

Finally, service updates that affect communication protocols usually require updates of the client software as well, even if the high-level service interface is unaffected by the update. While a new service additionally can implement the old protocol, the benefits of the new features cannot be utilised in backward compatibility mode. Smart proxies, in contrast, are developed along with the server, and simply need to be replaced when updating a service without affecting the actual client application.

3   Proxy Shipping

In general, smart proxies and clients can be shipped either *statically* or *dynamically*. With the static approach, the smart proxy is somehow sent to the client developer out of band (e. g., via email) and linked with the application. Hence, all smart proxies that a client might need must be present before the service is accessed. NETSCAPE plug-ins [3], for instance, work in a similar way. While this is a more systematic approach than integrating smart-proxy functionality directly into the client software, it only partially realises the benefits of smart proxies.

Dynamic proxy shipping, in contrast, is much more flexible. The most appropriate server, and then the most appropriate smart proxy of this server can be chosen and shipped to the client during binding establishment, taking the current resource availability into account. Moreover, as long as the service interface remains stable, server updates become completely transparent to the client: the updated smart proxy is simply sent and communicates with the new server version. At the client side, only smart proxies currently in use need to be present at the client.

However, regardless how a smart proxy is shipped, in an heterogeneous environment it must be available in several versions. If a server has m different types of smart proxies supporting different types of network connections, and n types of client applications run on p platforms, the service developer effectively must implement $m \times p$ smart proxies, where p is typically small. Note that there is still a lot less effort than implementing the same functionality in $n \times m \times p$ client versions. Furthermore, since smart proxies are implemented by the service developer, often only a recompile or minor modifications are needed for different platforms. If the development is spread among the client developers, in contrast, the same functionality generally would have to be re-invented and implemented over and over again.

To implement dynamic loading of smart proxies, code must be shipped from the server to the client. One way to allow this is using a virtual machine (such as provided by Java) for running the smart proxies. In this case, proxies need to be programmed only for the virtual machine, but not for each possible client platform in an heterogeneous environment. Yet, since smart proxies are meant to perform computationally intensive tasks such as decoding video frames and dealing with real-time constraints, run-time efficiency and predictability are important issues. Although considerable effort is being spent on improving virtual machines to this respect, the current state of the art is hardly satisfactory. Hence, we have explored a different approach. Many systems allow dynamic linking of shared libraries at run time. Then, smart proxies can be built as native-code shared libraries that are sent over the network and are dynamically linked to the client. While this mechanism requires a different smart proxy version for each supported client platform, language heterogenity is achieved to a certain extent since many languages share the same object-code format (e. g., ELF shared libraries [19]) and, thus, can be linked to libraries written in another language.

Code shipping in general, however, also causes serious security risks which are far easier to control with a virtual machine that 'sandboxes' smart proxies and, thus, protects the client process from malicious operations. With native-code libraries the problem is much more difficult and requires future research. For now, the problems may be mitigated by using only trusted servers and signing smart proxies cryptographically, or restricting the use of smart proxies to security domains such as a cluster of computers.

4   Platform Support

Smart proxies as a structuring mechanism can be used without any particular support from an underlying middleware platform. Developing services as a combination of a server and smart proxies first of all is a reasonable way of building distributed services. The smart proxies define the interface to the service from a client developer's point of view and only need to be linked to clients that want to use it.

For dynamic proxy shipping, in contrast, client and server at least must be able to transmit the proxy at connection setup and link it to the client application. With Java, the virtual machine handles downloading the byte code of smart proxies and running it, whereas the use of shared libraries with a language such as C or C++ is slightly more difficult. Since the function definitions are not available at compile time of the client, functions of smart proxies must be called via function pointers. The machinery required for these indirections, however, can be generated automatically from the header file of a smart proxy for which we have developed a tool. Apart from this, there needs to be a standardized way of retrieving the smart proxy from the server. The client may open, for example, a TCP/IP connection to the server and download the smart-proxy code to a local disk prior to linking it to the application code using the operating system's default dynamic-linking facilities such as `dlopen` under Unix. We have implemented this mechanism on LINUX and extended `dlopen` to read the code to be linked directly from the network rather than from a file.

However, the functionality required for dynamically downloading and linking smart proxies should be integrated with a middleware platform to be readily available. The middleware platform then is responsible for the handling of service references and locating the respective servers as well as performing the the actual shipping and linking of smart proxies. For choosing the best-suited smart proxy for a given client, the middleware platform automatically would report the client's operating system, hardware platform, and network technology to server, possibly complemented by status information such as the current processing load. It may also be useful to establish smart-proxy repositories to keep smart proxy and server implementations consistent. Finally, a middleware platform could provide some security in loading proxies such as checking their integrity.

To this end, we are currently investigating how smart proxy support can be integrated with CORBA. The ability to access objects by value [15] provides some prerequisites for proxy shipping and allows the development of a CORBA service for this task. For continuous-media transmission, smart proxies can be built along the lines of the CORBA telecoms stream-management specification [16], which provides services with the ability to exploit protocols not directly supported by the ORB itself. To fully utilise the potential of smart proxies with respect to QoS, however, the underlying operating environment including the operating system, the networking subsystem, and the middleware platform must support some resource management. The system should at least provide mechanisms for smart proxies and servers to reserve elementary resources such as CPU cycles and memory buffers on the respective node, and to specify connection properties such as guaranteed bandwidth and maximum latency. In this context, we are currently developing an open low-level foundation for QoS-supporting middleware in combination with appropriate operating-system-level support [6,7,8,9].

5   Case Study

To demonstrate the benefits of using smart proxies, we have implemented a live-video service providing access to a camera and to be used by, for example, video-conferencing and video-surveillance clients. With this example application we can demonstrate the following important features of smart proxies:

▷ Different service implementations that use different communication mechanisms can be accessed transparently by clients through a uniform interface.
▷ Different QoS management strategies can be encapsulated in proxies.
▷ Different client applications using the same service all can utilise the set of protocols supported by the service's smart proxies without re-implementing endpoint functionality in each client.

Right now, we have not implemented the example on a middleware platform, but have used the modified **dlopen** mentioned above to prove the general feasibility of smart proxies.

The video server runs on x86 PCs with Linux 2.2 using a Hauppauge framegrabber card with a camera as the video source. Clients and smart proxies have been implemented in C++, according to the following service interface:

```
class live_video {
    public:
        void start(int frame_rate);
        void stop();
        void get_frame(char* &frame, struct timeval &when);
        void free_frame(char* frame);
        int request(int frame_rate);
};
```

Calling the **start** method initiates the transmission of video frames with a given frame rate, calling **stop** terminates the transmission. Frame data can be read by calling **get_frame** which blocks until a frame becomes available and also reports the recording time of each frame returned. Finally, frames need to be freed with `free_frame`. The only QoS parameter controlled by this simple example is the frame rate. A client can try to make a reservation for some level of QoS using the `request` method. The frame rate returned can then be guaranteed by the system with a return value of 0 indicating that only best-effort access is supported.

5.1 Various Communication Mechanisms

We have implemented smart proxies and servers for four ways of communication. A simple UDP transmission just sends the frames over the network. Since UDP is unreliable and does not preserve order, packet losses and out-of-order delivery must be handled correctly. A second proxy-server pair also uses UDP but employs JPEG compression to save network bandwidth at the expense of higher computational load. The third version uses the B_{EAT} protocol for local networks [6], which is reliable and provides some level of QoS guarantees discussed in more detail below. Finally, proxy and server can efficiently communicate via shared memory if client and server happen to be co-located on the same node. Based on information submitted by the client, the server chooses the smart proxy which most closely matches the client requirements and is compatible with the processing time and network bandwidth available.

The various performance characteristics of the different communication protocols are illustrated in Fig. 4. Transmitting video frames over an idle 10 Mbps Ethernet peaks at 8.5 fps (frames per second) for raw images and 12.8 fps for JPEG-encoded images, independently of the network protocol used. For a colocated client/server pair, finally, shared memory reaches the expected frame rate of 25 fps.

5.2 QoS Management

The B_{EAT} protocol provides deterministic network access on an Ethernet and a means for bandwidth reservation, which is used as a simple example for QoS management. When a client application requests a particular frame rate from its service, a best-effort smart proxy (i.e., one that relies on UDP) would simply return 0 to indicate that there are no guarantees available. With B_{EAT}, in contrast, a smart proxy could map the high-level parameter 'frame rate' to the low-level parameter 'bandwidth'. This mapping can be done as part of the service logic since the smart proxy knows the size of the frames used. Then, the smart proxy tries to reserve this bandwidth with the transport protocol and checks with the server what frame rate can be delivered from the video source. Finally, the frame rate that can be guaranteed by server and network is reported to the client, which is unaware of the required low-level resource reservation and mechanisms used to guarantee the frame rate.

The advantage of using a resource-reservation protocol shows when transmitting video frames in competition with a synthetically generated load of 4 Mbps (Fig 5). Plain UDP peaks at a frame rate of only 4.3 fps for raw images, whereas B_{EAT} still allows up to 6 fps for raw images and about 12 fps for JPEG encoded

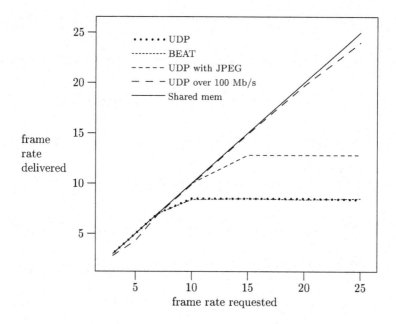

Fig. 4. Different Communication Protocols

ones. While JPEG encoding induces an additional computational load it allows to submit a reasonable frame rate even if the available network bandwidth would not allow an uncompressed transmission.

In a similar manner, reservations with RSVP or other protocols could be encapsulated. For this case study, we have also assumed that network bandwidth is the only potentially scarce resource. More elaborate smart proxy/server combinations would also control other resources on the client and the server side such as processing time or buffer space, as well as additional QoS parameters such as jitter and latency bounds.

Even if there is no support for reservations, smart proxies can improve QoS. Advanced best-effort transport protocols for continuous media typically employ some feedback mechanism to adjust the send rate of the server to the resources actually available [1,18]. The client-side code required for these features again can be provided by smart proxies without modifying the client.

5.3   Proxy Reuse for Several Clients

As one example for the versatility of our smart proxies, we have used the live-video service twice in our teleconferencing clients. A local server shows the picture of the person running the client while a remote server shows the person he or she is talking to. The client accesses both servers in the same way, relying on the smart proxies to take care of finding the best way of transmitting the video frames.

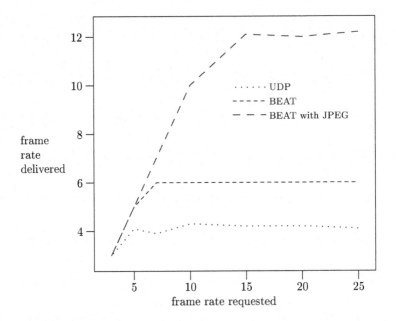

Fig. 5. Reservation with Smart Proxies

Furthermore, we have implemented a surveillance tool re-using the live-video server and its smart proxies. This tool connects to a remote video service and compares adjacent frames, raising an alarm when the picture changes. Regardless of what type of connection is best, the same service as for the teleconferencing can be used. Without smart proxies, all client-side functionality for the respective connection types would have been to be re-implemented. Even for this rather rudimentary example this would have resulted in a considerable effort in developing each client.

6   Related Work

The notion of smart proxies is most closely related to the work on *fragmented* or *distributed objects* as proposed by Makpangou et al. [12] and, more recently, within the GLOBE [20,21] and ASPECTIX [5] projects. The fundamental idea is to allow objects to be physically distributed and to consist of fragments at several nodes; distribution and communication between fragments are hidden from other (client) objects.

GLOBE is a middleware platform that employs distributed objects to provide scalability to wide-area distributed applications such as replication and caching for web documents. Middleware services are used to locate and download fragments, through which the object is accessed. The ASPECTIX project, in contrast, while also being based on distributed objects, is focussed on enhanced

QoS support, extending CORBA by support for mobile and reconfigurable object fragments.

Smart proxies can be seen as a particular way of using distributed objects and represent a simpler and more elementary model. In contrast to the symmetric model of fragments in a distributed object, however, smart proxies and servers have distinct roles. This approach is more similar to the familiar client and server model and, hence, may be more easily adopted by programmers than the development of servers as distributed objects. In addition, less platform support is needed. For instance, proxies do not have persistent state, are selected by the server, and need not be located independently of the server. Moreover, while we try to provide QoS support for applications such as continuous media streaming services, GLOBE focusses on scalability. It is not obvious, for instance, whether complex transmission mechanisms such as compression or feedback can easily be integrated with GLOBE's object fragments.

The QuO architecture [11,22] takes a different approach to hiding QoS management issues from the client application. Separately from the IDL defining the functional interface of an object, QoS parameters and adaptive behaviour are specified by QuO description languages. From these QDL so called delegates are generated and linked to the client application in a similar way as stubs are generated from the IDL. Hence, the delegates are basically a kind of statically shipped smart proxies. Compared to our approach, on the one hand, the QuO architecture and the automatic code generation facilitate integration of functionality such as resource reservation, QoS monitoring, and adaptation. On the other hand, complex delegate functionality not provided by the platform can only be added to the QDL as source code in the implementation languages of the clients, when the service interface is designed.

Within a more narrow context, the concept of embedding service-specific code within client applications has also been explored by Yoshikawa et al. with so-called *smart clients* [24]. These smart clients were primarily used to implement caching and prefetching as a means for increasing the scalability of Internet services in terms of performance, load balancing, and fault tolerance. Of course, these tasks can also be encapsulated in smart proxies.

Proxies are also an important concept in Sun's JINI environment [13,23], in which services are defined in terms of Java interfaces. To access a service, a lookup service returns sort of a smart proxy to the client that communicates with the server. JINI mainly uses this mechanism to allow devices and services to be dynamically added to and removed from the system. Of course, it also allows server and proxy to choose their own protocol for communicating with each other. Since JINI is based on Java, it inherits the advantages of security, ease of code shipping, and platform independence, as well as the drawbacks of being restricted to one language and the potential performance penalties and unpredictability of a virtual machine.

Furthermore, there are several ongoing efforts to develop QoS supporting middleware platforms in general and to improve real-time and QoS properties of CORBA in particular. Specifically related to QoS for continuous-media transmission are implementations of the CORBA telecoms specification [16] such as the audio/video streaming service built on top of TAO [14]. Work on configurable middleware platforms, finally, is related to our work since these platforms open a wider range of infrastructural support to smart proxies. TAO's pluggable protocol framework [10] is only one example of ongoing efforts in this context.

7   Conclusions

In this paper we have introduced the notion of smart proxies as an effective means for structuring QoS-sensitive services. The benefits of this approach are threefold. Firstly, service-specific client code is separated from the client application-code and encapsulated in self-contained modules. This leads to a clear separation of functionality as a prerequisite for dynamically substituting modules that adhere to the same high-level interface. Secondly, all low-level service-specific development efforts are shifted to the service developer, while the client developer merely interacts with a high-level interface in the same way as he does with QoS-unaware services. As a consequence, instead of developing low-level client-side functionality over and over again for each client application anew, with smart proxies this functionality is only developed once by the service developer who knows the internals of his service best anyway. Thirdly, dynamic shipping of smart proxies allows for the seamless introduction of improved service functionality or completely new service implementations without requiring modifications of the client applications. Only the functionality actually used must be available at the client.

To demonstrate the viability of smart proxies, we have implemented a video service that supports a small range of different communication protocols, namely unreliable UDP with and without compression, $B_{E\!A\!T}$ with explicit resource reservation, and shared memory for co-located client and servers. The video service is used both in a video-conferencing tool and a video-surveillance tool which only interact with the high-level interface of the video service. The use of smart proxies for low-level networking significantly reduced the development of both services and both services automatically would benefit from adding another smart proxy implementing, for example, a feedback loop over UDP.

As part of our future work we will integrate smart proxies with CORBA, making use of and possibly expanding on the recent *objects-by-value* specification. Furthermore, support for smart proxies will be integrated with our own QoS-supporting middleware under development [6,7,8,9].

Acknowledgements

We are indebted to Marcus Demker for implementing parts of the case study. Moreover, we thank the anonymous reviewers for their helpful comments.

References

1. S. Cen, C. Pu, R. Staehli, C. Cowan, and J. Walpole. A distributed real-time mpeg video audio player. In *Proceedings of the Fifth International Workshop on Network and Operating Systems Support for Digital Audio and Video*, volume 1018 of *Lecture Notes in Computer Science*, pages 142–153. Springer Verlag, April 1995. 283

2. Microsoft Corp. *Distributed Component Object Model Protocol*, 1998. 273

3. Netscape Communications Corporation. Plug-in guide. http://developer.netscape.com/docs/manuals/communicator/plugin/index.htm, January 1998. 279

4. The Open Group. *Introduction to OSF DCE 1.2.2*, November 1997. 273

5. F. Hauck, U. Becker, M. Geier, E. Meier, U. Rastofer, and M. Steckermeier. AspectIX, an aspect-oriented and CORBA-compliant ORB architecture. Technical Report TR-I4-98-08, Friedrich-Alexander-University, Erlangen-Nürnberg, September 1988. 284

6. R. Koster. Design of a real-time communication service for local-area networks. Diplom thesis, Department of Computer Science, University of Kaiserslautern, May 1998. 281, 282, 286

7. T. Kramp and G. Coulson. The design of a flexible communications framework for next-generation middleware. Technical Report SFB 501 12/99 and MPG-99-25, Dept. of Computer Science, University of Kaiserslautern, and Dept. of Computing, Lancaster University, 1999. 281, 286

8. T. Kramp and R. Koster. A service-centred approach to QoS-supporting middleware. Work-in-Progress Paper presented at *Middleware '98 (IFIP International Conference on Distributed Systems Platforms and Open Distributed Processing)*, September 1998. 281, 286

9. T. Kramp and R. Koster. Flexible event-based threading for QoS-supporting middleware. In *Proceedings of the Second International Working Conference on Distributed Applications and Interoperable Systems (DAIS)*. IFIP, July 1999. 281, 286

10. F. Kuhns, C. O'Ryan, D. C. Schmidt, O. Othman, and J. Parsons. The design and performance of a pluggable protocols framework for object request broker middleware. In *Proceedings of the sixth IFIP International Workshop on Protocols for High-Speed Networks (PfHSN)*, August 1999. 286

11. J. P. Loyall, D. E. Bakken, R. E. Schantz, J. A. Zinky, D. A. Karr, R. Vanegas, and K. R. Anderson. QoS aspect languages and their runtime integration. In *Proceedings of the Fourth Workshop on Languages, Compilers, and Run-time Systems for Scalable Computers (LCR98)*, volume 1511 of *Lecture Notes in Computer Science*. Springer Verlag, May 1998. 285

12. M. Makpangou, Y. Gourhant, J.-P. Le Narzul, and M. Shapiro. Fragmented objects for distributed abstractions. In T. L. Casavant and M. Singhal, editors, *Readings in Distributed Computing Systems*, pages 170–186. IEEE Computer Society Press, July 1994. 284

13. Sun Microsystems. Jini architectural overview, 1999. Technical White Paper. 285

14. S. Mungee, N. Surendran, and D. C. Schmidt. The design and performance of a CORBA audio/video streaming service. In *HICSS-32 International Conference on System Sciences, minitrack on Multimedia DBMS and WWW*, January 1999. 286

15. OMG. CORBA objects by value. http://www.omg.org/cgi-bin/doc?orbos/98-01-18, 1998. orbos/98-01-18. 280

16. OMG. CORBA telecoms specification. http://www.omg.org/corba/ctfull.html, June 1998. formal/98-07-12. 274, 276, 281, 286

17. OMG. *The Common Object Request Broker: Architecture and Specification (Release 2.2)*, February 1998. 273

18. L. A. Rowe and B. C. Smith. A continuous media player. In *Proceedings of the third International Workshop on Network and Operating Systems Support for Digital Audio and Video*, volume 712 of *Lecture Notes in Computer Science*, pages 376–386. Springer Verlag, November 1992. 283

19. SunSoft. SunOS 5.3 Linker and Libraries Manual, 1993. 279

20. M. van Steen, P. Homburg, and A. S. Tanenbaum. Globe: A wide-area distributed system. *IEEE Concurrency*, pages 70–78, January-March 1999. 284

21. M. van Steen, A. S. Tanenbaum, I. Kuz, and H. J. Sips. A scalable middleware solution for advanced wide-area web services. In *Proceedings of Middleware '98 (IFIP International Conference on Distributed Systems Platforms and Open Distributed Processing)*, pages 37–53. Springer Verlag, September 1998. 284

22. R. Vanegas, J. A. Zinky, J. P. Loyall, D. A. Karr, R. E. Schantz, and D. E. Bakken. QuO's runtime support for quality of service in distributed objects. In *Proceedings of the IFIP International Conference on Distributed Systems Platforms and Open Distributed Processing (Middleware'98)*. Springer Verlag, September 1998. 285

23. J. Waldo. The Jini architecture for network-centered computing. *Communications of the ACM*, 42(7):76–82, July 1999. 285

24. C. Yoshikawa, B. Chun, P. Eastham, A. Vahdat, T. Anderson, and D. Culler. Using smart clients to build scalable services. In *Proceedings of the USENIX 1997 Annual Technical Conference*, January 1997. 285

Trading and Negotiating Stream Bindings

H. O. Rafaelsen[1] and F. Eliassen[2]

[1]University of Tromsø
Dept of Computer Science, 9037 Tromsø, Norway
`hansr@cs.uit.no`
[2]University of Oslo, Dept of Informatics,
P.O.Box 1080, 0316 Oslo, Norway
`frank@ifi.uit.no`

Abstract. Distributed multimedia information systems require a range of different interaction styles ranging from simple remote operation interaction to complex patterns of interaction involving both discrete and continuous data. The standardized reference model for Open Distributed Processing (ODP) defines a binding model that encapsulates different interaction styles within explicit binding objects. In this paper we discuss mechanisms for selecting and negotiating appropriate explicit stream bindings as required by the application. We describe the notion of explicit bindings and introduce the idea of using a trading-like facility for selecting potential binding types. We show how an earlier proposed type model for stream interfaces can be used as a basis for binding type selection, and extended to support automatic negotiation of binding properties.

1 Introduction

The notion of stream interface has been proposed as the preferred means to convey media streams in distributed multimedia systems [3]. A stream interface consists of a collection of source and/or sink media flows. The act of stream binding establishes a logical association between compatible stream interfaces for the purpose of exchanging continuous flows as dictated by the type and direction of the flows. During binding interfaces to be bound must be type-checked for compatibility. Informally, type-checking means ensuring that the properties of each source flow are as expected by the corresponding sink flow.

In the reference model for Open Distributed Processing (RM-ODP) stream bindings are explicit. This supports direct client control of the binding during its lifetime. Furthermore, bindings are first class objects and are created, managed and invoked in the same way as other objects [1]. The result of the binding action is a control interface through which the binding object can be controlled. In figure 1, the binding model is illustrated where a binding object connects four interfaces by means of local bindings that associate the interfaces of the objects with the interfaces of the binding object.

J. Sventek and G. Coulson (Eds.): Middleware 2000, LNCS 1795, pp. 289-307, 2000.

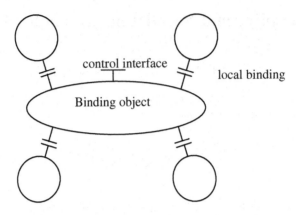

Fig. 1. The explicit binding model

Depending on the type of the binding object, new interfaces can be added to the binding, and existing ones can be removed. After a new (stream) interface has been added to the binding, it can be locally bound to a suitable application (stream) interface. Hence, for example, binding objects of the appropriate type can describe dynamic groups in which membership can change during the lifetime of the binding. The main rationale for explicit bindings is to support QoS management in terms of QoS specification, monitoring and control [1]. For example, the binding control interface of a stream binding can be used to control and monitor the QoS of ongoing streams.

A binding type (or template) defines a particular class of binding objects by identifying the type of interfaces which can participate in the binding, the roles they play, and the way behaviour at the various binding interfaces are linked [9]. For example, a multicast video binding would typically support a producer role and a consumer role. In some cases the binding will support operations for adding interfaces to a binding in a named role (e.g. a new multicast receiver), and for removing interfaces from the binding (e.g. remove a multicast receiver from the binding).

Binding factories are objects that create bindings. In our model, a binding factory is associated to a binding type such that by invoking the factory object's `create` method, a new binding of the associated type is created.

Through the local bindings the binding object receives and delivers information for binding participants according to the causality and type of the bound interfaces. Type checking as explained above, is applied when creating the binding and when adding a new interface to the binding. When creating the binding, type information about the application object interfaces to be initially bound and the corresponding roles they will fulfill in the binding, is provided as parameters of the `create` method call. Corresponding interfaces with the appropriate roles are as a result added to the binding. If an application object interface α is offered to fulfil a role β, then the type of α must be compatible with the type of β.

In this paper we present an approach for applications to select binding types and associated binding factories according to their needs based on a trading model. In this scheme a set of binding factories are located based on a specification of the required properties of the binding. The located set of binding factories are all capable of instantiating binding objects with properties conforming to those specified by the trading client. Furthermore, in those cases where binding objects specify alternative stream behaviour (e.g. alternative encodings, resolutions, or frame rates) at its supported interfaces, we also show how the notion *of policy specification* supports automatic negotiation to choose the actual stream interface behaviour to be used.

In general terms, a trading facility as indicated above, supports the reuse of binding factories. More specifically, it will allow evolution of supported binding types in a distributed computing environment without sacrificing support of existing applications. This can be ensured by requiring that a new version of a binding type must *conform* to the older version. Run time trading of binding types is also required for multimedia databases. In this case the required properties of the binding to be used to present a query result are generally not statically known, but rather depends on the specifics of each query [18].

The remainder of the paper is organized as follows. In section 2, we offer an overview of the model of bindings and streams that we base our work on. Following that, in section 3 we present a trading model for selecting binding types from binding type requirement specifications and introduces a simple middleware architecture illustrating the application of a binding type trader. Section 4 presents our approach to automatic negotiation of binding properties for those cases where binding objects specify alternative behaviour at its supported interfaces. In section 5 we discuss some related work while section 6 concludes with an outlook to further work.

2   Model of Bindings and Streams (MBS)

For the explicit binding and stream abstractions, we have developed a generic model called MBS (Model of Bindings and Streams). MBS will constitute a part of the foundation for the programming model of an adaptive multimedia ORB called MULTE-ORB [15]. The engineering of MULTE-ORB is based on the flexible protocol system Da CaPo [17]. MBS is based on a proposed generic type model for stream flows and associated type checking rules earlier proposed in [6]. This model is open-ended and can in principle support any set of flow parameters. It also includes compatibility rules ensuring the correctness of binding attempts of flow endpoints, and conformance rules expressing conditions for substitutability [7]. An implementation of the flow type model and examples of its application are described in [8].

2.1   Flow Type Model

In the flow type model a flow type is specified by indicating the media type of the flow such as audio or video, its causality (source or sink), and a set of quality attributes such as rate and resolution. Furthermore, an attribute value is specified as a set of "atomic" values. This will in general enhance the chances of successful binding.

For example when a sink flow type specifies a set of different names on the video encoding attribute, it actually declares that it can accept flows where the video can have any of the indicated formats.

The following example of an H.261 video flow type features optional playback rates.

```
flow videoPhone {
    video V {encoding:H.261, rate:2..24)};
    audio A {encoding:PCM, rate:{8000,16000}};
    constraint (V & A) | A };
```

This specification states that a VideoPhone flow consists of two different element types labeled V and A respectively. Each element type includes a declaration of the generic media type such as Video or Audio, and a specific set of attributes, referred to as a media descriptor, specifying quality properties of the element type. The expression (V & A) | A is referred to as the structural constraints of the flow [8]. It specifies legal configurations of flow elements that may occur in an instance of the flow. The above structural constraint indicates that an instance of a flow can consist of video and audio elements, or audio elements only. Hence, we may think of the specification as modeling an adaptable flow endpoint.

A flow type specification is interpreted as a set of potential flow qualities (QI) and flow configurations (SI) that can be produced by a source flow endpoint or is acceptable to a sink flow endpoint. This interpretation of a flow type allows us to define a variety of flow type relationships based on set theory. The quality interpretation of a flow type is defined as the combination of the interpretation I of each of its element types (for further details see e.g. [6]).

Flow quality subtype relationship. A flow type M is a *subtype* of the flow type N if both the quality and structural interpretation of M is a subset of the corresponding interpretations of N. Suppose A, B and C, D are element types of flows M and N, respectively. We derive that $M = \text{Flow}[A;B]$ is a *strict quality subtype* of $N = \text{Flow}[C;D]$, denoted $M <_q N$, if $I(A) \subseteq I(C)$ and $I(B) \subseteq I(D)$. On the other hand, a *relaxed quality subtype* may support fewer element types than the super type such that, for example, $M = \text{Flow}[A]$ is a relaxed quality subtype of $N = \text{Flow}[B;C]$, denoted $M <\sim_q N$, when $I(A) \subseteq I(B)$.

Flow structure subtype relationship. A flow type M is a *structural subtype* of N denoted $M <_s N$, if $SI(M) \subseteq SI(N)$. This means that the subtype supports a sub-set of the configurations supported by the supertype. Suppose b & c is the structural constraint of M and (a | b) & c is the structural constraint of N. The $SI(M) = \{\{b,c\}\}$ and $SI(N) = \{\{a,c\},\{b,c\}\}$. Clearly we have $SI(M) \subseteq SI(N)$.

Flow quality compatibility relationship. Compatibility is determined by computing the set of common flow qualities and configurations supported by the two endpoints. Compatibility requires that this set is not empty. If the two endpoints can support more than one common flow quality and flow configuration, a flow property negotiation protocol may be employed to choose the actual flow quality to be used. Our approach for type checking binding attempts is to require that the source and the sink can at least support one common flow quality. This relationship we refer to as quality compatibility. Informally, two flow types are strict quality compatible (denoted $<>_q$) if there exist a bijection between their respective sets of element types such that each pair in the bijection have non-empty set intersection of their respective interpretations. We may for example conclude that `Flow[A;B]` $<>_q$ `Flow[C;D]` if $I(A) \cap I(C) \neq \varnothing$ and $I(B) \cap I(D) \neq \varnothing$. Two flow types M and N are relaxed flow quality compatible (denoted $<\sim>_q$) if there exist a bijection between subsets of their respective element types such that each pair in the bijection is compatible. Thus if $I(A) \cap I(C) \neq \varnothing$, `Flow[A;B]` $<\sim>_q$ `Flow[C;D]` even if B and D are incompatible, i.e. $I(B) \cap I(D) = \varnothing$.

Flow structure compatibility relationship. Two flows of type M and N are structural compatible, denoted M $<>_s$ N, if their structural interpretations have non-empty intersection. This means that they support a least one common flow configuration. Suppose $(a \mid d) \& c$ is the structural constraint of M and $(a \mid b) \& c$ is the structural constraint of N. Then $SI(M) = \{\{a,c\},\{d,c\}\}$ and $SI(N) = \{\{a,c\},\{b,c\}\}$. Clearly we have $SI(M) \cap SI(N) \neq \varnothing$.

Different variants of the compatibility relationship where some variants are weaker than others, are the following:
i)   fully strict compatible, if M $<>_q$ N and M $<_s$ N.
ii)   partially strict compatible, if M $<>_q$ N and M $<>_s$ N.
iii) fully relaxed compatible, if M $<\sim>_q$ N and M $<_s$ N.
iv)   partially relaxed compatible, if M $<\sim>_q$ N and M $<>_s$ N

For example, fully strict compatible is a stronger relationship than partially strict compatible in the sense that the former logically implies the latter. These different kinds of compatibility can be used by applications to state their requirement to the degree of *matching* that must be fulfilled when an application object interface is locally bound to a corresponding interface provided by the binding object.

2.2   Stream Type Model

In [6] a stream interface is simply specified as a collection of flows. In MBS we extend this specification by adding the notion of configuration constraint which is a specification of alternative combinations of flows that may be configured in a stream binding. For example, a stream interface modeling an access point to a video conference provider, may exploit this feature to express the alternative audio and video flow configurations and qualities that can be supported.

A stream configuration constraint is written as a structural constraint over flow labels. The set of alternative configurations of flows of a stream interface is referred to as its structural interpretation SI.

Stream compatibility relationship. Two stream interfaces **S** and **T** are *compatible*, denoted **S** $<>$ **T**, if **S** and **T** have a common configuration of flows and there exist a bijection between the set of flows in these configurations of **S** and **T** such that for each pair of flows in the bijection, the pair is compatible. The kind of compatibility required we assume is specified by the application. Consider, for example, the following stream interface type of a video conference binding type

```
stream videoConfProducer {
   sink flow a {
      audio a1 {encoding:PCMA,
            rate:{8000,16000}};};
   sink flow v {
         v1: Video[encoding:H.261,
            rate:(2..24)};};
   constraint a|(a&v) }; //end stream
```

and the interface type `audioTalk` offered by a potential participant of the binding

```
stream audioTalk {
   source flow a {
      audio a1 {encoding:{PCMA,GSM},
         rate: 8000 }; }; //end flow
   constraint a }; //end stream
```

The absence of a flow configuration constraint means that all element types of the flow are required. The above interface types are compatible because they have a common configuration {{a}} where the label a refers the audio flow in both stream interfaces, and the two audio flows are compatible. By closer inspection it can be seen that the audio flow of `audioTalk` is fully strict compatible to the audio flow of `videoConfProducer`.

Stream conformance relationship. The MBS *conformance rules* express conditions for substitutability of stream interfaces. If the stream interface **T** *conforms* to the stream interface **S**, then **S** may be replaced transparently by **T**. A stream interface **T** conforms to a stream interface **S** if and only if $SI(S) \subseteq SI(T)$ and for each stream configuration of **T** that is also a stream configuration of **S** there exists a bijection between the set of flows in the two configurations such that for each pair in the bijection the flow of **S** is a subtype of the flow of **T**.

The kind of flow subtype relationship required is subject to application policy. For example, when trading for binding types, the client of the trader must specify the required relationship as a parameter to the `look_up` method of the trader.

The following example illustrates a case where a video source `mpgSource` is upgraded to support additional playback rates, video encodings and audio, all encapsulated in the stream interface `mpg_mjpgSource` such that `mpg_mjpgSource` conforms to `mpgSource`.

```
stream mpgSource {
   source flow mpgFlow {
      video h {encoding:mpeg,rate:{20,25};}; };
   constraint mpgFlow }; //end stream

stream mpg_mjpgSource {
   source flow  mpgFlow {
      video h {encoding:mpeg,rate:{20,25,30};};};
   source flow  mjpgFlow {
      video hj {encoding:mjpeg,rate:{20,25,30};};
      audio au {encoding:{PCMA,GSM},rate:8000};};
   constraint mpgFlow | mjpgFlow }; //end stream
```

The stream interface `mpg_mjpgSource` conforms to `mpgSource` because the structural interpretation of `mpgSource` (which is{{mpgFlow}}) is a subset of the

structural   interpretation   of   `mpg_mjpgSource`   (which   is
$\{\{$`mpgFlow`$\},\{$`mjpgFlow`$\}\}$), and the video flow labeled `mpgFlow` in the stream
interface `mpgSource` is a (strict) flow subtype of the video flow labeled `mpgFlow`
in the stream interface `mpg_mjpgSource`.

2.3   Binding Types

Our approach for specifying binding types is similar to the RIVUS template language
[9], the main difference being that binding requirements are specified using the stream
flow type model referred to above.

A binding type is defined as a 5-tuple $\langle T,P,M,\Delta,E \rangle$ where T denotes a set of role
types, P a set of roles, M a set role matching requirements (one for each role), Δ a set
of role causalities, and E a set of role cardinality requirements.

A *role type* τ is defined as a set of stream interface types, i.e. $\tau = \{T_1, ..., T_n\}$. A *role*
defines binding object roles and is specified as a role name and a role type, $r : \tau$. For
example, a video conference binding type could define the roles `talk` and `listen`
where the role `talk` could be of the role type $\{$`videoConfProducer`$\}$.

Role matching requirements apply to local bindings and specify for each role of the
binding type the kind of type matching required when an interface is offered to fulfil
the role. The kind of matching that can be specified is either a subtype or a
compatibility relationship. Thus we model role matching requirements as a set of pairs
$\{<r_1, m_1>, ..., <r_n, m_n>\}$ where r_i is a role name an m_i is a match kind.

A binding type may support several instances of each role. Binding behaviour
defines *causalities* between instances of roles. We model role causality as a tuple
$<C, r_1, r_2, m>$ where C specifies a causality option, r_1 and r_2 are roles, and m specifies
whether conversion between r_1 and r_2 is supported by the binding. Conversion is
supported if $m=$`conv`, otherwise $m=$`no_conv`. Conversion is required if the roles r_1
and r_2 have incompatible roles types. Conversion may be required in those cases
where alternative behaviour is specified at the corresponding interfaces (e.g.
alternative encodings) and the behaviour of r_1 is allowed to be incompatible with the
behaviour of r_2 as a result of local binding negotiation. For example, suppose the type
of r_1 and r_2 is both `video`, and the type `video` specifies a flow with the two
alternative encodings `mpeg` and `mjpeg`. If during local binding of r_1 to an
application object interface a configuration with `mpeg` is negotiated, and during local
binding of r_2 to another application object interface a configuration with `mjpeg` is
negotiated, then a conversion between `mpeg` and `mjpeg` is needed. This might, for
example, be realized as a suitable transcoder running within an active network.

As in [9] we define three options for how roles can be mapped together. Specifying
$<$`ONE-ONE`$, r_1, r_2, m>$ means that the binding object creates a one to one mapping
between a single instance of role r_1 and a single instance of role r_2, while $<$`ONE-`
`MANY`$, r_1, r_2, m>$ means that the binding object creates a one to many mapping
between a single instance of role r_1 and all instances of role r_2. Finally, $<$`MANY-`
`MANY`$, r_1, r_2, m>$ means that the binding object creates a mapping between all
instances of role r_1 and r_2.

Role cardinality is a specification of the number of instances of a particular role the binding object can support [9]. It is modeled as a pair `<r,i>` where `r` is a role and `i` is a range where the minimum value states the number of instances of the role that is needed for the binding object to make sense, while the maximum states the largest number of instances of the role the binding object is willing to support. An example is the specification `<talk,2..10>`.

Example: The following is an example of a specification of a binding type supporting audio/video conferencing. We will later refer to this specification by the name AVConf. The specification defines two role types AVConfProducer={AVTalk} and AVConfConsumer={AVListen} where

```
stream  AVTalk =   {
        sink flow  a {
            audio a1  {encoding:{PCMA,GSM};
                       rate:{8000,16000};};};
        sink flow v {
            video v1 {encoding:H.261;
                      rate:(2..24);};
        constraint a|(a&v) }; //end stream

stream AVListen {
        source flow a {
            audio a1 {encoding:{PCMA,GSM};
                      rate:{8000,16000};};};
        source flow  v {
            video v1 {encoding:H.261;
        constraint a|(a&v) }; //end stream
```

Note that the causalities of the flows are specified as they are provided by the binding. This means that a source flow of an audio conference participant (a talker) must locally bind to a corresponding sink flow offered by the binding (in this case to the flows of AVTalk)

The binding roles of the specification are

```
gen : AVConfProducer
rcv : AVConfConsumer
```

The role matching requirements are

```
<gen,fully_strict_compatible>
<rcv,fully_strict_compatible>,
```

while the role causality requirement of the binding type offer is

```
<MANY-MANY,gen,rcv,conv>,
```

and the role cardinality requirements are `<gen,2..20>` and `<rcv,2..20>`.

3   Trading Binding Types

In this section we present a trading model for selecting binding types from binding type requirement specifications. The trading model is based on the notion conformance between binding types.

3.1   Binding Type Conformance

An application selects a binding type by stating *binding type requirements* to a trader that compares the requirements to *binding type offers*. A binding type requirement specification is with one exception only, identical to a definition of a binding type as outlined above, while a binding type offer is simply a binding type specification. Selection is based on a conformance relationship between binding type requirements and binding type offers. The result of the selection is the identification of a set of binding factories that are all capable of instantiating binding objects with properties conforming to those specified by the client. A conformance relationship for binding types must be based on conformance of stream interfaces and notions of role matching, role causality, and role cardinality satisfaction.

While a role matching requirement of a binding type offer is specified as a pair $<r, m>$, the role matching requirement of a binding type requirement is specified as a triple $<r, m, \sigma>$ where σ indicates whether a stricter role matching requirement than m is acceptable (σ=narrow) or not (σ=no_narrow). It is easy to show that strict subtype logically implies ($\Rightarrow$) all other match kinds, relaxed subtype logically implies fully and partially relaxed compatibility, full compatibility logically implies partial compatibility, and strict compatibility logically implies relaxed compatibility. Thus, $<r, \texttt{full\_compatibility}>$ satisfies $<r, \texttt{relaxed\_compatibility}, \texttt{narrow}>$.

Definition 1 (*role matching satisfaction*) A role matching requirement $<r_1, m_1>$ of a binding type offer, satisfies a role matching requirement $<r_2, m_2, \sigma>$ of a binding type requirement if and only if $m_1 = m_2$, or $\sigma = \texttt{narrow}$ and $m_1 \Rightarrow m_2$. $\square$

Definition 2 (*role causality satisfaction*) A role causality $<C, r_1, r_2, m>$ is satisfied by a role causality $<C', s_1, s_2, n>$ if and only if $C = C'$, s_1 conforms to r_1, s_2 conforms to r_2, and if $m \neq n$, then $n = \texttt{conv}$. $\square$

Definition 3 (*role type conformance*) A role type $\tau = \{T_1, ..., T_n\}$ conforms to a role type $\sigma = \{S_1, ..., S_n\}$ if and only if there exists a bijection β between τ and σ such that for all $(T_i, S_j) \in \beta$, T_i conforms to S_j. $\square$

Definition 4 (*binding type conformance*) A binding type offer $B_1 = \langle T_1, P_1, M_1, \Delta_1, E_1 \rangle$ conforms to a binding type requirement $B_2 = \langle T_2, P_2, M_2, \Delta_2, E_2 \rangle$ if and only if there exists a bijection β between the sets of role causalities Δ_1 and Δ_2 such that for all $(\delta, \varepsilon) \in \beta$ with $\delta = <C_1, r_1, s_1, m_1>$ and $\varepsilon = <C_2, r_2, s_2, m_2>$, δ satisfies ε, and the role cardinality requirements $<r_1, i_1>$ and $<s_1, j_1>$ in E_1 satisfies the corresponding role cardinality requirements $<r_2, i_2>$ and $<s_2, j_2>$ in E_2 such that $i_2 \subseteq i_1$ and $j_2 \subseteq j_1$, and the role matching requirements $<r_1, m_1>$ and $<s_1, n_1>$ in M_1 satisfies the corresponding role matching requirements $<r_2, m_2, \sigma_2>$ and $<s_2, n_2, \mu_2>$ in M_2. $\square$

The kind of binding type conformance described above may be characterized as *structural* since conformance largely is determined by comparing the syntactic structure of binding type specifications (although for flows, attribute values are also compared). The analogy to this approach in the world of operational interfaces is signature matching [20]. A drawback of pure signature matching is that we might get false positives since semantics is not taken into account. This can be compensated in the case of stream bindings by "standardizing" the names of generic element types and their attributes. This is the approach taken, for example, by the Internet Engineering Task Force on a real time transport protocol [23] in which profiles standardize sets of attributes for certain media types and specific payload types such as audio and video encodings, are assigned unique names by an appropriate Internet authority.

3.2   Example

The following is a simple specification of a binding type requirement for an audio conference binding. We will later refer to this binding type by the name audioConf. We define two role types audioConfProducer={audioTalk} and audioConfConsumer= {audioListen} where

```
stream  audioTalk {
        sink flow a {
          audio a1 {encoding:{PCMA};rate: 8000};};
        constraint a }; //end stream

stream audioListen {
        source flow a {
          audio a1 {encoding:{PCMA};rate: 8000};};
        constraint a }; //end stream
```

The corresponding binding roles are

```
talk : audioConfProducer
listen : audioConfConsumer
```

The role matching requirements are

```
   <talk,partially_relaxed,narrow>
   <listen,partially_relaxed,narrow>,
```

while the role causality required by the audio conference application is

```
   <MANY-MANY,talk,listen,no_conv>,
```

and the role cardinality requirements are <talk,2..6> and <listen,2..6>.

Taken as a binding type offer, it is easy to show that the binding type specification referred to as AVConf in section 2.3, satisfies the above binding type requirement AudioConf according to definition 4. We basically need to show that the role causality requirements of the binding type offer, <MANY-MANY,gen,rcv,conv>, satisfies the role causality requirements of the binding type requirement, <MANY-MANY,talk,listen,conv>, and that role cardinality and role matching requirements of corresponding roles are satisfied.

3.3   Architecture of Trading Binding Types

Architecturally a binding trader can be considered as an object service of middleware platforms. The basic idea is that developers of binding factories register their implementations at the binding trader. The information that must be registered includes a specification of the binding type offer together with information on how to activate the corresponding binding factory.

An application may interrogate the trader to inquire about binding factories that may create bindings satisfying the requirements of the application. For example, a multimedia database may automatically generate the specification of the binding type requirement based on meta-data describing the result of the query and QoS requirements of the corresponding database clients [18]. Parameters of the inquire operation to the trader must include a specification of a binding type requirement.

The result of the inquire operation will typically be a reference to (the service interface of) a binding factory that is capable of instantiating bindings with properties conforming to the specified requirements. The application may now call the `create` method of the binding factory. Parameters of the method call include specifications of the interfaces to be bound, and the roles in which the interfaces are offered by the application. Upon completing the execution of the method, the binding factory returns a reference to the control interface of the binding.

3.4   Trader Implementation Issues

The main challenge of our approach is its computational complexity. Although a full implementation of a binding trader has not been made yet, some earlier results might indicate its complexity. In [8] is presented an algorithm that determines compatibility and subtype relationships between flows. The algorithm has polynomial complexity in the number of element types of a flow. On a Sun Ultra 2 workstation running Solaris 2.5.1 the execution time is demonstrated to be in the order of 1 ms to determine the presence of a flow type relationship for flow types with 5 element types or less, while flow types with 30 element types require about 50 ms execution time. It is expected, though, that flow types with more than 5 element types will not be very common.

Determining binding type conformance means matching $r \times s$ binding roles for "correspondence" where r and s are the number of different role types in each binding type. For each pair of role types to be compared, $m \times n$ flow types need to be compared for some flow type relationship where m and n are the number of flows in each stream interface. In an attempt to estimate the required execution time on the Sun Ultra for determining the presence of binding type conformance, suppose each binding type is composed of 4 different role types, and each role type is composed of one stream interface having 4 flow types. Then a rough estimate of the required execution time is in the order of a few hundreds of ms.

The performance of the trader task of finding a first conforming binding type offer now largely depends on the efficiency with which binding type offers likely to conform to the requirements can be located in the trader's database. This will narrow down the set of candidates that will be considered in detail such that all members of the set have a similar structure as the binding type requirement. In our future work we will investigate whether this can be efficiently achieved through proper indexing based on a classification of the most discriminating properties of stream bindings.

An alternative to comparing syntactic structure as part of the trader `look_up` operation, is *declared conformance*. This is the approach taken by the ODP/CORBA

Trader [22] in which service type offers and corresponding interface types are (manually) registered in a service type repository as unique *names*. The registration also encompasses information about which already registered service types the new service type conforms to. One advantage of this approach is the obvious reduced computational complexity. However, disadvantages are that only pre-registered conformance relationships can be detected by the trader, and that importers can only refer to registered service type offers in the trader look_up method, i.e. all applications have to know in advance the kind of stream bindings they potentially may need.

In our future work we will therefore look for ways to combine the above two approaches to trader implementations.

4   Negotiating Local Binding Behaviour

After having traded a binding type and corresponding binding factory (BF) as outlined in section 3.2, the BF type checks each application interface and the corresponding role of the binding type. The type checking is performed by computing the common flow properties of each pair of corresponding flows in the two interfaces. The result is a new interface specification representing the common behaviour supported by both interfaces [8]. We refer to this interface as the *intersection interface*.

In those cases where the intersection interface specifies alternative behaviours, it becomes necessary to choose the (initial) interface behaviour to be used for each local binding. The intersection interface may specify alternative behaviours with respect to stream interface configurations (see section 2.2), for each flow alternative flow configurations (see section 2.1), and for each possible flow configuration alternative quality behaviour (c.f. set valued attributes described in section 2.1).

If the selected binding type does not support conversion between causally related interfaces, the negotiations at one local binding will be constrained by the alternative behaviours that are possible at causally connected interfaces. Otherwise, it is a matter of BF policy how the negotiation at causally related interfaces are mutually constrained.

In the following we focus on the issue of negotiating individual flow quality behaviour.

4.1   Policy Specification

In order to support *automatic* negotiation of flow quality behaviour, we extend the flow type model of [6] with *policy specifications* that can be associated to each flow of a stream interface. A policy specification effectively specifies an order on the quality interpretation of a flow type. This ordering can be taken to represent user priorities with respect to desirable properties of the flow. The ordering is used as a basis for negotiation of the (initial) flow quality behaviour to be used for the local binding.

The alternative quality behaviours of a flow configuration is given by the set of quality attribute values associated to the flow elements of the flow. Given a set of attributes $A_1, .., A_n$ such that the value of A_i is a set of values $\{v_1, .., v_m\}$. The Cartesian product $A_1 \times ... \times A_n$ gives the total set of possible behaviours of the flow with respect to the properties $A_1, ... , A_n$ as a set of n-tuples. This we refer to as the interpretation of $A_1, .., A_n$. A policy specification specifies a priority order on this set of n-tuples.

For example, suppose after type checking two interfaces to be bound, the intersection includes a flow having the following alternative behaviours with respect to the attributes depth, framerate, and size:

```
depth {24,16,8};
framerate {30,25,20,15};
size {800x600,640x480,320x200};
```

A language for specifying policies of flow quality should allow the specification of arbitrary orderings of the Cartesian product of depth, framerate and size. On the other hand, such a language should not force a user to enumerate explicitly the ordering of all possible combinations of attribute values. The Cartesian product of the above attributes, for example, will give a total of 36 possible unordered (or arbitrary ordered) combinations.

Hence such a language should allow the users to specify orderings in a simple, yet expressive way. Our policy specification language is an attempt to achieve this. The language specifies value ranges for attributes assuming that attribute domains are totally ordered (either implicitly or explicitly specified). If no policy is specified for a flow, a default ordering is assumed derived from the ordering of the attribute domains. Otherwise the default ordering can be overridden with fine granularity, by specifying short attribute ranges, or with coarser granularity by specifying larger attribute ranges. In the extreme case a user could explicitly specify the complete ordering by consistently applying value ranges of length 1.

In our first version of a flow policy language, a policy specification is given by a list of selection statements. Each selection statement defines an ordered partition of the interpretation of the attributes. The total ordering is then achieved by concatenating each partition in the order given by the list of selection statements. A typical policy specification will have a structure as shown below.

$$A_{11}r_{11}, \ A_{12}r_{12}, \ ... \ , \ A_{1j}r_{1j};$$
$$A_{21}r_{21}, \ A_{22}r_{12}, \ ... \ , \ A_{2j}r_{2j};$$
$$...$$
$$A_{i1}r_{i1}, \ A_{i2}r_{i2}, \ ... \ , \ A_{ij}r_{ij};$$

A_{ij} denotes an attribute name, while r_{ij} denotes an attribute value range. A range is written as (v,w) where v and w are atomic attribute values. The position of the same attribute name might vary from selection element to selection element in the list.

The ordering implied by each selection statement is obtained by looping through a set of nested loops, where the left most attribute given corresponds to the outer most loop, and the right most corresponds to the inner most loop. Thus, all attribute values of $A_{i,j+1}$ will be used before starting to using "lower" values of $A_{i,j}$. The range (v,w) for a given attribute, specifies the range of values to be used for this attribute in this selection. For example, the selection statement

```
Depth(24, 16), size(800x600,800x600), framerate(25,20)
```

specifies that we first want to select qualities with depth between 24 and 16, size of 800x600 and framerate between 25 and 20. Since framerate is listed rightmost, the selector will first try out combination with lower frame rates, before starting to reduce the depth.

Example: Below we show an example of a policy specification and the corresponding ordering of the interpretation of the flow attributes given above.

```
1: size(800x600, 640x480), depth(24, 16),
                           framerate(30, 20);
2: size(640x480, 320x200), framerate(30, 15),
                           depth(24, 16);
3: depth(16, 8), framerate([20, 15),
                           size(320x200, 320x200);
```

Gives,

	depth	framerate	size
1:	24	30	800x600
	24	25	800x600
	24	20	800x600
	16	30	800x600
	16	25	800x600
	16	20	800x600
	24	30	640x480
	24	25	640x480
	24	20	640x480
	16	30	640x480
	16	25	640x480
	16	20	640x480
2:	24	30	640x480
	. . .		
3:			
	. . .		
	8	15	320x200

4.2   Negotiation

In this section we consider policy specifications as a foundation for QoS. In general, a variety of possible QoS negotiation protocols can be considered. In the MULTE-ORB architecture, QoS negotiation protocols are embedded within binding factories. Thus different BFs might support different negotiation protocols. In the following we discuss policy specification in the context of a simple, hypothetical negotiation protocol. For the sake of the discussion, we do not pay any attention to the efficiency of the protocol, but rather approach the issues in a principled manner. Possible optimizations are addressed in section 4.3 below.

Our approach to QoS negotiation is to take the ordering of alternative flow QoS behaviours implied by a policy specification as the users priorities in the negotiation. In the example above, the user gives priority to 24 bits pr pixel, 30 frames pr second, and a frame size of 800x600 pixels. The main principle of the QoS negotiation protocol is first to suggest a QoS level corresponding to the users first priority of QoS. If this can not be achieved, then the second priority of QoS is tried, and so on.

This simple protocol is sufficient for application scenarios where a single user retrieves a stream form a server, e.g. a video on demand server. In this case alternative QoS parameter configurations will be tried. Configurations might be rejected due to lack of resources. Alternatives are tried until either one configuration achieves enough resources to create the binding, or all the configurations fails. In the latter case, the binding attempt fails.

In other situations, when there are multiple receivers, there has to be a negotiation in order to agree on a common QoS parameter configuration (assuming no conversion such as scaling or transcoding of flows is supported). Below we outline such a negotiation protocol.

The negotiation protocol aims at finding a QoS parameter configuration that satisfies all the participants of the binding. In general, the various binding participants will specify different policies of flow QoS behaviour. Hence, in this case the goal of the protocol should be to find a QoS parameter configuration that is a "best fit" according to some metric. Again one might consider many different metrics for balancing the QoS parameter configuration between conflicting requirements. In the following we describe one possible metric that could be used as a basis for the negotiation.

Given that the negotiation is to be over a set of QoS attributes $A_1, .., A_n$, the starting point for the negotiation is the interpretation of $A_1, .., A_n$. Additionally, each participant specifies its own ordering of this interpretation as a flow QoS policy. Each QoS parameter configuration has a distance from the top of the list. A given QoS parameter's aggregated distance, is the sum of its distances from the top of the priority list over all participants lists. One possible metric to determine the "best fit" QoS parameter configuration, is to choose the configuration for which the aggregated distance to the top of the priority list is the shortest for all participants. If some configurations have the same aggregated distance, then the aggregated relative distance from the top is computed for these configurations. Relative distance is computed as a configuration's distance from the top in percents. This relative distance is used to find the inter distance between the configurations. The configuration with the shortest inter distance is considered the best. This corresponds to those configurations which have a relative height closest to each other. If there still are more than one candidate, one of them can be selected at random.

Below we give an example of the negotiation protocol for two receivers. Suppose user A and user B have the following flow QoS policies:

	A			B	
depth	rate	size	depth	rate	size
24	30	800x600	16	30	640x480
24	25	800x600	16	25	640x480
16	30	800x600	16	20	640x480
16	25	800x600	16	30	320x200
16	30	640x480	16	25	320x200
16	25	640x480	16	20	320x200
. . .					

From the above priorities and a "best fit" metric as described above, we see that the best configuration is (16,30,640x480), having an aggregated height of 6 while the second best is (16,25,640x480), having an aggregated height of 8. Thus, a binding supporting the quality (16,30,640x480) will be tried created first. If the BF is unable to create this binding, due to lack of available resources, a binding supporting (16,25,640x480) will then be tried created. This will continue until either the BF is able to create the binding, or it fails to create any binding due to lack of resources.

4.3   Design Issues of Negotiation Protocol

The above approach to a QoS negotiation protocol for a single flow did not consider efficiency. The protocol as it stands might result in several rounds of message exchanges in order to find a QoS parameter configuration. The reason for this is the way resources are handled. The protocol finds a possible candidate configuration, and then tries to allocate resources to support the binding for each of the binding parties. If there is insufficient resources at any of the participants, the binding attempt for this configuration will fail, and a new attempt has to be made.

The scalability of the negotiation protocol can be measured by the complexity of the algorithms and the number of messages which have to be sent. The number of messages exchanged will depend on how fast a "best fit" can be found. For this reason, it will be important to develop a negotiation protocol which takes the current resource situation into account when creating priority lists. Thus, an optimization of the above protocol would be to have participants reserve sufficient resources before they announce their policies. This might lead to participants having to remove some of their configurations, due to lack of resources, before they start the negotiation protocol. We may refer to the resulting policy at a *resource adapted policy* (RAP). The result of this requirement will be that once the participants find a configuration, they will have enough resources to create the binding.

With this new approach, a two-party negotiation for a single flow requires a two-way handshake. One participant announces its RAP, and the other participant subsequently intersects its RAP with the received RAP and communicates back its selected configuration provided the intersection was non-empty. For a multi-party negotiation a three-way handshake is required. First the initiator has to ask participants for their RAPs. Once the result of all participants have been collected, the initiator will select the configuration that is the "best fit" for all of the participants, if such a configuration can be found. Then it will inform the participants of the selected configuration, or it will inform that it failed to create the binding. Thus, using RAP specifications, the protocol will scale linearly to the number of participants, with regard to message exchanges. A challenge for further work will be to develop an efficient algorithm to calculate RAP specifications. Since the calculation of RAPs is done at each participant's node, scalability will not depend on this algorithm.

The scalability of the protocol will also depend on the efficiency of the "best fit" algorithm. Thus, it is important to design an algorithm that scales well with the number of participants. We are currently in the process of designing such an algorithm. The results of this work will be reported elsewhere.

5   Related Work

Stream interfaces have been adopted in the work on Open Distributed Processing [11], TINA-DPE [12] and OMG [13]. Compatibility and subtyping rules for stream interfaces, however, have been deemed outside the scope of the RM-ODP standard [11]. In the work of TINA-C, the need for a compatibility relationship for stream flows that is more relaxed than equivalence, is recognized, but no definition is offered [12]. A recent proposal for audio/video support in CORBA [14], also introduces the notion of flow end-point compatibility. QoS parameters beyond media encoding are not considered.

Microsoft's ActiveMovie framework [10] also includes the notion of "compatibility negotiation" between "pins" (connection points that carry flows between different processing objects). The subject of this negotiation is data compatibility rather than QoS. There is no support for distribution.

QML is a recent proposal for a QoS specification language [5]. The semantics of QML is similar to our stream and flow type model, and from our judgement should be capable of specifying quality properties of stream interfaces. Its applicability has been demonstrated for operational interfaces only. This work does not consider automatic support of QoS negotiation from QML specifications.

Other work that considers QoS specifications and/or negotiations includes [16], [2], [4], [19] and [21]. However, the focus of our work is different. These works do not provide anything corresponding to a type model of streams and bindings, including type relationships such as subtype, compatibility and conformance, and the derivation of automatic systems support such as QoS negotiation from high-level interface specifications.

6   Conclusions and Future Work

In this paper we introduced a trading model for selecting appropriate explicit stream bindings based on statements of binding type requirements provided by the application. We showed how an earlier proposed type model for stream flows can be extended to support binding type selection based on a notion of binding type conformance. In this scheme a set of binding factories are located based on a specification of the required properties of the binding. The located binding factories are all capable of instantiating binding objects with properties conforming to those specified by the client.

Furthermore, in those cases where binding objects specify alternative behaviour at its supported interfaces, we also introduced the notion of *policy specification* supporting automatic negotiation to choose the actual interface behaviour to be used at each interface. Finally, we demonstrated the usefulness of a trading facility and policy specifications as indicated above, through a number of examples.

In our future work we will address some of the limitations of the current model. In particular this includes automatic negotiation of stream interface configurations and flow configurations. Furthermore, the integration of resource management into the binding framework is a matter of high priority. In our current work we assume the availability of a resource manager that only supports simple reservation requests that can either be accepted or rejected depending on the availability of resources. This might force binding factories to make repeated reservation requests corresponding to different QoS parameter configurations. When one request is rejected, the binding factory will have to try again with a different QoS requirement. In future work we will give binding factories the possibility to examine the resource situation through the resource managers. Knowledge of available resources can be used by binding factories to reason about which QoS parameter configurations can currently be supported before making reservation requests.

References

1. Blair, G. S. et al. (1997) Adaptive Middleware for Mobile Multimedia Applications. *Network and Operating System Support for Digital Audio and Video (NOSSDAV '97)*, St Louis, USA, 1997.
2. Campbell, T. (1996) A Quality of Service Architecture. *PhD Thesis*, Lancaster University.
3. Coulson, G., Blair G. S., Stefani, J. B., , Horn, F., Hazard, L. (1992) Supporting the Real-Time Requirements of Continuous Media in Open Distributed Processing. *Technical Report MPG-92-35*, Lancaster University.
4. Dini, P., Hafid, A. (1997) Towards Automatic Trading of QoS Parameters in Multimedia Distributed Applications, *In proceedings of IEEE/IFIP ICODP/ICDP Conference*, Toronto, Canada, 166 – 179.
5. Frølund,, S., Koistinen, J (1998) Quality-of-Service Specification in Distributed Object Systems, *Distributed Systems Engineering Journal*, Vol.5, No.4
6. Eliassen, F., Nicol, J. R. (1996) Supporting Interoperation of Continuous Media Objects. *Theory and Practice of Object Systems: special issue on Distributed Object Management* (ed. G. Mitchell), Vol.2, No.2, Wiley, 1996, 95-117.

7. Eliassen, F. (1997) A Conformance Relationship for Stream Interfaces, 2nd Int'l Conf on Formal Methods in Open Object-based Distributed Systems (FMOODS'97), Canterbury July 21-23, Chapman & Hall.

8. Eliassen, F., Mehus, S. (1998) Type Checking Stream Flow Endpoints. *Middleware'98*, The Lake District, England, 16-18 Sept, Chapman & Hall, 305 - 322.

9. Lindsey, D., Linington, P.F. (1995) RIVUS: A Stream Template Language for Capturing Multimedia Requirements, *Lecture Notes in Computer Science (LNCS 1052)*, Springer Verlag, pp. 259 – 277.

10. Microsoft (1996), Microsoft ActiveMovie: Software Development Kit, Beta Release, June 1996.

11. ITU-T X.901 | ISO/IEC 10746-1 (1995) ODP Reference Model Part 1: Overview. *Draft International Standard.*

12. TINA-C (1995) TINA Object-Definition Language, Version 1.3. *TINA-C Deliverable.*

13. Object Management Group (1996) Control and Management of A/V Streams Request for Proposal. *OMG Document*: telecom/96-08-01.

14. IONA Technologies, Plc, Lucent Technologies, Inc, Siemens-Nixdorf, AG (1997) Control and Management of A/V Streams Request for Proposal. OMG RFP Submission, *OMG Document*: telecom/97-05-07.

15. Kristensen, T., Plagemann, T. (1999) Extending the Object Request Broker COOL with Flexible QoS Support, Technical Report UniK – Center for Technology, University of Oslo.

16. Nahrstedt, K., Smith, J. M. (1995) The QoS Broker, *IEEE Multimedia*, 2(1), pp. 53-67.

17. Plagemann, T. (1994), A Framework for Dynamic Protocol Configuration", *Dissertation at Swiss Federal Institute of Technology*, Computer Engineering and Networks Laboratory, Zurich, Switzerland, Sept. 1994.

18. Plagemann, T., Eliassen, F., Goebel, V., Kristensen, T., Rafaelsen, H. O. (1999), Adaptive QoS Aware Binding of Persistent Objects, in IEEE *Proceedings of International Symposium on Distributed Objects and Applications (DOA'99)*, Edinburgh, Scotland.

19. Vogt C., Wolf, L. C., Herrtwitch, R. G., Wittig, H. (1998), HeiRAT - Quality of Service management for distributed multimedia systems, *Multimedia systems*, 6(3), ACM/Springer, pp. 152-166.

20. Zaremski, A.M., Wing, J. M. (1995), Signature matching: a tool for using software libraries, ACM Trans. Softw. Eng. Methodol., Vol.4, No.2, pp. 146-170.

21. Zinky, A., Bakken, D.E., Schantz, R.D. (1997), Architectural Support for Quality-of-Service for CORBA Objects, *Theory and Practice of Object Systems,* Vol.3, No.1, Wiley.

22. ISO/IEC 13235-1 (1998) Information technology - Open Distributed Processing - Trading function: Specification.

23. Schulzrinne, H., Casner, R., Frederick, R., Jacobsen, V. (1996), RTP: A transport protocol for real-time applications, *IETF*, rfc 1889.

Strategies for Integrating Messaging and Distributed Object Transactions

Stefan Tai and Isabelle Rouvellou

IBM T.J. Watson Research Center, New York, USA
{stai,rouvello}@us.ibm.com

Abstract. Messaging, and distributed transactions, describe two important models for building enterprise software systems. Distributed object middleware aims to support both models by providing messaging and transaction services. But while the concept of distributed object transactions is well-understood, support for messaging in distributed object environments is still in its early stages, and not nearly as readily perceived. Integrating messaging into distributed object environments, and in particular with distributed object transactions, describes a novel and complex software design problem. This paper details this problem, presenting first results from our project of developing a messaging and transaction integration facility. The first contribution of this paper is a comprehensive messaging classification framework, which defines messaging concepts and terminology, and enables us to compare different messaging architectures. Second, we analyze sample messaging middleware using this framework, and identify the architectural messaging styles that they induce. Third, we derive four different strategies for integrating messaging and distributed object transactions. We discuss each of these integration strategies, and outline the open research issues that need to be solved. Overall, this paper advances our understanding of the motivation for, the problems of, the current state-of-the-art in, and future models for integrating messaging and distributed object transactions.

1 Introduction

Messaging, and distributed transactions, are among the most demanded and important models that distributed object middleware is required to support.

Transactions, as known from database systems and transaction processing monitors [1] [5], guarantee that a set of operations transforms the shared state of a system from one consistent state to another consistent state. Standards like the CORBA Object Transaction Service OTS [13] address transaction processing in distributed object environments, and with CORBA Object Transaction Monitors [15], or component technologies like Enterprise Java Beans [11], the middleware for building transactional distributed object systems is available today. Distributed object transactions are considered essential for the development of industrial-scale n-tier distributed object systems, where some server layers manage a persistent store [16].

J. Sventek and G. Coulson (Eds.): Middleware 2000, LNCS 1795, pp. 308–330, 2000.

Distributed object messaging, on the other hand, is not nearly as well-understood and readily perceived as distributed object transactions. There exists no common notion of messaging, and support for messaging in distributed object environments is more in its experimental, than adopted stage. In general, messaging refers to the communication model of asynchronous, possibly multicast message exchange for event notification, or request processing. In addition, messaging refers to the system development paradigm associated with messaging middleware like message queueing (MQ) systems [2] [8]. This paradigm is based on the strong decoupling of clients and servers using message queues as intermediators. Messaging is considered beneficial to enhancing system reliability, stability, and flexibility for system evolution [2].

Distributed object middleware that supports both distributed transaction processing, and messaging, promises to allow for addressing a large problem domain of software systems. Consequently, messaging service specifications, including CORBA Messaging [14], or the Java Messaging Service (JMS) [17], have recently been proposed. These messaging services are intended to be used in addition to the existing and already employed distributed object transaction services, and are different from existing event notification services like CORBA Events [13], or CORBA Notification [13].

The emergence, respective availability, of distributed object messaging and transaction services now inaugurates the question, and potential, of *distributed objects integrating messaging and transactions*. While middleware services in general attempt to mimic the Bauhaus principle of clear separation of functionality and concern to enable service integration, the integration of messaging and distributed transactions describes a more fundamental, complex problem. We need to better understand messaging and different models of messaging in order to approach integration with distributed transactions, and we need to identify the different objectives of integration, and how these objectives can be achieved in an efficient way.

We have begun to design a new middleware facility for integrating messaging and distributed transactions in a distributed object environment. We aim to integrate two advanced distributed object messaging and transaction services, which are currently being developed in two related projects. In this paper, we present the results from our first step in this design process, exploring the problem of integrating messaging and distributed transactions in detail.

The paper is structured as follows. In Section 2, we present a novel messaging classification framework, which defines messaging concepts and terminology. The framework establishes a common language to communicate about messaging, and enables us to compare different messaging architectures. In Section 3, we analyze sample messaging middleware using this framework, identifying the architectural messaging styles that they induce. Though we will eventually focus on a particular middleware and service environment for our integration facility, the objective in our first step has been to study messaging across different messaging middleware. In Section 4, we present four strategies for integrating messaging and distributed object transactions. We discuss each of these integration strategies, and outline the open research issues that need to be solved. Section 5 concludes with a summary of the work presented, and discusses our plans for future work.

2   Messaging Classification Framework

This section presents the *messaging classification framework* that is central to understanding and discussing different strategies for the integration of messaging and distributed transactions.

The framework is organized around three models: *message delivery model, message processing model*, and *message failure model*. The message delivery model defines fundamental properties of message delivery. The message processing model extends the delivery model with properties additional to message processing. The message failure model defines properties of message failure, with respect to message delivery or message processing.

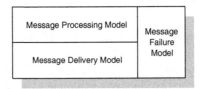

Fig. 1. Messaging Classification Framework

The framework is quite comprehensive, and deliberately addresses a variety of messaging aspects. Each model defines a number of messaging properties, and for each model property, we describe different possible values. Combinations of such values characterize a messaging architecture. Not all combinations of property values can be implemented using currently existing messaging middleware, and some combinations may not be feasible at all.

The properties that we define in each model represent those aspects of messaging that we find important to capture differences between messaging models and understandings. We have experienced practitioners and researchers to refer to messaging as "programs communicating by putting messages on queues", as "multicast event notification", or as "processing requests asynchronously". The classification framework aims to establish a common language to better communicate about messaging. We selected the properties based on communication with colleagues, including [9].

2.1   Message Delivery Model

The *message delivery model* defines the properties related to exchanging (sending and receiving) messages between message producers and message consumers.

Message delivery is not concerned with the processing of messages, i.e., the effects resulting from message exchange. Message delivery essentially is about *event notification*: ways to inform interested consumers about the occurence of some state transition.

The message delivery model comprises the following properties:

Representation defines how a message is represented in the system. A message may be represented as an *object*, or as a *data* element (possibly following a standard message format of message header and message body). Messages that are represented as either objects or data can be passed as parameters to operations for message exchange. In lieue, a message may have no representation as an entity, but corresponds to an (asynchronous) *operation invocation* on an object only.

Messaging API defines whether application-independent, or application-specific operations (or, the combination of both) are used for messaging. An *application-independent* messaging API describes generic operations for sending, receiving, or administering messages. An *application-specific* messaging API, on the other hand, is an interface of application functionality defined by the application developer.

Message representation, and messaging API, are the two most fundamental aspects that distinguish different messaging middleware.

Table 1. Message Delivery Model (1)

1. Representation	2. Messaging API
1. as object	1. application-independent
2. as data	2. application-specific
3. operation invocation	3. combination of 1. and 2.

The property of **initiation** defines who causes a message delivery to happen. The delivery can either be initiated by a producer who sends a message (*push*), or by a consumer who queries for a message (*pull*). *Mixed initiation* refers to the case where the same message is both pushed and pulled by different consumers. Pull and mixed initiation require that a message is represented as an entity.

Intermediation defines whether or not *intermediators* such as message queues or channel objects are part of the message exchange. There may be none, exactly one, or a set of intermediators involved for a single message delivery. Intermediators are used when messages are represented as own entities in the system, and they are essential to realize a messaging model on top of a synchronous object invocation model.

The **multiplicity of ultimate recipients** defines the number of the final (not intermediate) consumers of a message sent. If there is only one such ultimate recipient, the message delivery is *unicast*, or point-to-point. The message delivery is *multicast*, if there are multiple ultimate recipients. *Broadcast* is a special case of multicast delivery, where the message is sent to all consumers on the network.

The **anonimity of ultimate recipients** defines whether the final consumers are all known, partly known, or all unknown to the message sender. The consumers typically are known to the messaging middleware, or to an intermediator that is part of the message exchange.

The property of **subscription** defines whether consumers have declared their interest in receiving messages by subscribing according to some subscription mechanism, or whether no subscription was necessary for message exchange. Consumers may subscribe to intermediators, or to message producers directly. Subscription commonly is required for push event notification, and may address all messages that a producer or intermediator publishes, or only selected messages, for example based on message types.

Synchronicity defines the model of synchronization that is used for message delivery between a sender and its *direct* consumers (intermediators, or ultimate recipients, if no intermediator exists).

Messaging in general implements an *asynchronous* communication model between a message producer and its *ultimate* recipients. However, as illustrated in Figure 2, this asynchronicity may be implemented using synchronous communication via an intermediator. Alternatively, direct asynchronous calls (e.g., CORBA IDL oneways [12], or CORBA AMI and TII [14]) may be used.

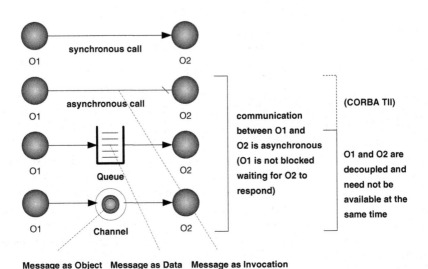

Fig. 2. Event Notification

The property of **delivery guarantee** defines the level of guarantee that is assured for message delivery. The *best-effort* delivery semantics is the lowest level of guarantee, and essentially describes no guarantee. With *at-most-once*, we refer to the semantics of basic delivery guarantee, and with *exactly-once*, to the highest level of delivery guarantee. The exactly-once delivery guarantee may be implicit (is transparently assured by the middleware), or may be explicit (is visible in the form of acknowledgments to the sender).

Table 2. Message Delivery Model (2)

3. Initiation	4. Intermediation	5. Multiplicity	6. Anonimity
1. by producer	1. none	1. unicast	1. known set
2. by consumer	2. exactly one	2. multicast	2. unkown set
3. push and pull	3. multiple	3. broadcast	3. mixed

7. Subscription	8. Synchronicity	9. Delivery Guarantee
1. subscription	1. synchronous	1. best effort
2. no subscription	2. asynchronous	2. at-most-once
3. mixed		3. implicit/explicit exactly-once
		4. either 2. or 3.

In addition, there are also the following properties of message delivery that are typically associated with intermediation ("queue-management"):

Persistence defines whether a message is persistent, or transient. *Persistent* messages are messages that are copied to a persistent store (of the intermediator), in order for the messages to survive failures such as system crashes. *Transient* messages, on the other hand, are kept temporarily, based on message birth and expiry times.

The **ordering** property defines the sequence in which a message is delivered w.r.t. other messages. Intermediators may implement a temporal-based ordering (*first-in-first-out (FIFO)*, or *last-in-first-out (LIFO)*), a *random* ordering, or a *priority-based* message delivery. Message priorities may include, for example, the specification of an allowed time window of start time and end time inside of which the message must be delivered.

Filtering defines whether a message is subject to a selection mechanism by intermediators in order to be further distributed to consumers. Filters may be defined for all kinds of selection, for example based on message timestamps, message size, or message content. We subsume these under filtering based on message *headers* (message properties), and filtering based on message *bodies* (message content).

Filters allow a single intermediator to handle various messages for a set of consumers with different interests. Filtering typically involves a prior subscription of consumers to the intermediator.

Table 3. Message Delivery Model (3)

10. Persistence	11. Ordering	12. Filtering
1. persistent	1. FIFO	1. none
2. transient	2. LIFO	2. header/type
3. either 1. or 2.	3. random	3. body/content
	4. priority-based	4. 2. and 3.

2.2   Message Processing Model

The *message processing model* defines the properties related to communicating back the results that are consequences of a message delivery. Message processing goes one step further than event notification, as it is essentially about *asynchronous request processing*: ways to asynchronously request results from a remote server.

There are two major roles that software components play for asynchronous communication: the role of a *client*, i.e., a sender of a request message and a consumer of a reply message, and the role of a *processing server*, i.e., an ultimate consumer of the request message and a sender of the reply message.

The message processing model defines the properties that characterize a *processing result*, and how the result is *communicated* from a processing server to the requesting client. These properties are in addition to those captured in the message delivery model.

Processing result defines whether the result of a message sent is a *single return value*, a *single integrated return value*, or a *set of individual return values*. The latter two address multicast or broadcast messages, where multiple recipients process the same message, and multiple acknowledgments of processing and/or processing results have to be communicated back. An intermediator is needed in order to integrate multiple returns.

Communication defines how the client receives the processing result. The client may receive a *separate reply message* to the request message, for which a message correlation mechanism (for example, using message ids) to associate the two messages as one request/reply message pair is needed. Two other, common patterns for returning processing results are the callback approach and the polling approach. With the *callback* approach, the client passes a callback object reference with the request, which in turn is invoked by the server when the results are ready. With the *polling* approach, a poller object is returned by the request, which the client can query for results.

In all three of these cases, the client can continue its processing independent of the request sent, but still expects a result of processing to be communicated back to him. Using the polling approach, the client may become blocked until a response is available to the poller. This model is also referred to as the *deferred synchronous* model.

Table 4. Message Processing Model

13. Processing Results	14. Communication
1. single return value	1. separate reply message
2. single integrated return value	2. callback
3. set of individual return values	3. polling

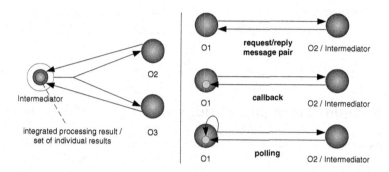

Fig. 3. Asynchronous Request Processing

2.3   Message Failure Model

The *message failure model* defines the properties related to message failures. The message failure model is of predominant importance for integrating messaging and distributed transactions, as any failure of a message affects the *acidity* ("all-or-nothing") property of transactions. But what constitutes a message failure (respective success), and how is the failure detected?

The **failure level** defines whether a message success is based on its successful *delivery only*, or whether a message success is based on the successful delivery and the successful *processing* of the message as well. For example, a `debit(account, value)` message can be considered successful if the message is successfully delivered, or, if the message is successfully delivered *and* the actual debit for the specified account is successful, too.

With **failure scope**, we distinguish whether the success of a message is based on *a defined set of particular, ultimate recipients* (for example, one specific recipient, or a defined list of recipients), *a defined number or range of any recipients* (for example, exactly one, at least one, or 2-5 recipients), or *all ultimate recipients*. The failure scope thus describes how the messaging property of multiplicity relates to message failure definition.

The property of **failure detection** finally defines how a messaging failure is discovered. *Acknowledgments* of message reception are necessary for the message delivery failure level, and actual *results of processing* are necessary for the message processing failure level. *System* and *user-defined exceptions*, a *timeout* for the acknowledgments/replies that is specified and monitored, or the combination of both may be used for failure detection.

Table 5. Message Failure Model

F1. Failure Level	F2. Failure Scope	F3. Failure Detection
1. delivery	1. particular recipients	1. exceptions
2. processing	2. number of any recipients	2. timeout of ack/reply
	3. all recipients	3. combination of 1. and 2.

3   Sample Messaging Middleware and Architectures

In this section, we analyze selected examples of messaging middleware: *CORBA Messaging*, *CORBA Events* and *CORBA Notification*, *Java Messaging*, and *Message Queueing (MQ)* systems.

The purpose of this section is not to evaluate each middleware regarding its strengths and weaknesses, but to identify the *messaging architectural styles* that they induce, and the commonalities and differences that exist between the different styles. The notion of an *architectural style* has been introduced in software architecture research to describe the communication and cooperation, and composition and design rules that a set of software systems shares. A middleware has an impact on the architecture of a system that is implemented on top of it, and implicitly defines an architectural style, or sub-style. [3] discuss event-notification styles as defined by event-based middleware. Our work focuses on messaging middleware for use in distributed object environments, and uses our more comprehensive classification framework for this purpose.

We aim to understand the different notions of messaging that are suggested by these middleware. Therefore, we focus on the messaging programming models that the technologies offer to developers, but we are not concerned with internal details of messaging middleware realization. The messaging classification framework introduced in the previous section allows us to describe each technology very briefly, by repeatedly looking at the same common messaging properties as defined in the framework.

3.1   CORBA Messaging

CORBA Messaging refers to the messaging style based on *asynchronous method invocations (AMI)* as proposed with the OMG CORBA Messaging service [14].

A message corresponds to an application-specific AMI on an object, which can either be a callback- or a poller-based request. Callback-based AMIs work on behalf of `ReplyHandler` CORBA object references, and poller-based AMIs on `Poller` objects that are instances of a CORBA value type. AMIs introduce a truly asynchronous invocation model in addition to the standard synchronous CORBA invocation model[1].

With CORBA Messaging, an application-specific, standard CORBA IDL server interface is mapped to an AMI "implied-IDL" interface, a client-side view of the interface containing either callback or poller-based operation signatures. In this way, servers need not be modified to serve asynchronous requests. Each message (AMI) is client-initiated (push-model), and no intermediator is used. Thus, the current CORBA messaging model does not support multicast, but is unicast, and targeted (the server is nonimous).

CORBA AMIs are asynchronous calls with at-most-once delivery semantics. For target servers that are not active (or, activatable) at the time the request is issued, CORBA Messaging introduces the notion of a *time-independent invocation (TII)* as a special kind of AMI. TIIs can outlive client and server process lifetimes (can be persistent, and have exactly-once delivery semantics). For both AMIs and TIIs, priorities can be specified, otherwise the message delivery is temporal, based on the time that the request is issued (FIFO). There is no filtering supported.

CORBA Messaging addresses message processing (not only event notification), and results are single return values due to CORBA AMIs being unicast. Results are communicated back to a client using the callback, or polling approach, alternatively. The failure level of messages is the processing level, and the failure scope are particular servers. CORBA Messaging does not support user-defined exceptions for AMIs, but message failure detection is based on system exceptions and processing results only (messages returning no results are successful if they return without an exception).

3.2 CORBA Events and Notification

CORBA Events and Notification refers to the messaging style based on the CORBA Events service [13], and its successor, the CORBA Notification service [13]. A variety of CORBA products currently support both services.

CORBA Events distinguishes generic (untyped), and typed event architectures. In the untyped case, a message corresponds to data that is passed in the form of the CORBA IDL type `any`. In the typed case, a message corresponds to an operation invocation of an application-specific IDL interface. In both cases, an application-independent messaging API is used, which defines standard interfaces for either push- or pull-based consumers and suppliers. Any number of event channels (being standard CORBA objects) may be used as intermediators

---

[1] CORBA also defines two other models of asynchronous invocation: IDL oneway operations, and deferred synchronous invocations. IDL oneways are, however, of unreliable best-effort delivery semantics, and serve only for event notification, but not for request processing returning results. CORBA deferred synchronous invocations, on the other hand, are only available with the CORBA dynamic invocation interface DII, which is a very complex, and thus less practical model.

for event notification, and a standard subscription mechanism for consumers and suppliers is defined. Using channels, multicast message distribution based on subscription is supported. All communication partners are known to the intermediator, but suppliers and consumers are anonymous to each other.

Asynchronicity is obtained using synchronous calls via an intermediator. If no intermediator is used, the communication is synchronous. With typed events, the application-specific interfaces contain standard synchronous CORBA operations, which in addition must not have any return values and out/inout-parameters. The delivery guarantee is at-most-once (standard CORBA). Messages may be persistent in the untyped case, if the intermediator (the service implementation) used supports persistence as a feature. The message delivery order is undefined for CORBA Events, but CORBA Notification supports per-consumer priority-specified message ordering. Message filtering, both header (type)-based, or content-based, is supported as well with CORBA Notification, but not with CORBA Events.

CORBA Events and Notification address event notification, but not message processing. Messages are parameters to standard CORBA requests, and results of message processing would need to be communicated back as parameters of separate reply requests. However, this is outside the scope of the services.

Figure 4 illustrates examples of channel-based messaging using the CORBA Events or Notification service.

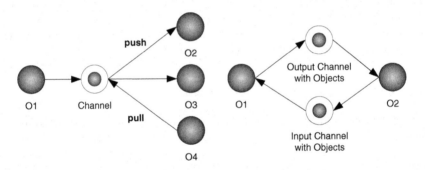

Fig. 4. Channel-based Messaging

3.3   Java Messaging

Java Messaging refers to the messaging style based on the *Java Messaging Service (JMS)* [17]. JMS addresses the integration of *message-oriented middleware (MOM)* to support messaging in Java object systems.

A message is an object of one of five JMS message types (`BytesMessage`, `TextMessage`, `MapMessage`, `StreamMessage`, or `ObjectMessage`), which are all specializations of the general JMS `Message` type, defining common message header fields, properties, and operations. The JMS messaging API is application-independent, and comprises a set of interfaces for point-to-point (PTP) messaging, and for publish/subscribe messaging. PTP is the model of sending a message to a `Queue` object as an intermediator. A `Queue` encapsulates a specific, single MOM message queue in order to integrate MOM-based applications. Publish/subscribe is the model of sending a message to a `Topic` object. A `Topic` is an object in a content-based hierarchy, and serves as an intermediator to which interested Java consumers can subscribe to. `Queue` objects and `Topic` objects are specializations of the JMS `Destination` type.

Both models support multicast communication (to either MOM-based consumers, or Java consumers), with the set of consumers being anonymous to the message producer. A subscription mechanisms exists for the publish/subscribe model. Asynchronicity is achieved using synchronous calls to `Destination` objects. Messages can be declared to be persistent, or transient. Persistent messages are guaranteed to be delivered exactly-once, whereas delivery for non-persistent messages is at-most-once. Messages are delivered in the order they were sent (FIFO), however, message priorities can be specified. In addition, consumers may select messages from intermediators.

JMS describes a message processing model, where results of message processing are communicated back as separate reply messages (messages carry ids and can be correlated). The failure level of messages is the processing level, and the failure scope are specific servers. The combination of exceptions, processing results, and/or timeouts can be used for message failure detection.

3.4 MQ Messaging

MQ Messaging refers to the messaging style as suggested by message queueing (MQ) systems [2] [7].

A message corresponds to data that is structured according to a standard format of message header and message body. Messages are exchanged using (multiple, input and output) message queues as intermediators. On each processor in the network, a queue manager exists, and clients and servers use an application-independent message queue interface for exchanging messages, i.e., to put messages on queues (push), or to read messages from queues (pull). Target queues must be specified, but ultimate message consumers (unicast, or multicast) are anonymous to the sender. There is no subscription mechanism to queues, as clients and servers always decide themselves when and if to take a message from a queue[2].

Asynchronicity is realized using synchronous calls to queues. Message delivery is guaranteed to be exactly-once, when messages are declared to be persistent. Delivery is FIFO, or priority-specified, and message selection is the responsibility of the program reading from the queue.

---

[2] The exception are *MQ trigger queues*, which notify an application about the arrival of a message in a queue. The message itself is, however, not automatically pushed by the queue to the application, but must be read by the application itself.

MQ Messaging addresses event notification, but also message processing using separate reply messages with correlated ids. If the request/reply message
model is selected, the message failure level is the processing level. Message failures are detected by queue managers and applications using exceptions and
timeouts. Figure 5 illustrates a common queue-based messaging architecture.

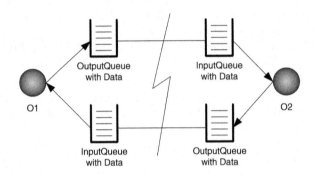

Fig. 5. Queue-based Messaging

3.5   Comparison

CORBA Messaging is the only messaging middleware that introduces an asynchronous invocation model for distributed objects. All other middleware represent messages as objects or data that is send as parameters of requests, and
asynchronicity is achieved using synchronous communication via intermediators
and an application-independent messaging API. Message initiation is commonly
push and pull, but CORBA Events is the only model where messages can also
be pushed by intermediators. With all middleware except CORBA Messaging,
multicast (as well as unicast), and anonimity of ultimate recipients is supported.
Subscription models vary. Exactly-once message delivery guarantees are provided with persistent messages only, the at-most-once semantics is the common
case otherwise. Standard message ordering is FIFO (time the request is issued),
or priority-specified. Filtering by intermediators is only supported with CORBA
Notification. JMS and MQ provide, however, message selection features for applications connecting to an intermediator. None of the middleware provides a
feature to return a single, integrated processing result of a multicast message,
but results of a multicast message are returned as a set of individual reply
messages. All models except CORBA Events/Notification address message processing, and not only event notification. The message failure level thus is the
processing level in these cases. The failure scope is in any case a defined set of
particular servers (or, intermediators) only (typically a single server). Failure
detection commonly is the combination of exceptions, processing results, and/or
timeouts.

Table 6. Messaging Comparison Table

Middleware	1. Representation	2. Messaging API
CORBA Messaging	3. invocation	2. specific
CORBA Events untyped	2. data	1. independent
CORBA Events typed	3. invocation	3. combination
CORBA Notification	2. data	1. independent
JMS Messaging	1. object	1. independent
MQ Messaging	2. data	1. independent

3. Initiation	4. Intermediation	5. Multiplicity	6. Anonimity
1. by producer	1. none	1. unicast	1. known set
3. push and pull	3. multiple	3. both	2. unknown set
3. push and pull	3. multiple	3. both	2. unknown set
3. push and pull	3. multiple	3. both	2. unknown set
3. push and pull	3. multiple	3. both	3. mixed
3. push and pull	3. multiple	3. both	2. unknown set

7. Subscription	8. Synchronicity	9. Delivery Guarantee	10. Persistence
2. no subscription	2. asynchronous	4. either 2. or 3.	3. either 1. or 2.
1. subscription	1. synchronous	2. at-most-once	2. transient (*)
1. subscription	1. synchronous	2. at-most-once	2. transient (*)
1. subscription	1. synchronous	2. either 2. or 3.	3. either 1. or 2.
3. mixed	1. synchronous	4. either 2. or 3.	3. either 1. or 2.
2. no subscription	1. synchronous	4. either 2. or 3.	3. either 1. or 2.

11. Ordering	12. Filtering	13. Proc. Results	14. Communication
1. FIFO/4. priority	1. none	1. single value	2. callback/3. polling
undefined	1. none	n/a	n/a
undefined	1. none	n/a	n/a
any/4. priority	4. 2. and 3.	n/a	n/a
1. FIFO/4. priority	2. header/type	3. set of values	1. separate message
1. FIFO/4. priority	2. header/type	3. set of values	1. separate message

F1. Failure Level	F2. Failure Scope	F3. Failure Detection
2. processing	1. particular	3. combination
1. delivery	n/a	n/a
1. delivery	n/a	n/a
1. delivery	n/a	n/a
2. processing	1. particular	3. combination
2. processing	1. particular	3. combination

(*) Persistence may be supported by service implementations

4   Integration Strategies

There is no single approach to integrating messaging and distributed transactions, due to different integration objectives, and the variety of the messaging models existing. In the following, we present four integration strategies, which all follow a distinct flavor of messaging set in the context of distributed object transactions. The strategies include a discussion of the initial integration models that are currently proposed by the JMS and CORBA Messaging.

The distributed transaction model that we use as a basis here is the two-phase commit transaction model as proposed, for instance, by the CORBA OTS, the transaction standard for distributed objects [13], and as specified by the X/Open XA distributed transaction processing model [18]. The OTS is a common and well-accepted transaction model, used by many modern middleware like CORBA OTMs, and the Java transaction service JTS, the Java mapping of the OTS.

4.1   MQ-Integrating Transactions

The first strategy is called *MQ-Integrating Transactions*. This integration strategy is the only one of the four strategies that is readily supported with current messaging and distributed object transaction middleware.

Intent. The intent is to integrate message queues of common MQ-systems as *resource managers* into the distributed object transaction. The distributed object system can in this way make use and incorporate the quality-of-services that are associated with message queues and MQ-systems.

Concept. MQ-integrating transactions integrate messaging in the sense that messages are transactional data that are managed by persistent message queues acting as resource managers. Data get() and put() calls on queues are made within a transaction scope. The following simple example illustrates this.

```
try {
   tx.begin();
   {
      data = inputQueue.getData();
      result = distributedObject.process(data);
      outputQueue.putData(result);
   }
   tx.commit();
} catch (Exception e)
{
   tx.rollback();
}
```

The transactional semantics here is that the dequeuing of the data from the input queue, the processing of the data by the distributed object, and the enqueuing of the data in the output queue, are executed as *one atomic* action.

Integrating message queues as resource managers basically compares to integrating a server that uses an XA-based database resource manager. Note that all put- and get-calls on the queues are local calls, and not remote. With MQ-integrating transactions, distributed message exchange is *not* part of the transaction. The transaction begins after a message has arrived in a local input queue, and the transaction commits when data is written to a local output queue.

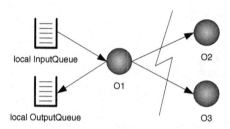

local InputQueue

local OutputQueue

O1

O2

O3

Fig. 6. MQ-Integrating Transactions

Implementation All major MQ-systems support the X/Open XA interface, which allows a message queue to be easily integrated as a resource manager into an OTS-like transaction.

4.2   Message Delivery Transactions

Message Delivery Transactions refers to the approach of integrating a *message delivery model* into distributed object transactions.

Intent. The intent is to enable *event notification* between remote communication partners: a message is send from a client to one or multiple distributed servers within the scope of a transaction, and among other, synchronous transactional requests (to the same or different servers). The ACID properties of the transaction must still be guaranteed, i.e., failure of message delivery must cause the transaction to abort, and if the transaction fails for some reason after a message has been sent out, a compensation strategy is needed to back out all messages sent.

A typical scenario and use of message delivery transactions is illustrated in Figure 7. The transactional client begins the transaction, sends out a message m1 to a defined set of direct consumers, does some distributed transaction processing, and sends out another message m2 to the same (or, a different) set of consumers. If this transaction were to be implemented as a non-messaging, standard OTS-transaction, each message must be mapped to a number of individual, synchronous, and blocking calls, leading to a more complex and time-consuming transaction.

The main purpose and benefit of message delivery transactions is the ability to send messages during the course of the transaction. Asynchronous event notification is particularly useful for long-running transactions. Message delivery transactions allow a client to begin or continue distributed transaction processing without being blocked when sending notification messages.

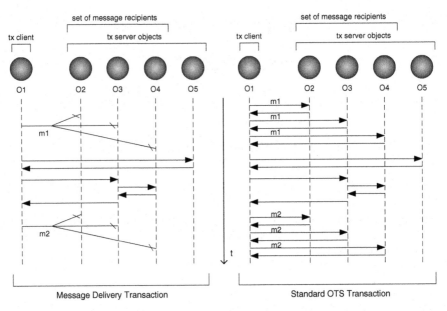

Fig. 7. Message Delivery Transactions Example

Concept. Message delivery transactions extend the standard transaction model in that

1. messages can be send in addition to synchronous object invocations, at any point in the transaction,
2. message delivery success is observed, and delivery failure can cause a transaction to abort, and
3. messages that are sent prior to a transaction failure are compensated.

Messages become part of the *atomic sphere*, the set of operations that make up the transaction. Compensation can be achieved by dequeing an original message from the intermediators that the message was sent to, if the message has not been read by consumers from the intermediators at the point of transaction rollback. Otherwise, a separate message to undo the effects of the original message is sent out to the same consumers, which requires the definition of a *compensation* sphere, the set of compensating operations that are part of the transaction [10].

Table 7 describes the messaging model for message delivery transactions.

Table 7. Messaging Model for Message Delivery Transactions

1. Representation	any
2. Messaging API	any
3. Initiation	push-model: the message delivery is caused by the transactional client as the message producer (the pull-model is not desired, as this would require the transactional client to wait for a message pull and impact the transaction control flow)
4. Intermediators	any
5. Multiplicity	any
6. Anonimity	any
7. Subscription	any, if subscription is with intermediators (subscription to the transactional client itself does not affect the transaction)
8. Synchronicity	any
9. Delivery Guarantee	exactly-once semantics
10. Persistence	persistent (exactly-once delivery guarantee)
11. Ordering	any
12. Filtering	any
13. Processing Results	n/a
14. Communication	n/a
F1. Failure Level	delivery
F2. Failure Scope	any
F3. Failure Detection	combined model of exceptions and timeouts for delivery acknowledgments

Implementation. Message delivery transactions are not readily supported with current messaging and transaction services, as the integration model proposed by messaging services does not conform to the model of message delivery transactions. Most notably, current messaging middleware does not allow to send messages at any point of a transaction, but if they allow to include messages in a transaction, the messages are only send after and in case of a successful commit the transaction. Consequently, message failure as well as message compensation are not addressed at all.

For example, the JMS talks about *transacted sessions*, which allows to group a set of produced messages and consumed messages as one atomic unit of work [17]. However, transacted sessions are not distributed transactions, but local, and the produced messages are sent out to distributed partners only in case of a successful commit. JMS does not address distributed transactions, but suggests to use the JMS-supported XA resource manager interface in the case of distributed transactions. Thus, JMS distributed transactions essentially are MQ-integrating transactions.

To implement message delivery transactions with current messaging and transaction middleware, two principal options exist:

1. Messages are declared to be outside the scope of the transaction, and sent concurrently to the running transaction. Message delivery observation, as well as message compensation, must be implemented at own costs.
2. A series of transactions is defined. Each subtransaction represents a synchronization point at which messages are sent. The series of transactions is a saga transaction with a corresponding set of compensating transactions [4]. Sagas must be hand-coded as well.

Both solutions are unsatisfactory, as they are very costly to be implemented, and even more, to be maintained. By matching Table 6 and Table 7, we can further identify that none of the current messaging middleware allows for a flexible message failure scope definition. Ideally, any cardinality specification for message recipients is useful, especially as ultimate consumers are anonimous.

4.3   Message Processing Transactions

Message Processing Transactions refers to the approach of integrating a *message processing model* into distributed object transactions.

Intent. The intent is to enable *asynchronous request processing* between transactional distributed objects. A transactional client requests some distributed processing within the scope of a transaction, but is not blocked until the processing results for the request return. In addition, message processing transactions do not require transactional servers to be available at the time that the request is issued by the client. The ACID properties must still be guaranteed to the transaction.

A typical scenario and use of message processing transactions is illustrated in Figure 8. A transactional client begins a transaction, invokes on a distributed transactional server O2 asynchronously, continues its processing, and eventually receives a processing result from O2 prior to committing the transaction. This transaction model cannot be mapped to a standard OTS transaction, due to the fact that a standard OTS transaction requires all servers to be available at the times that the client issues the request.

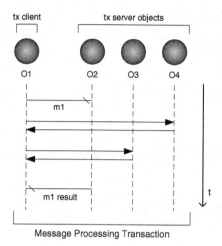

Fig. 8. Message Processing Transactions Example

Concept. Message processing transactions extend the conventional transaction model in that the atomic sphere of the transaction includes asynchronous requests. Different to message delivery transactions, this requires that the *transaction context* is shared between all transaction participants, i.e., the transaction context must be propagated from the client to the processing server[3]. The processing server is nonymous to the client, but need not be available at the time the client request is issued. The main purpose and benefit is the ability to process requests asynchronously, and to allow for independent client and server process lifetimes.

The messaging model for message processing transactions must meet the criteria as described in Table 8.

Implementation. The CORBA Messaging specification briefly addresses a special, CORBA-specific case of message processing transactions. CORBA Messaging refers to this transaction model as *unshared transactions*.

CORBA unshared transactions involve CORBA TIIs (time-independent requests), and thus do not have end-to-end transaction semantics (transaction contexts are not propagated from client to server at the time the request is made). Unshared transactions are different from CORBA messaging *shared transactions*, which involve CORBA AMIs only, and therefore can be mapped to standard OTS transactions that have an end-to-end transaction semantics.

CORBA unshared transactions describe a new transaction semantics. In principle, they may be implemented using three separate transactions: (1) the send-

---

[3] Transaction context propagation is not necessarily required for message delivery transactions, due to the client declaring a lack of interest in the consequences and processing of the message sent.

Table 8. Messaging Model for Message Processing Transactions

1. Representation	any
2. Messaging API	any
3. Initiation	push-model
4. Intermediators	any
5. Multiplicity	unicast or multicast
6. Anonimity	known set
7. Subscription	any, if subscription is with intermediators
8. Synchronicity	any
9. Delivery Guarantee	exactly-once semantics
10. Persistence	persistent
11. Ordering	any
12. Filtering	any
13. Processing Results	any
14. Communication	any
F1. Failure Level	processing
F2. Failure Scope	defined set of particular recipients
F3. Failure Detection	combined model of exceptions and timeouts

ing of the request by the client, (2) the delivery of the request, and the reception of the processing result, by the middleware, and (3) the propagation of the processing result to the client. (This model corresponds to the non-object-oriented notion of transactions as proposed with MQ systems.) However, such an implementation requires an ordering guarantee for requests, and a concept to identify a set of ordered requests as a single entity. Both is not defined and supported with CORBA and CORBA Messaging.

The problems described for CORBA unshared transactions apply to message processing transactions in general. Table 8 also reveals other open issues. For example, for communicating back processing results, a mechanism that supports the integration of a set of results of a multicast request is highly desired.

4.4   Full Messaging Transactions

With *Full Messaging Transactions*, we refer to the approach of a complete distributed object transaction model that allows for message delivery transactions and message processing transactions at the same time.

The intent is to enable *event notification* and *asynchronous request processing*, alternatively, and in addition to synchronous object invocations, between remote components and within the scope of a single transaction.

Full messaging transactions combine message delivery transactions and message processing transactions. Thus, they require an even more flexible model for defining messages and message failures, as they must distinguish the messaging models and conflicting values such as failure scope definition (property F2 in Table 7 and Table 8).

4.5   Related Work

The ACS object communication protocol of the KAROS system [6] is a notable previous work in this field. With ACS, a request message is associated to an atomic action, which may comprise other messages. ACS thus provides transactional semantics to nested actions through asynchronous communication. Three different kinds of messages with different failure recovery semantics for asynchronous request processing (apply, call), and for event notification (send), are supported. ACS addresses reliable distributed object messaging using an implicit atomic operation execution semantics, as opposed to explicit transaction demarcation as proposed with distributed transaction services like the OTS. The ACS protocol can thus not directly be adopted for distributed object messaging/transaction architectures as discussed in this paper. Also, we aim at supporting asynchronous communication in addition to synchronous communication, but not as an exclusive alternative.

5   Conclusion

In this paper, we addressed the problem of integrating messaging and distributed object transactions. We stated the need for a common language to communicate about messaging and different models of messaging, and introduced a comprehensive messaging classification framework that serves for this purpose. The framework defines messaging properties and property values organized around three models: message delivery model, message processing model, and message failure model.

We demonstrated the use of this framework for two purposes: to study and compare different messaging architectural styles as induced by messaging middleware, and to characterize the messaging models behind different strategies to integrate messaging and distributed object transactions. The messaging middleware comparison revealed a number of important differences between the notions of messaging currently supported, including fundamental differences, for example, regarding message representation, synchronicity, or message delivery guarantees, and more subtle differences, for example, regarding the support for multicast communication, or for message filtering by intermediators.

We derived four strategies for integrating messaging and distributed object transactions, each serving for a specific integration objective and following a distinct flavor of messaging: MQ-integrating transactions, message delivery transactions, message processing transactions, and full messaging transactions. We described the intent and concept for each of these strategies, and identified open issues for future integration support. These include, most notably, the ability to send messages at any point within the scope of the transaction, to support message compensation, to allow for time-independent transaction context propagation, and to support flexible message failure definition w.r.t. message delivery and/or message processing.

Our plans for the future are to step-wise address the issues discussed for each integration strategy, and to eventually provide a middleware support for full messaging transactions. The basis for our integration facility are a novel distributed object messaging, and an advanced distributed object transaction model that are currently being developed in two related projects at IBM Watson. We expect future work to expose additional, and more specialized aspects in the problem domain of integrating messaging and distributed transactions in distributed object environments, which we will need to address. The classification framework and the integration strategies presented in this paper are the first step towards our project goal.

References

1. Bernstein, P., Newcomer, E.: Principles of Transaction Processing. Morgan Kaufman. (1997) 308
2. Blakeley, B., Harris, H., Lewis, R.: Messaging and Queuing Using the MQI. McGraw-Hill. (1995) 309, 319
3. Carzaniga, A., DiNitto, E., Rosenblum, D., Wolf, A.: Issues in Supporting Event-based Architectural Styles. Proc. ISAW3, ACM. (1998) 316
4. Garcia-Molina, H., Salem, K.: Sagas. Proc. ACM SIGMOD. (1987) 326
5. Gray, R., Reuter, A.: Transaction Processing: Concepts and Techniques. Morgan Kaufman. (1993) 308
6. Guerraoui, R., Capobianchi, R., Lanusse, A., Roux, P.: Nesting Actions through Asynchronous Message Passing: the ACS Protocol. Proc. ECOOP'92, LNCS 615, Springer-Verlag. (1992) 329
7. IBM Corp.: MQSeries Application Programming Guide, 10th ed. IBM Corp. (1999) 319
8. IBM Corp.: An Introduction to Messaging and Queueing, 2nd ed. IBM Corp. (1995) 309
9. Jacobson,H. A., Olken, F., MacParland, C.: A Taxanomy of Event Services for Internet-Scale Monitoring and Control Applications (Draft). Technical Communication. (1998) 310
10. Leymann, F., Roller, D.: Production Workflow: Concepts and Techniques. Prentice-Hall. (1999) 325
11. Monson-Haefel, R.: Enterprise JavaBeans. O'Reilly. (1999) 308
12. The Common Object Request Broker: Architecture and Specification. OMG. (1995) http://www.omg.org 312
13. CORBAServices: The Common Object Service Specifications. OMG. (1997) http://www.omg.org 308, 309, 317, 322
14. CORBA Messaging (Joint Revised Submission). OMG TC Document orbos/98-05-05. (1998) http://www.omg.org 309, 312, 316
15. Orfali, R., Harkey, D.: Client/Server Programming with Java and CORBA, 2nd ed. Wiley. (1998) 308
16. Slama, D., Garbis, J., Russell, P.: Enterprise CORBA. Prentice-Hall (1999) 308
17. Sun Microsystems: Java Message Service, version 1.0.1. (1998) http://java.sun.com/products/jms/docs.html 309, 318, 326
18. X/Open Guide Distributed Transaction Processing: Reference Model, version 3. X/Open Ltd. (1996) 322

A Distributed Object Oriented Framework to Offer Transactional Support for Long Running Business Processes

Brian Bennett[1], Bill Hahm[2], Avraham Leff[1], Thomas Mikalsen[1],
Kevin Rasmus[2], James Rayfield[1], and Isabelle Rouvellou[1]

[1] IBM Research, T. J. Watson Research Center
P. O. Box 704, Yorktown Heights, NY 10598, USA,
{bennett,avraham,tommi,jtray,isabelle}@watson.ibm.com
[2] Country Companies Insurance,
Bloomington, IL, USA

Abstract. Many business processes are both long running and transactional in nature. They are also mostly multi-user processes. Implementations such as the CORBA OTS (Object Transaction Services) modeled on the lock-based systems used for classic transactions do not fully support the requirements of such processes, and as a result, application developers must develop custom-built infrastructure – on an application-by-application basis – to support users' transactional expectations. This paper presents a novel approach to implementing long-lived transactions within distributed object environments. We propose the use of the unit-of-work (UOW) transaction model and framework, an advanced nested transaction model that enables concurrent access to shared data without locking resources. The UOW approach describes a well-structured distributed object architecture that can easily be integrated with distributed object systems. The framework offers uniform (i.e., application independent) structural transaction support for long running business processes and provides them with the semantics of traditional, short, transactions. Use of the framework enables object developers to focus on business logic, with the framework infrastructure providing functions required to support the desired semantics. We discuss the framework programming model, how it provides transactional behavior to long running business processes and some of the research challenges still ahead of us.

1 Introduction

Many business processes, such as mortgage application processing or insurance policy underwriting, can run for several days to a month or even longer. Typically, more than one person is involved in the business process. The process may start with data that is not fully validated, and that will be "cleaned up" over the course of the process; in such cases a business often does not wish to allow other processes to see the new information until it is sufficiently correct. If a customer

J. Sventek and G. Coulson (Eds.): Middleware 2000, LNCS 1795, pp. 331–348, 2000.

backs out or changes her mind, the business may want the capability to easily throw away unfinished work which it does not want cluttering its database.

The *Long Running Unit Of Work* (or LRUOW) framework provides structural transactional support for such long running business processes (LRBP). A principal contribution of the framework is that a LRBP is treated as a single long running transaction, rather than as a series of loosely connected short transactions (the approach often used to implement business processes today). Framework users interact with units of work (or UOW) that represent an application-level structure following the structure of work done at a given enterprise. Once started, a UOW may be suspended (with its state stored persistently) and subsequently resumed. It continues to exist until it completes, which it may do by committing or by rolling back. The current version of the LRUOW framework has been implemented as a set of container managed, entity, Enterprise Java Beans [1] running on top of the IBM Websphere Advanced platform [2].

Traditional transaction processing (TP) monitors such as CICS, Encina, and Tuxedo, and databases such as DB2 and Oracle have successfully abstracted an application design philosophy that separates the business logic of a flat transaction from the transactional function (ACID[1]) provided by the underlying system. However, an LRBP cannot be naively implemented on a traditional TP system because of the interaction between the following important LRBP characteristics:

- long duration (in contrast to traditional, short, transactions)
- concurrent access (in contrast to batch jobs or single-user systems)

Batch systems (in which a job is the equivalent of a long transaction) and single-user systems (such as a spread sheet application, in which the time between saves corresponds to a non-ACID transaction) do lock resources and files for moderate lengths of time (minutes to hours). Such exclusive usage is acceptable because nobody else competes for the resources. While TP monitors and databases allow concurrent usage, concurrency is provided by locking out other users when another user accesses the resource. If one application locks data for a long time, other applications that need the data must wait until the first application completes and releases its lock. Long running applications (anything over a few seconds) are thus unacceptable for a traditional transaction system.

Because an LRBP is multi-user it must be able to deal with concurrent access, and because it is long, no single user can be permitted to lock the data for the duration of the business process. Traditional TP monitors and databases,

---

[1] The ACID properties are

Atomicity = the transaction is either executed entirely or not executed at all

Consistency= transactions transform a persistent data store from one consistent state to another

Isolation= transactions do not read intermediate results of other non-committed transactions

Durability = once a transaction is committed, its effects are guaranteed to endure despite failures

in other words, do not fully support an LRBP's requirements, and as a result, application developers must develop custom-built infrastructure – on an application-by-application basis – to support users' transactional expectations. Such infrastructures typically intermingle business logic with transactional function. By analogy to traditional TP monitors, the goal of the LRUOW framework is to provide infrastructure that implements common transactional functions for long running business processes. By providing LRBP developers with a consistent set of transactional methods that are independent of business logic, development and maintenance effort is reduced. Note that the LRUOW framework does not intend by itself to provide full support for long running business processes, but only to provide transactional functionalities (see Section 6).

The LRUOW framework provides three major pieces of functionality to the LRBP application developer.

- packaging control of business activities into a UOW so the set of activities can be committed or rolled-back as a unit
- visibility control so that the objects created or updated are only visible within well defined scopes rather than visible to everyone
- concurrency control that manages the possibility that two users might add or change the same data in conflicting ways

The paper starts with an example of a long running business process. This example is used throughout the paper to illustrate our presentation of the LRUOW framework. The way a LRBP is divided into UOWs is explained in Section 3. Section 4 discusses how we control the visibility of the work done within the scope of a UOW. Section 5 shows how transactional behavior is provided by the framework. We conclude with a discussion on other components needed to fully support LRBPs and how they relate to our framework.

2   Example of a Long Running Business Process

This section presents a (greatly simplified) LRBP example in which an insurance company underwrites car policies. This example will be used in the next sections to illustrate the different features of the framework. The LRBP begins when a customer calls the company and requests coverage for her car. For its part, the company must create a new Policy object; it will contain relationships to new Car and Customer objects. The agent can get some information at the time of the call (Car VIN, make, model and Customer name and address), but much information can be collected only after various long running activities have completed: e.g., a credit check (Customer credit status), a car inspection (Car image), and a Department of Motor Vehicle (DMV) driver violations check. The object model and task dependency graph are shown in Figure 1. The application developers want the ACID properties that UOWs, like traditional, short running transactions, provide. Thus, in our example, the insurance company:

- wants the Policy object, comprised of the Car and Customer objects, to be created in "all or nothing" fashion (atomicity).

- wants the state of the business to move only from one valid state (valid states are defined by the business) to another (consistency).
- does not want the intermediate states of the new Car and Customer objects to be visible to other parts of the business as the information has not been validated yet (isolation).
- wants the final and intermediate results to be permanent in spite of failures (durability).

We will use this example to illustrate the LRUOW programming model and implementation in the following sections.

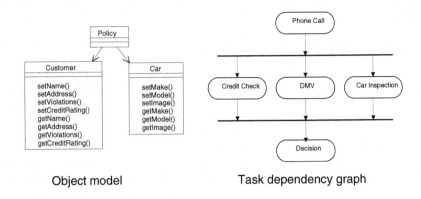

Object model   Task dependency graph

Fig. 1. Example: Object Model and Task Dependency Graph

3   Programming Model Overview

A key feature of the LRUOW programming model is that business logic is separated from the long running transaction semantics. Business object providers, in other words, concentrate on developing the function required by the long running business process: the framework is responsible for ensuring that long running transaction semantics are provided when the objects are actually deployed. In the client (application writer) view of the programming model, a LRBP contains only two types of object: the unit of work (or UOW) object which represents a nestable long running transaction (provided by the framework), and various base objects (arbitrary, non UOW-aware, objects provided by business developers). The framework takes those base objects and creates versions that are associated with the UOWs. It transparently maps method invocations under a given UOW context onto the set of objects associated with the UOW.

The LRUOW framework regards a LRBP as a directed, acyclic graph, whose nodes consist of units of work (or UOW), each of which is a nestable long running transaction [3]. Each UOW has one parent UOW (except for the root UOW

refered to as *enterprise level* UOW) and may have multiple children UOWs. The
enterprise UOW owns all objects in the system and is never committed. Each
sub-task of the LRBP shown in the task dependency graph of Figure 1 is mapped
to a node in the uow tree (Figure 2).

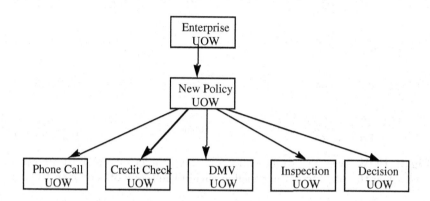

Fig. 2. UOW Tree: Note that, at a given time, only some of the leaf nodes may
exist. Figure 3 and Figure 4 show snapshots of the UOW tree at different times

All activities done within the course of a LRBP are done within the context
of some UOW. The UOW context is established when the client either obtains,
or creates a new UOW, and joins the UOW using join() on the UOW object.
Subsequent method invocations are performed within the scope of that UOW.
This compares to a conventional transaction begin, or, to calling begin() on
the Current object in a CORBA OTS transaction [4]. A transaction can be
committed or rolled back by invoking the respective method on the UOW object.
In our example, the *new policy* LRBP is initiated by requesting that the parent
(or enterprise level) UOW create a child *new policy* UOW. Isolation is provided
during the course of the LRBP because nodes in the UOW tree obey the following
visibility rules [5]:

- The state of all objects in the scope of a parent UOW is visible to all children
  of that parent.
- When a child UOW commits, state changes done to all objects within the
  scope of the child UOW become visible to the parent UOW.
- State changes performed by a child UOW are not visible to its siblings until
  the child UOW commits.

An object's state and its visibility are modified over time as UOWs are
created, committed, or rolled back. Continuing our example, Figure 3 represents
a snapshot of the UOW tree as the *phone call* UOW (a child of the *new policy*
UOW) commits. As a result, the Car and Customer objects that were created
in the course of the customer's phone call become visible (and made persistent).

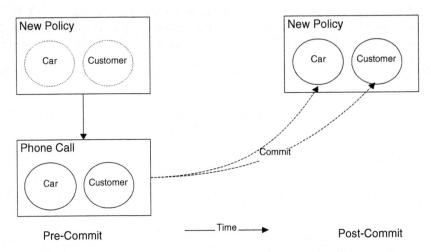

Fig. 3. UOW Tree: Effect of committing the Phone Call UOW (dotted lines are used when the objects are not visible within the scope of the given UOW)

Figure 4 is a snapshot of the LRUOW tree as one of the 2nd-level tasks (the car inspection) completes: the changes made to its version of the car (Car.image) are propagated to the parent's version. The car image was not visible to the *inspection* UOW's siblings until the commit.

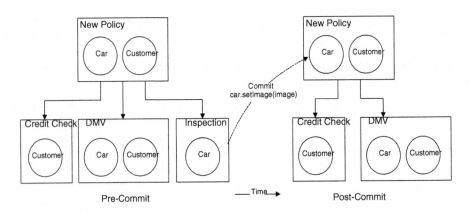

Fig. 4. UOW Tree: Effect of committing the Inspection UOW

4   Visibility and Isolation Enforcement: Facade & Version Objects

The framework uses a client/server model. In the client view of the LRUOW programming model, user interactions occur only with UOW objects and base objects; they rely on the framework to transparently map method invocations onto the set of objects associated with their UOW. The framework must enforce the protection implied by the visibility rules and, when a participant commits, must propagate the objects' state changes to the parent UOW.

The server implements this transparent mapping by ensuring that the client never actually accesses a base object instance. Instead, the client accesses a facade object that, in turn, delegates the client's method invocations to version objects that are associated with individual UOWs. The transaction context (UOW context) is implicitly propagated between the distributed EJB components that participate in the transaction, using request interceptors. UOW context propagation compares to propagation of transactional contexts in CORBA OTS transactions using implicit propagation mode.

As shown in Figure 5, each instance of a base object (e.g., a Car with VIN = 42) is associated with an instance of a facade object which wraps the set of version object instances. Each currently active UOW in which a client has referenced a facade object instance has an associated version object in the facade's version set. Through use of reflection techniques, the framework automatically generates facade and version objects from the base object. Users input the base objects as a Jar file containing, for example, Car and CarHome interfaces and CarBean and CarKey implementations. Based on this input, the framework generates the corresponding CarFacade and CarVersion EJBs, deploying them into a relational database container.

The fact that a client actually invokes methods on a facade requires the facade to extend the Car interface (as shown in Figure 5): the facade then maps from the client's UOW context (e.g., *inspection UOW*) to the corresponding Car version to which it delegates the method invocation. A Car version identity is determined by the specific Car semantics and a UOW identifier. A Car version has the Car interface, and uses the framework-independent implementation of the car (CarImpl) that is provided by the business developer (see Figure 5). The framework's task of generating the server-side facade and version objects on behalf of the client is made easier when base objects follow the *Bridge* design pattern [6]. Since clients code to an interface (e.g., Car in Figure 5), the server-side (facade) objects need only provide a shallow wrapping implementation to satisfy the contract with the client. At run-time, the server substitutes a facade for the base object.

4.1   Lifecycle

Although Figure 5 shows how the client view of a base object is actually implemented on the server by facade and version objects, it does not explain how the client gets a reference to a facade in the first place.

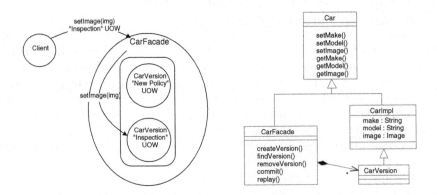

Fig. 5. Delegation of client methods / Facade and Version Car Objects

In addition to providing the base object interface and implementation (the *Car* and *CarImpl* objects), the LRUOW programming model requires the business object provider to supply an interface specifying how base object instances are created, located (queried), and removed. Our implementation follows the factory design pattern [6], so that clients access base object lifecycle function by invoking methods on the associated factory class. The LRUOW framework extends the base factory interface (e.g., with a *CarFacadeFactory*) such that the server returns facade objects to the client instead of the base object.

The challenge addressed by the framework is how the programming model used by LRBP participants – in which a single user accesses single instances of base objects – is supplied in an environment of concurrent, multi-user, access to sets of version objects. Users should be able to program as if there is only a single instance of a given object (e.g., a car with VIN = 42 where VIN is a unique key), even though the object accessed is actually one of a set of versions whose relationships are determined by the structure of the LRBP unit of work tree.

The key concept is that a business object's existence is defined relative to a specific UOW, so that an object may exist with respect to UOW_1 and not exist with respect to UOW_2. The reason for this has to do with the visibility rules discussed in Section 3 which we can now restate in terms of facade objects:

A business object exists with respect to UOW_i if and only if a non-deleted version, associated with UOW_i, exists in the facade's set of versions or the business object exists with respect to the parent of UOW_i in the LRUOW tree.

In our implementation, the facade and factory collaborate to provide business objects to clients. A client can get a reference to a facade in one of two ways: through object creation and through query (object location). Often, however, a child UOW will invoke business methods on an object whose reference was obtained in a *parent* UOW. The facade transparently creates a new version (to be associated with the child UOW) the first time that one of its business methods are invoked. If the business object does not exist with respect to the client's UOW, the facade throws an exception. This code path (unlike the ones for creation and location through query) is managed entirely by the facade, and does not involve the factory object.

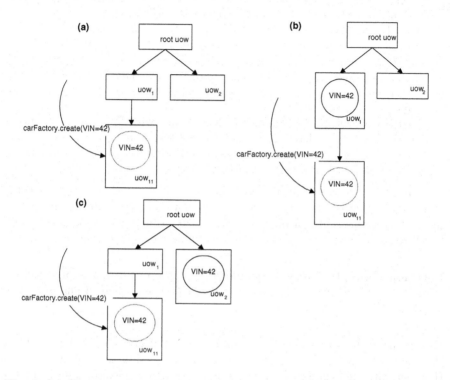

Fig. 6. (a) Client creation of a car, no pre-existing Facade car. (b) Client creation of a car, with a pre-existing version visible to client. This is an illegal state that results in an exception (c) Client creation of a car, with a pre-existing version that is not visible to the client. The resulting clash on commit is dealt with in Section 5

Creation Suppose that the base Car semantics specify that a new Car is created when a client invokes *CarFactory.create(VIN = 42)*. Figure 6 shows how the framework deals with various scenarios; note that, in these figures, the client is associated with UOW_{11}.

- No CarFacade with the specified VIN exists with respect to *any* UOW: i.e., there are no versions of a car with the specified VIN in existence (Figure 6a).
  - the CarFactory creates a FacadeCar with (VIN = 42).
  - the CarFacade creates a CarVersion that will be associated with UOW_{11}, and inserts it into the set of version objects.

- A CarFacade with the specified VIN exists with respect to UOW_{11} (Figure 6b), because a version is associated with its parent UOW_1 – even though it does not exist with respect to UOW_2.
  - the CarFactory determines that CarFacade with (VIN = 42) exists.
  - the CarFacade determines that it is visible to UOW_{11}. Since the object already exists, the facade must therefore throw a creation exception; this will be rethrown by the factory to the client.
- A CarFacade with the specified VIN does not exist with respect to UOW_{11} – even though the facade object *exists* (Figure 6c). Even though sibling UOW_2 has already created a car with the specified VIN, because UOW_2 has not yet committed (and propagated its state into UOW_0) the car does not yet exist with respect to UOW_{11}. The impending clash when the last child commits is discussed in Section 5.
  - the CarFactory determines that CarFacade with (VIN = 42) exists.
  - the CarFacade determines that it is not visible to UOW_{11}.
  - the CarFacade creates a CarVersion that will be associated with UOW_{11}, and inserts it into the set of version objects.

In order to separate a client's UOW context (which can change over the course of a LRBP) from the specific version object that is accessed at any given time, the factory returns the facade – which is responsible for mapping the client's UOW to a specific version – instead of returning the newly created version.

Location through Query Object location is the mirror image of object creation: i.e., a facade object instance can be located by a client if and only if the facade is visible to the client's UOW.

Removal A client can remove a business object if and only if it is visible to the client's UOW. Object removal is, in this sense, similar to object location. However, although the facade object cannot be actually removed until the top-level UOW commits, from the client's viewpoint once the remove method is invoked, the object no longer exists. For example, in Figure 6c, if UOW_2 deletes the CarFacade with (VIN = 42), and commits into UOW_0, the facade no longer exists with respect to UOW_1 and UOW_{11}. It is therefore valid for UOW_{11} to subsequently create a car with (VIN = 42).

To deal with such situations, whenever a client removes an object, the facade marks the associated version as *deleted* but does not remove the object from its set of versions (nor does it remove it from persistent storage). This tag allows the framework to recognize when an existing, but deleted, object actually exists with respect to a specific UOW.

5   UOW Transactional Behavior and Concurrency Management

The challenge faced in providing transactional behavior for a LRBP is that locking resources on behalf of one LRBP participant prevents other participants from accomplishing their portion of work. On the other hand, not locking resources is unacceptable because it implies that participants cannot be given any guarantees about resource consistency. Our framework uses the following approach to provide UOW transactional behavior.

A UOW executes in two phases: a long-running phase (termed the *rehearsal*), and a short-running phase (termed the *performance*). Users accomplish work during UOW rehearsal; but, as its name suggests, no work is actually committed (in a transactional sense) during this phase. More precisely, although user work can be made persistent (so that if the system crashes, user activity will resume from the last syncpoint), the UOW does not commit and make its work visible to a parent UOW context until the user invokes UOW.commit(). If a participant instead invokes UOW.rollback(), her work will be rolled back in traditional "all or none" fashion. The purpose of the rehearsal phase is to allow long running, concurrent, activity to occur *without* locking resources – while, at the same time, the system creates a persistent copy of the information needed to resolve conflicts at commit time (performance time). Because each UOW operates on a private set of data (the versions discussed in Section 4), protection from concurrent activity is automatically provided, making lock constraints unnecessary. The performance phase is in effect a *short*, traditional transaction (with ACID properties) which modifies the versions of the objects in the parent UOW. Thus, the LRUOW framework can be implemented on top of existing transaction middleware products: the only requirement is that the system support external transactional coordination (e.g., theX/Open XA interface).

During the performance phase, the framework must deal with the concurrency issues which were ignored during the rehearsal phase. We have included two different concurrency control mechanisms. Both mechanisms seek to minimize the possibility of not being able to commit because of irreconcilable concurrent activity. Both mechanisms include the concept that not all differences between rehearsal and performance results are irreconcilable. The mechanisms vary in whether the work needs to be on the front end or on the back end, their impact on analysis and design, the types of problems they can be applied to, and the way you go about manually resolving a concurrency problem if the system can't resolve it.

5.1   Predicate & Transform Approach

As mentioned above, the framework creates during the rehearsal phase of the UOW a persistent copy of the information needed to resolve conflict at commit time. In this first approach, the information kept is the user activity or *operational log*. Facade objects record method invocations in an operational log; entries contain sufficient information to enable subsequent method replay (see Figure 7). Object state changes are preserved by logging method invocations; arguments to these methods are recorded in the log using serialization techniques. The original method invocation is later replayed using dynamic method invocation. We must deal with one subtlety: if a client invokes method1 and that method, in turn, calls method2, we log only method1 rather than logging both methods. Replay of method1 implicitly replays method2: if method2 were to also be logged, the system would incorrectly apply method2 twice. To prevent such behavior, the system associates a *logging depth* with a given uow which is incremented each time a method is logged within that uow's scope. Log depth is decremented when the logging operation completes. An operational log record is created only if a uow's log depth corresponds to a top-level logging operation. One benefit of this approach is that facade objects are independently responsible for determining that an operation should be logged: the LRUOW framework is responsible for determining the runtime nesting of method invocations, and thus whether an individual invocation should be explicitly or implicitly logged.

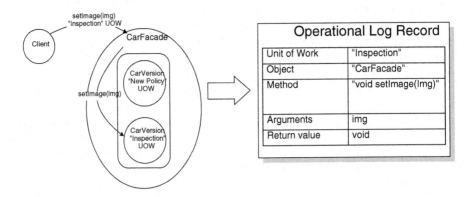

Fig. 7. Operational Log Record (there is one record per highest level transform invoked)

The operational log is a compressed copy of the LRBP in the sense that user think time, business process time, and other activities that add to the UOW's clock time (in contrast to actual business method execution time) are omitted. At performance time, the system begins a short transaction, replays the operational log, and commits the transaction to the underlying datastore if the replay is successful. Operational log replay is done with respect to a UOW's parent's data. For example, when the *inspection* UOW of Figure 4 commits, the set of methods that were invoked against its *Car* object are reinvoked against the Car version associated with the *new policy* UOW. After the UOW commits, the state of the parent UOW's versions has been updated, and reflects the state of the child UOW's versions. So, although concurrency is not an issue during rehearsal (because the *inspection* UOW manipulated its private Car version), the framework must deal with concurrency during performance since it is at this time that the *inspection* UOW Car version must be resolved with its parent *new policy* UOW Car version. Although the framework allows state changes to be applied only from within leaf UOWs, we must potentially resolve conflicts between sibling UOWs.

One approach is to log *all* methods (and their results) and allow a UOW to commit only if the rehearsal phase result matches the performance phase result. This has the advantage of being straightforward: a transaction is clearly not affected by concurrent activity if the state of all of its objects is determined only by the transaction's activity. Unfortunately, this semantic – equivalent to that of *optimistic* transactions [7] – can result in unnecessary transaction rollbacks. For example, in a debit transaction, what is important is that there are sufficient funds to cover the withdrawal – not the precise amount of funds in the account. As long as an account can cover all concurrent withdrawals, we do not want to rollback the transactions. Under the optimistic semantics, if the performance phase replays the fund withdrawals in a sequence that differs from the rehearsal phase, the difference in state (e.g., balance = getBalance()) is detected and the transaction aborted. Such behavior is especially unacceptable in the case of long running transactions: users will not be happy to be told that several weeks of work must be aborted despite the fact that the state transformations are *compatible*!

To achieve greater concurrency than what is offered by optimistic semantics, the LRUOW uses the concept of predicates and transforms. This approach is based on the concept of *field calls*. Field calls are a mechanism for increasing concurrency of short transactions by reducing the "product" of the amount of data and length of time, in which transaction locks must be held[5]. Field calls are more general (and allow more concurrency) than either *optimistic* or *timestamp* locking schemes. A field call consists of a predicate/transform pair consisting of (1) a *predicate*, which is checked at the time of the call and at commit time, and (2) a *transform*, which modifies transaction data in some way. The predicate test uses a shared-mode lock, and the lock is released as soon as the predicate is tested, thus allowing other transactions to read or update the data. If the predicate is false at the time of the field call, the transaction aborts. Otherwise, when the transaction is at phase 1 commit, it acquires exclusive locks on data involved in transforms, and the predicate is tested again. If it is false, the transaction aborts (no need to undo the transaction); otherwise the transform is applied (phase 2 of the commit), and the locks are released.

The LRUOW predicate/transform approach extends the field calls concept to long running processes. The application programmer has to code in terms of predicates and transforms (see below). Programmers must therefore be more aware of the fact that the LRUOW is running as a concurrent, transactional, program. This contrasts with the programming model of classic, short, transactions where application developers are almost completely oblivious of the transaction framework: all that is required is transaction demarcation and code to deal with situations where the transaction fails to commit. Note, however, that classic transactions often relax classic serializability semantics so as to achieve greater performance. Techniques such as cursor stability give greater concurrency at the cost of similarly forcing programmers to be aware of, and deal with the fact, that their application executes concurrently with other applications [5]. Different techniques to alleviate the strictness of serializability by allowing some degree of inconsistency have been investigated before. One of them, epsilon serializability (ESR) allows read-only transactions that can handle a certain amount of inconsistency to exploit that property in order to increase concurrency [8,9]. Update transactions must be serializable amongst themselves. ESR works through a high-level specification of inconsistency whereas our approach allows fine-grained specifications of inconsistency that can be coded in many cases within the methods of the object itself and can be exploited by update transactions.

What is a LRUOW Transform? A transform is any state transforming method on an object. State transforming methods are replayed so as to transform the parent version to reflect the transforms applied to the child version.

What is a LRUOW Predicate? A LRUOW predicate is a piece of code checking some arbitrarily complex condition on a number of objects. It protects and validates one or several transform invocations. The simplest case of LRUOW predicates are classic predicates that perform pre-condition or post-condition validation. For example, a debit method on an account object will include a test of the account balance.

```
Account::debit(x) {
If (this.balance < x)   throw exception;
Else  this.balance -= x;}
```

The business developer will use such predicates to validate the single-pass code logic (by single pass, we refer to code execution that, in order to be valid, executes only once). This predicate will implicitly be logged as part of the debit transform and replayed during the performance phase. The replay will be successful if the current parent UOW account version has sufficient balance. So, as long as there are sufficient funds in the account, sibling UOWs can invoke the *debit* method, and still successfully commit to the parent UOW. The key idea is that a UOW will be rolled back [2] by the system only if a transform cannot be replayed (against its parent's state) because an associated predicate is no longer true. Transforms are therefore logged with the best performance achieved when the programmer specifies the least restrictive set of predicates. Concurrency will not be a problem – i.e., the replay will succeed – as long as the predicates associated with the child's transforms are not violated by the current state of the parent's version. For example, since the *phone call* UOW of Figure 3 creates new Customer and Car objects, there is no conflict between the parent's state (which does not contain these Customer and Car objects): the performance phase simply recreates the objects in the parent *new policy* UOW's scope. Of course one could imagine that there is a limit in the number of customers that an insurance company wants to consider. In this case, a predicate on createCustomer() will assert that the total number of current customers is less than the maximum

---

[2] Note that a non successful replay may also result in compensating actions needing to be initiated (see Section 6).

allowed. Only the business developer with knowledge of the desired semantics can specify which predicates, if any, should be associated with the transform.

In addition to regular pre/post conditions, predicates may have to be used to protect code with respect to two pass issues: i.e., issues that arise because of the way that performance-phase code derives from rehearsal-phase code and because of the manner in which state is derived during performance. For example, selectors of branch conditions that determine execution (i.e., values which control the sequencing of logged transforms) may need to be protected. The default assumption made by the framework is that differences between get results do not matter – and thus need not be replayed – since read operations cannot cause conflict among concurrent applications. But, when read-only data might affect the outcome of a UOW (e.g., the application path differs based on an attribute value, so that the commit does require that the attribute have a specified relationship to some value), the corresponding get methods can be specified as a predicate. The framework recognizes special *ApplicationPredicate* objects (APO) whose methods are always logged when invoked (like transforms). This enables the framework to supply persistence for predicates in exactly the same way that it provides persistence for transforms. An example is:

```
long  netWorth = aCustomer.getNetWorth();
//invocation of a read method
CustomerAPO.assertGetNetWorth(netWorth, aCustomer);
```

where CustomerAPO.assertGetNetWorth() is a utility transform that throws an exception if the result of invoking GetNetWorth on the customer object and netWorth are not equal in value. During rehearsal, the value of netWorth is (trivially) equal to that of getNetWorth since netWorth was just derived from that method. During performance, this transform will be replayed among all the other transforms, and the stored (rehearsal) value of netWorth compared against the current value of getNetWorth. If the values do not match, the uow predicate detects that the rule is violated, and an exception is thrown. Note that the framework will generate a generic FooApplicationPredicate object for every class Foo provided by the application writer. In particular, for every non-void method x() of Foo, the generic FooApplicationPredicate has a corresponding method assertX() to assert that invoking x() on Foo returns the same value at rehearsal and performance time (as illustrated by the customer example above). Less generic predicates will be coded by the application developer.

5.2   Conflict Detection/Resolution Approach

The second concurrency mechanism the framework offers is *conflict detection and resolution* (CD/R). The information kept by the framework in this case is not an operational log, but snapshots of the objects as they are first versioned in the child UOW (see Section 4). Upon commit, a process goes through and checks to see if any data in the parent UOW has changed since the object was copied to the child UOW. If no changes are found, the parent versions are updated to reflect the data in the leaf UOW. If any changes are found, a *conflict* has been detected. A *conflict manager* is then invoked. The conflict manager is passed a list of participants in conflict. Its job is to select the *resolution manager(s)* that will be charged with resolving the conflict. As resolution managers are invoked, they apply the business logic necessary to resolve conflicts and arrive at the desired parent data state (in a similar way to what the manual procedures accomplish in a single-threaded multi-user system). Conflict and resolution managers have to implement an interface defined by the framework. A given uow is associated to one conflict manager and one or more resolution managers.

6   Further Challenges

The LRUOW framework provides structural transactional support for long running business processes. There are other aspects/issues however with LRBPs. Workflow systems [10] for example are concerned with the routing and sequencing of work among individuals and groups. The workflow system assists in defining resources, assigning resources, or initiating tasks. It acts as the controller of the overall business process. It takes a business process and breaks it into tasks (nodes in a process network), and defines a list of persons or programs that can perform tasks. Workflow systems manage recovery of the state of the workflow by reliably knowing which tasks have started and which have completed. They do not address recovery of resources manipulated in workflow tasks, nor provide an approach for handling contention when different tasks concurrently access shared data. The LRUOW framework addresses precisely these issues by providing transactional properties (including concurrency and durability) as well as an application model that is familiar to developers. This functionality can be programmed into workflow, but generally requires considerable custom work with high associated development and maintenance costs. Currently, the difficulty in custom coding of transactional constructs often leads developers to change natural workflow task definition or task relationships. For instance, because locking and visibility are complicated issues, a process – which may actually contain much parallel activity – will be serialized so as to sidestep the problem. Or, to avoid making "in process" data visible to other processes, much data will be inserted into separate containers instead of writing to a common database. The LRUOW framework greatly assists with such transactional concerns. Use of the LRUOW framework within a workflow can thus lead to a simplified workflow network, smaller workflow containers, a greater degree of parallelism, and less custom work.

Another issue with long running business processes is that some of the actions performed in the context of such processes (e.g., sending a letter to a customer) cannot be rolled-back. They can at best be *compensated* (e.g., sending a second letter to the customer asking to ignore the first one). The concept of compensation has been widely used in another approach to the problem of long running activities referred to as sagas [11]. A saga consists of a sequence of subtransactions $T_1,..., T_n$ and a corresponding sequence of compensation transactions $C_1,..., C_{n-1}$ such that if the desired full sequence $T_1,...,T_n$ fails in T_i then, by aborting T_i and executing $C_{i-1},..., C_1$, all trace of the overall transaction is removed. Like the LRUOW approach, sagas do not hold long term locks on data; unlike the LRUOW approach, sagas do not enforce visibility rules with the result that other transactions see intermediate results of any subsequence of $T_1,..., T_n$. Compensating transactions are a convenient and easily understood way of backing out transactions in simple systems. But they often need to be hand-coded, which makes it impractical to deploy sagas in large, complex, business systems. Also since humans must occasionally participate in the compensation process, the recovery process cannot be fully automated. The LRUOW framework by restricting the visibility of the work done in the course of the LRBP, and allowing to rollback (in case of failure) many of the actions performed, simplify the design of the compensation scheme.

Both the integration with workflow system and compensating schemes are currently being investigated.

Another area of investigation are strategies to integrate *legacy systems*. In order to provide ACID semantics to long running business processes, the framework makes a basic assumption: namely, that (during the performance phase) all resources used in the LRUOW can be externally coordinated to run in a single, short-running, classic transaction. A large set of systems meet this requirement – e.g., those that support the X/Open XA interface. However, many legacy datastores cannot be coordinated externally, and may not even supply transactions internally. One challenge that we must address, therefore, is whether precise semantics can be assigned to long running business processes that run on such systems.

References

1. Enterprise JavaBean Specification Version 1.0, http://java.sun.com/products/ejb/docs.html. 332
2. IBM Websphere Application Server, http://www.software.ibm.com/webservers/appserv/. 332
3. J. E. B. Moss. : Nested Transactions: An Approach to Reliable Distributed Computing. MIT Press. (1985). 334
4. Transaction Service Specification, in CORBA Services: Common Object Services Specification. http://www.omg.org. 335
5. J. Gray and A. Reuter. Transaction Processing Concepts and Techniques. Morgan Kaufmann, 1993. 335, 343
6. E. Gamma, R. Helm, R. Johnson, and J. Vlissides. Design Pattern, Elements of Reusable Object-Oriented Software. Addison-Wesley, 1994. 337, 338
7. H. T. Kung and J.T. Robinson, On Optimistic Methods for Concurrency Control, ACM Trans. on Database Sys., Vol 6., No. 2, June 1981, pp. 213-226. 343
8. K. Wu, P.S Yu, and C. Pu, Divergence Control Algorithms for Epsilon Serializability, IEEE Transactions on Knowledge and Data Engineering, Vol. 9, No. 2, March-April 1997, pp. 262-274. 344
9. C. Pu et al., Divergence Control for Distributed Database Systems, Distributed and Parallel Databases, Vol. 3, No. 1, Jan. 1995, pp. 85-109. 344

10. Workflow   Management   Coalition   (WfMC),   http://www.aiim.org/wfmc/
    mainframe.htm. 346
11. Modeling Long-Running Activities as Nested Sagas, H. Garcia-Molina, D. Gawlick,
    J. Klein, K. Kleissner, and K. Salem. Data Engineering, Vol. 14, No. 1, March 1991.
    346

Active Middleware Services in a Decision Support System for Managing Highly Available Distributed Resources

Sameh A. Fakhouri[1], William F. Jerome[1], Vijay K. Naik[1], Ajay Raina[2], and Pradeep Varma[3]

[1] IBM T. J. Watson Research Center, Hawthorne, NY 10532
{sameh,wfj,vkn}@us.ibm.com
[2] IBM Global Services, Bangalore, India
rajay@in.ibm.com
[3] IBM India Research Laboratory, New Delhi, India
pvarma@in.ibm.com

Abstract. We describe a decision support system called Mounties that is designed for managing applications and resources using rule-based constraints in scalable mission-critical clustering environments. Mounties consists of four active service components: (1) a repository of resource proxy objects for modeling and manipulating the cluster configuration; (2) an event notification mechanism for monitoring and controlling interdependent and distributed resources; (3) a rule evaluation and decision processing mechanism; and (4) a global optimization service for providing decision making capabilities. The focus of this paper is on the design of the first three services that together connect and coordinate the distributed resources with the decision making component. We discuss the overall architecture and design of these services. We describe in some detail the asynchronous, concurrent, and pipelined nature of their interactions and the fault tolerance designed in the system. We also describe a general programming paradigm that we have followed in designing these services.

1 Introduction

A cluster is a collection of resources (such as nodes, disks, adapters, databases, etc.) that collectively provide scalable services to end users and to their applications while maintaining a consistent, uniform, and single system view of the cluster services. By design, a cluster is supposed to provide a single point of control for cluster administrators and at the same time it is supposed to facilitate addition, removal, or replacement of individual resources without significantly affecting the services provided by the entire system. On one side, a cluster has a set of distributed, heterogeneous physical resources and, on the other side, it projects a seamless set of services that are supposed to have a look and feel (in terms of scheduling, fault tolerance, etc.) of services provided by a single large virtual resource. Obviously, this implies some form of continuous coordination

J. Sventek and G. Coulson (Eds.): Middleware 2000, LNCS 1795, pp. 349–371, 2000.

and mapping of the physical distributed resources and their services onto a set of virtual resources and their services.

Typically, such coordination and mappings are handled by the resource management facilities, with the bulk of the work done manually by the cluster administrators. Despite the advances in distributed operating systems and middleware technology, the cluster management is highly human administrator bound (and hence expensive, error-prone, and non scalable beyond a certain cluster size). Primary reasons for such a state-of-the-art is that existing resource management systems adopt a static resource-centric view where the physical resources in the cluster are considered to be static entities, that are either available or not available and are managed using predetermined strategies. These strategies are applied to provide reliable system-wide services, in the presence of highly dynamic conditions such as variable load, faults, application failures, and so on. The coordination and mapping using such an approach is too complex and tedious to make it amenable to any form of automation.

To overcome these difficulties, we take an approach that is different from the traditional resource management approach. In this approach, resources are considered as services whose availability and quality-of-service depends on the availability and the quality-of-service provided by one or more other services in the cluster. For this, to state it informally, the cluster and its resources are represented by two dimensions. The first dimension captures the semi-static nature of each resource; e.g., the type and quality of the supporting services needed to enable its services. Typically, these requirements are defined (explicitly or implicitly) by the designers of the resource or the application. These may be further qualified by the cluster administrators. These are formalized as simple rules that can be dynamically and programatically evaluated, taking into account the current state of the cluster. The second dimension is the dynamic state of the various services provided by the cluster. The dynamic changes are captured by events. Finally, all the coordination and mapping is done at a logically centralized place, where the events are funneled in and the rules are evaluated. This helps in isolating and localizing all the heterogeneity and associated complexity. By separating the dynamic part (the events) from the semi-static parts (the rules), and combining these in a systematic manner only when needed, the desired level of automation in the coordination and mapping of resources and services can be achieved.

While the general principles outlined above are fairly straightforward, there is a nontrivial amount of complexity in managing the choreography. To show the proof of concept, we have designed and implemented a system called Mounties based on the above described general principles. The Mounties architecture itself is composed of multiple components, a primary component being the modeling and decision making engine. The remaining components together form an active and efficient resource management layer between the actual cluster resources and the decision-making component. This layer continuously transports the state information to the decision maker and commands from the decision maker to the cluster resources, back-and-forth in a fault-tolerant manner. In this paper, we describe in detail the architecture and design of the services that form this middleware.

The remainder of the paper is organized as follows. First we define some terms and cluster concepts and then, in Sect. 3, briefly describe the overall Mounties approach. Following that, in Sect. 3.3, we present a small example to illustrate some of the key concepts. An overview of the Mounties architecture and its design is described in Sect. 4. Described in Sect. 5 are the salient features of the three main services that coordinate the actions between the cluster resources and the decision making component. In Sect. 6, we describe the programming paradigm that we have followed in designing these services. Finally, we conclude the paper after reviewing the related work, in Sects. 7 and 8, respectively.

2   Definitions and Basic Cluster Concepts

In a cluster managed by Mounties, hardware components such as nodes, adapters, memory, disks, and software components such as applications, database servers, web servers are all treated as cluster *resources*. When there is no ambiguity, in this paper, we use the terms resource and the service it provides, interchangeably. A *location* is a unique place in the cluster where a resource or service physically resides and makes its service available. Typically it is identified by the node (or the processing element), but it could be any uniquely identifiable location (such as an URL). To provide its intended services, a resource may need services provided by one or more other resources. These are referred to as the *dependencies*. In addition to the dependencies, a resource may have other limitations and restrictions such as capacity (defined in the following) or location in the cluster where it can provide its services. Some of these may be because of the physical limitations of the resource while others may be imposed by the cluster administrators. The dependencies and the specified limitations together form a set of *constraints* that must be satisfied for making a service available. Usually the cluster administrator satisfies these constraints by *allocating* appropriate resources. Typically, a cluster is expected to support multiple services. To achieve this, constraints for multiple resources must be satisfied simultaneously, by judiciously allocating lower level supporting resources and services. This hierarchical allocation of resources (i.e., one level of resources supporting the next level of resources) gives rise to a particular *cluster configuration* where dependency relations are defined among cluster resources. Note that there may be more than one possible cluster configuration to provide the same set of services. When there are only a limited number of resources or when the constraints among resources are complex, there may only be a small number of ways in which cluster can be configured to satisfy all the constraints. Determining such unique configurations is a hard problem.

Resources have attributes that distinguish them from one another. These include Name, Type, Capacity, Priority, and State. Each resource has a unique *Name* and resources are classified into multiple *Types* based on the functionality they provide. *Capacity* of a resource is the number of dependent resources that it can serve simultaneously. The capacity may be inherent in the design of a resource or it may be imposed by cluster administrators for performance or testing purposes. All allocations of a resource must ensure that its capacity constraints are not violated. *Priority* denotes the relative importance of a resource or a service. In Mounties, the Priority is a number (on a scale of 1 to 10, 1 being the lowest) to indicate its relative value. It is used in more than one way. For example, if two resources depend on a resource that can only support one of them, then one way to resolve the conflict is to allocate the scarce resource to the resource with higher priority. Similarly, in a cluster there may be more than one resource of a certain type and a resource or service that depends that type of resource may have a choice in satisfying that dependency. Here Priority of the supporting resources may be used to make the choice. The Priority field can also be used in stating the goals or objectives for cluster operation; e.g., resources may be allocated such that the sum of the Priorities of all services made available is maximized. The *State* of a resource indicates the readiness of its availability. In Mounties, the State of a resources is abstracted as ONLINE, OFFLINE, or FAILED. An ONLINE resource is ready and is available for immediate allocation, provided its capacity is not exhausted; An OFFLINE resource could be made ONLINE after its constraints are satisfied. A FAILED resource cannot be made available just by satisfying its constraints. The FAILED state is indicative of either a failure because of an error condition or unavailability because of administrative servicing requirements.

Finally, we note that throughout the paper we use the term *end users* to mean the cluster administrators, the applications that use the cluster services, or the end users in the conventional sense. In practice, cluster administrators and high level applications tend to be the real users of the services provided by Mounties.

3   The Mounties Approach

As described in the introductory section, Mounties introduces a constraint-based methodology for the cluster configuration, startup and recovery of applications and other higher level resources. The constraints are used to build relationships among supporting and dependent resources/services. Under this approach, the heterogeneity and nonuniformity of the physical cluster are replaced by the consistent and single-system like service views. This is further enhanced by providing higher-level abstractions that allow end users to express requirements and objectives that are tailored to a particular cluster and the organization using the cluster.

3.1   Basic Rules and Abstractions

In a cluster, certain services are expected to be normally available. In Mounties, this is expressed by means of a resource attribute called the *NominalState*. The NominalState acts as a constraint for one or more resources in the cluster and this information becomes a part of the cluster definition. To indicate the normal availability of the services of a resource, the NominalState of that resource is set to ONLINE. This constraint is satisfied when the State of that resource is ONLINE. Furthermore, the ONLINE NominalState implies that every effort must be made to keep that service ONLINE. Similarly, a NominalState of OFFLINE is sometimes desirable; e.g., for servicing a resource or when the cost of keeping a resource on-line all the time is too high.

When a resource or service has an ONLINE NominalState, the cluster management system needs to be informed about how the resource or service can be brought on-line. Typically, most services or applications depend on other lower level services or resources. Mounties provides two main abstractions for expressing the inter-resource dependencies: the *DependsOn* relationship and the *CollocatedWith* relationship. Resource A DependsOn B if services of Resource B are needed for the liveliness of A. Note that a resource or an application may require services of more than one type of other resources. Generally these services may be available anywhere in the cluster. In certain cases, only the services provided by local resources can be used. To express such a location specific constraint a CollocatedWith relationship is used. For example, Resource A CollocatedWith B means Resource A must have the same location as that of B; i.e., they must reside on the same node. Note that services of B may be available at more than one location. In that case, there is a choice and a decision has to be made about the location that is to be picked. Similarly, sometimes it is desirable not to locate two resources on the same node. This is expressed by the Anti-CollocatedWith constraint.

Mounties provides a new resource abstraction called an Equivalency. Informally, an equivalency is a set of resources with similar functionality, but possibly with different performance characteristics. It has a run-time semantics of "choose one of these". Since the selection of the most appropriate resource from an equivalency depends on the cluster-state, the concept of equivalencies provides Mounties with a strong and flexible method to meet the service goals of the cluster. With this abstraction, the end-user is freed from making ad-hoc decisions and allows Mounties to choose the most appropriate resource based on the conditions at run-time. An equivalency can also be associated with a weighting function, called a policy. A policy can guide, but not force, the decision- making mechanism within Mounties towards a particular selection based on end-user preferences or advanced knowledge about the system. Since an equivalency can be treated as a resource, it maintains uniformity in specifying constraints and at the same time allows specification of multiple options that can be utilized at run-time.

Finally, Mounties provides abstractions for defining *business objectives* or goals of how the resources in the cluster are to be managed and configured. These objectives typically consist of maintaining availability of cluster services and of individual resources in a prioritized manner, allocation of resources so as to balance the load or services, or delivering a level of service within a specified range, and so on.

3.2   Management and Coordination of Resources

At the lowest levels, all resources are manipulated in a programmable manner or from the command line. Mounties divides the work such that the decision making and resource allocation processes (which require global knowledge about the cluster) are distinct from the resource monitoring, controlling, and manipulating processes (which require resource specific information) such as the resource managers. This encapsulation of resource manipulation gives flexibility and requires no special programming in order to add an application into the cluster once its resource manager is available. For the purpose of this paper, we will not focus on the topic of resource managers.

Mounties gathers and maintains information about the cluster configuration and the dependency information for each resource at cluster startup or whenever a new resource or application is introduced in the cluster. A continuous event notification and heartbeat mechanisms are also needed for monitoring cluster-wide activities. Using these mechanisms, Mounties continuously monitors the cluster-wide events and compares the current cluster-state with the desired state. Whenever there are discrepancies between the two, the best possible realignment of resources is sought after taking into account the conditions existing in the cluster and the desired cluster-wide objectives. If a new realignment of resources can lead to a better configuration, commands are issued to the resources to bring about the desired changes.

We now illustrate these concepts using a simple, but realistic example.

3.3   An Example

Our example involves a cluster of three nodes shown in Fig. 1. Both Node 0 and Node 1 have disk adapters that connect them to a shared disk which holds a database. Each node has a network adapter which connects it to the network. The services of this cluster are used by a Web Server as shown in Fig. 2.

The hardware and software components shown the Fig. 1 are defined to Mounties along with their attributes and are treated as resources. For example, the disk adapter 0 has the following attributes:

```
Disk Adapter 0 Attributes
    {
        Capacity = 1
        Priority = 2.0
    }
```

The nodes and other adapters in the system are defined to Mounties in a similar manner. Using these basic resources, a set of equivalencies are defined. As explained earlier, an equivalency is a grouping of the same type of resources and is treated as an abstract resource. In our example, Equivalency 1 groups the two disk adapters into one new resource. Similarly, Equivalency 2 groups the three network adapters into one new resource.

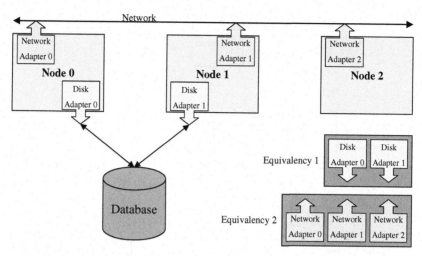

Fig. 1. An example cluster configuration managed by Mounties

The database itself has two engines that can be brought on-line only on the nodes with both disk and network adapters. Figure 2 shows the dependencies for the two database management engines. Database engine 0 has the following attributes:

```
Database 0 Attributes
    {
        NominalState = ONLINE
        Priority     = 8.0
        DependsOn     = Equivalency 1, Equivalency 2
        CollocatedWith = Equivalency 1,Equivalency 2
    }
```

Database engine 1 is defined in the same manner. Aside from having a relatively high priority of 8, both engines have a NominalState of ONLINE. This indicates to Mounties that it should try an keep them both ONLINE at all times. In addition, the database engines have dependencies and collocation constraints on both Equivalency 1 and 2. Both constraints are represented in Fig. 2 by the bi-directional arrows linking the Database engines to the Equivalencies.

Mounties represents these constraints as follows: For each Database engine to be online we need a Disk Adapter, a Network Adapter and they must be located on the same node as the Database engine. So, if Mounties were to pick Disk Adapter 0 from Equivalency 1 to satisfy the requirements of Database 1 for a disk adapter, the collocation constraint will force it to also pick Network Adapter 0 from the Equivalency 2. So, to make Database 1 ONLINE, Mounties would perform the following allocations:

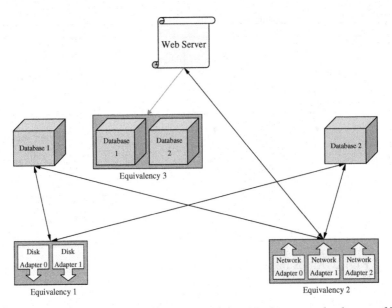

Fig. 2. Dependencies for a Web Server supported by the example cluster of Fig. 1

```
Database 1
    {
        From Equivalency 1 = Disk Adapter 0
        From Equivalency 2 = Network Adapter 0
        Node Assignment    = Node 0
    }
```

These allocations satisfy all the constraints of Database 1, therefore it can be brought ONLINE. When allocating resources for Database 2, neither Disk Adapter 0 nor Network Adapter 0 are eligible because their capacity is exhausted. Mounties cannot allocate Network Adapter 2 from Equivalency 2, since there is no Disk Adapter on Node 2 that would satisfy the collocation constraint. The only choice then is the following allocations for Database 2:

```
Database 2
    {
        From Equivalency 1 = Disk Adapter 1
        From Equivalency 2 = Network Adapter 1
        Node Assignment    = Node 1
    }
```

These allocations satisfy all the constraints of Database 2, therefore it can be brought ONLINE.

Figure 2 also shows Equivalency 3, which contains both Database engines. Shown also is a new resource, Web Server which has the following attributes:

```
Web Server Attributes
    {
        Nominal State = ONLINE
        Priority      = 6.0
        DependsOn     = Equivalency 2, Equivalency 3
        CollocatedWith = Equivalency 2
    }
```

The dependency and collocation constraints are shown with the bi-directional arrows linking the Web Server to Equivalency 2. The dependency is shown with the uni-directional arrow linking the Web Server to Equivalency 3.

Given the previous assignments that Mounties made to bring the Database engines up (i.e., make their State ONLINE), the only available Network Adapter from Equivalency 2 is Network Adapter 2. To satisfy the Web Server's dependency on Equivalency 3, Mounties could pick Database 1. So, to bring the Web Server to the ONLINE state, Mounties would perform the following allocations:

```
Web Server
    {
        From Equivalency 2 = Network Adapter 2
        From Equivalency 3 = Database 1
        Node Assignment    = Node 2
    }
```

This completes the resource allocations necessary to bring all resources to the ONLINE state. While running, if Database 1 should fail for any reason, Mounties would switch the Web Server over to Database 2 and thus keep it ONLINE.

We note here that in the above, we have described the decision making process in an intuitive manner. In Mounties, this process is formalized by modeling the problem as an optimization problem with specific objective functions defined by cluster administrators. The optimization problem encapsulates all the relevant constraints for the cluster resources along with desired cluster objective. Good solution techniques invariable involve performing global optimization.

4 Mounties Design Overview

In previous section, we have discussed the resource management concepts used in Mounties. We now describe the Mounties architecture and its design in some detail, and provide rationale for our design decisions where appropriate.

A cluster is a dynamically evolving system and is constantly subject to changes in its state because of the spontaneous and concurrent behavior of the cluster resources, random and unpredictable nature of the demands on the services, and the interactions with end users. At the same time, a cluster is expected to respond in a well-defined manner to events that seek to change the cluster-state. Some of these events are:

1. Individual resource related events such as: resource is currently unavailable; unavailable resource has become available; a new resource has joined the cluster; a resource has (permanently) left the cluster.
2. Feedback response to a cluster manager command: successful execution of a command such as go online or go offline; failure to execute such a command.
3. End user interactions and directives: cluster startup and shutdown; resource isolation and shutdown; manual overrides for cluster configurations; movement of individual and/or a group of resources; changes in dependency definitions and constraint definitions among resources; updates to business objectives; requests leading to what-if type of analysis, and status queries.
4. Resource groups related events, or virtual events, which arise from a combination of events/feedback related to individual resources.
5. Alerts and alarms from service and load monitors.

With these dynamic changes taking place in the background, a cluster manager such as Mounties is required to make resource allocation and other changes such that the predefined global objectives are met in the best possible manner, while resource specific constraints are obeyed. The resource specific constraints usually limit the number of ways in which the resources in the cluster can be configured. These constraints include capacity constraints, dependency constraints, location constraints, and so on. The objectives and the constraints lead to a solution of a global optimization problem that must be solved in soft real-time. This requires an efficient decision making component and a set of services that form an efficient middleware connecting the resources with the decision making component. Before describing how these components can be designed, first we describe the overall clustering environment in which a system like Mounties operates.

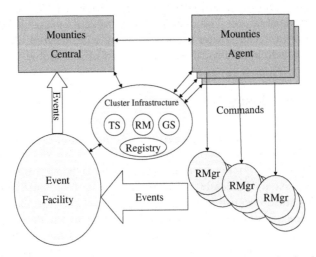

Fig. 3. Mounties design and its relationship cluster services for high availability

4.1   Cluster Infrastructure

The Mounties system as described here can be used as an application/resource management system or as a subsystem for guaranteeing high availability and quality-of-service for other components in the cluster. When used an application/resource management system, the Mounties system described here can basically be used in a stand-alone mode. When used as a guarantor of dependable services, a few other cluster services are required. In Fig. 3, we illustrate a conceptual design of Mounties on the top of basic high availability services. Using these services, Mounties can then be used as an intelligent mechanism for guaranteeing high availability. Note that the basic cluster services that Mounties would depend on are provided as standard services in state-of-the-art clusters such as IBM's SP-2 System [6,7]. As shown in Fig. 3, four additional cluster services are needed to ensure high availability: (1) a persistent Cluster Registry (CR) to store and retrieve the configuration of the resources; (2) a mechanism called Topology Services (TS) for detecting node and communication adapter failures; (3) a mechanism for Reliable Messaging (RM) for important communication between Mounties Central and all the other Mounties Agents; and (4) a Group Services (GS) facility for electing a leader (i.e., Mounties Central) at cluster initialization and whenever an existing leader is unable to provide its services (because of a node failure, for example). We note here that the Mounties Repository and the Event Notification services (described in the next section) can be embellished to incorporate the functions provided by Cluster Registry and Reliable Messaging. Similarly, a customized version of Group Services can be designed into the Mounties architecture to monitor and elect Mounties Central.

4.2   Internals of Mounties Design

Overview and the Ideal. In brief terms, designing the internals of the manager described thus far is an exercise in coming up with software that can coordinate the following choreography: Events arise asynchronously, throughout the cluster. They are delivered to the coordinator (such as an ideal version of Mounties) using pipelined communication channels. The coordinator is programmed to respond to events in the context of a semi-static definition of the cluster, that consists of dependencies, constraints, objective functions etc. The coordinator's decision-making component, basically an optimizer, has to combine the dynamic events with the semi-static definition in order to arrive at a response to events. The response has to translate into simple commands to resources such as go ONLINE and go OFFLINE. The coordinator sends its commands to resources at the same time as when various events arise and traverse the cluster. The commands are also sent using pipelined communication channels. Thus there is a basic dichotomy in the activity of coordinating the choreography. At the one end there is the cluster of resources and the events it generates. At the other end there is the decision-making optimizer. In between the two is middleware that along one path, collects, transports, and fine-tunes events for the decision-maker, and on the reverse path, decomposes the decisions of the decision-maker into commands that are then transported to the individual cluster resources.

Ideally, the coordinator reacts to the events instantaneously. It is able to account for faults in command execution–not all commands may succeed–along with being able to respond to events and command feedback in a real-time manner. Suppose the ideal coordinator is an infinitely fast computation engine. In this case, the choreography becomes a seamless movement of events, commands, and commands feedback in a pipelined/systolic manner throughout the cluster. Events and feedback upon arrival at the coordinator get transformed instantaneously into commands that in turn get placed on channels to various resources. The coordinator is able to ensure that globally-optimal solutions get deployed in the cluster in response to cluster events.

In Mounties, the ideal coordinator as described above is approximated by one active Mounties Central that resides on one node to which all events and command feedback get directed. Mounties Central can change or migrate in response to say node failure. However, at one time, only one Mounties Central is active.

Command Execution Model. The next definition we add in deriving our practical system from the ideal alluded to above is a command execution model. The model builds fault tolerance and simplicity in the execution of commands by sacrificing pipelining. It uses the following protocol: A command contains all the state needed for its execution by a resource manager. A command is only a simple directive to a resource manager; e.g., "go ONLINE using X, Y, Z resources", or "go OFFLINE", and no more. A resource manager does not need a computation engine to handle conditional behavior or context evaluation at its site. To achieve this, no new command is sent out until Mounties is aware of the positive outcome of the commands that the execution of the new command depends on. It is up to Mounties Central to make the best use of the command feedback it receives in order to minimize command failure. So for example, after receiving an "go ONLINE" command, a resource manager need not find out whether its supporting resources are actually up. The resource manager should simply assume that to be the case. In general, the more effective Mounties is in managing such assumptions, more efficient is the overall resource coordination. Clearly, one of the things Mounties Central has to do is to issue the commands in the partial order given by dependencies. Thus, in order for a resource to be asked to go on-line, its planned supporting resources have to be brought up first. Only after that the resource is to be asked to go on-line using the specific supporting resources. Similarly, before bringing down a resource, all the resources dependent on that resource must be brought down first. The existing and the planned dependencies in the cluster thus enforce a *dataflow* or partial order on the execution of the commands.

The above command execution model imposes minimal requirements on resource managers. This allows our system to coordinate heterogeneous and variously-sourced resources without requiring unnecessary standardization on the implementation of resource managers. The command execution proceeds in a dataflow or frontier-by-frontier manner. Within a frontier, commands do not depend on one another, and thus can proceed concurrently. A preceding frontier comprises of commands whose execution results are needed for the succeeding frontier. For bringing up resources, the frontiers are arranged bottom up, from the leaves to root(s), while for bringing down resources, the order is reversed. For example, in shutting down the cluster in the example of Sect. 3.3, the first the web server has to be brought down. The next frontier comprises of the two databases and either can be brought down before the other. On the other hand, in bringing up the same cluster, the order of the frontiers is reversed and the web server is the last entity on which an up command gets executed. Note that ordering of the frontiers does not imply synchronized execution. Individual commands in a frontier are issued as soon as the corresponding commands in the preceding frontiers are executed successfully. Although commands across frontiers are not pipelined, no artificial serialization is introduced either. The system remains as asynchronous and concurrent as it can within the bounds of the commands model described above.

Realizable Decision Making. An infinitely-fast or zero-time computation engine is not realizable. Since the optimization decisions involve solution of NP-hard problems [9], even an attempt at approximating zero time, or say hard real time, for solving the optimization problem is not possible. The approach we follow embraces global heuristic solutions that can be arrived at in soft real time. The computationally intensive nature of the decision making component predisposes us towards persisting with a previously derived global solution even when there are a limited number of command failures. It is not computationally-efficient to chart a totally new global course every time there is a command failure. So for example, when a resource refuses to go ONLINE, Mounties looks for an auxiliary solution from within the proposed solution that can substitute for the failed resource. For example, a lightly-loaded resource can (and does) replace a failed resource in case the two belong to the same equivalency. Auxiliary solutions are local in nature. If the finally deployed solution turns out to have too many auxiliary solutions, then the quality of the solution is expected to suffer. To avoid the configuration to deviate too far from the globally optimal solution, Mounties recomputes a global solution whenever the objective value of the deployed solution is below a certain value as compared to the proposed solution. This is done by feeding back an artificially-generated event that forces recomputing the global solution. In summary, Mounties does not attempt to maintain a globally-optimal cluster configuration at all times. Instead, Mounties looks for global approximations for the same. The obvious tradeoff here is using a suboptimal solution versus keeping one or more cluster services unavailable while the optimal solution is being computed. The tradeoff could be unfavorable for Mounties in a relatively uneventful and simple clusters where resources take relatively long time to execute "go ONLINE" and "go OFFLINE" commands as compared to the time spent in determining optimal solution. For such clusters, it would be of merit to recompute a globally optimal cluster configuration.

Computing a globally optimal solution based on the constraints and the current state of cluster, is a significant function of Mounties. The resulting optimization problem can be cast as an abstract optimization problem that can be solved using many well known techniques such as combinatorial optimization methods, mathematical programming and genetic/evolutionary methods. For that reason and to bring modularity to the design, in Mounties, we treat that as a separate module and is called, the Global Optimizer or simply, the Optimizer. It is designed with a purely functional interface to the rest of the system. A detailed discussion of the Optimizer is beyond the purview of this paper and is discussed elsewhere [9,10]. The interface to the Optimizer module completely isolates it from effects of concurrent cluster events on its input. A *snapshot* of the current cluster-state, which incorporates all events that have been recorded till the time of the snapshot, is created and handed over to the Optimizer. The metaphor *snapshot* is meaningful since once taken, the snapshot does not change even if new events occur in the cluster. The snapshot is thus referentially transparent, i.e., purely functional and non-imperative, and references to a particular snapshot return the same data time after time. Given a snapshot, the Optimizer proceeds with its work of proposing an approximately optimal cluster configuration that takes into account the current context and the long-term objectives defined for the cluster.

Just as the Optimizer is not invoked whenever a new cluster event arrives, it may not be interrupted if a new event arrives while it is computing a new global solution. This is primarily to maintain simplicity in the design and implementation. Thus, when the Optimizer returns a solution, the state of the cluster, as perceived by Mounties, may not be the same as the state at the time the optimizer is invoked and that the results produced may be stale. Our system however does try to make up for exclusion of newer events by aligning the solutions proposed by the optimizer with any events that may have arrived during the time the solutions were being created. Such an alignment however, is local in nature. Over longer time intervals, the effects of newer events get reflected in the global solutions computed subsequently.

Because of the nature of the problem, simple rule-based heuristics can be used to make local optimization decisions prior to invoking the Optimizer. Such preprocessing can significantly reduce the turnaround time in responding to events. The preprocessing step is also necessary for isolating the Optimizer from the on going changes in the system. This is referred to as the Preprocessor. Specifically, the Preprocessor waits on a queue of incoming events and then processes an eligible event all by itself or hands down a preprocessed version of the problem to the Optimizer. The decisions from the Optimizer or the Preprocessor are directed to a module called the Postprocessor, which is the center of the command generation and execution machinery. Figure 4 shows the interactions among the Preprocessor, the Optimizer, the Postprocessor, and other modules. These modules are discussed in detail next.

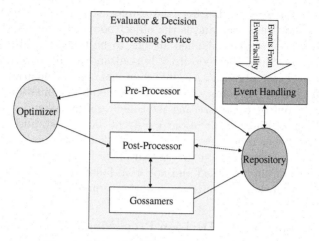

Fig. 4. Mounties Central: internal design

5   Main Services

5.1   The Resource Repository

The Repository of resource objects provides a local, somewhat minimal, and abstract representation of the cluster. The repository cache is coherent with the actual cluster to the extent that cluster events are successfully generated and reported to Mounties. Mounties does safe/conservative cluster management without any assumptions of: (a) completeness of the set of events received by it; (b) correctness of any of the events received by it; and (c) (firm) significance of the temporal ordering of the events received by it. Generally, the effectiveness and efficiency of management depends upon the completeness, correctness, and speed with which events are reported to Mounties, but Mounties does not become unsafe even if event reporting degrades. Within the above event-reporting context, Mounties does assume ownership of the management process, so resources are not expected to configure themselves independently of Mounties. If the context requires say human intervention and direct configuration of resources, then either this can be routed through Mounties, or the semantics of the events reported to Mounties modified so that Mounties remains conservative in its actions.

Regardless of its current state, the repository is updated with an event before the preprocessor is informed. The updating of the repository is an atomic act: readers of the repository either see the update fully, or not at all. The repository is partitioned, and individual resource objects can be accessed individually, so the synchronization requirements of such updating are limited. Partitioning of the repository serves many purposes, including permitting higher concurrent access and better memory use and reduced traversal and searching costs.

Resource objects in the repository contain only a few fields representing necessary information such as current status, desired status, and the current supports of the resource, etc. Snapshot related information (e.g., a time-stamp when the last snapshot was taken and is the object now ready for another snapshot) as well information on the planned actions to be taken are also stored in the resource objects. Since the repository is read and modified concurrently, it is mandatory to reason about all possible combinations of concurrent actions that can take place in the repository so that no erroneous combination slips through. This is carried out by (a) restricting the concurrent access and modifications to only a small set of states in the resource objects, and (b) establishing/identifying invariants and other useful properties of these fields such as monotonicity. For example, we know that cluster events can only change the state of a resource from on-line to off-line or failed and not from failed to on-line since the change to on-line from any state requires a Mounties command.

5.2   The Evaluator and Decision Processing Mechanisms

The Preprocessor. As shown in Fig. 4, events arrive from the cluster and are recorded in the repository module. If an event needs attention by the Preprocessor, then the event is also placed in the input queue of the Preprocessor after it has been recorded in the repository. When there are one or more events in its input queue, the Preprocessor creates a snapshot of the relevant cluster-state by identifying and making a copy of the affected part of the repository. While the repository is constantly updated by new events, the snapshot remains unaffected. Any further processing, in response to the event, takes place using the information encapsulated in the snapshot. Note that the snapshot may capture some of the events that are yet to show up in the Preprocessor queue. Since the repository is more up-to-date, the Preprocessor treats the snapshot as representative of all the events received so far. Note also that because of the atomic nature of the updates to the repository, a snapshot captures an atomic event entirely, or leaves it out completely. For identifying the part of the repository affected by an event, the Preprocessor partitions the cluster resources into disjoint components, called islands, by using the constraint graphs formed by the resource dependencies and collocation constraints. Clearly, an event cannot directly, or indirectly affect resources outside its own island. Such partitioning also serves the purpose as an optimization step prior to applying the global optimization step, by creating multiple smaller size problems, which are less expensive to solve. This is especially beneficial at cluster startup time, when each island can be processed as a small cluster.

Preprocessing includes many more activities: excluding ineligible events (an event can be ineligible for reasons like Mounties is busy with processing a previous snapshot comprising the event's related resources, and thus processing the same resources in another snapshot may lead to divergent action plans which cannot be reconciled); clubbing multiple events (in conjunction with the repository's predisposition) into a larger event; optimizing the snapshot associated with one or more events so that either the event can be handled directly by the Preprocessor, or can be posed as an optimization problem to the Optimizer. A somewhat advanced, but optional treatment of the Preprocessor is to partially evaluate an event using a basic set of rules so as to reduce the amount of processing done by the Optimizer. In general, this can lead to globally non-optimal solutions, but in many instances simple rules can be constructed and embedded in the Preprocessor so as to keep the solutions globally optimal while reducing the load on the Optimizer.

5.3   The Postprocessor

Using the cluster status contained in a snapshot, a new cluster configuration is created by either the preprocessor alone, or by the preprocessor and the optimizer jointly . The configuration primarily indicates the supporting resources to be used in on-lining the resources in the snapshot. The solution is in the form of a graph, outlining the choices to be made in bringing up the resources in the snapshot. Note that, in the cluster, some of these resources may be yet to be configured; some other resources may already be configured and up, as desired by the solution, while the remaining resources may be configured differently and may require alterations. The postprocessor takes this into account and partitions this solution graph into one or more disjoint components that are then handled by simple finite-automaton like machines called the *up-* and *down-gossamers*. Commands within a disjoint region are executed in a pipelined or concurrent manner, as discussed earlier. Across disjoint regions these can be carried out concurrently.

When the Postprocessor picks up a solution to translate into commands and control machinery (one or more gossamers), the Postprocessor notes into the repository the availability of the resources comprising the solution for new analysis. This makes events related to these resources eligible for preprocessing (see above). For Mounties Central supported by a single-processor node, a convenient task size for the Postprocessor is from picking up a solution to the creation of gossamers related to the solution. The Postprocessor can make auxiliary solutions available to a gossamer as the following. If a resource cannot come up because of a failure of one or more issued commands and a suitable alternative resource exists (with spare capacity to support another dependent resource) then that alternative is treated as an auxiliary solution.

The Gossamers. Each gossamer is a simple finite-automaton like machine, which is responsible for changing the state of its set of resources to ONLINE or OFFLINE and follows the dataflow order. Simultaneous execution by multiple gossamers brings a high-degree of concurrency to the execution process. The simplicity in their design allows these entities to be spawned just like auxiliary devices while the more interesting and "thinking" work is kept within the other modules (e.g., the Postprocessor). A gossamer executes its commands by "wiring up" the relevant part of the repository with the solution-set assigned to it. Mounties attempts to bring down a resource only after it has confirmed that all resources dependent on such a resource are currently down. A "go ONLINE" command for a resource is dispatched only after receiving positive acknowledgements for all the supporting resources, and checking that the supporting resources have enough capacity for the upcoming resource (i.e. all necessary resource downs have occurred). This naturally leads to the execution of the commands in a dataflow manner.

The process of on-lining and off-lining of resources in unrelated parts of a solution can proceed simultaneously in a distributed manner. If a resource fails to come up after being asked to do so, the related gossamer asks (the Postprocessor) for auxiliary solutions for the same resource in trying to bring dependent resources of the same up, upon their individual turns.

5.4   Other Services

The Event Notification and Event Handler Mechanisms. Mounties Central and Mounties Agents are associated with a component of the Event Handler. We use Java RMI layer as the event notification mechanism. The central handler gets requests from the agents, which are serialized automatically by Java RMI and communicates back with the agents, again using Java RMI. Because we use the standard services provided by Java RMI, we do not describe those in detail here. We note here that the more reliable event notification mechanisms can replace the RMI-based event notification layer, in a straightforward manner. All resource managers in the cluster, various Mounties agents, and Mounties Central, as well as Mounties GUI all are glued together by the event notification mechanism. We describe the GUI component in some details here.

Mounties GUI. The GUI displays various graphical views of the cluster to the end user, in response to the submitted queries and commands. These requests are routed through the Event Notification mechanism. Java's EventDespatcher thread writes the request in the form of an event in an input queue of the EventHandler. The EventHandler then requests for the required data from Mounties Central. When the necessary information is received, the EventHandler communicates the same to the Mounties agent that local to the node where the initial request came from. The actual rendering is then done by the GUI. The two-way communication between the local Mounties agent and the Mounties Central is done over a layer of Java RMI. Using the GUI, the user can view many of the important characteristics of the resources being managed.

6   Structuring Mounties Implementation

Implementation of Mounties architecture and design imposes a challenging requirement for the software developer–the challenge being how to ensure that the software developed is correct, robust, extensible, maintainable, and efficient enough to meet soft real-time constraints. In this section, we describe a programming paradigm that is well suited to meet these requirements.

A concurrent specification is naturally suited to Mounties and is more likely to yield a verifiably correct and robust implementation of the system. A simple and concurrent implementation of Mounties would comprise of a CSP-style process [5] for each functional block described earlier. Each such process would then communicate with other processes via communication channels, and the entire operation would then proceed in a pipelined manner. Such a specification however can suffer from two problems: (a) complexities associated with managing parallelism including state sharing and synchronization, and (b) inefficiency of fine-grained parallelism. Both of these problems can be addressed by using a different approach than the CSP approach, as described in the following. The approach described here enables a variable-concurrency specification of Mounties and is consistent with the overall operational semantics of Mounties described previously. The paradigm also provides a few additional benefits such as: efficiency and ease in performance tuning; simple extensions to simulate events using cloned copies of the repository; flexibility and amenability to changes in functionality (e.g., adding more Preprocessor smarts).

6.1 Efficient and Flexible Concurrent Programming

The paradigm comprises of an approach of defining relatively short lived, dynamic, concurrent tasks wherein the tasks can be in-lined. In the limit of this approach, all of the tasks can be in-lined, resulting in a sequential implementation of the system. The key issue in this approach is not to compromise on the natural concurrency in the description of the system while defining the dynamic, concurrent tasks, and task in-lining.

In this paradigm, computations are broken into a set of atomic tasks. Tasks are defined such that (a) each task is computationally significant as compared to the bookkeeping costs of managing parallelism; and (b) each task forms a natural unit of computation so that its specification is natural and straightforward. In initial prototyping, (b) can overrule (a), so that correctness considerations of initial work can override performance considerations. Each atomic computation described in a detailed Mounties semantics has to be contained in a task from this set of atomic tasks. Although this is an optimization and not a requirement, for reducing context-switching costs, the computation of a task should proceed with thread-preemption/task-preemption disabled.

Under this paradigm, the operations within Mounties can proceed as follows. Each event from the event handler results in the creation of one or more tasks, to be picked by the one or more threads implementing Mounties. The tasks wait in an appropriate queue prior to being picked. In processing a task, the thread/processor will compute it to completion, without switching to another task. The task execution can result in one or more new tasks getting created, which the thread will compute as and when it gets around to dealing with them. So for example, say an event arises, that creates a Preprocessor-task. The Preprocessor-task can end up creating an Optimizer-task, and a Postprocessor-task. The Postprocessor-task can create gossamer-related tasks, and so on. Allowing for performance tuning and also for later extensions, it may be desirable for the Preprocessor to inline the Postprocessor task within itself and to create the gossamer-related tasks directly, which can be done straightforwardly in this paradigm since tasks are explicit and not tied to the executing threads.

In this programming paradigm, computation and communication are merged. Generally a task is a procedure call, with its arguments representing the communicated, inter-process, channel data from the CSP model. In general inter-module communication is carried out by task queues connecting the modules, wherein, the scheduler is given the charge of executing a task for a module by causing a thread to pick it up from the module's incoming queue. Since in this paradigm, just one thread can implement all the modules, it becomes possible to continue thinking in terms of a purely sequential computation, and to avoid concurrency complexity such as synchronization and locks. If this sequential exercise using this paradigm is carried out in consistence with the Mounties choreography described earlier, then a straightforward extension of the work to multi-threaded implementation with thread safety is guaranteed. The accompanying complexity of lock management and synchronization is straightforward.

7   Related Work

The Mounties system described here is of relevance to both the commercial state-of-the-art products as well as to academic research in this area. First we describe and compare the Mounties System with three important systems that can be considered as the state-of-the-art: IBM's HA/CMP, Microsoft's MSCS, Tivoli's AMS system, and Sun's Jini technology.

Application management middleware has traditionally been used for products that provide high availability such as IBM's HA/CMP and Microsoft's Cluster Services (MSCS). HA/CMP's application management requires cluster resource configuration. Custom recovery scripts that are programmed separately for each cluster installation are needed. Making changes to the recovery scheme or to basic set of resource in the cluster requires these scripts to be re-programmed. Finally, HA/CMP recovery programs are stored and executed synchronously on all nodes of the cluster. MSCS provides a GUI-driven application manager across a two-node cluster with a single shared resource: a shared disk [11]. These two nodes are configured as a primary node and a backup node; the backup node is used normally pure backup node and no service-oriented processing is performed on it. Configuration and resource management is simplified with MSCS: there is only one resource to manage with limited management capabilities.

Tivoli offers an Application Management Specification (AMS) mechanism, which provides an ability to define and configure applications using the Tivoli Application Response Measurement (ARM) API layer [12]. These applications are referred to as instrumented applications. The information gathered from the instrumented applications can be used to drive scripts by channeling the information through the Tivoli Event Console (TEC). The TEC can be configured to respond to specific application notification and initiate subsequent actions upon application feedback. The current version of ARM application monitoring is from a single system's perspective. Future versions may include correlating events among multiple systems.

Over the last few years several new efforts towards coordinating and managing services provided by heterogeneous set of resources in dynamically changing environments. The examples of these include TSpaces [14] and the Jini Technology [3]. The TSpaces technology provides messaging and database style repository services that can be used by other higher level services to manage and coordinate resources in a distributed environment. Jini, on the other hand is a collection of services for dynamically acquiring and relinquishing services of other resources, for notifying availability of services, and for providing a uniform means for interacting among a heterogeneous set of resources. Both TSpaces and Jini technologies are complimentary to Mounties in the sense that they both lack any systematic decision making and decision execution component. However, the services provided by the Repository and Event Notification mechanisms in Mounties do overlap in functionality with the similar services provided in TSpaces and Jini. Finally, there are several resource management systems for distributed environments with decision-making capabilities. Darwin is an example of such a system that performs resource allocations taking into account application requirements [1]. Although there are similarities between Darwin and Mounties, Mounties provides a much richer set of abstractions for expressing complex dependency information among resources. Also, the Mounties system is geared towards optimizing the allocation of services such that overall objectives are met; in Darwin the goal seems to be more geared towards optimizing the requirements of an application or of a service.

The Mounties services described here have some similarities with the *Workflow management systems* that are typically used in automating and coordinating business processes such as customer order processing, product support, etc. As in Mounties, workflow systems also involve coordination and monitoring of multiple tasks that interact with one another in a complex manner [4]. Thus, the task and data choreography can have similar implementation features. However, workflow systems typically do not involve any type of global decision making component, much less solution of an optimization problem resulting in commands for the components of the system.

At the implementation level, Mounties software structuring approach or programming paradigm provides a contrast with approaches such as CSP [5], and Linda [2,13]. Briefly, in comparison to CSP, instead of defining static, concurrent tasks, our paradigm works with relatively short lived, dynamic, atomic tasks that can be inlined. Since tasks in our approach are delinked from threads, our approach has the advantage of allowing greater flexibility and control in software development including variable and controlled concurrency, and a finer level of control over task priority and data priority. In contrast to CSP, the Linda approach and futures [8] provide a handle on dynamic threads, [8] provides a method of dynamic thread in-lining, and Linda in particular provides a handle on a coordination structure, a tuplespace, that can straightforwardly emulate and provide the equivalent of CSP channels for data communication. Our paradigm is different from all these programming language approaches in that it is an informal framework wherein implementation issues/idioms relevant to Mounties-like systems find a convenient, and top-down expression, beyond what these generic language approaches with their compiler/run-time support provide. We leave a formalization of our paradigm as a language/framework for say building domain-specific compilers as an exercise for the future.

8 Conclusions

In this paper, we have described the Mounties system that is designed to support a diverse set of objectives including support for global cluster startup, resource failure and recovery, guarantees for quality-of-service, load-balance, application farm management, plug-and-configure style of management for the cluster resources, and so on. The system itself is composed of multiple services and we describe the design of the key services. The services described here are designed to be general purpose and scalable. This modularity allows for substitution, at run-time, by alternate services including alternate decision making components. Moreover, the system is flexible enough to operate in a full auto pilot mode or a human operator can control it partially or fully. The three services described here (the repository services, the evaluation and execution services, and the event notification services) are adaptable to changes in the system. New resources, constraints, and even new rules or policies can be defined and the system adjusts the cluster-state around these changes. In that sense, these services are active and dynamic components of the middleware. A fourth component of the system, the Optimizer, is also capable of adjusting to such changes in the system. The Optimizer, which is not described here, will be a topic of a separate publication.

Finally, we note here that the decision making capabilities and associated support services are general enough to be applied in other scenarios including in environments that are much more loosely coupled than clusters and that are highly distributed such those encountered in mobile and pervasive computing environments. In such environments, multiple independent decision support systems can co-exist in a cooperative and/or hierarchical manner. This is an area we intend to explore in the future.

Acknowledgements

Many individuals have contributed to the concepts that lead to the Mounties system as described in this paper. In particular the authors would like to thank Peter Badovinatz, Tushar Chandra, and John Pershing, Jr. for many insightful discussions. Many thanks to Rob Strom for his help in improving the style of the paper.

References

1. P. Chandra, A. Fisher, C. Kosak, E. Ng, P. Steenkiste, E. Takahashi, and H. Zhang, *Darwin: Customizable Resource Management for Value-Added Network Services,* Proceedings of 6th International Conference on Network Protocols, pp. 177–188, Oct. 1998. 369

2. N. Carriero, and D. Gelernter, *Linda in Context,* Communications of the ACM, vol. 32, pp. 444–458, April 1989. 369

3. K. Edwards, Core JINI, The Sun Microsystems Press Java Series, 1999. 369

4. J. Halliday, S. Shrivastava, and S. Wheater, *Implementing Support for Work Activity Coordination within a Distributed Workflow System,* Proceedings of 3rd IEEE/OMG International Enterprise Distributed Object Computing Conference, pp. 116–123, September, 1999. 369

5. C. Hoare, *Communicating Sequential Processes,* Prentice Hall International (U.K.) Ltd., 1985. 367, 369

6. IBM Corp., RS/6000 SP High Availability Infrastructure, IBM Publication SG24–4838, 1996. 359

7. IBM Corp., RS/6000 SP Monitoring: Keeping It Alive, IBM Publication SG24–4873, 1997. 359

8. D. Kranz, R. Halstead, and E. Mohr, *Mul-T: A High Performance Parallel Lisp,* Proceedings of the ACM Symposium on Programming Language Design and Implementation, pages 81–91, June 1989. 369

9. K. Krishna and V. Naik, *Application of Evolutionary Algorithms in Controlling Semi-autonomous Mission-Critical Distributed Systems* Proceedings of the Workshop on Frontiers in Evolutionary Algorithms (FEA200), Feb, 2000. 361, 362

10. V. Kumar and V. Naik, *Modeling the Global Optimization Problem in Highly Available Cluster Environments* Submitted for publication, 2000. 362

11. M. Sportack, Windows NT Clustering BluePrints, SAMS Publishing, Indianapolis, IN 46290, 1997. 368

12. Tivoli Corp., Tivoli and Application Management, http://www.tivoli.com/products/documents/whitepapers/body_map_wp.html, 1999. 368

13. P. Varma, Compile-time analyses and run-time support for a higher order, distributed data-structures based, parallel language, University Microfilms International, Ann Arbor, Michigan, 1995. 369

14. P. Wyckoff, S. McLaughry, T. Lehman, and D. Ford, *T Spaces,* IBM Systems Journal, pp. 454–474, vol. 37, 1998. 369

The Design and Performance of a Pluggable Protocols Framework for Real-Time Distributed Object Computing Middleware*

Carlos O'Ryan, Fred Kuhns, Douglas C. Schmidt,
Ossama Othman, and Jeff Parsons

Department of Computer Science, Washington University
St. Louis, MO 63130, USA
{coryan,fredk,schmidt,othman,parsons}@cs.wustl.edu

Abstract. To be an effective platform for performance-sensitive real-time and embedded applications, off-the-shelf CORBA middleware must preserve the communication-layer quality of service (QoS) properties of applications end-to-end. However, the standard CORBA GIOP/IIOP interoperability protocols are not well suited for applications that cannot tolerate the message footprint size, latency, and jitter associated with general-purpose messaging and transport protocols. It is essential, therefore, to develop standard pluggable protocols frameworks that allow custom messaging and transport protocols to be configured flexibly and used transparently by applications.

This paper provides three contributions to research on pluggable protocols frameworks for performance-sensitive distributed object computing (DOC) middleware. First, we outline the key design challenges faced by pluggable protocols developers. Second, we describe how we resolved these challenges by developing a pluggable protocols framework for TAO, which is our high-performance, real-time CORBA-compliant ORB. Third, we present the results of benchmarks that pinpoint the impact of TAO's pluggable protocols framework on its end-to-end efficiency and predictability.

Our results demonstrate how the application of optimizations and patterns to DOC middleware can yield both highly flexible/reusable designs and highly efficient/predictable implementations. In particular, the overall roundtrip latency of a TAO two-way method invocation using the standard inter-ORB protocol and using a commercial, off-the-self Pentium II Xeon 400 MHz workstation running in loopback mode is ~189 μsecs. The ORB middleware accounts for approximately 48% or ~90 μsecs of the total roundtrip latency. Using the specialized POSIX local IPC protocol reduces roundtrip latency to ~125 μsecs. These results illustrate that (1) DOC middleware performance is largely an implementation detail and (2) the next-generation of optimized, standards-based CORBA middleware can replace ad hoc and proprietary solutions.

Subject areas: Frameworks; Design Patterns; Distributed and Real-Time Systems

* This work was supported in part by Boeing, DARPA contract 9701516, GDIS, NSF grant NCR-9628218, Nortel, Siemens, and Sprint.

J. Sventek and G. Coulson (Eds.): Middleware 2000, LNCS 1795, pp. 372–395, 2000.

1   Introduction

Current trends and limitations: Three trends are shaping the future of communication application and system development. First, there is a movement away from *programming* applications from scratch, using low-level protocols and operating system APIs, to *integrating* applications, using reusable components [1], such as ActiveX, Enterprise Java Beans (EJB), and CORBA components. Second, there is great demand for *DOC middleware* that provides remote method invocation and/or message-oriented middleware to simplify application component collaboration [2]. Third, there are increasing efforts to define *standard* DOC middleware, such as CORBA [3], that permits applications to interoperate seamlessly throughout *heterogeneous* networks and endsystems.

Standard DOC middleware now available off-the-shelf allows clients to invoke operations on distributed components without concern for component location, programming language, OS platform, communication protocols and interconnects, or hardware [4]. However, off-the-shelf DOC middleware generally lacks (1) support for QoS specification and enforcement, (2) integration with high-speed networking technology, and (3) efficiency, predictability, and scalability optimizations [5]. These omissions have limited the rate at which performance-sensitive applications, such as video-on-demand, teleconferencing, and avionics mission computing, have been developed to leverage advances in DOC middleware.

Overcoming DOC middleware limitations with pluggable protocols: To address the shortcomings of DOC middleware described above, we have developed *The ACE ORB* (TAO) [5]. TAO is open-source,[1] standards-based, high-performance, real-time ORB endsystem DOC middleware that supports applications with deterministic and statistical QoS requirements, as well as "best-effort" requirements. TAO is the first ORB to support end-to-end QoS guarantees over ATM/IP networks [6,7] and embedded backplanes [8,9].

We have used TAO to research many dimensions of high-performance and real-time ORB endsystems, including static [5] and dynamic [10] scheduling, request demultiplexing [11], event processing [8], ORB Core connection and concurrency architectures [12], IDL compiler stub/skeleton optimizations [13], systematic benchmarking of multiple ORBs [14], I/O subsystem integration [7], and patterns for ORB extensibility [15]. This paper focuses on a previously unexamined dimension in the high-performance and real-time ORB endsystem design space: *the design and implementation of a high-performance pluggable protocols framework for real-time communications middleware* that can efficiently and flexibly support high-speed protocols and networks, real-time embedded system interconnects, and standard TCP/IP protocols over the Internet.

At the heart of TAO's pluggable protocols framework is its patterns-oriented OO design [16], which decouples TAO's ORB messaging and transport interfaces from its transport-specific protocol components. This design allows custom ORB

---

[1] TAO is available at `www.cs.wustl.edu/~schmidt/TAO.html`.

messaging and transport protocols to be configured flexibly and used transparently by CORBA applications. For example, if ORBs communicate over a high-speed networking infrastructure, such as ATM AAL5 or specialized protocols like HPPI, then simpler ORB messaging and transport protocols can be configured to optimize unnecessary features and overhead of the standard CORBA General Inter-ORB Protocol (GIOP) and Internet Inter-ORB Protocol (IIOP). Likewise, TAO's pluggable protocols framework makes it straightforward to support customized embedded system interconnects, such as CompactPCI or VME, under standard CORBA inter-ORB protocols like GIOP.

For OO researchers and practitioners, the results in this paper are important, because they demonstrate concretely that the ability of standards-based DOC middleware to support high-performance, real-time systems is largely an *implementation detail*, rather than an inherent liability. For instance, TAO's end-to-end latency overhead is only ~110 μsecs using commercial off-the-self 200 MHz PowerPCs, a 320 Mbps VMEbus, and VxWorks, which is as fast, or faster, than many *ad hoc*, proprietary solutions [9]. These results motivate the use of well-tuned, standards-based DOC middleware, even for real-time embedded applications with very stringent QoS requirements. The paper also explores how patterns can be applied to resolve key design challenges. Our pattern-oriented OO design can also be extended to other pluggable protocol frameworks, either in standard middleware or in distributed applications using proprietary middleware.

Paper organization: The remainder of this paper is organized as follows: Section 2 motivates the requirements for standard CORBA pluggable protocols and outlines TAO's pluggable protocols framework; Section 3 describes the patterns that guide the architecture of TAO's pluggable protocols framework and resolve key design challenges. Section 4 illustrates the performance characteristics of TAO's pluggable protocols framework; Section 5 compares TAO with related work; and Section 6 presents concluding remarks.

2   The Design of a CORBA Pluggable Protocols Framework

The CORBA specification provides a standard for general-purpose DOC middleware. Within the scope of this specification, however, ORB implementors are free to optimize internal data structures and algorithms [11]. Moreover, ORBs may use specialized inter-ORB protocols and ORB services and still comply with the CORBA specification.[2] This section identifies contemporary limitations of and requirements for protocol support in CORBA ORBs and describes how TAO's pluggable protocols framework is designed to overcome these limitations.

---

[2] An ORB *must* implement GIOP/IIOP, however, to be interoperability-compliant.

2.1   Protocol Limitations of Conventional ORBs

CORBA's standard GIOP/IIOP protocols are well suited for conventional request/response applications with best-effort QoS requirements [13]. They are not well suited, however, for high-performance real-time and/or embedded applications that cannot tolerate the message footprint size of GIOP or the latency, overhead, and jitter of the TCP/IP-based IIOP transport protocol. For instance, TCP functionality, such as adaptive retransmissions, deferred transmissions, and delayed acknowledgments, can cause excessive overhead and latency for real-time applications [17]. Likewise, networking protocols, such as IPv4, lack the functionality of packet admission policies and rate control, which can lead to excessive congestion and missed deadlines in networks and endsystems.

Therefore, applications with more stringent QoS requirements need optimized protocol implementations, QoS-aware interfaces, custom presentations layers, specialized memory management (*e.g.*, shared memory between ORB and I/O subsystem), and alternative transport programming APIs (*e.g.*, sockets vs. VIA [18]). Domains where highly optimized ORB messaging and transport protocols are particularly important include (1) multimedia applications running over high-speed networks, such as Gigabit Ethernet or ATM, and (2) real-time applications running over embedded system interconnects, such as VME or CompactPCI.

Conventional CORBA implementations have the following limitations that make it hard for them to support performance-sensitive applications effectively:

1. Static protocol configurations: Conventional ORBs support a limited number of statically configured protocols, typically only GIOP/IIOP over TCP/IP.

2. Lack of protocol control interfaces: Conventional ORBs do not allow applications to configure key protocol policies and properties, such as peak virtual circuit bandwidth or cell pacing rate.

3. Single protocol support: Conventional ORBs do not support simultaneous use of multiple inter-ORB messaging or transport protocols.

4. Lack of real-time protocol support: Conventional ORBs have limited or no support for specifying and enforcing real-time protocol requirements across a backplane, network, or Internet end-to-end.

2.2   Pluggable Protocols Framework Requirements

The limitations of conventional ORBs described in Section 2.1 make it hard for developers to leverage existing implementations, expertise, and ORB optimizations across projects or application domains. Defining a standard *pluggable protocols framework* for CORBA ORBs is an effective way to address this problem. The requirements for such a pluggable protocols framework for CORBA include the following:

1. Define standard, unobtrusive protocol configuration interfaces: To address limitations of conventional ORBs, a pluggable protocols framework should define a standard set of APIs to install ESIOPs and their transport-dependent components. Most applications need not use this interface directly. Therefore, the pluggable protocol interface should be exposed only to application developers interested in defining new protocols or in configuring existing protocol implementations in new ways.

2. Use standard CORBA programming and control interfaces: To ensure application portability, clients should program to standard application interfaces defined in CORBA IDL, even if pluggable ORB messaging or transport protocols are used. Likewise, object implementors need not be aware of the underlying framework. Developers should be able to set policies, however, that control the ORB's choice of protocols and protocol properties. Moreover, these interfaces should transparently support certain real-time ORB features, such as scatter/gather I/O, optimized memory management, and strategized concurrency models [11].

3. Simultaneous use of multiple ORB messaging and transport protocols: To address the lack of support for multiple inter-ORB protocols in conventional ORBs, a pluggable protocols framework should support different messaging and transport protocols *simultaneously* within an ORB endsystem. The framework should transparently configure inter-ORB protocols either statically, *i.e.*, during ORB initialization [19], or dynamically, *i.e.*, during ORB run-time [20].

4. Support for multiple address representations: This requirement addresses the lack of support for multiple Inter-ORB protocols and dynamic protocol configurations in conventional ORBs. For example, each pluggable protocol implementation can potentially have a different profile and object addressing scheme. Therefore, a pluggable protocols framework should provide a general mechanism to represent these disparate address formats transparently, while also supporting standard IOR address representations efficiently.

5. Support CORBA 2.3 features and future enhancements: A pluggable protocol framework should support CORBA 2.3 [21] features, such as object reference forwarding, connection transparency, preservation of foreign IORs and profiles, and the GIOP 1.2 protocol, in a manner that does not degrade end-to-end performance and predictability. Moreover, a pluggable protocols framework should accommodate future changes and enhancements to the CORBA specification, such as (1) fault tolerance [22], which supports group communication, (2) real-time CORBA [19], which includes features to reserve connection and threading resources on a per-object basis, (3) asynchronous messaging [23], which exports QoS policies to application developers, and (4) wireless access and mobility [24], which defines lighterweight Inter-ORB protocols for low-bandwidth links.

6. Optimized inter-ORB bridging: A pluggable protocols framework should ensure that protocol implementors can create efficient, high-performance inter-ORB *in-line bridges.* An in-line bridge converts inter-ORB messages or requests from one type of IOP to another. This makes it possible to bridge disparate ORB domains efficiently without incurring unnecessary context switching, synchronization, or data movement.

7. Provide common protocol optimizations and real-time features: A pluggable protocols framework should support features required by real-time CORBA applications [19], such as resource pre-allocation and reservation, end-to-end priority propagation, and mechanisms to control properties specific to real-time protocols. These features should be implemented without modifying the standard CORBA programming APIs used by applications that do not possess real-time QoS requirements.

8. Dynamic protocol bindings: To address the limitation of static protocol bindings in conventional ORBs, a pluggable protocols frameworks should support dynamic binding of specific ORB messaging protocols with specific instances of ORB transport protocols. This design permits efficient and predictable configurations for both standard and customized IOPs.

2.3 Architectural Overview of TAO's Pluggable Protocols Framework

To meet the requirements outlined in Section 2.2, we identified logical communication component layers within TAO, factored out common features, defined general framework interfaces, and implemented components to support different concrete inter-ORB protocols. Higher-level services in the ORB, such as stubs, skeletons, and standard CORBA pseudo-objects, are decoupled from the implementation details of particular protocols, as shown in Figure 1. This decoupling

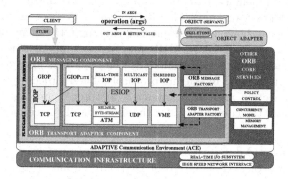

Fig. 1. TAO's Pluggable Protocols Framework Architecture

is essential to resolve several limitations of conventional ORBs outlined in Section 2.1, as well as to meet the requirements set forth in Section 2.2.

In general, the higher-level components and services of TAO use a facade [25] interface to access the mechanisms provided by its pluggable protocols framework. Thus, applications can (re)configure custom protocols without requiring global changes to the ORB. Moreover, because applications typically access only the standard CORBA APIs, TAO's pluggable protocols framework can be entirely transparent to CORBA application developers.

Figure 1 also illustrates the key components in TAO's pluggable protocols framework: (1) the ORB messaging component, (2) the ORB transport adapter component, and (3) the ORB policy control component, which are outlined below.

ORB Messaging Component This component is responsible for implementing ORB messaging protocols, such as the standard CORBA GIOP ORB messaging protocol, as well as custom ESIOPs. An ORB messaging protocol must define a data representation, an ORB message format, an ORB transport protocol or transport adapter, and an object addressing format. Within this framework, ORB protocol developers are free to implement optimized Inter-ORB protocols and enhanced transport adaptors, as long as the ORB interfaces are respected.

Each ORB messaging protocol implementation inherits from a common base class that defines a uniform interface. This interface can be extended to include new capabilities needed by special protocol-aware policies. For example, ORB end-to-end resource reservation or priority negotiation can be implemented in an ORB messaging component. TAO's pluggable protocols framework ensures consistent operational characteristics and enforces general IOP syntax and semantic constraints, such as error handling.

In general it is not necessary to re-implement all aspects of an ORB messaging protocol. For example, TAO has a highly optimized CDR implementation that can be used by new protocols [11]. TAO's CDR implementation contains highly optimized memory allocation strategies and data type translations. Thus, protocol developers can simply identify new memory or connection management strategies that can be configured into the existing CDR components.

Another key part of TAO's ORB messaging component is its message factories. During connection establishment, these factories instantiate objects that implement various ORB messaging protocols. These objects are associated with a specific connection and ORB transport adapter component, *i.e.*, the object that implements the component, for the duration of the connection.

ORB Transport Adapter Component This component maps a specific ORB messaging protocol, such as GIOP or DCE-CIOP, onto a specific instance of an underlying transport protocol, such as TCP or ATM. Figure 1 shows an example in which TAO's transport adapter maps the GIOP messaging protocol onto TCP (this standard mapping is called IIOP). In this case, the ORB transport adapter combined with TCP corresponds to the transport layer in the Internet reference model. However, if ORBs are communicating over an embedded interconnect, such as a VME bus, the bus driver and DMA controller provide the "transport layer" in the communication infrastructure.

TAO's ORB transport component accepts a byte stream from the ORB messaging component, provides any additional processing required, and passes the resulting data unit to the underlying communication infrastructure. Additional processing that can be implemented by protocol developers includes (1) concurrency strategies, (2) endsystem/network resource reservation protocols, (3) high-performance techniques, such as zero-copy I/O, shared memory pools, periodic I/O, and interface pooling, (4) enhancement of underlying communications protocols, *e.g.*, provision of a reliable byte stream protocol over ATM, and (5) tight coupling between the ORB and efficient user-space protocol implementations, such as Fast Messages [26].

ORB Policy Control Component This component allows applications to control the QoS attributes of configured ORB transport protocols explicitly. It is not possible to determine *a priori* all attributes defined by all protocols. Therefore, TAO's pluggable protocols framework provides an extensible *policy control* component, which implements the QoS framework defined in the CORBA Messaging [23] and Real-time CORBA [19] specifications.

The CORBA QoS framework allows applications to specify various *policies* to control the QoS attributes in the ORB. The CORBA specification uses policies to define semantic properties of ORB features precisely without (1) over-constraining ORB implementations or (2) increasing interface complexity for common use cases. Example policies relevant for pluggable protocols include buffer pre-allocations, fragmentation, bandwidth reservation, and maximum transport queue sizes.

Policies in CORBA can be set at the ORB, thread, or object level. Thus, application developers can set global policies that take effect for any request issued in a particular ORB. Moreover, these global settings can be overridden on a per-thread basis, a per-object basis, or even before a particular request. In general, CORBA's Policy framework provides very fine-grained control over the ORB behavior, while providing simplicity for the common case.

Certain policies, such as timeouts, can be shared between multiple protocols. Other policies, such as ATM virtual circuit bandwidth allocation, may apply to a single protocol. Each configured protocol can query TAO's policy control component to determine its policies and use them to configure itself for user needs. Moreover, protocol implementations can simply ignore policies that do not apply to it.

TAO's policy control component enables applications to select their protocol(s). This choice can be controlled by the `ClientProtocolPolicy` defined in the Real-time CORBA specification [19]. Using this policy, an application can indicate its preferred protocol(s) and TAO's policy control component attempts to match that preference with the set of available protocols. TAO provides other policies that control the behavior of the ORB if an application's preferences cannot be satisfied. For example, an exception can be raised or another available protocol can be selected transparently.

3   Key Design Challenges and Pattern-Based Resolutions

The architecture overview in Section 2.3 outlines *how* TAO's pluggable protocols framework is designed. However, it does not motivate *why* this particular design was selected. In this appendix, we explore each feature in TAO's pluggable protocols framework and show how they achieve the goals described in Section 2.2. To clarify and generalize our approach, the discussion below focuses on the patterns [25] we applied to resolve the key design challenges we faced during the development process.

3.1   Adding New Protocols Transparently

Context: The QoS requirements of many applications can be supported solely by using default static protocol configurations, *i.e.*, GIOP/IIOP, described in section 2.1. However, applications with more stringent QoS requirements often require custom protocol configurations. Implementations of these custom protocols require several related classes, such as Connectors, Acceptors, Transports, and Profiles. To be integrated into a common framework, all these classes must be created consistently. In addition, many embedded and deterministic real-time systems require protocols to be configured *a priori*, with no additional protocols required once the application is configured statically. These types of systems typically cannot afford to incur the footprint overhead associated with dynamic protocol configurations.

Problem: It must be possible to add new protocols to the pluggable protocols framework without making *any* changes to the rest of the ORB. Thus, the framework must be open for extensions, but closed to modifications, *i.e.*, the Open-Closed principle [27]. Ideally, creating the new protocol and configuring it into the ORB is all that should be required.

Solution: Use a Registry to maintain a collection of *Abstract Factories* [25]. In the Abstract Factory pattern, a single class defines an interface for creating families of related objects, without specifying their concrete types. Subclasses of the Abstract Factory are responsible for creating concrete classes that collaborate among themselves. In the context of pluggable protocols, each Abstract Factory can create the `Connector`, `Acceptor`, `Profile`, and `Transport` classes for a particular protocol.

Applying the solution in TAO: In TAO, the role of the protocol registry is played by the `Connector_Registry` for the client and the `Acceptor_Registry` on the server. This registry is created by TAO's Resource Factory, which is a more general Abstract Factory that creates all the ORB's strategies and policies [15]. Figure 2 depicts the connector registry and its relation to the abstract factories.

Note that TAO does not use these Abstract Factories directly, however. Instead, these factories are accessed via the *Facade* [25] pattern in order to hide the complexity of manipulating multiple factories behind a simpler interface. The Registry described above plays the Facade role. As shown below, these patterns provide sufficient flexibility to add new protocols transparently to the ORB.

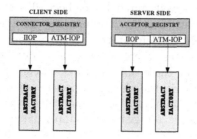

Fig. 2. TAO Connector and Acceptor Registries

Establishing connections, manipulating profiles, and creating endpoints are delegated to the connector and acceptor registries respectively. Clients will simply provide the connector registry with an opaque profile, which corresponds to an object address for a particular protocol instance. The registry is responsible for locating the correct concrete factory, to which it then delegates the responsibility for establishing the connection. The concrete factory establishes the connection using the corresponding specific protocol instance, notifying the client of its success or failure. Thereafter, the client simply invokes method invocations using the selected protocol.

The server delegates endpoint creation to the acceptor registry in a similar manner. The registry is passed an opaque endpoint representation, which it provides to the corresponding concrete factory for the indicated protocol instance. The concrete acceptor factory creates the endpoint and enables the ORB to receive requests on the new endpoint.

3.2   Adding New Protocols Dynamically

Context: When developing new pluggable protocols, it is inconvenient to recompile the ORB and applications just to validate a new protocol implementation. Moreover, it is often useful to experiment with different protocols, *e.g.*, systematically compare their performance, footprint size, and QoS guarantees. Moreover, in 24×7 systems with high availability requirements, it is important to configure protocols dynamically, even while the system is running. This level of flexibility helps simplify upgrades and protocol enhancements.

Problem: How to populate the registry *dynamically* with the correct objects.

Solution: Use the Service Configurator [28] pattern, which decouples the implementation of a service from its configuration into the application. This pattern can be applied in either of the following ways:

1. The Service Configurator pattern can be used to dynamically load the registry class, which is a Facade that knows how to configure a particular set of protocols. To add new protocols, we must either implement a new Registry class or derive from an existing one.

This alternative is well suited for embedded systems with tight memory footprint constraints, because it minimizes the number of objects that are loaded dynamically. Implementations of the Service Configurator pattern can optimize for use cases where objects are configured statically. Embedded systems can exploit these optimizations to eliminate the need for loading objects dynamically in the pluggable protocols framework.

2. Use the Service Configurator to dynamically load the set of entries in the Registry. For instance, a registry can simply parse a configuration script and dynamically link the services listed in it. This is the most flexible approach, but it requires more code, *e.g.*, to parse the configuration script, load the objects dynamically, etc.

Applying the solution in TAO: TAO implements a class that maintains all parameters specified in a configuration script. Adding a new parameter to represent the list of protocols is straightforward, *i.e.*, the default registry simply examines this list and links the services into the address-space of the application, using the ACE[3] Service Configurator implementation [29] . Figure 3 depicts the connector registry and its relation to the Service Configurator.

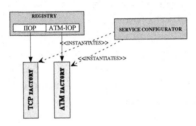

Fig. 3. TAO Connector Registry and the Service Configurator

3.3   Actively Establishing Connections

Context: When a client references an object, the ORB must obtain the corresponding profile list, which is derived from the IOR and a profile ordering policy, and transparently establish a connection to the server.

Problem: There can be one or more combinations of inter-ORB and transport protocols available in an ORB. For a given profile, the ORB must verify the presence of the associated IOP and transport protocol, if available. It must then locate the applicable `Connector` and delegate it to establish the connection.

Solution: We use the Connector pattern [31] to actively establish a connection to a remote object. This pattern decouples the connection establishment from the processing performed after the connection is successful. As before, the `Connector Registry` shown in Figure 4 is used to locate the right `Connector` for the current

---

[3] ACE provides a rich set of reusable and efficient components for high-performance, real-time communication, and forms the portability layer of TAO.

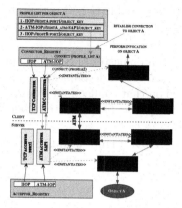

Fig. 4. Connection Establishment Using Multiple Pluggable Protocols

profile. The actual profile selected for use will depend on the set of Policies active at the time of connection establishment. However, once a profile is selected, the connector registry matches the profile type, represented by a well known tag, with an instance of a concrete `Connector`.

Applying the solution in TAO: TAO `Connectors` are adapters for the ACE implementation of the Connector pattern. Thus, they are typically lightweight objects that simply delegate to a corresponding ACE component.

Figure 5 shows the base classes and their relations for IIOP. This figure shows an explicit co-variance between the `Profile` and the `Connectors` for each protocol. In general, a `Connector` must downcast the `Profile` to its specific type. This downcast is safe because profile creation is limited to the `Connector` and `Acceptor` registries. In both cases, the profile is created with a matching tag. The tag is used by the Connector Registry to choose the `Connector` that can handle each profile.

As shown in the same figure, the Connector Registry manipulates only the base classes. Therefore, new protocols can be added without requiring any modification to the existing pluggable protocols framework. When a connection is successfully established, the `Profile` is passed a pointer to the particular IOP object and to the `Transport` objects that were created.

3.4 Passively Accepting Connections

Context: A server can accept connections at one or more endpoints, potentially using the same protocol for all endpoints. The set of protocols that an ORB uses to play the client role need not match the set of protocols used for the server role. Moreover, the ORB can even be a "pure client", *i.e.*, a client that only makes requests, in which case it can use several protocols to make requests, but receive no requests from other clients.

Problem: The server must generate an IOR that includes all possible inter-ORB and transport-protocol-specific profiles for which the object can be accessed. As with the client, it should be possible to add new protocols without changing the ORB.

Solution: We use the Acceptor pattern [31] to accept the connections. As with the Connector pattern, an Acceptor decouples the connection establishment from the processing performed on that connection. However, in the Acceptor pattern, the connection is accepted *passively,* rather than being initiated *actively.*

Applying the solution to TAO: Figure 5 illustrates how TAO's pluggable pro-

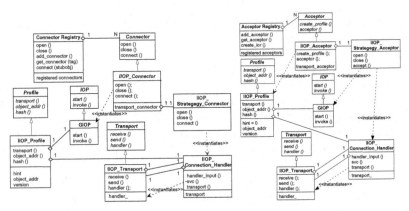

Fig. 5. Client and Server Pluggable Protocol Class Diagram

tocols framework leverages the design presented in Section 3.1. The concrete ACE `Service Handler` created by the ACE `Acceptor` is responsible for implementing the External Polymorphism pattern and encapsulating itself behind the `Transport` interface defined in our pluggable protocols framework.

TAO uses the Adapter pattern to leverage the ACE implementation of the Acceptors. This pattern also permits a seamless integration with the lower levels of the ORB. In the Acceptor pattern, the `Acceptor` object is a factory that creates `Service Handlers`. `Service Handlers` are responsible for performing I/O with their connected peers. In TAO's pluggable protocol framework, the `Transport` objects are `Service Handlers` implemented as abstract classes. This design shields the ORB from variations in the `Acceptors`, `Connectors`, and `Service Handlers` for each particular protocol.

When a connection is established, the concrete `Acceptor` creates the appropriate `Connection Handler` and IOP objects. The `Connection Handler` also creates a `Transport` object that functions as a bridge. As with the `Connector`, the `Acceptor` also acts as a bridge object, hiding the transport- and strategy-specific details of the acceptor.

4 The Performance of TAO's Pluggable Protocols Framework

Despite the growing demand for off-the-shelf middleware in many application domains, a widespread belief persists in the embedded systems community that OO techniques are not suitable for real-time systems due to performance penalties attributed to the OO paradigm [8]. In particular, the dynamic binding properties of OO programming languages and the indirection implied in OO designs seem antithetical to real-time systems, which require low latency and jitter. The results presented in this section are significant, therefore, because they illustrate empirically how the choice of patterns described in Section 3, allowed us to meet non-functional requirements, such as portability, flexibility, reusability, and maintainability, without compromising overall system efficiency, predictability, or scalability.

To quantify the benefits and costs of TAO's pluggable protocols framework, we conducted several benchmarks using two different ORB messaging protocols, GIOP and GIOPlite, and two different transport protocols, POSIX local IPC (also known as UNIX-domain sockets) and TCP/IP. These benchmarks are based on our experience developing DOC middleware for avionics mission computing applications [8] and multimedia applications [32].

Note that POSIX local IPC is not a traditional high-performance networking environment. However, it does provide the opportunity to obtain an accurate measure of ORB and pluggable protocols framework overhead. Based on these measurements, we have isolated the overhead associated with each component, which provides a baseline for future work in high-performance protocol development and experimentation.

4.1 Hardware/Software Benchmarking Platform

All benchmarks in this section were run on a Quad-CPU Intel Pentium II Xeon 400 MHz workstation, with one gigabyte of RAM. The operating system used for the benchmarking was Debian GNU/Linux "potato" (glibc 2.1) with Linux kernel version 2.2.10. GNU/Linux is an open-source operating system that supports true multi-tasking, multi-threading, and symmetric multiprocessing.

For these experiments, we used the GIOP and GIOPlite [11] messaging protocols. GIOPlite is a streamlined version of GIOP that removes ≥ 15 extraneous bytes from the standard GIOP message and request headers.[4] These bytes include the GIOP magic number (4 bytes), GIOP version (2 bytes), flags (1 byte), Request Service Context (at least 4 bytes), and Request Principal (at least 4 bytes).

Our benchmarks were run using the standard GIOP ORB messaging protocol, as well as TAO's GIOPlite messaging protocol. For the TCP/IP tests,

---

[4] The request header size is variable. Therefore, it is not possible to precisely pinpoint the proportional savings represented by these bytes. In many cases, however, the reduction is as large as 25%.

the GIOP and GIOPlite ORB messaging protocols were run using the standard CORBA IIOP transport adapter along with the Linux TCP/IP socket library and the loopback interface.

For the local IPC tests, GIOP and GIOPlite were used along with the optimized local IPC transport adapter. This resulted in four different Inter-ORB Protocols: GIOP over TCP (IIOP), GIOPlite over TCP, GIOP over local IPC (UIOP [5]) and GIOPlite over local IPC. No changes were required to our standard CORBA benchmarking tool, called IDL_Cubit [12], for either of the ORB messaging and transport protocol implementations.

4.2   Blackbox Benchmarks

Blackbox benchmarks measure the end-to-end performance of a system from an external application perspective. In our experiments, we used blackbox benchmarks to compute the average two-way response time incurred by clients sending various types of data using the four different Inter-ORB transport protocols.

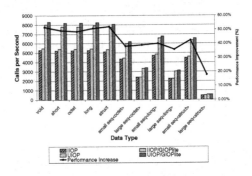

Fig. 6. TAO's Pluggable Protocols Framework Performance Over Local IPC and TCP/IP

Measurement technique: A single-threaded client is used in the IDL_Cubit benchmark to issue two-way IDL operations at the fastest possible rate. The server performs the operation, which cubes each parameter in the request. For two-way calls, the client thread waits for the response and checks that it is correct. Interprocess communication is performed over selected IOPs, as described above.

We measure throughput for operations using a variety of IDL data types, including void, sequence, and struct types. The void data type instructs the server not to perform any processing other than that necessary to prepare and

---

[5] For historical reasons, TAO retains the expression "UNIX-domain" in its local IPC pluggable protocol implementation, which is where the name "UIOP" derives from.

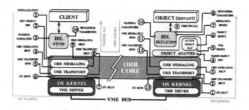

Fig. 7. Timeprobe Locations for Whitebox Experiment

send the response, *i.e.*, it does not cube any input parameters. The `sequence` and `struct` data types exercise TAO's (de)marshaling engine. The `struct` contains an `octet`, a `long`, and a `short`, along with padding necessary to align those fields. We also measure throughput using long and short sequences of the `long` and `octet` types. The `long` sequences contain 4,096 bytes (1,024 four byte `long`s or 4,096 `octet`s) and the short sequences are 4 bytes (one four byte `long` or four `octet`s).

Blackbox results: The blackbox benchmark results are shown in Figure 6. All blackbox benchmarks were averaged over 100,000 two-way operation calls for each data type, as shown in Figure 6.

UIOP performance surpassed IIOP performance for all data types. The benchmarks show UIOP improves performance from 20% to 50% depending on the data type and size. For smaller data sizes and basic types, such as `octet` and `long`, the performance improvement is approximately 50%. However, for larger data payload sizes and more complex data types, the performance improvements are reduced. This is a direct result of the increasing cost of both the data copies associated with performing I/O and the increasing complexity of marshaling structures other than the basic data types.

For certain data types, additional improvements are obtained by reducing the number of data copies required. Such a situation exists when marshaling and demarshaling data of type `octet` and `long`. For complicated data types, such as a large `sequence` of `struct`s, ORB overhead is particularly prevalent. Large ORB overhead implies lower efficiency, which accounts for the smaller performance improvement gained by UIOP over IIOP for complex data types.

GIOPlite outperformed GIOP by a small margin. For IIOP, GIOPlite performance increases over GIOP ranged from 0.36% to 4.74%, with an average performance increase of 2.74%. GIOPlite performance improvements were slightly better over UIOP due to the fact that UIOP is more efficient than IIOP. GIOPlite over UIOP provided improvements ranging from 0.37% to 5.29%, with an average of 3.26%.

Our blackbox results suggest that more substantial changes to the GIOP message protocol are required to achieve significant performance improvements. However, these results also illustrate that the GIOP message footprint has a relatively minor performance impact over high-speed networks and embedded interconnects. Naturally, the impact of the GIOP message footprint for lower-speed links, such as second-generation wireless systems or low-speed modems, is more significant.

4.3   Whitebox Benchmarks

Whitebox benchmarks measure the performance of specific components or layers in a system from an internal perspective. In our experiments, we used whitebox benchmarks to pinpoint the time spent in key components in TAO's client and server ORBs. The ORB's logical layers, or components, are shown in Figure 7 along with the timeprobe locations used for these benchmarks.

Measurement Techniques

One way to measure performance overhead of operations in complex DOC middleware is to use a profiling tool like Quantify [33]. Quantify instruments an application's binary instructions and then analyzes performance bottlenecks by identifying sections of code that dominate execution time. Quantify is useful because it can measure the overhead of system calls and third-party libraries without requiring source code access.

Unfortunately, Quantify is not available for Linux kernel-based operating systems on which whitebox measurement of TAO's performance was performed. Moreover, Quantify modifies the binary code to collect timing information. Therefore, it is most useful for measuring *relative* overhead of different operations in a system, rather than measuring *absolute* run-time performance.

To avoid the limitations of Quantify, we therefore used a lightweight timeprobe mechanism provided by ACE to precisely pinpoint the amount of time spent in various ORB components and layers. The ACE timeprobe mechanism provides highly accurate, low-cost timestamps that record the time spent between regions of code in a software system. These timeprobes have minimal performance impact, *e.g.*, 1-2 μsec overhead per timeprobe, and no binary code instrumentation is required.

Depending on the underlying platform, ACE's timeprobes are implemented either by high-resolution OS timers or by high-precision timing hardware. An example of the latter is the VMEtro board, which is a VME bus monitor. VMEtro writes unique ACE timeprobe values to an otherwise unused VME address. These values record the duration between timeprobe markers across multiple processors using a single clock. This enables TAO to collect synchronized timestamps and accurately measure communication delays end-to-end across distributed CPUs.

Below, we examine the client and server whitebox performance in detail.

Whitebox Results

Figure 7 shows the points in a two-way operation request path where timeprobes were inserted. Each labeled number in the figure corresponds to an entry in Table 1 and Table 2 below. The results presented in the tables and figures which follow were averaged over 1,000 samples.

Client performance: Table 1 depicts the time in microseconds (μs) spent in each sequential activity that a TAO client performs to process an outgoing operation request and its reply.

Table 1. μseconds Spent in Each Client Processing Step

Direction	Client Activities	Absolute Time (μs)
Outgoing	1. *Initialization*	6.30
	2. *Get object reference*	15.6
	3. *Parameter marshal*	0.74 (param. dependent)
	4. *ORB messaging send*	7.78
	5. *ORB transport send*	1.02
	6. *I/O*	8.70 (op. dependent)
	7. *ORB transport recv*	50.7
	8. *ORB messaging recv*	9.25
	9. *Parameter demarshal*	op. dependent

Server performance: Table 2 depicts the time in microseconds (μs) spent in each activity as a TAO server processes a request.

Table 2. μseconds Spent in Each Server Processing Step

Direction	Server Activities	Absolute Time (μs)
Incoming	1. *I/O*	7.0 (op. dependent)
	2. *ORB transport recv*	24.8
	3. *ORB messaging recv*	4.5
	4. *Parsing object key*	4.6
	5. *POA demux*	1.39
	6. *Servant demux*	4.6
	7. *Operation demux*	4.52
	8. *User upcall*	3.84 (op. dependent)
Outgoing	9. *ORB messaging send*	4.56
	10. *ORB transport send*	93.6

Depending on the type and number of operation parameters, the *ORB transport recv* step typically requires the most ORB processing time. This time is dominated by the required data copies. By using a transport adapter which implements a shared buffer strategy these costs can be reduced significantly.

Component costs: Figure 8 compares the relative overhead attributable to the

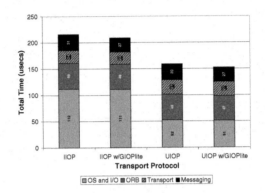

Fig. 8. Comparison of ORB and Transport/OS Overhead Using Timeprobes

ORB messaging component, transport adaptor, ORB and OS for two-way IDL_Cubit calls to the cube_void operation for each possible protocol combination. This figure shows that when using IIOP the I/O and OS overhead accounts for just over 50% of the total round trip latency.

It also shows that the difference in performance between IIOP and UIOP is primarily due to the larger OS and I/O overhead that TCP/IP has, as compared to local IPC.

The only overhead that depends on size is *(de)marshaling*, which depends on the type complexity, number, and size of operation parameters, and *data copying*, which depends on the size of the data. In our whitebox experiment, only the parameter size changes, *i.e.*, the sequences vary in length. Moreover, TAO's (de)marshaling optimizations [13] incur minimal overhead when running between homogeneous ORB endsystems.

In Figure 9, the parameter size is varied and the above test is repeated. It shows that as the size of the operation parameters increases, I/O overhead grows faster than the overall ORB overhead (including messaging and transport). This result illustrates that the overall ORB overhead is largely independent of the request size. In particular, demultiplexing a request, creating message headers, and invoking an operation upcall are not affected by the size of the request.

TAO employs standard buffer size and data copy tradeoff optimizations. This optimization is demonstrated in Figure 9 by the fact that there is a slight increase in the time spent both in the transport component and in the ORB itself when the sequence size is greater than 256 bytes. The data copy tradeoff optimization is fully configurable via run-time command line options, so it is possible to

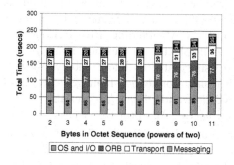

Fig. 9. ORB and Transport/OS Overhead Versus Parameter Size

configure TAO to further improve performance above the 256 byte data copy threshold.

For the operations tested in the IDL_Cubit benchmark, the overhead of the ORB is dominated by memory bandwidth limitations. Both the loopback driver and local IPC driver copy data within the same host. Therefore, memory bandwidth limitations should essentially be the same for both IIOP and UIOP. This result is illustrated in Figure 8 by the fact that the time spent in the ORB is generally constant for the four protocol combinations shown.

In general, the use of UIOP demonstrates the advantages of this framework and how optimized, domain-specific protocols can be deployed.

5   Related Work

The design of TAO's pluggable protocols framework is influenced by prior research on the design and optimization of protocol frameworks for communication subsystems. This section outlines that research and compares it with our work.

Configurable communication frameworks: The x-kernel [34], Conduit+ [30], System V STREAMS [35], ADAPTIVE [36], and F-CSS [37] are all configurable communication frameworks that provide a protocol backplane consisting of standard, reusable services that support network protocol development and experimentation. These frameworks support flexible composition of modular protocol processing components, such as connection-oriented and connectionless message delivery and routing, based on uniform interfaces.

The frameworks for communication subsystems listed above focus on implementing various protocol layers beneath relatively low-level programming APIs, such as sockets. In contrast, TAO's pluggable protocols framework focuses on implementing and/or adapting to transport protocols beneath a higher-level DOC middleware API, i.e., the standard CORBA programming API. Therefore, existing communication subsystem frameworks can provide building block protocol components for TAO's pluggable protocols framework.

Patterns-based communication frameworks: An increasing number of communication frameworks are being designed and documented using patterns[15,30]. In particular, Conduit+ [30] is an OO framework for configuring network protocol software to support ATM signaling. Key portions of the Conduit+ protocol framework, e.g., demultiplexing, connection management, and message buffering, were designed using patterns like Strategy, Visitor, and Composite [25]. Likewise, the concurrency, connection management, and demultiplexing components in TAO's ORB Core and Object Adapter also have been explicitly designed using patterns like Reactor, Acceptor-Connector, and Active Object [15].

CORBA pluggable protocol frameworks: The architecture of TAO's pluggable protocols framework is based on the ORBacus [38] Open Communications Interface (OCI) [39]. The OCI framework provides a flexible, intuitive, and portable interface for pluggable protocols. The framework interfaces are defined in IDL, with a few special rules to map critical types, such as data buffers.

Defining pluggable protocol interfaces with IDL permits developers to familiarize themselves with a single programming model that can be used to implement protocols in different languages. In addition, the use of IDL makes it possible to write pluggable protocols that are portable among different ORB implementations and platforms.

However, using IDL also limits the the degree to which various optimizations can be applied at the ORB and transport protocol levels. For example, efficiently handling locality constrained objects, optimizing profile handling, strategized buffer allocation, or interfacing with optimized OS abstraction layers/libraries are not generally supported by existing IDL compilers. Additionally, changes to an IDL compiler's mapping rules on a per protocol basis is prohibitive.

In our approach we use C++ classes and optimized framework interfaces to allow protocol developers to exploit new strategies or available libraries. TAO uses the ACE framework [29] to isolate itself from non-portable aspects of underlying operating systems. This design leverages the testing, optimizations, implemented by ACE, enabling us to focus on the particular problems of developing a high-performance, real-time ORB.

6   Concluding Remarks

To be an effective development platform for performance-sensitive applications, OO middleware must preserve communication layer QoS properties of applications end-to-end. It is essential, therefore, to define a pluggable protocols framework that allows custom inter-ORB messaging and transport protocols to be configured flexibly and transparently by CORBA applications.

This paper identifies the protocol-related limitations of current ORBs and describes a CORBA-based pluggable protocols framework we developed and integrated with TAO to address these limitations. TAO's pluggable protocols framework contains two main components: an ORB messaging component and an ORB transport adapter component. These two components allows applications developers and end-users to transparently extend their communication infrastructure to support the dynamic and/or static binding of new ORB messaging and transport protocols. Moreover, TAO's patterns-oriented OO design makes it straightforward to develop custom inter-ORB protocol stacks that can be optimized for particular application requirements and endsystem/network environments.

This paper illustrates empirically the performance of TAO's pluggable protocols framework when running CORBA applications over high-speed interconnects, such as VME. Our benchmarking results demonstrate that applying appropriate optimizations and patterns to DOC middleware can yield highly efficient and predictable implementations, without sacrificing flexibility or reuse. These results support our contention that DOC middleware performance is largely an implementation issue. Thus, well-tuned, standard-based DOC middleware like TAO can replace *ad hoc* and proprietary solutions that are still commonly used in traditional distributed applications and embedded real-time systems.

Most of the performance overhead associated with pluggable protocols framework described in this paper stem from "out-of-band" creation operations, rather operations in the critical path. We have shown how patterns can resolve key design forces to flexibly create and control the objects in the framework. Simple and efficient wrapper facades can then be used to isolate the rest of the application from low-level implementation details, without significantly affecting end-to-end performance.

We are currently developing pluggable protocols for high-speed networks such as ATM and Myrinet. One focus of our future work is to determine effective patterns for supporting advanced I/O features, such as buffer management schemes using intelligent I/O interfaces and shared memory, available in current high-speed network adaptors. In addition, we are exploring the integration of high-speed messaging protocols, such as Fast Messages [26], with standard CORBA DOC middleware.

References

1. R. Johnson, "Frameworks = Patterns + Components," *Communications of the ACM*, vol. 40, Oct. 1997. 373

2. S. Vinoski, "CORBA: Integrating Diverse Applications Within Distributed Heterogeneous Environments," *IEEE Communications Magazine*, vol. 14, February 1997. 373

3. Object Management Group, *The Common Object Request Broker: Architecture and Specification*, 2.2 ed., Feb. 1998. 373

4. M. Henning and S. Vinoski, *Advanced CORBA Programming With C++*. Addison-Wesley Longman, 1999. 373

5. D. C. Schmidt, D. L. Levine, and S. Mungee, "The Design and Performance of Real-Time Object Request Brokers," *Computer Communications*, vol. 21, pp. 294–324, Apr. 1998. 373

6. G. Parulkar, D. C. Schmidt, and J. S. Turner, "$a^m athrmIt^P$m: a Strategy for Integrating IP with ATM," in *Proceedings of the Symposium on Communications Architectures and Protocols (SIGCOMM)*, ACM, September 1995. 373

7. F. Kuhns, D. C. Schmidt, and D. L. Levine, "The Design and Performance of a Real-time I/O Subsystem," in *Proceedings of the 5th IEEE Real-Time Technology and Applications Symposium*, (Vancouver, British Columbia, Canada), pp. 154–163, IEEE, June 1999. 373

8. T. H. Harrison, D. L. Levine, and D. C. Schmidt, "The Design and Performance of a Real-time CORBA Event Service," in *Proceedings of OOPSLA '97*, (Atlanta, GA), ACM, October 1997. 373, 385

9. F. Kuhns, C. O'Ryan, D. C. Schmidt, and J. Parsons, "The Performance of TAO's Pluggable Protocols Framework on High-speed Embedded Interconnects," Department of Computer Science, Technical Report WUCS-99-12, Washington University, St. Louis, 1999. 373, 374

10. C. D. Gill, D. L. Levine, and D. C. Schmidt, "The Design and Performance of a Real-Time CORBA Scheduling Service," *The International Journal of Time-Critical Computing Systems*, special issue on Real-Time Middleware, 2000. 373

11. I. Pyarali, C. O'Ryan, D. C. Schmidt, N. Wang, V. Kachroo, and A. Gokhale, "Applying Optimization Patterns to the Design of Real-time ORBs," in *Proceedings of the 5th Conference on Object-Oriented Technologies and Systems*, (San Diego, CA), USENIX, May 1999. 373, 374, 376, 378, 385

12. D. C. Schmidt, S. Mungee, S. Flores-Gaitan, and A. Gokhale, "Software Architectures for Reducing Priority Inversion and Non-determinism in Real-time Object Request Brokers," *Journal of Real-time Systems*, To appear 2000. 373, 386

13. A. Gokhale and D. C. Schmidt, "Optimizing a CORBA IIOP Protocol Engine for Minimal Footprint Multimedia Systems," *Journal on Selected Areas in Communications special issue on Service Enabling Platforms for Networked Multimedia Systems*, vol. 17, Sept. 1999. 373, 375, 390

14. A. Gokhale and D. C. Schmidt, "Measuring the Performance of Communication Middleware on High-Speed Networks," in *Proceedings of SIGCOMM '96*, (Stanford, CA), pp. 306–317, ACM, August 1996. 373

15. D. C. Schmidt and C. Cleeland, "Applying Patterns to Develop Extensible ORB Middleware," *IEEE Communications Magazine*, vol. 37, April 1999. 373, 380, 392

16. F. Buschmann, R. Meunier, H. Rohnert, P. Sommerlad, and M. Stal, *Pattern-Oriented Software Architecture - A System of Patterns*, Wiley and Sons, 1996. 373

17. R. S. Madukkarumukumana and H. V. Shah and C. Pu, "Harnessing User-Level Networking Architectures for Distributed Object Computing over High-Speed Networks," in *Proceedings of the 2nd Usenix Windows NT Symposium*, August 1998. 375

18. Compaq, Intel, and Microsoft, "Virtual Interface Architecture, Version 1.0." http://www.viarch.org, 1997. 375

19. Object Management Group, *Realtime CORBA Joint Revised Submission*, OMG Document orbos/99-02-12 ed., March 1999. 376, 377, 379

20. F. Kon and R. H. Campbell, "Supporting Automatic Configuration of Component-Based Distributed Systems," in *Proceedings of the 5th Conference on Object-Oriented Technologies and Systems*, (San Diego, CA), USENIX, May 1999. 376

21. Object Management Group, *The Common Object Request Broker: Architecture and Specification*, 2.3 ed., June 1999. 376

22. Object Management Group, *Fault Tolerance CORBA Using Entity Redundancy RFP*, OMG Document orbos/98-04-01 ed., April 1998. 376

23. Object Management Group, *CORBA Messaging Specification*, OMG Document orbos/98-05-05 ed., May 1998. 376, 379

24. Object Management Group, *Telecom Domain Task Force Request For Information Supporting Wireless Access and Mobility in CORBA - Request For Information*, OMG Document telecom/98-06-04 ed., June 1998. 376

25. E. Gamma, R. Helm, R. Johnson, and J. Vlissides, *Design Patterns: Elements of Reusable Object-Oriented Software*, Reading, MA: Addison-Wesley, 1995.   377, 380, 392

26. M. Lauria, S. Pakin, and A. Chien, "Efficient Layering for High Speed Communication: Fast Messages 2.x.," in *Proceedings of the 7th High Performance Distributed Computing (HPDC7) conference*, (Chicago, Illinois), July 1998. 379, 393

27. B. Meyer, *Object Oriented Software Construction*. Englewood Cliffs, NJ: Prentice Hall, 1989. 380

28. P. Jain and D. C. Schmidt, "Service Configurator: A Pattern for Dynamic Configuration of Services," in *Proceedings of the 3rd Conference on Object-Oriented Technologies and Systems*, USENIX, June 1997. 381

29. D. C. Schmidt and T. Suda, "An Object-Oriented Framework for Dynamically Configuring Extensible Distributed Communication Systems," *IEE/BCS Distributed Systems Engineering Journal (Special Issue on Configurable Distributed Systems)*, vol. 2, pp. 280–293, December 1994. 382, 392

30. H. Hueni, R. Johnson, and R. Engel, "A Framework for Network Protocol Software," in *Proceedings of OOPSLA '95*, (Austin, Texas), ACM, October 1995. 391, 392

31. D. C. Schmidt, "Acceptor and Connector: Design Patterns for Initializing Communication Services," in *Pattern Languages of Program Design* (R. Martin, F. Buschmann, and D. Riehle, eds.), Reading, MA: Addison-Wesley, 1997. 382, 384

32. S. Mungee, N. Surendran, and D. C. Schmidt, "The Design and Performance of a CORBA Audio/Video Streaming Service," in *Proceedings of the Hawaiian International Conference on System Sciences*, Jan. 1999. 385

33. P. S. Inc., *Quantify User's Guide*. PureAtria Software Inc., 1996. 388

34. N. C. Hutchinson and L. L. Peterson, "The x-kernel: An Architecture for Implementing Network Protocols," *IEEE Transactions on Software Engineering*, vol. 17, pp. 64–76, January 1991. 391

35. D. Ritchie, "A Stream Input–Output System," *AT&T Bell Labs Technical Journal*, vol. 63, pp. 311–324, Oct. 1984. 391

36. D. C. Schmidt, D. F. Box, and T. Suda, "ADAPTIVE: A Dynamically Assembled Protocol Transformation, Integration, and eValuation Environment," *Journal of Concurrency: Practice and Experience*, vol. 5, pp. 269–286, June 1993. 391

37. M. Zitterbart, B. Stiller, and A. Tantawy, "A Model for High-Performance Communication Subsystems," *IEEE Journal on Selected Areas in Communication*, vol. 11, pp. 507–519, May 1993. 391

38. I. Object Oriented Concepts, "ORBacus." www.ooc.com/ob. 392

39. I. Object-Oriented Concepts, "ORBacus User Manual - Version 3.1.2." www.ooc.com/ob, 1999. 392

Customizing IDL Mappings and ORB Protocols

Girish Welling and Maximilian Ott

C&C Research Laboratories, NEC-USA, Inc.
4 Independence Way, Princeton, NJ 08540, USA
{welling,max}@ccrl.nj.nec.com

Abstract. Current mappings of IDL to implementation languages such as C++ or Java use CORBA specific data-types, which makes it imperative for an object implementation to be CORBA-compliant. While being completely CORBA-compliant ensures portability *and* interoperability, several classes of enterprise applications may *only* require interoperability with other CORBA applications. Other applications may be constrained by such factors as a large existing code-base or a widely used communication protocol. In many cases, these applications can benefit from the concise expressiveness of IDL without committing to the overhead of using a general-purpose CORBA ORB. To aid this process, we propose a new approach to ORB design where the IDL mapping and ORB protocol is completely configurable. As a motivation, we present our use of IDL in the development of a large in-house application. In this application, all interfaces are specified using IDL, which is mapped to C++ using a custom mapping. We then present an architecture for a template-driven IDL compiler and describe the implementation of a prototype we built. With this compiler architecture, an IDL mapping can easily be specified and customized by writing an appropriate template.

1 Introduction

CORBA [1] is an enabling technology for building distributed systems, permitting the integration of distributed components at a higher level of communication than traditional byte-streams. This is achieved by providing the communication infrastructure for heterogeneous, distributed collections of objects, for which CORBA presents the communication abstraction of a method call on remote CORBA objects. The benefits derived are akin to the benefits of utilizing object oriented programming for building non-distributed programs.

In order to promote language and platform independence, CORBA encourages the use of an Interface Definition Language (IDL) specified by the Object Management Group (OMG). OMG IDL can only be utilized to specify the *interface* of a CORBA object, enforcing the separation of interface specification from object implementation. This also ensures that a client of a CORBA object remains unconcerned with the implementation of the object. Moreover, the client is also unconcerned with the implementation language of the CORBA object, simplifying the integration of distributed components that are implemented in different languages.

J. Sventek and G. Coulson (Eds.): Middleware 2000, LNCS 1795, pp. 396–414, 2000.

Current mappings of IDL to implementation languages like C, C++ or Java use data-types that are CORBA or ORB-vendor specific. Moreover, in the IDL-C++ or IDL-Java mappings, the inheritance relations between the generated stub/skeleton classes and implementation classes are usually fixed by the IDL compiler. These factors impose additional constraints on the implementation of applications that utilize IDL. The problem is especially acute in legacy applications, which are already associated with a large, well-established code-base.

In order to enable applications to benefit from the concise expressiveness of IDL without committing to being completely CORBA compliant, the mapping of IDL to a particular implementation language should be decoupled from the IDL parser and code-generation engine. This makes it possible to customize the bridge between the application and the underlying ORB, introducing ample flexibility for building both, the application and the ORB. To aid this process, we propose a template-driven IDL compiler architecture. This compiler architecture not only permits the customization of an IDL mapping and generated code, but also enables all aspects of the underlying ORB to be configured. This approach can be considered to introduce the flexibility of tuning middleware to existing code-bases rather than the more common other way around.

The rest of this paper is organized as follows: Section 2 describes the benefits of customizing IDL mappings. Section 3 motivates our approach by presenting the custom IDL to C++ mapping we utilize in HEIDI, an existing in-house application. Section 4 presents the architecture and implementation of our proposed template-driven IDL compiler. Section 5 compares our approach with other approaches to customize ORBs, and Section 6 concludes this paper.

2   The Benefits of Customizing a Mapping

Among the important goals of the CORBA specification are *portability* and *interoperability* of CORBA compliant application code with different ORB implementations. Towards this end, CORBA defines mappings from OMG IDL to various programming languages including Java, C, C++, Smalltalk, COBOL and Modula 3. The mapping process is automated in an IDL compiler, which generates the framework for implementing a CORBA object from the IDL specification of its interface. In addition, the IDL compiler also generates client-side *stubs* and server-side *skeletons*, which collaborate with the underlying ORB to implement such activities as object registration, method call parameter marshaling and unmarshaling, and call dispatching. Usually, stubs and skeletons utilize an abstract interface to the underlying ORB functionality so that the same generated code can be utilized with ORBs that implement different *on-the-wire* protocols. The portability of a CORBA compliant object implementation across IDL compilers from different vendors is ensured in theory by each compiler conforming to the specified IDL to implementation language data-type mapping (Table 1) and object model. The interoperability between applications that utilize ORBs from different vendors is guaranteed by each ORB conforming to such a standard ORB protocol as the Internet Inter-ORB Protocol (IIOP).

Table 1. IDL to C++ Type Mappings

IDL Type	Prescribed C++ Type	Alternate C++ Mapping
long	CORBA::Long	long
boolean	CORBA::Boolean	XBool
float	CORBA::Float	float

The CORBA specification also provides guidelines for generating stubs and skeletons from an IDL interface. A typical inheritance hierarchy for C++ stubs and skeletons is shown in Fig. 1, where the non-shaded classes are generated by the IDL compiler and the shaded classes implemented by the application programmer. In this hierarchy, the implementation of a CORBA object can inherit from the generated skeleton, or remain unrelated to the generated classes, utilizing a *tie* class as a bridge to/from the ORB. Most IDL compilers generate stubs and skeletons conforming to a variation of this inheritance hierarchy.

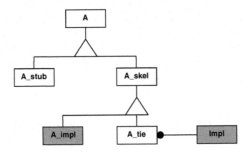

Fig. 1. Inheritance Hierarchy for C++ Stubs and Skeletons

Although portability and large-scale interoperability are important concerns of building software for distributed systems, there are several situations when it is useful to customize the code generated by an IDL compiler:

– **Using legacy code for CORBA-object implementations:** While being completely CORBA-compliant ensures portability across different ORBs and interoperability with other CORBA-compliant applications, several classes of enterprise applications may only require interoperability with other CORBA applications. This is especially true with legacy applications, which are often constrained by such factors as a large existing code-base or a widely used communication protocol. With most current IDL compilers, these applications can benefit from the concise expressiveness of IDL only by becoming completely CORBA compliant. However, a legacy application may utilize the C++ usages shown in Table 2, while the CORBA specification for mapping an IDL interface *A* to a C++ interface class *A* states that it is non-compliant to declare either an instance, pointer or reference to A. As this shows, it can be an expensive, time-consuming process to integrate a legacy application into a CORBA-based distributed system.

Table 2. CORBA-prescribed and Legacy C++ Usages

CORBA-prescribed	Legacy
A_var a;	A a;
A_ptr p;	A* p;
void f(A_ptr& r);	void f(A& r);

- **Customizing the ORB:** An ORB that fully implements the CORBA specification is usually very big in terms of code size. For many classes of applications, this can be the major reason to decide against utilizing CORBA. This issue has motivated a recent OMG effort towards identifying an irreducible set of capabilities and characteristics for a minimal ORB. Such an ORB would implement a CORBA subset that is useful and acceptable for the applications in consideration. Keeping with this trend, we believe that it is also useful to permit the customization of the ORB to implement exactly the subset of CORBA functionality that is necessary for a particular class of applications.

- **Customizing the ORB Protocol and Messaging Formats:** Utilizing a standard inter-ORB protocol guarantees that an application can easily interoperate with other applications. However, such protocols are often expensive to use because they are designed for generality. Moreover, for many applications, a simple protocol or messaging format may suffice.

  To address this issue, most IDL compilers generate stubs and skeletons that utilize an abstract interface to the ORB. This keeps the IDL compiler, and hence the generated code independent of any particular ORB protocol, permitting the utilization of alternate protocols. With such an approach, utilizing a particular protocol involves choosing the appropriate ORB run-time library.

- **Incorporating Custom Optimizations:** Often, the code generated by an IDL compiler is not well suited for optimization. For instance, many IDL compilers use string comparisons to implement the dispatching logic in the skeleton. Such a scheme can be very expensive for interfaces with a large number of methods with long names. Alternate schemes that utilize nested comparisons [2], or a hash-table can result in faster dispatching.

  Marshaling/Unmarshaling code is typically associated with format conversions and copying. As pointed out in the Universal Stub Compiler (USC) work by O'Malley, et al [3], a user-level specification of the byte-level representations of data types can be effectively utilized to optimize copying operations, and therefore marshaling and unmarshaling code. It is clearly beneficial to introduce such optimizations in generated stubs and skeletons in order to improve the performance of a remote call.

3   HEIDIRMI

In order to demonstrate that it is indeed useful to customize an IDL mapping, we consider the motivation, design and implementation of HEIDIRMI, the control-messaging infrastructure for HEIDI. HEIDI is a large in-house project currently being used to build and test prototype multimedia software systems [4]. In early versions of HEIDI, all control messaging between distributed software components utilized a simple text-based request-response protocol over dedicated TCP/IP connections. This approach sufficed for the simple initial prototype applications we built. However, as more complicated prototypes were developed, it clearly became necessary to automate the process of generating control messaging support. OMG IDL was an available alternative, and was well suited to describe the control messaging interfaces in HEIDI.

Using IDL along with a general-purpose ORB in HEIDI was associated with problems that arose from the large amount of legacy code that was not CORBA-compliant, and the non-blocking nature of communication in a HEIDI application. The large existing code-base clearly needed wide-spread changes before it could be integrated with a general-purpose ORB. Even if this were done, it would still be difficult to utilize a general purpose ORB because of the non-preemptive computation model of HEIDI.

To avoid the wide-spread changes necessary to make existing HEIDI code CORBA-compliant, we modified the OmniBroker[1] IDL compiler [5] to generate an alternate C++ mapping that conforms to existing HEIDI code. The HEIDIRMI mapping only utilizes HEIDI defined data types, which simplifies the use of legacy HEIDI code. Besides utilizing only existing HEIDI data-types, the mapping also implements a delegation based relation between the skeleton and implementation classes as shown in Fig. 2. This approach ensures that no re-structuring of the existing HEIDI class hierarchy is necessary.

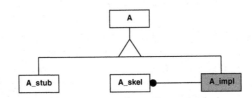

Fig. 2. IDL to C++ Mapping in HEIDIRMI

The delegation model of the HEIDIRMI mapping is similar to the *tie* approach in the CORBA-prescribed IDL to C++ mapping. A *tie* is usually im-

---

[1] OmniBroker is now called ORBacus.

plemented as a template to which the implementation class of the target object must be specified. This approach makes it unnecessary for the implementation class to depend on any of the classes generated by the IDL compiler. Although this simplifies the utilization of legacy code, there still is the dependency on CORBA-specific data types because method signatures in the implementation class must exactly match method signatures in the interface class. We therefore believe that *ties* alone are largely insufficient to address the problem of utilizing legacy code. Our approach of using a custom mapping on the other hand, provides the desired flexibility while maintaining a simpler relation between the implementation class and the skeleton. Moreover, such coding conventions as class naming can be easily customized, saving large amounts of otherwise mundane, but time consuming changes.

3.1   Implementation Details

We extended the IDL syntax in support of default parameters and passing parameters by value. Since legacy HEIDI code extensively utilized the ability to specify default parameters to a method in C++, we added support for the specification of default parameters in IDL. Default parameters are indicated as shown in the IDL interface presented in Fig. 3, and have the same effect as that of default parameters in C++ class specifications. Each default parameter to a method in an IDL interface is mapped to an appropriate default parameter in the generated C++ interface class.

In order to support passing parameters by value, we introduced the new *incopy* keyword, which is used as a qualifier for a method parameter. For simple data types, the effect of *incopy* is identical to that of *in*. However, object references passed *incopy* are copied across the IDL interface, if possible. The ORB run-time utilizes marshaling/unmarshaling primitives that the object implementation may have provided. Whether a particular object has actually implemented the required marshaling/unmarshaling primitives is determined by testing if it implements the *HdSerializable* interface. The dynamic type checking support that is implemented in HEIDI is utilized for this purpose. The semantics of passing parameters by value in HEIDIRMI are identical to the effect of passing a *Serializable* object that is not *Remote* as a parameter to a remote method in Java RMI [6].

Also shown in Fig. 3 are the relevant portions of the abstract C++ interface class generated by our customized HEIDIRMI IDL compiler. It can be seen that no CORBA-specific types are utilized: primitive IDL data-types are mapped to primitive C++ types, while **sequence** and **boolean** are mapped to the HEIDI specific *HdList* and *XBool* data types. Also, default parameters are mapped to appropriate C++ constants. Note that the IDL interfaces HEIDI::*A* and HEIDI::*S* are respectively mapped to the C++ interface classes *HdA* and *HdS*. This unconventional mapping facilitates the integration with legacy code, assuming that *HdA* and *HdS* were existing HEIDI interface classes.

Not shown in Fig. 3 is the generated support for dynamic type checking, which all HEIDI classes provide. Methods for marshaling and unmarshaling ob-

```
/* File A.idl */                    /* File A.hh */
module Heidi {                      // IDL:Heidi/Status:1.0
  // External declaration of Heidi::S   enum HdStatus { Start, Stop };
  interface S;                      // IDL:Heidi/SSequence:1.0
  // Heidi::Status                  typedef HdList<HdS> HdSSequence;
  enum Status {Start, Stop};        typedef HdListIterator<HdS>
  // Heidi::SSequence                              HdSSequenceIter;
  typedef sequence<S> SSequence;    // IDL:Heidi/A:1.0
  // Heidi::A                       class HdA : virtual public HdS
  interface A : S                   {
  {                                 public:
    void f(in A a);                   virtual void f(HdA*) = 0;
    void g(incopy S s);               virtual void g(HdS*) = 0;
    void p(in long l = 0);            virtual void p(long l = 0) = 0;
    void q(in Status s = Heidi::Start);  virtual void q(HdStatus s = Start) = 0;
    readonly attribute Status button;   virtual void s(XBool b = XTrue) = 0;
    void s(in boolean b = TRUE);      virtual void t(HdSSequence*) = 0;
    void t(in SSequence s);           virtual HdStatus GetButton() = 0;
  };                                  virtual ~HdA() {}
};                                  };
```

Fig. 3. Example IDL Interface and Generated C++ Interface Class

jects that implement the generated interface have also been omitted. These methods implement the logic for determining if a given object also implements *HdSerializable*, and passing control to the implementation object specific methods for marshaling/unmarshaling object state. This simplifies generated code for stubs and skeletons by putting together what would otherwise be redundantly generated marshaling/unmarshaling code.

In HEIDIRMI, each object is associated with a stringified object reference. An object reference is composed of three parts: the bootstrap URL, the object identifier, and the object type. The bootstrap URL consists of a protocol-hostname-port tuple that provides a means to open a communication channel to the object. The object identifier uniquely identifies the object in a particular address space, while the type information ensures that the correct stub and skeleton is utilized in accessing the object. A typical stringified object reference is *@tcp:galaxy.nec.com:1234#9876#IDL:*HEIDI*/A:1.0*. Although a HEIDIRMI object reference may be considered minimal, it is not unlike an object reference in CORBA or any other remote object system.

The interaction diagram on the client-side of a remote method invocation is shown in Fig. 4. When a stub method is invoked, a new *Call* object that provides the generic functionality for making a remote method call is created. The stringified object reference of the target remote object forms the header of the *Call*. After any parameters to the remote method are marshaled into the *Call* object, the *Call* is *invoked*, resulting in the call request being sent to the server-side.

An *ObjectCommunicator* provides the abstraction of a communication channel on which individual requests can be demarcated. The current implementation of *Call* and *ObjectCommunicator* utilize a newline terminated string of ASCII characters to implement the on-the-wire protocol. The *Call* object provides the functions for marshaling and unmarshaling all primitive data types, as well as additional *begin* and *end* functions that permit structuring of the call request so that such composite data types as *structs* or *sequences* can be easily represented.

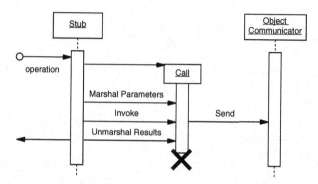

Fig. 4. Remote Method Invocation in HEIDIRMI

The interaction at the server-side is shown in Fig. 5. The bootstrap port in each address space serves as means to initiate a communication channel. When a client connects to the bootstrap port (1), a new *ObjectCommunicator* is wrapped around the resulting connection. Connections are cached and reused in HEIDIRMI, and only if there is no available connection is a new connection opened. The *ObjectCommunicator* reads in an incoming request (2) and encapsulates it in a *Call* object. The *Call* header contains the stringified object reference, whose type information and object identifier permit the selection of the appropriate *Skeleton*. Control is passed to the *dispatch* method of the selected *Skeleton*, where the remote method call parameters are unmarshaled. The *skeleton* then calls the desired method of the target object implementation, marshals any return value into the *Call* object, and sends the result back to the client-side.

An important aspect of HEIDIRMI is that an implementation object is unconcerned with being remote accessible. The skeleton for a particular object is only created when a reference to it is being passed as either the parameter to, or the result of a remote call. Moreover, if the implementation object is *Serializable* and is being passed-by-value, then no *skeleton* is ever created. In this case, the marshaling method defined by the object is utilized to copy the object. At the receiving end, the type information contained in the object reference is utilized to create a stub of the appropriate type. Both stubs and skeletons are cached in each address-space in order to minimize the overhead of their creation.

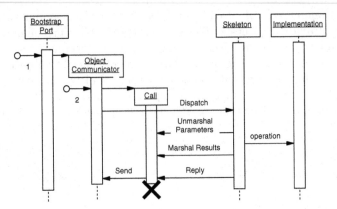

Fig. 5. Server-side Method Call Dispatching in HEIDIRMI

The implementation of stubs and skeletons for an IDL interface is straight-forward. All stubs inherit from a base *HdStub* class which provides the generic stub functionality. A stub also implements the C++ mapping of the IDL inter-face, and reflects the IDL inheritance structure appropriately. For the running example, the stub *A_stub* for the IDL interface *A* inherits functionality from the stub *S_stub* for the IDL interface *S*, and in addition implements the methods of interface *A*.

In HEIDIRMI, skeletons do not share any inheritance relation with the ab-stract interface class. However, similar to generated stubs, skeletons also reflect the IDL inheritance structure. For the running example, the skeleton *A_skel* for interface *A* inherits from the skeleton *S_skel* for interface *S*. The *dispatch* method of *A_skel* first attempts to dispatch an incoming request to methods defined in the interface *A*. If this fails, then dispatching is delegated to the dis-patch method of *S_skel*, continuing recursively up the skeleton class hierarchy. If *A* inherits from more than one interface, then dispatching is delegated to each of the corresponding skeleton super-classes in order.

3.2   Shortcomings of This Approach

Early use of our compiler involved reverse-engineering existing C++ interfaces into suitable IDL interfaces. However, the ease with which our approach per-mitted us to quickly build HEIDI components led us to begin specifying their interfaces in IDL. HEIDIRMI has thus become an integral part of the HEIDI de-velopment environment, and our custom compiler has evolved into a key tool to build the system. Extensive utilization of HEIDIRMI has strengthened our belief that IDL is indeed a powerful tool for specifying the interfaces of mod-ules in a large application. By customizing the IDL compiler for HEIDIRMI, we have succeeded in separating the utilization of IDL from the necessity of using a complete CORBA-compatible ORB.

However, the evolution of the HEIDIRMI IDL compiler has also raised concerns regarding the limitations of the customization approach. It is evident that even a minor change in the IDL to C++ mapping requires compiler source code changes and recompilation. This concern led us to consider the alternative of template-based code-generation. Here, details of the IDL to implementation mapping are specified in a template, which the IDL compiler utilizes to drive its code generation. This greatly simplifies customization of the IDL compiler to generate code conforming to a desired mapping. Moreover, the very same compiler can be utilized with alternate templates to generate code in different implementation languages.

It should be noted, though, that our extensions for default parameters and passing parameters by value required IDL syntax changes. Such syntax enhancements must be reflected in the IDL parser, and is outside the scope of any template scheme for code-generation.

4   Architecture of a Customizable IDL Compiler

As with OmniBroker, most current IDL compilers hard-code the IDL mapping. Although this approach serves well to ensure CORBA-conformance, the inflexibility restricts the ability to customize generated code. In order to overcome this restriction, we propose the compiler architecture shown in Fig. 6. In this architecture, an IDL compiler consists of a generic parser that creates an *enhanced syntax tree* (EST) representation of the IDL source, and a template driven code-generator that utilizes the EST to generate stub/skeleton code. Figure 6 also shows the languages utilized in our prototype implementation.

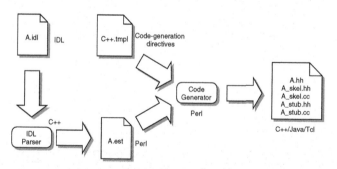

Fig. 6. Template-driven IDL Compiler Architecture

The key point to note in this compiler architecture is that the generated code no longer depends on anything that is hard-coded in the compiler modules. While both modules clearly must understand the EST representation, the parser must additionally understand the IDL syntax, while the code-generator must understand the syntax for specifying a template. The generated code now depends only on the template that is provided to the code-generator. This makes it possible to tune generated code by only changing the template specification. Moreover, this approach also makes it is possible to generate code for an IDL mapping to any implementation language.

4.1   Prototype Implementation

In order to determine the feasibility of the template approach, we built a hybrid two-stage IDL compiler using the OmniBroker compiler to parse IDL, and a template-driven back-end code-generator that is based on Jeeves [7].

   We modified the Omnibroker compiler to generate a perl program that encodes the EST representation of the IDL source. An EST representation is a parse tree that is organized so that similar elements are grouped together. For instance, IDL permits interspersing of attributes and methods in an interface. This can be seen in the example of Fig. 3 where the attribute *button* occurs between the methods *q* and *s*. The children of a node corresponding to an interface in a regular IDL parse tree would therefore be ordered exactly as the corresponding order of attributes and methods in the IDL. On the other hand, an EST would be constructed so that nodes corresponding to all the attributes are grouped, as are those corresponding to all the methods. This can be seen in Fig. 7, where the EST for the IDL interface presented in Fig. 3 maintains the node corresponding to the *button* attribute in a separate sub-tree of the node corresponding to the interface *A*. Irrelevant parts of the EST have been omitted from Fig. 7 for simplicity. A portion of the actual perl program that encodes the EST is shown in Fig. 8.

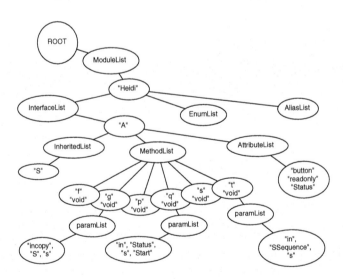

Fig. 7. Extended Syntax Tree for A.idl

```perl
#!/usr/bin/perl
use Ast;
use JeevesUtil;
$ROOT = $n0 = Ast::New("Root");
#
# IDL:Heidi:1.0
#
$n1 = Ast::New("Heidi", "Module", $n0);
    #
    # IDL:Heidi/Status:1.0
    #
    $n2 = Ast::New("Status", "Enum", $n1);
    @m = [ Start, Stop ];
    $n2→AddProp("members", @m);
    #
    # IDL:Heidi/SSequence:1.0
    #
    $n2 = Ast::New("SSequence", "Alias", $n1);
    $n2→AddProp("type", "sequence");
    #————————
        $n3 = Ast::New("", "Sequence", $n2);
        $n3→AddProp("type", "objref");
        $n3→AddProp("typeName", "Heidi_S");
        $n3→AddProp("IsVariable", true);
    #
    # IDL:Heidi/A:1.0
    #
    $n2 = Ast::New("A", "Interface", $n1);
    $n2→AddProp("Parent", "Heidi_S");
        #
        # IDL:Heidi/A/f:1.0
        #
        $n3 = Ast::New("f", "Operation", $n2);
        $n3→AddProp("type", "void");
        #————————————
            $n4 = Ast::New("a", "Param", $n3);
            $n4→AddProp("type", "objref");
            $n4→AddProp("typeName", "Heidi_A");
            $n4→AddProp("getType", "in");
    . . .
```

Fig. 8. Portion of the generated Perl program representing the EST

Grouping similar nodes in the EST simplifies the specification of a template that drives the code-generator back-end. This can be seen in Fig. 9, which presents a template for the C++ interface class header as defined in the HEIDIRMI mapping. The template syntax is straightforward: the '@' character serves as an escape for code-generation commands, while the other lines are just printed out with appropriate substitutions. The '$' indicates the name of an attribute of the node under current consideration, and is substituted by its text value before being printed out. The use of a *map* makes it possible to convert an IDL name into one that is suitable in the context of the code that is being generated, changing HEIDI::*A* to *HdA*, for instance. The *foreach* command walks through a list of nodes, examining each node in sequence. Since the EST has already classified the nodes into separate sub-trees according to their types, using the *foreach* command will in fact exhaustively enumerate all elements of the lists of methods, attributes, or parameters.

In our current implementation, code-generation is a two-step process. In the first step, a perl program that represents the actual code generator is automatically produced from the given template. A modified version of Jeeves [7] is utilized for this process. This program is then executed together with the perl program generated in the IDL parse stage to produce the desired IDL mapping. The latter program essentially rebuilds the EST within the perl interpreter, while the former uses the EST to generate the desired code based on the template.

Although the two-step code-generation stage is akin to recompiling the compiler, it is possible to merge the two code-generation steps as we plan to do in the future. It can also be noted that the first step of the code-generation stage need only be performed once for a particular code-generation template. Moreover, evaluating a perl program that directly rebuilds the EST, as we do in the second code-generation step, is certainly more efficient than parsing an external representation of the EST.

4.2   Experience

Our template approach to generating code introduces the flexibility of quickly building an ORB to suit an existing application. For instance, it took us about two weeks and 700 lines of **tcl** code to build an IIOP compatible **tcl** ORB. This exercise enabled the integration of an existing **tcl** management GUI application with a CORBA-based distributed system. We utilized our template-driven IDL compiler to generate an IDL-**tcl** mapping that suited the existing **tcl** code (Fig. 10). Our experience goes to show that the template approach has introduced the option of quickly developing an ORB to suit an existing application, as opposed to only having the option of making the existing application CORBA-compliant.

We have also utilized our hybrid compiler to generate an experimental HEIDIRMI compatible IDL-Java mapping. The goal of this work was to enable the use of HEIDIRMI to configure a generic HEIDI engine from within a Java program. The class inheritance structure in our IDL-Java mapping was similar to the HEIDIRMI C++ mapping, but expanded multiple super-classes in order to get

```
@foreach interfaceList -map interfaceName CPP::MapClassName
@openfile ${interfaceName}.hh
/* File ${interfaceName}.hh */
class ${interfaceName} :
@foreach inheritedList -ifMore ',' -map inheritedName CPP::MapClassName
        virtual public ${inheritedName} ${ifMore}
@end inheritedList
{
@foreach attributeList -map attributeType CPP::MapType
        ${attributeType} ${attributeName};
@end attributeList
public:
@foreach methodList -map returnType CPP::MapReturnType
   virtual ${returnType} ${methodName}(
@foreach paramList -ifMore ',' -map paramType CPP::MapType
@if ${defaultParam} == ""
                ${paramType} ${ifMore}
@else
                ${paramType} ${paramName} = ${defaultParam} ${ifMore}
@fi
@end parameterList
                ) = 0;
@end methodList
   virtual ~${interfaceName}() {}

   // Attribute access methods
@foreach attributeList -map attributeType CPP::MapType
        ${attributeType} Get${attributeName}() const = 0;
@if ${attributeQualifier} ≠ "readonly"
        void Set${attributeName}(${attributeType}) = 0;
@fi
@end attributeList

};
@end interfaceList
```

Fig. 9. Template for Generation of C++ Interface Class Header

```
if {[info vars "IDL:Receiver:1.0"] ≠ ""} return
set IDL:Receiver:1.0 1

BOA::addIdlMapping ::Receiver "IDL:Receiver:1.0"

class ReceiverStub {
  inherit Stub

  constructor {ior connector} {
    Stub::constructor $ior $connector
  } {}

  public method print {text} {
    set c [$pb_connector_ getRequestCall $this "print" 0]
    $c insertString $text
    $c send
    # void return
    $c release
  }
}

class ReceiverSkel {
  inherit Skel

  constructor {implObj} {
    Skel::constructor $implObj
  } {}

  public method print {c} {
    set text [$c extractString]
    $pb_obj_ print $text
    # void return
  }
}
```

Fig. 10. Sample **tcl** stub and skeleton code

around the unavailability of multiple inheritance in Java. The IDL-Java mapping we implemented also does not support default parameters as the corresponding C++ mapping does.

The template approach also makes it easy to customize primitive ORB functionality and protocols. Assuming that all generated code utilizes generic ORB functionality provided by an ORB library, it is possible to write templates for stubs and skeletons that only use portions of the ORB library to minimize the ORB footprint as may be required for small embedded devices. HEIDIRMI itself utilizes an entirely text-based wire-protocol that suffices for the control messaging needed in HEIDI. Utilizing such a text-based protocol permitted a *"human"* client to telnet into the bootstrap port of a HEIDI application and type in simple HEIDIRMI requests to debug the system. This was made possible by writing templates that utilized a custom *Call* object that implemented the appropriate marshaling/unmarshaling functionality.

5   Related Work

Although ORB customization has received the attention of many researchers, current work has mostly concentrated on finding an appropriate balance between ORB functionality, code-size and efficiency, while preserving a fixed, conforming programming interface. By addressing the problem of customizing the ORB interface, our approach can be considered to add an additional degree of flexibility to ORB design. We first compare our approach with other approaches to ORB customization, and then with other approaches to building configurable IDL compilers.

One approach to customizing an ORB is to synthesize it from primitive components. For instance, *Quarterware* [8] provides the core components required for middleware implementations: data marshaling/unmarshaling, object references, transport, dispatching, invocation policy, and wire protocol. Specific middleware like CORBA or Java RMI are implemented by suitably selecting and customizing these *Quarterware* components. Similarly, *Jonathan* [9] provides interface references, binding types, and binding factories using which a CORBA or RMI *personality* can be implemented. While this approach can clearly be utilized to customize ORB functionality to fit application requirements, it does not simplify customizing the language interface presented by the ORB to the application. Our template driven code-generation can therefore be considered to complement the synthesis approach. Moreover, the availability of primitive components will certainly simplify designing suitable templates for a particular class of applications.

A less flexible approach to synthesizing an ORB is for it to expose certain object patterns and interfaces. With this approach, certain aspects of a core ORB engine can be customized by attaching a custom module. For instance a *strategy* may be attached in TAO [10] and *dynamicTAO* [11,12], a *subcontract* in Spring [13], or a *policy* in the extensions to RMI suggested in [14]. The CORBA standard [1] provides the Object Adaptor (OA) through which server objects interact with the ORB. An OA can make such services as a database appear as an object. ORB implementations too provide features based on this approach: Orbix [15] provides *filters* that are triggered in the dispatch path, and *smart proxies* that can cache object state. Visibroker [16] provides similar features called *interceptors* and *smart stubs*. Java RMI [6] permits the customization of its reference layer so that alternate invocation semantics can be implemented. While this approach certainly permits the customization of ORB functionality, the degree of flexibility introduced is clearly limited to only those aspects of the ORB that are actually exposed.

Our two-stage compiler architecture is not unlike that of the Omnibroker compiler itself. The Omnibroker parser stores an abstract representation of the IDL source in a possibly persistent global *Interface Repository* (IR) in support of a distributed development environment. The code-generation stage then queries the IR for details of each required IDL interface, generating code as it walks the IDL parse tree. We believe our own code generator would integrate well with the OmniBroker framework to directly utilize the OmniBroker IR. The EST that our template code-generation requires could either be generated on the fly from the parse tree in the IR, or the IR could modified to store the EST instead of the parse tree.

An extensive effort towards modularizing IDL compilers has been made in the *Flick* project at the University of Utah [2]. Although the *Flick* compiler framework has been designed with the goal of supporting multiple IDLs, implementation languages and protocols, the flexibility that has been introduced does not simplify the tuning of generated code. Each new IDL mapping would typically require the design and development of a new *Flick* back-end module, which in turn would require recompilation for every change in the mapping. In contrast, our approach of specifying the IDL mapping in a template clearly simplifies the customization of a mapping. However, our approach of building an IDL compiler is consistent with that of *Flick* and we believe that it is possible to incorporate the template approach into the *Flick* framework by writing a suitable template-driven back-end.

We believe *Flick* is superior at providing certain sophisticated optimizations, especially those involving marshal buffer management and parameter management. However, code-generation optimizations involving inlining code or nested message demultiplexing can easily be accomplished with the template approach. A good strategy may be to utilize the template approach when code-generation flexibility is desired, but resort to writing a custom *Flick* back-end for incorporating sophisticated optimizations.

Although the ILU project at XEROX, Palo Alto Research Center [17] also emphasizes customizability, the customizability is restricted to primitive ORB functionality rather than IDL mappings. For instance new messaging protocols, URL parsing functions, or authentication and accounting schemes can be specified to the ILU kernel. Many different target languages including C, C++, Java, and Modula-3 are supported, but the code-generation for each of these is based on fixed mappings of ILU's native IDL to the target language. This limitation makes it hard to utilize ILU to generate code that is compliant with legacy application code.

6   Conclusions

Most ORBs are designed to provide features that satisfy a large class of applications. However, not all available features are necessary for all applications. Moreover, a particular set of features may not suffice for certain classes of applications. This makes it necessary for an ORB to be customizable and tunable to the requirements of a particular class of applications.

In this paper, we first illustrated that there do indeed exist several classes of applications where it is useful to customize the code that is generated to bridge application code with the underlying ORB. We then presented a flexible template-driven code-generator where the mapping of IDL to the implementation language is specified in a template. This approach simplifies tuning the IDL mapping, and can be used to complement other approaches of ORB customization. Extensive utilization of this approach suggests that it is a powerful technique for tailoring an ORB to application requirements. Moreover, the template approach can also be utilized to quickly generate the framework for object implementations, which are often associated with fixed code *patterns.*

We have already strengthened our belief in the template approach by building support for an IDL-Java mapping for HEIDIRMI (without support for default parameters), and a new IDL-**tcl** mapping that utilizes a custom **tcl** ORB. In the future, we plan to further consolidate our position by considering the design of IDL mappings for minimal, real-time ORBs based on IIOP.

References

1. Object Management Group, Inc., *The Common Object Request Broker: Architecture and Specification*, Aug. 1996. Document PTC/96-08-04, Revision 2.0. 396, 411
2. E. Eide, K. Frei, B. Ford, J. Lepreau, and G. Lindstrom, "Flick: A flexible, optimizing compiler," in *Proceedings of the ACM SIGPLAN Conference on Programming Language Design and Implementation*, (Las Vegas, Nevada, USA), June 1997. 399, 412
3. S. O'Malley, T. Proebsting, and A. Montz, "USC: A universal stub compiler," in *Proceedings of the Conference on Communication Architectures, Protocols and Applications (SIGCOMM)*, (London, UK), Aug. 1994. 399
4. M. Ott, G. Michelitsch, D. Reininger, and G. Welling, "An architecture for adaptive QoS and its application to multimedia systems design," *Computer Communications*, vol. 21, pp. 334–349, Feb. 1998. 400
5. Object Oriented Concepts, Inc., *OmniBroker*. http://www.ooc.com/ob/. 400
6. Sun Microsystems, Inc., *Java Remote Method Invocation Specification*. http://java.sun.com/products/jdk/rmi/index.html. 401, 412
7. S. Srinivasan, "Template-driven code generation," in *Advanced Perl Programming*, ch. 17, O'Reilly Associates, Inc., Aug. 1997. 406, 408

8. A. Singhai, A. Sane, and R. H. Campbell, "Quarterware for middleware," in *Proceedings of the International Conference on Distributed Computing Systems*, (Amsterdam, The Netherlands), May 1998. 411

9. B. Dumant, F. Horn, F. D. Tran, and J.-B. Stefani, "Jonathan: An open distributed processing environment in Java," in *Proceedings of the IFIP International Conference on Distributed Systems Platforms and Open Distributed Processing (Middleware '98)*, (The Lake District, England), Sept. 1998. 411

10. D. C. Schmidt and C. Cleeland, "Applying patterns to develop extensible and maintainable ORB middleware," *Communications of the ACM*, vol. 40, no. 12, 1997. 411

11. F. Kon and R. H. Campbell, "Supporting automatic configuration of component-based distributed system," in *Proceedings of the USENIX Conference on Object-Oriented Technologies (COOTS)*, (San Diego, California, USA), May 1999. 411

12. M. Roman, F. Kon, and R. H. Campbell, "Design and implementation of runtime reflection in communication middleware: the *dynamicTAO* case," in *Proceedings of the ICDCS '99 Workshop on Middleware*, (Austin, Texas, USA), May 1999. 411

13. G. Hamilton, M. L. Powell, and J. G. Michell, "Subcontract: A flexible base for distributed programming," in *Proceedings of the 14th ACM Symposium on Operating Systems Principles*, (Asheville, North Carolina, USA), Dec. 1993. 411

14. G. Welling and M. Ott, "Structuring remote object systems for mobile hosts with intermittent connectivity," in *Proceedings of the 18th International Conference on Distributed Computing Systems*, (Amsterdam, The Netherlands), May 1998. 411

15. IONA Technologies, *The ORBIX Architecture*.
http://www.iona.com/products/orbix/. 412

16. Visigenic, Inc., *The New Application Architecture, Version 3.0*, 1997. 412

17. XEROX Corporation, *ILU Reference Manual*.
http://pubweb.parc.xerox.com/hypertext/ilu/index.html. 412

Hierarchical Architecture for Real-Time Adaptive Resource Management

Ionut Cardei[1], Rakesh Jha[2], Mihaela Cardei[1], Allalaghatta Pavan[2]

Honeywell Technology Center
3660 Technology Drive, Minneapolis, MN 55418, USA
[1]{ionut, mihaela}@cs.umn.edu, [2]{jha, pavan}@htc.honeywell.com

Abstract. This paper presents the Real Time Adaptive Resource Management system (RTARM[1]), developed at the Honeywell Technology Center. RTARM supports provision of integrated services for real-time distributed applications and offers management services for end-to-end QoS negotiation, QoS adaptation, real-time monitoring and hierarchical QoS feedback adaptation. In this paper, we focus on the hierarchical architecture of RTARM, its flexibility, internal mechanisms and protocols that enable management of resources for integrated services. The architecture extensibility is emphasized with the description of several service managers, including an object wrapper build around the NetEx real-time network resource management. We use practical experiments with a distributed Automatic Target Recognition application and a synthetic pipeline application to illustrate the impact of RTARM on the application behavior and to evaluate the system performance.

1   Introduction

Current distributed mission-critical environments employ heterogeneous resources that are shared by a host of diverse applications cooperating towards a common mission goal. These applications are generally a mix of hard-, soft- and non-real-time applications with different levels of criticality and have a variety of structures, ranging from periodic independent tasks, multimedia streams and parallel pipelines, to event-driven method-invocation communicating components. The applications usually tolerate a range of Quality of Services (QoS) and are ready to trade off QoS in favor of the most critical functions they perform. The distributed systems must be able to evolve and adapt to the high variability in resource demands and criticality of the applications as well as to the changing availability of resources.

The current industry trend is to build distributed environments for mission-critical applications using "Common-Off-The-Shelf" (COTS) commercial hardware and software components. A middleware layer above the COTS components provides consistent management for the system resources, decreases complexity and development costs.

This paper presents the Real Time Adaptive Resource Management system (RTARM), developed at the Honeywell Technology Center, that implements a

---

[1] Funded by DARPA under NRaD Contract number N66001-97-C-8524.

J. Sventek and G. Coulson (Eds.): Middleware 2000, LNCS 1795, pp. 415-434, 2000.
© Springer-Verlag Berlin Heidelberg 2000

general middleware architecture/framework for adaptive management for integrated services aimed to real-time mission-critical distributed applications.

The RTARM system has the following basic features [5]: (1) scalable end-to-end criticality-based QoS contract negotiation that allows distributed applications to share common resources while maximizing their utilization and execution quality; (2) end-to-end QoS adaptation that dynamically adjusts application resource utilization according to their availability while optimizing application QoS; (3) integrated services for CPU and network resources with end-to-end QoS guarantees; (4) real-time application QoS monitoring for integrated services and (5) plug-and-play architecture components for easy extensibility for new services.

The resource management architecture for RTARM uses an innovative approach that unifies heterogeneous resources and their management functions into a hierarchical uniform abstract service model [5]. The building block of the architecture is the Service Manager (SM). It encapsulates a set of services and their management functions and exports a common interface to clients and other service managers. This facilitates recursive hierarchies, in which heterogeneous services are integrated bottom-up. A higher-level service manager aggregates services provided by itself and its lower-level SMs and provides clients with a higher-level QoS representation.

In this paper, we focus on the architecture, protocols and implementation of an RTARM prototype that supports integrated services for real-time distributed applications. It runs as a middleware on a network of workstations and uses CORBA for portable communication. A major contribution of our work is the hierarchical feedback adaptation mechanism [1] that provides efficient dynamic QoS control for distributed data-flow applications. We illustrate the RTARM capabilities with a practical experiment with an Automatic Target Recognition (ATR) distributed application [9] and with a synthetic pipeline demonstration application.

The DARPA Quorum program [11] provides an extensive framework for QoS-related research projects. Similar efforts for building adaptive management systems for heterogeneous resources are GRMS [6,7], ARA [9,12], and QualMan [10]. GRMS is a precursor of RTARM. It introduced the uniform resource model and the atomic ripple scheduling protocol. Its hierarchical architecture reflects the application data flow and does not offer feedback adaptation. ARA considers a discrete set of runtime configurations for distributed applications and does feedback adaptation by resource reallocation. The ARA architecture is non-recursive and differs considerably from the uniform RTARM architecture by using proxies for specific service providers. QualMan is designed for multimedia applications and defines two basic resource management components, the resource scheduler and the QoS broker, that adhere to a uniform resource model without considering deeper recursive structures and QoS composition. [2] introduces a portable and QoS-enabled middleware platform suitable for building multimedia and real-time distributed applications.

The rest of this paper is organized as follows. Section 2 describes the RTARM hierarchical architecture, system models and interfaces. Section 3 presents the architecture of a Service Manager and describes the CPU, network and a higher-level SM. Section 4 continues with experiments involving an ATR application and synthetic pipeline applications that emphasize the RTARM capabilities. The paper concludes in Section 5 with a discussion and future plans.

2   The RTARM System Architecture

We have designed and implemented the RTARM system prototype as a middleware layer above the operating system and network resources. The middleware approach provides the benefit of flexibility and portability but the increased distance to the basic resources makes fine-grained control difficult. The RTARM servers, developed in C++, run as user-level processes on Windows NT workstations and export a CORBA (Orbix [8]) interface to clients and applications. The RTARM model differentiates between clients and applications. A client is any entity that issues a request for services and negotiates a QoS contract that defines the allocated services. An application consumes services reserved by a client on its behalf and continuously cooperates with the resource management system to achieve the best available QoS while maintaining its runtime parameters within the contracted region. The QoS contract may change during the application lifetime.

2.1   The Service Manager Hierarchy

The RTARM system employs a hierarchical resource management architecture that facilitates provision of integrated services over heterogeneous resources. The uniform resource model [5] defines a recursive structural entity called Service Manager (SM) that encapsulates a set of resources and their management mechanism. At the bottom of the hierarchy are SMs that provide management functions for basic resources, such as CPU or network resources, and directly control resource utilization by application components. Higher level services are assembled on top of lower-level services, giving rise to a service hierarchy.

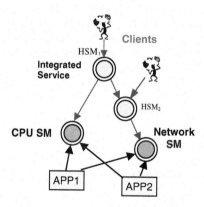

Fig. 1. Sample RTARM hierarchy consisting of one network SM, one CPU SM and two integrated service managers

Resources as well as negotiation requests are treated uniformly across the entire hierarchy. Higher-level service managers (HSM) may act as clients for lower-level SMs (LSM). The hierarchy allows dynamic configuration as new service managers can join the system at any time. A request for an integrated service sent to an HSM may require resources from lower-level service providers. The admission protocol builds a virtual reservation tree over the SM hierarchy that remains valid for the entire application lifetime. The SM hierarchy forms a directed acyclic graph, with SM as nodes and edges represented by the "uses-services-from" relation.

Figure 1 illustrates a simple RTARM hierarchy with two LSMs, a CPU and a Network SM, at the bottom of the hierarchy. Two clients request services from the two HSMs while applications are consuming CPU and network resources. Section 3 describes the service managers in more detail.

There are several benefits from a hierarchical, recursive, resource management architecture. First, services with complex, composite QoS representations are easier to implement on top of basic services. Complex distributed applications benefit from a richer representation of QoS. It simplifies the application design and facilitates consistent resource management for QoS-incompatible applications. Regardless of how complex the application architecture and QoS semantics are at the top of the SM hierarchy, at the bottom of the hierarchy everything translates to QoS requests for basic services (CPU and network in our prototype).

The hierarchical architecture of RTARM scales well with large distributed environments. Many SMs grouped in clusters may benefit from service localization and avoid communication bottlenecks. Sharing of LSMs between HSMs adds redundancy, fault tolerance and load balancing. In contrast, the centralized approach for heterogeneous resource management in distributed environments may introduce the drawbacks of a central controller: communication and processing bottleneck, one point of failure and decreased flexibility, but has certain performance benefits and lower latency.

A potential shortcoming for deep RTARM hierarchies derives from the increased distance between the top-most-level SM and bottom layer in the hierarchy. This may cause high latency for time sensitive RTARM functions, such as feedback adaptation and application control in case of deep SM hierarchies.

Issues related to deadlock prevention and distributed SM synchronization have been studied for the GRMS project [6,7] and can be easily extended to the RTARM model.

2.2   RTARM System Models

2.2.1   QoS Model and Translation

The quality of the interaction of a mission-critical application with a dynamic environment directly reflects its performance. The wide magnitude of this interaction requires a range for the quality measures. RTARM supports a multidimensional QoS representation, each dimension specifying an acceptable range $[Q_{min}, Q_{max}]$ of a quality parameter for the application. A set of range specifications, one per dimension, defines a QoS region. This QoS model facilitates resource negotiation and makes resource management more flexible.

In the RTARM recursive hierarchy, the QoS representation at a SM reflects the type of services provided by that SM. An HSM translates a QoS request for integrated services into individual QoS requests for services provided by itself and its lower-level SMs. When the SM receives replies from its LSMs, it reassembles the returned QoS into its own QoS representation in a process called QoS reverse-translation.

RTARM uses a unique implementation for QoS, which is independent of the addressed service. We define a QoS parameter as a set of name-value pairs, where the value part is a sequence of one or more scalar primitive data values (string, short, double, etc.) and the name indicates the specific QoS dimension, such as "rate", "workload", "latency", etc..

2.2.2   Adaptation Model

RTARM recognizes three situations when application QoS may be changed after admission [5]: (1a) QoS shrinking/reduction of lower criticality applications when a new application comes; (1b) QoS expansion/improvement when applications depart and release resources, and (2) feedback adaptation. While (1a) and (1b) imply contract changes and involve other applications, feedback adaptation does not change the contract but only varies the current operational point of the application within the contracted QoS region. Feedback adaptation is like closed loop control. It relies on monitoring of delivered QoS and uses the difference between delivered and desired QoS to adapt the application behavior.

2.3   RTARM Interfaces

Each SM implements and exports three interfaces: (1) *Negotiator* for admission control, collateral adaptation, QoS expansion and application control, such as suspend, resume and end; (2) *Service Manager* for SM hierarchy set up (register/deregister SM) and (3) *Monitor* for application monitoring and event propagation.

For admission control and adaptation RTARM uses a modified version of the GRMS Ripple Scheduling algorithm [6,7]. A detailed description with examples follows in Section 3.4. Briefly said, RTARM admission and adaptation employ a transaction-based two-phase commit protocol applied recursively at each SM. The first phase executes a service availability test starting from the SM that received the admission request, down on the reservation tree that resulted from the QoS translation and request dispatch process. The available, reserved QoS propagates back to the initiator SM from the lowest SM layer, being reverse-translated along the way. In the second phase, the initiator SM assesses the success status of the reservation phase and the transaction is committed or aborted, implying service reservations along the spanning tree to be committed, or to be cancelled, respectively. If not enough resources are available, a SM will try to adapt lower criticality applications to their minimum contracted QoS and use the released resources for the new application. Later, when resources become available, the SM expands the QoS for the most critical applications.

Sometimes in order to admit a new, more critical application, it is enough to squeeze the QoS of only a part of an existing distributed application. Then, changes in the high-level QoS may require collateral adaptation of other components of the application that do not directly impact admission of the new application. For instance, for a multimedia stream application having frame rate as QoS parameter, if one processing stage is adapted to the minimum rate, than all other stages will run at the same low rate, too.

The next section presents the object architecture of the SM and details the implementation of a CPU, a Network and a Higher-level SM.

3   RTARM Service Managers

3.1   The Service Manager Architecture and Implementation

The unified resource model provides the benefits of a uniform internal architecture for all service managers (Figure 2) and a common interface between them.

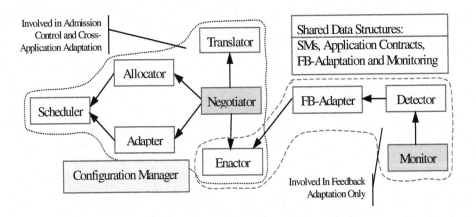

Fig. 2. The internal object architecture of a service manager

The arrows in the figure indicate object service requests. The components in a SM are as follows:

- *Negotiator:* brokers contract admission, delegates responsibilities to other components and exports the external RTARM CORBA interface.
- *Translator:* translates higher-layer integrated QoS into lower-layer QoS representation.
- *Allocator:* handles resource allocation/release when no adaptation is necessary.
- *Adapter:* handles resource allocation/release with adaptation and QoS expansion/contraction.
- *Scheduler:* determines whether allocation of resources and expansion of application QoS are feasible.

- *Enactor:* enforces changes in application QoS or status.
- *Monitor:* keeps an eye on applications in execution and passes status information and QoS usage to the Detector. Exports external RTARM CORBA interface.
- *Detector:* uses application runtime information (e.g. current QoS operational point) to detect significant changes in application operation (e.g. overload, underutilization, contract violation). Triggers Feedback Adapter actions.
- *Feedback Adapter:* decides corrective actions for applications when their runtime status changes significantly.

Additional data structures exist to hold information regarding application contracts, other service managers and available services.

Applications implement a simple CORBA interface that allows SMs to change their QoS and status. LSMs keep proxies for the application CORBA server objects. All RTARM CORBA servers and applications are started in the shared, multi-client activation mode.

A SM component class has the same object interface regardless of the SM position in the hierarchy or the resources the SM controls. For instance, the Adapter object implements the same functions in all SMs, but in a way that depends actually on the scope of the SM. Not all components are required within a SM. For example, a Translator may exist only inside an HSM.

RTARM provides a common object oriented execution framework that allows users to dynamically load SM components from shared libraries during runtime configuration. A configuration manager uses a mechanism similar to a *Factory Method* [4] to instantiate SM components. It also passes configuration information extracted from a configuration file to the SM components during their initialization.

For all SMs there is a single executable program that originally contains the empty SM framework and the configuration manager. By loading specialized components from shared libraries, the configuration manager practically starts different SMs. We use this technique when we initialize the CPU, Network and Higher-level SMs with components from specific Windows NT DLLs.

The flexibility of this plug-and-play feature permits implementation of a new SM by just replacing a set of components that realize a particular SM component interface, without rewriting the whole program. Writing a new SM component only requires the header file with the object interface, the executable program (common execution framework) and its corresponding library.

3.2   The CPU Service Manager

The CPU SM provides periodic applications access to a processor resource. Each computing node has a CPU SM, allowing concurrent applications to share a CPU. The application QoS is bi-dimensional: application execution rate (R) and iteration execution time (W) (Figure 3). The COP (Current Operational Point) represents the current values for the multidimensional QoS.

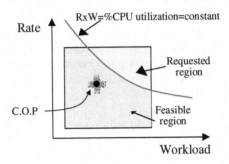

Fig. 3. CPU Service Manager QoS representation

3.2.1   Admission and Adaptation

The specific CPU scheduling policy is isolated within the Scheduler object and the Monitor keeps track of application CPU utilization. The invariant condition for admission and schedulability for n applications is $\Sigma_{i=1..n}R_iW_i < 100\%$ processor utilization. A more sophisticated CPU SM can be implemented at any time, by just using the plug-and-play feature, replacing the default Scheduler component with one specific to the scheduling discipline used.

The CPU SM service allocation unit for each periodic application is the fraction of CPU utilization (R x W). The CPU SM communicates this information to applications and assumes they are well behaved and keep their process utilization below the allocated limits. The SM scheduler only assigns application rates and does not control the underlying OS scheduler. This policy works fine on a larger time scale and for our experimental purposes. For real-time performance one solution is to implement a soft real-time CPU scheduling server above the OS scheduler [10]. Commercial operating systems with soft real-time capabilities, like Windows NT and Solaris, limit the scheduler granularity to 10-20ms.

The CPU SM implements the Ripple Scheduling admission protocol. Because it is at the bottom of the SM hierarchy and has no LSMs, it does not make any other recursive calls. Adaptation and collateral adaptation reduce the application rate to the minimum contracted value. QoS expansion increases the application contracted QoS (rate) to the best available value.

3.2.2   Feedback Adaptation

The CPU SM controls the task rate in real-time. It cannot change the workload, which is left exclusively under application control. Applications send their current QoS operational point as events to the CPU SM monitor at the end of each periodic iteration. At any moment, the QoS COP may vary so that R x W ≤ L, where L is the fraction of the contracted processor utilization. The CPU SM adjusts the COP as follows: (1) increase rate when workload decreases; (2) decrease rate on overload, when the workload pushes the COP outside the contracted region.

3.3   The Network Service Manager

We integrated the NetEx real-time network management system [3,13] from Texas A&M University into the RTARM system. NetEx runs as middleware and provides connection-oriented real-time communication with guaranteed delay and bandwidth over COTS network infrastructure, such as ATM and switched 10/100 Mbps Ethernet. NetEx uses a tri-dimensional QoS: period, delay and message size and adds the connection source and destination network addresses to the connection contract. The NetEx resource management interface is, however, incompatible with the RTARM interfaces. It has different semantics and it does not export the two-phase commit protocol.

We built an object-oriented *wrapper* [4] around NetEx that hides the incompatibilities and exports the RTARM interface to clients, applications and HSMs (Figure 4). The wrapper method can be used to integrate any service provider in the RTARM architecture.

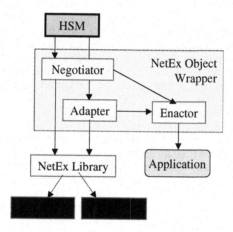

Fig. 4. The object wrapper for NetEx communication manager

The wrapper implements three SM components, Negotiator, Adapter and Enactor, that map the RTARM interface calls for admission, adaptation and expansion to the native NetEx API. NetEx does not provide feedback adaptation for connections, so the wrapper SM does not implement feedback adaptation either. It is important to note, however, that our HSM for integrated services for parallel pipeline applications implements hierarchical feedback adaptation. This is detailed in the next section.

3.4   The Higher-Level Service Manager for Integrated Services

Within the RTARM service manager hierarchy, HSMs aggregate services from LSMs (CPU, Network or any other type of SM) and provide RTARM services to applications that need a more complex QoS representation. The unified resource model enables recursive deployment of HSMs. Our HSM implementation is generic and is able to support various types of distributed applications with arbitrary QoS representations that map to available LSM QoS. The only restriction is that the Ripple Scheduling admission and adaptation procedure and the hierarchical feedback adaptation must not contradict the application semantics. The QoS Translator SM component inside an HSM is responsible for translating a QoS request into something the LSMs understand. Replacing the translator component with a different one (for a different QoS representation) produces a HSM capable of supporting different integrated services.

3.4.1   Admission and Adaptation

The Negotiator implements the recursive two-phase admission protocol that runs at the heart of each HSM. The code for the first phase, reservation, follows next:

```
test_reservation(in reqQos, out avQos, in candidates,
                 out adaptedApps)
// reqQoS is the requested QoS region
// avQoS is the returned (acceptable) QoS region
// candidates is the list of applications that may be
// adapted in order to accommodate the current request
// adaptedApps is the list of adapted applications
{
  translate reqQos into:
    LS - list of requested services from LSMs, and
    LreqQos - corresponding QoS per service.
  for each service S from LS {
    for each LSM lsm that provides service S {
      success = lsm->test_reservation(LreqQoS[lsm],
                        lsmAvQos[S],
                        candidates that run on lsm,
                        lsmAdaptedApps[S])
      if success then mark admitted service
                 and continue with next service S from LS
    }
    if service S was not admitted then {
      cancel all previous successful reservations
      return false
    }
  }
  // now all services from LS have been admitted
  reverse-translate and maximize the returned QoS from
                                 lsmAvQos into avQos
  perform collateral adaptation if necessary
  return true
}
```

The second phase that commits the resource reservation from phase I is implemented like this:

```
commit_reservation(in committedQos, in adaptedApps)
// commitedQos is the QoS region to commit
// adaptedApps is a list of applications (adapted in phase
// I) whose adaptations have to be committed
{
  translate commitedQos into:
              Llsm - list of LSMs and
              LcommittedQos - committed QoS per service
  for each lsm from Llsm {
    lsm->commit_reservation(LcommitedQos[lsm],
                            adaptedApps that run on lsm)
  }
  save committedQos into the application contract
}
```

The `cancel_reservation()` call is similar to `commit_reservation()` and is omitted here.

Figures 5 and 6 illustrate examples of admission of a new application with id 3 at an HSM H that has 3 LSMs, L_1, L_2, L_3.

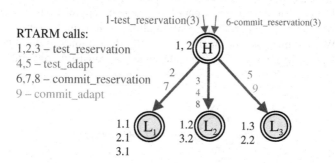

Fig. 5. Example of successful admission of application 3 at the HSM "H"

Applications 1 and 2 are already running at H and use services from L_1, L_2, L_3. For example, application 1 (denoted with 1 at H) runs also at L_1 (1.1), at L_2 (1.2) and L_3 (denoted 1.3). The new application 3 requires two services and maps to 3.1 and 3.2. In example a) both 3.1 and 3.2 are admitted at L_1 and L_2. Admission for 3.1 needs adaptation of application 1.1 on L_1. This triggers collateral adaptations for 1.2 as well as 1.3, as the entire application 1 must be adapted. Calls 4 and 5 (`test_adapt`) ask L_2 and L_3 to adapt collaterally application 1. During the execution of `commit_reservation` on H (call number 6), the collateral adaptation of 1 is committed on L_1 and L_2 with the two `commit_reservation` calls plus the extra `commit_adapt` call (9) to L_3. The example from Figure 6 shows the call sequence

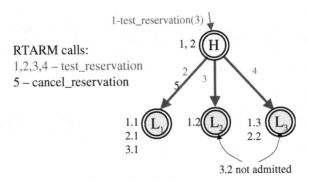

Fig. 6. Example of failed admission of application 3 at the HSM "H". Stage 3.2 is denied by both L_1 and L_2

when application 3 is accepted by L_1, but rejected both by L_2 and L_3. HSM H finally rejects 3 and returns false to the `test_reservation` call 1.

We have implemented a Pipeline Service Manager (PSM), an HSM that aggregates services from lower-level SMs (CPU, Network, other HSMs) into a higher-level integrated representation suited for pipeline applications. Our PSM supports periodic independent tasks and periodic parallel pipeline applications, consisting of communicating stages in an arbitrary configuration, with a single source and a single sink node. We assume a sensor enters periodically data frames in the pipeline. Each frame is processed by a stage or a composite stage [1] (consisting of parallel strings of

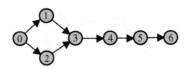

Fig. 7. Sample parallel pipeline application with 7 stages

elementary stages) and then sent to the next stage. Such a pipeline application is depicted in Figure 7.

For periodic pipeline applications, we use a QoS consisting of end-to-end message latency and rate for the final stage. The admission contract also contains execution time for each stage as well as the message size for each inter-stage connection. It is the job of the pipeline translator to decompose the integrated-service pipeline request into CPU and network admission requests. We assume all stages use the same range for rate. The pipeline QoS (end-to-end latency, frame rate plus state workloads and message sizes) translates into CPU QoS parameters for all stages and Network QoS for all network connections. The CPU QoS rate range is the same as that for the pipeline frame rate. The pipeline translator uses the same rate range and a fraction of the end-to-end pipeline latency to generate the Network QoS parameters.

3.4.2   Hierarchical Feedback Adaptation for Parallel Data-Flow Applications

We have implemented an innovative and efficient hierarchical feedback adaptation mechanism for parallel pipeline applications [1]. It performs feedback adaptation at two levels in the SM hierarchy. The pipeline end-to-end latency is controlled at the HSM level while the CPU SMs perform CPU feedback adaptation independent of the HSM.

The pipeline QoS parameter we consider critical and want to control is the end-to-end latency. As the pipeline evolves in time, rates of intermediate stages may change as a result of CPU SM feedback adaptation. In normal circumstances, the input sensor period is maintained at a value greater than the current period of any stage/substage of the parallel pipeline application, but it can get lower because of independent CPU feedback adaptation. When accumulation of queues between stages increases the end-to-end latency beyond a maximum threshold, the PSM sets the input sensor period at the maximum value from the pipeline contract. A finite state machine in the PSM maintains this maximal period for a fixed time, allowing the queues to empty. Then, the PSM sets again the input sensor period to the maximal current period of all stages, typically lower than maximum period from the contract. We have proved in [1] that the end-to-end latency decreases, and that after a finite number of frames the pipeline enters a region of stability where the end-to-end latency and the output frame rate are within the contracted region.

This method is simple and quite efficient, as the only parameter to be adjusted is the sensor input period, while the pipeline stages are controlled only by the corresponding CPU SM. This mechanism avoids costly communication and coordination between the HSM and all the CPU SMs. The information required for pipeline feedback adaptation is minimal: the end-to-end latency for the current frame and the maximal current period of all stages.

In the next section we present experiments with synthetic pipeline applications and an Automatic Target Recognition application and we give performance estimates for the RTARM system.

4   Experiments and Performance Evaluations

In this section we present two preliminary experiments that reflect our current research progress. We need further work to fully assess the implication of the hierarchical architecture to the overall system performance. The first experiment deals with synthetic pipeline applications and yields performance numbers for admission, adaptation and QoS expansion for the CPU, Network and Pipeline SMs. The second experiment tests feedback adaptation for parallel pipeline applications. The Forward Looking Infrared Automatic Target Recognition application provides an excellent testbed to prove the efficiency of our hierarchical feedback adaptation technique.

The runtime environment for these experiments consists of three 450MHz Dell Workstation-400 machines, running Windows NT, connected via a Fore ATM switch with OC-3c (155Mbps) links. Each machine hosts a CPU SM. Both the network SM that controls the inter-stage communication and the pipeline SM run on one of the three machines. We consider their own CPU resource consumption negligible. All inter-SM CORBA communication uses a secondary Fast Ethernet network, so the ATM lines remain 100% available for inter-stage communication. We used the NT performance counter for precise time measurements.

4.1   Performance for Admission and Adaptation

For evaluating admission, adaptation and expansion performance for pipeline applications we devised two scenarios.

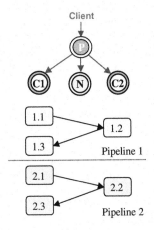

Fig. 8. Scenario 1. SM configuration and stage mapping

Scenario 1.
1. We tested admission of three-stage pipelines on a SM hierarchy with one HSM (P), one NSM (N) and two CPU SMs (C$_1$, C$_2$), as illustrated in Figure 8. The sequence of events is:
2. admit pipeline 1; no adaptation required.
3. admit pipeline 2 with higher criticality; stage 1.1 is adapted due to CPU constraints on SM C1; stages 1.2, 1.3 and network connections are adapted collaterally.
4. terminate pipeline 2; pipeline 1 is expanded back to its original QoS (all stages and the network connections).
5. try admission for pipeline 3 with lower criticality than 1; not enough CPU resources, admission is denied.
6. terminate pipeline 1.

Scenario 2 runs on the same environment as Scenario 1 and is similar, except the pipeline applications now have two stages and adaptation is caused only by network bandwidth constraints, not by CPU resource insufficiency.

Throughout the tests we measured the time required to complete the RTARM interface calls for admission, adaptation and expansion for the CPU, Network and Pipeline SM. The measured time consists of the actual processing overhead and time to complete nested calls to: (1) application CORBA servers for the CPU SM; (2) the NetEx management subsystem and application CORBA servers for the Network SM (NetEx wrapper) and (3) LSMs for the Pipeline SM.

The performance measurements for the Pipeline SM are listed in Table 1, for the CPU SM in Table 2 and for the Network SM in Table 3. All values are expressed in milliseconds.

Table 1. Performance measurements for the Pipeline Service Manager

	w/o Adaptation		with Adaptation	
	Total time	Processing time	Total time	Processing time
test_reservation	99.159	17.972	118.344	18.899
commit_reservation	2239.02	6.366	2376.34	11.338
cancel_reservation	7.102	0.313		
test_expansion			212.751	4.508
commit_expansion			39.987	4.921
end_app	252.325	1.414	460.348	4.145

Table 2. Performance measurements for the CPU Service Manager

	w/o Adaptation		with Adaptation	
	with CORBA	w/o CORBA	with CORBA	w/o CORBA
test_reservation		0.447		0.707
commit_reservation	525.165	0.474	544.796	1.397
cancel_reservation		0.146		0.168
test_adapt				0.234
test_expansion				0.189
commit_expansion			3.132	0.112
end_app	4.619	0.846		

Table 3. Performance measurements for the Network Service Manager

	w/o Adaptation				with Adaptation			
	Total time	Processing time	CORBA time	NETEX time	Total time	Processing time	CORBA time	NETEX time
test_reservation	22.475	3.147	0	19.328	48.414	3.901	0	44.513
commit_reservation	45.434	0.637	44.797	0	49.962	1.105	48.857	0
test_adapt					0.056	0.056	0	0
test_expansion					33.093	0.355	0	32.738
commit_expansion					0.697	0.697	0	0
end_app	10.08	0.289	0	9.791				

For the PSM the "Total Time" columns include the sequence of recursive RTARM CORBA calls to the LSMs and the algorithm processing overhead. Some calls may require adaptation of lower criticality applications, such as `test_reservation()` at step 2 in scenario 1; other calls, like the expansion operations, are 100% with adaptation. From Table 1 we notice that the reservation operations and `end_app()` require extra processing work if adaptation is involved. Also the processing time for `test_reservation()` is considerably larger than all other calls since it involves back-and-forth QoS translation and reverse-translation. But what stands out is the large total time consumed for `commit_reservation()` for a three stage pipeline application, approximately 2.3 seconds. This time includes the duration for `commit_reservation()` calls to the CPU SM that take more than 500ms for each pipeline stage (see Table 2). A CPU `commit_reservation()` call actually generates a `set_qos()` call with the committed application QoS to the application stage CORBA server. The stages are not up and running when admission happens.

The Orbix daemon [8] starts the stage process and passes the CORBA server IIOP TCP port number and IP address to the CPU SM. Only after the stage is up and initialized it is able to respond to the `set_qos()` CORBA call from the CPU SM. The time to start a Windows GUI application (the pipeline stage) on Windows NT 4.0 is around half a second for our test configuration.

Table 3 shows time measurements for the Nework SM These are more complex since the NetEx wrapper communicates through TCP/IP with the NetEx Host Traffic Manager [3,13] and stages through `set_qos()` CORBA calls (only during `commit_reservation()`). The communication latency overhead caused by NetEx is comparable to CORBA communication overhead, between 10 and 45ms.

We conclude that operation of the RTARM system is efficient, except the `commit_reservation()` call for CPU applications. This major delay can be completely avoided by pre-loading the applications before the client submits the pipeline contract to the HSM. The overall system performance may further improve by using a faster CORBA implementation that guarantees real-time operation deadlines.

4.2   Performance for Hierarchical Feedback Adaptation

4.2.1.1   The Automatic Target Recognition Experiment

We tested the RTARM feedback adaptation mechanism on a true mission-critical application. The ATR application, schematically shown in Figure 9, processes video frames captured by a camera and displays recognized targets on a display. Stage 0 (the sensor) generates frames that are passed through a series of filters and processing elements up to stage 6, which displays the original image and the identified targets. The frames are 8-bit, 360x360 pixels, monochrome images, and contain a variable number of targets (from 3 to 50), depending on the frame. Stages 4, 5 and 6 expose a variable workload, proportional to the number of targets, that without feedback adaptation would cause queue accumulations with negative effect on the end-to-end frame latency.

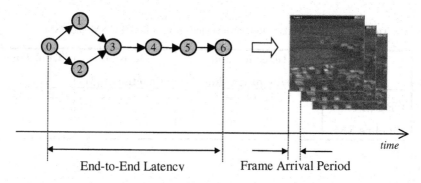

Fig. 9. ATR pipeline application and its high-level QoS

4.2.2 Performance Metrics and Evaluation

The ATR pipeline contract requires an acceptable output frame period interval of [1,5] s, and a frame latency of 0.7-13 s. The seven ATR stages run at a variable workload between 0.02s and 1.5s and within the same period interval [1,5] s. We first present timing measurements for the feedback adaptation at the CPU SM and PSM SM level (Figure 10). We measured the processing overhead of the feedback

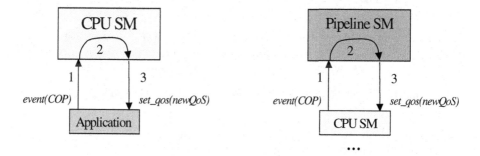

Fig. 10. Measuring feedback adaptation performance

adaptation code (part 2 in Figure 10) and the time it takes the SM to react from the moment it receives the current QoS from the application until its adaptation command is enforced (part 2 + part 3).

The measured times are displayed in Table 4. For the CPU feedback adaptation, detection and enforcing the QoS adaptation takes around 4.4ms. Most of the time, 3.9ms, is spent in a `set_qos()` operation, a two-way normal, local CORBA call. The pipeline adaptation enforcement includes a `set_qos()` call to the CPU SM that controls the sensor (or first stage) that calls directly the first stage with a `set_qos()` call. This explains why enacting pipeline QoS adaptation takes almost double than for CPU SM QoS.

Table 4. Feedback adaptation performance results for CPU SM and PSM

	Detection and decision processing (2)	Decision Enactment (3)	Total Time (2+3)
CPU SM	0.508 ms	3.914 ms	4.422 ms
Pipeline SM	0.859 ms	6.816 ms	7.675 ms

Figure 11 displays CPU feedback adaptation for stage 4 in the ATR pipeline. The stage has variable workload that triggers its CPU SM to change its rate. Points A

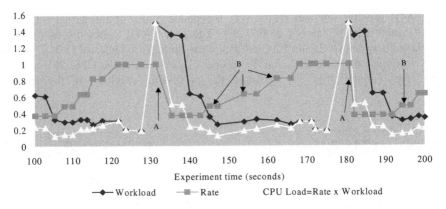

Fig. 11. CPU SM feedback adaptation for a task with variable workload

indicate overload that triggers rate decrease and points B indicate chronic underutilization that determines rate increase.

While running the ATR application, the pipeline feedback adaptation mechanism makes sure the end-to-end latency and rate stay in the contracted range (Figure 12). In order to practically demonstrate its effectiveness, we disabled the pipeline feedback adaptation after some time while keeping the sensor input period at a sustained low value of 1.48s (0.67Hz). This caused accumulation of frames in stage queues that translated into an increasing end-to-end frame latency. While feedback adaptation was disabled we actually did not get latency measurements, so we drew a dotted line between points A and B. When the latency reached 30s, way above the contracted value, we re-enabled pipeline feedback adaptation. Immediately the PSM sensor increased the sensor input period up to 5s. The latency went rapidly down (B → C), below the threshold, after a brief spike caused by the inertia of the more than 23 frames already in transit through the pipeline.

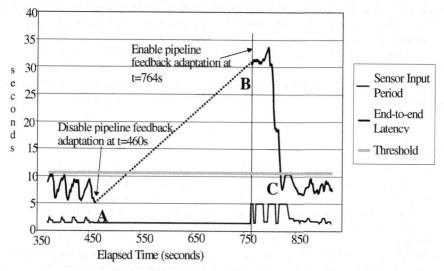

Fig. 12. Latency variation for ATR with and without pipeline feedback adaptation

The feedback adaptation algorithm we implemented tends to keep the intermediary stage queues empty while changing the input sensor period only. This is effective but introduces high oscillations for latency. Further research will use control theory to design more efficient algorithms that use target history and prediction, able to smooth down the end-to-end latency oscillations without compromising overall performance and response time.

Our hierarchical feedback adaptation algorithm proved to be effective and efficient. Detection, decision and enforcement take less than 8ms and involve only the CPU SMs for the sensor and the last stage that actually reports the latency and rate.

5   Conclusions

This paper presents the middleware architecture and implementation of the RTARM system. We have first focused on the architectural elements that enable RTARM support for integrated services: (1) the uniform service management recursive hierarchy and protocols, (2) the common architecture of a Service Manager that facilitates rapid object-oriented prototyping, massive code reuse and features plug-and-play support for SM components. Then we detailed the specific service managers that constitute the RTARM hierarchy. The clean and flexible architecture of a SM allowed us to integrate quickly a new service provider in the RTARM hierarchy. We built an object wrapper around the incompatible interface of the NetEx network management system that provided the same CORBA interface implemented by all RTARM service managers.

Finally, we presented experiments that illustrate the practical use of the RTARM system and its effectiveness for a real-world Automatic Target Recognition application. We demonstrated that our hierarchical feedback adaptation mechanism is able to efficiently control in real time the dynamic behavior of a parallel pipeline distributed application.

We plan to port RTARM to a real-time CORBA implementation, such as WUStL TAO [14] and to optimize its performance. We also intend to develop more sophisticated feedback adaptation mechanisms with prediction features which would further decrease the system reaction time while optimizing the application QoS.

References

1. Cardei, M., Cardei, I., Jha, R., Pavan, A., "Hierarchical Feedback Adaptation For Real-Time Sensor-based Distributed Applications", to appear in the Proceedings of the 3rd IEEE International Symposium on Object-Oriented Real-time distributed Computing, 2000
2. Coulson, G., "A Configurable Multimedia Middleware Platform", IEEE Multimedia, Vol 6, No 1, 1999
3. Devalla, B., Sahoo, A., Guan, Y., Li,C., Bettati, R., Zhao, W., "Adaptive Connection Admission Control for Mission Critical Real-Time Communication Networks", to appear in International Journal of Parallel and Distributed Systems and Networks, Special Issue On Network Architectures for End-to-end Quality-of-Service Support
4. Gamma, E., Helm, R., Johnson, R., Vlissides, J., "Design Patterns. Elements of Reusable Object-Oriented Software", Addison-Wesley, 1994
5. Huang, J., Jha, R., Heimerdinger, W., Muhammad, M., Lauzac, S., Kannikeswaran, B., Schwan, K., Zhao, W., Bettati, R.. "RT-ARM: A Real-Time Adaptive Resource Management System for Distributed Mission-Critical Applications", Proceedings of the IEEE Workshop on Middleware for Distributed Real-Time Systems and Services, December 1997
6. Huang, J., Wang, Y., Cao, F., "On Developing Distributed Multimedia Services for QoS and Criticality Based Resource Negotiation and Adaptation", Journal of Real-Time Systems, May 1999
7. Huang, J., Wang, Y., Vaidyanathan, N.R., Cao, F., "GRMS: A Global Resource Management System for Distributed QoS and Criticality Support", Proceedings of the 4th IEEE International Conference on Multimedia Computing and Systems, June 1997
8. IONA Technologies, "The Orbix Programmer's Guide", 1997
9. Jha, R., Muhammad, M., Yalamanchili, S., Schwan, K., Rosu, D., deCastro, C., "Adaptive Resource Allocation for Embedded Parallel Applications", Proceedings of the 3rd International Conference on High Performance Computing, December 1996
10. Nahrstedt, K., Chu, H., Narayan., S., "QoS-aware Resource Management for Distributed Multimedia Applications", to appear in Journal on High-Speed Networking, Special Issue on Multimedia Networking
11. Quorum, http://www.darpa.mil/ito/research/quorum
12. Rosu, D., Schwan, K., Yalamanchili, S., "FARA – A Framework for Adaptive Resource Allocation in Complex Real-Time Systems", Proceedings of the 4th IEEE Real-Time Technology and Applications Symposium, June 1998
13. Sahoo, A., Li, C., Devalla, B., Zhao, W., "Design and Implementation of NetEx: A Toolkit for Delay Guaranteed Communications", Proceedings of Milcom, December 1997
14. Schmidt, D., Levine D., Mungee S., "The Design of the TAO Real-Time Object Request Broker", Computer Communications Special Issue on Building Quality of Service into Distributed Systems, Elsevier Science, 1998

Author Index

Lecture Notes in Computer Science

For information about Vols. 1–1713
please contact your bookseller or Springer-Verlag